Resolutions and Decisions of the Security Council

1 August 2014 – 31 July 2015

Security Council
Official Records

United Nations • New York, 2016

NOTE

The present volume of *Resolutions and Decisions of the Security Council* contains the resolutions adopted and the decisions taken by the Council on substantive questions during the period from 1 August 2014 to 31 July 2015, as well as decisions on some of the more important procedural matters. The resolutions and decisions are set out in parts I and II, under general headings indicating the questions under consideration. In each part, the questions are arranged according to the date on which they were first taken up by the Council, and under each question the resolutions and decisions appear in chronological order.

The resolutions are numbered in the order of their adoption. Each resolution is followed by the result of the vote. Decisions are usually taken without a vote.

S/INF/70

ISSN 0257–1455

Contents

Membership of the Security Council in 2014 and 2015

In 2014 and 2015, the membership of the Security Council was as follows:

2014	2015
Argentina	Angola
Australia	Chad
Chad	Chile
Chile	China
China	France
France	Jordan
Jordan	Lithuania
Lithuania	Malaysia
Luxembourg	New Zealand
Nigeria	Nigeria
Republic of Korea	Russian Federation
Russian Federation	Spain
Rwanda	United Kingdom of Great Britain and Northern Ireland
United Kingdom of Great Britain and Northern Ireland	United States of America
United States of America	Venezuela (Bolivarian Republic of)

Resolutions adopted and decisions taken by the Security Council from 1 August 2014 to 31 July 2015

Part I. Questions considered by the Security Council under its responsibility for the maintenance of international peace and security

THE SITUATION IN CYPRUS[1]

Decisions

On 22 August 2014, the President of the Security Council addressed the following letter to the Secretary-General:[2]

I have the honour to inform you that your letter dated 21 August 2014 concerning your intention to designate Mr. Espen Barth Eide, of Norway, as your Special Adviser on Cyprus at the Under-Secretary-General level[3] has been brought to the attention of the members of the Security Council. They take note of the intention expressed in your letter.

At its 7370th meeting, on 29 January 2015, the Council considered the item entitled:

"The situation in Cyprus

"Report of the Secretary-General on the United Nations operation in Cyprus (S/2015/17)".

Resolution 2197 (2015) of 29 January 2015

The Security Council,

Welcoming the report of the Secretary-General of 9 January 2015 on the United Nations operation in Cyprus,[4]

Noting that the Government of Cyprus has agreed that, in view of the prevailing conditions on the island, it is necessary to keep the United Nations Peacekeeping Force in Cyprus beyond 31 January 2015,

Noting also the intention of the Secretary-General to report on his good offices in the next reporting period, echoing the Secretary-General's firm belief that the responsibility for finding a solution lies first and foremost with the Cypriots themselves, and reaffirming the primary role of the United Nations in assisting the parties to bring the Cyprus conflict and division of the island to a comprehensive and durable settlement,

Expressing its support for the ongoing efforts of the Special Adviser to the Secretary-General on Cyprus, Mr. Espen Barth Eide, noting the importance of a conducive environment, calling for the resumption of structured negotiations without delay, in a results-oriented manner as agreed to in the joint declaration adopted by the Greek Cypriot and Turkish Cypriot leaders on 11 February 2014, and stressing the need for renewed efforts of the leaders and negotiators to reach a comprehensive settlement as soon as possible,

Recalling the importance that the international community attaches to all parties engaging fully, flexibly and constructively in the negotiations, noting that the negotiations have not yet resulted in an enduring, comprehensive and just settlement based on a bicommunal, bizonal federation with political equality, as set out in the relevant Security Council resolutions, encouraging the sides to intensify the substantive negotiations on the unresolved core issues interdependently, and stressing that the status quo is unsustainable,

Noting the need to advance the consideration of and discussions on military confidence-building measures, and calling for renewed efforts to implement all remaining confidence-building measures and for agreement on and implementation of further steps to build trust between the communities,

---

[1] Resolutions or decisions on this question were first adopted by the Security Council in 1963.

[2] S/2014/619.

[3] S/2014/618.

[4] S/2015/17.

Reaffirming the importance of continued crossings of the Green Line by Cypriots, and encouraging the opening by mutual agreement of other crossing points,

Convinced of the many important benefits, including economic benefits, for all Cypriots that would flow from a comprehensive and durable Cyprus settlement, urging the two sides and their leaders to foster positive public rhetoric, and encouraging them clearly to explain the benefits of the settlement, as well as the need for increased flexibility and compromise in order to secure it, to both communities well in advance of any eventual referendums,

Highlighting the importance of the supporting role of the international community, and in particular that of the parties concerned in taking practical steps towards helping the Greek Cypriot and Turkish Cypriot leaders to exploit fully the current opportunity,

Taking note of the assessment of the Secretary-General that the security situation on the island and along the Green Line remains stable, and urging all sides to avoid any action, including violations of the military status quo, which could lead to an increase in tension, undermine the progress achieved so far or damage the goodwill on the island,

Recalling the Secretary-General's firm belief that the situation in the buffer zone would be improved if both sides accepted the 1989 aide-memoire used by the United Nations,

Noting with regret that the sides are withholding access to the remaining minefields in the buffer zone, and that demining in Cyprus must continue, noting the continued danger posed by mines in Cyprus, noting also recent proposals and discussions on demining, and urging rapid agreement on facilitating the recommencement of demining operations and clearance of the remaining minefields,

Commending the work of the Committee on Missing Persons in Cyprus, highlighting the importance of intensifying its activities, noting that half of all missing persons have yet to be located and more than 70 per cent have yet to be identified, urging the opening up of access to all areas expeditiously to allow the Committee to carry out its work, and trusting that this process will promote reconciliation between the communities,

Agreeing that active participation of civil society groups, including women's groups, is essential to the political process and can contribute to making any future settlement sustainable, recalling that women play a critically important role in peace processes, welcoming all efforts to promote bicommunal contacts and events, including on the part of all United Nations bodies on the island, and urging the two sides to promote the active engagement of civil society and the encouragement of cooperation between economic and commercial bodies and to remove all obstacles to such contacts,

Stressing the need for the Council to pursue a rigorous, strategic approach to peacekeeping deployments,

Welcoming the intention of the Secretary-General to keep all peacekeeping operations under close review to ensure efficiency and effectiveness, including a review of the Force when appropriate, and noting the importance of contingency planning in relation to the settlement, including recommendations, as appropriate, for further adjustments to the mandate, force levels and other resources and concept of operations of the Force, taking into account developments on the ground and the views of the parties,

Noting with appreciation the efforts of Ms. Lisa Buttenheim as the Special Representative of the Secretary-General in Cyprus and the Force Commander, Major General Kristin Lund, and welcoming the appointment by the Secretary-General of his Special Adviser, Mr. Espen Barth Eide,

Echoing the Secretary-General's gratitude to the Government of Cyprus and the Government of Greece for their voluntary contributions to the funding of the Force and his request for further voluntary contributions from other countries and organizations, and expressing appreciation to Member States that contribute personnel to the Force,

Welcoming and encouraging efforts by the United Nations to sensitize peacekeeping personnel in the prevention and control of HIV/AIDS and other communicable diseases in all its peacekeeping operations,

1. *Acknowledges* the progress made so far in the fully fledged negotiations, but notes that this has not been sufficient and has not yet resulted in a comprehensive and durable settlement, and calls for an urgent resumption of structured negotiations to reach decisive progress on the core issues;

2. *Takes note* of the report of the Secretary-General;[4]

3. *Recalls* Security Council resolution 2026 (2011) of 14 December 2011, and calls upon the two leaders:

(*a*) To put their efforts behind further work on reaching convergences on the core issues;

(*b*) To continue to work with the technical committees with the objective of improving the daily lives of the Cypriots;

(*c*) To improve the public atmosphere for the negotiations, including by focusing public messages on convergences and the way ahead and delivering more constructive and harmonized messages;

(*d*) To increase the participation of civil society in the process, as appropriate;

4. *Urges* the implementation of confidence-building measures, and looks forward to agreement on and implementation of further such mutually acceptable steps, including military confidence-building measures and the opening of other crossing points, that can contribute to a conducive environment for a settlement;

5. *Welcomes* all efforts to accommodate the exhumation requirements of Committee on Missing Persons in Cyprus, and calls upon all parties to provide more expeditious, full access to all areas, given the need to intensify the work of the Committee;

6. *Reaffirms* all its relevant resolutions on Cyprus, in particular resolution 1251 (1999) of 29 June 1999 and subsequent resolutions;

7. *Expresses its full support* for the United Nations Peacekeeping Force in Cyprus, and decides to extend its mandate for a further period ending 31 July 2015;

8. *Calls upon* both sides to continue to engage, as a matter of urgency and while respecting the mandate of the Force, in consultations with the Force on the demarcation of the buffer zone and on the United Nations 1989 aide-memoire, with a view to reaching early agreement on outstanding issues;

9. *Calls upon* the Turkish Cypriot side and Turkish forces to restore in Strovilia the military status quo which existed there prior to 30 June 2000;

10. *Calls upon* both sides to allow access to deminers and to facilitate the removal of the remaining mines in Cyprus within the buffer zone, and urges both sides to extend demining operations outside the buffer zone;

11. *Requests* the Secretary-General to submit a report on the implementation of the present resolution, including on contingency planning in relation to the settlement, by 10 July 2015 and to keep the Council updated on events as necessary;

12. *Welcomes* the efforts being undertaken by the Force to implement the Secretary-General's zero-tolerance policy on sexual exploitation and abuse and to ensure full compliance of its personnel with the United Nations code of conduct, requests the Secretary-General to continue to take all necessary action in this regard and to keep the Council informed, and urges troop-contributing countries to take appropriate preventive action, including conducting predeployment awareness training, and to take disciplinary action and other action to ensure full accountability in cases of such conduct involving their personnel;

13. *Decides* to remain seized of the matter.

Adopted unanimously at the 7370th meeting.

Decisions

On 30 June 2015, the President of the Security Council addressed the following letter to the Secretary-General:[5]

> I have the honour to inform you that your letter dated 26 June 2015[6] has been brought to the attention of the members of the Security Council. They take note of the information contained in your letter and the intention expressed therein.

[5] S/2015/495.

[6] S/2015/494.

At its 7496th meeting, on 29 July 2015, the Council considered the item entitled:

"The situation in Cyprus

"Report of the Secretary-General on the United Nations operation in Cyprus (S/2015/517)".

Resolution 2234 (2015) of 29 July 2015

The Security Council,

Welcoming the report of the Secretary-General of 2 July 2015 on the United Nations operation in Cyprus,[7]

Noting that the Government of Cyprus has agreed that, in view of the prevailing conditions on the island, it is necessary to keep the United Nations Peacekeeping Force in Cyprus beyond 31 July 2015,

Noting also the intention of the Secretary-General to report on his good offices in the next reporting period, echoing the Secretary-General's firm belief that the responsibility for finding a solution lies first and foremost with the Cypriots themselves, and reaffirming the primary role of the United Nations in assisting the parties to bring the Cyprus conflict and division of the island to a comprehensive and durable settlement,

Welcoming the re-launching of negotiations, the positive momentum and the commitment expressed by the leaders to work tirelessly to reach a comprehensive settlement as soon as possible, in a results-oriented manner as agreed to in the joint declaration adopted by the Greek Cypriot and Turkish Cypriot leaders on 11 February 2014, and the support provided by the Special Adviser to the Secretary-General on Cyprus, Mr. Espen Barth Eide,

Recalling the importance that the international community attaches to all parties engaging fully, flexibly and constructively in the negotiations, noting that the negotiations have not yet resulted in an enduring, comprehensive and just settlement based on a bicommunal, bizonal federation with political equality, as set out in the relevant Security Council resolutions, encouraging the sides to intensify the substantive negotiations on the unresolved core issues interdependently, and stressing that the status quo is unsustainable,

Noting the need to advance the consideration of and discussions on military confidence-building measures, and calling for renewed efforts to implement all remaining confidence-building measures and for agreement on and implementation of further steps to build trust between the communities,

Reaffirming the importance of continued crossings of the Green Line by Cypriots, and encouraging the opening by mutual agreement of other crossing points,

Convinced of the many important benefits, including economic benefits, for all Cypriots that would flow from a comprehensive and durable Cyprus settlement, urging the two sides and their leaders to foster positive public rhetoric, and encouraging them clearly to explain the benefits of the settlement, as well as the need for increased flexibility and compromise in order to secure it, to both communities well in advance of any eventual referendums,

Highlighting the importance of the supporting role of the international community, and in particular that of all parties concerned in taking practical steps towards helping the Greek Cypriot and Turkish Cypriot leaders to exploit fully the current opportunity,

Taking note of the assessment of the Secretary-General that the security situation on the island and along the Green Line remains stable, and urging all sides to avoid any action, including violations of the military status quo, which could lead to an increase in tension, undermine the progress achieved so far or damage the goodwill on the island,

Recalling the Secretary-General's firm belief that the situation in the buffer zone would be improved if both sides accepted the 1989 aide-memoire used by the United Nations,

Noting with regret that the sides are withholding access to the remaining minefields in the buffer zone, and that demining in Cyprus must continue, noting the continued danger posed by mines in Cyprus, noting also recent proposals and discussions as well as positive initiatives on demining, and urging rapid agreement on facilitating the recommencement of demining operations and clearance of the remaining minefields,

[7] S/2015/517.

Commending the work of the Committee on Missing Persons in Cyprus, highlighting the importance of intensifying its activities, noting that half of all missing persons have yet to be located and more than 70 per cent have yet to be identified, urging the opening up of access to all areas expeditiously to allow the Committee to carry out its work, and trusting that this process will promote reconciliation between the communities,

Agreeing that active participation of civil society groups, including women's groups, is essential to the political process and can contribute to making any future settlement sustainable, recalling that women play a critically important role in peace processes, welcoming all efforts to promote bicommunal contacts and events including on the part of all United Nations bodies on the island, and urging the two sides to promote the active engagement of civil society and the encouragement of cooperation between economic and commercial bodies and to remove all obstacles to such contacts,

Stressing the need for the Council to pursue a rigorous, strategic approach to peacekeeping deployments,

Welcoming the intention of the Secretary-General to keep all peacekeeping operations under close review to ensure efficiency and effectiveness, including a review of the Force when appropriate, and noting the importance of contingency planning in relation to the settlement, including recommendations, as appropriate, for further adjustments to the mandate, force levels and other resources and concept of operations of the Force, taking into account developments on the ground and the views of the parties,

Noting with appreciation the efforts of Ms. Lisa Buttenheim as the Special Representative of the Secretary-General in Cyprus and the Force Commander, Major General Kristin Lund, and the appointment by the Secretary-General of his Special Adviser on Cyprus, Mr. Espen Barth Eide,

Echoing the Secretary-General's gratitude to the Government of Cyprus and the Government of Greece for their voluntary contributions to the funding of the Force and his request for further voluntary contributions from other countries and organizations, and expressing appreciation to Member States that contribute personnel to the Force,

Welcoming and encouraging efforts by the United Nations to sensitize peacekeeping personnel in the prevention and control of HIV/AIDS and other communicable diseases in all its peacekeeping operations,

1. *Welcomes* the resumption of the negotiations led by the leaders as well as the progress achieved so far and the ongoing efforts of the leaders and their negotiators to reach a comprehensive and durable settlement, and encourages the sides to grasp the current opportunity with determination to secure a comprehensive settlement;

2. *Takes note* of the report of the Secretary-General;[7]

3. *Recalls* Security Council resolution 2026 (2011) of 14 December 2011, and calls upon the two leaders:

(*a*) To put their efforts behind further work on reaching convergences on the core issues;

(*b*) To continue to work with the technical committees with the objective of improving the daily lives of the Cypriots;

(*c*) To improve the public atmosphere for the negotiations, including by focusing public messages on convergences and the way ahead and delivering more constructive and harmonized messages;

(*d*) To increase the participation of civil society in the process, as appropriate;

4. *Urges* the implementation of confidence-building measures, and looks forward to agreement on and implementation of further such mutually acceptable steps, including military confidence-building measures and the opening of other crossing points, that can contribute to a conducive environment for a settlement;

5. *Welcomes* all efforts to accommodate exhumation requirements of the Committee on Missing Persons in Cyprus, as well as the joint appeal for information issued by the two leaders on 28 May 2015, and calls upon all parties to provide more expeditious, full access to all areas, given the need to intensify the work of the Committee;

6. *Reaffirms* all its relevant resolutions on Cyprus, in particular resolution 1251 (1999) of 29 June 1999 and subsequent resolutions;

7. *Expresses its full support* for the United Nations Peacekeeping Force in Cyprus, and decides to extend its mandate for a further period ending 31 January 2016;

8. *Calls upon* both sides to continue to engage, as a matter of urgency and while respecting the mandate of the Force, in consultations with the Force on the demarcation of the buffer zone and on the United Nations 1989 aide-memoire, with a view to reaching early agreement on outstanding issues;

9. *Calls upon* the Turkish Cypriot side and Turkish forces to restore in Strovilia the military status quo which existed there prior to 30 June 2000;

10. *Calls upon* both sides to allow access to deminers and to facilitate the removal of the remaining mines in Cyprus within the buffer zone, and urges both sides to extend demining operations outside the buffer zone;

11. *Requests* the Secretary-General to submit a report on the implementation of the present resolution, including on contingency planning in relation to the settlement, by 10 January 2016 and to keep the Council updated on events as necessary;

12. *Welcomes* the efforts being undertaken by the Force to implement the Secretary-General's zero-tolerance policy on sexual exploitation and abuse and to ensure full compliance of its personnel with the United Nations code of conduct, requests the Secretary-General to continue to take all necessary action in this regard and to keep the Council informed, and urges troop-contributing countries to take appropriate preventive action, including conducting predeployment awareness training, and to take disciplinary action and other action to ensure full accountability in cases of such conduct involving their personnel;

13. *Decides* to remain seized of the matter.

Adopted unanimously at the 7496th meeting.

ITEMS RELATING TO THE SITUATION IN THE MIDDLE EAST

A. The situation in the Middle East[8]

Decision

At its 7248th meeting, on 26 August 2014, the Security Council decided to invite the representatives of Italy, Lebanon and Spain to participate, without vote, in accordance with rule 37 of its provisional rules of procedure, in the discussion of the item entitled:

"The situation in the Middle East

> "Letter dated 31 July 2014 from the Secretary-General addressed to the President of the Security Council (S/2014/554)".

Resolution 2172 (2014) of 26 August 2014

The Security Council,

Recalling all its previous resolutions on Lebanon, in particular resolutions 425 (1978) and 426 (1978) of 19 March 1978, 1559 (2004) of 2 September 2004, 1680 (2006) of 17 May 2006, 1701 (2006)) of 11 August 2006, 1773 (2007) of 24 August 2007, 1832 (2008) of 27 August 2008, 1884 (2009) of 27 August 2009, 1937 (2010) of 30 August 2010, 2004 (2011) of 30 August 2011, 2064 (2012) of 30 August 2012 and 2115 (2013) of 29 August 2013, as well as the statements by its President on the situation in Lebanon,

Responding to the request of the Government of Lebanon to extend the mandate of the United Nations Interim Force in Lebanon for a new period of one year, without amendment, presented in the letter dated 25 July 2014 from the Minister for Foreign Affairs and Emigrants of Lebanon to the Secretary-General, and welcoming the letter dated 31 July 2014 from the Secretary-General to the President of the Security Council recommending this extension,[9]

Reiterating its strong support for the territorial integrity, sovereignty and political independence of Lebanon,

---

[8] Resolutions or decisions on this question were first adopted by the Security Council in 1967.

[9] S/2014/554.

Reaffirming its commitment to the full implementation of all provisions of resolution 1701 (2006), and aware of its responsibilities to help to secure a permanent ceasefire and a long-term solution as envisioned in the resolution,

Calling upon all parties concerned to strengthen their efforts to fully implement all provisions of resolution 1701 (2006) without delay,

Expressing deep concern at all violations in connection with resolution 1701 (2006), and looking forward to the rapid finalization of the investigations by the Force with a view to preventing such violations in the future,

Welcoming the constructive role played by the tripartite mechanism in de-escalating tensions, and expressing its support for the efforts of the Force to engage with both parties to further develop liaison and coordination arrangements,

Emphasizing the importance of full compliance with the prohibition on sales and supply of arms and related materiel established by resolution 1701 (2006),

Recalling the utmost importance that all parties concerned respect the Blue Line in its entirety, welcoming the continued progress in the marking of the Blue Line, and encouraging the parties to accelerate their efforts in coordination with the Force to visibly mark the Blue Line in its entirety, as well as to move forward on the marking of its points of contention, as recommended by the strategic review of the Force,

Condemning in the strongest terms all attempts to threaten the security and stability of Lebanon, reaffirming its determination to ensure that no such acts of intimidation will prevent the Force from implementing its mandate in accordance with resolution 1701 (2006), and recalling the necessity for all parties to ensure that Force personnel are secure and their freedom of movement is fully respected and unimpeded,

Recalling the relevant principles contained in the Convention on the Safety of United Nations and Associated Personnel,[10]

Commending the active role and dedication of the personnel of the Force, expressing its strong appreciation to Member States that contribute to the Force, and underlining the necessity that the Force have at its disposal all necessary means and equipment to carry out its mandate,

Recalling the request of the Government of Lebanon to deploy an international force to assist it to exercise its authority throughout the territory, and reaffirming the authority of the Force to take all necessary action, in areas of operations of its forces and as it deems within its capabilities, to ensure that its area of operations is not utilized for hostile activities of any kind and to resist attempts by forceful means to prevent it from discharging its mandate,

Welcoming the efforts of the Secretary-General to keep all peacekeeping operations, including the Force, under close review, and stressing the need for the Council to pursue a rigorous, strategic approach to peacekeeping deployments,

Expressing its full support for the strategic priorities and recommendations identified by the Secretary-General in his letter dated 12 March 2012 to the President of the Security Council as a result of the strategic review of the Force,[11] and requesting the Secretary-General to continue to update the Council on the implementation of the strategic review,

Calling upon Member States to assist the Lebanese Armed Forces as needed to enable them to perform their duties in line with resolution 1701 (2006),

Determining that the situation in Lebanon continues to constitute a threat to international peace and security,

1. *Decides* to extend the present mandate of the United Nations Interim Force in Lebanon until 31 August 2015;

2. *Commends* the positive role of the Force, whose deployment together with the Lebanese Armed Forces has helped to establish a new strategic environment in southern Lebanon, welcomes the expansion of coordinated activities between the Force and the Lebanese Armed Forces, and calls for further enhancement of this cooperation;

[10] United Nations, *Treaty Series*, vol. 2051, No. 35457.

[11] S/2012/151.

3. *Welcomes*, in this regard, the engagement of the Force and the Lebanese Armed Forces in the strategic dialogue, which aims at carrying out analysis of ground forces and maritime assets and setting a series of benchmarks reflecting the correlation between the capacities and responsibilities of the Force vis-à-vis those of the Lebanese Armed Forces, with a view to identifying Lebanese Armed Forces requirements for implementing tasks mandated in resolution 1701 (2006), and in this regard is encouraged by the progress made in the formalization of a regular strategic dialogue mechanism between the Lebanese Armed Forces and the Force;

4. *Commends*, in this context, the Lebanese Armed Forces for their efforts regarding their wider capabilities development plan, of which the strategic dialogue plan forms a separate but integral component, consistent with the relevant recommendations of the strategic review of the Force,[11] encourages Member States to support the Lebanese Armed Forces, in particular through the established coordination tools of international assistance to build up Lebanese Armed Forces capabilities, including through training, as these forces are a central pillar of the country's stability; and recognizes in this regard the importance of the International Support Group for Lebanon and the related meetings held in Paris and Rome, as well as substantial contributions already made by some donors;

5. *Strongly calls upon* all parties concerned to respect the cessation of hostilities, to prevent any violation of the Blue Line and to respect it in its entirety and to cooperate fully with the United Nations and the Force;

6. *Welcomes*, in this regard, the constructive role played by the tripartite mechanism in facilitating coordination and in de-escalating tensions, and expresses support for the efforts of the Force to engage with both parties to further develop liaison and coordination arrangements;

7. *Urges* all parties to abide scrupulously by their obligation to respect the safety of the Force and other United Nations personnel and to ensure that the freedom of movement of the Force is fully respected and unimpeded, in conformity with its mandate and its rules of engagement, including by avoiding any course of action which endangers United Nations personnel, and in this regard calls for further cooperation between the Force and the Lebanese Armed Forces, in particular regarding coordinated and adjacent patrols, welcomes the commitment of the Lebanese authorities to protect the movements of the Force, and reiterates its call for the rapid finalization of the investigation launched by Lebanon regarding the attacks of 27 May, 26 July and 9 December 2011 in order to bring to justice the perpetrators of those attacks;

8. *Also urges* all parties to cooperate fully with the Security Council and the Secretary-General to make tangible progress towards a permanent ceasefire and a long-term solution as envisioned in resolution 1701 (2006), and emphasizes that more work remains to be done by the parties to advance the full implementation of resolution 1701 (2006);

9. *Urges* the Government of Israel to expedite the withdrawal of its army from northern Ghajar without further delay in coordination with the Force, which has actively engaged Israel and Lebanon to facilitate such a withdrawal;

10. *Reaffirms its call upon* all States to fully support and respect the establishment between the Blue Line and the Litani River of an area free of any armed personnel, assets and weapons other than those of the Government of Lebanon and the Force;

11. *Welcomes* the efforts being undertaken by the Force to implement the Secretary-General's zero-tolerance policy on sexual exploitation and abuse and to ensure full compliance of its personnel with the United Nations code of conduct, requests the Secretary-General to continue to take all necessary action in this regard and to keep the Council informed, and urges troop-contributing countries to take preventive and disciplinary action to ensure that such acts are properly investigated and punished in cases involving their personnel;

12. *Requests* the Secretary-General to continue to report to the Council on the implementation of resolution 1701 (2006) every four months or at any time as he deems appropriate;

13. *Stresses* the importance of, and the need to achieve, a comprehensive, just and lasting peace in the Middle East, based on all its relevant resolutions, including resolutions 242 (1967) of 22 November 1967, 338 (1973) of 22 October 1973, 1515 (2003) of 19 November 2003 and 1850 (2008) of 16 December 2008;

14. *Decides* to remain actively seized of the matter.

Adopted unanimously at the 7248th meeting.

Decisions

At its 7252nd meeting, on 28 August 2014, the Security Council considered the item entitled:

"The situation in the Middle East

"Report of the Secretary-General on the implementation of Security Council resolutions 2139 (2014) and 2165 (2014) (S/2014/611)".

At the same meeting, the Council decided to extend an invitation, in accordance with rule 39 of its provisional rules of procedure, to Ms. Kyung-wha Kang, Assistant Secretary-General for Humanitarian Affairs and Deputy Emergency Relief Coordinator.

At its 7255th meeting, on 29 August 2014, the Council decided to invite the representative of Yemen to participate, without vote, in accordance with rule 37 of its provisional rules of procedure, in the discussion of the item entitled "The situation in the Middle East".

At the same meeting, following consultations among members of the Security Council, the President made the following statement on behalf of the Council:[12]

The Security Council welcomes the recent progress in Yemen's political transition, in line with the Gulf Cooperation Council initiative and implementation mechanism, including the recent meeting of the National Authority for Monitoring the Implementation of the National Dialogue Conference Outcomes held on 11 August 2014; and the economic reform agenda. The Security Council supports the President of Yemen, Mr. Abd Rabbuh Mansour Hadi, in his efforts to address the concerns of all parties within the framework of the National Dialogue Conference outcomes, urging the Yemeni authorities to expedite the process of reforms, including army and security sector reform.

The Council urges all the parties in Yemen to adhere to resolving their differences through dialogue and consultation, reject acts of violence to achieve political goals, refrain from provocation and fully abide by resolutions 2014 (2011), 2051 (2012) and 2140 (2014). Furthermore, the Council calls upon all Member States to refrain from external interference which seeks to foment conflict and instability and instead to support the political transition.

The members of the Council note with concern that the Houthis and others continue to stoke the conflict in the north in an attempt to obstruct the political transition. The Council recalls that resolution 2140 (2014) introduced targeted sanctions measures against individuals or entities engaging in or providing support for acts that threaten the peace, security or stability of Yemen. The Council supports the efforts of the Panel of Experts on Yemen in gathering and analysing information regarding the implementation of these measures, in particular incidents of undermining the political transition.

The Council expresses grave concern about the deterioration of the security situation in Yemen in the light of the action taken by the Houthis, led by Mr. Abdul Malik al-Houthi, and those who support them, to undermine the political transition and the security of Yemen. These actions include their escalating campaign to bring down the Government of Yemen; establishing camps in and around Sana'a; seeking to supplant the authority of the State by installing checkpoints on strategic routes into Sana'a; as well as ongoing fighting in Al Jawf. The Council calls upon all armed groups to refrain from any action which might exacerbate this already fragile situation.

The Council condemns the actions of Houthi forces commanded by Mr. Abdullah Yahya Al Hakim (Abu Ali al Hakim), who overran Amran, including the Yemeni Army Brigade headquarters, on 8 July 2014.

The Council calls upon the Houthis:

(*a*) To withdraw their forces from Amran and return Amran to Government of Yemen control;

(*b*) To cease all armed hostilities against the Government of Yemen in Al Jawf; and

(*c*) To remove the camps and dismantle the checkpoints they have erected in and around Sana'a.

[12] S/PRST/2014/18.

The Council condemns the growing number of attacks carried out or sponsored by Al-Qaida in the Arabian Peninsula, and expresses its determination to address this threat in accordance with the Charter of the United Nations and international law, including applicable human rights, refugee and humanitarian law, and, in this regard, through the Al-Qaida sanctions regime administered by the Security Council Committee pursuant to resolutions 1267 (1999) and 1989 (2011), and reiterates its readiness, under the above-mentioned regime, to sanction further individuals, groups, undertakings and entities who do not cut off all ties to Al-Qaida and associated groups.

The Council stresses the need for an initial draft of the constitution to be passed to the National Authority review in a timely manner in order to conduct a referendum on the constitution without undue delay.

The Council reiterates its call for comprehensive, independent and impartial investigations, consistent with international standards, into alleged human rights violations and abuses in line with the outcomes of the National Dialogue Conference and the Gulf Cooperation Council initiative and implementation mechanism. The Security Council recalls its reference in resolution 2140 (2014) to the early adoption of a law on transitional justice and national reconciliation.

The Council notes the formidable economic, security and social challenges confronting Yemen, which continue to leave many Yemenis in acute need of humanitarian assistance. It reaffirms the need to expedite economic reforms, which are a necessary part of achieving macroeconomic stability, fighting poverty and addressing the chronic humanitarian consequences of the crisis in a sustainable manner. It encourages rapid implementation of Government of Yemen plans to improve social protection, as well as urging the international community to support the humanitarian response plan, which remains underfunded. The Council also urges all parties to facilitate safe and unhindered access for humanitarian actors to reach people in need of humanitarian assistance. It also reaffirms the need for all parties to ensure the safety of civilians, including those receiving assistance, as well as the need to ensure the security of humanitarian personnel and United Nations and associated personnel.

The Council remains closely engaged on the situation in Yemen and will continue to closely follow the next steps towards a peaceful political transition. In this regard, it welcomes the continued and coordinated efforts of the Gulf Cooperation Council, the Group of Ten Ambassadors, the Secretary-General's good offices, including through his Special Adviser on Yemen, Mr. Jamal Benomar, the wider diplomatic community and the next meeting of the Friends of Yemen that will take place on 24 September 2014 in New York. The Council underscores the need for continued international support for Yemen's political transition, including through the fulfilment of commitments made by donors to support Yemen.

At its 7270th meeting, on 19 September 2014, the Council considered the item entitled:

"The situation in the Middle East

"Report of the Secretary-General on the United Nations Disengagement Observer Force for the period from 29 May to 3 September 2014 (S/2014/665)".

At the same meeting, following consultations among members of the Security Council, the President made the following statement on behalf of the Council:[13]

The Security Council reaffirms the importance of maintaining the disengagement of forces agreement of 31 May 1974 between Israel and the Syrian Arab Republic. The Council stresses that, despite the latest security challenges and the United Nations Disengagement Observer Force's temporary relocation of the majority of its personnel across the Alpha line, both parties must remain committed to the terms of the disengagement of forces agreement and scrupulously observe the ceasefire and the separation of forces. The Council also urges both parties to continue to offer support to the Force during this period of heightened security threats, and to offer the Force and the United Nations Truce Supervision Organization-Observer Group Golan safe passage and resupply when requested.

[13] S/PRST/2014/19.

The Council also reaffirms its unconditional support for the Force and the importance of maintaining the Force as a vital contributor to peace and security in the Middle East. The Council notes with concern the deteriorating security situation in the area of operation of the Force due to the ongoing Syrian conflict and the activities of several non-State armed actors, including Al-Nusrah Front, and the risk it poses to the disengagement of forces agreement and to United Nations peacekeepers serving there. In this connection, the Council recognizes the necessity of efforts to flexibly adjust the posture of the Force to minimize risk to United Nations personnel as the Force continues to implement its mandate, while emphasizing that the ultimate goal is for the peacekeepers to return to their positions in the area of operation of the Force as soon as practicable.

The Council condemns recent hostile acts against United Nations peacekeepers in the area of operation of the Force by terrorist groups and non-State armed actors designated by the Council and stresses that there can never be any justification for these attacks on and detention of United Nations peacekeepers. The Council is deeply concerned that firing in close proximity to United Nations positions and camps also significantly increases risk to United Nations personnel. To this end, the Council demands that all groups other than the Force must abandon all Force positions and the Qunaytirah crossing point and return the peacekeepers' vehicles, weapons and other equipment. The Council reiterates that the mandate, impartiality, operations, safety and security of the Force must be respected. The Council calls upon all parties to allow the Force to operate freely and to ensure full security of its personnel and full implementation of the 1974 agreement.

The Council commends peacekeepers of the Force and the United Nations Truce Supervision Operation-Observer Group Golan for their bravery in facing the threats and challenges in their area of operation, and extends its appreciation to the troop-contributing countries. The Council notes the importance of maintaining the force strength and self-defence resources of the Force at the level necessary to carry out its important mandate and to retain its quick reaction and counter-improvised explosive device capabilities, which have proved indispensable in the face of a changing security environment.

The Council urges Member States with influence to convey strongly to non-State armed actors in this area the need to halt immediately all activities that endanger United Nations peacekeepers on the ground and impede them in the implementation of their duties as mandated by the Council. The Council recalls the obligation of all Member States to ensure that any person who participates in the financing, planning, preparation or perpetration of terrorist acts or in supporting terrorist acts is brought to justice and notes the importance of this obligation with respect to terrorist acts directed against United Nations peacekeepers.

The Council requests that the Secretary-General provide an update within 30 days on steps necessary to maintain the ability of the Force to carry out its mandate, including options for monitoring the ceasefire and the separation of forces even under circumstances when security conditions constrain the Force from fully operating in the area of separation and the area of limitation on the Bravo side, and to keep the Council updated on ways it can support the continuation of this vital mission.

At its 7273rd meeting, on 30 September 2014, the Council considered the item entitled:

"The situation in the Middle East

> "Report of the Secretary-General on the implementation of Security Council resolutions 2139 (2014) and 2165 (2014) (S/2014/696)".

At the same meeting, the Council decided to extend an invitation, in accordance with rule 39 of its provisional rules of procedure, to Ms. Valerie Amos, Under-Secretary-General for Humanitarian Affairs and Emergency Relief Coordinator.

At its 7293rd meeting, on 30 October 2014, the Council considered the item entitled:

"The situation in the Middle East

> "Report of the Secretary-General on the implementation of Security Council resolutions 2139 (2014) and 2165 (2014) (S/2014/756)".

At the same meeting, the Council decided to extend an invitation, in accordance with rule 39 of its provisional rules of procedure, to Ms. Kyung-wha Kang, Assistant Secretary-General for Humanitarian Affairs and Deputy Emergency Relief Coordinator.

At its 7324th meeting, on 25 November 2014, the Council considered the item entitled:

"The situation in the Middle East

"Report of the Secretary-General on the implementation of Security Council resolutions 2139 (2014) and 2165 (2014) (S/2014/840)".

At the same meeting, the Council decided to extend an invitation, in accordance with rule 39 of its provisional rules of procedure, to Ms. Valerie Amos, Under-Secretary-General for Humanitarian Affairs and Emergency Relief Coordinator.

On 28 November 2014, the President of the Security Council addressed the following letter to the Secretary-General:[14]

I have the honour to inform you that your letter dated 25 November 2014 concerning your intention to appoint Ms. Sigrid Kaag, of the Netherlands, as the United Nations Special Coordinator for Lebanon[15] has been brought to the attention of the members of the Security Council. They take note of the intention expressed in your letter.

At its 7336th meeting, on 11 December 2014, the Council considered the item entitled:

"The situation in the Middle East

"Briefing by the Chair of the Security Council Committee established pursuant to resolution 2140 (2014)".

At its 7342nd meeting, on 15 December 2014, the Council considered the item entitled "The situation in the Middle East".

At the same meeting, the Council decided to extend an invitation, in accordance with rule 39 of its provisional rules of procedure, to Ms. Valerie Amos, Under-Secretary-General for Humanitarian Affairs and Emergency Relief Coordinator.

At its 7344th meeting, on 17 December 2014, the Council considered the item entitled "The situation in the Middle East".

Resolution 2191 (2014) of 17 December 2014

The Security Council,

Recalling its resolutions 2042 (2012) of 14 April 2012, 2043 (2012) of 21 April 2012, 2118 (2013) of 27 September 2013, 2139 (2014) of 22 February 2014, 2165 (2014) of 14 July 2014 and 2175 (2014) of 29 August 2014, and the statements by its President of 3 August 2011,[16] 21 March[17] and 5 April 2012[18] and 2 October 2013,[19]

Reaffirming its strong commitment to the sovereignty, independence, unity and territorial integrity of the Syrian Arab Republic and to the purposes and principles of the Charter of the United Nations,

Expressing outrage at the unacceptable and escalating level of violence and the killing of more than 191,000 people, including well over 10,000 children, as a result of the Syrian conflict, as reported by the Secretary-General and his Special Representative for Children and Armed Conflict,

Gravely distressed by the continued deterioration of the devastating humanitarian situation in the Syrian Arab Republic and by the fact that now more than 12.2 million people in the Syrian Arab Republic – of whom 7.6 million are internally displaced, 4.5 million are living in hard-to-reach areas and 212,000 are trapped in besieged areas,

[14] S/2014/861.

[15] S/2014/860.

[16] S/PRST/2011/16.

[17] S/PRST/2012/6.

[18] S/PRST/2012/10.

[19] S/PRST/2013/15.

including Palestinian refugees – require urgent humanitarian assistance, including medical assistance, and noting with concern that approximately one million more people have been displaced within the Syrian Arab Republic since the adoption of resolution 2165 (2014),

Gravely concerned at the lack of effective implementation of its resolutions 2139 (2014) and 2165 (2014) by the parties to the Syrian domestic conflict, recalling in this regard their legal obligations under international humanitarian law and international human rights law, as well as all the relevant decisions of the Security Council, including by ceasing all attacks against civilians and civilian objects, including those involving attacks on schools and medical facilities and the deliberate interruptions of water supply, the indiscriminate use of weapons, including artillery, barrel bombs and air strikes, indiscriminate shelling by mortars, car bombs, suicide attacks and tunnel bombs, as well as the use of starvation of civilians as a method of combat, including by the besiegement of populated areas, and the widespread use of torture, ill-treatment, arbitrary executions, extrajudicial killings, enforced disappearances and sexual and gender-based violence as well as all grave violations and abuses committed against children,

Expressing its grave concern that areas of the Syrian Arab Republic are under the control of Islamic State in Iraq and the Levant and Al-Nusrah Front and about the negative impact of their presence, violent extremist ideology and actions on stability in the Syrian Arab Republic and the region, including the devastating humanitarian impact on the civilian populations which has led to the displacement of hundreds of thousands of people, reaffirming its resolve to address all aspects of the threat posed by Islamic State in Iraq and the Levant, Al-Nusrah Front and all other individuals, groups, undertakings and entities associated with Al-Qaida, and calling for the implementation of Council resolutions 2170 (2014) of 15 August 2014 and 2178 (2014) of 24 September 2014 and the statement by its President of 28 July 2014,[20]

Strongly condemning the arbitrary detention and torture of civilians in the Syrian Arab Republic, notably in prisons and detention facilities, as well as the kidnappings, abductions, hostage-taking and forced disappearances, and demanding the immediate end of these practices and the release of all arbitrarily detained persons starting with women and children, as well as sick, wounded and elderly people, including United Nations and humanitarian personnel and journalists,

Recalling its strong condemnation in resolution 2175 (2014) of all forms of violence and intimidation to which those participating in humanitarian operations are increasingly exposed, as well as attacks on humanitarian convoys and acts of destruction and looting of their assets, and its urging of all parties involved in an armed conflict to promote the safety, security and freedom of movement of humanitarian personnel and United Nations and associated personnel and their assets, and urging that all parties to the Syrian domestic conflict must take all appropriate steps to ensure the safety and security of United Nations and associated personnel, those of its specialized agencies and all other personnel engaged in humanitarian relief activities,

Noting that, despite all the challenges, the United Nations and its implementing partners continue to deliver life-saving assistance to millions of people in need, and taking note that hard-to-reach locations in Aleppo, Idlib, Qunaytirah and Dar'a have been reached since the adoption of resolution 2165 (2014) through humanitarian aid delivered across borders, stressing, however, in this regard that most people in hard-to-reach and besieged areas remain difficult for the United Nations and its implementing partners to reach with humanitarian assistance,

Expressing deep concern at the continuing and new impediments to the delivery of humanitarian assistance across borders and across conflict lines, encouraging the United Nations humanitarian agencies and their implementing partners to take steps to scale up humanitarian deliveries into hard-to-reach and besieged areas, including by using, as effectively as possible, border crossings under resolution 2165 (2014), and noting that the United Nations monitoring mechanism is operational and is continuing its activities, including monitoring shipments and confirming their humanitarian nature, in accordance with resolution 2165 (2014),

Reaffirming the need to support the United Nations humanitarian agencies and their implementing partners in their efforts to expand the delivery of humanitarian assistance to reach all people in need in the Syrian Arab Republic, and further reaffirming its decision in resolution 2165 (2014) that all Syrian parties to the conflict shall enable the immediate and unhindered delivery of humanitarian assistance directly to people throughout the Syrian

[20] S/PRST/2014/14.

Arab Republic by the United Nations humanitarian agencies and their implementing partners, on the basis of United Nations assessments of need and devoid of any political prejudices and aims, including by immediately removing all impediments to the provision of humanitarian assistance,

Noting the role that ceasefire agreements which are consistent with humanitarian principles and international humanitarian law can play in facilitating the delivery of humanitarian assistance in order to help to save civilian lives,

Recalling the need for all parties to respect the relevant provisions of international humanitarian law and the United Nations guiding principles of humanitarian emergency assistance,

Expressing grave concern at the more than 3.2 million refugees, including more than 2.5 million women and children, who have fled the Syrian Arab Republic as a result of ongoing violence, and recognizing that the continued deterioration of the humanitarian situation in the Syrian Arab Republic is further contributing to the movement of refugees and poses risks to regional stability,

Reiterating its deep appreciation for the significant and admirable efforts that have been made by the countries of the region, notably Lebanon, Jordan, Turkey, Iraq and Egypt, to accommodate Syrian refugees, including the approximately 400,000 refugees who have fled the Syrian Arab Republic since the adoption of resolution 2165 (2014), and mindful of the immense costs and social challenges incurred by these countries as a consequence of the crisis,

Noting with concern that the international response to the Syrian and regional crisis continues to fall short of meeting the needs as assessed by host Governments and the United Nations, therefore urging once again all Member States, based on burden-sharing principles, to support the United Nations and the countries of the region, including by adopting medium- and long-term responses to alleviate the impact on communities, providing increased, flexible and predictable funding as well as increasing resettlement efforts, and taking note in this regard of the Berlin Communiqué on solidarity with refugees and their hosts of 28 October 2014,[21]

Noting with grave concern that impunity in the Syrian Arab Republic contributes to widespread violations and abuses of human rights and violations of international humanitarian law, stressing the need to end impunity for these violations and abuses, and re-emphasizing in this regard the need for those who have committed or are otherwise responsible for such violations and abuses in the Syrian Arab Republic to be brought to justice,

Emphasizing that the humanitarian situation will continue to deteriorate further in the absence of a political solution to the crisis,

Determining that the deteriorating humanitarian situation in the Syrian Arab Republic continues to constitute a threat to peace and security in the region,

Underscoring that Member States are obligated under Article 25 of the Charter to accept and carry out the decisions of the Council,

1. *Demands* that all parties to the Syrian domestic conflict, in particular the Syrian authorities, immediately comply with their obligations under international humanitarian law and international human rights law, and fully and immediately implement all the provisions of Security Council resolutions 2139 (2014) and 2165 (2014) and the statement by its President of 2 October 2013,[19] and recalls that some of the violations and abuses committed in the Syrian Arab Republic may amount to war crimes and crimes against humanity;

2. *Decides* to renew the decisions in paragraphs 2 and 3 of resolution 2165 (2014) for a period of 12 months, that is, until 10 January 2016;

3. *Also decides* to conduct, six months after the renewal of these decisions, a review of the implementation of paragraph 2 of the present resolution;

4. *Expresses its full support* for the Special Envoy of the Secretary-General for Syria, Mr. Staffan de Mistura, looks forward in particular to further advice from the Special Envoy concerning his proposals aimed at reducing violence, including through the implementation of freeze zones, emphasizes that if the violence in the

[21] A/69/630, enclosure.

Syrian Arab Republic continues to escalate, the humanitarian situation will continue to worsen, and reiterates that the only sustainable solution to the current crisis in the Syrian Arab Republic is through an inclusive and Syrian-led political process that meets the legitimate aspirations of the Syrian people, with a view to full implementation of the Geneva communiqué of 30 June 2012 endorsed in its resolution 2118 (2013) and contained in annex II thereto;

5. *Requests* the Secretary-General to report to the Council on the implementation of the present resolution and on compliance by all parties to the Syrian domestic conflict, within the framework of his reporting on resolutions 2139 (2014) and 2165 (2014);

6. *Reaffirms* that it will take further measures under the Charter of the United Nations in the event of non-compliance with the present resolution or resolution 2139 (2014) or 2165 (2014) by any party to the Syrian domestic conflict;

7. *Decides* to remain actively seized of the matter.

Adopted unanimously at the 7344th meeting.

Decision

At its 7346th meeting, on 18 December 2014, the Security Council considered the item entitled:

"The situation in the Middle East

"Report of the Secretary-General on the United Nations Disengagement Observer Force for the period from 4 September to 19 November 2014 (S/2014/859)".

Resolution 2192 (2014) of 18 December 2014

The Security Council,

Noting with concern that the situation in the Middle East is tense and is likely to remain so, unless and until a comprehensive settlement covering all aspects of the Middle East problem can be reached,

Having considered the report of the Secretary-General of 28 November 2014 on the United Nations Disengagement Observer Force,[22] and reaffirming its resolution 1308 (2000) of 17 July 2000,

Stressing that both parties must abide by the terms of the disengagement of forces agreement of 31 May 1974 between Israel and the Syrian Arab Republic and scrupulously observe the ceasefire,

Concurring with the findings of the Secretary-General that the ongoing military activities conducted by any actor in the area of separation continue to have the potential to escalate tensions between Israel and the Syrian Arab Republic, jeopardize the ceasefire between the two countries, and pose a risk to the local civilian population and United Nations personnel on the ground,

Expressing grave concern at all violations of the disengagement of forces agreement,

Stressing that there should be no military forces in the area of separation other than those of the Force,

Strongly condemning the recent intense fighting in the area of separation, calling upon all parties to the Syrian domestic conflict to cease military actions in the area of operation of the Force and to respect international humanitarian law, and further condemning the use by armed Syrian extremist groups of improvised explosive devices in the area of operation of the Force,

Condemning the use of heavy weapons by both the Syrian armed forces and armed groups in the ongoing Syrian conflict in the area of separation, including the use of tanks by the Syrian armed forces and opposition during clashes,

Echoing the Secretary-General's call upon all parties to the Syrian domestic conflict to cease military actions throughout the country, including in the area of operation of the Force,

[22] S/2014/859.

Strongly condemning the incidents threatening the safety and security of United Nations personnel in recent months, including the detention of 45 Force peacekeepers by Al-Nusrah Front, stressing that there can never be any justification for these attacks on and detention of United Nations peacekeepers, and emphasizing the need to hold those responsible accountable,

Reaffirming its readiness to consider listing individuals, groups, undertakings and entities providing support to Islamic State in Iraq and the Levant or to Al-Nusrah Front, including those who are financing, arming, planning or recruiting for Islamic State in Iraq and the Levant or Al-Nusrah Front and all other individuals, groups, undertakings and entities associated with Al-Qaida under the Al-Qaida sanctions regime pursuant to resolutions 1267 (1999) of 15 October 1999 and 1989 (2011) of 17 June 2011, including those participating in or otherwise supporting attacks against United Nations peacekeepers,

Recognizing the necessity of efforts to flexibly adjust the posture of the Force on a temporary basis to minimize the security risk to United Nations personnel as the Force continues to implement its mandate, while emphasizing that the ultimate goal is for the peacekeepers to return to their positions in the area of operation of the Force as soon as practicable,

Underscoring the need for the Force to have at its disposal all means and resources necessary to carry out its mandate safely and securely, and recalling that the theft of United Nations weapons and ammunition, vehicles and other assets and the looting and destruction of United Nations facilities are unacceptable,

Expressing its profound appreciation to the military and civilian personnel of the Force, including those from Observer Group Golan, for their service and continued contribution in an increasingly challenging operating environment, underscoring the important contribution that the continued presence of the Force makes to peace and security in the Middle East, welcoming steps taken to enhance the safety and security of personnel of the Force, including Observer Group Golan personnel, and stressing the need for continued vigilance to ensure the safety and security of Force and Observer Group Golan personnel,

1. *Calls upon* the parties concerned to implement immediately its resolution 338 (1973) of 22 October 1973;

2. *Stresses* the obligation on both parties to scrupulously and fully respect the terms of the disengagement of forces agreement of 31 May 1974, calls upon the parties to exercise maximum restraint and prevent any breaches of the ceasefire and the area of separation, and underscores that there should be no military activity of any kind in the area of separation, including military operations by the Syrian Arab Armed Forces;

3. *Underlines* that there should be no military activity of the armed opposition groups in the area of separation, and urges Member States to convey strongly to the Syrian armed opposition groups in the area of operation of the United Nations Disengagement Observer Force the need to halt all activities that endanger United Nations peacekeepers on the ground and to accord the United Nations personnel on the ground the freedom to carry out their mandate safely and securely;

4. *Calls upon* all groups other than the Force to abandon all Force positions and the Qunaytirah crossing point and to return the peacekeepers' vehicles, weapons and other equipment;

5. *Calls upon* all parties to cooperate fully with the operations of the Force, to respect its privileges and immunities and to ensure its freedom of movement, as well as the security of and unhindered and immediate access for the United Nations personnel carrying out their mandate, including the unimpeded delivery of Force equipment and the temporary use of alternative ports of entry and departure, as required, to ensure safe and secure troop rotation and resupply activities, in conformity with existing agreements, and urges prompt reporting by the Secretary-General to the Security Council and troop-contributing countries of any actions that impede the ability of the Force to fulfil its mandate;

6. *Welcomes* the efforts being undertaken by the Force to implement the Secretary-General's zero-tolerance policy on sexual exploitation and abuse and to ensure full compliance of its personnel with the United Nations code of conduct, requests the Secretary-General to continue to take all necessary action in this regard and to keep the Council informed, and urges troop-contributing countries to take preventive and disciplinary action to ensure that such acts are properly investigated and punished in cases involving their personnel;

7. *Decides* to renew the mandate of the Force for a period of six months, that is, until 30 June 2015, and requests the Secretary-General to ensure that the Force has the required capacity and resources to fulfil the mandate in a safe and secure way;

8. *Requests* the Secretary-General to report every 90 days on developments in the situation and the measures taken to implement resolution 338 (1973).

Adopted unanimously at the 7346th meeting.

Decisions

On 26 December 2014, the President of the Security Council addressed the following letter to the Secretary-General:[23]

> I have the honour to inform you that your letter dated 23 December 2014,[24] in which you express your intention to extend the mandate of the Special Tribunal for Lebanon for a period of three years from 1 March 2015, in accordance with article 21, paragraph 2, of the annex to Security Council resolution 1757 (2007), has been brought to the attention of the members of the Council. They take note of the intention expressed in your letter.

On 15 January 2015, the President of the Security Council addressed the following letter to the Secretary-General:[25]

> I have the honour to inform you that your letter dated 13 January 2015 concerning your intention to appoint Major General Purna Chandra Thapa, of Nepal, as the Head of Mission and Force Commander of the United Nations Disengagement Observer Force[26] has been brought to the attention of the members of the Security Council. They take note of the intention expressed in your letter.

At its 7369th meeting, on 28 January 2015, the Council decided to invite the representative of the Syrian Arab Republic to participate, without vote, in accordance with rule 37 of its provisional rules of procedure, in the discussion of the item entitled:

"The situation in the Middle East

> "Report of the Secretary-General on the implementation of Security Council resolutions 2139 (2014), 2165 (2014) and 2191 (2014) (S/2015/48)".

At the same meeting, the Council also decided to extend an invitation, in accordance with rule 39 of its provisional rules of procedure, to Ms. Kyung-wha Kang, Assistant Secretary-General for Humanitarian Affairs and Deputy Emergency Relief Coordinator.

At its 7381st meeting, on 12 February 2015, the Council decided to invite the representatives of Qatar and Yemen to participate, without vote, in accordance with rule 37 of its provisional rules of procedure, in the discussion of the item entitled "The situation in the Middle East".

At the same meeting, the Council also decided to extend an invitation, in accordance with rule 39 of its provisional rules of procedure, to Mr. Jamal Benomar, Special Adviser to the Secretary-General on Yemen.

At its 7382nd meeting, on 15 February 2015, the Council considered the item entitled "The situation in the Middle East".

Resolution 2201 (2015)
of 15 February 2015

The Security Council,

Recalling its resolutions 2014 (2011) of 21 October 2011, 2051 (2012) of 12 June 2012 and 2140 (2014) of 26 February 2014 and the statements by its President of 15 February 2013[27] and 29 August 2014,[12]

---

[23] S/2014/950.

[24] S/2014/949.

[25] S/2015/30.

[26] S/2015/29.

[27] S/PRST/2013/3.

Reaffirming its strong commitment to the unity, sovereignty, independence and territorial integrity of Yemen, and its commitment to stand by the people of Yemen,

Supporting the efforts of the Gulf Cooperation Council, and commending its engagement in assisting the political transition in Yemen,

Deploring the unilateral actions taken by the Houthis to dissolve parliament and take over Yemen's government institutions, which have seriously escalated the situation, expressing alarm at the acts of violence committed by the Houthis and their supporters, which have undermined the political transition process in Yemen and jeopardized the security, stability, sovereignty and unity of Yemen,

Emphasizing that the political transitional process agreed upon by the parties in the Gulf Cooperation Council initiative and its implementation mechanism, the outcomes of the comprehensive National Dialogue Conference and the Peace and National Partnership Agreement has been undermined,

Expressing grave concern that the Houthis are holding officials of the Government of Yemen, including the President, Mr. Abd Rabbuh Mansour Hadi, the Prime Minister, Mr. Khalid Bahah, and members of the Cabinet, under house arrest,

Expressing grave concern also over reports of the use of child soldiers by Houthi forces, Ansar al-Sharia and government forces,

Underscoring the importance of all parties allowing all Yemenis to assemble peacefully without fear of attack, injury, arrest or retaliation,

Noting the formidable economic, security and social challenges confronting Yemen, which have left many Yemenis in acute need of humanitarian assistance,

Emphasizing the need for the return to the implementation of the Gulf Cooperation Council initiative and its implementation mechanism and the outcomes of the comprehensive National Dialogue Conference, including drafting a new constitution, electoral reform, the holding of a referendum on the draft constitution and timely general elections, to avoid further deterioration of the humanitarian and security situation in Yemen,

Reiterating the need for comprehensive, independent and impartial investigations consistent with international standards into alleged human rights violations and abuses in line with the outcomes of the comprehensive National Dialogue Conference and the Gulf Cooperation Council initiative and its implementation mechanism, to ensure full accountability,

Stressing that the solution to the situation in Yemen is through a peaceful, inclusive, orderly and Yemeni-led political transition process that meets the legitimate demands and aspirations of the Yemeni people for peaceful change and meaningful political, economic and social reform, as set out in the Gulf Cooperation Council initiative and its implementation mechanism, the outcomes of the comprehensive National Dialogue Conference and the Peace and National Partnership Agreement, and in this regard reaffirms its full support for, and commitment to, the efforts of the Special Adviser to the Secretary-General on Yemen, Mr. Jamal Benomar,

Condemning the growing number of attacks carried out or sponsored by Al-Qaida in the Arabian Peninsula, and expresses its determination to address this threat in accordance with the Charter of the United Nations and international law, including applicable human rights, refugee and humanitarian law and, in this regard, through the Al-Qaida sanctions regime administered by the Security Council Committee pursuant to resolutions 1267 (1999) and 1989 (2011), and reiterates its readiness, under the above-mentioned regime, to sanction further individuals, groups, undertakings and entities who do not cut off all ties to Al-Qaida and associated groups,

Expressing concern at the ability of Al-Qaida in the Arabian Peninsula to benefit from the deterioration of the political and security situation in Yemen, mindful that any acts of terrorism are criminal and unjustifiable regardless of their motivation, whenever, wherever and by whomsoever committed,

Recalling its determination in resolution 2140 (2014) that the situation in Yemen constitutes a threat to international peace and security,

1. *Strongly deplores* actions taken by the Houthis to dissolve parliament and take over Yemen's government institutions, including acts of violence;

2. *Reiterates its call* for all parties in Yemen to adhere to resolving their differences through dialogue and consultation, reject acts of violence to achieve political goals and refrain from provocation and all unilateral actions to undermine the political transition;

3. *Expresses grave concern* over the takeover by the Houthis of State media outlets, and rejects the use of the media to incite violence;

4. *Strongly calls upon* all parties, in particular the Houthis, to abide by the Gulf Cooperation Council initiative and its implementation mechanism, the outcomes of the comprehensive National Dialogue Conference and the Peace and National Partnership Agreement and its security annex, which provide for a Yemeni-led democratic transition;

5. *Urges* all parties, in particular the Houthis, to accelerate inclusive United Nations-brokered negotiations, to continue the political transition in order to reach a consensus solution in accordance with the Gulf Cooperation Council initiative and its implementation mechanism, the outcomes of the comprehensive National Dialogue Conference and the Peace and National Partnership Agreement and its security annex and to implement it;

6. *Also urges* all parties to agree upon and announce publicly dates for completing the constitutional consultation process, to hold a referendum on the constitution and to conduct elections under the new electoral law pursuant to the new constitution;

7. *Demands* that the Houthis immediately and unconditionally:

(*a*) Engage in good faith in the United Nations-brokered negotiations;

(*b*) Withdraw their forces from government institutions, including in the capital, Sana'a, and normalize the security situation in the capital and other provinces, and relinquish government and security institutions;

(*c*) Safely release President Hadi, Prime Minister Bahah, members of the Cabinet and all individuals under house arrest or arbitrarily detained;

(*d*) Refrain from further unilateral actions that could undermine the political transition and the security of Yemen;

8. *Also demands* that all parties in Yemen cease all armed hostilities against the people and the legitimate authorities of Yemen and relinquish the arms seized from Yemen's military and security institutions, in accordance with the Peace and National Partnership Agreement and its security annex;

9. *Calls upon* all Member States to refrain from external interference which seeks to foment conflict and instability and instead to support the political transition;

10. *Calls upon* all parties to abide by commitments to ensure the security of the diplomatic community and its premises;

11. *Requests* the Secretary-General to continue his good offices role, notes with appreciation the work of his Special Adviser on Yemen, Mr. Jamal Benomar, stresses the importance of the United Nations' close coordination with international partners, including the Gulf Cooperation Council, the Group of Ambassadors in Sana'a and other actors, in order to contribute to the successful transition;

12. *Also requests* the Secretary-General to continue to coordinate assistance from the international community in support of the transition, and to propose options for strengthening the Office of the Special Adviser to enable him to fulfil his mandate, including on United Nations assistance for finalizing and adopting the draft constitution, undertaking electoral reform, holding general elections and creating mechanisms for disarmament, demobilization and reintegration as well as security sector reform;

13. *Further requests* the Secretary-General to report on the implementation of the present resolution and to continue to report on developments in Yemen, including on the implementation of the Gulf Cooperation Council initiative and its implementation mechanism, the outcomes of the comprehensive National Dialogue Conference and the Peace and National Partnership Agreement and its security annex, within 15 days of the date of adoption of the present resolution and every 60 days thereafter;

14. *Declares its readiness* to take further steps in case of non-implementation by any Yemeni party of the present resolution, in particular paragraphs 5 to 8 above;

15. *Decides* to remain actively seized of the matter.

Adopted unanimously at the 7382nd meeting.

Decision

At its 7390th meeting, on 24 February 2015, the Security Council considered the item entitled:

"The situation in the Middle East

"Letter dated 20 February 2015 from the Panel of Experts on Yemen established pursuant to resolution 2140 (2014) addressed to the President of the Security Council (S/2015/125)".

Resolution 2204 (2015) of 24 February 2015

The Security Council,

Recalling its resolutions 2014 (2011) of 21 October 2011, 2051 (2012) of 12 June 2012, 2140 (2014) of 26 February 2014 and 2201 (2015) of 15 February 2015 and the statements by its President of 15 February 2013[27] and 29 August 2014[12] concerning Yemen,

Reaffirming its strong commitment to the unity, sovereignty, independence and territorial integrity of Yemen,

Expressing concern at the ongoing political, security, economic and humanitarian challenges in Yemen, including the ongoing violence, and threats arising from the illicit transfer, destabilizing accumulation and misuse of weapons,

Reiterating its call for all parties in Yemen to adhere to resolving their differences through dialogue and consultation, reject acts of violence to achieve political goals, and refrain from provocation,

Expressing its support for and commitment to the work of the Special Adviser to the Secretary-General on Yemen, Mr. Jamal Benomar, in support of the Yemeni transition process,

Recalling the listing of Al-Qaida in the Arabian Peninsula and associated individuals on the Al-Qaida Sanctions List established by the Security Council Committee pursuant to resolutions 1267 (1999) and 1989 (2011), and stressing in this regard the need for robust implementation of the measures in paragraph 1 of resolution 2161 (2014) of 17 June 2014 as a significant tool in combating terrorist activity in Yemen,

Noting the critical importance of effective implementation of the sanctions regime imposed pursuant to resolution 2140 (2014), including the key role that Member States from the region can play in this regard, and encouraging efforts to further enhance cooperation,

Determining that the situation in Yemen continues to constitute a threat to international peace and security,

Acting under Chapter VII of the Charter of the United Nations,

1. *Reaffirms* the need for the full and timely implementation of the political transition following the comprehensive National Dialogue Conference, in line with the Gulf Cooperation Council initiative and implementation mechanism and the Peace and National Partnership Agreement and in accordance with resolutions 2014 (2011), 2051 (2012) and 2140 (2014), and with regard to the expectations of the Yemeni people;

2. *Decides* to renew until 26 February 2016 the measures imposed by paragraphs 11 and 15 of resolution 2140 (2014), and reaffirms the provisions of paragraphs 12 to 14 and 16 of resolution 2140 (2014);

Designation criteria

3. *Reaffirms* that the provisions of paragraphs 11 and 15 of resolution 2140 (2014) shall apply to individuals or entities designated by the Security Council Committee established pursuant to paragraph 19 of resolution 2140 (2014) (the Committee) as engaging in or providing support for acts that threaten the peace, security or stability of Yemen;

Reporting

4. *Decides* to extend until 25 March 2016 the mandate of the Panel of Experts on Yemen as set out in paragraph 21 of resolution 2140 (2014), expresses its intention to review the mandate and take appropriate action regarding further extension no later than 25 February 2016, and requests the Secretary-General to take the necessary administrative measures as expeditiously as possible to re-establish the Panel of Experts, in consultation with the Committee, for a period of 13 months from the date of the present resolution, drawing, as appropriate, on the expertise of the members of the Panel established pursuant to resolution 2140 (2014);

5. *Requests* the Panel of Experts to provide a midterm update to the Committee no later than 24 September 2015, and a final report no later than 24 January 2016 to the Council, after discussion with the Committee;

6. *Directs* the Panel of Experts to cooperate with other relevant expert groups established by the Council to support the work of its sanctions committees, in particular the Analytical Support and Sanctions Monitoring Team whose mandate was established by resolution 1526 (2004) of 30 January 2004 and extended by resolution 2161 (2014);

7. *Urges* all parties and all Member States, as well as international, regional and subregional organizations, to ensure cooperation with the Panel of Experts, and further urges all Member States involved to ensure the safety of the members of the Panel and unhindered access, in particular to persons, documents and sites, in order for the Panel to execute its mandate;

8. *Emphasizes* the importance of holding consultations with concerned Member States, as may be necessary, in order to ensure full implementation of the measures set forth in the present resolution;

9. *Calls upon* all Member States to report to the Committee within 90 days of the adoption of the present resolution on the steps they have taken with a view to implementing effectively the measures imposed by paragraphs 11 and 15 of resolution 2140 (2014);

10. *Reaffirms* its intention to keep the situation in Yemen under continuous review and its readiness to review the appropriateness of the measures contained in the present resolution, including the strengthening, modification, suspension or lifting of the measures, as may be needed at any time in the light of developments;

United Nations involvement

11. *Requests* the Secretary-General to continue his good offices role, notes with appreciation the work of his Special Adviser on Yemen, Mr. Jamal Benomar, and stresses the importance of the United Nations' close coordination with international partners, including the Gulf Cooperation Council, the Group of Ambassadors in Sana'a and other actors, in order to contribute to the successful transition;

12. *Also requests* the Secretary-General to continue to coordinate assistance from the international community in support of the transition and to propose options for strengthening the Office of the Special Adviser to enable him to fulfil his mandate, including on United Nations assistance for finalizing and adopting the draft constitution, undertaking electoral reform, holding general elections and creating mechanisms for disarmament, demobilization and reintegration as well as security sector reform;

13. *Decides* to remain actively seized of the matter.

Adopted unanimously at the 7390th meeting.

Decisions

At its 7394th meeting, on 26 February 2015, the Security Council decided to invite the representatives of Lebanon, the Syrian Arab Republic and Turkey to participate, without vote, in accordance with rule 37 of its provisional rules of procedure, in the discussion of the item entitled:

"The situation in the Middle East

"Report of the Secretary-General on the implementation of Security Council resolutions 2139 (2014), 2165 (2014) and 2191 (2014) (S/2015/124)".

At the same meeting, the Council also decided to extend invitations, in accordance with rule 39 of its provisional rules of procedure, to Ms. Kyung-wha Kang, Assistant Secretary-General for Humanitarian Affairs and Deputy Emergency Relief Coordinator, and Mr. António Guterres, United Nations High Commissioner for Refugees.

At its 7401st meeting, on 6 March 2015, the Council decided to invite the representatives of Albania, Australia, Austria, Belgium, Bulgaria, Canada, Croatia, Cyprus, the Czech Republic, Denmark, Estonia, Finland, Germany, Hungary, Iceland, Ireland, Israel, Italy, Latvia, Luxembourg, Malta, Montenegro, the Netherlands, Norway, Poland, Portugal, the Republic of Korea, Romania, Serbia, Slovakia, Slovenia and Sweden to participate, without vote, in accordance with rule 37 of its provisional rules of procedure, in the discussion of the item entitled:

"The situation in the Middle East

"Letter dated 25 February 2015 from the Secretary-General addressed to the President of the Security Council (S/2015/138)".

Resolution 2209 (2015)
of 6 March 2015

The Security Council,

Recalling the Protocol for the Prohibition of the Use in War of Asphyxiating, Poisonous or Other Gases, and of Bacteriological Methods of Warfare,[28] and the Convention on the Prohibition of the Development, Production, Stockpiling and Use of Chemical Weapons and on Their Destruction,[29] and Security Council resolutions 1540 (2004) of 28 April 2004 and 2118 (2013) of 27 September 2013,

Recalling also that in resolution 2118 (2013), the Council decided that the Syrian Arab Republic shall not use, develop, produce, otherwise acquire, stockpile or retain chemical weapons, or transfer, directly or indirectly, chemical weapons to other States or non-State actors and that the Council underscored that no party in the Syrian Arab Republic should use, develop, produce, acquire, stockpile, retain or transfer chemical weapons,

Recalling further that the Syrian Arab Republic acceded to the Convention, noting that the use of any toxic chemical, such as chlorine, as a chemical weapon in the Syrian Arab Republic is a violation of resolution 2118 (2013), and further noting that any such use by the Syrian Arab Republic would constitute a violation of the Convention,

Noting that chlorine was the chemical first used as a chemical weapon on a large scale in the Battle of Ypres in April 1915,

Noting also the first, second and third reports of the Organization for the Prohibition of Chemical Weapons fact-finding mission, which was mandated to establish the facts surrounding allegations of the use of toxic chemicals for hostile purposes in the Syrian Arab Republic,[30]

Noting further the decision of 4 February 2015 of the Executive Council of the Organization for the Prohibition of Chemical Weapons,[31] in which the Executive Council, while stating diverse views on these reports, expressed serious concern regarding the findings of the fact-finding mission, made with a high degree of confidence, that chlorine has been used repeatedly and systematically as a weapon in the Syrian Arab Republic,

Noting that this is the first ever documented instance of the use of toxic chemicals as weapons within the territory of a State party to the Convention,

Reaffirming that the use of chemical weapons constitutes a serious violation of international law, and reiterating that those individuals responsible for any use of chemical weapons must be held accountable,

---

[28] League of Nations, *Treaty Series*, vol. XCIV, No. 2138.

[29] United Nations, *Treaty Series*, vol. 1974, No. 33757.

[30] S/2015/138, enclosures II–IV.

[31] S/2015/95, enclosure.

1. *Condemns in the strongest terms* any use of any toxic chemical, such as chlorine, as a weapon in the Syrian Arab Republic;

2. *Expresses deep concern* that toxic chemicals have been used as a weapon in the Syrian Arab Republic as concluded with a high degree of confidence by the Organization for the Prohibition of Chemical Weapons fact-finding mission, and notes that such use of toxic chemicals as a weapon would constitute a violation of resolution 2118 (2013) and of the Convention on the Prohibition of the Development, Production, Stockpiling and Use of Chemical Weapons and on Their Destruction;[29]

3. *Recalls* its decision that the Syrian Arab Republic shall not use, develop, produce, otherwise acquire, stockpile or retain chemical weapons, or transfer, directly or indirectly, chemical weapons to other States or non-State actors;

4. *Reiterates* that no party in the Syrian Arab Republic should use, develop, produce, acquire, stockpile, retain or transfer chemical weapons;

5. *Expresses support* for the decision of 4 February 2015 of the Executive Council of the Organization for the Prohibition of Chemical Weapons to continue the work of the fact-finding mission, in particular to study all available information relating to allegations of use of chemical weapons in the Syrian Arab Republic,[31] and welcomes the intention of the Director-General of the Organization to include further reports of the mission as part of his monthly reports to the Security Council;

6. *Stresses* that those individuals responsible for any use of chemicals as weapons, including chlorine or any other toxic chemical, must be held accountable, and calls upon all parties in the Syrian Arab Republic to extend their full cooperation to the fact-finding mission;

7. *Recalls* the decisions made by the Security Council in resolution 2118 (2013), and in this context decides, in the event of future non-compliance with resolution 2118 (2013), to impose measures under Chapter VII of the Charter of the United Nations;

8. *Decides* to remain actively seized of the matter.

Adopted at the 7401st meeting
by 14 votes to none, with 1 abstention
(Bolivarian Republic of Venezuela).

Decisions

At its 7409th meeting, on 19 March 2015, the Security Council decided to invite the representative of Lebanon to participate, without vote, in accordance with rule 37 of its provisional rules of procedure, in the discussion of the item entitled:

"The situation in the Middle East

"Report of the Secretary-General on the implementation of Security Council resolution 1701 (2006) (S/2015/147)".

At the same meeting, following consultations among members of the Security Council, the President made the following statement on behalf of the Council:[32]

The Security Council has been briefed by the United Nations Special Coordinator for Lebanon, Ms. Sigrid Kaag, and the Assistant-Secretary-General for Peacekeeping Operations, Mr. Edmond Mulet, following the report of the Secretary-General on the implementation of Security Council resolution 1701 (2006).[33] The Council expresses its appreciation for the work of Mr. Derek Plumbly as the Special Coordinator from 2012 to 2014 and welcomes the appointment and initial efforts of Ms. Kaag as the new Special Coordinator.

[32] S/PRST/2015/7.

[33] S/2015/147.

The Council recalls all its previous resolutions and the statements by its President on the situation in Lebanon. The Council reaffirms its strong support for the territorial integrity, sovereignty and political independence of Lebanon.

The Council expresses its deep concern following the recent incidents which occurred across the Blue Line and in the area of operation of the United Nations Interim Force in Lebanon. The Council stresses that such violence and the presence of unauthorized weapons in the area of operation of the Force violates resolution 1701 (2006) and the cessation of hostilities. It underlines the risk that such events could lead to a new conflict that none of the parties or the region can afford. It urges all parties to make every effort to ensure that the cessation of hostilities is sustained, exercise maximum calm and restraint and refrain from any action or rhetoric that could jeopardize the cessation of hostilities or destabilize the region.

The Council recalls its statement to the press on Lebanon of 4 February 2015. The Council urges all parties to abide scrupulously by their obligation to respect the safety of personnel of the Force and other United Nations personnel and to ensure that the freedom of movement of the Force is fully respected and unimpeded, in conformity with its mandate and rules of engagement.

The Council urges all parties to make every effort to ensure that the cessation of hostilities is sustained, and emphasizes the need for them to continue working with the Special Coordinator and the Force, including through the tripartite mechanism, to continue working in the ongoing process to delineate and mark the Blue Line in its entirety, to focus again on the goal of a permanent ceasefire and to reflect positively on ways forward on all outstanding issues in the implementation of resolutions 1701 (2006), 1680 (2006) and 1559 (2004) and other relevant Council resolutions.

The Council expresses deep concern at all violations of Lebanon's sovereignty and calls upon all parties to fully respect Lebanon's sovereignty, territorial integrity and political independence within its internationally recognized borders, in accordance with the relevant Council resolutions.

The Council expresses its concern at the 10-month stalemate in the election of the President of the Republic, which has undermined Lebanon's ability to address the security, economic and social challenges it faces and has jeopardized the normal functioning of Lebanese institutions. The Council urges Lebanese leaders to adhere to Lebanon's Constitution and National Pact and calls upon all parties to act responsibly and put Lebanon's stability and national interests ahead of partisan politics and to show the necessary flexibility and sense of urgency to apply mechanisms provided for by the Lebanese Constitution with regard to the election. It calls upon the members of parliament to uphold Lebanon's longstanding democratic tradition and to convene to elect a President without further delay. The Council supports the efforts of the Prime Minister, Mr. Tammam Salam, to govern under difficult circumstances and calls upon all parties in Lebanon to enable the Government to function effectively.

The Council expresses its deep concern at the increasing and negative impact of the Syrian crisis on the stability of Lebanon and the immediate threat to its security. It underscores its concern at the continued cross-border fire and shelling from the Syrian Arab Republic into Lebanon, which has caused death and injury among the Lebanese population, as well as incursions, abductions and arms trafficking across the Lebanese-Syrian border.

The Council also notes with deep concern all other border violations, including the presence of terrorist and violent extremist groups in Lebanese territory, the deepening involvement of some Lebanese parties in the fighting in the Syrian Arab Republic and the risks this poses for the stability of Lebanon and for the Lebanese people. The Council underscores its call upon all Lebanese parties to recommit to Lebanon's policy of disassociation and to step back from any involvement in the Syrian crisis, consistent with their commitment in the ministerial declaration of the current Government and in the Baabda Declaration of 11 June 2012.[34]

The Council condemns in the strongest terms acts of terrorism, including hostage-taking by terrorist and violent extremist groups, including Islamic State in Iraq and the Levant, also known as Da'esh, and Al-Nusrah Front, on Lebanese territory and commends the Lebanese Armed Forces and security forces for their

[34] S/2012/477, annex.

commitment and critical role played in preventing and combating terrorism within Lebanon. The Council expresses concern at the rising risk of radicalization across the region and the threat it poses to Lebanon. It also expresses concern at the abduction of Lebanese soldiers by Islamic State in Iraq and the Levant, also known as Da'esh, and Al-Nusrah Front and calls for their immediate release.

The Council encourages all parties in Lebanon to demonstrate renewed unity and determination to resist a slide into violence and conflict and notes with appreciation the messages of moderation made by Lebanon's leaders, including ongoing dialogues and recent calls to defuse sectarian tensions and to develop a national strategy to combat terrorism in Lebanon.

The Council welcomes the crucial role played by the Lebanese Armed Forces and security forces in extending and sustaining the authority of the State and responding to new security challenges. The Council further welcomes the strong international commitment to support the Lebanese Armed Forces through its capabilities development plan, including the agreement for the 3 billion United States dollars of assistance provided by Saudi Arabia in cooperation with France and the additional 1 billion dollars pledged by Saudi Arabia in 2014, the more than 1 billion dollars in security assistance by the United States of America since 2006, and the support from other Member States which has helped to strengthen the capability of the Lebanese Armed Forces to provide security for Lebanon. It also urges additional and expedited assistance in areas where the Lebanese Armed Forces are most critically in need of support, including counter-terrorism and border protection. It calls upon Lebanon's leaders and Lebanese of all communities to offer support to the Lebanese Armed Forces.

The Council also stresses the need to support the Lebanese security and judicial authorities to combat impunity. It welcomes the renewal of the mandate of the Special Tribunal for Lebanon and recalls the need to put an end to impunity in Lebanon for the long-term stability and security of Lebanon. The Council urges the Lebanese authorities to continue to meet their international obligations in this regard, including on financial matters, and also urges Member States to provide voluntary contributions as necessary. The Council calls upon all parties to fully cooperate with the Tribunal.

The Council is gravely concerned by the impact of hosting over 1,180,000 Syrian refugees registered with the Office of the United Nations High Commissioner for Refugees in Lebanon, which represents more refugees in proportion to Lebanon's national population than any other country, and its impact on host communities, on the stability and security of Lebanon and in the wider region. The Council acknowledges the extraordinary challenges that Lebanon and the Lebanese people continue to face in this regard and Lebanon's efforts to host, assist and protect those refugees and the importance of upholding human rights and humanitarian principles. It notes the recent decisions of the Government of Lebanon concerning its Syrian refugee policy and encourages the Government to continue to work closely with the United Nations, especially the Office of the High Commissioner, and partners.

The Council underscores that support to Lebanon's efforts to manage the impact of the influx of refugees, including on essential services such as education and health, is crucial to preserving the stability and security of Lebanon. The Council urges the international community to urgently disburse existing pledges and meaningfully increase assistance to Lebanon, consistent with the Lebanon Crisis Response Plan, in particular at the Third International Humanitarian Pledging Conference for Syria, to be held in Kuwait on 31 March 2015.

The Council appreciates the work of the International Support Group for Lebanon under the stewardship of the Secretary-General and its role in ensuring strong, coordinated international support for Lebanon to help the country to withstand the multiple challenges to its security and stability. The Council urges the Group to continue its work in coordination with the Special Coordinator and seek opportunities to help to address rising challenges to the security and stability of Lebanon, including the consequences of regional crises and the impact of hosting millions of refugees.

At its 7411th meeting, on 22 March 2015, the Council decided to invite the representatives of Qatar and Yemen to participate, without vote, in accordance with rule 37 of its provisional rules of procedure, in the discussion of the item entitled "The situation in the Middle East".

At the same meeting, the Council also decided to extend an invitation, in accordance with rule 39 of its provisional rules of procedure, to Mr. Jamal Benomar, Special Adviser to the Secretary-General on Yemen.

At the same meeting, following consultations among members of the Security Council, the President made the following statement on behalf of the Council:[35]

The Security Council recalls its resolutions 2014 (2011), 2051 (2012), 2140 (2014), 2201 (2015) and 2204 (2015) and the statements by its President of 15 February 2013[27] and 29 August 2014.[12]

The Council reaffirms its strong commitment to the unity, sovereignty, independence and territorial integrity of Yemen and its commitment to stand by the people of Yemen.

The Council reiterates its support for the efforts of the Gulf Cooperation Council and commends its engagement in assisting the political transition in Yemen.

The Security Council supports the legitimacy of the President of Yemen, Mr. Abd Rabbuh Mansour Hadi, and calls upon all parties and Member States to refrain from taking any actions that undermine the unity, sovereignty, independence and territorial integrity of Yemen and the legitimacy of the President of Yemen.

The Council reaffirms its full support for, and commitment to, the efforts of the Special Adviser to the Secretary-General on Yemen, Mr. Jamal Benomar, and the United Nations-brokered negotiations.

The Council condemns the ongoing unilateral actions taken by the Houthis, which undermine the political transition process in Yemen and jeopardize the security, stability, sovereignty and unity of Yemen and expresses deep concern at the insufficient implementation of resolution 2201 (2015).

The Council deplores that the Houthis have not implemented its demands in resolution 2201 (2015) to withdraw their forces from government institutions, including in the capital, Sana'a, and normalize the security situation in the capital and other provinces, and relinquish government and security institutions.

The Council expresses serious concern over continued arbitrary detention, by all parties, in particular by Houthis, contrary to resolution 2201 (2015), and reiterates its demand for the unconditional and safe release of all persons arbitrarily detained.

The Council welcomes that the Prime Minister of Yemen, Mr. Khalid Bahah, and other members of the Cabinet are no longer under the house arrest imposed by the Houthis.

The Council urges non-State actors to withdraw from government institutions, including in the south of Yemen, and to refrain from any attempt to take over such institutions.

The Council condemns in the strongest terms the airstrikes against the presidential palace in Aden and attacks at Aden International Airport. The Council condemns in the strongest terms the horrific bomb attacks of 20 March 2015 at the two mosques in Sana'a and in Saada, Yemen, which killed at least 126 and injured many more. The Council urges all sides to refrain from any further use of military force, any offensive military actions and other uses of violence.

The Council reiterates its call urging all parties to agree upon and announce publicly dates for completing the constitutional consultation process, to hold a referendum on the constitution, and to conduct elections under the new electoral law pursuant to the new constitution and in this regard demands that the parties take all actions conducive to this process, including by the full implementation of resolution 2201 (2015).

The Council reiterates its concern at the ability of Al-Qaida in the Arabian Peninsula to benefit from the deterioration of the political and security situation in Yemen, mindful that any acts of terrorism are criminal and unjustifiable regardless of their motivation, whenever, wherever and by whomsoever committed.

The Council reiterates that the solution to the situation in Yemen is through a peaceful, inclusive, orderly and Yemeni-led political transition process that meets the legitimate demands and aspirations of the Yemeni people for peaceful change and meaningful political, economic and social reform, as set out in the Gulf Cooperation Council initiative and its implementation mechanism, the outcomes of the comprehensive National Dialogue Conference and the Peace and National Partnership Agreement and its security annex.

[35] S/PRST/2015/8.

The Security Council strongly calls upon all parties, in particular the Houthis, to abide by the Gulf Cooperation Council initiative and its implementation mechanism, the outcomes of the comprehensive National Dialogue Conference and the Peace and National Partnership Agreement and its security annex and the relevant Security Council resolutions and to accelerate inclusive United Nations-brokered negotiations, including on issues relating to governance, to continue the political transition in order to reach a consensus solution and stresses the importance of full implementation of agreements reached and commitments made towards that goal.

The Council emphasizes its call for all parties in Yemen, including the Houthis, government officials, leaders of political parties and movements, and members of so-called "popular committees", to adhere to resolving their differences through dialogue and consultation, reject acts of violence to achieve political goals and refrain from provocation and all unilateral actions to undermine the political transition. The Council stresses that all parties should take concrete steps to agree and implement a consensus-based political solution to Yemen's crisis in accordance with the Gulf Cooperation Council initiative and its implementation mechanism, the outcomes of the comprehensive National Dialogue Conference and the Peace and National Partnership Agreement and its security annex.

The Security Council welcomes the intention of the President of Yemen, Mr. Abd Rabbuh Mansour Hadi, to engage in good faith in the United Nations-brokered negotiations.

The Council welcomes the intention of the Gulf Cooperation Council to convene a conference in Riyadh, upon the request of the President of Yemen, with the participation of all Yemeni parties to further support the political transition in Yemen and to complement and support the United Nations-brokered negotiations.

The Security Council reiterates the importance of all parties allowing all Yemenis to assemble peacefully without fear of attack, injury, arrest or retaliation.

The Council calls upon all parties to comply with their obligations under international law, including applicable international humanitarian law and human rights law.

The Council reiterates its demand that all parties in Yemen cease all armed hostilities against the people and the legitimate authorities of Yemen and relinquish the arms seized from Yemen's military and security institutions, in accordance with the Peace and National Partnership Agreement and its security annex.

The Council also urges all parties to facilitate safe and unhindered access for humanitarian actors to reach people in need of humanitarian assistance. It also reaffirms the need for all parties to ensure the safety of civilians, including those receiving assistance, as well as the need to ensure the security of humanitarian personnel and United Nations and associated personnel.

The Council notes with appreciation the work of the Special Adviser to the Secretary-General on Yemen, Mr. Jamal Benomar, and stresses the importance of the United Nations' close coordination with international partners, including the Gulf Cooperation Council, the Group of Ambassadors in Sana'a and other actors, in order to contribute to the successful transition.

The Security Council calls upon all Member States to refrain from external interference which seeks to foment conflict and instability and instead to support the political transition.

The Council demands that all parties fully implement all Council resolutions on Yemen, including resolution 2201 (2015).

The Council reaffirms its readiness to take further measures against any party in case of non-implementation of its resolutions on Yemen, in particular resolution 2201 (2015).

At its 7418th meeting, on 26 March 2015, the Council decided to invite the representative of the Syrian Arab Republic to participate, without vote, in accordance with rule 37 of its provisional rules of procedure, in the discussion of the item entitled:

"The situation in the Middle East

"Report of the Secretary-General on the implementation of Security Council resolutions 2139 (2014), 2165 (2014) and 2191 (2014) (S/2015/206)".

At the same meeting, the Council also decided to extend an invitation, in accordance with rule 39 of its provisional rules of procedure, to Ms. Valerie Amos, Under-Secretary-General for Humanitarian Affairs and Emergency Relief Coordinator.

At its 7419th meeting, on 27 March 2015, the Council decided to invite the representatives of Argentina, Armenia, Australia, Austria, Bahrain, Belgium, Botswana, Brazil, Bulgaria, Canada, Colombia, Croatia, Cyprus, Egypt, Germany, Greece, Guatemala, Hungary, India, Iran (Islamic Republic of), Iraq, Ireland, Israel, Italy, Japan, Kazakhstan, Latvia, Lebanon, Luxembourg, Morocco, the Netherlands, Pakistan, Poland, Portugal, the Republic of Korea, Romania, Saudi Arabia, Slovakia, Slovenia, South Africa, Sweden, Switzerland, the Syrian Arab Republic, Thailand, Turkey, Ukraine and the United Arab Emirates to participate, without vote, in accordance with rule 37 of its provisional rules of procedure, in the discussion of the item entitled:

"The situation in the Middle East

"The victims of attacks and abuses on ethnic or religious grounds in the Middle East

"Letter dated 12 March 2015 from the Chargé d'affaires a.i. of the Permanent Mission of France to the United Nations addressed to the Secretary-General (S/2015/176)".

At the same meeting, the Council also decided to extend an invitation, in accordance with rule 39 of its provisional rules of procedure, to Mr. Zeid Ra'ad Al Hussein, United Nations High Commissioner for Human Rights.

At the same meeting, the Council further decided to extend invitations, in accordance with rule 39 of its provisional rules of procedure, to His Beatitude Louis Raphaël I Sako, Patriarch of Babylon of the Chaldeans, and Ms. Vian Dakhil, member of the Iraqi parliament.

At the same meeting, the Council decided to extend invitations, in accordance with rule 39 of its provisional rules of procedure, to Mr. Stavros Lambrinidis, European Union Special Representative for Human Rights, and Mr. Ufuk Gokcen, Permanent Observer for the Organization of Islamic Cooperation to the United Nations.

At the same meeting, the Council also decided to extend an invitation to the Permanent Observer of the Observer State of the Holy See to the United Nations, in accordance with the provisional rules of procedure of the Council and its previous practice in that regard.

At its 7426th meeting, on 14 April 2015, the Council decided to invite the representative of Yemen to participate, without vote, in accordance with rule 37 of its provisional rules of procedure, in the discussion of the item entitled "The situation in the Middle East".

Resolution 2216 (2015)
of 14 April 2015

The Security Council,

Recalling its resolutions 2014 (2011) of 21 October 2011, 2051 (2012) of 12 June 2012, 2140 (2014) of 26 February 2014, 2201 (2015) of 15 February 2015 and 2204 (2015) of 24 February 2015 and the statements by its President of 15 February 2013,[27] 29 August 2014[12] and 22 March 2015,[35]

Noting the letter dated 24 March 2015 from the Permanent Representative of Yemen to the United Nations transmitting a letter from the President of Yemen, in which he informed the President of the Security Council that "he has requested from the Cooperation Council for the Arab States of the Gulf and the League of Arab States to immediately provide support, by all necessary means and measures, including military intervention, to protect Yemen and its people from the continuing aggression by the Houthis", and noting the letter dated 26 March 2015 from the Permanent Representative of Qatar to the United Nations transmitting a letter from the representatives of Bahrain, Kuwait, Qatar, Saudi Arabia and the United Arab Emirates,[36]

[36] S/2015/217.

Recalling the resolution of the twenty-sixth summit of the League of Arab States on the developments in Yemen,[37] stressing, inter alia, the necessity to resume Yemen's political transition process with the participation of all Yemeni parties in accordance with the Gulf Cooperation Council initiative and its implementation mechanism and the outcomes of the comprehensive National Dialogue Conference,

Reaffirming its strong commitment to the unity, sovereignty, independence and territorial integrity of Yemen, and its commitment to stand by the people of Yemen,

Condemning the growing number of and scale of the attacks by Al-Qaida in the Arabian Peninsula,

Expressing concern at the ability of Al-Qaida in the Arabian Peninsula to benefit from the deterioration of the political and security situation in Yemen, mindful that any acts of terrorism are criminal and unjustifiable regardless of their motivation, whenever, wherever and by whomsoever committed,

Reiterating its support for the efforts of the Gulf Cooperation Council in assisting the political transition in Yemen, and commending its engagement in this regard,

Reaffirming its support for the legitimacy of the President of Yemen, Mr. Abd Rabbuh Mansour Hadi, and reiterating its call to all parties and Member States to refrain from taking any actions that undermine the unity, sovereignty, independence and territorial integrity of Yemen and the legitimacy of the President of Yemen,

Expressing grave alarm at the significant and rapid deterioration of the humanitarian situation in Yemen, and emphasizing that the humanitarian situation will continue to deteriorate in the absence of a political solution,

Recalling that arbitrary denial of humanitarian access and depriving civilians of objects indispensable to their survival, including wilfully impeding relief supply and access, may constitute a violation of international humanitarian law,

Emphasizing the need for the return to the implementation of the Gulf Cooperation Council initiative and its implementation mechanism and the outcomes of the comprehensive National Dialogue Conference, including drafting a new constitution, electoral reform, the holding of a referendum on the draft constitution and timely general elections, to avoid further deterioration of the humanitarian and security situation in Yemen,

Reaffirming its full support for, and commitment to, the efforts of the United Nations and the Special Adviser to the Secretary-General on Yemen, in particular to the United Nations-brokered negotiations, and its support for the efforts of the Group of Ambassadors in Sana'a,

Alarmed at the military escalation by the Houthis in many parts of Yemen, including in the governorates of Ta'iz, Marib, Al Jawf and Albayda, their advance towards Aden and their seizure of arms, including missile systems, from Yemen's military and security institutions,

Condemning in the strongest terms the ongoing unilateral actions taken by the Houthis and their failure to implement the demands in resolution 2201 (2015) to immediately and unconditionally withdraw their forces from government institutions, including in the capital, Sana'a, normalize the security situation in the capital and other provinces, relinquish government and security institutions, and safely release all individuals under house arrest or arbitrarily detained, and reiterating its call upon all non-State actors to withdraw from government institutions across Yemen and to refrain from any attempts to take over such institutions,

Deploring any attempt by the Houthis to take actions that are exclusively within the authority of the legitimate Government of Yemen, and noting that such actions are unacceptable,

Expressing alarm that such actions taken by the Houthis undermine the political transition process in Yemen and jeopardize the security, stability, sovereignty and unity of Yemen,

Noting with concern the destabilizing actions taken by the former President of Yemen, Mr. Ali Abdullah Saleh, including supporting the actions of the Houthis, which continue to undermine the peace, security and stability of Yemen,

---

[37] S/2015/232, annex, resolution 625.

Welcoming the intention of the Gulf Cooperation Council to convene a conference in Riyadh, upon the request of the President of Yemen, with the participation of all Yemeni parties to further support the political transition in Yemen and to complement and support the United Nations-brokered negotiations,

Recalling its resolution 2117 (2013) of 26 September 2013, and expressing grave concern at the threat to peace and security in Yemen arising from the illicit transfer, destabilizing accumulation and misuse of small arms and light weapons,

Recognizing that the continuing deterioration of the security situation and escalation of violence in Yemen poses an increasing and serious threat to neighbouring States, and reaffirming its determination that the situation in Yemen constitutes a threat to international peace and security,

Acting under Chapter VII of the Charter of the United Nations,

1. *Demands* that all Yemeni parties, in particular the Houthis, fully implement resolution 2201 (2015) and refrain from further unilateral actions that could undermine the political transition in Yemen, and further demands that the Houthis immediately and unconditionally:

(*a*) End the use of violence;

(*b*) Withdraw their forces from all areas they have seized, including the capital, Sana'a;

(*c*) Relinquish all additional arms seized from military and security institutions, including missile systems;

(*d*) Cease all actions that are exclusively within the authority of the legitimate Government of Yemen;

(*e*) Refrain from any provocation or threats to neighbouring States, including through acquiring surface-to-surface missiles and stockpiling weapons in any bordering territory of a neighbouring State;

(*f*) Safely release Major General Mahmoud al-Subaihi, the Minister of Defence of Yemen, all political prisoners and all individuals under house arrest or arbitrarily detained; and

(*g*) End the recruitment and use of children and release all children from their ranks;

2. *Requests* the Secretary-General to report on the implementation of the present resolution and resolution 2201 (2015), in particular paragraph 1 of the present resolution, in 10 days from the adoption of the present resolution; and in case of further non-implementation expresses its intent to consider designating additional individuals and entities who are engaged in or providing support for acts that threaten the peace, security or stability of Yemen, to be subject to the measures imposed by paragraphs 11 and 15 of resolution 2140 (2014);

3. *Decides* that the individuals listed in the annex to the present resolution shall be subject to the measures imposed by paragraphs 11 and 15 of resolution 2140 (2014);

4. *Reiterates* the importance of the implementation of all measures imposed by resolution 2140 (2014), as extended in resolution 2204 (2015);

5. *Calls upon* all Yemeni parties, in particular the Houthis, to abide by the Gulf Cooperation Council initiative and its implementation mechanism, the outcomes of the comprehensive National Dialogue Conference and the relevant Security Council resolutions and to resume and accelerate inclusive United Nations-brokered negotiations, including on issues relating to governance, to continue the political transition in order to reach a consensus solution and stresses the importance of full implementation of agreements reached and commitments made towards that goal, and calls upon the parties in this regard to agree on the conditions leading to an expeditious cessation of violence, in accordance with the Charter of the United Nations and relevant Council resolutions, including the present resolution and resolution 2201 (2015);

6. *Demands* that all Yemeni parties adhere to resolving their differences through dialogue and consultation, reject acts of violence to achieve political goals, and refrain from provocation and all unilateral actions to undermine the political transition, and stresses that all parties should take concrete steps to agree and implement a consensus-based political solution to Yemen's crisis in accordance with the Gulf Cooperation Council initiative and its implementation mechanism and the outcomes of the comprehensive National Dialogue Conference;

7. *Urges* all Yemeni parties to respond positively to the request of the President of Yemen to attend a conference in Riyadh, under the auspices of the Gulf Cooperation Council, to further support the political transition in Yemen and to complement and support the United Nations-brokered negotiations;

8. *Calls upon* all parties to comply with their obligations under international law, including applicable international humanitarian law and human rights law;

9. *Reaffirms*, consistent with international humanitarian law, the need for all parties to ensure the safety of civilians, including those receiving assistance, as well as the need to ensure the security of humanitarian personnel and United Nations and associated personnel, and urges all parties to facilitate the delivery of humanitarian assistance, as well as rapid, safe and unhindered access for humanitarian actors to reach people in need of humanitarian assistance, including medical assistance;

10. *Calls upon* all parties to facilitate the evacuation by concerned States and international organizations of their civilians and personnel from Yemen, and commends steps already taken in this regard;

11. *Reaffirms* the principle of the inviolability of diplomatic and consular premises and the obligations of host Governments, including under the Vienna Convention on Diplomatic Relations of 1961[38] and under the Vienna Convention on Consular Relations of 1963,[39] to take all appropriate steps to protect diplomatic and consular premises against any intrusion or damage and to prevent any disturbance of the peace of these missions or impairment of their dignity;

12. *Requests* the Secretary-General to intensify his efforts in order to facilitate the delivery of humanitarian assistance and evacuation, including the establishment of humanitarian pauses, as appropriate, in coordination with the Government of Yemen, and calls upon Yemeni parties to cooperate with the Secretary-General to deliver humanitarian aid to those in need;

13. *Also requests* the Secretary-General to intensify his good offices role in order to enable a resumption of a peaceful, inclusive, orderly and Yemeni-led political transition process that meets the legitimate demands and aspirations of the Yemeni people, including women, for peaceful change and meaningful political, economic and social reform, as set out in the Gulf Cooperation Council initiative and its implementation mechanism and the outcomes of the comprehensive National Dialogue Conference, and stresses the importance of the United Nations' close coordination with international partners, in particular the Gulf Cooperation Council, the Group of Ambassadors in Sana'a and other actors, in order to contribute to a successful transition;

Arms embargo

14. *Decides* that all Member States shall immediately take the measures necessary to prevent the direct or indirect supply, sale or transfer to or for the benefit of Ali Abdullah Saleh, Abdullah Yahya Al Hakim, Abd Al-Khaliq Al-Huthi, and the individuals and entities designated by the Security Council Committee established pursuant to paragraph 19 of resolution 2140 (2014) (hereinafter referred to as "the Committee") pursuant to paragraph 20 (*d*) of the present resolution, the individuals and entities listed in the annex to the present resolution and those acting on their behalf or at their direction in Yemen, from or through their territories or by their nationals, or using their flag vessels or aircraft, of arms and related materiel of all types, including weapons and ammunition, military vehicles and equipment, paramilitary equipment and spare parts for the aforementioned, and technical assistance, training, financial or other assistance related to military activities or the provision, maintenance or use of any arms and related materiel, including the provision of armed mercenary personnel, whether or not originating in their territories;

15. *Calls upon* Member States, in particular States neighbouring Yemen, to inspect, in accordance with their national authorities and legislation and consistent with international law, in particular the law of the sea and relevant international civil aviation agreements, all cargo to Yemen in their territory, including seaports and airports, if the State concerned has information that provides reasonable grounds to believe the cargo contains items the supply, sale or transfer of which is prohibited by paragraph 14 of the present resolution for the purpose of ensuring strict implementation of those provisions;

16. *Decides* to authorize all Member States to, and that all Member States shall, upon discovery of items the supply, sale or transfer of which is prohibited by paragraph 14 of the present resolution, seize and dispose (such as

[38] United Nations, *Treaty Series*, vol. 500, No. 7310.

[39] Ibid., vol. 596, No. 8638.

through destruction, rendering inoperable, storage or transferring to a State other than the originating or destination States for disposal) of such items, and decides further that all Member States shall cooperate in such efforts;

17. *Requires* any Member State, when it undertakes an inspection pursuant to paragraph 15 of the present resolution, to submit promptly an initial written report to the Committee containing, in particular, an explanation of the grounds for the inspections, the results of such inspections and whether or not cooperation was provided, and, if prohibited items for supply, sale or transfer are found, further requires such Member States to submit to the Committee within 30 days a subsequent written report containing relevant details on the inspection, seizure and disposal, and relevant details of the transfer, including a description of the items, their origin and intended destination, if this information is not in the initial report;

Additional designation criteria

18. *Reaffirms* the designation criteria set out in paragraph 17 of resolution 2140 (2014) and the measures imposed by paragraphs 11 and 15 of the same, and stresses the importance of their full implementation;

19. *Also reaffirms* paragraph 18 of resolution 2140 (2014), and underscores that acts that threaten the peace, security or stability of Yemen may also include violations of the arms embargo imposed by paragraph 14 above or obstructing the delivery of humanitarian assistance to Yemen or access to, or distribution of, humanitarian assistance in Yemen;

Mandate of the sanctions committee

20. *Decides* that the Committee established pursuant to paragraph 19 of resolution 2140 (2014) shall also undertake the following tasks:

(*a*) Monitoring implementation of the measures imposed in paragraph 14 of the present resolution;

(*b*) Seeking from all States whatever information it may consider useful regarding the actions taken by them to implement effectively the measures imposed by paragraph 14 above;

(*c*) Examining and taking appropriate action on information regarding alleged non-compliance with the measures contained in the present resolution;

(*d*) Designating as may be necessary additional individuals and entities subject to the measures imposed by paragraph 14 above;

Mandate of the Panel of Experts

21. *Decides* that the mandate of the Panel of Experts on Yemen established pursuant to paragraph 21 of resolution 2140 (2014) and renewed by resolution 2204 (2015) shall also include monitoring implementation of the measures imposed by paragraph 14 above;

22. *Requests* the Secretary-General, having due regard for the increased mandate of the Panel of Experts, to increase the Panel to five members and to make the financial and security arrangements necessary to support the work of the Panel;

23. *Calls upon* the Panel of Experts to cooperate actively with other panels or groups of experts established by the Council, including the Analytical Support and Sanctions Monitoring Team of the Security Council Committee pursuant to resolutions 1267 (1999) and 1989 (2011), as relevant to the implementation of its mandate;

Commitment to review

24. *Reaffirms its readiness* to take further measures in case of non-implementation by any Yemeni party of the present resolution and resolution 2201 (2015);

25. *Decides* to remain actively seized of the matter.

Adopted unanimously at the 7426th meeting
by 14 votes to none, with 1 abstention
(Russian Federation).

Annex

1. Abdulmalik al-Houthi

Abdul Malik al-Houthi is a leader of a group that has engaged in acts that threaten the peace, security or stability of Yemen.

In September 2014, Houthi forces captured Sana'a and in January 2015 they attempted to unilaterally replace the legitimate government of Yemen with an illegitimate governing authority that the Houthis dominated. Al-Houthi assumed the leadership of Yemen's Houthi movement in 2004 after the death of his brother, Hussein Badredden al-Houthi. As leader of the group, al-Houthi has repeatedly threatened Yemeni authorities with further unrest if they do not respond to his demands and detained President Hadi, the Prime Minister and key cabinet members. Hadi subsequently escaped to Aden. The Houthis then launched another offensive towards Aden assisted by military units loyal to former president Saleh and his son, Ahmed Ali Saleh.

2. Ahmed Ali Abdullah Saleh

Ahmed Ali Saleh has engaged in acts that threaten the peace, security and stability of Yemen.

Ahmed Ali Saleh has been working to undermine President Hadi's authority, thwart Hadi's attempts to reform the military, and hinder Yemen's peaceful transition to democracy. Saleh played a key role in facilitating the Houthi military expansion. As of mid-February 2013, Ahmed Ali Saleh had issued thousands of new rifles to Republican Guard brigades and unidentified tribal shaykhs. The weapons were originally procured in 2010 and reserved to purchase the loyalties of the recipients for political gain at a later date.

After Saleh's father, former Republic of Yemen President Ali Abdullah Saleh, stepped down as President of Yemen in 2011, Ahmed Ali Saleh retained his post as commander of Yemen's Republican Guard. A little over a year later, Saleh was dismissed by President Hadi but he retained significant influence within the Yemeni military, even after he was removed from command. Ali Abdullah Saleh was designated by the United Nations under Security Council resolution 2140 (2014) in November 2014.

Decisions

At its 7433rd meeting, on 24 April 2015, the Security Council decided to invite the representatives of Lebanon, the Syrian Arab Republic and Turkey to participate, without vote, in accordance with rule 37 of its provisional rules of procedure, in the discussion of the item entitled:

"The situation in the Middle East

> "Report of the Secretary-General on the implementation of Security Council resolutions 2139 (2014), 2165 (2014) and 2191 (2014) (S/2015/264)".

At the same meeting, the Council also decided to extend invitations, in accordance with rule 39 of its provisional rules of procedure, to Ms. Valerie Amos, Under-Secretary-General for Humanitarian Affairs and Emergency Relief Coordinator, Mr. António Guterres, United Nations High Commissioner for Refugees, Ms. Angelina Jolie Pitt, Special Envoy of the United Nations High Commissioner for Refugees, and Ms. Ertharin Cousin, Executive Director of the United Nations World Food Programme.

At the same meeting, following consultations among members of the Security Council, the President made the following statement on behalf of the Council:[40]

> The Security Council recalls its resolutions 2042 (2012), 2043 (2012), 2139 (2014), 2165 (2014), 2175 (2014) and 2191 (2014) and the statements by its President of 3 August 2011[16] and 2 October 2013.[19]

> The Council reaffirms its strong commitment to the sovereignty, independence, unity and territorial integrity of the Syrian Arab Republic and all other States affected by the Syrian conflict, and to the purposes and principles of the Charter of the United Nations.

[40] S/PRST/2015/10.

The Council expresses grave alarm at the significant and rapid deterioration of the humanitarian situation in the Syrian Arab Republic, including at the fact that over 220,000 people have been killed, including well over 10,000 children, since the beginning of the conflict; about half of the population have been forced to flee their homes, including over 3.9 million who have sought refuge in neighbouring countries, among whom are nearly 2.1 million children; and that more than 12.2 million people in the Syrian Arab Republic require urgent humanitarian assistance, including 440,000 civilians in besieged areas.

The Council demands that all parties to the Syrian domestic conflict immediately put an end to all forms of violence and reiterates that all parties to the Syrian domestic conflict, in particular the Syrian authorities, must comply with their applicable obligations under international humanitarian law and international human rights law and respect human rights, and reiterates its demand that they fully and immediately implement the provisions of its resolutions 2139 (2014), 2165 (2014) and 2191 (2014), particularly through facilitating the expansion of humanitarian relief operations and the immediate delivery of humanitarian assistance to hard-to-reach and besieged areas across borders and conflict lines.

The Council is alarmed that the Syrian crisis has become the largest humanitarian emergency crisis in the world today, threatening peace and security in the region with diverse implications for the neighbouring countries and the displacement of millions of Syrians into those countries, and calls for further spillover of the conflict in the Syrian Arab Republic into the neighbouring countries to be addressed.

The Council further calls for coordinated international support to the neighbouring countries hosting Syrian refugees, at their request, in addressing legitimate security concerns and ensuring the safety and security of host communities and refugees and countering radicalization, through, inter alia, the provision of support for effective border management and internal security measures.

The Council reiterates its deep appreciation for the significant and admirable efforts that have been made by the countries of the region, notably Lebanon, Jordan, Turkey, Iraq and Egypt, to accommodate Syrian refugees and is mindful of the immense costs and multifaceted challenges incurred by these countries as a consequence of the crisis.

The Council notes with deep concern that the crisis in the Syrian Arab Republic has had social, demographic, environmental and economic effects on neighbouring countries; which have exacerbated vulnerabilities; overstretched limited resources and basic social services such as health, water, sanitation, housing capacities, energy and education; aggravated unemployment; diminished trade and investment; and affected regional stability and security.

The Council emphasizes the strain placed on host country education systems by the inflow of refugees and that additional resources will be required to help the 600,000 children outside the school system to access quality education.

The Council underlines the risk of further regional destabilization if the conflict, the refugee crisis and the needs of the host countries are not adequately addressed. The Council stresses the importance of funding the humanitarian and development responses to the refugee crisis, providing support for national response plans, addressing the humanitarian needs of refugees, in particular women and children, both in camps and urban areas and through capacity-building and technical support, strengthening the resilience of host countries and communities as components of stabilizing the region, preventing radicalization and countering the threat of terrorism and foreign terrorist fighters.

The Council notes with concern that the international response to the Syrian and regional crisis continues to fall short of meeting the needs as assessed by host Governments and the United Nations, and urges all Member States, based on burden-sharing principles, to support the United Nations and the countries of the region, including by adopting medium- and long-term responses to alleviate the impact on communities, providing increased, flexible and multi-year predictable funding as well as increasing resettlement efforts, and taking note in this regard of the Berlin Communiqué on solidarity with refugees and their hosts of 28 October 2014.[21]

The Council urges donors, international financial institutions and United Nations agencies to consider financing instruments that effectively meet the unique needs of middle-income countries impacted by the Syrian conflict and address its massive structural impact on neighbouring countries.

The Council emphasizes the importance of complying with applicable international humanitarian law and refugee law, promoting and protecting the human rights of all people affected by the crisis and respecting the United Nations guiding principles of humanitarian emergency assistance, welcomes efforts by host countries in this regard and urges Member States to continue to help them in this effort.

The Council welcomes the convening of the Third International Humanitarian Pledging Conference for Syria, generously hosted by Kuwait on 31 March 2015, and the 3.6 billion United States dollars in pledges made and calls upon all Member States to ensure the timely disbursement of pledges.

The Council emphasizes that the humanitarian situation will continue to deteriorate in the absence of a political solution, expresses its full support for the Special Envoy of the Secretary-General for Syria, Mr. Staffan de Mistura, and reiterates that the only sustainable solution to the current crisis in the Syrian Arab Republic is through an inclusive and Syrian-led political process that meets the legitimate aspirations of the Syrian people, with a view to full implementation of the Geneva communiqué of 30 June 2012, endorsed by the Council and contained in annex II to its resolution 2118 (2013).

On 25 April 2015, the President of the Security Council addressed the following letter to the Secretary-General:[41]

I have the honour to inform you that your letter dated 23 April 2015 concerning your intention to appoint Mr. Ismail Ould Cheikh Ahmed, of Mauritania, as your Special Envoy for Yemen at the level of Under-Secretary-General[42] has been brought to the attention of the members of the Security Council. They take note of the intention expressed in your letter.

At its 7452nd meeting, on 28 May 2015, the Council decided to invite the representative of the Syrian Arab Republic to participate, without vote, in accordance with rule 37 of its provisional rules of procedure, in the discussion of the item entitled:

"The situation in the Middle East

"Report of the Secretary-General on the implementation of Security Council resolutions 2139 (2014), 2165 (2014) and 2191 (2014) (S/2015/368)".

At the same meeting, the Council also decided to extend an invitation, in accordance with rule 39 of its provisional rules of procedure, to Ms. Valerie Amos, Under-Secretary-General for Humanitarian Affairs and Emergency Relief Coordinator.

At its 7476th meeting, on 29 June 2015, the Council decided to invite the representative of the Syrian Arab Republic to participate, without vote, in accordance with rule 37 of its provisional rules of procedure, in the discussion of the item entitled:

"The situation in the Middle East

"Report of the Secretary-General on the implementation of Security Council resolutions 2139 (2014), 2165 (2014) and 2191 (2014) (S/2015/468)".

At the same meeting, the Council also decided to extend an invitation, in accordance with rule 39 of its provisional rules of procedure, to Ms. Kyung-wha Kang, Assistant Secretary-General for Humanitarian Affairs and Deputy Emergency Relief Coordinator.

At its 7477th meeting, on 29 June 2015, the Council considered the item entitled:

"The situation in the Middle East

"Report of the Secretary-General on the United Nations Disengagement Observer Force for the period from 3 March to 28 May 2015 (S/2015/405)".

---

[41] S/2015/284.

[42] S/2015/283.

Resolution 2229 (2015)
of 29 June 2015

The Security Council,

Noting with concern that the situation in the Middle East is tense and is likely to remain so, unless and until a comprehensive settlement covering all aspects of the Middle East problem can be reached,

Having considered the report of the Secretary-General of 3 June 2015 on the United Nations Disengagement Observer Force,[43] and reaffirming its resolution 1308 (2000) of 17 July 2000,

Stressing that both parties must abide by the terms of the disengagement of forces agreement of 31 May 1974 between Israel and the Syrian Arab Republic and scrupulously observe the ceasefire,

Concurring with the findings of the Secretary-General that the ongoing military activities conducted by any actor in the area of separation continue to have the potential to escalate tensions between Israel and the Syrian Arab Republic, jeopardize the ceasefire between the two countries, and pose a risk to the local civilian population and United Nations personnel on the ground,

Expressing grave concern at all violations of the disengagement of forces agreement,

Stressing that there should be no military forces in the area of separation other than those of the Force,

Strongly condemning the continued fighting in the area of separation, and calling upon all parties to the Syrian domestic conflict to cease military actions in the area of operation of the Force and to respect international humanitarian law,

Condemning the use of heavy weapons by both the Syrian armed forces and armed groups in the ongoing Syrian conflict in the area of separation, including the use of tanks by the Syrian armed forces and opposition during clashes,

Echoing the Secretary-General's call upon all parties to the Syrian domestic conflict to cease military actions throughout the country, including in the area of operation of the Force,

Reaffirming its readiness to consider listing individuals, groups, undertakings and entities providing support to Islamic State in Iraq and the Levant or to Al-Nusrah Front, including those who are financing, arming, planning or recruiting for Islamic State in Iraq and the Levant or Al-Nusrah Front and all other individuals, groups, undertakings and entities associated with Al-Qaida under the Al-Qaida sanctions regime pursuant to resolutions 1267 (1999) of 15 October 1999 and 1989 (2011) of 17 June 2011, including those participating in or otherwise supporting attacks against United Nations peacekeepers,

Recognizing the necessity of efforts to flexibly adjust the posture of the Force on a temporary basis to minimize the security risk to United Nations personnel as the Force continues to implement its mandate, while emphasizing that the ultimate goal is for the peacekeepers to return to their positions in the area of operation of the Force as soon as practicable,

Underscoring the need for the Force to have at its disposal all means and resources necessary to carry out its mandate safely and securely, and recalling that the theft of United Nations weapons and ammunition, vehicles and other assets and the looting and destruction of United Nations facilities are unacceptable,

Expressing its profound appreciation to the military and civilian personnel of the Force, including those from Observer Group Golan, for their service and continued contribution in an increasingly challenging operating environment, underscoring the important contribution that the continued presence of the Force makes to peace and security in the Middle East, welcoming steps taken to enhance the safety and security of personnel of the Force, including Observer Group Golan personnel, and stressing the need for continued vigilance to ensure the safety and security of Force and Observer Group Golan personnel,

Strongly condemning the incidents threatening the safety and security of United Nations personnel in recent months, including the cases of injury to four United Nations peacekeepers as a result of the ongoing Syrian conflict,

---

[43] S/2015/405.

1. *Calls upon* the parties concerned to implement immediately its resolution 338 (1973) of 22 October 1973;

2. *Stresses* the obligation on both parties to scrupulously and fully respect the terms of the disengagement of forces agreement of 31 May 1974, calls upon the parties to exercise maximum restraint and prevent any breaches of the ceasefire and the area of separation, and underscores that there should be no military activity of any kind in the area of separation, including military operations by the Syrian Arab Armed Forces;

3. *Underlines* that there should be no military activity of the armed opposition groups in the area of separation, and urges Member States to convey strongly to the Syrian armed opposition groups in the area of operation of the United Nations Disengagement Observer Force the need to halt all activities that endanger United Nations peacekeepers on the ground and to accord the United Nations personnel on the ground the freedom to carry out their mandate safely and securely;

4. *Calls upon* all groups other than the Force to abandon all positions of the Force and the Qunaytirah crossing point and to return the peacekeepers' vehicles, weapons and other equipment;

5. *Calls upon* all parties to cooperate fully with the operations of the Force, to respect its privileges and immunities and to ensure its freedom of movement, as well as the security of and unhindered and immediate access for the United Nations personnel carrying out their mandate, including the unimpeded delivery of Force equipment and the temporary use of alternative ports of entry and departure, as required, to ensure safe and secure troop rotation and resupply activities, in conformity with existing agreements, and urges prompt reporting by the Secretary-General to the Security Council and troop-contributing countries of any actions that impede the ability of the Force to fulfil its mandate;

6. *Welcomes* the efforts being undertaken by the Force to implement the Secretary-General's zero-tolerance policy on sexual exploitation and abuse and to ensure full compliance of its personnel with the United Nations code of conduct, requests the Secretary-General to continue to take all necessary action in this regard and to keep the Council informed, and urges troop-contributing countries to take preventive and disciplinary action to ensure that such acts are properly investigated and punished in cases involving their personnel;

7. *Decides* to renew the mandate of the Force for a period of six months, that is, until 31 December 2015, and requests the Secretary-General to ensure that the Force has the required capacity and resources to fulfil the mandate in a safe and secure way;

8. *Requests* the Secretary-General to report every 90 days on developments in the situation and the measures taken to implement resolution 338 (1973).

Adopted unanimously at the 7477th meeting.

Decisions

On 16 July 2015, the President of the Security Council addressed the following letter to the Secretary-General:[44]

> I have the honour to inform you that your letter dated 14 July 2015 concerning your intention to appoint Major General Arthur Davis Gawn, of New Zealand, as the Head of Mission and Chief of Staff of the United Nations Truce Supervision Organization[45] has been brought to the attention of the members of the Security Council. They take note of the intention expressed in your letter.

At its 7493rd meeting, on 28 July 2015, the Council considered the item entitled:

"The situation in the Middle East

> "Report of the Secretary-General on the implementation of Security Council resolutions 2139 (2014), 2165 (2014) and 2191 (2014) (S/2015/561)".

[44] S/2015/542.

[45] S/2015/541.

At the same meeting, the Council decided to extend an invitation, in accordance with rule 39 of its provisional rules of procedure, to Mr. Stephen O'Brien, Under-Secretary-General for Humanitarian Affairs and Emergency Relief Coordinator.

At its 7494th meeting, on 28 July 2015, the Council decided to invite the representative of Yemen to participate, without vote, in accordance with rule 37 of its provisional rules of procedure, in the discussion of the item entitled "The situation in the Middle East".

At the same meeting, the Council also decided to extend an invitation, in accordance with rule 39 of its provisional rules of procedure, to Mr. Stephen O'Brien, Under-Secretary-General for Humanitarian Affairs and Emergency Relief Coordinator.

At its 7497th meeting, on 29 July 2015, the Council considered the item entitled "The situation in the Middle East".

At the same meeting, the Council decided to extend an invitation, in accordance with rule 39 of its provisional rules of procedure, to Mr. Staffan de Mistura, Special Envoy of the Secretary-General for Syria .

B. The situation in the Middle East, including the Palestinian question[46]

Decisions

At its 7243rd meeting, on 18 August 2014, the Security Council considered the item entitled "The situation in the Middle East, including the Palestinian question".

At the same meeting, the Council decided to extend an invitation, in accordance with rule 39 of its provisional rules of procedure, to Mr. Robert H. Serry, United Nations Special Coordinator for the Middle East Peace Process and Personal Representative of the Secretary-General to the Palestine Liberation Organization and the Palestinian Authority.

At its 7266th meeting, on 16 September 2014, the Council considered the item entitled "The situation in the Middle East, including the Palestinian question".

At the same meeting, the Council decided to extend an invitation, in accordance with rule 39 of its provisional rules of procedure, to Mr. Robert H. Serry, United Nations Special Coordinator for the Middle East Peace Process and Personal Representative of the Secretary-General to the Palestine Liberation Organization and the Palestinian Authority.

At its 7281st meeting, on 21 October 2014, the Council decided to invite the representatives of Algeria, Bahrain, Belize, Brazil, Cuba, Egypt, Guatemala, Iceland, India, Indonesia, Iran (Islamic Republic of), Israel, Japan, Kazakhstan, Kuwait, Lebanon, Malaysia, Maldives, Morocco, Namibia, Nicaragua, Norway, Pakistan, Peru, the Philippines, Qatar, Saudi Arabia, South Africa, Sri Lanka, the Syrian Arab Republic, Tunisia, Turkey, Ukraine and Zimbabwe to participate, without vote, in accordance with rule 37 of its provisional rules of procedure, in the discussion of the item entitled "The situation in the Middle East, including the Palestinian question".

At the same meeting, the Council also decided to extend invitations to the Permanent Observer of the Observer State of Palestine to the United Nations and the Permanent Observer of the Observer State of the Holy See to the United Nations, in accordance with the provisional rules of procedure of the Council and its previous practice in that regard.

At the same meeting, the Council further decided to extend an invitation, in accordance with rule 39 of its provisional rules of procedure, to Mr. Thomas Mayr-Harting, Head of the Delegation of the European Union to the United Nations.

At the same meeting, the Council decided to extend an invitation, in accordance with rule 39 of its provisional rules of procedure, to Mr. Fodé Seck, Chair of the Committee on the Exercise of the Inalienable Rights of the Palestinian People.

[46] Resolutions or decisions on this question were first adopted by the Security Council in 2000.

At its 7291st meeting, on 29 October 2014, the Council decided to invite the representative of Israel to participate, without vote, in accordance with rule 37 of its provisional rules of procedure, in the discussion of the item entitled "The situation in the Middle East, including the Palestinian question".

At the same meeting, the Council also decided to extend an invitation to the Permanent Observer of the Observer State of Palestine to the United Nations, in accordance with the provisional rules of procedure of the Council and its previous practice in that regard.

At the same meeting, the Council further decided to extend an invitation, in accordance with rule 39 of its provisional rules of procedure, to Mr. Jeffrey Feltman, Under-Secretary-General for Political Affairs.

At its 7312th meeting, on 17 November 2014, the Council considered the item entitled "The situation in the Middle East, including the Palestinian question".

At the same meeting, the Council decided to extend an invitation, in accordance with rule 39 of its provisional rules of procedure, to Mr. Jens Anders Toyberg-Frandzen, Assistant Secretary-General ad interim for Political Affairs.

At its 7339th meeting, on 15 December 2014, the Council considered the item entitled "The situation in the Middle East, including the Palestinian question".

At the same meeting, the Council decided to extend an invitation, in accordance with rule 39 of its provisional rules of procedure, to Mr. Robert H. Serry, United Nations Special Coordinator for the Middle East Peace Process and Personal Representative of the Secretary-General to the Palestine Liberation Organization and the Palestinian Authority.

At its 7354th meeting, on 30 December 2014, the Council decided to invite the representative of Israel to participate, without vote, in accordance with rule 37 of its provisional rules of procedure, in the discussion of the item entitled "The situation in the Middle East, including the Palestinian question".

At the same meeting, the Council also decided to extend an invitation to the Permanent Observer of the Observer State of Palestine to the United Nations, in accordance with the provisional rules of procedure of the Council and its previous practice in that regard.

At the same meeting, the Council voted on a draft resolution contained in document S/2014/916. The result of the voting was as follows: 8 votes in favour (Argentina, Chad, Chile, China, France, Jordan, Luxembourg and Russian Federation), 2 against (Australia and United States of America) and 5 abstentions (Lithuania, Nigeria, Republic of Korea, Rwanda and United Kingdom of Great Britain and Northern Ireland). The draft resolution failed to receive the affirmative vote of nine members and was therefore not adopted.

At its 7360th meeting, on 15 January 2015, the Council decided to invite the representatives of Botswana, Brazil, Cuba, Egypt, Guatemala, Iceland, India, Indonesia, Iran (Islamic Republic of), Israel, Japan, Kazakhstan, Kuwait, Lebanon, Liechtenstein, Morocco, Pakistan, Peru, Qatar, the Republic of Korea, Saudi Arabia, South Africa, Sri Lanka, the Syrian Arab Republic, Tunisia, Turkey and Zimbabwe to participate, without vote, in accordance with rule 37 of its provisional rules of procedure, in the discussion of the item entitled "The situation in the Middle East, including the Palestinian question".

At the same meeting, the Council also decided to extend invitations, in accordance with rule 39 of its provisional rules of procedure, to Mr. Jens Anders Toyberg-Frandzen, Assistant Secretary-General ad interim for Political Affairs, and Mr. Fodé Seck, Chair of the Committee on the Exercise of the Inalienable Rights of the Palestinian People.

At the same meeting, the Council further decided to extend an invitation to the Permanent Observer of the Observer State of Palestine to the United Nations, in accordance with the provisional rules of procedure of the Council and its previous practice in that regard.

At the same meeting, the Council decided to extend an invitation, in accordance with rule 39 of its provisional rules of procedure, to Mr. Ioannis Vrailas, Deputy Head of the Delegation of the European Union to the United Nations.

On 3 February 2015, the President of the Security Council addressed the following letter to the Secretary-General:[47]

> I have the honour to inform you that your letter dated 30 January 2015 concerning your intention to appoint Mr. Nickolay Mladenov, of Bulgaria, as the United Nations Special Coordinator for the Middle East Peace Process and your Personal Representative to the Palestine Liberation Organization and the Palestinian Authority[48] has been brought to the attention of the members of the Security Council. They take note of the intention expressed in your letter.

At its 7386th meeting, on 18 February 2015, the Council considered the item entitled "The situation in the Middle East, including the Palestinian question".

At the same meeting, the Council decided to extend an invitation, in accordance with rule 39 of its provisional rules of procedure, to Mr. Jeffrey Feltman, Under-Secretary-General for Political Affairs.

At its 7417th meeting, on 26 March 2015, the Council considered the item entitled "The situation in the Middle East, including the Palestinian question".

At the same meeting, the Council decided to extend an invitation, in accordance with rule 39 of its provisional rules of procedure, to Mr. Robert H. Serry, United Nations Special Coordinator for the Middle East Peace Process and Personal Representative of the Secretary-General to the Palestine Liberation Organization and the Palestinian Authority.

At its 7430th meeting, on 21 April 2015, the Council decided to invite the representatives of Bahrain, Bangladesh, Brazil, Costa Rica, Cuba, Egypt, Guatemala, India, Indonesia, Iran (Islamic Republic of), Israel, Japan, Kazakhstan, Lebanon, Maldives, Mexico, Morocco, Namibia, Norway, Pakistan, Qatar, the Republic of Korea, Saudi Arabia, South Africa, Sri Lanka, the Syrian Arab Republic, Turkey, Ukraine and Zimbabwe to participate, without vote, in accordance with rule 37 of its provisional rules of procedure, in the discussion of the item entitled "The situation in the Middle East, including the Palestinian question".

At the same meeting, the Council also decided to extend invitations to the Deputy Permanent Observer of the Observer State of Palestine to the United Nations and the Permanent Observer of the Observer State of the Holy See to the United Nations, in accordance with the provisional rules of procedure of the Council and its previous practice in that regard.

At the same meeting, the Council further decided to extend an invitation, in accordance with rule 39 of its provisional rules of procedure, to Mr. Fodé Seck, Chair of the Committee on the Exercise of the Inalienable Rights of the Palestinian People.

At the same meeting, the Council decided to extend an invitation, in accordance with rule 39 of its provisional rules of procedure, to Mr. Thomas Mayr-Harting, Head of the Delegation of the European Union to the United Nations.

At its 7446th meeting, on 19 May 2015, the Council considered the item entitled "The situation in the Middle East, including the Palestinian question".

At the same meeting, the Council decided to extend an invitation, in accordance with rule 39 of its provisional rules of procedure, to Mr. Nickolay Mladenov, United Nations Special Coordinator for the Middle East Peace Process and Personal Representative of the Secretary-General to the Palestine Liberation Organization and the Palestinian Authority.

At its 7470th meeting, on 24 June 2015, the Council considered the item entitled "The situation in the Middle East, including the Palestinian question".

At the same meeting, the Council decided to extend an invitation, in accordance with rule 39 of its provisional rules of procedure, to Mr. Jeffrey Feltman, Under-Secretary-General for Political Affairs.

---

[47] S/2015/89.

[48] S/2015/88.

At its 7490th meeting, on 23 July 2015, the Council decided to invite the representatives of Bangladesh, Brazil, Cuba, Egypt, Guatemala, Iceland, India, Indonesia, Iran (Islamic Republic of), Israel, Japan, Kazakhstan, Kuwait, Lebanon, Maldives, Morocco, Namibia, Norway, Pakistan, Saudi Arabia, Sri Lanka, the Syrian Arab Republic, Turkey, Ukraine, the United Arab Emirates and Zimbabwe to participate, without vote, in accordance with rule 37 of its provisional rules of procedure, in the discussion of the item entitled "The situation in the Middle East, including the Palestinian question".

At the same meeting, the Council also decided to extend invitations to the Permanent Observer of the Observer State of Palestine to the United Nations and the Deputy Permanent Observer of the Observer State of the Holy See to the United Nations, in accordance with the provisional rules of procedure of the Council and its previous practice in that regard.

At the same meeting, the Council further decided to extend invitations, in accordance with rule 39 of its provisional rules of procedure, to Mr. Nickolay Mladenov, United Nations Special Coordinator for the Middle East Peace Process and Personal Representative of the Secretary-General to the Palestine Liberation Organization and the Palestinian Authority, and Mr. Fodé Seck, Chair of the Committee on the Exercise of the Inalienable Rights of the Palestinian People.

At the same meeting, the Council decided to extend an invitation, in accordance with rule 39 of its provisional rules of procedure, to Mr. Carl Hallergard, Minister Counsellor of the Delegation of the European Union to the United Nations.

THE SITUATION CONCERNING WESTERN SAHARA[49]

Decision

At its 7435th meeting, on 28 April 2015, the Security Council considered the item entitled:

"The situation concerning Western Sahara

"Report of the Secretary-General on the situation concerning Western Sahara (S/2015/246)".

Resolution 2218 (2015) of 28 April 2015

The Security Council,

Recalling and reaffirming all its previous resolutions on Western Sahara,

Reaffirming its strong support for the efforts of the Secretary-General and his Personal Envoy for Western Sahara to implement resolutions 1754 (2007) of 30 April 2007, 1783 (2007) of 31 October 2007, 1813 (2008) of 30 April 2008, 1871 (2009) of 30 April 2009, 1920 (2010) of 30 April 2010, 1979 (2011) of 27 April 2011, 2044 (2012) of 24 April 2012, 2099 (2013) of 25 April 2013 and 2152 (2014) of 29 April 2014,

Reaffirming its commitment to assist the parties to achieve a just, lasting and mutually acceptable political solution, which will provide for the self-determination of the people of Western Sahara in the context of arrangements consistent with the principles and purposes of the Charter of the United Nations, and noting the role and responsibilities of the parties in this respect,

Reiterating its call upon the parties and the neighbouring States to cooperate more fully with the United Nations and with each other and to strengthen their involvement to end the current impasse and to achieve progress towards a political solution,

Recognizing that achieving a political solution to this long-standing dispute and enhanced cooperation between the States members of the Arab Maghreb Union would contribute to stability and security in the Sahel region,

---

[49] Resolutions or decisions on this question were first adopted by the Security Council in 1975.

Welcoming the efforts of the Secretary-General to keep all peacekeeping operations, including the United Nations Mission for the Referendum in Western Sahara, under close review, and reiterating the need for the Security Council to pursue a rigorous, strategic approach to peacekeeping deployments, and effective management of resources,

Expressing concern about the violations of existing agreements, and calling upon the parties to respect their relevant obligations,

Taking note of the proposal presented by Morocco to the Secretary-General on 11 April 2007[50] and welcoming serious and credible Moroccan efforts to move the process forward towards resolution, and taking note also of the proposal presented by the Frente Popular para la Liberación de Saguía el-Hamra y de Río de Oro to the Secretary-General on 10 April 2007,[51]

Encouraging the parties, in this context, to demonstrate further political will towards a solution, including by expanding upon their discussion of each other's proposals,

Taking note of the four rounds of negotiations held under the auspices of the Secretary-General, and welcoming the commitment of the parties to continue the negotiations process,

Encouraging the parties to continue to cooperate with the Office of the United Nations High Commissioner for Refugees in implementing the January 2012 updated plan of action on confidence-building measures,

Stressing the importance of improving the human rights situation in Western Sahara and the Tindouf refugee camps, and encouraging the parties to work with the international community to develop and implement independent and credible measures to ensure full respect for human rights, bearing in mind their relevant obligations under international law,

Encouraging the parties to continue in their respective efforts to enhance the promotion and protection of human rights in Western Sahara and the Tindouf refugee camps, including freedom of expression and of association,

Recognizing and welcoming, in this regard, the recent steps and initiatives taken by Morocco to strengthen the National Council on Human Rights regional commissions operating in Dakhla and Laayoune, and Morocco's ongoing interaction with special procedures of the United Nations Human Rights Council, including those planned for 2015, as well as the planned visit of the Office of the United Nations High Commissioner for Human Rights in 2015,

Welcoming the implementation of the enhanced refugee protection programme developed by the Office of the United Nations High Commissioner for Refugees in coordination with the Frente Popular para la Liberación de Saguía el-Hamra y de Río de Oro, which includes refugee and human rights training and awareness initiatives,

Reiterating its request for consideration of refugee registration in the Tindouf refugee camps, and inviting efforts in this regard,

Welcoming the commitment of the parties to continue the process of negotiations through the United Nations-sponsored talks,

Recognizing that the consolidation of the status quo is not acceptable, and noting further that progress in the negotiations is essential in order to improve the quality of life of the people of Western Sahara in all its aspects,

Affirming its full support for the Personal Envoy of the Secretary-General, Mr. Christopher Ross, and his work in facilitating negotiations between the parties, and welcoming to that effect his recent initiatives and ongoing consultations with the parties and neighbouring States,

Affirming its full support also for the Special Representative of the Secretary-General for Western Sahara and Head of the United Nations Mission for the Referendum in Western Sahara, Ms. Kim Bolduc,

Having considered the report of the Secretary-General of 10 April 2015,[52]

---

[50] See S/2007/206, annex.

[51] S/2007/210, annex.

[52] S/2015/246.

1. *Decides* to extend the mandate of the United Nations Mission for the Referendum in Western Sahara until 30 April 2016;

2. *Reaffirms* the need for full respect of the military agreements reached with the Mission with regard to the ceasefire, and calls upon the parties to adhere fully to those agreements;

3. *Calls upon* all parties to cooperate fully with the operations of the Mission, including its free interaction with all interlocutors, and to take the steps necessary to ensure the security of, as well as unhindered movement and immediate access for, the United Nations and associated personnel carrying out their mandate, in conformity with existing agreements;

4. *Welcomes* the commitment of the parties to continue the process of preparation for a fifth round of negotiations, and recalls its endorsement of the recommendation in the report of the Secretary-General of 14 April 2008 that realism and a spirit of compromise by the parties are essential to achieve progress in negotiations;[53]

5. *Calls upon* the parties to continue to show political will and to work in an atmosphere propitious for dialogue in order to enter into a more intensive and substantive phase of negotiations, thus ensuring the implementation of resolutions 1754 (2007), 1783 (2007), 1813 (2008), 1871 (2009), 1920 (2010), 1979 (2011), 2044 (2012), 2099 (2013) and 2152 (2014) and the success of negotiations;

6. *Affirms its full support* for the commitment of the Secretary-General and his Personal Envoy for Western Sahara towards a solution to the question of Western Sahara in this context, and calls for renewed meetings and strengthening of contacts;

7. *Calls upon* the parties to continue negotiations under the auspices of the Secretary-General without preconditions and in good faith, taking into account the efforts made since 2006 and subsequent developments, with a view to achieving a just, lasting and mutually acceptable political solution, which will provide for the self-determination of the people of Western Sahara in the context of arrangements consistent with the principles and purposes of the Charter of the United Nations, and notes the role and responsibilities of the parties in this respect;

8. *Invites* Member States to lend appropriate assistance to these talks;

9. *Requests* the Secretary-General to brief the Security Council on a regular basis, and at least twice a year, on the status and progress of these negotiations under his auspices, on the implementation of the present resolution and on challenges to the operations of the Mission and steps taken to address them, expresses its intention to meet to receive and discuss his briefings, and in this regard further requests the Secretary-General to provide a report on the situation in Western Sahara well before the end of the mandate period;

10. *Welcomes* the commitment of the parties and the neighbouring States to hold periodic meetings with the Office of the United Nations High Commissioner for Refugees to review and, where possible, expand confidence-building measures;

11. *Urges* Member States to provide voluntary contributions to fund confidence-building measures agreed upon between the parties, including those that allow for visits between separated family members, as well as food programmes to ensure that the humanitarian needs of refugees are adequately addressed;

12. *Requests* the Secretary-General to continue to take the measures necessary to ensure full compliance in the Mission with the United Nations zero-tolerance policy on sexual exploitation and abuse and to keep the Council informed, and urges troop-contributing countries to take appropriate preventive action, including predeployment awareness training, and other action to ensure full accountability in cases of such conduct involving their personnel;

13. *Decides* to remain seized of the matter.

Adopted unanimously at the 7435th meeting.

---

[53] S/2008/251, para. 66.

UNITED NATIONS PEACEKEEPING OPERATIONS[54]

Decisions

At its 7275th meeting, on 9 October 2014, the Security Council considered the item entitled "United Nations peacekeeping operations".

At the same meeting, the Council decided to extend invitations, in accordance with rule 39 of its provisional rules of procedure, to Lieutenant General Maqsood Ahmed, Military Adviser for Peacekeeping Operations, Lieutenant General Carlos Alberto dos Santos Cruz, Force Commander of the United Nations Organization Stabilization Mission in the Democratic Republic of the Congo, Major General Jean Bosco Kazura, Force Commander of the United Nations Multidimensional Integrated Stabilization Mission in Mali, and Lieutenant General Iqbal Singh Singha, Force Commander of the United Nations Disengagement Observer Force.

At its 7317th meeting, on 20 November 2014, the Council considered the item entitled:

"United Nations peacekeeping operations

"The role of policing in peacekeeping and post-conflict peacebuilding

"Letter dated 4 November 2014 from the Permanent Representative of Australia to the United Nations addressed to the Secretary-General (S/2014/788)".

At the same meeting, the Council decided to extend invitations, in accordance with rule 39 of its provisional rules of procedure, to Mr. Hervé Ladsous, Under-Secretary-General for Peacekeeping Operations, Mr. Greg Hinds, Police Commissioner of the United Nations Mission in Liberia, Mr. Fred Yiga, Police Commissioner of the United Nations Mission in South Sudan, and Mr. Luis Miguel Carrilho, Police Commissioner of the United Nations Multidimensional Integrated Stabilization Mission in the Central African Republic.

Resolution 2185 (2014) of 20 November 2014

The Security Council,

Recalling its primary responsibility under the Charter of the United Nations for the maintenance of international peace and security,

Recalling also its resolutions 2151 (2014) of 28 April 2014 on security sector reform, 2167 (2014) of 28 July 2014 and 2086 (2013) of 21 January 2013 on United Nations peacekeeping operations, 1894 (2009) of 11 November 2009 on the protection of civilians in armed conflict, 1325 (2000) of 31 October 2000 and all subsequent resolutions on women and peace and security, 2143 (2014) of 7 March 2014 and previous resolutions on children and armed conflict and 2117 (2013) of 26 September 2013 on small arms and light weapons, and the statements by its President of 21 February 2014 on the rule of law[55] and 20 December 2012 on post-conflict peacebuilding,[56] as well as other relevant resolutions and statements by its President,

Reiterating the need for a comprehensive approach to conflict prevention and sustainable peace, which comprises operational and structural measures for the prevention of armed conflict and addresses its root causes, including through strengthening the rule of law at international and national levels and promoting sustained economic growth, poverty eradication, social development, sustainable development, national reconciliation, good governance, democracy, gender equality and respect for and protection of human rights,

Stressing that the success of the mandates of peacekeeping operations and special political missions requires close cooperation between the different elements of these missions under the overall leadership of the Head of Mission,

[54] Resolutions or decisions on this question were first adopted by the Security Council in 1990.

[55] S/PRST/2014/5.

[56] S/PRST/2012/29.

Reaffirming its commitment to uphold the purposes and principles of the Charter, including its commitment to and respect for the principles of political independence, sovereign equality and territorial integrity of all States, in conducting all peacekeeping activities and the need for States to comply with their obligations under international law,

Reaffirming also that respect for the basic principles of peacekeeping, including consent of the parties, impartiality and non-use of force except in self-defence and defence of the mandate, is essential to the success of peacekeeping operations,

Recognizing that the mandate of each peacekeeping operation and special political mission is specific to the needs and situation of the country concerned,

Reaffirming the principles of impartiality, consent of the parties, national ownership and national responsibility, and stressing the significance of the views of and dialogue with countries hosting special political missions,

Noting that host State policing institutions are often the primary link between the Government and the communities on security issues, and reiterating that professional, effective, accountable and accessible law enforcement, corrections and judicial institutions are necessary to lay the foundation for sustainable peace and national development,

Acknowledging the significant growth in the role of police components as an integral part of United Nations peacekeeping operations and special political missions, and the increasingly diverse and complex policing-related tasks in the mandates of such operations and missions, noting that police components can include both uniformed United Nations police officers and civilian policing experts, noting also the distinct roles performed by individual police officers and formed police units and the increasing demand for these different capacities, stressing that use of these capacities should be based on the situation and the needs of the host State, and noting the necessity of aligning tasks of United Nations police components with the mandated tasks of missions,

Stressing that United Nations policing-related work makes an invaluable contribution to peacekeeping, post-conflict peacebuilding, security, the rule of law and the creation of a basis for development,

Recalling that policing-related aspects of mandates of United Nations peacekeeping operations and special political missions may include support for the reform, restructuring and development of host State policing and other law enforcement institutions, providing operational support to host State policing and other law enforcement institutions, and conducting interim policing and other law enforcement,

Underlining the importance of close coordination of the range of United Nations policing activities, both at Headquarters and in the field, in particular between Security Council-mandated missions and the United Nations country team, as appropriate, and encouraging relevant United Nations entities mandated to undertake policing activities to work through existing coordination mechanisms, as appropriate,

Noting that United Nations police components face a range of challenges, including a need for specialized skills and equipment and to ensure a unified policing approach, given the various policing models across police-contributing countries,

Recalling reports of the Special Committee on Peacekeeping Operations of the General Assembly which have provided guidance to the Secretariat on the subject of United Nations policing, including the development of a United Nations standardized approach to policing, and recognizing the inclusive consultative process undertaken by the Police Division of the Department of Peacekeeping Operations of the Secretariat in the development of the Strategic Guidance Framework for International Police Peacekeeping,

Emphasizing the importance of Member States contributing police with professional skills, experience and expertise to carry out the mandated tasks who are appropriately trained and vetted and, where appropriate, operationally ready and deployed with the full complement of contingent-owned equipment, welcoming cooperation between the United Nations, police-contributing countries, other Member States and relevant regional and international organizations to help to ensure that formed police units are properly trained and equipped, and underscoring the importance of such cooperation,

Noting the increasing use of modern technologies by United Nations police components, including information and communications technologies such as closed circuit television, specialized crime data software and geographic information mapping systems, and other technologies such as advanced metal detectors, laboratory equipment and drug, explosive and ballistic detection and analysis systems, to increase their abilities to carry out their mandates efficiently and effectively and to enhance their safety and security, and encouraging the Secretariat to ensure that these technologies, when deployed, are integrated effectively into United Nations policing work consistent with the purposes and principles of the Charter and the basic principles of peacekeeping and that the confidentiality of all data gathered by such assets is preserved as detailed in relevant specific procedures,

Welcoming the announcement by the Secretary-General of a comprehensive review of United Nations peacekeeping operations and special political missions, and taking note of the announcement by the Secretary-General of the establishment of a high-level independent panel to conduct the review,

Noting the designation of the Department of Peacekeeping Operations and the United Nations Development Programme as the joint global focal point for the police, justice and corrections areas,

Recalling the sovereign right and the primary responsibility of the State concerned to determine the national approach and priorities of security sector reform, including reform of policing and other law enforcement institutions, and recognizing that such reform should be a nationally owned process that is rooted in the particular needs and conditions of the country in question, and encouraging the development of expertise in the field of security sector reform at the national level,

Noting the important role that United Nations police components can play in supporting, and coordinating international support for, reform of host State policing institutions and building policing capacity in a comprehensive way that emphasizes a community-oriented approach and is integrated with other areas of security sector reform and the rule of law,

Emphasizing that good governance and oversight of policing and law enforcement services, within the framework of a functional justice and corrections system, are important in ensuring that those services are accountable, responsive and capable of serving the population,

Highlighting the important role that United Nations police components can play, where mandated, in consultation with the host State and in collaboration with other components, in supporting host States in upholding their primary responsibility to protect civilians as well as to respect and ensure the human rights of all individuals within their territory and subject to their jurisdiction, including through monitoring and deterrence, early warning and prevention, support for basic safety and security, physical protection, creating protective environments, assisting national security sector reform programmes, capacity-building and political engagement with host State counterparts,

Reaffirming the important role of women in the prevention and resolution of conflicts and in peacebuilding, and stressing the importance of their equal participation and full involvement in all efforts for the maintenance and promotion of peace and security, and the need to increase their role in decision-making with regard to conflict prevention and resolution, including in relation to policing and the rule of law,

Taking note of and encouraging the increased participation of female police officers in United Nations peacekeeping operations and special political missions, thereby contributing to the effectiveness of relevant mandate implementation, including by providing diverse perspectives that can assist in building trust with local communities, improving the protection of women and children from violence and abuse and facilitating gender-sensitive police approaches and mentoring,

Recalling the launch of the United Nations Global Effort in 2009 to promote an increase in the percentage of female police officers in United Nations peacekeeping missions to 20 per cent by 2014, welcoming the increase in female police officers in peacekeeping operations since the launch of the United Nations Global Effort, and encouraging States and the Secretary-General to strengthen efforts to support the realization of the 20 per cent goal,

Recognizing innovative practices to improve the success of United Nations policing in recognizing specific needs of women in conflict and post-conflict environments, including the need for protection from sexual and gender-based violence and for community strategies that reflect women's needs, such as the deployment of women within formed police units and the establishment of special protection units,

Reiterating that the protection of children in armed conflict should be an important aspect of any comprehensive strategy to resolve conflict and build peace, reiterating also in this regard the importance of providing United Nations police components with specialized predeployment and in-mission training on mission-specific child protection and on appropriate comprehensive child-sensitive prevention and protection responses, as well as on the monitoring and reporting of violations and abuses committed against children, and stressing the importance of enhancing coordination between police components and child protection advisers as well as gender and women's protection advisers,

Highlighting the important role that United Nations police components can play in building the capacity of host State policing and other law enforcement institutions, as mandated, to address organized crime, particularly through support in the areas of border, immigration and maritime security and crime prevention, response and investigation,

Highlighting also that impartial, responsive, accountable, community-oriented police institutions with well-trained personnel can help to counter violent extremism, including through building trust and dialogue between State authorities and communities,

Noting the role that police components can play in assisting host Governments in the implementation and compliance monitoring of Council-mandated sanctions measures, including, where mandated, through the provision of advice and assistance,

Recognizing the role that regional and subregional organizations can play in post-conflict peacebuilding, including security sector reform and disarmament, demobilization and reintegration, rule of law, recovery, reconstruction and development processes, including through support for host State policing and other law enforcement institutions, and affirming the importance of interaction and cooperation between peacekeeping operations and special political missions and regional and subregional organizations and arrangements,

Paying tribute to the memory of United Nations peacekeepers who have lost their lives in the cause of peace, and in this regard underscoring the importance of the safety and security of United Nations peacekeepers, expressing grave concern about the security threats and targeted attacks against United Nations peacekeepers in many peacekeeping missions, which constitute a major challenge to United Nations peacekeeping operations, condemning in the strongest terms the killing of and all acts of violence against United Nations peacekeeping personnel, and emphasizing that perpetrators of such attacks must be brought to justice,

Reaffirming that the primary responsibility for the security and protection of personnel employed by the United Nations system organizations rests with the host Government, and noting that complementary to the host Government responsibility, the safety and security of individually deployed police personnel in United Nations peacekeeping operations and special political missions, including but not limited to United Nations police officers, or members of formed police units when not deployed with their unit, falls under the security arrangements of the United Nations security management system,

1. *Resolves* to include, as appropriate, policing as an integral part of the mandates of United Nations peacekeeping operations and special political missions, and to give clear, credible and achievable mandates for policing-related activities, matched by appropriate resources;

2. *Stresses* the importance of strong cooperation and coordination between United Nations police components and other elements of peacekeeping operations and special political missions, in support of the mandate and under the overall leadership of the Head of Mission;

3. *Urges* police-contributing countries to continue to contribute professional police personnel with the necessary skills, equipment and experience to implement mission mandates, including, where relevant, multidimensional peacekeeping mandates, underlining the importance of appropriate language skills at relevant levels to fulfil the mandate and of gender expertise, and urges prospective police-contributors to also contribute such personnel to help to ensure that the demand for professional police personnel in United Nations peacekeeping operations and special political missions is fully met;

4. *Requests* the Secretary-General to further promote professionalism, effectiveness and system-wide coherence in the policing-related work of the United Nations, including, in close consultation, as appropriate, with Member States and the Special Committee on Peacekeeping Operations in full respect of its vital role, through:

(*a*) The development and implementation of standards and guidance for United Nations policing-related work, through the Strategic Guidance Framework for International Police Peacekeeping;

(*b*) The development of comprehensive, standardized training for United Nations police components, including predeployment, induction and in-service training;

(*c*) The provision of senior police leadership training, including through the Senior Mission Leaders' Course;

(*d*) The development of strong processes for evaluating the effectiveness of United Nations policing-related work;

(*e*) The streamlining and improvement of recruitment and deployment procedures for United Nations police and civilian policing experts, recognizing that the Fifth Committee is the appropriate Main Committee of the General Assembly entrusted with administrative and budgetary matters;

(*f*) The coordination of work within the United Nations system on reform of policing and law enforcement institutions;

5. *Recognizes* that political leadership and the will of national authorities are critical to reforming host State policing and other law enforcement services, emphasizes the lead role of the host State authorities in developing, as part of an inclusive national vision for its security sector, a strategy for policing and other law enforcement that promotes the rule of law and respects human rights, coordinating the implementation of the vision, dedicating national resources towards policing, law enforcement and other security institutions, and monitoring the impact of security sector reform processes, including policing reform;

6. *Urges* Member States and international partners to support, upon request, host State efforts to professionalize policing and other law enforcement agencies, within the context of broader security sector reform, and to ensure that international policing support is well coordinated in support of a nationally agreed plan, and underscores that such support should be tailored to the needs of the host State;

7. *Recognizes* that reform of police and other law enforcement institutions needs to be in support of, and informed by, inclusive political processes and agreements, to enhance the legitimacy of the institutions concerned and ensure wide ownership of such reform;

8. *Notes* the important role that United Nations police components can play, where mandated, in strengthening the rule of law in conflict and post-conflict situations by, inter-alia, providing operational support to host State policing and other law enforcement institutions and supporting the reform, restructuring and rebuilding of such institutions, including through technical assistance, co-location, training and mentoring programmes, in the context of broader efforts to strengthen the rule of law and reform the security sector, where mandated;

9. *Requests* the Secretary-General, in this regard, to consider, as appropriate, security sector reform, including reform of policing and other law enforcement institutions, in the overall strategic planning of peacekeeping operations and special political missions in each country-specific context, and to work with Member States to enhance the capabilities and expertise of United Nations police components in relation to capacity development and institution building, including in the areas of:

(*a*) Operational policing, including community-oriented policing and information-based policing;

(*b*) Administration, management and leadership;

(*c*) Governance, oversight and evaluation;

(*d*) Policy formulation and strategic planning;

(*e*) Coordination with partners;

10. *Emphasizes* the role of peacekeeping operations and special political missions in supporting host State policing institutions in their preparation to transition to function self-sufficiently, and underlines that this preparation for transition should be based on a timely analysis of need, in consultation with the host State, of any assistance beyond the duration of the presence of the peacekeeping operation or special political mission, to enable United Nations peacebuilding and development actors, including the United Nations country team, to undertake the necessary strategic planning and resource mobilization, working in close partnership with host State authorities, and to transfer skills and expertise to host State officials and experts as quickly as possible in order to ensure a successful and durable transition;

11. *Encourages* the Special Representatives and Envoys of the Secretary-General to fully take into account the strategic value of security sector reform, including reform of host State policing and other law enforcement institutions, in their work, as appropriate, in the context of broader security sector reform efforts, including through their good offices where mandated;

12. *Welcomes* the work of the United Nations Standing Police Capacity in providing expertise across the broad range of policing activities and providing a rapid, coherent, effective and responsive start-up capability for the police components of United Nations peacekeeping operations and special political missions, and assisting existing missions through the provision of advice, expertise, baseline assessments and evaluation;

13. *Requests* the Secretariat to continue refining the composition of the United Nations Standing Police Capacity to ensure that it includes skill sets to meet contemporary demands, including through enabling partnerships with Member States and regional organizations;

14. *Notes with appreciation* the efforts made by the Police Division of the Department of Peacekeeping Operation of the Secretariat to continue to explore the use of "specialized police teams" for police capacity-building, and requests the Secretary-General to report on this use, as appropriate;

15. *Notes* the efforts of the Secretariat to enhance inter-mission cooperation, including through the rapid redeployment of formed police units, recognizes that such cooperation can provide timely responses for critically needed capacity as an interim, short-term measure, notes the logistical challenges that can undermine the effectiveness of inter-mission cooperation, and encourages the Secretariat, in consultation with police-contributing countries, to continue to assess the practice of inter-mission cooperation with a view to streamlining standing operating procedures and improving the effectiveness of such cooperation;

16. *Also notes* the importance of the deployment of civilian policing experts, with adequate and appropriate skills and expertise, to United Nations peacekeeping operations and special political missions;

17. *Affirms* the central role of the protection of civilians, where mandated, in the work undertaken by United Nations police components;

18. *Also affirms* the importance of the role that United Nations police components can play, where mandated, in supporting the efforts of host authorities in the protection of civilians, particularly those under imminent threat of physical violence, including all forms of sexual and gender-based violence, and in this regard, while recognizing that the protection of civilians is the primary responsibility of the host State, helping to build and reform policing and law enforcement institutions of the host State so that they are able to sustainably and consistently protect civilians;

19. *Highlights* the critical role that United Nations police components can play in facilitating the participation and inclusion of women in dialogue on conflict resolution and peacebuilding, including on rule of law and security issues;

20. *Encourages* police-contributing countries to increase the percentage of women police in deployments to United Nations peacekeeping operations, in particular senior officers, including in leadership roles, and requests the Secretary-General to continue to support innovative efforts to encourage such deployment of women police and to enhance coordination between police components and child protection advisers as well as gender and women's protection advisers;

21. *Also encourages* police-contributing countries to provide all police personnel with adequate training to carry out their responsibilities in relation to sexual and gender-based violence and child protection, and further encourages relevant United Nations entities to make available appropriate guidance and training modules, including in particular the United Nations predeployment scenario-based training on prevention of sexual and gender-based violence and on children and armed conflict;

22. *Requests* the Secretary-General to continue and strengthen efforts to implement the policy of zero tolerance of sexual exploitation and abuse by United Nations personnel, as well as the policy on prohibition of child labour in United Nations peacekeeping operations, and urges police-contributing countries to take appropriate preventative action, including predeployment and in-mission awareness training and other action to ensure full accountability, including prosecutions, in cases of such conduct involving their nationals;

23. *Notes* the importance of United Nations policing-related support to non-United Nations security forces adhering to the United Nations human rights due diligence policy;[57]

[57] S/2013/110, annex.

24. *Reiterates* that United Nations peacekeeping operations and special political missions, including police components, located in a host State with a Security Council-mandated sanctions regime, may, if deemed necessary by the Council, provide appropriate expertise to the host Government, the relevant sanctions committee and relevant expert groups in the implementation and the compliance monitoring of that sanctions regime, and further notes the importance of appropriate training for United Nations police components in this regard;

25. *Also reiterates* that United Nations peacekeeping operations and special political missions, including police components, may, if mandated by the Council, assist in capacity-building for host Governments, as requested, to implement commitments under existing global and regional instruments and to address the illicit trafficking in small arms and light weapons, including through weapons collection, disarmament, demobilization and reintegration programmes, enhancing physical security and stockpile management practices, record-keeping and tracing capacities, development of national export and import control systems, enhancement of border security, and strengthening of judicial institutions, policing and other law enforcement capacities;

26. *Encourages* information-sharing, where relevant and appropriate, between Special Representatives of the Secretary-General, the Department of Peacekeeping Operations, including its Police Division, the Department of Political Affairs of the Secretariat, the Counter-Terrorism Committee Executive Directorate, the United Nations Office on Drugs and Crime, the Counter-Terrorism Implementation Task Force and the United Nations Development Programme, within existing mandates and resources, when considering means to address, in a comprehensive and integrated manner, transnational organized crime, terrorism and violent extremism that can be conducive to terrorism;

27. *Encourages* the Counter-Terrorism Committee Executive Directorate to enhance its dialogue and information-sharing with Special Envoys, the Department of Political Affairs and the Department of Peacekeeping Operations, with respect to policing activities, including during the planning stages of missions, as appropriate, in relation to the implementation of Council resolutions 1373 (2001) of 28 September 2001 and 1624 (2005) of 14 September 2005, and requests the Executive Directorate to identify the principal gaps in the capacities of Member States, including the capacities of their policing and other law enforcement institutions, to implement resolutions 1373 (2001) and 1624 (2005);

28. *Affirms* that United Nations police components, deployed as part of a United Nations peacekeeping operation, may, if mandated by the Council, provide support, in consultation with the host State, as feasible and where appropriate, to the efforts of national authorities, without prejudice to the responsibilities of those authorities, to bring to justice those responsible for serious international crimes;

29. *Encourages* closer coordination and cooperation on policing issues between the Secretariat and international, regional and subregional organizations, the International Criminal Police Organization (INTERPOL) and regional police organizations, including through training, the sharing and exchange of information, thematic expertise and operational support, as appropriate;

30. *Reiterates* the need to further strengthen cooperation and consultation with police-contributing countries, including through triangular cooperation between the Council, troop- and police-contributing countries and the Secretariat, to foster a spirit of partnership, cooperation, confidence and mutual trust;

31. *Expresses its intention* to consider holding an annual meeting on policing issues with the heads of United Nations police components;

32. *Encourages* the Secretary-General to consider the increasing role of policing, along with the many other critical issues related to peacekeeping operations and special political missions, in his upcoming strategic review of United Nations peacekeeping operations and special political missions, as appropriate;

33. *Requests* the Secretary-General to submit a report by the end of 2016 on the role of policing as an integral part of peacekeeping and post-conflict peacebuilding, with particular focus on the challenges faced by police components of United Nations peacekeeping operations and special political missions, and making recommendations on how best to strengthen their contribution to the achievement of mission mandates.

Adopted unanimously at the 7317th meeting.

Decisions

At its 7464th meeting, on 17 June 2015, the Security Council considered the item entitled "United Nations peacekeeping operations".

At the same meeting, the Council decided to extend invitations, in accordance with rule 39 of its provisional rules of procedure, to Mr. Hervé Ladsous, Under-Secretary-General for Peacekeeping Operations, Lieutenant General Yohannes Gebremeskel Tesfamariam, Force Commander of the United Nations Mission in South Sudan, Major General Michael Lollesgaard, Force Commander of the United Nations Multidimensional Integrated Stabilization Mission in Mali, and Major General Michael Finn, Chief of Staff of the United Nations Truce Supervision Organization.

THE SITUATION IN LIBERIA[58]

Decisions

On 2 September 2014, the President of the Security Council addressed the following letter to the Secretary-General:[59]

> I have the honour to inform you that your letter dated 28 August 2014 concerning your recommendation of a technical rollover of the mandate of the United Nations Mission in Liberia for a period of three months, until 30 December 2014,[60] has been brought to the attention of the members of the Security Council. They take note of the proposal contained in your letter.

At its 7260th meeting, on 9 September 2014, the Council decided to invite the representative of Liberia to participate, without vote, in accordance with rule 37 of its provisional rules of procedure, in the discussion of the item entitled:

"The situation in Liberia

> "Twenty-eighth progress report of the Secretary-General on the United Nations Mission in Liberia (S/2014/598)
>
> "Letter dated 28 August 2014 from the Secretary-General addressed to the President of the Security Council (S/2014/644)".

At the same meeting, the Council also decided to extend invitations, in accordance with rule 39 of its provisional rules of procedure, to Ms. Karin Landgren, Special Representative of the Secretary-General for Liberia and Head of the United Nations Mission in Liberia, and Mr. Mårten Grunditz, Permanent Representative of Sweden to the United Nations, in his capacity as Chair of the Liberia configuration of the Peacebuilding Commission.

At its 7263rd meeting, on 15 September 2014, the Council considered the item entitled:

"The situation in Liberia

> "Twenty-eighth progress report of the Secretary-General on the United Nations Mission in Liberia (S/2014/598)
>
> "Letter dated 28 August 2014 from the Secretary-General addressed to the President of the Security Council (S/2014/644)".

---

[58] Resolutions or decisions on this question were first adopted by the Security Council in 1991.

[59] S/2014/645.

[60] S/2014/644.

Resolution 2176 (2014)
of 15 September 2014

The Security Council,

Recalling its previous resolutions concerning the situation in Liberia, in particular resolutions 1509 (2003) of 19 September 2003, 2066 (2012) of 17 September 2012 and 2116 (2013) of 18 September 2013, and its statement to the press of 9 July 2014,

Expressing grave concern about the extent of the outbreak of the Ebola virus in West Africa, in particular in Liberia, Guinea and Sierra Leone,

Affirming that the Government of Liberia bears primary responsibility for ensuring peace, stability and the protection of the civilian population in Liberia, and stressing that lasting stability in Liberia will require the Government to sustain well-functioning and accountable government institutions, particularly in the rule of law and security sectors,

Welcoming the launch of the Liberia Operational Plan for Accelerated Response to Recurrence of Ebola Epidemic, taking note of the efforts of the national security forces, notably the Liberia National Police and the Armed Forces of Liberia, to respond promptly to the outbreak through undertaking public awareness and prevention activities in conformity with established safety protocols and procedures, and urging the national security forces, when responding to security incidents, to use proportionate force,

Welcoming also the convening of the Mano River Union Extraordinary Summit, held in Guinea on 1 August 2014, and the commitments expressed by the Heads of State of Côte d'Ivoire, Guinea, Liberia and Sierra Leone and the Head of the World Health Organization to combat the Ebola outbreak in the region, including by strengthening treatment services and measures to prevent the outbreak spreading across borders, and also welcoming the commitment of the African Union and the Economic Community of West African States, as well as bilateral partners and multilateral organizations, to support efforts to combat the further spread of the Ebola virus,

Expressing appreciation for the appointments by the Secretary-General of Dr. David Nabarro as the United Nations System Senior Coordinator for Ebola Virus Disease and of Mr. Anthony Banbury as the Deputy Ebola Coordinator and Operation Crisis Manager operating from the United Nations Operations and Crisis Centre, in order to assist Governments in the region to address the Ebola outbreak,

Urging the international community to respond swiftly to the shortage of qualified medical professionals and appropriate equipment and preventive measures necessary to address the Ebola outbreak in West Africa,

Expressing deep appreciation for and commending the continued contribution and commitment of United Nations personnel, especially the troop- and police-contributing countries of the United Nations Mission in Liberia, to assist in consolidating peace and stability in Liberia, and the efforts of the Special Representative of the Secretary-General for Liberia,

Noting the possible delays in the conduct of the special senatorial election scheduled for October 2014,

Taking note of the report of the Secretary-General of 15 August 2014,[61] and taking note also of the letter dated 28 August 2014 from the Secretary-General[60] and his recommendation to defer consideration of the proposals for the extension of the mandate of the Mission, outlined in his report,

Determining that the situation in Liberia continues to constitute a threat to international peace and security in the region,

Acting under Chapter VII of the Charter of the United Nations,

1. *Decides* to extend the mandate of the United Nations Mission in Liberia until 31 December 2014;

2. *Endorses* the recommendation of the Secretary-General, in his letter dated 28 August 2014,[60] to defer consideration of the proposals on adjustments to the mandate of the Mission, outlined in his report of 15 August 2014;[61]

[61] S/2014/598.

3. *Expresses its intention* to further extend the mandate of the Mission to 30 September 2015 after consideration of the proposals of the Secretary-General;

4. *Requests* the Secretary-General to keep the Security Council updated on the situation in Liberia no later than 15 November 2014;

5. *Decides* to remain actively seized of the matter.

Adopted unanimously at the 7263rd meeting.

Decisions

At its 7310th meeting, on 12 November 2014, the Security Council decided to invite the representative of Liberia to participate, without vote, in accordance with rule 37 of its provisional rules of procedure, in the discussion of the item entitled "The situation in Liberia".

At the same meeting, the Council also decided to extend invitations, in accordance with rule 39 of its provisional rules of procedure, to Mr. Hervé Ladsous, Under-Secretary-General for Peacekeeping Operations, and Mr. Per Thöresson, of Sweden, in his capacity as representative of the Chair of the Liberia configuration of the Peacebuilding Commission.

At its 7328th meeting, on 9 December 2014, the Council considered the item entitled:

"The situation in Liberia

"Letter dated 29 September 2014 from the Secretary-General addressed to the President of the Security Council (S/2014/707)

"Letter dated 19 November 2014 from the Panel of Experts on Liberia established pursuant to resolution 2128 (2013) addressed to the President of the Security Council (S/2014/831)".

Resolution 2188 (2014)
of 9 December 2014

The Security Council,

Recalling its previous resolutions and the statements by its President on the situation in Liberia,

Welcoming the sustained progress made by the Government of Liberia in rebuilding Liberia for the benefit of all Liberians, with the support of the international community,

Taking note of the report of the Panel of Experts on Liberia,[62]

Taking note also of the letter dated 29 September 2014 from the Secretary-General to the President of the Security Council,[63] and welcoming the recommendations to the Council in the annex thereto, regarding the assessment mission concerning the Liberia sanctions regime,

Expressing grave concern about the outbreak of the Ebola virus in, and its impact on, West Africa, including Liberia,

Recognizing that the peacebuilding and development gains in Liberia could be reversed in the light of the Ebola outbreak, and, in the light of these factors, expressing its intent to scale back and terminate the remaining sanctions in a prudent manner,

Affirming that the Government of Liberia bears primary responsibility for ensuring peace, stability and the protection of the civilian population in Liberia, and stressing that lasting stability in Liberia will require the Government to sustain well-functioning and accountable government institutions, particularly in the rule of law and security sectors,

[62] S/2014/831.

[63] S/2014/707.

Stressing the need for continued progress on security sector reform in Liberia to ensure that Liberia's military, police and border security forces are self-sufficient, capable and adequately prepared to protect the Liberian people,

Underlining that the transparent and effective management of natural resources is critical for Liberia's sustainable peace and security,

Underlining its determination to support the Government of Liberia in its efforts to meet the conditions of resolution 1521 (2003) of 22 December 2003, welcoming the engagement of the Peacebuilding Commission, and encouraging all stakeholders, including donors, to support the Government in its efforts,

Determining that the situation in Liberia remains fragile and constitutes a threat to international peace and security in the region,

Acting under Chapter VII of the Charter of the United Nations,

1. *Reaffirms* that the measures imposed by paragraph 1 of resolution 1532 (2004) of 12 March 2004 remain in force;

2. *Decides*, for a period of nine months from the date of adoption of the present resolution:

(*a*) To renew the measures on travel imposed by paragraph 4 of resolution 1521 (2003);

(*b*) To renew the measures on arms, previously imposed by paragraph 2 of resolution 1521 (2003) and modified by paragraphs 1 and 2 of resolution 1683 (2006) of 13 June 2006, by paragraph 1 (*b*) of resolution 1731 (2006) of 20 December 2006, by paragraphs 3 to 6 of resolution 1903 (2009) of 17 December 2009, by paragraph 3 of resolution 1961 (2010) of 17 December 2010 and by paragraph 2 (*b*) of resolution 2128 (2013) of 10 December 2013;

3. *Also decides* to maintain all of the above measures under continuous review with a view to modifying or lifting all or part of the measures of the sanctions regime dependent upon Liberia's progress towards meeting the conditions set out in resolution 1521 (2003) for terminating those measures and in the light of the threat to peace and security in Liberia posed by the Ebola virus;

4. *Requests* the Secretary-General to provide an update to the Security Council by 1 August 2015 on progress made by the Government of Liberia in implementing the recommendations on the proper management of arms and ammunition, including enacting the necessary legislative frameworks, and on facilitating the effective monitoring and management of the border regions between Liberia and Côte d'Ivoire;

5. *Decides* to extend the mandate of the Panel of Experts on Liberia appointed pursuant to paragraph 9 of resolution 1903 (2009) for a period of 10 months from the date of adoption of the present resolution to undertake the following tasks in close collaboration with the Government of Liberia and the Group of Experts on Côte d'Ivoire:

(*a*) To conduct a follow-up assessment mission to Liberia and neighbouring States, as feasible, given conditions on the ground, to investigate and compile a final report on the implementation, and any violations, of the measures on arms as amended by resolutions 1903 (2009), 1961 (2010) and 2128 (2013), including the various sources of financing for the illicit trade in arms, on progress in the security and legal sectors with respect to the ability of the Government of Liberia to effectively monitor and control arms and border issues, and on the progress of the Government in meeting notification requirements;

(*b*) To provide to the Security Council, after discussion with the Security Council Committee established pursuant to resolution 1521 (2003), no later than 1 August 2015, a final report on all the issues listed in the present paragraph, and to provide to the Committee no later than 23 April 2015, an update on the status of legislation in Liberia related to the ability of the Government of Liberia to effectively monitor and control arms and border issues, and any other informal updates to the Committee as appropriate;

(*c*) To cooperate actively with other relevant panels of experts, in particular the Group of Experts on Côte d'Ivoire re-established by paragraph 24 of resolution 2153 (2014) of 29 April 2014;

6. *Requests* the Secretary-General to take the necessary administrative measures, as expeditiously as possible, to re-establish the Panel of Experts, in consultation with the Committee, for a period of 10 months from the date of the present resolution, drawing, as appropriate, on the expertise of the members of the Panel of Experts established pursuant to previous resolutions;

7. *Calls upon* all States and the Government of Liberia to cooperate fully with the Panel of Experts in all aspects of its mandate;

8. *Recalls* that responsibility for controlling the circulation of small arms within the territory of Liberia and between Liberia and neighbouring States rests with the relevant governmental authorities in accordance with the Economic Community of West African States Convention on Small Arms and Light Weapons, Their Ammunition and Other Related Materials of 2006;

9. *Urges* the Government of Liberia to expedite the adoption and implementation of appropriate legislation and take other necessary and appropriate steps to establish the legal framework necessary to combat illicit trafficking in arms and ammunition;

10. *Decides* to remain actively seized of the matter.

Adopted unanimously at the 7328th meeting.

Decision

At its 7340th meeting, on 15 December 2014, the Security Council considered the item entitled "The situation in Liberia".

Resolution 2190 (2014)
of 15 December 2014

The Security Council,

Recalling its previous resolutions, in particular resolutions 1509 (2003) of 19 September 2003, 2066 (2012) of 17 September 2012, 2116 (2013) of 18 September 2013, 2176 (2014) of 15 September 2014, 2177 (2014) of 18 September 2014 and 2188 (2014) of 9 December 2014, the statements by its President concerning the situation in Liberia and the subregion, and resolution 2162 (2014) of 25 June 2014 on the situation in Côte d'Ivoire,

Affirming its strong commitment to the sovereignty, independence, territorial integrity and unity of Liberia, and recalling the principles of good-neighbourliness, non-interference and regional cooperation,

Affirming that the Government of Liberia bears primary responsibility for ensuring peace, stability and the protection of the civilian population in Liberia and for reforming the security sector, particularly the Liberia National Police, stressing that lasting stability in Liberia will require the Government to sustain well-functioning and accountable government institutions, especially in the security and justice sectors, to build the confidence of all Liberians, and urging the Government to demonstrate substantive progress in the reform, restructuring and effective functioning of the security and justice sectors to provide for the protection of all Liberians,

Welcoming the overall progress toward restoring peace, security and stability in Liberia, commending the enduring commitment of the people and Government of Liberia to peace and to developing democratic processes and institutions and initiating important reform efforts, and calling upon all Liberian stakeholders to intensify momentum toward achieving greater social cohesion,

Reiterating grave concern about the unprecedented extent of the Ebola outbreak in Africa, and the impact of the Ebola virus on West Africa, including Liberia,

Recognizing the role of the Government of Liberia in continuing to lead the ground-level response against the Ebola outbreak in Liberia, as well as to address the wider impact of the Ebola outbreak on communities and to plan for the longer-term recovery, including with the support of the Peacebuilding Commission, taking note of the Liberia Economic Stabilization and Recovery Plan, and commending those Member States which, in concert with other actors on the ground, continue to provide crucial support to assist the efforts of the Government of Liberia to prevent, respond to, isolate and mitigate suspected cases of Ebola,

Recognizing also that the Ebola outbreak in Liberia has slowed the efforts of the Government of Liberia to advance certain governance and national reform priorities,

Extolling the continued contribution, commitment and resolve of United Nations personnel, especially from the troop- and police-contributing countries of the United Nations Mission in Liberia, to assist in consolidating peace and stability in Liberia, and the efforts of the Special Representative of the Secretary-General for Liberia, particularly during the Ebola outbreak, and expressing appreciation to the international community, including the Economic Community of West African States, the African Union and the Mano River Union, for their continuing support to consolidate peace, security and stability in Liberia,

Welcoming the efforts undertaken by the United Nations Mission for Ebola Emergency Response to provide overall leadership and direction to the operational work of the United Nations system, and underscoring the need for relevant United Nations system entities, including the United Nations peacekeeping operations in West Africa, in close collaboration with the Mission and within their existing mandates and capacities, to provide immediate assistance to the Governments of the most affected countries, including Liberia,

Noting with concern the potential for conflict over Liberia's natural resources and disputes related to land ownership, and noting also that issues related to corruption continue to threaten to undermine stability and the effectiveness of government institutions,

Recognizing the extension provided by the Government of Liberia to the Constitution Review Committee, looking forward to a comprehensive, inclusive constitutional review process as well as the development of the national human rights action plan and the implementation of the National Reconciliation Road Map, and urging efforts to strengthen the Independent National Commission on Human Rights, which could play a key role as a publicly accessible human rights institution and as a mechanism to monitor and follow up on the implementation of the recommendations of the Truth and Reconciliation Commission,

Welcoming the contributions of the Peacebuilding Commission to security sector reform, the rule of law and national reconciliation in Liberia, and emphasizing the need for coherence between, and integration of, peacekeeping, peacebuilding and development to achieve an effective response to post-conflict situations,

Commending the cooperation between, and the significant efforts of, the Government of Liberia and the United Nations Mission in Liberia to plan, manage and implement the phased military drawdown of the Mission, and expressing concern that the Government has not provided predictable and sustainable funding to shoulder the continuing costs of deploying security personnel and resources, including to operate and maintain the sites vacated by the Mission,

Noting the postponement from October 2014 of the senatorial elections,

Expressing appreciation for the continued assistance provided by both the Government and the people of Liberia to Ivorian refugees in eastern Liberia and toward their voluntary repatriation to Côte d'Ivoire,

Commending the continued efforts of the Government of Liberia to strengthen security cooperation in the subregion, notably with the Governments of Guinea, Sierra Leone and Côte d'Ivoire, and recognizing that the instability in western Côte d'Ivoire continues to pose cross-border security challenges for Liberia and Côte d'Ivoire,

Recognizing the significant challenges that remain across all sectors, including continuing problems with violent crime, in particular the high rates of sexual and gender-based violence, especially involving children, recalling its resolutions 1325 (2000) of 31 October 2000, 1820 (2008) of 19 June 2008, 1888 (2009) of 30 September 2009, 1889 (2009) of 5 October 2009, 1960 (2010) of 16 December 2010, and 2106 (2013) of 24 June 2013 on women and peace and security, welcoming the renewed efforts of the Government of Liberia to promote and protect human rights, in particular of women and children, and emphasizing that persistent barriers to full implementation of resolution 1325 (2000) will only be dismantled through dedicated commitment to women's empowerment, participation and human rights, and through concerted leadership, consistent information and action, and support, to build women's engagement in all levels of decision-making,

Taking note of the report of the Secretary-General of 15 August 2014[61] and the recommendations contained therein on the adjustments to the mandate and reconfiguration of the Mission, his letter dated 28 August 2014[60] and his update to the Security Council on 12 November 2014,

Determining that the situation in Liberia continues to constitute a threat to international peace and security in the region,

Acting under Chapter VII of the Charter of the United Nations,

Governance, rule of law, security sector reform and national reconciliation

1. *Emphasizes* that the Government of Liberia bears primary and ultimate responsibility for security and the protection of its population, and urges the Government to prioritize the effective and rapid development of the

security agencies, especially the Liberia National Police, which is the priority law enforcement agency tasked with civilian policing responsibilities, including through the timely provision of sufficient financial resources and other support;

2. *Encourages* the Government of Liberia to prioritize its efforts to further national reconciliation and economic recovery, to combat corruption and to promote efficiency and good governance, in particular by continuing to strengthen Government transparency and accountability, including by managing effectively Liberia's natural resources, emphasizes the importance of pursuing a national reconciliation and social cohesion strategy, through concrete measures to promote national healing, justice and reconciliation at all levels and involving all Liberian stakeholders, and calls upon the Government to continue to support the participation of women in conflict prevention, conflict resolution and peacebuilding, including in decision-making roles in post-conflict governance institutions and the broad range of reform efforts;

3. *Emphasizes* the need for continued progress by the Liberian authorities on constitutional and institutional reforms, especially of the rule of law and security sectors, and the national reconciliation processes, particularly in the light of the wider political, security, socioeconomic and humanitarian impact of the Ebola outbreak on communities and the need to plan for the longer-term recovery of Liberia, in this regard requests the Special Representative of the Secretary-General for Liberia to assist such efforts through the use of good offices and political support, including in view of the senatorial elections, and stresses that the responsibility for the preparation, security and conduct of free, fair, transparent and safe elections, including measures to mitigate the potential negative impact of the holding of elections on the spread of Ebola, rests with the Liberian authorities;

4. *Urges* the Government of Liberia to intensify its efforts toward achieving progress on the transition of security responsibilities from the United Nations Mission in Liberia to the national authorities, particularly with regard to prioritizing and resourcing the critical gaps to facilitate a successful transition, improving the capacity and capability of the Liberia National Police and the Bureau of Immigration and Naturalization as well as the justice sector, including courts and prisons, enabling the promotion of human rights and reconciliation, effective oversight, professionalism, transparency and accountability across all security institutions and strengthening democratic institutions and extension of State authority and services throughout the country for the benefit of all Liberians;

5. *Affirms its expectation* that the Government of Liberia will assume fully its complete security responsibilities from the Mission no later than 30 June 2016, and also affirms its intention to consider accordingly, consistent with paragraphs 16 and 17 below, the continued and future reconfiguration of the Mission;

6. *Stresses* the importance of the Government of Liberia formulating a concrete plan, with timelines and benchmarks, for building the security sector in coordination with the reconfiguration of the Mission, detailing leadership, coordination, monitoring and resources, oversight mechanisms, early passage of the draft Police Act and further reform of the promotion and manpower policies, with a view to decentralizing the national security institutions, particularly the Liberia National Police;

7. *Underscores* the importance of the Government of Liberia, in coordination with the Mission, the United Nations country team and international partners, continuing to develop national security and rule of law institutions that are fully and independently operational, and to this end encourages accelerated coordinated progress on the development and implementation of the security and justice development plans and the national human rights action plan, urges the effective, transparent and efficient management by the Government of assistance, including from bilateral and multilateral partners, to support the reform of the justice and security sectors, and further urges the Government to redouble its efforts to register and track arms and related materiel used and imported by its security forces;

Sexual and gender-based violence

8. *Expresses its continued concern* that women and girls in Liberia continue to face a high incidence of sexual and gender-based violence, reiterates its call upon the Government of Liberia to continue to combat sexual violence, particularly against children, and gender-based violence, to aggressively combat impunity for perpetrators of such crimes, to provide redress, support and protection to victims, including through public information campaigns and by continuing to strengthen national police capacity in this area, and to raise awareness of existing national legislation on sexual violence, and encourages the Government to reinforce its commitment in this regard, including by funding the implementation of its national action plan on sexual and gender-based violence and improving women and girls' access to justice;

Mandate of the United Nations Mission in Liberia

9. *Decides* to extend the mandate of the Mission until 30 September 2015;

10. *Also decides* that the mandate of the Mission shall be the following, in priority order:

(*a*) *Protection of civilians*

To protect, without prejudice to the primary responsibility of the Liberian authorities, the civilian population from threat of physical violence, within its capabilities and areas of deployment;

(*b*) *Humanitarian assistance support*

(i) To facilitate the provision of humanitarian assistance, including in collaboration with the Government of Liberia, and those supporting it, and by helping to establish the necessary security conditions;

(ii) To coordinate with the United Nations Mission for Ebola Emergency Response, as appropriate;

(*c*) *Reform of justice and security institutions*

(i) To assist the Government of Liberia in developing and implementing, as soon as possible and in close coordination with bilateral and multilateral partners, its national strategy on security sector reform;

(ii) To advise the Government of Liberia on security sector reform and on the organization of the Liberia National Police and the Bureau of Immigration and Naturalization to provide technical assistance, co-location and mentoring programmes for the National Police and the Bureau, with a particular focus on developing the leadership and internal management systems of the National Police and the Bureau, as well as for justice and corrections;

(iii) To assist the Government of Liberia in extending national justice and security sector services throughout the country through capacity-building and training;

(iv) To assist the Government of Liberia to coordinate these efforts with all partners, including bilateral and multilateral donors;

(*d*) *Electoral support*

To assist the Government of Liberia with the senatorial elections by providing logistical support, particularly to facilitate access to remote areas, coordinating international electoral assistance and supporting Liberian institutions and all Liberian stakeholders, including political parties, in creating an atmosphere conducive to the conduct of peaceful elections, including through UNMIL Radio;

(*e*) *Human rights promotion and protection*

(i) To carry out human rights promotion, protection and monitoring activities in Liberia, with special attention to violations and abuses committed against children and women, notably sexual and gender-based violence;

(ii) To support the strengthening of efforts by the Government of Liberia to combat sexual and gender-based violence, including its efforts to combat impunity for perpetrators of such crimes;

(*f*) *Protection of United Nations personnel*

To protect United Nations personnel, installations and equipment and ensure the security and freedom of movement of United Nations and associated personnel;

11. *Further decides* that the Mission, in accordance with paragraphs 4 to 6 and 10 (*c*) above, shall put renewed focus on supporting the Government of Liberia to achieve a successful transition of complete security responsibility to the Liberia National Police by strengthening its capacity to manage existing personnel and to improve training programmes to expedite their readiness to assume security responsibilities throughout Liberia;

12. *Requests* the Mission to ensure that any support provided to non-United Nations security forces is provided in strict compliance with the human rights due diligence policy on United Nations support to non-United Nations security forces;[64]

[64] S/2013/110, annex.

13. *Requests* the Secretary-General to ensure that the Mission has the requisite qualified specialist advisers with the professional skills and experience appropriate to this transition phase in order to enhance mentoring with the aim of increasing the capacity of the Government of Liberia, particularly the Liberia National Police and the Bureau of Immigration and Naturalization, to accelerate the implementation of sustainable rule of law, justice, governance and security sector reform programmes, including mechanisms to hold perpetrators of sexual and gender-based violence accountable;

14. *States* the importance of the Mission, within its capabilities and areas of deployment, and without prejudice to its mandate, continuing to assist the Government of Liberia, the Security Council Committee established pursuant to paragraph 21 of resolution 1521 (2003) and the Panel of Experts on Liberia and to carry out its tasks in this regard, as set forth in previous resolutions, including resolution 1683 (2006) of 13 June 2006;

Force structure

15. *Decides* that the authorized strength of the Mission shall remain at up to 4,811 military and 1,795 police personnel;

16. *Recalls* its endorsement, in its resolution 2066 (2012), of the recommendation of the Secretary-General to decrease the military strength of the Mission in three phases between August 2012 and July 2015, and affirms its intention to resume the phased drawdown once it has been determined that Liberia has made significant progress in combatting the Ebola outbreak, which represents a threat to the peace and stability of Liberia;

17. *Requests* the Secretary-General to provide an update no later than 15 March 2015 on the situation in Liberia, especially an assessment of the impact of the Ebola outbreak on the stability of Liberia and options for resuming the drawdown in line with the objective of completing the security transition as referred to in paragraph 5 above, and recognizes that the modalities for the resumption of the phased drawdown, referred to in paragraph 16 above, may require adjustments in the light of this update;

Regional and inter-mission cooperation

18. *Recognizes* that the Ebola outbreak has put on hold the joint activities between the Governments of Liberia and Côte d'Ivoire, as well as between the United Nations Mission in Liberia and the United Nations Operation in Côte d'Ivoire, calls upon these Governments to continue reinforcing their cooperation, particularly with respect to the border area, including through increased monitoring, information-sharing, and coordinated actions, and in implementing the shared border strategy, inter alia, to support the disarmament and repatriation of armed elements on both sides of the border and the voluntary return of refugees in safety and dignity, as well as to address the root causes of conflict and tension, and in this regard calls upon all United Nations entities in Côte d'Ivoire and Liberia, including all relevant components of the Operation and the Mission, within their respective mandates, capabilities and areas of deployment, as well as the two United Nations country teams, where relevant and appropriate, to support the Ivorian and Liberian authorities;

19. *Affirms* the importance of inter-mission cooperation arrangements as the United Nations Mission in Liberia and the United Nations Operation in Côte d'Ivoire downsize, reaffirms the inter-mission cooperation framework set out in its resolution 1609 (2005) of 24 June 2005, recalls its endorsement in its resolution 2062 (2012) of 26 July 2012 of the recommendation of the Secretary-General to transfer three armed helicopters from the Mission to the Operation to be used in both Côte d'Ivoire and Liberia along and across their border, and also recalls its decision in its resolution 2162 (2014) of 25 June 2014 that all military utility helicopters of the Operation and the Mission shall be utilized in both Côte d'Ivoire and Liberia in order to facilitate rapid response and mobility, while not affecting the area of responsibility of either mission;

20. *Recalls* the proposal by the Secretary-General as set out in his report of 15 May 2014,[65] to establish, in the context of inter-mission cooperation arrangements between the United Nations Mission in Liberia and the United Nations Operation in Côte d'Ivoire, for an initial period of one year and within the authorized military strength of the Operation, a quick reaction force to implement the mandate of the Operation and to support the Mission, while reiterating that this unit will remain primarily an asset of the Operation;

[65] S/2014/342.

21. *Also recalls* its authorization, pursuant to its resolution 2162 (2014), to the Secretary-General to deploy this unit to Liberia, subject to the consent of the troop-contributing countries concerned and the Government of Liberia, in the event of a serious deterioration of the security situation on the ground in order to temporarily reinforce the Mission with the sole purpose of implementing its mandate, and further recalls its requests to the Secretary-General to take steps to ensure that this unit reaches full operational capability as soon as possible, and no later than May 2015, and to inform the Council immediately of any deployment of this unit to Liberia and to obtain Council authorization for any such deployment for a period that exceeds 90 days;

Reports of the Secretary-General

22. *Requests* the Secretary-General to keep the Council regularly informed of the situation in Liberia and the implementation of the mandate of the Mission and to provide to it a midterm report no later than 30 April 2015 and a final report no later than 15 August 2015 on the situation on the ground and implementation of the present resolution;

23. *Decides* to remain seized of the matter.

Adopted unanimously at the 7340th meeting.

Decisions

On 8 January 2015, the President of the Security Council addressed the following letter to the Secretary-General:[66]

> I have the honour to inform you that your letter dated 6 January 2015, concerning your intention to appoint Major General Salihu Zaway Uba, of Nigeria, as Force Commander of the United Nations Mission in Liberia,[67] has been brought to the attention of the members of the Security Council. They take note of the intention expressed in your letter.

At its 7423rd meeting, on 2 April 2015, the Council considered the item entitled "The situation in Liberia".

Resolution 2215 (2015) of 2 April 2015

The Security Council,

Recalling its previous resolutions concerning the situation in Liberia and the subregion, in particular resolutions 1509 (2003) of 19 September 2003, 2066 (2012) of 17 September 2012, 2116 (2013) of 18 September 2013, 2176 (2014) of 15 September 2014, 2177 (2014) of 18 September 2014 and 2190 (2014) of 15 December 2014,

Commending the Government of Liberia for responding effectively to the Ebola outbreak in Liberia, and recognizing in this regard the resilience of the people and Government of Liberia, and its security institutions, especially the Armed Forces of Liberia and the Liberia National Police,

Welcoming the efforts of Member States, bilateral partners and multilateral organizations, including the United Nations, the African Union and the Economic Community of West African States, to support the Government of Liberia in its response to the Ebola outbreak, further welcoming the contributions of the international community, including the Peacebuilding Commission, to assist Liberia in its comprehensive development commitment in the post-Ebola recovery period, and strongly encouraging further steps forward in this regard,

Recalling its endorsement, in resolution 2066 (2012), of the recommendation of the Secretary-General to decrease the military strength of the United Nations Mission in Liberia in three phases between August 2012 and July 2015,

[66] S/2015/13.

[67] S/2015/12.

Taking note of the report of the Secretary-General of 15 August 2014,[61] as well as his update to the Security Council on 16 March 2015 and recommendations on the resumption of the drawdown of the Mission,

Determining that the situation in Liberia continues to constitute a threat to international peace and security in the region,

Acting under Chapter VII of the Charter of the United Nations,

1. *Endorses* the recommendation of the Secretary-General in his update of 16 March 2015 on the drawdown of uniformed personnel of the United Nations Mission in Liberia, and, consistent with resolution 2190 (2014), authorizes the Secretary-General to implement the third phase of the phased drawdown to arrive at a new military ceiling of 3,590 personnel and to reduce the police ceiling to 1,515 personnel, with both ceilings to be reached by September 2015;

2. *Decides* that the mandate of the Mission shall no longer include the task set forth in paragraph 10 (*d*) of resolution 2190 (2014);

3. *Reaffirms its expectation* that the Government of Liberia will assume fully its complete security responsibilities from the Mission no later than 30 June 2016, and also reaffirms its intention to consider the continued and future reconfiguration of the Mission accordingly;

4. *Requests* the Secretary-General to continue to streamline the activities of the Mission across its civilian, police and military components to fully reflect the downsizing of the police and military components and narrowing of the mandate decided in resolution 2190 (2014) and the present resolution, and further requests the Secretary-General to consolidate the civilian, police and military presence of the Mission in line with the security transition noted in paragraph 3 above;

5. *Calls upon* the Governments of Liberia and Côte d'Ivoire to continue reinforcing their cooperation, particularly with respect to the border area, and in this regard calls upon all United Nations entities in Côte d'Ivoire and Liberia, including all relevant components of the United Nations Operation in Côte d'Ivoire and the United Nations Mission in Liberia, within their respective mandates, capabilities and areas of deployment, as well as the two United Nations country teams, where relevant and appropriate, to support the Ivorian and Liberian authorities;

6. *Reaffirms* the importance of inter-mission cooperation arrangements as the United Nations Mission in Liberia and the United Nations Operation in Côte d'Ivoire downsize, as well as the inter-mission cooperation framework set out in resolution 1609 (2005) of 24 June 2005, and recalls the relevant provisions of resolution 2162 (2014) of 25 June 2014 in this regard;

7. *Decides* to remain seized of the matter.

Adopted unanimously at the 7423rd meeting.

Decisions

At its 7438th meeting, on 5 May 2015, the Security Council decided to invite the representative of Liberia to participate, without vote, in accordance with rule 37 of its provisional rules of procedure, in the discussion of the item entitled:

"The situation in Liberia

"Twenty-ninth progress report of the Secretary-General on the United Nations Mission in Liberia (S/2015/275)".

At the same meeting, the Council also decided to extend invitations, in accordance with rule 39 of its provisional rules of procedure, to Ms. Karin Landgren, Special Representative of the Secretary-General for Liberia and Head of the United Nations Mission in Liberia, and Mr. Olof Skoog, Permanent Representative of Sweden to the United Nations, in his capacity as Chair of the Liberia configuration of the Peacebuilding Commission.

THE SITUATION IN SOMALIA[68]

Decisions

At its 7278th meeting, on 14 October 2014, the Security Council decided to invite the representative of Somalia to participate, without vote, in accordance with rule 37 of its provisional rules of procedure, in the discussion of the item entitled:

"The situation in Somalia

"Report of the Secretary-General on Somalia (S/2014/699)".

At the same meeting, the Council also decided to extend an invitation, in accordance with rule 39 of its provisional rules of procedure, to Mr. Nicholas Kay, Special Representative of the Secretary-General for Somalia and Head of the United Nations Assistance Mission in Somalia.

At the same meeting, the Council further decided to extend an invitation, in accordance with rule 39 of its provisional rules of procedure, to Mr. Maman Sidikou, Special Representative of the Chairperson of the African Union Commission for Somalia and Head of the African Union Mission in Somalia.

At its 7284th meeting, on 22 October 2014, the Council decided to invite the representative of Somalia to participate, without vote, in accordance with rule 37 of its provisional rules of procedure, in the discussion of the item entitled:

"The situation in Somalia

"Report of the Secretary-General on the situation with respect to piracy and armed robbery at sea off the coast of Somalia (S/2014/740)".

At the same meeting, the Council also decided to extend an invitation, in accordance with rule 39 of its provisional rules of procedure, to Mr. Jeffrey Feltman, Under-Secretary-General for Political Affairs.

At its 7286th meeting, on 24 October 2014, the Council decided to invite the representative of Somalia to participate, without vote, in accordance with rule 37 of its provisional rules of procedure, in the discussion of the item entitled:

"The situation in Somalia

"Report of the Secretary-General on Somalia (S/2014/699)

"Letters dated 10 October 2014 from the Chair of the Security Council Committee pursuant to resolutions 751 (1992) and 1907 (2009) concerning Somalia and Eritrea addressed to the President of the Security Council (S/2014/726 and S/2014/727)".

Resolution 2182 (2014) of 24 October 2014

The Security Council,

Recalling all its previous resolutions and the statements by its President on the situation in Somalia and Eritrea, in particular resolutions 733 (1992) of 23 January 1992, 1844 (2008) of 20 November 2008, 1907 (2009) of 23 December 2009, 2023 (2011) of 5 December 2011, 2036 (2012) of 22 February 2012, 2093 (2013) of 6 March 2013, 2111 (2013) of 24 July 2013, 2124 (2013) of 12 November 2013, 2125 (2013) of 18 November 2013 and 2142 (2014) of 5 March 2014,

Taking note of the final reports of the Monitoring Group on Somalia and Eritrea[69] and the conclusions contained therein on the situations in both Somalia and Eritrea,

Reaffirming its respect for the sovereignty, territorial integrity, political independence and unity of Somalia, Djibouti and Eritrea, respectively,

[68] Resolutions or decisions on this question were first adopted by the Security Council in 1992.

[69] See S/2014/726 and S/2014/727.

Condemning flows of weapons and ammunition supplies to and through Somalia in violation of the arms embargo on Somalia and to Eritrea in violation of the arms embargo on Eritrea, as a serious threat to peace and stability in the region,

Somalia

Welcoming the recent high-level event on Somalia, chaired by the Secretary-General, and looking forward to all participants following up on their commitments,

Highlighting, in particular, the commitment of the Federal Government of Somalia to establish interim regional administrations by the end of 2014, which is an essential step under the Vision 2016 programme, and emphasizing the importance of this being an inclusive and consultative process,

Underlining the importance of full and effective participation in the peace and reconciliation process across Somali society, including women, youth and minority groups,

Welcoming the establishment of the Independent Constitutional Review and Implementation Commission, and emphasizing the importance of establishing the Boundaries and Federation Commission within the upcoming parliamentary session,

Welcoming also the commitment of the Federal Government of Somalia to a credible electoral process in 2016, emphasizing the need for legislation to establish the National Independent Electoral Commission as soon as possible, underlining the importance of all partners supporting a Somali-led process, and looking forward in particular to the upcoming United Nations electoral assessment mission,

Underlining the importance of capacity-building of the Somali security forces, and in this regard reaffirming the importance of re-establishing training, equipping and retention in the Security Forces of the Federal Government of Somalia, which is vital for the long-term stability and security of Somalia, expressing its support for the ongoing European Union Training Mission and other capacity-building programmes, and emphasizing the importance of increased coordinated, timely and sustained support from the international community,

Underlining also the need for greater effort in improving the institutional transparency and accountability of public financial management in Somalia, welcoming the establishment of a Financial Governance Committee, encouraging the Federal Government of Somalia to use the Committee effectively, and underlining the need for increased mutual transparency and accountability between the Federal Government and the donor community,

Welcoming the intention of the Secretary-General and the World Bank to develop an initiative aimed at promoting economic development in the Horn of Africa, and looking forward to the results of the initiative,

Recalling the total ban on the export and import of charcoal from Somalia, irrespective of whether such charcoal originated in Somalia, as set out in resolution 2036 (2012),

Expressing concern at the continuing violations and abuses of human rights, including extrajudicial killings, violence against women, children and journalists, arbitrary detention and pervasive sexual violence in Somalia, including in camps for internally displaced persons, underscoring the need to end impunity, promote and protect human rights and hold accountable those who commit such crimes, welcoming the efforts of the Federal Government of Somalia to address violations and abuses of human rights, including by implementing the two action plans signed on children and armed conflict and by developing a national action plan to combat sexual violence, and encouraging the Federal Government to establish its National Human Rights Commission and to take concrete measures to implement fully the post-transition human rights road map of August 2013,

Recalling the arms embargo on Somalia, and in particular the need for all supplies of weapons and military equipment destined for the Security Forces of the Federal Government of Somalia to be notified to the Security Council Committee pursuant to resolutions 751 (1992) and 1907 (2009) (the Committee), and further recalling that improved arms and ammunition management in Somalia is a fundamental component of greater peace and stability for the region,

Stressing that any decision to continue or end the partial suspension of the arms embargo on the Federal Government of Somalia will be taken in the light of the thoroughness of the Federal Government's implementation of its requirements as set out in the present resolution and other relevant Council resolutions,

Stressing also the need for all Member States to respect and implement, in accordance with relevant Council resolutions, their obligations with respect to preventing unauthorized deliveries of weapons and military equipment to Somalia and to prevent the direct or indirect import of charcoal from Somalia in violation of the relevant Council resolutions,

Recalling that international law, as reflected in the United Nations Convention on the Law of the Sea of 10 December 1982,[70] sets out the legal framework applicable to activities in the ocean,

Taking note of the Monitoring Group's continued assessment that the illegal charcoal trade continues to generate significant funding for Al-Shabaab, reiterating that charcoal exports from Somalia are a significant revenue source for Al-Shabaab and also exacerbate the humanitarian crisis, and deploring the continued violation of the ban,

Expressing concern that destination countries for Somali charcoal have not yet taken sufficient steps to prevent the importation of charcoal from Somalia,

Taking note of the letter dated 8 October 2014 from the President of Somalia to the Council requesting Member States to provide military assistance to prevent the export of charcoal from Somalia and to prevent the import of weapons into Somalia in violation of the arms embargo,

Encouraging the Federal Government of Somalia, in consultation with all levels of government in Somalia, to mitigate properly against the petroleum sector in Somalia becoming a source of increased tension in Somalia, including through respecting the provisions of the constitution, and stressing the need to resolve issues of resource management and ownership as part of ongoing discussions around federalism,

Eritrea

Welcoming the meetings between representatives of the Government of Eritrea and the Monitoring Group held in Paris and Cairo and by telephone conference from New York, encouraging further cooperation, and underlining its expectation that this cooperation will deepen during the mandate of the Monitoring Group, including through regular visits to Eritrea by the Monitoring Group,

Stressing its demand that Eritrea make available information pertaining to Djiboutian combatants missing in action since the clashes of June 2008 so that those concerned may ascertain the presence and conditions of the Djiboutian prisoners of war,

Underlining the importance of full cooperation between the Monitoring Group and the Government of Eritrea,

African Union Mission in Somalia

Expressing its gratitude to the African Union Mission in Somalia for its work in bringing greater peace and stability to Somalia,

Welcoming the recent joint operations of the African Union Mission with the Somali National Army, and paying tribute to the extraordinary bravery and sacrifices made by both Mission and National Army personnel in the fight against Al-Shabaab,

Recognizing the importance of effective coordination among the United Nations Support Office for the African Union Mission in Somalia, the African Union Mission, troop-contributing countries and donors in order for the Support Office to effectively plan, budget and provide authorized logistics for the operations of the Mission, and underscoring the necessity of enablers and force multipliers to address key limiting factors to Mission operations such as timely maintenance of key equipment, maintenance of logistical supply lines and availability of water,

Recalling and welcoming the efforts of the African Union Mission to assist in the provision of training to the Somali National Army, and underlining the importance of the Federal Government of Somalia taking on increased responsibility and ownership of the security sector, which is an essential part of the eventual exit strategy of the Mission,

---

[70] United Nations, *Treaty Series,* vol. 1833, No. 31363.

Expressing concern at the reports of sexual violence and exploitation allegedly perpetrated by some African Union Mission troops, reminding the Mission of the United Nations human rights due diligence policy,[71] underscoring in this context the importance of the United Nations zero-tolerance policy on sexual exploitation and abuse in the context of peacekeeping, welcoming the deployment by the African Union of a team to conduct a full investigation into these allegations, and underlining the importance of holding to account those responsible for such abuses,

Welcoming the support of the international community to peace and stability in Somalia, in particular the European Union, for its substantial contribution in supporting the African Union Mission, and emphasizing the importance of new contributors sharing the financial burden of supporting the Mission,

Monitoring Group on Somalia and Eritrea

Taking note of the letter dated 7 February 2014 from the Monitoring Group recommending an exemption to the arms embargo to improve reporting on security operations for commercial shipping,

Determining that the situation in Somalia, Eritrea's influence in Somalia, as well as the dispute between Djibouti and Eritrea, continue to constitute a threat to international peace and security in the region,

Acting under Chapter VII of the Charter of the United Nations,

Arms embargo

1. *Reaffirms* the arms embargo on Somalia, imposed by paragraph 5 of resolution 733 (1992) and further elaborated upon in paragraphs 1 and 2 of resolution 1425 (2002) of 22 July 2002 and modified by paragraphs 33 to 38 of resolution 2093 (2013), paragraphs 4 to 17 of resolution 2111 (2013), paragraph 14 of resolution 2125 (2013) and paragraph 2 of resolution 2142 (2014) (hereinafter referred to as "the arms embargo on Somalia");

2. *Notes with concern* that some deliveries of weapons and military equipment have not been notified to the Committee in accordance with the relevant Security Council resolutions, underlines the fundamental importance of timely and detailed notifications to the Committee as set out in paragraphs 3 to 7 of resolution 2142 (2014), notes with concern reports of the diversion of arms and ammunition, and encourages supplying Member States to assist the Federal Government of Somalia in improving its notifications to the Committee;

3. *Decides* to renew the provisions set out in paragraph 2 of resolution 2142 (2014) until 30 October 2015, and in that context reiterates that the arms embargo on Somalia shall not apply to deliveries of weapons, ammunition or military equipment or the provision of advice, assistance or training intended solely for the development of the Security Forces of the Federal Government of Somalia, to provide security for the Somali people, except in relation to deliveries of the items set out in the annex to resolution 2111 (2013);

4. *Welcomes* the steps taken by the Federal Government of Somalia to establish effective mechanisms in managing its weapons and military equipment, including the Arms and Ammunition Steering Committee, and notes with regret that these structures are not functioning with the required level of efficiency or at all levels of government;

5. *Expresses its disappointment* that a weapons marking and registration process has not yet commenced, despite the appeal by the Council in the statement by its President of 22 May 2014,[72] and urges the Federal Government of Somalia to implement this process without further delay;

6. *Requests* the Somali National Army and the African Union Mission in Somalia to document and register all military equipment captured as part of offensive operations or in the course of carrying out their mandates, including recording the type and serial number of the weapon and/or ammunition, photographing all items and relevant markings and facilitating inspection by the Monitoring Group on Somalia and Eritrea of all military items before their redistribution or destruction;

7. *Reiterates its request* to the Federal Government of Somalia, with the support of international partners, to establish a joint verification team which would conduct routine inspections of government security forces'

[71] S/2013/110, annex.

[72] S/PRST/2014/9.

stockpiles, inventory records and the supply chain of weapons, and requests that any such group provide its findings to the Committee, for the purpose of mitigating the diversion of arms and ammunition to entities outside of the security services of the Federal Government;

8. *Reiterates* that weapons or military equipment sold or supplied solely for the development of the Security Forces of the Federal Government of Somalia may not be resold to, transferred to, or made available for use by, any individual or entity not in the service of the Security Forces;

9. *Urges* the Federal Government of Somalia to implement fully all its requirements as set out in the present resolution and other relevant Council resolutions, and requests the Federal Government to report to the Council by 30 March 2015, and then by 30 September 2015, on:

(*a*) The current structure of the Security Forces of the Federal Government of Somalia;

(*b*) The infrastructure in place to ensure the safe storage, registration, maintenance and distribution of military equipment by the Security Forces of the Federal Government of Somalia;

(*c*) The procedures and codes of conduct in place for the registration, distribution, use and storage of weapons by the Security Forces of the Federal Government of Somalia, and on training needs in this regard;

10. *Takes note* of the recommendation of the Monitoring Group that weapons on board vessels engaged in commercial activity in Somali ports be granted an exemption to the arms embargo, expresses its willingness to take such a proposal forward, in close consultation with the Federal Government of Somalia, and requests the Federal Government and the Monitoring Group to work together and formulate a proposal which should be communicated to the Council by 27 February 2015;

Maritime interdiction of charcoal and arms

11. *Reaffirms* the ban on the import and export of Somali charcoal, as set out in paragraph 22 of resolution 2036 (2012) (the charcoal ban), reiterates that the Somali authorities shall take the measures necessary to prevent the export of charcoal from Somalia, and reiterates its requests in paragraph 18 of resolution 2111 (2013) that the African Union Mission support and assist the Somali authorities in doing so, as part of the implementation by the Mission of its mandate set out in paragraph 1 of resolution 2093 (2013);

12. *Condemns* the ongoing export of charcoal from Somalia, in violation of the total ban on the export of charcoal from Somalia reaffirmed above;

13. *Urges* all Member States, including those contributing police and troop contingents to the African Union Mission, to respect and implement their obligations to prevent the direct or indirect import of charcoal from Somalia, whether or not such charcoal originated in Somalia, as set out in paragraph 22 of resolution 2036 (2012), and affirms that this includes taking the measures necessary to prevent the use of their flag vessels for such importing;

14. *Condemns* the flow of weapons and military equipment to Al-Shabaab and other armed groups which are not part of the Security Forces of the Federal Government of Somalia, and expresses serious concern at the destabilizing impact of such weapons;

15. *Authorizes*, for a period of 12 months from the date of the present resolution, Member States, acting nationally or through voluntary multinational naval partnerships, such as the Combined Maritime Forces, in cooperation with the Federal Government of Somalia and which the Federal Government has notified to the Secretary-General and which the Secretary-General has subsequently notified to all Member States, in order to ensure strict implementation of the arms embargo on Somalia and the charcoal ban, to inspect, without undue delay, in Somali territorial waters and on the high seas off the coast of Somalia extending to and including the Arabian Sea and Persian Gulf, vessels bound to or from Somalia which they have reasonable grounds to believe are:

(i) Carrying charcoal from Somalia in violation of the charcoal ban;

(ii) Carrying weapons or military equipment to Somalia, directly or indirectly, in violation of the arms embargo on Somalia;

(iii) Carrying weapons or military equipment to individuals or entities designated by the Committee pursuant to resolutions 751 (1992) and 1907 (2009);

16. *Calls upon* all flag States of such vessels to cooperate with such inspections, requests Member States to make good-faith efforts to first seek the consent of the vessel's flag State prior to any inspections pursuant to paragraph 15 above, authorizes Member States conducting inspections pursuant to paragraph 15 to use all necessary measures commensurate with the circumstances to carry out such inspections and in full compliance with international humanitarian law and international human rights law, as may be applicable, and urges Member States conducting such inspections to do so without causing undue delay to or undue interference with the exercise of the right of innocent passage or freedom of navigation;

17. *Authorizes* Member States to seize and dispose of (such as through destruction, rendering inoperable or unusable, storage or transferring to a State other than the originating or destination States for disposal) any items identified in inspections pursuant to paragraph 15 above, the delivery, import or export of which is prohibited by the arms embargo on Somalia or the charcoal ban, authorizes Member States to collect evidence directly related to the carriage of such items in the course of such inspections, and decides that charcoal seized in accordance with the present paragraph may be disposed of through resale which shall be monitored by the Monitoring Group;

18. *Emphasizes* the importance of all Member States, including Somalia, taking the measures necessary to ensure that no claim shall lie at the instance of Somalia, or of any person or entity in Somalia, or of persons or entities designated for measures set out in resolutions 1844 (2008), 2002 (2011) of 29 July 2011 or 2093 (2013), or any person claiming through or for the benefit of any such person or entity, in connection with any contract or other transaction where its performance was prevented by reason of the measures imposed by the present resolution or previous resolutions;

19. *Requests* Member States to dispose of any charcoal, weapons or military equipment seized pursuant to paragraph 17 above in an environmentally responsible manner, taking into account the letter dated 4 September 2013 from the United Nations Environment Programme to the Chair of the Committee and the implementation assistance notice adopted by the Committee on 7 May 2014, calls upon all Member States in the region to cooperate in the disposal of such charcoal, weapons or military equipment, affirms that the authorization provided for in paragraph 15 above includes the authority to divert vessels and their crews to a suitable port to facilitate such disposal, with the consent of the port State, affirms that the authorization in paragraph 15 includes the authority to use all necessary measures to seize items pursuant to paragraph 17 in the course of inspections, and decides that any Member State cooperating in the disposal of items identified in inspections pursuant to paragraph 15, the delivery, import or export of which is prohibited by the arms embargo on Somalia or the charcoal ban, shall provide a written report to the Committee, no later than 30 days after such items enter its territory, on the steps taken to dispose of or destroy them;

20. *Decides* that any Member State that undertakes an inspection pursuant to paragraph 15 above shall promptly notify the Committee and submit a report on the inspection containing all relevant details, including an explanation of the grounds for and the results of the inspection and, where possible, including the flag of the vessel, the name of the vessel, the name and identifying information of the master of the vessel, the owner of the vessel and the original seller of the cargo, and efforts made to seek the consent of the vessel's flag State, requests the Committee to notify the flag State of the inspected vessel that an inspection has been undertaken, notes the prerogative of any Member State to write to the Committee concerning the implementation of any aspect of the present resolution, and further encourages the Monitoring Group to share relevant information with Member States operating under the authorization set out in the present resolution;

21. *Affirms* that the authorizations provided in the present resolution apply only with respect to the situation in Somalia and shall not affect the rights or obligations or responsibilities of Member States under international law, including any rights or obligations under the United Nations Convention on the Law of the Sea,[70] including the general principle of exclusive jurisdiction of a flag State over its vessels on the high seas, with respect to any other situation, underscores in particular that the present resolution shall not be considered as establishing customary international law, and notes further that such authorizations have been provided only following receipt of the letter dated 8 October 2014 conveying the request of the President of Somalia;

22. *Decides* to review after six months from the date of the present resolution the provisions set out in paragraphs 11 to 21 above;

African Union Mission in Somalia

23. *Decides* to authorize the States members of the African Union to maintain the deployment of the African Union Mission as set out in paragraph 1 of resolution 2093 (2013) until 30 November 2015, in line with the request of the Council to the African Union for a maximum level of 22,126 troops, which shall be authorized to take all measures necessary, in full compliance with the obligations of its Member States under international humanitarian law and human rights law, and in full respect of the sovereignty, territorial integrity, political independence and unity of Somalia, to carry out its mandate;

24. *Recalls* the benchmarks for the deployment of a United Nations peacekeeping operation as set out in both the letter dated 11 October 2013 from the Chairperson of the African Union Commission to the Secretary-General[73] and the subsequent letter, dated 14 October 2013, from the Secretary-General to the President of the Security Council,[74] requests that the Secretary-General keep these benchmarks under continuous review in close consultation with the African Union, and further requests the Secretary-General and the African Union to review jointly the impact of the temporary surge authorized in resolution 2124 (2013) and to set out recommendations on the next steps in the military campaign by 30 May 2015, taking into due consideration the political situation in Somalia;

25. *Also recalls* that, in line with the joint African Union-United Nations review of the African Union Mission, the increases in the force strength decided in resolution 2124 (2013) are to provide a short-term enhancement of the military capacity of the Mission, for a period of 18 to 24 months and as part of an overall exit strategy for the Mission, after which a decrease in the force strength of the Mission will be considered;

26. *Reiterates* paragraphs 4 and 14 of resolution 2124 (2013) and paragraphs 4 and 5 of resolution 2093 (2013) with regard to the logistical support package for the African Union Mission;

27. *Requests* the Secretary-General to continue to work closely with and provide technical expertise to the African Union as set out in paragraph 9 of resolution 2124 (2013), in particular by improving the efficiency in the planning and strategic management of the African Union Mission, including strengthening command and control structures and improving the coordination between troop contingents, sectors and joint operations with the Somali National Army;

28. *Welcomes* the recent joint African Union Mission and Somali National Army offensive operations, which have had a significant impact in reducing territory held by Al-Shabaab, underlines the importance of such operations continuing, further underlines that it is essential that military operations be followed immediately by national efforts to establish or improve governance structures in recovered areas and by the delivery of basic services, including security, and in that regard encourages the timely delivery of quick-impact projects in support of stabilization efforts of the Federal Government of Somalia;

29. *Underlines* the imperative of securing key supply routes to areas recovered from Al-Shabaab in view of the deteriorating humanitarian situation in Somalia, requests the African Union Mission and the Somali National Army to ensure that they give the utmost priority to securing key supply routes essential to improve the humanitarian situation in the most affected areas, and requests the Secretary-General to report, in consultation with the Federal Government of Somalia and the Mission, on progress in this regard in his written reports to the Council as set out in paragraph 15 of resolution 2158 (2014) of 29 May 2014;

30. *Strongly urges* Member States to provide helicopters to the African Union Mission for the authorized aviation component of up to 12 military helicopters, provided for in paragraph 6 of resolution 2036 (2012), as well as providing the enablers and force multipliers which were identified as necessary in the 2013 joint United Nations-African Union benchmarking assessment;

31. *Reiterates its request*, and that of the African Union Peace and Security Council for the African Union Mission to develop further an effective approach to the protection of civilians, notes with concern that the Mission has not yet established a Civilian Casualty Tracking, Analysis and Response Cell, as requested in resolutions 2093 (2013) and 2124 (2013), and requests the African Union to conclude the deployment of this Cell without any further delay;

[73] S/2013/620, annex.

[74] S/2013/606.

32. *Looks forward* to the results of both the investigation by the African Union and investigations by troop-contributing countries concerning acts of sexual exploitation and abuse allegedly perpetrated by some African Union Mission soldiers, underlines the importance of accountability and transparency in this regard, requests the African Union to review and endorse the draft African Union policy on prevention and response to sexual exploitation and abuse, and requests the African Union and the Secretary-General to make public the outcomes of these investigations;

33. *Underlines* the need for African Union Mission troops to continue to receive appropriate information and predeployment training in relation to human rights principles, including gender equality and sexual violence, and for Mission personnel to be properly informed of the accountability mechanisms in place should any abuse be committed;

34. *Encourages* the African Union Mission to strengthen the mechanisms to prevent and respond to sexual violence and sexual exploitation and abuse, such as introducing a centralized database for the efficient and independent receipt, preliminary assessment and tracking of investigations into allegations of sexual and gender-based violence and sexual exploitation and abuse, including through the institution of protective measures for complainants in order to prevent the redeployment of any individual who has been involved in serious violations of international humanitarian law and international human rights law, including those related to sexual violence;

35. *Condemns* all violations and abuses committed against children by all parties in Somalia, calls for the immediate cessation of such violations and abuses and for those responsible to be held to account, and requests the Federal Government of Somalia and the African Union Mission to protect and treat as victims those children who have been released or otherwise separated from armed forces and armed groups, including through the full implementation of standard operating procedures for the protection and handover of those children;

36. *Reiterates* the need for the African Union Mission to ensure that any detainees in its custody, including disengaged combatants, are treated in strict compliance with applicable obligations under international humanitarian law and human rights law, including ensuring their humane treatment, and further reiterates its request for the Mission to allow appropriate access to detainees by a neutral body;

37. *Reiterates its call* for new donors to support the African Union Mission through the provision of additional funding for troop stipends, equipment, technical assistance and uncaveated funding for the Mission to the United Nations trust fund for the Mission, calls upon the African Union to consider how to provide sustainable funding for the Mission, such as through its own assessed costs as it did for the African-led International Support Mission in Mali, and underlines the African Union's call for its member States to provide financial support to the African Union Mission;

Public financial management in Somalia

38. *Expresses its concern* that corruption continues to undermine both security in the country and the efforts of the Federal Government of Somalia to rebuild Somalia's institutions, and urges the Federal Government to fight corruption and tighten financial governance procedures in order to improve transparency and accountability of public financial management, and also urges the Federal Government to ensure that assets recovered from overseas and revenue raised, including through the ports, are documented transparently and channelled through the national budget;

39. *Underlines* the importance of ensuring that international aid is also delivered in a transparent manner, and encourages all Member States to use the structures currently being established between the Federal Government of Somalia and donors, particularly on recurrent financing;

Humanitarian situation in Somalia

40. *Expresses serious concern* at the deterioration of the humanitarian situation in Somalia, condemns in the strongest terms increased attacks against humanitarian actors and any misuse of donor assistance and the obstruction of the delivery of humanitarian aid, and reiterates paragraph 10 of resolution 2158 (2014) in this regard;

41. *Decides* that, until 30 October 2015 and without prejudice to humanitarian assistance programmes conducted elsewhere, the measures imposed by paragraph 3 of resolution 1844 (2008) shall not apply to the payment of funds, other financial assets or economic resources necessary to ensure the timely delivery of urgently

needed humanitarian assistance in Somalia, by the United Nations, its specialized agencies or programmes, humanitarian organizations having observer status in the General Assembly that provide humanitarian assistance and their implementing partners, including bilaterally or multilaterally funded non-governmental organizations participating in the United Nations Consolidated Appeal for Somalia;

42. *Requests* the Emergency Relief Coordinator to report to the Council by 1 October 2015 on the delivery of humanitarian assistance in Somalia and on any impediments to the delivery of humanitarian assistance in Somalia, and requests relevant United Nations agencies and humanitarian organizations having observer status in the General Assembly and their implementing partners that provide humanitarian assistance in Somalia to increase their cooperation and willingness to share information with the United Nations Resident and Humanitarian Coordinator for Somalia in the preparation of such reports and in the interest of increasing transparency and accountability;

Monitoring Group on Somalia and Eritrea

43. *Recalls* resolution 1844 (2008), by which it imposed targeted sanctions, and resolutions 2002 (2011) and 2093 (2013), by which it expanded the listing criteria, and notes that one of the listing criteria under resolution 1844 (2008) is engaging in acts that threaten the peace, security and stability of Somalia;

44. *Reiterates its willingness* to adopt targeted measures against individuals and entities on the basis of the above-mentioned criteria;

45. *Requests* Member States to assist the Monitoring Group in its investigations, and reiterates that obstructing the investigations or work of the Monitoring Group is a criterion for listing under paragraph 15 (*e*) of resolution 1907 (2009);

46. *Decides* to extend until 30 November 2015 the mandate of the Monitoring Group as set out in paragraph 13 of resolution 2060 (2012) of 25 July 2012 and updated in paragraph 41 of resolution 2093 (2013), expresses its intention to review the mandate and take appropriate action regarding the further extension no later than 30 October 2015, and requests the Secretary-General to take the necessary administrative measures, as expeditiously as possible, to re-establish the Monitoring Group, in consultation with the Committee, for a period of 13 months from the date of the present resolution, drawing, as appropriate, on the expertise of the members of the Monitoring Group established pursuant to previous resolutions;

47. *Requests* the Monitoring Group to submit, for the consideration of the Council, through the Committee, two final reports, one focusing on Somalia, the other on Eritrea, covering all the tasks set out in paragraph 13 of resolution 2060 (2012) and updated in paragraph 41 of resolution 2093 (2013), not later than 30 September 2015;

48. *Requests* the Committee, in accordance with its mandate and in consultation with the Monitoring Group and other relevant United Nations entities, to consider the recommendations in the reports of the Monitoring Group and recommend to the Council ways to improve the implementation of and compliance with the Somalia and Eritrea arms embargoes, the measures regarding the import and export of charcoal from Somalia, as well as implementation of the measures imposed by paragraphs 1, 3 and 7 of resolution 1844 (2008) and paragraphs 5, 6, 8, 10, 12 and 13 of resolution 1907 (2009), taking into account paragraph 15 above, in response to continuing violations;

49. *Requests* the Monitoring Group to report on the implementation of the authorization set out in paragraph 15 above, as part of its regular reporting to the Committee;

50. *Encourages* Member States from East Africa to appoint focal points for the purpose of coordinating and exchanging information with the Monitoring Group on regional investigations into Al-Shabaab;

51. *Underlines* the importance of a constructive relationship between the Monitoring Group and the Federal Government of Somalia, welcomes efforts made by both so far, and emphasizes the need for this to continue and deepen during the course of this mandate;

52. *Welcomes* the ongoing and significant efforts of the Monitoring Group to engage with the Government of Eritrea and the Government's cooperation with the Monitoring Group, emphasizes that this must continue and strengthen, and reiterates its expectation that the Government will facilitate the entry of the Monitoring Group to Eritrea, as requested in paragraph 31 of resolution 2111 (2013);

53. *Urges* Eritrea to make available information pertaining to Djiboutian combatants missing in action since the clashes of 10 to 12 June 2008;

54. *Decides* to remain actively seized of the matter.

Adopted at the 7286th meeting by 13 votes to none, with 2 abstentions (Jordan and Russian Federation).

Decision

At its 7309th meeting, on 12 November 2014, the Security Council decided to invite the representatives of Croatia, Cyprus, Denmark, Italy, the Netherlands, Somalia and Spain to participate, without vote, in accordance with rule 37 of its provisional rules of procedure, in the discussion of the item entitled:

"The situation in Somalia

"Report of the Secretary-General on the situation with respect to piracy and armed robbery at sea off the coast of Somalia (S/2014/740)".

Resolution 2184 (2014)
of 12 November 2014

The Security Council,

Recalling its previous resolutions concerning the situation in Somalia, especially resolutions 1814 (2008) of 15 May 2008, 1816 (2008) of 2 June 2008, 1838 (2008) of 7 October 2008, 1844 (2008) of 20 November 2008, 1846 (2008) of 2 December 2008, 1851 (2008) of 16 December 2008, 1897 (2009) of 30 November 2009, 1918 (2010) of 27 April 2010, 1950 (2010) of 23 November 2010, 1976 (2011) of 11 April 2011, 2015 (2011) of 24 October 2011, 2020 (2011) of 22 November 2011, 2077 (2012) of 21 November 2012 and 2125 (2013) of 18 November 2013, as well as the statements by its President of 25 August 2010[75] and of 19 November 2012,[76]

Welcoming the report of the Secretary-General of 16 October 2014, as requested in resolution 2125 (2013), on the implementation of that resolution and on the situation with respect to piracy and armed robbery at sea off the coast of Somalia,[77]

Reaffirming its respect for the sovereignty, territorial integrity, political independence and unity of Somalia, including Somalia's sovereign rights in accordance with international law, with respect to offshore natural resources, including fisheries,

While noting that the joint counter-piracy efforts of States, regions, organizations, the maritime industry, the private sector, think tanks and civil society have resulted in a sharp decline in pirate attacks as well as hijackings since 2011, continuing to be gravely concerned by the ongoing threat that piracy and armed robbery at sea pose to the prompt, safe and effective delivery of humanitarian aid to Somalia and the region, to the safety of seafarers and other persons, to international navigation and the safety of commercial maritime routes and to other ships, including fishing activities in conformity with international law, and also gravely concerned by the extended range of the piracy threat into the western Indian Ocean and adjacent sea areas and increased pirate capacities,

Expressing concern about the reported involvement of children in piracy off the coast of Somalia, reported sexual exploitation of women and girls in areas controlled by pirates, as well as their reported coercion to participate in activities that support piracy,

Recognizing the need to investigate and prosecute not only suspects captured at sea, but also anyone who incites or intentionally facilitates piracy operations, including key figures of criminal networks involved in piracy who plan, organize, facilitate or illicitly finance or profit from such attacks, reiterating its concern over persons

[75] S/PRST/2010/16.

[76] S/PRST/2012/24.

[77] S/2014/740.

suspected of piracy having been released without facing justice, and reaffirming that the failure to prosecute persons responsible for acts of piracy and armed robbery at sea off the coast of Somalia undermines anti-piracy efforts,

Further reaffirming that international law, as reflected in the United Nations Convention on the Law of the Sea of 10 December 1982,[70] sets out the legal framework applicable to activities in the ocean, including countering piracy and armed robbery at sea,

Underlining the primary responsibility of the Somali authorities in the fight against piracy and armed robbery at sea off the coast of Somalia, and noting the several requests from Somali authorities for international assistance to counter piracy off the coast of Somalia, including the letter dated 4 November 2014 from the Permanent Representative of Somalia to the United Nations expressing the appreciation of Somali authorities to the Security Council for its assistance, expressing their willingness to consider working with other States and regional organizations to combat piracy and armed robbery at sea off the coast of Somalia and requesting that the provisions of resolution 2125 (2013) be renewed for an additional 12 months,

Welcoming the participation of the Federal Government of Somalia and regional partners in the seventeenth plenary session of the Contact Group on Piracy off the Coast of Somalia, hosted by the United Arab Emirates in Dubai on 28 October 2014,

Recognizing the work of the Contact Group to facilitate the prosecution of suspected pirates and to promote the establishment of the Law Enforcement Task Force, an ongoing network and mechanism for sharing information and evidence between investigators and prosecutors, in accordance with international law, welcoming the work of the Working Group on Capacity-Building of the Contact Group to coordinate judicial, penal and maritime capacity-building efforts to enable regional States to better tackle piracy, and welcoming the work of the Working Group on Disrupting Pirate Networks Ashore of the Contact Group to disrupt illicit financial flows linked to piracy,

Welcoming the financing provided by the Trust Fund to Support Initiatives of States Countering Piracy off the Coast of Somalia (the Trust Fund) to strengthen regional ability to prosecute suspected pirates and imprison those convicted in accordance with applicable international human rights law, noting with appreciation the assistance provided by the United Nations Office on Drugs and Crime Maritime Crime Programme, and being determined to continue efforts to ensure that pirates are held accountable,

Commending the efforts of the European Union operation Atalanta, the North Atlantic Treaty Organization Operation Ocean Shield, the Combined Maritime Forces' Combined Task Force 151 commanded by the Republic of Korea, followed by New Zealand, as well as United States ships assigned to Combined Task Force 151 and North Atlantic Treaty Organization Task Force 508, the counter-piracy activities of the African Union onshore in Somalia and the naval activities of the Southern African Development Community and other States acting in a national capacity in cooperation with Somali authorities and each other to suppress piracy and to protect ships transiting through the waters off the coast of Somalia, and welcoming the Shared Awareness and Deconfliction initiative and the efforts of individual countries, including China, India, Iran (Islamic Republic of), Japan, the Republic of Korea and the Russian Federation, which have deployed naval counter-piracy missions in the region, as stated in the report of the Secretary-General,

Noting the efforts of flag States in taking measures to permit vessels sailing under their flag transiting the high-risk area to embark vessel protection detachments and privately contracted armed security personnel, and encouraging States to regulate such activities in accordance with applicable international law and permit charters to favour arrangements that make use of such measures,

Noting also the request of some Member States on the need to review the boundaries of the high-risk area on an objective and transparent basis, taking into account actual incidents of piracy, and noting that the high-risk area is set and defined by the insurance and maritime industry,

Welcoming the capacity-building efforts in the region made by the International Maritime Organization-funded Code of Conduct concerning the Repression of Piracy and Armed Robbery against Ships in the Western Indian Ocean and the Gulf of Aden (the Djibouti Code of Conduct), the Trust Fund and the activities of the European Union under its Mission on Regional Maritime Capacity-building in the Horn of Africa (EUCAP Nestor), which is working with the Federal Government of Somalia to strengthen its criminal justice system, and recognizing the need for all engaged international and regional organizations to coordinate and cooperate fully,

Supporting the development of a coastal police force, noting with appreciation the efforts made by the International Maritime Organization and the shipping industry to develop and update guidance, best management practices and recommendations to assist ships to prevent and suppress piracy attacks off the coast of Somalia, including in the Gulf of Aden, and the Indian Ocean area, and recognizing the work of the International Maritime Organization and the Contact Group in this regard, noting the efforts of the International Organization for Standardization, which has developed industry standards of training and certification for private maritime security companies when providing privately contracted armed security personnel on board ships in high-risk areas, and further welcoming the European Union's EUCAP Nestor, which is working to develop the sea-going maritime security capacities of Somalia, Djibouti, Seychelles and the United Republic of Tanzania,

Noting with concern that the continuing limited capacity and domestic legislation to facilitate the custody and prosecution of suspected pirates after their capture has hindered more robust international action against the pirates off the coast of Somalia, and too often has led to pirates being released without facing justice, regardless of whether there is sufficient evidence to support prosecution, and reiterating that, consistent with the provisions of the United Nations Convention on the Law of the Sea concerning the repression of piracy, the Convention for the Suppression of Unlawful Acts against the Safety of Maritime Navigation of 10 March 1988[78] provides for parties to create criminal offences, establish jurisdiction and accept delivery of persons responsible for or suspected of seizing or exercising control over a ship by force or threat thereof or any other form of intimidation,

Underlining the importance of continuing to enhance the collection, preservation and transmission to competent authorities of evidence of acts of piracy and armed robbery at sea off the coast of Somalia, welcoming the ongoing work of the International Maritime Organization, the International Criminal Police Organization (INTERPOL) and industry groups to develop guidance to seafarers on the preservation of crime scenes following acts of piracy, and noting the importance of enabling seafarers to give evidence in criminal proceedings to prosecute acts of piracy,

Recognizing that pirate networks continue to rely on kidnapping and hostage-taking to help generate funding to purchase weapons, gain recruits and continue their operational activities, thereby jeopardizing the safety and security of civilians and restricting the flow of commerce, and welcoming international efforts to coordinate the work of investigators and prosecutors, inter alia, through the Law Enforcement Task Force, and collect and share information to disrupt the pirate enterprise, as exemplified by INTERPOL's Global Database on Maritime Piracy, and taking note of the ongoing efforts of the Regional Fusion and Law Enforcement Centre for Safety and Security at Sea, hosted by Seychelles, to combat piracy and transnational organized crime,

Reaffirming international condemnation of acts of kidnapping and hostage-taking, including offences contained within the International Convention against the Taking of Hostages,[79] strongly condemning the continuing practice of hostage-taking by pirates operating off the coast of Somalia, expressing serious concern at the inhumane conditions that hostages face in captivity, recognizing the adverse impact on their families, calling for the immediate release of all hostages, and noting the importance of cooperation between Member States on the issue of hostage-taking and the prosecution of suspected pirates for taking hostages,

Commending Kenya, Mauritius, Seychelles and the United Republic of Tanzania for their efforts to prosecute suspected pirates in their national courts, and noting with appreciation the assistance provided by the United Nations Office on Drugs and Crime Maritime Crime Programme, the Trust Fund and other international organizations and donors, in coordination with the Contact Group, to support Kenya, Mauritius, Seychelles, the United Republic of Tanzania, Somalia and other States in the region with their efforts to prosecute, or incarcerate in a third State after prosecution elsewhere, pirates, including facilitators and financiers ashore, consistent with applicable international human rights law, and emphasizing the need for States and international organizations to further enhance international efforts in this regard,

Welcoming the readiness of the national and regional administrations of Somalia to cooperate with each other and with States that have prosecuted suspected pirates with a view to enabling convicted pirates to be repatriated back to Somalia under suitable prisoner transfer arrangements, consistent with applicable international law, including international human rights law, and acknowledging the return from Seychelles to Somalia of convicted prisoners willing and eligible to serve their sentences in Somalia,

[78] United Nations, *Treaty Series*, vol. 1678, No. 29004.

[79] Ibid., vol. 1316, No. 21931.

Recalling the reports of the Secretary General which illustrate the seriousness of piracy and armed robbery at sea off the coast of Somalia and provide useful guidance for the investigation and prosecution of pirates, including on specialized anti-piracy courts,[80]

Stressing the need for States to consider possible methods to assist the seafarers who are victims of pirates, and welcoming in this regard the efforts of the Hostage Support Programme and the new Piracy Survivor Family Fund launched at the recent Contact Group session to provide support to hostages during their release and return home, as well as to their families throughout the hostage situation,

Recognizing the progress made by the Contact Group and the United Nations Office on Drugs and Crime in the use of public information tools to raise awareness of the dangers of piracy and highlight the best practices to eradicate this criminal phenomenon,

Noting with appreciation the ongoing efforts of the United Nations Office on Drugs and Crime to support efforts to enhance Somalia's maritime security and law enforcement capacities, and noting efforts by the Office and the United Nations Development Programme and the funding provided by the Trust Fund, the European Union, the United Kingdom of Great Britain and Northern Ireland, the United States of America and other donors to develop regional judicial and law enforcement capacity to investigate, arrest and prosecute suspected pirates and to incarcerate convicted pirates consistent with applicable international human rights law,

Bearing in mind the Djibouti Code of Conduct, noting the operations of information-sharing centres in Yemen, Kenya and the United Republic of Tanzania and the regional maritime training centre in Djibouti, and recognizing the efforts of signatory States to develop the appropriate regulatory and legislative frameworks to combat piracy, enhance their capacity to patrol the waters of the region, interdict suspect vessels and prosecute suspected pirates,

Emphasizing that peace and stability within Somalia, the strengthening of State institutions, economic and social development and respect for human rights and the rule of law are necessary to create the conditions for a durable eradication of piracy and armed robbery at sea off the coast of Somalia, and further emphasizing that Somalia's long-term security rests with the effective development by Somali authorities of the Somali National Security Forces,

Taking note with appreciation of the work of the Indian Ocean Rim Association at the 14th meeting of its Council of Ministers to bolster maritime security and safety, including through the announcement of the second Indian Ocean Dialogue, which will continue to explore options to enhance counter-piracy cooperation, including through improved maritime information-sharing arrangements and stronger national legal capacity and laws, encouraging the Association to pursue efforts that are complementary to and coordinated with the ongoing work of the Contact Group, and welcoming Somalia's application for membership in the Association as an important step towards building closer regional cooperation on maritime security and other issues,

Recognizing that the ongoing instability in Somalia and the acts of piracy and armed robbery at sea off its coast are inextricably linked, and stressing the need to continue the comprehensive response by the international community to repress piracy and armed robbery at sea and tackle its underlying causes, recognizing the need to undertake long-term and sustainable efforts to repress piracy and the need to create adequate economic opportunities for the citizens of Somalia,

Determining that the incidents of piracy and armed robbery at sea off the coast of Somalia, as well as the activity of pirate groups in Somalia, are an important factor exacerbating the situation in Somalia, which continues to constitute a threat to international peace and security in the region,

Acting under Chapter VII of the Charter of the United Nations,

1. *Reiterates* that it condemns and deplores all acts of piracy and armed robbery at sea off the coast of Somalia;

2. *Recognizes* that the ongoing instability in Somalia is one of the underlying causes of the problem of piracy and contributes to the problem of piracy and armed robbery at sea off the coast of Somalia, while piracy in turn exacerbates instability by introducing large amounts of illicit cash that fuels additional crime and corruption in Somalia;

[80] S/2011/360 and S/2012/50.

3. *Stresses* the need for a comprehensive response to repress piracy and tackle its underlying causes by the international community;

4. *Underlines* the primary responsibility of Somali authorities in the fight against piracy and armed robbery at sea off the coast of Somalia, and urgently requests the Somali authorities, with assistance from the Secretary-General and relevant United Nations entities, to pass a comprehensive set of anti-piracy and maritime laws without further delay and establish security forces with clear roles and jurisdictions to enforce these laws, and to continue to develop, with international support as appropriate, the capacity of Somali courts to investigate and prosecute persons responsible for acts of piracy and armed robbery, including key figures of criminal networks involved in piracy who plan, organize, facilitate or illicitly finance or profit from such attacks, and notes the proclamation by the President of Somalia on 30 June 2014 of the exclusive economic zone of Somalia;

5. *Recognizes* the need to continue to investigate and prosecute those who plan, organize or illicitly finance or profit from pirate attacks off the coast of Somalia, including key figures of criminal networks involved in piracy, and urges States, working in conjunction with relevant international organizations, to adopt legislation to facilitate prosecution of suspected pirates off the coast of Somalia;

6. *Calls upon* the Somali authorities to interdict and, upon interdiction, to have mechanisms in place to safely return effects seized by pirates, to investigate and prosecute pirates and to patrol the territorial waters off the coast of Somalia to suppress acts of piracy and armed robbery at sea;

7. *Also calls upon* the Somali authorities to make all efforts to bring to justice those who are using Somali territory to plan, facilitate or undertake criminal acts of piracy and armed robbery at sea, and calls upon Member States to assist Somalia, at the request of Somali authorities and with notification to the Secretary-General, to strengthen maritime capacity in Somalia, including regional authorities, and stresses that any measures undertaken pursuant to the present paragraph shall be consistent with applicable international law, in particular international human rights law;

8. *Calls upon* States to cooperate also, as appropriate, on the issue of hostage-taking, and the prosecution of suspected pirates for taking hostages;

9. *Calls for* the immediate and unconditional release of all seafarers held hostage by Somali pirates, and further calls upon the Somali authorities and all relevant stakeholders to redouble their efforts to secure their safe and immediate release;

10. *Recognizes* the need for States, international and regional organizations and other appropriate partners to exchange evidence and information for anti-piracy law enforcement purposes with a view to ensuring effective prosecution of suspected, and imprisonment of convicted, pirates and with a view to the arrest and prosecution of key figures of criminal networks involved in piracy who plan, organize, facilitate or illicitly finance and profit from piracy operations, and keeps under review the possibility of applying targeted sanctions against individuals or entities that plan, organize, facilitate or illicitly finance or profit from piracy operations if they meet the listing criteria set out in paragraph 8 of resolution 1844 (2008); and calls upon all States to cooperate fully with the Monitoring Group on Somalia and Eritrea, including on information-sharing regarding possible violations of the arms embargo or charcoal ban;

11. *Renews its call upon* States and regional organizations that are able to do so to take part in the fight against piracy and armed robbery at sea off the coast of Somalia, in particular, consistent with the present resolution and international law, by deploying naval vessels, arms and military aircraft, by providing basing and logistical support for counter-piracy forces and by seizing and disposing of boats, vessels, arms and other related equipment used in the commission of piracy and armed robbery at sea off the coast of Somalia, or for which there are reasonable grounds for suspecting such use;

12. *Highlights* the importance of coordination among States and international organizations in order to deter acts of piracy and armed robbery at sea off the coast of Somalia, commends the work of the Contact Group on Piracy off the Coast of Somalia to facilitate such coordination, in cooperation with the International Maritime Organization, flag States and Somali authorities, and urges continued support of these efforts;

13. *Encourages* Member States to continue to cooperate with Somali authorities in the fight against piracy and armed robbery at sea, notes the primary role of Somali authorities in the fight against piracy and armed robbery at sea off the coast of Somalia, and decides to renew, for a further period of 12 months from the date of the present

resolution, the authorizations as set out in paragraph 10 of resolution 1846 (2008) and paragraph 6 of resolution 1851 (2008), as renewed by paragraph 7 of resolution 1897 (2009), paragraph 7 of resolution 1950 (2010), paragraph 9 of resolution 2020 (2011), paragraph 12 of resolution 2077 (2012) and paragraph 12 of resolution 2125 (2013), granted to States and regional organizations cooperating with Somali authorities in the fight against piracy and armed robbery at sea off the coast of Somalia, for which advance notification has been provided by Somali authorities to the Secretary-General;

14. *Affirms* that the authorizations renewed in the present resolution apply only with respect to the situation in Somalia and shall not affect the rights, obligations or responsibilities of Member States under international law, including any rights or obligations under the United Nations Convention on the Law of the Sea[70] with respect to any other situation, and underscores in particular that the present resolution shall not be considered as establishing customary international law; and affirms further that such authorizations have been renewed only following the receipt of the letter dated 4 November 2014 conveying the consent of Somali authorities;

15. *Decides* that the arms embargo on Somalia imposed by paragraph 5 of resolution 733 (1992) of 23 January 1992 and further elaborated upon in paragraphs 1 and 2 of resolution 1425 (2002) of 22 July 2002 and modified by paragraphs 33 to 38 of resolution 2093 (2013) of 6 March 2013 does not apply to supplies of weapons and military equipment or the provision of assistance destined for the sole use of Member States and international, regional and subregional organizations taking measures in accordance with paragraph 13 above;

16. *Requests* that cooperating States take appropriate steps to ensure that the activities they undertake pursuant to the authorizations in paragraph 13 above do not have the practical effect of denying or impairing the right of innocent passage to the ships of any third State;

17. *Calls upon* all States, in particular flag, port and coastal States, States of the nationality of victims and perpetrators of piracy and armed robbery and other States with relevant jurisdiction under international law and national legislation, to cooperate in determining jurisdiction and in the investigation and prosecution of all persons responsible for acts of piracy and armed robbery off the coast of Somalia, including key figures of criminal networks involved in piracy who plan, organize, facilitate or illicitly finance or profit from such attacks, consistent with applicable international law, including international human rights law, to ensure that all pirates handed over to judicial authorities are subject to a judicial process, and to render assistance by, among other actions, providing disposition and logistics assistance with respect to persons under their jurisdiction and control, such as victims, witnesses and persons detained as a result of operations conducted under the present resolution;

18. *Also calls upon* all States to criminalize piracy under their domestic law and to favourably consider the prosecution of suspected, and imprisonment of those convicted, pirates apprehended off the coast of Somalia, and their facilitators and financiers ashore, consistent with applicable international law, including international human rights law, and decides to keep these matters under review, including, as appropriate, the establishment of specialized anti-piracy courts in Somalia with substantial international participation and/or support, as set forth in resolution 2015 (2011), and encourages the Contact Group to continue its discussions in this regard;

19. *Welcomes*, in this context, the continued work of the United Nations Office on Drugs and Crime Maritime Crime Programme with authorities in Somalia and in neighbouring States to ensure that individuals suspected of piracy are prosecuted and that those convicted are imprisoned in a manner consistent with international law, including international human rights law;

20. *Urges* all States to take appropriate actions under their existing domestic law to prevent the illicit financing of acts of piracy and the laundering of its proceeds;

21. *Urges* States, in cooperation with INTERPOL and the European Police Office (Europol), to further investigate international criminal networks involved in piracy off the coast of Somalia, including those responsible for illicit financing and facilitation;

22. *Urges* all States to ensure that counter-piracy activities, particularly land-based activities, take into consideration the need to protect women and girls from exploitation, including sexual exploitation;

23. *Commends* INTERPOL for operationalizing the global piracy database that consolidates information about piracy off the coast of Somalia and facilitates the development of actionable analysis for law enforcement, and urges all States to share such information with INTERPOL for use in the database, through appropriate channels;

24. *Commends* the contributions of the Trust Fund and the International Maritime Organization-funded Djibouti Code of Conduct, and urges both State and non-State actors affected by piracy, most notably the international shipping community, to contribute to them;

25. *Urges* States parties to the United Nations Convention on the Law of the Sea and the Convention for the Suppression of Unlawful Acts against the Safety of Maritime Navigation[78] to implement fully their relevant obligations under these conventions and customary international law and to cooperate with the United Nations Office on Drugs and Crime, the International Maritime Organization and other States and international organizations to build judicial capacity for the successful prosecution of persons suspected of piracy and armed robbery at sea off the coast of Somalia;

26. *Acknowledges* the recommendations and guidance provided by the International Maritime Organization on preventing and suppressing piracy and armed robbery at sea, urges States, in collaboration with the shipping and insurance industries and the Organization, to continue to develop and implement avoidance, evasion and defensive best practices and advisories to take when under attack or when sailing in the waters off the coast of Somalia, and further urges States to make their citizens and vessels available for forensic investigation, as appropriate, at the first suitable port of call immediately following an act or attempted act of piracy or armed robbery at sea or release from captivity;

27. *Encourages* flag States and port States to further consider the development of safety and security measures on board vessels, including, where applicable, developing regulations for the use of privately contracted armed security personnel on board ships, aimed at preventing and suppressing piracy off the coast of Somalia, through a consultative process, including through the International Maritime Organization and the International Organization for Standardization;

28. *Invites* the International Maritime Organization to continue its contributions to the prevention and suppression of acts of piracy and armed robbery against ships, in coordination, in particular, with the United Nations Office on Drugs and Crime, the World Food Programme, the shipping industry and all other parties concerned, and recognizes the role of the Organization concerning privately contracted armed security personnel on board ships in high-risk areas;

29. *Notes* the importance of securing the safe delivery of World Food Programme assistance by sea, and welcomes the ongoing work by the World Food Programme, the European Union operation Atalanta and flag States with regard to vessel protection detachments on World Food Programme vessels;

30. *Requests* States and regional organizations cooperating with Somali authorities to inform the Security Council and the Secretary-General in nine months of the progress of actions undertaken in the exercise of the authorizations provided in paragraph 13 above, and further requests all States contributing through the Contact Group to the fight against piracy off the coast of Somalia, including Somalia and other States in the region, to report by the same deadline on their efforts to establish jurisdiction and cooperation in the investigation and prosecution of piracy;

31. *Requests* the Secretary-General to report to the Council within 11 months of the adoption of the present resolution on the implementation of the present resolution and on the situation with respect to piracy and armed robbery at sea off the coast of Somalia;

32. *Expresses its intention* to review the situation and consider, as appropriate, renewing the authorizations provided in paragraph 13 above for additional periods upon the request of Somali authorities;

33. *Decides* to remain seized of the matter.

Adopted unanimously at the 7309th meeting.

Decisions

At its 7375th meeting, on 4 February 2015, the Security Council decided to invite the representative of Somalia to participate, without vote, in accordance with rule 37 of its provisional rules of procedure, in the discussion of the item entitled:

"The situation in Somalia

"Report of the Secretary-General on Somalia (S/2015/51)".

At the same meeting, the Council also decided to extend an invitation, in accordance with rule 39 of its provisional rules of procedure, to Mr. Nicholas Kay, Special Representative of the Secretary-General for Somalia and Head of the United Nations Assistance Mission in Somalia.

At the same meeting, the Council further decided to extend an invitation, in accordance with rule 39 of its provisional rules of procedure, to Mr. Maman Sidikou, Special Representative of the Chairperson of the African Union Commission for Somalia and Head of the African Union Mission in Somalia.

On 2 April 2015, the President of the Security Council addressed the following letter to the Secretary-General:[81]

> I have the honour to inform you that your letter dated 31 March 2015 concerning your intention to increase the strength of the guard unit in Mogadishu to a total of 530 personnel[82] has been brought to the attention of the members of the Security Council. They take note of the information contained in your letter and the intention expressed therein.

At its 7445th meeting, on 19 May 2015, the Council decided to invite the representative of Somalia to participate, without vote, in accordance with rule 37 of its provisional rules of procedure, in the discussion of the item entitled:

"The situation in Somalia

"Report of the Secretary-General on Somalia (S/2015/331)".

At the same meeting, the Council also decided to extend an invitation, in accordance with rule 39 of its provisional rules of procedure, to Mr. Nicholas Kay, Special Representative of the Secretary-General for Somalia and Head of the United Nations Assistance Mission in Somalia.

At the same meeting, the Council further decided to extend an invitation, in accordance with rule 39 of its provisional rules of procedure, to Mr. Maman Sidikou, Special Representative of the Chairperson of the African Union Commission for Somalia and Head of the African Union Mission in Somalia.

At its 7449th meeting, on 26 May 2015, the Council decided to invite the representative of Somalia to participate, without vote, in accordance with rule 37 of its provisional rules of procedure, in the discussion of the item entitled:

"The situation in Somalia

"Report of the Secretary-General on Somalia (S/2015/331)".

Resolution 2221 (2015)
of 26 May 2015

The Security Council,

Recalling all its previous resolutions and the statements by its President on the situation in Somalia,

Reaffirming its respect for the sovereignty, political independence, territorial integrity and unity of Somalia,

Recalling the ongoing joint United Nations and African Union review, requested in resolution 2182 (2014) of 24 October 2014, of the temporary surge for the African Union Mission in Somalia authorized in resolution 2124 (2013) of 12 November 2013, and further recalling its request for the United Nations and the African Union to set out recommendations for the next steps in the military campaign in Somalia, taking into due consideration the political situation,

[81] S/2015/235.

[82] S/2015/234.

1. *Decides* to extend the mandate of the United Nations Assistance Mission in Somalia, as set out in paragraph 1 of resolution 2158 (2014) of 29 May 2014, until 7 August 2015, in order to consider fully the recommendations of the joint United Nations and African Union review of the temporary surge for the African Union Mission in Somalia, including any relevant recommendations connected to the mandate of the United Nations Assistance Mission in Somalia;

2. *Also decides* to remain actively seized of the matter.

Adopted unanimously at the 7449th meeting.

Decisions

At its 7487th meeting, on 16 July 2015, the Security Council decided to invite the representative of Somalia to participate, without vote, in accordance with rule 37 of its provisional rules of procedure, in the discussion of the item entitled "The situation in Somalia".

At the same meeting, the Council also decided to extend an invitation, in accordance with rule 39 of its provisional rules of procedure, to Mr. Edmond Mulet, Assistant Secretary-General for Peacekeeping Operations.

At its 7491st meeting, on 28 July 2015, the Council decided to invite the representative of Somalia to participate, without vote, in accordance with rule 37 of its provisional rules of procedure, in the discussion of the item entitled "The situation in Somalia".

Resolution 2232 (2015)
of 28 July 2015

The Security Council,

Recalling all its previous resolutions and the statements by its President on the situation in Somalia,

Underlining its respect for the sovereignty, territorial integrity, political independence and unity of Somalia,

Condemning recent Al-Shabaab attacks in Somalia and beyond, expressing serious concern at the ongoing threat posed by Al-Shabaab, and underlining its concern that Al-Shabaab continues to hold territory in Somalia,

Expressing outrage at the loss of civilian life in Al-Shabaab attacks, and paying tribute to the bravery and sacrifices made by the personnel of the African Union Mission in Somalia and the Somali National Army in the fight against Al-Shabaab, as well as to United Nations staff killed in the Garowe attack,

Reiterating its determination to support efforts to reduce the threat posed by Al-Shabaab in Somalia, and underlining its commitment to support a Somali-led political peace and reconciliation process,

African Union Mission in Somalia

Welcoming the report of the joint African Union–United Nations mission on the benchmarks for a United Nations peacekeeping operation in Somalia and recommendations on the next steps in the military campaign (the joint African Union-United Nations review) requested in resolution 2182 (2014) of 24 October 2014, and taking note of the recommendations of the joint review,

Welcoming also the constructive manner in which the United Nations and the African Union conducted the joint review,

Welcoming further the progress of the African Union Mission and the Somali National Army in the fight against Al-Shabaab, in particular through "Operation Indian Ocean" and "Operation Eagle", and underlining the importance of continuing offensive operations against Al-Shabaab,

Taking note of the communiqué issued by the African Union Peace and Security Council on 30 June 2015,[83] which endorsed the recommendations of the joint African Union-United Nations review, and underlining its call for

[83] See S/2015/556.

full adherence to the African Union Mission command and control architecture, which can help to ensure that the recommendations of the joint review are properly implemented,

Welcoming the support of the international community to peace and stability in Somalia, in particular the European Union, for its substantial contribution in supporting the African Union Mission, as well as the support from other key bilateral partners to both the African Union Mission and the Somali National Army, and emphasizing the importance of new contributors, in particular the African Union, sharing the financial burden of supporting the Mission,

Welcoming also the African Union's investigation of allegations of sexual violence allegedly perpetrated by some African Union Mission troops, underlining the importance of the African Union implementing the recommendations of the report, expressing its disappointment that the African Union did not receive full cooperation from all African Union Mission troop-contributing countries in carrying out its investigation, and calling upon the African Union and troop-contributing countries to ensure that allegations are properly investigated and appropriate follow-up action is taken, including full investigation of those cases of abuse evidenced by the African Union investigation team,

United Nations Assistance Mission in Somalia

Commending the role of the United Nations Assistance Mission in Somalia in supporting peace and reconciliation and the promotion and protection of human rights in Somalia,

Underlining the importance of the Assistance Mission consolidating its presence across Somalia in order to help to facilitate political dialogue between the centre and the regions and to support local peace and reconciliation processes,

Determining that the situation in Somalia continues to constitute a threat to international peace and security,

Acting under Chapter VII of the Charter of the United Nations,

African Union Mission in Somalia

1. *Agrees* with the Secretary-General that conditions in Somalia are not appropriate for the deployment of a United Nations peacekeeping mission until the end of 2016 at the earliest;

2. *Welcomes* the revised benchmarks as set out in the letter dated 2 July 2015 from the Secretary-General to the President of the Security Council, agrees with his conclusion that the achievement of the benchmarks could pave the way for the deployment of a United Nations peacekeeping operation which could help to consolidate the peace process in Somalia and the development of Somali security sector institutions, and requests the Secretary-General to keep these benchmarks under continuous review, in consultation with the African Union;

3. *Decides* to authorize the States members of the African Union to maintain the deployment of the African Union Mission in Somalia, as set out in paragraph 1 of resolution 2093 (2013) of 6 March 2013, until 30 May 2016, in line with the request of the Security Council to the African Union for a maximum level of 22,126 uniformed personnel, and as part of an overall exit strategy for the African Union Mission, after which a decrease in the force strength of the Mission will be considered, and further decides that the Mission shall be authorized to take all measures necessary, in full compliance with the obligations of its Member States under international humanitarian law and human rights law, and in full respect of the sovereignty, territorial integrity, political independence and unity of Somalia, to carry out its mandate;

4. *Requests* the Secretary-General to continue to provide a logistical support package for the African Union Mission, referred to in paragraphs 10 to 12 of resolution 2010 (2011) of 30 September 2011, paragraphs 4 and 6 of resolution 2036 (2012) of 22 February 2012, paragraph 2 of resolution 2073 (2012) of 7 November 2012, paragraph 4 of resolution 2093 (2013) and paragraph 26 of resolution 2182 (2014), ensuring the accountability and transparency of expenditure of United Nations funds as set out in paragraph 4 of resolution 1910 (2010) of 28 January 2010, and consistent with the requirements of the Secretary-General's human rights due diligence policy;[71]

5. *Underlines* that the security strategy for the next 18 months should aim to create and preserve an enabling environment for the political and peace and reconciliation processes to unfold in Somalia, and agrees with the Secretary-General's assessment that the security strategy in Somalia should be guided by three objectives:

(i) Continuing offensive operations against Al-Shabaab strongholds;

(ii) Enabling the political process at all levels, including through securing critical political processes throughout Somalia;

(iii) Enabling stabilization efforts through supporting the delivery of security for the Somali people to facilitate the wider process of peacebuilding and reconciliation, including through the gradual handing over of security responsibilities from the African Union Mission to the Somali National Army and subsequently to the Somali police force;

6. *Requests* that, in line with the recommendations of the joint African Union-United Nations review, the African Union undertake a structured and targeted reconfiguration of the African Union Mission to enable a surge in its efficiency, in particular by strengthening command and control structures, enhancing cross-sector operations, examining sector boundaries, generating a dedicated special forces capability under the authority of the Force Commander, which should operate alongside existing Somali special forces, generating all the requisite specialized units recommended in the letter from the Secretary-General dated 14 October 2013[74] and authorized in paragraph 3 of resolution 2124 (2013) of 12 November 2013, ensuring that all force enablers and multipliers operate under the authority of the Special Representative of the Chairperson of the African Union Commission for Somalia and the Force Commander, and taking into account progress achieved in offensive operations against Al-Shabaab and other terrorist organizations, by gradually, and in a limited manner, and where appropriate, reconfiguring Mission uniformed personnel in favour of police personnel within the authorized Mission personnel ceiling, welcomes in this regard the intention of the African Union to develop a new concept of operations for the Mission, and requests the African Union to develop this concept in close collaboration with the United Nations by 30 October 2015;

7. *Welcomes* the commitment of the Secretary-General to work with the Chairperson of the African Union Commission, the troop-contributing countries and the Federal Government of Somalia to help to ensure that this surge in efficiency materializes and is sustained over time, and requests the Secretary-General to monitor the implementation of the surge, including through performance indicators, and in this regard to keep the Council updated in his regular reporting;

8. *Requests* the Secretary-General to work closely with the African Union in supporting the implementation of the present resolution, paying particular attention to the provisions of paragraph 6 of the present resolution, further requests the Secretary-General to continue to provide technical and expert advice to the African Union on the planning, deployment and strategic management of the African Union Mission through the United Nations Office to the African Union, and reiterates its request to the Secretary-General, in view of the need to increase the efficiency of the Mission, to enhance the provision of technical advice to the African Union through existing United Nations mechanisms;

9. *Agrees* with the Secretary-General that a joint African Union Mission–United Nations–Somali planning mechanism should assess and facilitate the delivery of the strategy set out in paragraph 5 of the present resolution, as well as the implementation of stabilization priorities, and ensuring, in particular, thorough coordination and consultation ahead of, during and after offensive operations;

10. *Underlines* that it is essential that military operations be followed immediately by national efforts to establish or improve governance structures in recovered areas and by the delivery of basic services, including security;

11. *Also underlines* the imperative of securing key supply routes to areas recovered from Al-Shabaab, requests the African Union Mission and the Somali National Army to ensure that they give the utmost priority to securing key supply routes essential to improve the humanitarian situation in the most affected areas, and as a critical condition for logistical support to the Mission, and requests the Secretary-General to report, in consultation with the Federal Government of Somalia and the Mission, on progress in this regard in his written reports to the Council;

12. *Agrees* with the Secretary-General that there have been gaps in the integrated provision of logistical support to African Union Mission and Somali National Army troops, underscores that the delivery of logistical support remains a joint responsibility between the United Nations and the African Union, and underlines its determination to seek improvements to the support provided to the Mission, and that provided by the United Nations Support Office for the African Union Mission in Somalia to the Somali National Army, as funded through the United Nations trust fund;

13. *Requests* the Secretary-General, in consultation with all stakeholders, to carry out a strategic review of the Support Office, including a thorough review of support provided to the African Union Mission by all partners, and set out a wide range of options on how to improve overall support to the Mission, in the context of the efficiency surge outlined in paragraph 6 above, including through making improvements to the performance, management and structures of the Support Office, bearing in mind the imperative of responsible cost control and taking into account the availability of resources, and further requests the Secretary-General to present these options to the Council no later than 30 September 2015;

14. *Stresses* the critical need to source contingent-owned equipment, including force enablers and multipliers as provided for in paragraph 6 of resolution 2036 (2012), either from existing troop-contributing countries to the African Union Mission or other Member States, emphasizes in particular the need for an appropriate aviation component of up to 12 military helicopters, welcomes the progress made in the partial generation of this component, and encourages Member States to respond to African Union efforts to mobilize such equipment urgently;

15. *Welcomes* the commencement of activities establishing a Civilian Casualty Tracking Analysis and Response Cell as requested in resolutions 2093 (2013) and 2124 (2013), and underlines the importance of making the Cell operational and effective without further delay, in collaboration with humanitarian, human rights and protection actors, and ensuring that information is shared with relevant actors, including the United Nations;

16. *Reiterates its call* for new donors to support the African Union Mission through the provision of additional funding for troop stipends, equipment, technical assistance and uncaveated funding for the Mission to the United Nations trust fund for the Mission, calls upon the African Union to consider how to provide sustainable funding for the Mission, such as through its own assessed costs as it did for the African-led International Support Mission in Mali, and underlines the African Union's call for its member States to provide financial support to the Mission;

Somali National Security Forces

17. *Stresses* the importance of accelerating the strengthening and improved coordination of the Somali security institutions and of initiating efforts to move towards the eventual handover of security responsibilities to the Somali security services, including through the establishment of a forum between the Federal Government of Somalia, the African Union and the United Nations to specifically plan for and regularly monitor the handover of security responsibilities, which is an essential part of the eventual exit strategy of the African Union Mission, and further calls for the rapid completion of the Somali national security sector architecture, including a definition of the roles of relevant national security sector institutions as a way of improving coordination between the Somali National Army and the Mission;

18. *Welcomes* the adoption of the Guulwade (Victory) Plan as a critical step towards the development of the capacity of a more effective and sustainable Somali National Army, including the initial priority of supporting and developing the 10,900 National Army troops, welcomes the efforts taken so far by the Federal Government of Somalia in establishing an integrated army, and urges the Federal Government to complete this process across Somalia as soon as possible, notes the importance for implementing the Guulwade Plan of provision by the African Union Mission of training and mentoring to the National Army, and underscores the importance of bilateral partners delivering on any pledged support as well as supporting the United Nations Assistance Mission in Somalia in implementing its mandate to assist the Federal Government in coordinating international donor support on security sector assistance, and in this regard emphasizes the importance of the mandate of the Assistance Mission to assist the Federal Government in coordinating international donor support on security sector assistance;

19. *Also welcomes* efforts to develop a realistic police plan linked with medium-term rule of law programmes and in line with the federal vision, taking into account existing plans for the development of the Somali National Police Force, and emphasizes the importance of substantially contributing to the development and

sustenance of the regional police forces, while continuing police initiatives in Mogadishu, welcomes the Federal Government of Somalia's initial draft Heegan (Readiness) Plan for the police, and looks forward to its finalization by the end of October 2015, and in this regard takes note of the recommendation of the Secretary-General to establish a non-lethal support package for the Somali police force, further stresses that an appropriate United Nations trust fund or voluntary funding arrangement should be used to fund such support if authorized by the Council, requests further details from the Secretary-General for implementation and delivery of such support by 30 September 2015, and underlines that such support should be provided in accordance with the human rights due diligence policy on United Nations support to non-United Nations security forces;[71]

20. *Expresses concern* over the increasing activities of Al-Shabaab in Puntland and the security implications of the situation in Yemen for Somalia, takes note of the recommendation of the Secretary-General to extend the Somali National Army non-lethal support package authorized in paragraph 14 of resolution 2124 (2013) to 3,000 Puntland forces on an exceptional basis upon the completion of their integration process and inclusion into the Guulwade Plan, recalls the criteria established in paragraph 14 of resolution 2124 (2013) with respect to the provision of non-lethal logistical support to the National Army, recalls the mandate of the United Nations Support Office for the African Union Mission in Somalia, and underlines its current areas of operations and limitations to its capacity, and requests the Secretary-General to explore the feasibility of implementing this recommendation and to report to the Council no later than 30 September 2015;

United Nations Assistance Mission in Somalia

21. *Decides* to extend the mandate of the United Nations Assistance Mission in Somalia, as set out in paragraph 1 of resolution 2158 (2014) of 29 May 2014, until 30 March 2016;

22. *Underscores* the importance of the Assistance Mission's support to the political process, in particular supporting the preparation of an inclusive, realistic and legitimate electoral process in 2016;

23. *Welcomes* the strong relationship between the Assistance Mission and the African Union Mission, welcomes in particular the key role played by the Special Representative of the Secretary-General for Somalia and the Special Representative of the Chairperson of the African Union Commission for Somalia in ensuring that the organizations work closely together, and underlines the importance of both entities further strengthening that relationship to ensure that the activities of both entities support the political process;

24. *Requests* the Assistance Mission, subject to strict adherence to United Nations security requirements and in the context of the evolving security situation, to strengthen its presence in all capitals of interim regional administrations to support strategically the political and peace and reconciliation processes, including by engaging with the interim regional administrations in support of a federal structure, taking into account operational and security constraints, and in this context takes note of the importance of keeping security arrangements under constant review, encourages regional engagement to be carried out jointly by African Union Mission-Assistance Mission teams, agrees with the conclusion of the Secretary-General that deployment of civilian planning capacity in regional capitals should be a priority in order to improve joint planning between military and civilian components, and requests the African Union Mission, in accordance with its existing mandate, and the Somali National Security Forces to take appropriate measures to protect Assistance Mission personnel, facilities, installations, equipment and mission and to ensure the security and freedom of movement of its personnel;

Somalia

25. *Welcomes* the commitment of President Hassan Sheikh and of the Federal Government of Somalia to an inclusive and credible electoral process in 2016, underlines the Council's expectation that there should not be an extension of electoral process timelines for either the executive or legislative branches, and underlines the importance of implementing this commitment, including through an inclusive process to agree on the model for the electoral process, and ensuring that the National Independent Electoral Commission and Boundaries and Federation Commission are operational without further delay, and emphasizes the importance of reconciliation across the country as the basis of any long-term approach to stability;

26. *Underlines* the need to ensure progress in the constitutional review process without further delay in order to establish an effective federal political system and a comprehensive reconciliation process that brings about national cohesion and integration, and underlines in this regard the importance of supporting the peaceful and

inclusive completion of the state formation process and providing effective mediation when necessary, and encourages close dialogue between the Federal Government of Somalia, regional administrations, civil society and the Somali public in this regard;

27. *Calls upon* all key actors and institutions in Somalia, including Parliament, to engage constructively to ensure progress on Vision 2016 before an electoral process in 2016;

28. *Underlines* the importance of governing in a spirit of national unity in an inclusive manner, in order to ensure no further delays in the political process;

29. *Expresses concern* at continued violations and abuses of human rights and violations of international humanitarian law in Somalia and underscores the need to end impunity, uphold human rights and hold accountable those responsible for such crimes, and encourages the Federal Government of Somalia to finalize its human rights road map and establish its National Human Rights Commission and to pass legislation, including legislation aimed at protecting human rights and ensuring investigations and prosecutions of perpetrators of human rights violations;

30. *Also expresses concern* at the increase in forced evictions of internally displaced persons from public and private infrastructure in major towns in Somalia, stresses that any eviction should be consistent with relevant national and international frameworks, and calls upon the Federal Government of Somalia and all relevant actors to strive to provide concrete durable solutions for internal displacement;

31. *Further expresses concern* at the ongoing humanitarian crisis in Somalia and its impact on the people of Somalia, commends the efforts of the United Nations humanitarian agencies and other humanitarian actors to deliver life-saving assistance to vulnerable populations, condemns any misuse or obstruction of humanitarian assistance, and reiterates its demand that all parties allow and facilitate full, safe and unhindered access for the timely delivery of aid to persons in need across Somalia; and underlines the importance of proper accounting in international humanitarian support, and encourages national disaster management agencies in Somalia to scale up capacity with support from the United Nations to take a stronger leadership role in the coordination of humanitarian response;

32. *Underlines* the importance of respect for international humanitarian law and the protection of civilians, especially women and children, by all armed groups in Somalia;

33. *Reaffirms* the important role of women and youth in the prevention and resolution of conflicts and in peacebuilding, stresses the importance of their participation in all efforts for the maintenance and promotion of peace and security, notes that women are not adequately represented in the assemblies of the new interim regional administrations, and urges the Federal Government of Somalia and interim regional administrations to continue to promote increased representation of women at all decision-making levels in Somali institutions, and encourages the Assistance Mission to enhance its interaction across Somali civil society, including women, youth and religious leaders, in order to ensure that the views of civil society are incorporated in the various political processes;

34. *Welcomes* Somalia's progress towards ratifying the Convention on the Rights of the Child of 1989,[84] and calls for increased implementation of the two action plans signed in 2012 and strengthening of the legal framework for the protection of children, especially in the light of continued abductions and recruitment of children as detailed in the report of the Secretary-General of 5 June 2015 on children and armed conflict;[85]

35. *Requests* the Secretary-General to keep the Council regularly informed on the implementation of the present resolution, including through oral updates and no fewer than three written reports, with the first written report by 12 September 2015, and every 120 days thereafter;

36. *Decides* to remain actively seized of the matter.

Adopted unanimously at the 7491st meeting.

---

[84] United Nations, *Treaty Series*, vol. 1577, No. 27531.

[85] S/2015/409.

ITEMS RELATING TO THE SITUATION IN THE FORMER YUGOSLAVIA

A. The situation in Bosnia and Herzegovina[86]

Decision

At its 7307th meeting, on 11 November 2014, the Security Council decided to invite the representative of Bosnia and Herzegovina to participate, without vote, in accordance with rule 37 of its provisional rules of procedure, in the discussion of the item entitled:

"The situation in Bosnia and Herzegovina

"Letter dated 30 October 2014 from the Secretary-General addressed to the President of the Security Council (S/2014/777)".

Resolution 2183 (2014) of 11 November 2014

The Security Council,

Recalling all its previous relevant resolutions concerning the conflicts in the former Yugoslavia and the relevant statements by its President, including resolutions 1031 (1995) of 15 December 1995, 1088 (1996) of 12 December 1996, 1423 (2002) of 12 July 2002, 1491 (2003) of 11 July 2003, 1551 (2004) of 9 July 2004, 1575 (2004) of 22 November 2004, 1639 (2005) of 21 November 2005, 1722 (2006) of 21 November 2006, 1764 (2007) of 29 June 2007, 1785 (2007) of 21 November 2007, 1845 (2008) of 20 November 2008, 1869 (2009) of 25 March 2009, 1895 (2009) of 18 November 2009, 1948 (2010) of 18 November 2010, 2019 (2011) of 16 November 2011, 2074 (2012) of 14 November 2012 and 2123 (2013) of 12 November 2013,

Reaffirming its commitment to the political settlement of the conflicts in the former Yugoslavia, preserving the sovereignty and territorial integrity of all States there within their internationally recognized borders,

Emphasizing its full support for the continued role in Bosnia and Herzegovina of the High Representative for Bosnia and Herzegovina,

Underlining its commitment to support the implementation of the General Framework Agreement for Peace in Bosnia and Herzegovina and the annexes thereto (collectively, the Peace Agreement),[87] as well as the relevant decisions of the Peace Implementation Council,

Recalling all the agreements concerning the status of forces referred to in appendix B to annex 1-A of the Peace Agreement, and reminding the parties of their obligation to continue to comply therewith,

Recalling also the provisions of its resolution 1551 (2004) concerning the provisional application of the status-of-forces agreements contained in appendix B to annex 1-A of the Peace Agreement,

Emphasizing its appreciation to the High Representative, the Commander and personnel of the multinational stabilization force (the European Union Force-Althea), the Senior Military Representative and personnel of the North Atlantic Treaty Organization Headquarters Sarajevo, the Organization for Security and Cooperation in Europe, the European Union and the personnel of other international organizations and agencies in Bosnia and Herzegovina for their contributions to the implementation of the Peace Agreement,

Emphasizing that a comprehensive and coordinated return of refugees and displaced persons throughout the region continues to be crucial to lasting peace,

Encouraging the authorities of Bosnia and Herzegovina, with the support of the international community, to accelerate their efforts to address the disposal of excess ammunition,

Recalling the declarations of the ministerial meetings of the Peace Implementation Council,

[86] Resolutions or decisions on this question were first adopted by the Security Council in 1992.

[87] See S/1995/999.

Recognizing that full implementation of the Peace Agreement is not yet complete, while paying tribute to the achievements of the authorities at State and entity level in Bosnia and Herzegovina and of the international community in the 19 years since the signing of the Peace Agreement,

Recognizing also that the security environment has remained calm and stable, and noting that the Bosnia and Herzegovina authorities have so far proven capable to deal with threats to the safe and secure environment,

Emphasizing the importance of Bosnia and Herzegovina's progress towards Euro-Atlantic integration on the basis of the Peace Agreement, while recognizing the importance of Bosnia and Herzegovina's transition to a functional, reform-oriented, modern and democratic European country,

Welcoming the steps taken by the international community to assist Bosnia and Herzegovina in the ongoing reconstruction efforts following unprecedented floods that hit the country in May 2014, and stressing the importance for its authorities to address the calls by citizens of Bosnia and Herzegovina to improve the social and economic situation,

Welcoming also the overall orderly conduct and the competitive environment of the elections, which took place in Bosnia and Herzegovina on 12 October 2014, while taking note of concerns expressed by the Organization for Security and Cooperation in Europe election observation mission, and underlining the crucial importance of swift government formation at all levels to address the multiple challenges ahead,

Taking note of the reports of the High Representative, including his latest report, transmitted on 31 October 2014,[88]

Determined to promote the peaceful resolution of the conflicts in accordance with the purposes and principles of the Charter of the United Nations,

Recalling the relevant principles contained in the Convention on the Safety of United Nations and Associated Personnel of 9 December 1994[89] and the statement by its President of 9 February 2000,[90]

Welcoming and encouraging efforts by the United Nations to sensitize peacekeeping personnel in the prevention and control of HIV/AIDS and other communicable diseases in all its peacekeeping operations,

Welcoming the continued presence of the European Union Force-Althea, successfully focusing on capacity-building and training while also retaining the capability to contribute to the deterrence capacity of the Bosnia and Herzegovina authorities if the situation so requires,

Welcoming also the readiness of the European Union, as confirmed in the conclusions of the Ministers for Foreign Affairs of the European Union on 20 October 2014, to continue at this stage an executive military role to support Bosnia and Herzegovina authorities to maintain the safe and secure environment, under a renewed United Nations mandate, and welcoming the agreement of the European Union to keep the operation under regular review, including on the basis of the situation on the ground, with a view to making progress on the conditions conducive to the delivery of its mandate,

Recalling the letters between the European Union and the North Atlantic Treaty Organization sent to the Security Council on 19 November 2004 on how those organizations will cooperate together in Bosnia and Herzegovina,[91] in which both organizations recognize that the European Union Force-Althea will have the main peace stabilization role under the military aspects of the Peace Agreement,

Recalling also the confirmation by the Presidency of Bosnia and Herzegovina, on behalf of Bosnia and Herzegovina, including its constituent entities, of the arrangements for the European Union Force-Althea and the North Atlantic Treaty Organization Headquarters presence,[92]

---

[88] See S/2014/777.

[89] United Nations, *Treaty Series*, vol. 2051, No. 35457.

[90] S/PRST/2000/4.

[91] See S/2004/915 and S/2004/916.

[92] See S/2004/917.

Welcoming the reaffirmed determination of the European Union to actively and intensively engage in support of Bosnia and Herzegovina's European Union integration process and the continued engagement of the North Atlantic Treaty Organization,

Reiterating its calls upon the competent authorities in Bosnia and Herzegovina to take the steps necessary to complete the 5 plus 2 agenda, which remains necessary for the closure of the Office of the High Representative, as confirmed in the Steering Board communiqués of the Peace Implementation Council, and noting the continued lack of progress in that regard,

Reiterating its calls upon all Bosnia and Herzegovina's political leaders to refrain from divisive rhetoric and to make further concrete and tangible progress towards European Union integration,

Determining that the situation in the region continues to constitute a threat to international peace and security,

Acting under Chapter VII of the Charter,

1. *Reaffirms once again its support* for the General Framework Agreement for Peace in Bosnia and Herzegovina and the annexes thereto (collectively, the Peace Agreement),[87] as well as for the Dayton Agreement on Implementing the Federation of Bosnia and Herzegovina of 10 November 1995,[93] and calls upon the parties to comply strictly with their obligations under the Agreements;

2. *Reiterates* that the primary responsibility for the further successful implementation of the Peace Agreement lies with the authorities in Bosnia and Herzegovina themselves and that the continued willingness of the international community and major donors to assume the political, military and economic burden of implementation and reconstruction efforts will be determined by the compliance and active participation by all the authorities in Bosnia and Herzegovina in implementing the Peace Agreement and rebuilding a civil society, in particular in full cooperation with the International Tribunal for the Prosecution of Persons Responsible for Serious Violations of International Humanitarian Law Committed in the Territory of the Former Yugoslavia since 1991 and the International Residual Mechanism for Criminal Tribunals in accordance with their respective obligations under resolutions 827 (1993) of 25 May 1993, 955 (1994) of 8 November 1994 and 1966 (2010) of 22 December 2010, in strengthening joint institutions, which foster the building of a fully functioning self-sustaining State able to integrate itself into the European structures, and in facilitating returns of refugees and displaced persons;

3. *Reminds* the parties once again that, in accordance with the Peace Agreement, they have committed themselves to cooperate fully with all entities involved in the implementation of this peace settlement, as described in the Peace Agreement, or which are otherwise authorized by the Security Council, including the International Tribunal and the Mechanism, in accordance with their respective obligations under resolutions 827 (1993), 955 (1994) and 1966 (2010), and recalls the obligation of States to cooperate with the Tribunal and the Mechanism and in particular to comply without undue delay with requests for assistance;

4. *Emphasizes its full support* for the role of the High Representative for Bosnia and Herzegovina in monitoring the implementation of the Peace Agreement and giving guidance to and coordinating the activities of the civilian organizations and agencies involved in assisting the parties to implement the Peace Agreement, and reaffirms that, under annex 10 of the Peace Agreement, the High Representative is the final authority in theatre regarding the interpretation of civilian implementation of the Peace Agreement and that, in case of dispute, he may give his interpretation and make recommendations, and make binding decisions as he judges necessary on issues as elaborated by the Peace Implementation Council in Bonn, Germany, on 9 and 10 December 1997;[94]

5. *Expresses its support* for the declarations of the ministerial meetings of the Peace Implementation Council;

6. *Reaffirms* its intention to keep implementation of the Peace Agreement and the situation in Bosnia and Herzegovina under close review, taking into account the reports submitted pursuant to paragraphs 18 and 20 below, and any recommendations those reports might include, and its readiness to consider the imposition of measures if any party fails significantly to meet its obligations under the Peace Agreement;

---

[93] S/1995/1021, annex.

[94] See S/1997/979, annex.

7. *Recalls* the support of the authorities of Bosnia and Herzegovina for the European Union Force-Althea and the continued North Atlantic Treaty Organization presence and their confirmation that both are the legal successors to the Stabilization Force for the fulfilment of their missions for the purposes of the Peace Agreement, its annexes and appendices and relevant Security Council resolutions and can take such actions as are required, including the use of force, to ensure compliance with annexes 1-A and 2 of the Peace Agreement and relevant Council resolutions;

8. *Pays tribute* to those Member States which participated in the multinational stabilization force (the European Union Force-Althea), and in the continued North Atlantic Treaty Organization presence, established in accordance with its resolution 1575 (2004) and extended by its resolutions 1639 (2005), 1722 (2006), 1785 (2007), 1845 (2008), 1895 (2009), 1948 (2010), 2019 (2011) 2074 (2012) and 2123 (2013), and welcomes their willingness to assist the parties to the Peace Agreement by continuing to deploy a multinational stabilization force (the European Union Force-Althea) and by maintaining a continued North Atlantic Treaty Organization presence;

9. *Welcomes* the intention of the European Union to maintain a European Union military operation (the European Union Force-Althea) in Bosnia and Herzegovina from November 2014;

10. *Authorizes* the Member States acting through or in cooperation with the European Union to establish for a further period of 12 months, starting from the date of the adoption of the present resolution, a multinational stabilization force (the European Union Force-Althea) as a legal successor to the Stabilization Force under unified command and control, which will fulfil its missions in relation to the implementation of annexes 1-A and 2 of the Peace Agreement in cooperation with the North Atlantic Treaty Organization Headquarters presence in accordance with the arrangements agreed between the North Atlantic Treaty Organization and the European Union as communicated to the Security Council in their letters of 19 November 2004,[91] which recognize that the European Union Force-Althea will have the main peace stabilization role under the military aspects of the Peace Agreement;

11. *Welcomes* the decision of the North Atlantic Treaty Organization to continue to maintain a presence in Bosnia and Herzegovina in the form of a North Atlantic Treaty Organization Headquarters in order to continue to assist in implementing the Peace Agreement in conjunction with the European Union Force-Althea, and authorizes the Member States acting through or in cooperation with the North Atlantic Treaty Organization to continue to maintain a North Atlantic Treaty Organization Headquarters as a legal successor to the Stabilization Force under unified command and control, which will fulfil its missions in relation to the implementation of annexes 1-A and 2 of the Peace Agreement in cooperation with the European Union Force-Althea in accordance with the arrangements agreed between the North Atlantic Treaty Organization and the European Union as communicated to the Security Council in their letters of 19 November 2004, which recognize that the European Union Force-Althea will have the main peace stabilization role under the military aspects of the Peace Agreement;

12. *Reaffirms* that the Peace Agreement and the provisions of its previous relevant resolutions shall apply to and in respect of both the European Union Force-Althea and the North Atlantic Treaty Organization presence as they have applied to and in respect of the Stabilization Force and that, therefore, references in the Peace Agreement, in particular in annex 1-A and the appendices thereto, and relevant resolutions to the Implementation Force and/or the Stabilization Force, the North Atlantic Treaty Organization and the North Atlantic Council shall be read as applying, as appropriate, to the North Atlantic Treaty Organization presence, the European Union Force-Althea, the European Union and the Political and Security Committee and Council of the European Union respectively;

13. *Expresses its intention* to consider the terms of further authorization as necessary in the light of developments in the implementation of the Peace Agreement and the situation in Bosnia and Herzegovina;

14. *Authorizes* the Member States acting under paragraphs 10 and 11 above to take all measures necessary to effect the implementation of and to ensure compliance with annexes 1-A and 2 of the Peace Agreement, and stresses that the parties shall continue to be held equally responsible for the compliance with those annexes and shall be equally subject to such enforcement action by the European Union Force-Althea and the North Atlantic Treaty Organization presence as may be necessary to ensure implementation of those annexes and the protection of the European Union Force-Althea and the North Atlantic Treaty Organization presence;

15. *Authorizes* Member States to take all necessary measures, at the request of either the European Union Force-Althea or the North Atlantic Treaty Organization Headquarters, in defence of the European Union Force-Althea or the North Atlantic Treaty Organization presence respectively, and to assist both organizations in carrying out their missions, and recognizes the right of both the European Union Force-Althea and the North Atlantic Treaty Organization presence to take all measures necessary to defend themselves from attack or threat of attack;

16. *Authorizes* the Member States acting under paragraphs 10 and 11 above, in accordance with annex 1-A of the Peace Agreement, to take all measures necessary to ensure compliance with the rules and procedures governing command and control of airspace over Bosnia and Herzegovina with respect to all civilian and military air traffic;

17. *Demands* that the parties respect the security and freedom of movement of the European Union Force-Althea, the North Atlantic Treaty Organization presence and other international personnel;

18. *Requests* the Member States acting through or in cooperation with the European Union and the Member States acting through or in cooperation with the North Atlantic Treaty Organization to report to the Security Council on the activity of the European Union Force-Althea and the North Atlantic Treaty Organization Headquarters presence respectively, through the appropriate channels and at least at six-monthly intervals;

19. *Invites* all States, in particular those in the region, to continue to provide appropriate support and facilities, including transit facilities, for the Member States acting under paragraphs 10 and 11 above;

20. *Requests* the Secretary-General to continue to submit to the Security Council reports of the High Representative, in accordance with annex 10 of the Peace Agreement and the conclusions of the Peace Implementation Conference held in London on 4 and 5 December 1996,[95] and later Peace Implementation Conferences, on the implementation of the Peace Agreement and in particular on compliance by the parties with their commitments under the Agreement;

21. *Decides* to remain seized of the matter.

Adopted at the 7307th meeting
by 14 votes to none, with 1 abstention
(Russian Federation).

Decisions

At its 7308th meeting, on 11 November 2014, the Security Council decided to invite the representatives of Bosnia and Herzegovina, Croatia and Serbia to participate, without vote, in accordance with rule 37 of its provisional rules of procedure, in the discussion of the item entitled:

"The situation in Bosnia and Herzegovina

"Letter dated 30 October 2014 from the Secretary-General addressed to the President of the Security Council (S/2014/777)".

At the same meeting, the Council also decided to extend invitations, in accordance with rule 39 of its provisional rules of procedure, to Mr. Valentin Inzko, High Representative for Bosnia and Herzegovina, and Mr. Thomas Mayr-Harting, Head of the Delegation of the European Union to the United Nations.

At its 7440th meeting, on 12 May 2015, the Council decided to invite the representatives of Bosnia and Herzegovina, Croatia and Serbia to participate, without vote, in accordance with rule 37 of its provisional rules of procedure, in the discussion of the item entitled:

"The situation in Bosnia and Herzegovina

"Letter dated 29 April 2015 from the Secretary-General addressed to the President of the Security Council (S/2015/300)".

At the same meeting, the Council also decided to extend invitations, in accordance with rule 39 of its provisional rules of procedure, to Mr. Valentin Inzko, High Representative for Bosnia and Herzegovina, and Mr. Thomas Mayr-Harting, Head of the Delegation of the European Union to the United Nations.

At its 7481st meeting, on 8 July 2015, the Council considered the item entitled "The situation in Bosnia and Herzegovina".

At the same meeting, the Council decided to extend an invitation, in accordance with rule 39 of its provisional rules of procedure, to Mr. Zeid Ra'ad Al Hussein, United Nations High Commissioner for Human Rights.

[95] S/1996/1012.

At the same meeting, the Council voted on a draft resolution contained in document S/2015/508. The result of the voting was as follows: 10 votes in favour (Chad, Chile, France, Jordan, Lithuania, Malaysia, New Zealand, Spain, United Kingdom of Great Britain and Northern Ireland and United States of America), 1 against (Russian Federation) and 4 abstentions (Angola, China, Nigeria and Venezuela (Bolivarian Republic of)). The draft resolution was not adopted, owing to the negative vote of a permanent member of the Council.

B. Security Council resolutions 1160 (1998), 1199 (1998), 1203 (1998), 1239 (1999) and 1244 (1999)[96]

Decisions

At its 7257th meeting, on 29 August 2014, the Security Council decided to invite the representative of Serbia to participate, without vote, in accordance with rule 37 of its provisional rules of procedure, in the discussion of the item entitled:

"Security Council resolutions 1160 (1998), 1199 (1998), 1203 (1998), 1239 (1999) and 1244 (1999)

"Report of the Secretary-General on the United Nations Interim Administration Mission in Kosovo (S/2014/558)".

At the same meeting, the Council also decided to extend an invitation, in accordance with rule 39 of its provisional rules of procedure, to Mr. Farid Zarif, Special Representative of the Secretary-General for Kosovo and Head of the United Nations Interim Administration Mission in Kosovo.

At the same meeting, the Council further decided to extend an invitation, in accordance with rule 39 of its provisional rules of procedure, to Mr. Enver Hoxhaj.

At its 7327th meeting, on 4 December 2014, the Council decided to invite the representative of Serbia to participate, without vote, in accordance with rule 37 of its provisional rules of procedure, in the discussion of the item entitled:

"Security Council resolutions 1160 (1998), 1199 (1998), 1203 (1998), 1239 (1999) and 1244 (1999)

"Report of the Secretary-General on the United Nations Interim Administration Mission in Kosovo (S/2014/773 and Corr.1)".

At the same meeting, the Council also decided to extend an invitation, in accordance with rule 39 of its provisional rules of procedure, to Mr. Farid Zarif, Special Representative of the Secretary-General for Kosovo and Head of the United Nations Interim Administration Mission in Kosovo.

At the same meeting, the Council further decided to extend an invitation, in accordance with rule 39 of its provisional rules of procedure, to Mr. Hashim Thaçi.

At its 7377th meeting, on 6 February 2015, the Council decided to invite the representative of Serbia to participate, without vote, in accordance with rule 37 of its provisional rules of procedure, in the discussion of the item entitled:

"Security Council resolutions 1160 (1998), 1199 (1998), 1203 (1998), 1239 (1999) and 1244 (1999)

"Report of the Secretary-General on the United Nations Interim Administration Mission in Kosovo (S/2015/74)".

At the same meeting, the Council also decided to extend an invitation, in accordance with rule 39 of its provisional rules of procedure, to Mr. Farid Zarif, Special Representative of the Secretary-General for Kosovo and Head of the United Nations Interim Administration Mission in Kosovo.

At the same meeting, the Council further decided to extend an invitation, in accordance with rule 39 of its provisional rules of procedure, to Mr. Hashim Thaçi.

[96] Resolutions or decisions on this question were first adopted by the Security Council in 1999.

At its 7448th meeting, on 26 May 2015, the Council decided to invite the representative of Serbia to participate, without vote, in accordance with rule 37 of its provisional rules of procedure, in the discussion of the item entitled:

"Security Council resolutions 1160 (1998), 1199 (1998), 1203 (1998), 1239 (1999) and 1244 (1999)

"Report of the Secretary-General on the United Nations Interim Administration Mission in Kosovo (S/2015/303)".

At the same meeting, the Council also decided to extend an invitation, in accordance with rule 39 of its provisional rules of procedure, to Mr. Farid Zarif, Special Representative of the Secretary-General for Kosovo and Head of the United Nations Interim Administration Mission in Kosovo.

At the same meeting, the Council further decided to extend an invitation, in accordance with rule 39 of its provisional rules of procedure, to Mr. Hashim Thaçi.

INTERNATIONAL TRIBUNAL FOR THE PROSECUTION OF PERSONS RESPONSIBLE FOR SERIOUS VIOLATIONS OF INTERNATIONAL HUMANITARIAN LAW COMMITTED IN THE TERRITORY OF THE FORMER YUGOSLAVIA SINCE 1991

INTERNATIONAL CRIMINAL TRIBUNAL FOR THE PROSECUTION OF PERSONS RESPONSIBLE FOR GENOCIDE AND OTHER SERIOUS VIOLATIONS OF INTERNATIONAL HUMANITARIAN LAW COMMITTED IN THE TERRITORY OF RWANDA AND RWANDAN CITIZENS RESPONSIBLE FOR GENOCIDE AND OTHER SUCH VIOLATIONS COMMITTED IN THE TERRITORY OF NEIGHBOURING STATES BETWEEN 1 JANUARY 1994 AND 31 DECEMBER 1994[96]

Decisions

At its 7332nd meeting, on 10 December 2014, the Security Council decided to invite the representatives of Bosnia and Herzegovina, Croatia and Serbia to participate, without vote, in accordance with rule 37 of its provisional rules of procedure, in the discussion of the item entitled:

"International Tribunal for the Prosecution of Persons Responsible for Serious Violations of International Humanitarian Law Committed in the Territory of the Former Yugoslavia since 1991

"International Criminal Tribunal for the Prosecution of Persons Responsible for Genocide and Other Serious Violations of International Humanitarian Law Committed in the Territory of Rwanda and Rwandan Citizens Responsible for Genocide and Other Such Violations Committed in the Territory of Neighbouring States between 1 January 1994 and 31 December 1994

"Report of the International Criminal Tribunal for Rwanda (S/2014/546)

"Report of the International Tribunal for the Former Yugoslavia (S/2014/556)

"Letter dated 19 November 2014 from the President of the International Residual Mechanism for Criminal Tribunals addressed to the President of the Security Council (S/2014/826)

"Letter dated 19 November 2014 from the President of the International Tribunal for the Prosecution of Persons Responsible for Serious Violations of International Humanitarian Law Committed in the Territory of the Former Yugoslavia since 1991, addressed to the President of the Security Council (S/2014/827)

"Letter dated 19 November 2014 from the President of the International Criminal Tribunal for Rwanda addressed to the President of the Security Council (S/2014/829 and Corr.1)".

At the same meeting, the Council also decided to extend invitations, in accordance with rule 39 of its provisional rules of procedure, to Judge Theodor Meron, President of the International Tribunal for the Former Yugoslavia and President of the International Residual Mechanism for Criminal Tribunals, Judge Vagn Joensen, President of the International Criminal Tribunal for Rwanda, Mr. Serge Brammertz, Prosecutor of the International Tribunal for the Former Yugoslavia, and Mr. Hassan Bubacar Jallow, Prosecutor of the International Criminal Tribunal for Rwanda and Prosecutor of the International Residual Mechanism for Criminal Tribunals.

At its 7348th meeting, on 18 December 2014, the Council considered the item entitled:

"International Tribunal for the Prosecution of Persons Responsible for Serious Violations of International Humanitarian Law Committed in the Territory of the Former Yugoslavia since 1991

"International Criminal Tribunal for the Prosecution of Persons Responsible for Genocide and Other Serious Violations of International Humanitarian Law Committed in the Territory of Rwanda and Rwandan Citizens Responsible for Genocide and Other Such Violations Committed in the Territory of Neighbouring States between 1 January 1994 and 31 December 1994

"Report of the International Criminal Tribunal for Rwanda (S/2014/546)

"Report of the International Tribunal for the Former Yugoslavia (S/2014/556)

"Letter dated 19 November 2014 from the President of the International Residual Mechanism for Criminal Tribunals addressed to the President of the Security Council (S/2014/826)

"Letter dated 19 November 2014 from the President of the International Tribunal for the Prosecution of Persons Responsible for Serious Violations of International Humanitarian Law Committed in the Territory of the Former Yugoslavia since 1991, addressed to the President of the Security Council (S/2014/827)

"Letter dated 19 November 2014 from the President of the International Criminal Tribunal for Rwanda addressed to the President of the Security Council (S/2014/829 and Corr.1)".

Resolution 2193 (2014)
of 18 December 2014[97]

The Security Council,

Reaffirming its determination to combat impunity for all those responsible for serious international crimes and the necessity of all persons indicted by the International Tribunal for the Former Yugoslavia (the International Tribunal) being brought to justice,

Taking note of the letters dated 31 October[98] and 3 December 2014[99] from the Secretary-General to the President of the Security Council attaching letters dated 1 October and 25 November 2014 from the President of the International Tribunal,

Recalling its resolutions 827 (1993) of 25 May 1993, 1503 (2003) of 28 August 2003 and 1534 (2004) of 26 March 2004 and, in particular, 1966 (2010) of 22 December 2010, in which it, inter alia, established the International Residual Mechanism for Criminal Tribunals (the Mechanism),

Taking into account the assessments by the International Tribunal in its completion strategy report,[100] and the updated trial and appeals schedule,

Noting the concerns expressed by the President of the International Tribunal about staffing, and reaffirming that staff retention is essential for the most expeditious completion of the work of the Tribunal,

[97] By a letter dated 22 December 2014 (A/69/678), the President of the Security Council drew the attention of the President of the General Assembly to the text of resolution 2193 (2014).

[98] S/2014/780.

[99] S/2014/865.

[100] See S/2014/827.

Recalling its previous resolutions on the extension of the terms of office of the permanent and ad litem judges at the International Tribunal, who are members of the Trial Chambers and the Appeals Chamber,

Recalling also its resolution 2007 (2011) adopted on 14 September 2011,

Having regard to article 16 of the statute of the International Tribunal,

Having considered the nomination by the Secretary-General of Mr. Serge Brammertz for reappointment as Prosecutor of the International Tribunal,[101]

Acting under Chapter VII of the Charter of the United Nations,

1. *Requests* the International Tribunal to complete its work and facilitate the closure of the Tribunal as expeditiously as possible with the aim of completing the transition to the Mechanism, and expresses its continued concern over delays in the conclusion of the work of the Tribunal, in the light of resolution 1966 (2010), in which the Security Council requested the Tribunal to complete its trial and appeals proceedings by 31 December 2014;

2. *Underlines* that States should cooperate fully with the International Tribunal, as well as with the Mechanism;

3. *Decides* to extend the term of office of the following permanent judge at the International Tribunal, who is a member of the Appeals Chamber, until 31 July 2015 or until the completion of the cases to which he is assigned, if sooner:

Mr. Patrick Lipton Robinson (Jamaica)

4. *Also decides* to extend the term of office of the following permanent and ad litem judges at the International Tribunal, who are members of the Trial Chambers and the Appeals Chamber, until 31 December 2015 or until the completion of the cases to which they are assigned, if sooner:

Mr. Koffi Kumelio A. Afande (Togo)

Mr. Carmel A. Agius (Malta)

Mr. Liu Daqun (China)

Mr. Theodor Meron (United States of America)

Mr. Fausto Pocar (Italy)

Mr. Jean-Claude Antonetti (France)

Mr. Guy Delvoie (Belgium)

Mr. Christoph Flügge (Germany)

Mr. Burton Hall (Bahamas)

Mr. O-gon Kwon (Republic of Korea)

Mr. Bakone Melema Moloto (South Africa)

Mr. Howard Morrison (United Kingdom of Great Britain and Northern Ireland)

Mr. Alphonsus Martinus Maria Orie (Netherlands)

Mr. Melville Baird (Trinidad and Tobago)

Ms. Flavia Lattanzi (Italy)

Mr. Antoine Kesia-Mbe Mindua (Democratic Republic of the Congo)

5. *Further decides* to reappoint Mr. Serge Brammertz as Prosecutor of the International Tribunal, notwithstanding the provisions of article 16, paragraph 4, of the statute of the International Tribunal related to the length of office of the Prosecutor, for a term with effect from 1 January 2015 until 31 December 2015, which is subject to an earlier termination by the Council upon the completion of the work of the Tribunal;

---

[101] See S/2014/781.

6. *Urges* the International Tribunal, in the light of resolution 1966 (2010), to redouble its efforts to review its projected case completion dates with a view towards shortening them as appropriate;

7. *Decides* to remain seized of the matter.

Adopted at the 7348th meeting by 14 votes to none, with 1 abstention (Russian Federation).

Resolution 2194 (2014) of 18 December 2014[102]

The Security Council,

Reaffirming its determination to combat impunity for all those responsible for serious international crimes and the necessity of all persons indicted by the International Criminal Tribunal for Rwanda (the International Tribunal) being brought to justice,

Taking note of the letter dated 31 October 2014 from the Secretary-General to the President of the Security Council attaching a letter dated 1 October 2014 from the President of the International Tribunal,[103]

Recalling its resolutions 955 (1994) of 8 November 1994, 1503 (2003) of 28 August 2003, 1534 (2004) of 26 March 2004 and, in particular, 1966 (2010) of 22 December 2010, in which it, inter alia, established the International Residual Mechanism for Criminal Tribunals (the Mechanism),

Taking into account the assessments by the International Tribunal in its completion strategy report,[104] and the updated appeal schedule,

Noting that the year 2014 marked the twentieth anniversary of the International Tribunal, established on 8 November 1994,

Noting also the referral of cases of Laurent Bucyibaruta, Wenceslas Munyeshyaka, Jean Uwinkindi and Bernard Munyagishari to national jurisdictions, pursuant to rule 11 bis of the Rules of Procedure and Evidence of the International Tribunal, and emphasizing the importance of continuing to monitor progress in referred cases, as well as the goal of achieving the completion of all Tribunal and referred cases at the earliest possible time,

Noting with concern that many genocide suspects continue to elude justice, including the remaining nine fugitives indicated by the International Tribunal,

Noting with concern also that the International Tribunal continues to face problems in the relocation of acquitted persons and convicted persons who have completed serving their sentences, emphasizing the importance of the successful relocation of such persons, and also noting the assumption of responsibility of the Mechanism for such persons from 1 January 2015,

Noting the concerns expressed by the President of the International Tribunal about staffing, and reaffirming that staff retention is essential for the most expeditious completion of the work of the International Tribunal,

Recalling its previous resolutions on the extension of the terms of office of the permanent and ad litem judges at the International Tribunal, who are members of the Trial Chamber and the Appeals Chamber,

Recalling also its resolution 2006 (2011) adopted on 14 September 2011,

Having regard to article 15 of the statute of the International Tribunal,

Having considered the nomination by the Secretary-General of Mr. Hassan Bubacar Jallow for reappointment as Prosecutor of the International Tribunal,[105]

[102] By a letter dated 22 December 2014 (A/69/679), the President of the Security Council drew the attention of the President of the General Assembly to the text of resolution 2194 (2014).

[103] S/2014/779.

[104] See S/2014/829 and Corr.1.

[105] See S/2014/778.

Acting under Chapter VII of the Charter of the United Nations,

1. *Requests* the International Tribunal to complete its work and facilitate the closure of the Tribunal as expeditiously as possible with the aim of completing the transition to the Mechanism, taking into account resolution resolution 1966 (2010), in which the Security Council requested the Tribunal to complete its trial and appeals proceedings by 31 December 2014;

2. *Underlines* that States should cooperate fully with the International Tribunal as well as with the Mechanism;

3. *Commends* States that have accepted the relocation of acquitted persons or convicted persons who have completed serving their sentences to their territories, and reiterates its call upon all States to cooperate with and render all necessary assistance to the International Tribunal and, from 1 January 2015, the Mechanism, for increased efforts towards the relocation of acquitted persons and convicted persons who have completed serving their sentences;

4. *Urges* all States, especially States where fugitives are suspected to be at large, to intensify their cooperation with and render all necessary assistance to the International Tribunal and the Mechanism, in particular to achieve the arrest and surrender of all remaining fugitives indicted by the Tribunal as soon as possible;

5. *Urges* the Mechanism to continue to monitor cases of Laurent Bucyibaruta, Wenceslas Munyeshyaka, Jean Uwinkindi and Bernard Munyagishari, which were referred to national jurisdictions;

6. *Decides* to extend the term of office of the following permanent judges at the International Tribunal, who are members of the Appeals Chamber, until 31 July 2015 or until the completion of the cases to which they are or will be assigned, if sooner:

Mr. Mehmet Güney (Turkey)

Mr. William H. Sekule (United Republic of Tanzania)

7. *Also decides* to extend the term of office of the following permanent judges at the International Tribunal, who are members of the Appeals Chamber, until 31 December 2015 or until the completion of the cases to which they are or will be assigned, if sooner:

Ms. Khalida Rachid Khan (Pakistan)

Mr. Mandiaye Niang (Senegal)

Ms. Arlette Ramaroson (Madagascar)

Mr. Bakhtiyar Tuzmukhamedov (Russian Federation)

8. *Further decides*, bearing in mind the expiry of his term of office on 31 December 2014, to extend the term of office of Judge Vagn Joensen (Denmark) until 31 December 2015 so that he may continue to perform the functions required of him as trial judge and President of the International Tribunal, to complete the work of the Tribunal;

9. *Decides* to reappoint Mr. Hassan Bubacar Jallow as Prosecutor of the International Tribunal, notwithstanding the provisions of article 15, paragraph 4, of the statute of the International Tribunal related to the length of office of the Prosecutor, for a term with effect from 1 January 2015 until 31 December 2015, which is subject to an earlier termination by the Council upon the completion of the work of the Tribunal;

10. *Also decides* to remain seized of the matter.

Adopted unanimously at the 7348th meeting.

Decisions

At its 7455th meeting, on 3 June 2015, the Security Council decided to invite the representatives of Bosnia and Herzegovina, Croatia, Rwanda and Serbia to participate, without vote, in accordance with rule 37 of its provisional rules of procedure, in the discussion of the item entitled:

"International Tribunal for the Prosecution of Persons Responsible for Serious Violations of International Humanitarian Law Committed in the Territory of the Former Yugoslavia since 1991

"International Criminal Tribunal for the Prosecution of Persons Responsible for Genocide and Other Serious Violations of International Humanitarian Law Committed in the Territory of Rwanda and Rwandan Citizens

Responsible for Genocide and Other Such Violations Committed in the Territory of Neighbouring States between 1 January 1994 and 31 December 1994

"Letter dated 15 May 2015 from the President of the International Criminal Tribunal for Rwanda addressed to the President of the Security Council (S/2015/340)

"Letter dated 15 May 2015 from the President of the International Residual Mechanism for Criminal Tribunals addressed to the President of the Security Council (S/2015/341)

"Letter dated 15 May 2015 from the President of the International Tribunal for the Prosecution of Persons Responsible for Serious Violations of International Humanitarian Law Committed in the Territory of the Former Yugoslavia since 1991, addressed to the President of the Security Council (S/2015/342)".

At the same meeting, the Council also decided to extend invitations, in accordance with rule 39 of its provisional rules of procedure, to Judge Theodor Meron, President of the International Tribunal for the Former Yugoslavia and President of the International Residual Mechanism for Criminal Tribunals, Judge Vagn Joensen, President of the International Criminal Tribunal for Rwanda, Mr. Serge Brammertz, Prosecutor of the International Tribunal for the Former Yugoslavia, and Mr. Hassan Bubacar Jallow, Prosecutor of the International Criminal Tribunal for Rwanda and Prosecutor of the International Residual Mechanism for Criminal Tribunals.

THE QUESTION CONCERNING HAITI[106]

Decisions

At its 7262nd meeting, on 11 September 2014, the Security Council decided to invite the representatives of Brazil, Canada, Colombia, Ecuador, Guatemala, Haiti, Mexico, Peru, Spain and Uruguay to participate, without vote, in accordance with rule 37 of its provisional rules of procedure, in the discussion of the item entitled:

"The question concerning Haiti

"Report of the Secretary-General on the United Nations Stabilization Mission in Haiti (S/2014/617)".

At the same meeting, the Council also decided to extend an invitation, in accordance with rule 39 of its provisional rules of procedure, to Ms. Sandra Honoré, Special Representative of the Secretary-General for Haiti and Head of the United Nations Stabilization Mission in Haiti.

At the same meeting, the Council further decided to extend an invitation, in accordance with rule 39 of its provisional rules of procedure, to Mr. Thomas Mayr-Harting, Head of the Delegation of the European Union to the United Nations.

At its 7277th meeting, on 14 October 2014, the Council decided to invite the representatives of Brazil, Canada, Ecuador, Guatemala and Uruguay to participate, without vote, in accordance with rule 37 of its provisional rules of procedure, in the discussion of the item entitled:

"The question concerning Haiti

"Report of the Secretary-General on the United Nations Stabilization Mission in Haiti (S/2014/617)".

Resolution 2180 (2014)
of 14 October 2014

The Security Council,

Reaffirming its previous resolutions on Haiti, in particular resolutions 1542 (2004) of 30 April 2004, 1576 (2004) of 29 November 2004, 1608 (2005) of 22 June 2005, 1658 (2006) of 14 February 2006, 1702 (2006) of 15 August 2006, 1743 (2007) of 15 February 2007, 1780 (2007) of 15 October 2007, 1840 (2008) of 14 October

[106] Resolutions or decisions on this question were first adopted by the Security Council in 1993.

2008, 1892 (2009) of 13 October 2009, 1908 (2010) of 19 January 2010, 1927 (2010) of 4 June 2010, 1944 (2010) of 14 October 2010, 2012 (2011) of 14 October 2011, 2070 (2012) of 12 October 2012 and 2119 (2013) of 10 October 2013,

Reaffirming its strong commitment to the sovereignty, independence, territorial integrity and unity of Haiti,

Recognizing that, over the past year, Haiti has taken steps towards stabilization, including the signing of the El Rancho Accord, which called for the conversion of the Transitional College of the Permanent Electoral Council into a new Provisional Electoral Council and provided for a period within which the 2013 electoral law would have been amended to allow for legislative, partial senatorial, municipal and local elections in 2014,

Noting with great concern that some elections have been postponed for three years and that Haiti still does not have an amended electoral law and that as a result the Provisional Electoral Council has concluded that it will not be possible to organize elections on 26 October 2014 as called for by the Government of Haiti,

Recognizing that the overall security situation remained relatively stable with some improvement since the adoption of resolution 2119 (2013), which allowed the United Nations Stabilization Mission in Haiti to continue to draw down and to adapt its configuration without undermining the security and stability of Haiti, and recognizing the importance of conditions-based security-related decisions about the future of the Mission,

Recognizing also the critical role of the Mission in ensuring stability and security in Haiti, commending the Mission for continuing to assist the Government of Haiti to ensure a secure and stable environment, expressing its gratitude to the personnel of the Mission and to their countries and paying tribute to those injured or killed in the line of duty, and commending also the wide range of reconstruction efforts in Haiti and the successful work achieved by the military engineering units of the Mission,

Underlining the need to further strengthen Haitian judicial and corrections systems in order to support a more integrated and cohesive Haitian security sector, noting the commitment by the Government of Haiti to strengthen the rule of law and to make further progress in security sector reform, and encouraging Haitian authorities to continue to pursue efforts in that regard,

Recognizing the interconnected nature of the challenges in Haiti, reaffirming that sustainable progress on security, the rule of law and institutional reform, national reconciliation and development, including the combat against unemployment and poverty, are mutually reinforcing, and welcoming the continuing efforts of the Government of Haiti and the international community to address these challenges, in line with the Government's priorities,

Reiterating the critical role of the Haitian National Police for the security and stability of Haiti, stressing the importance of the ongoing strengthening, professionalization and reform of the National Police in order to enable it to assume full responsibility for the security of Haiti, noting the progress made in the implementation of the five-year 2012–2016 Haitian National Police development plan, and reiterating the importance of maintaining support for it, especially in the area of recruitment and retention,

Underscoring the importance of adequately funding the Haitian National Police to enhance its logistic, administrative and operational capacities, encouraging the Government of Haiti to take advantage of the support being provided by the international community to guarantee the provision of adequate security for the Haitian people, and calling upon all international partners to strengthen their coordination in this regard,

Recognizing the steps taken by the Superior Council of the Judiciary, including the adoption of its internal rules of procedure in June 2014, to carry out its mandate and promote the strengthening of judicial independence, and expressing the need to further address human rights concerns that still remain in the corrections system, such as prolonged pretrial detentions, prison overcrowding and sanitary conditions,

Acknowledging that, while important progress has been made in 2014, Haiti continues to face significant humanitarian challenges, with approximately 85,432 internally displaced persons, whose living conditions in the remaining camps, which are characterized by malnutrition and uneven access to water and sanitation, affecting especially women and children, must be further addressed,

Welcoming the ongoing efforts of the Government of Haiti to control and eliminate the cholera epidemic and the progress made in reducing the incidence of cholera in Haiti, urging the United Nations country team, in coordination with other actors, to continue to support the Government in addressing the structural weaknesses, in particular in the water and sanitation systems, underscoring the importance of strengthening the Haitian national health institutions, and recognizing United Nations efforts to combat cholera, including through the initiative of the Secretary-General to support the National Plan for the Elimination of Cholera in Haiti, stressing the importance of adequate and sustainable support with particular attention to rapid and targeted medical responses to outbreaks designed to reduce the threat, welcoming the visit that the Secretary-General undertook in July 2014 to Haiti, and taking note that he, among other things, launched jointly with the Prime Minister of Haiti, Mr. Laurent Lamothe, the "Total Sanitation Campaign" as a key initiative against cholera, and of the creation of the High-level Committee for the Elimination of Cholera,

Emphasizing that progress in the reconstruction of Haiti, as well as in the social and economic development of Haiti, including through effective, coordinated, commendable international development assistance and increased Haitian institutional capacity to benefit from this assistance, are crucial to achieving lasting and sustainable stability, and reiterating the need for security to be accompanied by social and economic development, including efforts in risk reduction and preparedness that address the country's extreme vulnerability to natural disasters, efforts in which the Government of Haiti plays a leading role,

Welcoming the continued development of the Government of Haiti's External Aid Coordination Framework for the Development of Haiti as its preferred donor coordination mechanism and venue for supporting the development priorities of the Government, welcoming also the increased joint programming of the United Nations country team in Haiti in alignment and coordination with the government-endorsed Integrated Strategic Framework, and welcoming further the commitment to foster greater alignment of international assistance with national priorities, increase transparency and strengthen mutual accountability, as well as the need for stronger coordination,

Urging donors to complete the pledges made at the conference held in New York on 31 March 2010 in order, inter alia, to help to promote access to services and jobs for the most vulnerable, and underlining the responsibility of the Government of Haiti to provide clear guidance to donors on its priorities and to facilitate delivery of assistance to those most in need,

Emphasizing the role of regional organizations in the ongoing process of stabilization and reconstruction of Haiti, and calling upon the Mission to continue to work closely with international financial institutions, regional and subregional organizations and other stakeholders, in particular the Organization of American States, the Union of South American Nations and the Caribbean Community,

Welcoming the continued efforts of the Haitian National Police to patrol and enhance its presence and direct engagement with the population, recognizing the continued community policing efforts of the Mission, in close coordination with camp committees, in camps for internally displaced persons, and welcoming their engagement with the population,

Expressing serious concern that sexual and gender-based violence, especially against women and children, remains a substantial problem, particularly in marginalized districts of Port-au-Prince, in remaining camps for internally displaced persons and in remote areas of the country,

Recognizing that strengthening national human rights institutions as well as respect for human rights, including of children, and due process, combating criminality and sexual and gender-based violence, and putting an end to impunity and ensuring accountability are essential to ensuring the rule of law and security in Haiti, including access to justice,

Reaffirming the authority of the Special Representative of the Secretary-General for Haiti in the coordination and conduct of all activities of United Nations agencies, funds and programmes in Haiti, and reaffirming also its support for the role of the Special Representative in ensuring optimal coordination and collaboration between the Mission and the United Nations country team in connection with the aspects of their respective mandates that are correlated, particularly as part of the Mission's conditions-based consolidation plan,

Taking note of the report of the Secretary-General of 29 August 2014,[107]

Mindful of its primary responsibility for the maintenance of international peace and security under the Charter of the United Nations,

[107] S/2014/617.

Acting under Chapter VII of the Charter, as described in section I of paragraph 7 of resolution 1542 (2004),

1. *Decides* to extend the mandate of the United Nations Stabilization Mission in Haiti as contained in resolutions 1542 (2004), 1608 (2005), 1702 (2006), 1743 (2007), 1780 (2007), 1840 (2008), 1892 (2009), 1908 (2010), 1927 (2010), 1944 (2010), 2012 (2011) 2070 (2012), and 2119 (2013) until 15 October 2015, with the intention of further renewal;

2. *Also decides* that the overall force levels of the Mission will consist of up to 2,370 troops and of a police component composed of up to 2,601 personnel, the force levels recommended by the Secretary-General, and calls upon the Secretary-General to ensure that a force level close to the current level would remain in the country until his next report to the Security Council, and to alert the Council in that report of any major changes in the situation;

3. *Affirms* that adjustments to the force configuration should be based on the situation on the ground, compatible with the capacity of the Mission to maintain security in the context of impending parliamentary and local elections as well as presidential elections in 2015, taking into account the importance of maintaining a secure and stable environment and the impact of social and political realities on the stability and security of Haiti; the increasing development of Haitian State capabilities, in particular the ongoing strengthening of the Haitian National Police; and the national authorities' increasing exercise of the Haitian State's responsibility for the maintenance of stability and security in the country; and calls upon the Mission to maintain capacity, including appropriate air assets, to deploy troops rapidly throughout the country;

4. *Affirms its commitment* to act at any time to adapt the mandate and force levels of the Mission, if compelled by a change of conditions in Haiti, and if necessary to preserve the progress Haiti has made towards durable security and stability;

5. *Takes note* of the implementation of the conditions-based consolidation plan of the Mission, which focused the activities of the Mission on a core set of mandated tasks as agreed with the Government of Haiti;

6. *Recognizes* the ownership and primary responsibility of the Government and the people of Haiti over all aspects of the country's stabilization; and encourages the Mission to intensify its efforts to provide logistical and technical expertise, within available means and consistent with its mandate, and coordinating as appropriate with the United Nations country team and others active in stabilization efforts, to assist, as requested by the Government of Haiti, in continuing to implement decentralization efforts and build the capacity of its institutions at the national and local levels, with a view to enhancing further the ability of the Government to extend State authority throughout Haiti and promote good governance and rule of law at all levels;

7. *Strongly urges* Haiti's political actors to work cooperatively and without further delays to ensure the urgent holding of free, fair, inclusive and transparent legislative, partial senatorial, municipal and local elections, including those which are long overdue, in accordance with the Constitution of Haiti in order to ensure the continued functioning of the National Assembly and other elected bodies;

8. *Welcomes* the efforts of the Special Representative of the Secretary-General for Haiti to support the political process under way in Haiti, reaffirms its call upon the Mission to continue to support this process, and calls upon the Mission to deliver and coordinate, as appropriate, international electoral assistance to the Government of Haiti in cooperation with international stakeholders, including the Organization of American States, the Union of South American Nations and the Caribbean Community, as appropriate;

9. *Reaffirms* that Haiti is at an important juncture in the consolidation of stability and democracy, and the engagement of its political leaders and stakeholders in dialogue and compromise is vital to securing the gains made in recent years, in order to set Haiti firmly on a path towards lasting stability and economic development and to enable Haitians to assume even greater responsibility in that regard;

10. *Recalls* its resolutions 1325 (2000) of 31 October 2000 and 2122 (2013) of 18 October 2013, and encourages the Government of Haiti, with the support of relevant stakeholders, to promote increased political participation of women in Haiti, in accordance with the Constitution of Haiti;

11. *Reaffirms* that, in the framework of the improvement of the rule of law in Haiti, strengthening the capacity of the Haitian National Police is paramount for the Government of Haiti to take timely and full responsibility for the country's security needs, which is central to the overall stability and future development of Haiti;

12. *Reiterates* that the capacity-building of the Haitian National Police remains a most critical task for the Mission, requests the Mission to continue its efforts to strengthen the institutional and operational capacities of the National Police, in particular by renewed efforts to mentor and train police and corrections personnel, including at intermediate rank levels, and calls upon the Mission to align skills of United Nations police personnel to support these objectives and provide skilled trainers and technical advisers;

13. *Underlines* the need to ensure effective support from the Government of Haiti and its international and regional partners for the 2012–2016 Haitian National Police development plan, in order to achieve the goals of a minimum of 15,000 fully operational serving police officers by 2016, adequate logistic and administrative capacity, accountability and respect for human rights and the rule of law, a robust vetting process, enhanced recruitment procedures and training, strengthened land and maritime border control and improved deterrence of transnational organized crime;

14. *Stresses* the need for close coordination among the Mission, donors and the Government of Haiti to enhance the effectiveness and sustainability of Haitian National Police capacity-building efforts. and requests the Mission to facilitate this coordination and to continue to provide technical guidance to donor-funded projects, as requested, for the rehabilitation and construction of police and corrections facilities as well as for other projects aiming to support the institutional capacity of the National Police, as appropriate;

15. *Encourages* the Mission, in cooperation with the appropriate international actors, to assist the Government of Haiti in effectively tackling gang violence, organized crime, illegal arms trafficking, drug trafficking and trafficking in persons, especially children, as well as ensuring proper border management;

16. *Encourages* the Haitian authorities to continue to implement justice reform by taking the necessary steps, including through ongoing support to the Superior Council of the Judiciary, to ensure the independence and effectiveness of the judicial institutions, and to continue to address the issue of prolonged pretrial detentions and prison conditions and overcrowding, with special regard to women and children held in detention;

17. *Calls upon* all donors and partners, including international and non-governmental organizations as well as the United Nations country team, to better coordinate their efforts and work closely with the Government of Haiti through its External Aid Coordination Framework for the Development of Haiti, which is intended to help the Government to ensure increased transparency, national ownership and coordination of foreign assistance and to strengthen the capacity of the Government to manage external assistance;

18. *Requests* the United Nations country team, and calls upon all actors, to complement security and development operations undertaken by the Government of Haiti with the support of the Mission with activities aimed at effectively improving the living conditions of the concerned populations, in particular women and children;

19. *Requests* the Mission, working in coordination with the United Nations country team, to continue to implement quick-impact projects that contribute to building a secure and stable environment and enhance national ownership and the trust of the Haitian population in the Mission, particularly in the priority areas identified by the Mission's leadership and consistent with the priorities of the Government of Haiti, as appropriate;

20. *Strongly condemns* the grave violations against children affected particularly by criminal gang violence, as well as widespread rape and other sexual abuse of women and girls, calls upon the Government of Haiti, with the support of the Mission and the United Nations country team, to continue to promote and protect the rights of women and children as set out in Security Council resolutions 1325 (2000), 1612 (2005) of 26 July 2005, 1820 (2008) of 19 June 2008, 1882 (2009) of 4 August 2009, 1888 (2009) of 30 September 2009, 1889 (2009) of 5 October 2009, 2106 (2013) and 2122 (2013), encourages all actors in the Government, the international community and civil society to renew their efforts to eliminate sexual and gender-based violence in Haiti, as well as to improve response to rape complaints and access to justice for the victims of rape and other sexual crimes, and encourages national authorities to promote national legislation in this regard;

21. *Requests* the Mission to continue to pursue its community violence reduction approach, in close collaboration with the Government of Haiti, with a particular focus on at-risk youth, women, the displaced and those living in violence-affected neighbourhoods, and to ensure that this activity is coordinated with, and supports the work of, the United Nations country team to build local capacity in this area by taking into account Haitian priorities;

22. *Encourages* the Mission to continue to assist the Government of Haiti in providing adequate protection to the civilian population, with particular attention to the needs of internally displaced persons and other vulnerable

groups, especially women and children, including through joint community policing in the camps, in line with Council resolution 1894 (2009) of 11 November 2009;

23. *Requests* the Secretary-General to continue to take the measures necessary to ensure full compliance of all Mission personnel with the United Nations zero-tolerance policy on sexual exploitation and abuse, and to continue to keep the Council informed, and urges troop- and police-contributing countries to redouble efforts in preventing cases of misconduct and to ensure that acts involving their personnel are properly investigated and punished;

24. *Reaffirms* the human rights mandate of the Mission as an essential component of the Mission, and recognizes that respect for human rights is an essential element for the stability of Haiti, in particular attention to individual accountability for grave violations under past governments, urges the Government of Haiti to ensure with the support of the international community, as appropriate, the respect and protection of human rights by the Haitian National Police and the judiciary, and calls upon the Mission to provide monitoring and support in this regard;

25. *Encourages* the Mission, within its mandate, to continue to use existing means and capabilities, including its engineers, with a view to enhancing stability in Haiti while fostering greater Haitian ownership in the context of its conditions-based consolidation plan;

26. *Requests* the Mission to continue to support the Haitian authorities in their efforts to control the flow of small arms, the development of a weapons registry, the revision of current laws on the importation and possession of arms, reform of the weapons permit system and the development and implementation of a national community policing doctrine;

27. *Underscores* the importance of planning documents for the military and police components of the Mission, such as the concept of operations and rules of engagement, being regularly updated, as appropriate, and in line with the provisions of all its relevant resolutions, and requests the Secretary-General to fully report on them in a timely manner to the Council and troop- and police-contributing countries;

28. *Requests* the Secretary-General to keep the Council regularly informed and to report to the Council on the implementation of the mandate of the Mission, semi-annually and not later than 45 days prior to its expiration;

29. *Also requests* the Secretary-General to continue to include in his reports a comprehensive assessment of the situation in Haiti, to propose, as appropriate, options regarding the reconfiguration of the Mission based on conditions on the ground, and to continue to present a progress report on the consolidation plan as an annex to his next report;

30. *Decides* to remain seized of the matter.

Adopted unanimously at the 7277th meeting.

Decisions

At its 7408th meeting, on 18 March 2015, the Security Council decided to invite the representatives of Antigua and Barbuda, Argentina, Belize, Brazil, Canada, Colombia, Guatemala, Haiti, Japan, Mexico, Peru and Uruguay to participate, without vote, in accordance with rule 37 of its provisional rules of procedure, in the discussion of the item entitled:

"The question concerning Haiti

"Report of the Secretary-General on the United Nations Stabilization Mission in Haiti (S/2015/157)".

At the same meeting, the Council also decided to extend an invitation, in accordance with rule 39 of its provisional rules of procedure, to Ms. Sandra Honoré, Special Representative of the Secretary-General for Haiti and Head of the United Nations Stabilization Mission in Haiti.

At the same meeting, the Council further decided to extend an invitation, in accordance with rule 39 of its provisional rules of procedure, to Mr. Thomas Mayr-Harting, Head of the Delegation of the European Union to the United Nations.

THE SITUATION IN BURUNDI[108]

Decisions

At its 7236th meeting, on 6 August 2014, the Security Council decided to invite the representative of Burundi to participate, without vote, in accordance with rule 37 of its provisional rules of procedure, in the discussion of the item entitled:

"The situation in Burundi

"Report of the Secretary-General on the United Nations Office in Burundi (S/2014/550)".

At the same meeting, the Council also decided to extend an invitation, in accordance with rule 39 of its provisional rules of procedure, to Mr. Parfait Onanga-Anyanga, Special Representative of the Secretary-General for Burundi and Head of the United Nations Office in Burundi.

On 25 September 2014, the President of the Security Council addressed the following letter to the Secretary-General:[109]

> I have the honour to inform you that your letter dated 23 September 2014 concerning your intention to deploy immediately an advance team to commence preparations for the establishment of a United Nations electoral observer mission in Burundi[110] has been brought to the attention of the members of the Security Council. They take note of the intention expressed in your letter.

At its 7295th meeting, on 5 November 2014, the Council decided to invite the representative of Burundi to participate, without vote, in accordance with rule 37 of its provisional rules of procedure, in the discussion of the item entitled "The situation in Burundi".

At the same meeting, the Council also decided to extend invitations, in accordance with rule 39 of its provisional rules of procedure, to Mr. Parfait Onanga-Anyanga, Special Representative of the Secretary-General for Burundi and Head of the United Nations Office in Burundi, and Mr. Paul Seger, Permanent Representative of Switzerland to the United Nations, in his capacity as Chair of the Burundi configuration of the Peacebuilding Commission.

On 6 November 2014, the President of the Security Council addressed the following letter to the Secretary-General:[111]

> I have the honour to inform you that your letter dated 6 November 2014 concerning your intention to appoint Mr. Cassam Uteem, of Mauritius, as your Special Envoy and Head of the United Nations Electoral Observation Mission in Burundi[112] has been brought to the attention of the members of the Security Council. They take note of the intention expressed in your letter.

At its 7364th meeting, on 21 January 2015, the Council decided to invite the representative of Burundi to participate, without vote, in accordance with rule 37 of its provisional rules of procedure, in the discussion of the item entitled:

"The situation in Burundi

"Report of the Secretary-General on the United Nations Office in Burundi (S/2015/36)".

At the same meeting, the Council also decided to extend invitations, in accordance with rule 39 of its provisional rules of procedure, to Mr. Jeffrey Feltman, Under-Secretary-General for Political Affairs, and Mr. Paul Seger, Permanent Representative of Switzerland to the United Nations, in his capacity as Chair of the Burundi configuration of the Peacebuilding Commission.

[108] Resolutions or decisions on this question were first adopted by the Security Council in 1993.

[109] S/2014/701.

[110] S/2014/700.

[111] S/2014/800.

[112] S/2014/799.

At its 7388th meeting, on 18 February 2015, the Council considered the item entitled "The situation in Burundi".

At the same meeting, following consultations among members of the Security Council, the President made the following statement on behalf of the Council:[113]

In accordance with Security Council resolution 2137 (2014), the mandate of the United Nations Office in Burundi terminated on 31 December 2014. The Council commends the continued contribution of the Office to the peace, democracy and stability of Burundi in these last four years. The Council commends the role played by the Special Representative of the Secretary-General for Burundi, Mr. Parfait Onanga-Anyanga, in this regard, notably in the facilitation of dialogue between political actors in Burundi. The Council welcomes the final report of the Secretary-General on the Office.[114]

The Council welcomes the significant progress made by Burundi since the adoption of the Arusha Agreement in 2000, notably in the restoration of security and stability in the country. The Council notes that the spirit of Arusha helped to sustain almost a decade of peace in Burundi. The Council welcomes Burundi's contribution and active participation to United Nations and African Union peacekeeping operations, especially in Somalia and the Central African Republic.

The Council notes that there remain challenges to overcome to ensure that the significant progress is not reversed, especially in the context of the 2015 elections. The Council stresses, in this regard, the crucial need for a free, transparent, credible, inclusive and peaceful electoral process in 2015 and sustained attention to such a process. The Council welcomes continued engagement by international and regional partners, including the African Union, in support of the reform agenda and the electoral process in Burundi.

The Council expresses its concern regarding the recent events that occurred in the province of Cibitoke, strongly condemns such attempts to resort to violence for political means, and stresses the importance of guaranteeing a peaceful electoral process. The Council expresses its deep concern at the high number of reported victims resulting from this incident, looks forward to the outcome of an impartial investigation by the Government of Burundi, and stresses the need for it to be independent and impartial, led by competent national institutions.

The Council welcomes the unanimous adoption of the Electoral Code in 2014, as well as of the road map for the elections and the signing of the code of conduct for political parties and political actors, which was facilitated by the United Nations Office in Burundi.

The Council takes note of the engagement of the Government of Burundi to implement the code of conduct for political parties and political actors as well as the road map for the elections. The Council expresses concern about reports of intimidation, harassment, political violence, arbitrary arrest and detention and other curtailments of the enjoyment of the rights to freedom of peaceful assembly and expression. The Council encourages the Government of Burundi to make further efforts to ensure a space for all political parties, including from the extra-parliamentary opposition, and to improve dialogue between all political actors, with a view to ensuring a conducive, free and open environment for the run-up to the 2015 elections, and further calls upon the Government to ensure the full and effective participation of women at all stages of the electoral process.

The Council welcomes the efforts of the Independent National Electoral Commission and emphasizes the importance of guaranteeing the independence and impartiality of the Commission, as well as its provincial and communal organs, and their engagement with all partners to ensure inclusive participation in the electoral process throughout the country for all citizens and candidates.

The Council welcomes recent steps taken by the Independent National Electoral Commission to reach out to electoral stakeholders and address some of their concerns and stresses that it is critical that the Commission continue to undertake effective measures to strengthen the public's confidence in the electoral process. The Council also encourages the opposition to play its part and remain engaged throughout the electoral process and use peaceful and democratic means to address any electoral disputes.

---

[113] S/PRST/2015/6.

[114] S/2015/36.

The Council takes note of the electoral workshop held by the Independent National Electoral Commission in Bujumbura on 29 and 30 January 2015 with the participation of the Government of Burundi, political parties, civil society, religious entities as well as international technical and financial partners, to address the reports of significant irregularities during the voter registration process conducted between 24 November and 12 December 2014. The Council encourages the Government and the Commission to continue efforts to work with the interested parties to ensure the credibility and inclusivity of the upcoming elections.

The Council welcomes the deployment on 1 January 2015, immediately at the end of the mandate of the United Nations Office in Burundi, of the United Nations Electoral Observation Mission in Burundi under the leadership of Mr. Cassam Uteem as the Special Envoy of the Secretary-General and Head of the Mission. In accordance with its resolution 2137 (2014), the Council recalls that this mission has the mandate to follow and report on the electoral process in Burundi before, during and after the elections, and calls upon the Government of Burundi, the Independent National Electoral Commission and all relevant electoral stakeholders to ensure close cooperation with the Mission in this regard.

The Council notes the efforts made by the Government of Burundi to improve the human rights situation in Burundi and takes note of the reports of a reduction in extrajudicial killings, cases of torture and ill-treatment, as well as politically motivated acts of violence carried out by youth wings affiliated with political parties, while expressing concern about some recent developments and urging the Government to resume the previous trend.

The Council expresses concern about restrictions on freedom of expression and opinion, peaceful assembly and association, as well as continued threats against journalists and representatives of civil society, including those who work on human rights. The Council calls for the Government of Burundi to take all appropriate measures to ensure the exercise of these fundamental freedoms and to assure the protection of civil society, including those who work on human rights, in order to ensure an inclusive and credible electoral process. The Council further expresses its concern about the insufficient progress on the fight against impunity and calls for the Government to deploy greater efforts to ensure that all human rights violations and abuses are seriously investigated and that perpetrators are held accountable.

The Council commends the growing role played by the National Independent Human Rights Commission in leading a national effort to protect human rights and calls upon the Burundian authorities to guarantee the Commission's independence.

The Council welcomes the opening of a stand-alone office of the United Nations High Commissioner for Human Rights in Burundi with a comprehensive mandate to monitor and report on human rights violations and abuses and to support the Government of Burundi in upholding its obligations under international human rights law. The Council encourages the international community to support the Office, including through providing sufficient resources.

The Council notes that Burundi remains one of the poorest countries in the world and stresses the utmost importance of fighting against poverty. In this regard, the Council urges progress by Burundi towards development and ongoing economic reforms to enhance macroeconomic stability, including the policy on zero tolerance of corruption, and calls for these efforts to include holding accountable individuals who violate the zero-tolerance policy on corruption.

The Council emphasizes the need for the United Nations system and the international community, including the international financial institutions and Burundi's development partners, to maintain their support for peace consolidation and long-term development in Burundi. In this regard the Council welcomes the round table meeting held in Bujumbura on 11 and 12 December 2014, and calls upon the Government of Burundi and international and regional partners to fully implement the mutual commitments made in the joint communiqué adopted at the meeting.

The Council welcomes the continued engagement of the Burundi configuration of the Peacebuilding Commission, and encourages the continued constructive cooperation between the Government of Burundi and the Peacebuilding Commission, acknowledging the contribution that the Peacebuilding Fund has made to peacebuilding efforts in Burundi.

The Council reiterates its call upon the United Nations country team and its component United Nations agencies to scale up their activities and factor them into the United Nations Development Assistance

Framework and urges the Secretary-General to work toward a seamless transition to the Resident Coordinator and United Nations country team management model.

The Council emphasizes the need to address the implications of the departure of the United Nations Office in Burundi as identified in the Joint Transition Plan adopted by the Transition Steering Group, in particular in the areas of political dialogue, high-level facilitation and advocacy, as well as human rights. In accordance with its resolution 2137 (2014), the Council reiterates its request to the United Nations Electoral Observation Mission in Burundi, as may be required, to report to the Secretary-General and the Secretary-General to report to the Council before, during and after the elections, and further reiterates its request to the Secretary-General to report every six months to the Council until after the 2015 elections.

On 17 June 2015, the President of the Security Council addressed the following letter to the Secretary-General:[115]

I have the honour to inform you that your letter dated 11 June 2015 concerning your intention to seek additional staffing positions, including more long-term electoral observers and additional security staff, for the United Nations Electoral Observation Mission in Burundi[116] has been brought to the attention of the members of the Security Council, who took note of the information provided and the intention expressed therein.

They also emphasized that it was important for the Mission to play a more prominent, robust and visible role in following and reporting on the electoral process and, to that end, recalled their reporting requests under Security Council resolution 2137 (2014).

At its 7473rd meeting, on 26 June 2015, the Council decided to invite the representative of Burundi to participate, without vote, in accordance with rule 37 of its provisional rules of procedure, in the discussion of the item entitled "The situation in Burundi".

At the same meeting, following consultations among members of the Security Council, the President made the following statement on behalf of the Council:[117]

The Security Council reiterates its deep concern regarding the grave security and political situation in Burundi against the backdrop of the forthcoming communal, presidential and senatorial elections and for the impact of the crisis in the region. The Council strongly condemns all acts of violence and human rights violations and abuses and recalls that those responsible for such violence should be held accountable and brought to justice.

The Council welcomes the regional and subregional efforts aimed at addressing the crisis, and in this regard takes note of the conclusions of the East African Community summits held on 13 and 31 May 2015[118] in Dar es Salaam, United Republic of Tanzania, of the communiqué issued by the African Union Peace and Security Council after its summit held on 13 June 2015 in Johannesburg, South Africa,[119] and of the letters sent by the Government of Burundi to the Security Council.

The Council pays tribute to the Special Envoy of the Secretary-General for the Great Lakes Region, Mr. Saïd Djinnit, for his relentless efforts, and recalls that Burundian stakeholders had made some progress in a difficult dialogue thanks to Mr. Djinnit's able facilitation.

The Council takes note of the statement by the African Union that the political dialogue has not produced expected results and that the current situation could jeopardize the important gains recorded following the signing of the Arusha Agreement for Peace and Reconciliation in Burundi and the Global Ceasefire Agreement of 2003,[120] and affect the stability of the region.

The Council welcomes the resumption of the dialogue between all the Burundian parties, under the facilitation of the African Union, the United Nations, the East African Community and the International Conference on the Great Lakes Region. In this regard, the Council welcomes the appointment of Mr. Ibrahima

---

[115] S/2015/448.

[116] S/2015/447.

[117] S/PRST/2015/13.

[118] S/2015/407, annex.

[119] S/2015/483, annex, enclosure 1.

[120] S/2003/1105, annex.

Fall by the African Union as the new Special Representative of the Chairperson of the Commission for the Great Lakes Region and Head of the African Union Liaison Office in Bujumbura. The Council also welcomes the arrival in Bujumbura of Mr. Abdoulaye Bathily, Special Representative of the Secretary-General for Central Africa and Head of the United Nations Regional Office for Central Africa, which allows for the international mediation to immediately assist all Burundian parties to expedite the search for a consensual political solution to the crisis.

While acknowledging that further steps must continue to be taken by parties to adhere to the decisions taken by the East African Community and the Peace and Security Council, the Security Council calls upon the Burundian parties to urgently participate in an inclusive dialogue which should focus, in the spirit of the Arusha Agreement and the Constitution, on the measures to be taken to create conditions conducive to the organization of free, fair, transparent and credible elections.

The Security Council takes note of the statement in the Peace and Security Council communiqué of 13 June 2015 that the date of the election should be set by consensus between the Burundian parties, in the spirit of the East African Community communiqué of 31 May 2015 requesting a postponement of the elections, and on the basis of a technical assessment to be undertaken by the United Nations.

The Security Council emphasizes that the dialogue should address all matters on which the parties disagree. The Council further emphasizes that this dialogue should address concerns related to the reinstatement of private media; the protection of human rights and fundamental freedoms, in particular freedoms of expression and of peaceful assembly, including for members of the political opposition to campaign freely, as guaranteed by the Constitution of Burundi; the release of those arbitrarily detained following demonstrations; respect for the rule of the law; and the urgent disarmament of all armed youth groups allied with political parties, as reflected in the conditions of the East African Community communiqué of 31 May 2015, conditions to be met prior to the holding of elections.

The Council welcomes the commitment of the African Union and the Chairperson of the African Union Commission to fully assume the responsibilities stemming from its role as guarantor of the Arusha Agreement, as well as that of the region not to stand by in case the situation deteriorates.

In this regard, the Council welcomes the decision of the African Union to immediately deploy human rights observers and other civilian personnel; to deploy African Union military experts to verify the process of the disarming of all armed youth groups allied with political parties, who will submit regular reports on the implementation of the disarmament process; and to deploy an African Union election observer mission if conditions for the organization of free, fair, transparent and credible elections are met. The Council urges the Government of Burundi and other relevant actors to extend their full cooperation to these processes.

The Security Council also welcomes the decision of the Peace and Security Council to send, by the first week of July 2015, a ministerial delegation including the Commission, to assess the implementation of the conditions required by the East African Community, the African Union and the Security Council for the holding of the elections.

The Council calls upon the United Nations Electoral Observation Mission in Burundi to fully and actively pursue the implementation of its mandate in accordance with resolution 2137 (2014), including to swiftly report to the Council before, during and after the elections.

The Council reiterates its concern about the difficult situation of the Burundian refugees who fled their country into the neighbouring States, commends the host countries (the Democratic Republic of the Congo, Rwanda and the United Republic of Tanzania), as well as humanitarian agencies, for their support to the affected populations, and calls upon the international community to provide the necessary humanitarian assistance. The Council urges the Government of Burundi to create the conditions conducive to their early return.

The Council calls upon all actors in the region the preserve the safety and security of populations in the region.

At its 7482nd meeting, on 9 July 2015, the Council decided to invite the representative of Burundi to participate, without vote, in accordance with rule 37 of its provisional rules of procedure, in the discussion of the item entitled:

"The situation in Burundi

"Report of the Secretary-General on the United Nations Electoral Observation Mission in Burundi (S/2015/510)".

At the same meeting, the Council also decided to extend invitations, in accordance with rule 39 of its provisional rules of procedure, to Mr. Tayé-Brook Zerihoun, Assistant Secretary-General for Political Affairs, and Mr. Zeid Ra'ad Zeid Al Hussein, United Nations High Commissioner for Human Rights.

THE SITUATION IN AFGHANISTAN[121]

Decisions

On 17 September 2014, the President of the Security Council addressed the following letter to the Secretary-General:[122]

> I have the honour to inform you that your letter dated 15 September 2014 concerning your intention to appoint Mr. Nicholas Haysom, of South Africa, as your Special Representative for Afghanistan and Head of the United Nations Assistance Mission in Afghanistan[123] has been brought to the attention of the members of the Security Council. They take note of the intention expressed in your letter.

At its 7267th meeting, on 18 September 2014, the Council decided to invite the representatives of Afghanistan, Canada, Germany, India, Iran (Islamic Republic of), Italy, Japan, Pakistan, Poland, Slovakia, Spain and Turkey to participate, without vote, in accordance with rule 37 of its provisional rules of procedure, in the discussion of the item entitled:

"The situation in Afghanistan

> "Report of the Secretary-General on the situation in Afghanistan and its implications for international peace and security (S/2014/656)".

At the same meeting, the Council also decided to extend an invitation, in accordance with rule 39 of its provisional rules of procedure, to Mr. Ján Kubiš, Special Representative of the Secretary-General for Afghanistan and Head of the United Nations Assistance Mission in Afghanistan.

At the same meeting, the Council further decided to extend an invitation, in accordance with rule 39 of its provisional rules of procedure, to Mr. Thomas Mayr-Harting, Head of the Delegation of the European Union to the United Nations.

At its 7338th meeting, on 12 December 2014, the Council decided to invite the representative of Afghanistan to participate, without vote, in accordance with rule 37 of its provisional rules of procedure, in the discussion of the item entitled "The situation in Afghanistan".

Resolution 2189 (2014)
of 12 December 2014

The Security Council,

Reaffirming its strong commitment to the sovereignty, independence, territorial integrity and national unity of Afghanistan,

Recognizing Afghanistan's gains since the fall of the Taliban in 2001, in particular on democracy, governance, institution-building, economic development and human rights,

Condemning the ongoing violent and terrorist activities by the Taliban, Al-Qaida and other violent and extremist groups, illegal armed groups, criminals and those involved in the production of, trafficking in or trade in illicit drugs,

---

[121] Resolutions or decisions on this question were first adopted by the Security Council in 1994.

[122] S/2014/675.

[123] S/2014/674.

Reaffirming the importance of sustainable progress on security, development, human rights, in particular for women and children, democracy, governance, the fight against corruption, and economic development, taking all appropriate measures to ensure the protection of civilians, and of addressing the cross-cutting issue of counter-narcotics,

Underscoring the importance of continued international support for Afghanistan, and in this regard welcoming and emphasizing the importance of regional cooperation on Afghanistan, as well as the process by which Afghanistan and its regional and international partners are entering into long-term strategic partnership and other agreements, aimed at achieving a peaceful, stable and prosperous Afghanistan,

Emphasizing the important role that the United Nations continues to play in support of Afghanistan's full assumption of leadership and ownership in the areas of security, governance and development, welcoming in this regard the continued role of the United Nations Assistance Mission in Afghanistan, and noting that the Secretary-General reports to the Security Council every three months on developments in Afghanistan,

Acknowledging the contribution of Afghanistan's partners to peace and security in Afghanistan,

Welcoming the increased capacities and capabilities of the Afghan National Defence and Security Forces, looking forward to the completion of security transition at the end of 2014, after which Afghan authorities will assume full responsibility for security, noting the conclusion of the International Security Assistance Force at the end of 2014, and underscoring the importance of sustained international support to continue building the capacities and capabilities of the Afghan National Defence and Security Forces,

Taking note of the letter dated 28 November 2014 from the Secretary-General to the President of the Security Council transmitting the final report on the operations of the International Security Assistance Force in Afghanistan,[124]

Underlining the significance of the Lisbon, Bonn and Chicago declarations on Afghanistan, which stressed the long-term commitment, beyond 2014, to lasting peace, security and stability in Afghanistan,

Underlining also the significance of the North Atlantic Treaty Organization Wales Summit Declaration on Afghanistan of 5 September 2014 which outlined the role of the North Atlantic Treaty Organization and contributing partners in supporting lasting peace, security and stability in Afghanistan beyond 2014, including through the non-combat Resolute Support Mission to train, advise and assist the Afghan National Defence and Security Forces, the contribution to the financial sustainment of the Afghan National Defence and Security Forces and the long-term North Atlantic Treaty Organization-Afghanistan Enduring Partnership,

Noting the signing of the security and defence cooperation agreement between the United States of America and Afghanistan (bilateral security agreement) on 30 September 2014, and welcoming the signing of the status-of-forces agreement between Afghanistan and the North Atlantic Treaty Organization on 30 September 2014 and as ratified by the Parliament of Afghanistan on 27 November 2014,

Noting also that the bilateral agreement between the North Atlantic Treaty Organization and Afghanistan and the invitation of the Government of Afghanistan to the North Atlantic Treaty Organization to establish the Resolute Support Mission provide a sound legal basis for the Mission,

1. *Underscores* the importance of continued international support for the stabilization of the situation in Afghanistan and of further enhancing the capabilities and capacities of the Afghan National Defence and Security Forces in order for them to maintain security and stability throughout the country, and in this regard welcomes the agreement between the North Atlantic Treaty Organization and Afghanistan to establish the post-2014 non-combat Resolute Support Mission which will train, advise and assist the Afghan National Defence and Security Forces at the invitation of Afghanistan;

2. *Looks forward* to the leadership of the Resolute Support Mission working with the Government of Afghanistan and in close coordination and cooperation, where relevant, with the United Nations Assistance Mission in Afghanistan and the Special Representative of the Secretary-General for Afghanistan;

---

[124] S/2014/856.

3. *Welcomes* the commitment of the international community to continue to provide substantial support to the Government and the people of Afghanistan, and notes in this regard the long-term North Atlantic Treaty Organization-Afghanistan Enduring Partnership, Afghanistan's bilateral strategic partnership agreements and other bilateral agreements with other countries;

4. *Affirms its readiness* to revisit the present resolution in the context of the consideration by the Security Council of the situation in Afghanistan.

Adopted unanimously at the 7338th meeting.

Decisions

At its 7347th meeting, on 18 December 2014, the Security Council decided to invite the representatives of Afghanistan, Canada, Finland, Germany, India, Iran (Islamic Republic of), Italy, Japan, Pakistan, Slovakia, Spain, Sweden and Turkey to participate, without vote, in accordance with rule 37 of its provisional rules of procedure, in the discussion of the item entitled:

"The situation in Afghanistan

> "Report of the Secretary-General on the situation in Afghanistan and its implications for international peace and security (S/2014/876)".

At the same meeting, the Council also decided to extend invitations, in accordance with rule 39 of its provisional rules of procedure, to Mr. Nicholas Haysom, Special Representative of the Secretary-General for Afghanistan and Head of the United Nations Assistance Mission in Afghanistan, and Mr. Yury Fedotov, Executive Director of the United Nations Office on Drugs and Crime.

At the same meeting, the Council further decided to extend an invitation, in accordance with rule 39 of its provisional rules of procedure, to Mr. Ioannis Vrailas, Deputy Head of the Delegation of the European Union to the United Nations.

At its 7403rd meeting, on 16 March 2015, the Council decided to invite the representatives of Afghanistan, Australia, Germany, India, Iran (Islamic Republic of), Italy, Japan, Pakistan, Slovakia, Sweden and Turkey to participate, without vote, in accordance with rule 37 of its provisional rules of procedure, in the discussion of the item entitled:

"The situation in Afghanistan

> "Report of the Secretary-General on the situation in Afghanistan and its implications for international peace and security (S/2015/151)".

At the same meeting, the Council also decided to extend an invitation, in accordance with rule 39 of its provisional rules of procedure, to Mr. Nicholas Haysom, Special Representative of the Secretary-General for Afghanistan and Head of the United Nations Assistance Mission in Afghanistan.

At the same meeting, the Council further decided to extend an invitation, in accordance with rule 39 of its provisional rules of procedure, to Mr. Ioannis Vrailas, Deputy Head of the Delegation of the European Union to the United Nations.

Resolution 2210 (2015) of 16 March 2015

The Security Council,

Recalling its previous resolutions on Afghanistan, in particular resolution 2145 (2014) of 17 March 2014, in which it extended until 17 March 2015 the mandate of the United Nations Assistance Mission in Afghanistan as established by resolution 1662 (2006) of 23 March 2006,

Reaffirming its strong commitment to the sovereignty, independence, territorial integrity and national unity of Afghanistan,

Welcoming the completion, at the end of 2014, of the transition (Inteqal) process and the initiation of the transformation decade (2015–2024), with the assumption of full responsibility for the security sector by Afghan institutions, recognizing that transition is not only a security process but also entails the full assumption of Afghan leadership and ownership in governance and development, and affirming that the United Nations support in Afghanistan takes full account of the completion of the transition process in Afghanistan,

Emphasizing the Kabul Process towards the primary objective of reinforced Afghan leadership and ownership, strengthened international partnership and regional cooperation, improved Afghan governance, enhanced capabilities of Afghan security forces, economic growth, sustainable development and better protection for the rights of all Afghan citizens, including women and girls, and welcoming specifically the commitments made by the Government of Afghanistan,

Stressing the importance of a comprehensive approach to address the security, economic, governance and development challenges in Afghanistan, which are of an interconnected nature, and recognizing that there is no purely military solution to ensure the stability of Afghanistan,

Reaffirming its continued support for the Government and people of Afghanistan as they rebuild their country and strengthen the foundations of sustainable peace and development and constitutional democracy,

Welcoming the inauguration on 29 September 2014 of the new President of Afghanistan, marking the first democratic transition of power in the country's history, as well as the establishment of a National Unity Government, and emphasizing the importance of all parties in Afghanistan working within the framework of the National Unity Government in order to achieve a unified, peaceful and prosperous future for all the people of Afghanistan,

Welcoming also the strategic consensus between the Government of Afghanistan and the international community on a renewed and enduring partnership for the transformation decade based on firm mutual commitments, welcoming progress made towards meeting the mutual commitments set out in the Tokyo Mutual Accountability Framework[125] and reaffirmed at the 2014 London Conference on Afghanistan to support the sustainable economic growth and development of Afghanistan, and reaffirming the importance of continued efforts by the Government and the international community towards meeting their mutual commitments,

Affirming that sustainable progress on security, governance, human rights, including the rights of women and girls, the rule of law and development as well as the cross-cutting issues of counter-narcotics, anti-corruption and accountability are mutually reinforcing and that governance and development programmes should be consistent with the goals set forth in the Tokyo Declaration: Partnership for Self-Reliance in Afghanistan - From Transition to Transformation[126] and the national priority programmes of the Government of Afghanistan, and welcoming the continuing efforts of the Government and the international community to address these challenges through a comprehensive approach,

Reaffirming specifically in this context its support for the implementation, under the leadership and ownership of the Afghan people, of the commitments set out in the communiqués of the London Conference on Afghanistan, held on 28 January 2010,[127] and the Kabul International Conference on Afghanistan, held on 20 July 2010, of the Afghanistan National Development Strategy and the National Drug Control Strategy,[128] as part of the comprehensive implementation strategy to be taken forward by the Government of Afghanistan with the support of the region and the international community and with a central and impartial coordinating role for the United Nations among donors, consistent with the Kabul Process and in line with the national priority programmes,

Welcoming the reform programme of the Government of Afghanistan entitled "Realizing Self-Reliance: Commitments to Reforms and Renewed Partnership" that contains strategic policy priorities for Afghanistan towards realizing self-reliance in the transformation decade for improving security, political stability, economic and fiscal stabilization, advancing good governance, including electoral reform and strengthening democratic institutions, promoting the rule of law and respect for human rights, particularly in relation to women and girls, fighting corruption and the illicit economy, including narcotics, and paving the way for enhanced private sector

[125] S/2012/532, annex II.

[126] Ibid., annex I.

[127] S/2010/65, annex II.

[128] S/2006/106, annex.

investment and sustainable, social, environmental and economic development, and in this context affirming its support for the implementation of this reform programme under the leadership and ownership of the Government,

Stressing the crucial importance of advancing regional cooperation as an effective means to promote security, stability and economic and social development in Afghanistan, recalling the importance of the Kabul Declaration on Good-neighbourly Relations of 22 December 2002,[129] welcoming in this regard the continued commitment of the international community to support stability and development in Afghanistan, and noting international and regional initiatives such as the Heart of Asia-Istanbul Process on Regional Security and Cooperation for a Secure and Stable Afghanistan,[130] the quadrilateral summit of Afghanistan, Pakistan, Tajikistan and the Russian Federation, the trilateral summit of Afghanistan, the Islamic Republic of Iran and Pakistan, the trilateral summit of Afghanistan, Pakistan and Turkey and the trilateral summit of Afghanistan, Pakistan and the United Kingdom of Great Britain and Northern Ireland, as well as initiatives by the Shanghai Cooperation Organization, the Collective Security Treaty Organization and the South Asian Association for Regional Cooperation, and the Regional Economic Cooperation Conference on Afghanistan process,

Commending the outcome of the fourth Heart of Asia-Istanbul Process Ministerial Conference, which convened in Beijing on 31 October 2014, in which Afghanistan and its regional partners, while stating their belief that increased political mutual trust and deepened regional cooperation are the foundation for peace and prosperity in Afghanistan and the region, reaffirmed their commitment to pursue opportunities to enhance regional economic cooperation and called upon the rest of the international community to fulfil its commitments to the long-term development of Afghanistan, welcoming the confidence-building measures on counter-terrorism, counter-narcotics and trade, commerce and investment opportunity and those on education, disaster management and regional infrastructure, welcoming also the fifth Heart of Asia-Istanbul Process Ministerial Conference, to be held in Pakistan in 2015, and noting that the Heart of Asia-Istanbul Process is intended to complement and cooperate with, and not substitute for, existing efforts of regional organizations, particularly where they relate to Afghanistan,

Welcoming the outcome of the International Conference on the Solutions Strategy for Afghan Refugees to Support Voluntary Repatriation, Sustainable Reintegration and Assistance to Host Countries, held in Geneva on 2 and 3 May 2012, and looking forward to the further implementation of the joint communiqué of the Conference aimed at increased sustainability of returns and continued support for host countries, through sustained support and directed efforts of the international community,

Stressing the important role that the United Nations will continue to play in promoting peace and stability in Afghanistan by coordinating among international donors and supporting the efforts of the Government of Afghanistan in the role it plays in leading and coordinating between the Government and the international community consistent with the principle of Afghan leadership, ownership and sovereignty in governance and development and in line with the Kabul Process and the Tokyo Mutual Accountability Framework and based on the Government's national priority programmes, including, jointly with the Government, the coordination and monitoring of efforts in implementing the Kabul Process through the Joint Coordination and Monitoring Board in support of the priorities set up by the Government and affirmed at the Tokyo and London Conferences, and expressing its appreciation and strong support for the ongoing efforts of the Secretary-General, his Special Representative for Afghanistan and, in particular, the women and men of the United Nations Assistance Mission in Afghanistan who are serving in difficult conditions to help the people of Afghanistan,

Stressing the importance of a comprehensive and inclusive, Afghan-led and Afghan-owned political process in Afghanistan to support reconciliation for all those who are prepared to reconcile as laid down in the Kabul Conference communiqué on dialogue for all those who renounce violence, have no links to international terrorist organizations, including Al-Qaida, respect the Constitution, including its human rights provisions, notably the rights of women, and are willing to join in building a peaceful Afghanistan, and as further elaborated in the Bonn Conference conclusions,[131] supported by the Government of Afghanistan and the international community, with full respect for the implementation of measures and application of the procedures introduced by the Security Council in

---

[129] S/2002/1416, annex.

[130] S/2011/767, annex.

[131] S/2011/762, annex.

its resolutions 1267 (1999) of 15 October 1999, 1988 (2011) of 17 June 2011, 2082 (2012) of 17 December 2012 and 2160 (2014) of 17 June 2014, as well as other relevant resolutions of the Council,

Recalling the commitments made by the Government of Afghanistan at the Kabul, Tokyo and London Conferences to strengthen and improve Afghanistan's electoral process, including long-term electoral reform, in order to ensure that future elections will be transparent, credible, inclusive and democratic, and looking forward to preparations for the upcoming parliamentary elections,

Reaffirming that Afghanistan's peaceful future lies in building a stable, secure and economically sustainable State, free of terrorism and narcotics and based on the rule of law, strengthened democratic institutions, respect for the separation of powers, reinforced constitutional checks and balances and the guarantee and enforcement of citizens' rights and obligations, and welcoming the contribution of the International Contact Group on Afghanistan to the United Nations efforts in coordinating and broadening international support for Afghanistan,

Underlining the importance of operationally capable, professional, inclusive and sustainable Afghan National Defence and Security Forces for meeting Afghanistan's security needs, with a view to lasting peace, security and stability, stressing the long-term commitment, beyond 2014, and into the transformation decade, of the international community to support the further development, including training, and professionalization of the Afghan National Defence and Security Forces, and the recruitment and retention of women to the Afghan National Defence and Security Forces, acknowledging the contribution of Afghanistan's partners to peace and security in Afghanistan, noting the conclusion of the mission of the International Security Assistance Force at the end of 2014, and welcoming the agreement between the North Atlantic Treaty Organization and Afghanistan that led to the establishment, on 1 January 2015, of the non-combat Resolute Support Mission to train, advise and assist the Afghan National Defence and Security Forces at the invitation of Afghanistan, noting the responsibility of the Government of Afghanistan to sustain sufficient and capable Afghan National Defence and Security Forces, noting also the contribution of the North Atlantic Treaty Organization and contributing partners to the financial sustainment of the Afghan National Defence and Security Forces and the long-term North Atlantic Treaty Organization-Afghanistan Enduring Partnership, with a clear view to the assumption by the Government, no later than 2024, of full financial responsibility for its own security forces, and recalling in this context resolution 2189 (2014) of 12 December 2014,

Stressing the need for all United Nations agencies, funds and programmes, through the country team mechanism and a "One United Nations" approach, under the guidance of the Special Representative, in a manner that increases effectiveness, including through cost-effective mechanisms and aid information-sharing strategies, to further increase efforts, in full consultation and cooperation with the Government of Afghanistan, to achieve further greater coherence, coordination, efficiency and full alignment with the Government's national priority programmes,

Welcoming the efforts of countries that are sustaining their civilian efforts to assist the Government and the people of Afghanistan, and encouraging the international community to further enhance its contributions in a coordinated manner with the Afghan authorities and the United Nations Assistance Mission in Afghanistan, with a view to strengthening Afghan leadership and ownership, as reaffirmed in the Kabul Process and at the Tokyo Conference in July 2012 and the London Conference in December 2014,

Stressing the need to further improve the efficient and effective delivery of humanitarian assistance, including through enhanced coordination among the United Nations agencies, funds and programmes under the authority of the Special Representative and between the United Nations and other donors, especially where it is most needed, welcoming the establishment of the Common Humanitarian Fund, and supporting the essential role of the Government of Afghanistan in the coordination of humanitarian assistance to its citizens,

Emphasizing the need for all, within the framework of humanitarian assistance, of upholding and respecting the humanitarian principles of humanity, neutrality, impartiality and independence,

Reiterating its concern about the security situation in Afghanistan, in particular the ongoing violent and terrorist activities by the Taliban, Al-Qaida and other violent and extremist groups, illegal armed groups, criminals and those involved in the production of, trafficking in or trade in illicit drugs, and the strong links between terrorist activities and illicit drugs, resulting in threats to the local population, including women and children, national security forces and international military and civilian personnel, including humanitarian and development workers, and expressing also its deep concern about the increase in civilian casualties, including women and children, from conflict-related violence in Afghanistan, as noted in the report of the United Nations Assistance Mission in Afghanistan of 18 February 2015 on the protection of civilians in armed conflict,

Recognizing the continuously alarming threats posed by the Taliban, Al-Qaida and other violent and extremist groups and illegal armed groups, as well as the challenges related to the efforts to address such threats, and expressing its serious concern over the harmful consequences of violent and terrorist activities by the Taliban, Al-Qaida and other violent and extremist groups and illegal armed groups on the capacity of the Government of Afghanistan to guarantee the rule of law, to provide security and basic services to the Afghan people and to ensure the improvement and protection of their human rights and fundamental freedoms,

Recalling its resolutions 1674 (2006) of 28 April 2006, 1738 (2006) of 23 December 2006 and 1894 (2009) of 11 November 2009 on the protection of civilians in armed conflict, expressing its serious concern about the high number of civilian casualties in Afghanistan, in particular women and children, the increasingly large majority of which are caused by the Taliban, Al-Qaida and other violent and extremist groups and illegal armed groups, condemning the targeted killing of women and girls, in particular high-level female officials, reaffirming that all parties to armed conflict must take all feasible steps to ensure the protection of affected civilians, especially women, children and displaced persons, including from sexual violence and all other forms of gender-based violence, and that perpetrators of such violence must be held accountable, calling upon all parties to comply with their obligations under international law, including international humanitarian law and human rights law, and for all appropriate measures to be taken to ensure the protection of civilians, and recognizing the importance of the ongoing monitoring and reporting to the Security Council on the situation of civilians and in particular civilian casualties, taking note of the efforts made by Afghan and international forces in minimizing civilian casualties, and noting the report of the United Nations Assistance Mission in Afghanistan of 18 February 2015 on the protection of civilians in armed conflict,

Expressing concern about the serious threat that anti-personnel mines, remnants of war and improvised explosive devices pose to the civilian population, and stressing the need to refrain from the use of weapons and devices prohibited by international law,

Encouraging the international community and regional partners to further effectively support Afghan-led sustained efforts to address drug production and trafficking in a balanced and integrated approach, including through the working group on counter-narcotics of the Joint Coordination and Monitoring Board as well as regional initiatives, and recognizing the threat posed by the production of, trade in and trafficking in illicit drugs to international peace and stability in different regions of the world and the important role played by the United Nations Office on Drugs and Crime in this regard,

Expressing concern at the continuing increase in poppy production, as noted in the United Nations Office on Drugs and Crime Afghanistan Opium Survey 2014, noting the serious harm that opium cultivation, production and trafficking and consumption continue to cause to the stability, security, public health, social and economic development and governance of Afghanistan as well as to the region and internationally, and stressing the important role of the United Nations to continue to monitor the drug situation in Afghanistan,

Stressing the need for coordinated regional efforts to combat the drug problem, and in this regard welcoming the holding of the Regional Ministerial Conference on Counter-Narcotics, in Islamabad on 12 and 13 November 2012, aimed at enhancing regional cooperation to counter narcotics,

Welcoming the ongoing work of the Paris Pact initiative[132] as one of the most important frameworks in the fight against opiates originating in Afghanistan, taking note of the Vienna Declaration,[133] and emphasizing the aim of the Paris Pact to establish a broad international coalition to combat traffic in illicit opiates, as part of a comprehensive approach to peace, stability and development in Afghanistan, the region and beyond,

Recalling the declaration addressed to the International Narcotics Control Board by the Government of Afghanistan that there is no legal use for acetic anhydride in Afghanistan for the time being and that producing and exporting countries should abstain from authorizing the export of this substance to Afghanistan without a request

[132] See S/2003/641, annex.

[133] See E/CN.7/2012/17.

from the Government,[134] and encouraging, pursuant to resolution 1817 (2008) of 11 June 2008, Member States to increase their cooperation with the Board, notably by complying fully with the provisions of article 12 of the United Nations Convention against Illicit Traffic in Narcotic Drugs and Psychotropic Substances of 1988,[135] and encouraging further international and regional cooperation with a view to preventing the diversion of and trafficking in chemical precursors into Afghanistan,

Supporting the continued ban by the Government of Afghanistan of ammonium nitrate fertilizer, urging prompt action to implement regulations for the control of all explosive materials and precursor chemicals, thereby reducing the ability of insurgents to use them for improvised explosive devices, and calling upon the international community to support the efforts of the Government in this regard,

Recalling its resolutions 1265 (1999) of 17 September 1999, 1296 (2000) of 19 April 2000, 1674 (2006), 1738 (2006) and 1894 (2009) on the protection of civilians in armed conflict, its resolutions 1325 (2000) of 31 October 2000, 1820 (2008) of 19 June 2008, 1888 (2009) of 30 September 2009, 1889 (2009) of 5 October 2009, 1960 (2010) of 16 December 2010, 2106 (2013) of 24 June 2013 and 2122 (2013) of 18 October 2013 on women and peace and security, its resolutions 1612 (2005) of 26 July 2005, 1882 (2009) of 4 August 2009, 1998 (2011) of 12 July 2011, 2068 (2012) of 19 September 2012 and 2143 (2014) of 7 March 2014 on children and armed conflict and its resolution 2117 (2013) of 26 September 2013 on small arms and light weapons, and taking note of the reports of the Secretary-General on children and armed conflict[136] and on the protection of civilians in armed conflict,[137] as well as the conclusions of the Security Council Working Group on Children and Armed Conflict,[138]

1. *Welcomes* the report of the Secretary-General of 27 February 2015;[139]

2. *Expresses its appreciation* for the United Nations long-term commitment, including throughout the transformation decade (2015–2024), to support the Government and the people of Afghanistan, reiterates its full support for the work of the United Nations Assistance Mission in Afghanistan and the Special Representative of the Secretary-General for Afghanistan, and stresses the need to ensure continued adequate resourcing for the Mission to fulfil its mandate;

3. *Decides* to extend until 17 March 2016 the mandate of the United Nations Assistance Mission in Afghanistan, as defined in its resolutions 1662 (2006), 1746 (2007) of 23 March 2007, 1806 (2008) of 20 March 2008, 1868 (2009) of 23 March 2009, 1917 (2010) of 22 March 2010, 1974 (2011) of 22 March 2011, 2041 (2012) of 22 March 2012, 2096 (2013) of 19 March 2013 and 2145 (2014), and in paragraphs 4 to 7 below;

4. *Recognizes* that the renewed mandate of the United Nations Assistance Mission in Afghanistan takes full account of the completion of the transition process and the initiation of the transformation decade on 1 January 2015, and that the renewed mandate is in support of the full assumption by Afghanistan of leadership and ownership in the security, governance and development areas, consistent with the understandings reached between Afghanistan and the international community at the London, Kabul, Bonn and Tokyo Conferences and the Lisbon, Chicago and Wales summits;

5. *Calls upon* the United Nations, with the support of the international community, to support the Government of Afghanistan's national priority programmes covering the issues of security, governance, justice and economic and social development and to support the full implementation of mutual commitments made on these issues at international conferences, as well as on continuing implementation of the National Drug Control Strategy,[128] fully consistent with the principle of Afghan leadership, ownership and sovereignty reaffirmed at the Kabul, Tokyo and London Conferences;

6. *Decides* that the United Nations Assistance Mission in Afghanistan and the Special Representative, within their mandate and in a manner consistent with Afghan sovereignty, leadership and ownership, shall continue to lead and

[134] See S/2009/235, annex.

[135] United Nations, *Treaty Series*, vol. 1582, No. 27627.

[136] S/2014/339.

[137] S/2013/689.

[138] S/AC.51/2011/3.

[139] S/2015/151.

coordinate the international civilian efforts, in accordance with the London,[127] Kabul and Tokyo Conference communiqués and the Bonn Conference conclusions,[131] with a particular focus on the priorities laid down below:

(*a*) Promote, as co-chair of the Joint Coordination and Monitoring Board, more coherent support by the international community to the development and governance priorities of the Government of Afghanistan, including through supporting the ongoing development and sequencing of the national priority programmes, mobilization of resources, coordination of international donors and organizations, in a manner consistent with Afghan sovereignty, leadership and ownership, and direction of the contributions of United Nations agencies, funds and programmes, in particular for counter-narcotics, reconstruction and development activities; at the same time, coordinate also in a manner consistent with Afghan leadership, ownership and sovereignty, international partners for follow-up, in particular through information-sharing, prioritize efforts to increase the proportion of development aid delivered through the Government, in line with the commitments made at the Kabul and Tokyo Conferences, and support efforts to increase the mutual accountability and transparency and effectiveness of aid use in line with the commitments made at the Kabul and Tokyo Conferences, including cost-effectiveness in this regard;

(*b*) Support, at the request of the Afghan authorities, the organization of future Afghan elections, including the upcoming parliamentary elections, as well as strengthen, in support of the efforts of the Government of Afghanistan, the sustainability, integrity and inclusiveness of the electoral process, as agreed at the London, Kabul, Bonn and Tokyo Conferences and the Chicago summit, and provide capacity-building and technical assistance to the Afghan institutions involved in this process, in close consultation and coordination with the Government;

(*c*) Provide outreach as well as good offices to support, if requested by and in close consultation with the Government of Afghanistan, the Afghan-led and Afghan-owned process of peace and reconciliation, including through the implementation of the Afghan Peace and Reintegration Programme and proposing and supporting confidence-building measures, also in close consultation with the Government, within the framework of the Afghan Constitution and with full respect for the implementation of measures and application of the procedures introduced by the Security Council in its resolutions 1267 (1999), 1988 (2011), 1989 (2011) of 17 June 2011, 2082 (2012) and 2083 (2012) of 17 December 2012 as well as other relevant resolutions of the Council;

(*d*) Support regional cooperation, with a view to assisting Afghanistan to utilize its role at the heart of Asia to promote regional cooperation, and work towards a stable and prosperous Afghanistan, building on the achievements made;

(*e*) Continue, with the support of the Office of the United Nations High Commissioner for Human Rights, to cooperate with and strengthen the capacity of the Afghan Independent Human Rights Commission, to cooperate also with the Government of Afghanistan and relevant international and local non-governmental organizations to monitor the situation of civilians, to coordinate efforts to ensure their protection, to promote accountability and to assist in the full implementation of the fundamental freedoms and human rights provisions of the Afghan Constitution and international treaties to which Afghanistan is a State party, in particular those regarding the full enjoyment by women of their human rights, including the Convention on the Elimination of All Forms of Discrimination against Women;[140]

(*f*) Closely coordinate and cooperate, where relevant, with the non-combat Resolute Support Mission agreed upon between the North Atlantic Treaty Organization and Afghanistan, as well as with the Senior Civilian Representative of the North Atlantic Treaty Organization;

7. *Calls upon* the United Nations Assistance Mission in Afghanistan and the Special Representative to further increase efforts to achieve greater coherence, coordination and efficiency among relevant United Nations agencies, funds and programmes in Afghanistan based on a "One United Nations" approach in close cooperation with the Government of Afghanistan, with a view to maximizing their collective effectiveness in full alignment with the Government's national priority programmes, and continue to lead, in a manner consistent with Afghan leadership, ownership and sovereignty, international civilian efforts aimed at reinforcing the role of Afghan institutions to perform their responsibilities in the following priority areas:

(*a*) Support through an appropriate presence of the Mission, to be determined in full consultation and cooperation with the Government of Afghanistan, and in support of the Government's efforts, implementation of the

[140] United Nations, *Treaty Series*, vol. 1249, No. 20378.

Kabul Process throughout the country, including through enhanced cooperation with the United Nations Office on Drugs and Crime, in line with the Government's policies;

(*b*) Support the efforts of the Government of Afghanistan in fulfilling its commitments as stated at the London, Kabul, Bonn and Tokyo Conferences, to improve governance and the rule of law, including transitional justice, budget execution and the fight against corruption, throughout the country in accordance with the Kabul Process and the Tokyo Mutual Accountability Framework,[125] with a view to helping to bring the benefits of peace and the delivery of services in a timely and sustainable manner;

(*c*) Coordinate and facilitate the delivery of humanitarian assistance, including in support of the Government of Afghanistan and in accordance with humanitarian principles, with a view to reinforcing the Government's capacity, including by providing effective support to national and local authorities in assisting and protecting internally displaced persons, and to creating conditions conducive to the voluntary, safe, dignified and sustainable return of refugees from neighbouring and other countries and internally displaced persons;

8. *Calls upon* all Afghan and international parties to coordinate with the United Nations Assistance Mission in Afghanistan in the implementation of its mandate and in efforts to promote the security and freedom of movement of United Nations and associated personnel throughout the country;

9. *Reiterates* the need to ensure the security of United Nations staff and its support for the measures already taken by the Secretary-General in this regard;

10. *Stresses* the critical importance of a continued presence of the United Nations Assistance Mission in Afghanistan and other United Nations agencies, funds and programmes in the provinces, in close consultation and coordination with and in support of the Government of Afghanistan, in response to needs and with a view to security and including the objective of overall United Nations effectiveness, and strongly supports the authority of the Special Representative in the coordination of all activities of United Nations agencies, funds and programmes in Afghanistan based on a "One United Nations" approach;

11. *Encourages* the Secretary-General to continue his current efforts to take the measures necessary to address the security issues associated with the United Nations presence, and particularly encourages careful coordination with the Afghan National Defence and Security Forces;

12. *Underscores* the importance of a sustainable democratic development in Afghanistan with all Afghan institutions acting within their clearly defined areas of competence, in accordance with the relevant laws and the Afghan Constitution, welcomes in this regard the commitment of the Government of Afghanistan at the Kabul Conference, reaffirmed at the Bonn and Tokyo Conferences, to deliver further improvements to the electoral process, including addressing the sustainability of the electoral process, and, taking into account the commitments made by the international community and the Government at the London, Kabul, Bonn and Tokyo Conferences, reaffirms the supporting role of the United Nations Assistance Mission in Afghanistan, upon the request of the Government, in the realization of these commitments, and requests that, upon the request of the Government, the Mission provide assistance to the relevant Afghan institutions to support the integrity and inclusiveness of the electoral process, including measures to enable the full and safe participation of women, welcomes the participation of women in the electoral process as candidates, registered voters and campaigners, and further calls upon members of the international community to provide assistance as appropriate;

13. *Welcomes* the continuing efforts of the Government of Afghanistan to advance the peace and reconciliation process, including by the High Peace Council and the implementation of the Afghan Peace and Reintegration Programme, to promote an inclusive, Afghan-led and Afghan-owned dialogue on reconciliation and political participation, as laid down in the Kabul Conference communiqué on dialogue for all those who renounce violence, have no links to international terrorist organizations, including Al-Qaida, respect the Constitution, including its human rights provisions, notably the rights of women, and are willing to join in building a peaceful Afghanistan, and as further elaborated in the principles and outcomes of the Bonn Conference conclusions, and encourages the Government to make use of the good offices of the United Nations Assistance Mission in Afghanistan to support this process as appropriate, in full respect of the implementation of measures and procedures introduced by the Security Council in its resolutions 1267 (1999), 1988 (2011), 2082 (2012) and 2160 (2014), as well as other relevant resolutions of the Council;

14. *Also welcomes* the measures taken by the Government of Afghanistan, including the adoption, in October 2014, of the national action plan for the implementation of Council resolution 1325 (2000), and encourages

it to continue to increase the participation of women as well as minorities and civil society in outreach, consultation and decision-making processes, recalls that women play a vital role in the peace process, as recognized in resolution 1325 (2000) and related resolutions, therefore reiterates the need for the full, equal and effective participation of women at all stages of peace processes, and urges their involvement in the development and implementation of post-conflict strategies in order to take account of their perspectives and needs, as affirmed by the Bonn and Tokyo Conferences;

15. *Notes* the establishment of the Security Council Committee pursuant to resolution 1988 (2011), its methods and procedures, including procedures to facilitate and expedite requests for travel ban exemptions in support of the peace and reconciliation process, introduced in resolution 2082 (2012), welcomes the continuation of the cooperation of the Government of Afghanistan, the High Peace Council and the United Nations Assistance Mission in Afghanistan with the Committee, including its Analytical Support and Sanctions Monitoring Team, including by providing relevant information for updating the 1988 List, and by identifying individuals, groups, undertakings and entities associated with the Taliban in constituting a threat to the peace, stability and security of Afghanistan, in accordance with the designation criteria set out in resolution 2160 (2014), notes that means of financing or supporting these individuals, groups, undertakings and entities includes but is not limited to proceeds derived from the illicit cultivation of, production of and trafficking in narcotic drugs originating in and transiting through Afghanistan, trafficking in precursors into Afghanistan, the illegal exploitation of natural resources in Afghanistan, kidnapping for ransom, extortion and other criminal activities, and notes with concern the increasing cooperation of the Taliban with other organizations involved in criminal activities;

16. *Stresses* the role of the United Nations Assistance Mission in Afghanistan in supporting, if requested by and in close consultation with the Government of Afghanistan, an inclusive, Afghan-led and Afghan-owned process of peace and reconciliation, including the Afghan Peace and Reintegration Programme, while continuing to assess, including in collaboration with the Afghan Independent Human Rights Commission, its human rights and gender implications, including the promotion and protection of human rights, and encourages the international community to assist the efforts of the Government in this regard, including through continued support to the Peace and Reintegration Trust Fund;

17. *Reaffirms* support to the ongoing Afghan-led regional effort within the framework of the Heart of Asia-Istanbul Process on Regional Security and Cooperation for a Secure and Stable Afghanistan,[130] looks forward to the next ministerial conference, to be held in Pakistan in 2015, calls upon Afghanistan and its regional partners to keep up the momentum and continue their efforts to enhance regional dialogue and confidence through the Heart of Asia-Istanbul Process, and notes that the Heart of Asia-Istanbul Process is intended to complement and cooperate with, and not substitute for, existing efforts of regional organizations, particularly where they relate to Afghanistan;

18. *Welcomes* ongoing efforts by the Government of Afghanistan, its neighbouring and regional partners and international organizations, including the Organization of Islamic Cooperation, to foster trust and cooperation with each other, as well as recent cooperation initiatives developed by the countries concerned and regional organizations, including trilateral, quadrilateral, Shanghai Cooperation Organization and South Asian Association for Regional Cooperation summits;

19. *Calls for* the strengthening of the process of regional cooperation, including measures to facilitate regional trade and transit, including through regional and bilateral transit trade agreements, expanded consular visa cooperation and facilitation of business travel, to expand trade, to increase foreign investments and to develop infrastructure, including infrastructural connectivity, energy supply, transport and integrated border management, with a view to strengthening Afghanistan's role in regional economic cooperation and promoting sustainable economic growth and the creation of jobs in Afghanistan;

20. *Emphasizes*, in this regard, the importance of strengthening local and regional networks of transportation that will facilitate connectivity for economic development, stability and self-sustainability, particularly the completion and maintenance of local railroad and land routes, the development of regional projects to foster further connectivity and the enhancement of international civil aviation capabilities;

21. *Reaffirms* the central role played by the Joint Coordination and Monitoring Board, in a manner consistent with Afghan leadership, ownership and sovereignty, in coordinating, facilitating and monitoring the implementation of the Afghanistan National Development Strategy and the national priority programmes, and calls upon all relevant actors to enhance their cooperation with the Board in this regard, with a view to further improving its efficiency;

22. *Calls upon* international donors and organizations and the Government of Afghanistan to adhere to their commitments made at the Kabul and Tokyo Conferences and previous international conferences, and reaffirmed at the 2014 London Conference, and reiterates the critical importance of enhancing the predictability and effectiveness of aid by increasing on-budget assistance to the Government, in tandem with the improvements to Afghan budget and expenditure systems and improving aid coordination and effectiveness through ensuring transparency, combating corruption and enhancing the capacity of the Government to coordinate aid;

23. *Calls upon* the Government of Afghanistan, with the assistance of the international community, to continue to address the threat to the security and stability of Afghanistan posed by the Taliban, Al-Qaida and other violent and extremist groups, illegal armed groups, criminals and those involved in the production of, trafficking in or trade in illicit drugs;

24. *Reiterates* the importance of increasing, in a comprehensive framework, the functionality, professionalism and accountability of the Afghan security sector through appropriate vetting procedures, training, including on child rights, mentoring, equipping and empowerment efforts, for both women and men, in order to accelerate progress towards the goal of self-sufficient, ethnically balanced and women-inclusive Afghan security forces providing security and ensuring the rule of law throughout the country, and stresses the importance of the long-term commitment by the international community to ensure capable, professional and sustainable Afghan National Defence and Security Forces, and notes in this context the establishment of the non-combat Resolute Support Mission to train, advise and assist, based on the bilateral agreements between the North Atlantic Treaty Organization and Afghanistan and at the invitation of Afghanistan;

25. *Welcomes*, in this context, the continued progress in the development of the Afghan National Army and its improved ability to plan and undertake operations, and encourages sustained training efforts, including through the contribution of trainers, resources and advisory teams through the Resolute Support Mission, and advice in developing a sustainable defence planning process as well as assistance in defence reform initiatives;

26. *Takes note* of the ongoing efforts of the Afghan authorities to enhance the capabilities of the Afghan National Police, calls for further efforts towards that goal, and stresses the importance, in this context, of international assistance through financial support and the provision of trainers and mentors, including the contribution of the Resolute Support Mission, as agreed to and accepted by the Government of Afghanistan, the European Gendarmerie Force contribution to this mission and the European Union through the European Union Police Mission in Afghanistan, as well as the German Police Project Team, noting the importance of a sufficient and capable police force for Afghanistan's long-term security, welcomes the 10-year vision for the Ministry of the Interior and the Afghan National Police, including the commitment to develop an effective strategy for coordinating increased recruitment, retention, training and capacity development for women in the Afghan National Police, as well as furthering the implementation of their gender integration strategy, and welcomes the continued support of the United Nations Assistance Mission in Afghanistan for women police associations;

27. *Welcomes* the progress in the implementation by the Government of Afghanistan of the programme of disbandment of illegal armed groups and its integration with the Afghan Peace and Reintegration Programme, and calls for accelerated and harmonized efforts for further progress, with support from the international community;

28. *Condemns in the strongest terms* all attacks, including improvised explosive device attacks, suicide attacks, assassinations and abductions, targeting civilians and Afghan and international forces and their deleterious effect on the stabilization, reconstruction and development efforts in Afghanistan, and condemns further the use by the Taliban and other extremist groups of civilians as human shields;

29. *Notes with concern* the continued high incidence of attacks against humanitarian and development workers, including attacks on health-care workers and medical transports and facilities, condemns these attacks in the strongest terms, emphasizing that the attacks impede efforts to aid the people of Afghanistan, and calls upon all parties to ensure full, safe and unhindered access of all humanitarian actors, including United Nations staff and associated personnel, and to comply fully with applicable international humanitarian law, and to respect the United Nations guiding principles of emergency humanitarian assistance;

30. *Welcomes* the achievements to date in the implementation of the Mine Action Programme for Afghanistan, and encourages the Government of Afghanistan, with the support of the United Nations and all the relevant actors, to continue its efforts towards the removal and destruction of anti-personnel landmines, anti-tank landmines and explosive remnants of war in order to reduce the threats posed to human life and peace and security

in the country, and expresses the need to provide assistance for the care, rehabilitation and economic and social reintegration of victims, including persons with disabilities;

31. *Expresses its strong concern* about the recruitment and use of children by the Taliban, Al-Qaida and other violent and extremist groups in Afghanistan, as well as the killing and maiming of children as a result of the conflict, reiterates its strong condemnation of the recruitment and use of child soldiers in violation of applicable international law and all other violations and abuses committed against children in situations of armed conflict, in particular those involving attacks against schools and education and health-care facilities, including the burning and forced closure of schools and the intimidation, abduction and killing of education personnel, particularly those attacks targeting girls' education by illegal armed groups, including the Taliban, and noting in this context the listing of the Taliban in annex I to the report of the Secretary-General on children and armed conflict,[136] and the use of children in suicide attacks, and calls for those responsible to be brought to justice;

32. *Stresses*, in this context, the importance of implementing Council resolution 1612 (2005) on children and armed conflict and subsequent resolutions, supports the decree of 6 July 2011 by the Minister of the Interior reaffirming the commitment of the Government of Afghanistan to preventing violations of the rights of the child, welcomes the progress made on the implementation of the action plan, and the annex thereto, on children associated with the Afghan National Security Forces, signed in January 2011, in particular the establishment of the Afghan Inter-Ministerial Steering Committee on Children and Armed Conflict, the appointment of a focal point on child protection, the recent adoption of a new law prohibiting recruitment of children into military units and criminalizing any underage recruitment, and the endorsement by the Government of a road map to accelerate compliance with the action plan, and calls for the full implementation of the provisions of the action plan, in close cooperation with the United Nations Assistance Mission in Afghanistan, and requests the Secretary-General to continue to give priority to the child protection activities and capacity of the Mission and continue to include in his future reports the matter of children and armed conflict in the country in line with the relevant Council resolutions;

33. *Remains concerned* at the serious harm that opium cultivation, production and trafficking and consumption continue to cause to the security, development and governance of Afghanistan as well as to the region and internationally, takes note of the United Nations Office on Drugs and Crime Afghanistan Opium Survey 2014 released in November 2014, calls upon the Government of Afghanistan, with the assistance of the international community, to accelerate the implementation of the National Drug Control Strategy, including through alternative livelihood programmes, and to mainstream counter-narcotics throughout national programmes, encourages additional international support for the four priorities identified in the Strategy, and commends the support provided by the Office to the Triangular Initiative and the Central Asian Regional Information and Coordination Centre within the framework of the Paris Pact initiative[132] and the Rainbow Strategy and the regional programme of the Office for Afghanistan and neighbouring countries, as well as the contribution of the Domodedovo police academy of the Russian Federation;

34. *Welcomes* the continued efforts of the United Nations Office on Drugs and Crime in empowering the Afghan Ministry of Counter Narcotics-led implementation of the Afghan National Drug Control Strategy, including through the Counter-Narcotics Monitoring Mechanism of the Joint Coordination and Monitoring Board;

35. *Calls upon* States to strengthen international and regional cooperation to counter the threat to the international community posed by the production of, trafficking in and consumption of illicit drugs originating in Afghanistan, with a view to its progressive elimination, in accordance with the principle of common and shared responsibility in addressing the drug problem of Afghanistan, including through strengthening the law enforcement capacity and cooperation against the trafficking in illicit drugs and precursor chemicals and money-laundering and corruption linked to such trafficking, and calls for full implementation of its resolution 1817 (2008);

36. *Appreciates* the work of the Paris Pact initiative and its "Paris-Moscow" process in countering the production of, trafficking in and consumption of opium and heroin from Afghanistan and the elimination of poppy crops, drug laboratories and stores, as well as the interception of drug convoys, underlines the importance of border management cooperation, and welcomes the intensified cooperation of the relevant United Nations institutions with the Organization for Security and Cooperation in Europe and the Collective Security Treaty Organization in this regard;

37. *Reiterates* the importance of the completion of the National Priority Programme on Law and Justice for All by all the relevant Afghan institutions and other actors, in view of accelerating the establishment of a fair and transparent justice system, eliminating impunity and contributing to the affirmation of the rule of law throughout the country;

38. *Stresses*, in this context, the importance of further progress in the reconstruction and reform of the prison sector in Afghanistan, in order to improve the respect for the rule of law and human rights therein, emphasizes the importance of ensuring access for relevant organizations, as applicable, to all prisons and places of detention in Afghanistan, calls for full respect for relevant international law, including humanitarian law and human rights law, and notes the recommendations contained in the report of the United Nations Assistance Mission in Afghanistan of 25 February 2015 and the announcement by the Government of Afghanistan of a national plan on the elimination of torture;

39. *Notes with strong concern* the effects of corruption on security, good governance, counter-narcotics efforts and economic development, welcomes the anti-corruption commitments made by the Government of Afghanistan at the Tokyo Conference, as reinforced in the Tokyo Mutual Accountability Framework, welcomes the efforts of the Government in this regard, including the issuance of the presidential decree in July 2012, calls for continued action by the Government to fulfil those commitments in order to establish a more effective, accountable and transparent administration at the national, provincial and local levels of government, and also welcomes continued international support for Afghanistan's governance objectives;

40. *Encourages* all Afghan institutions, including the executive and legislative branches, to work in a spirit of cooperation, recognizes the continued efforts of the Government of Afghanistan in pursuing legislative and public administration reform in order to tackle corruption and to ensure good governance, as agreed at the Bonn Conference, with full representation of all Afghan women and men and accountability at both the national and subnational levels, welcoming the issuance of the presidential decree in July 2012, and stresses the need for further international efforts to provide technical assistance in this area, recognizes efforts by the Government in this regard, and reiterates the importance of the full, sequenced, timely and coordinated implementation of the National Priority Programme on National Transparency and Accountability;

41. *Calls for* full respect for and protection of all human rights and fundamental freedoms, including those of human rights defenders, and international humanitarian law throughout Afghanistan, welcomes the growth in Afghan free media, but notes with concern the continued restrictions on freedom of the media and attacks against journalists by terrorist as well as extremist and criminal groups, commends the Afghan Independent Human Rights Commission for its courageous efforts to monitor respect for human rights in Afghanistan as well as to foster and protect those rights and to promote the emergence of a pluralistic civil society, stresses the importance of full cooperation with the Commission by all relevant actors and of promoting their independence, as well as of ensuring their safety, and supports broad engagement across government agencies and civil society for the realization of the mutual commitments made, including the commitment to provide sufficient government financing for the Commission, reiterates the important role of the Commission, and supports the efforts of the Commission to strengthen its institutional capacity and independence within the framework of the Afghan Constitution;

42. *Recognizes* that, despite progress achieved on gender equality, enhanced efforts, including on measurable and action-oriented objectives, are necessary to secure the rights and full participation of women and girls and to ensure that all women and girls in Afghanistan are protected from violence and abuse, that perpetrators of such violence and abuse are held accountable, and that women and girls enjoy equal protection under the law and equal access to justice, welcomes the adoption, in October 2014, of the national action plan for the implementation of resolution 1325 (2000), emphasizes the importance of maintaining adequate legislative protections for women, strongly condemns discrimination and violence against women and girls, in particular violence aimed at preventing girls from attending school, and stresses the importance of implementing resolutions 1325 (2000), 1820 (2008), 1888 (2009), 1889 (2009), 1960 (2010), 2106 (2013) and 2122 (2013), and notes the mainstreaming commitments introduced therein, and of ensuring that women fleeing domestic violence are able to find safe and secure refuge;

43. *Welcomes* the commitment of the Government of Afghanistan to strengthen the participation of women in Afghan political life and in all Afghan governance institutions, including elected and appointed bodies and the civil service, notes the progress in this regard, welcomes its continued efforts to protect and promote the full participation of women in the electoral process, supports efforts to accelerate full implementation of the National Action Plan for the Women of Afghanistan and to integrate its benchmarks into the national priority programmes, calls upon the Government to urgently develop a strategy to implement fully the Law on Elimination of Violence against Women, including services to victims and access to justice, welcomes in this regard the launch, in November 2014, by the Ministry of Public Health, of the Gender-based Violence Treatment Protocol for Health-

care Providers, recalls that the promotion and protection of women's rights are an integral part of peace, reintegration and reconciliation, recalls that women play a vital role in the peace process, welcomes the commitment by the Government to developing, implementing and monitoring the National Action Plan on Women, Peace, and Security and identifying further opportunities to support the participation of women in the Afghan-led and Afghan-owned peace and reconciliation process, notes the report of the United Nations Assistance Mission in Afghanistan on the implementation of the Law on Elimination of Violence against Women in Afghanistan, and the importance of its full implementation, and requests the Secretary-General to continue to include in his reports to the Council relevant information on the process of integration of women into the political, economic and social life of Afghanistan;

44. *Recognizes* the importance of the voluntary, safe, orderly return and sustainable reintegration of the remaining Afghan refugees for the stability of the country and the region, and calls for continued and enhanced international assistance in this regard;

45. *Affirms* the importance of the voluntary, safe, orderly return and sustainable reintegration of internally displaced persons, and welcomes the inclusion of Afghanistan as a pilot country for the Secretary-General's initiative on durable solutions and the progress made on the development of an internally displaced persons policy for Afghanistan;

46. *Notes* the need to continue to strengthen, with the support of the international community, Afghanistan's absorption capacity for the full rehabilitation and reintegration of the remaining Afghan refugees and internally displaced persons;

47. *Requests* that the Secretary-General report to the Council every three months on developments in Afghanistan and include in his reports an evaluation of progress made against the benchmarks for measuring and tracking progress in the implementation of the mandate of the United Nations Assistance Mission in Afghanistan, including at the subnational level, and priorities as set out in the present resolution;

48. *Also requests* that the Secretary-General initiate a process to conduct, within six months of the renewal of this mandate, a full examination of the role, structure and activities of all United Nations entities in Afghanistan, in full consultation and engagement with the Government of Afghanistan and key stakeholders, including the donor community, in the light of the completion of transition and the beginning of the transformation decade, and in accordance with the principles of Afghan national sovereignty, national leadership and national ownership;

49. *Decides* to remain actively seized of the matter.

Adopted unanimously at the 7403rd meeting.

Decisions

At its 7467th meeting, on 22 June 2015, the Security Council decided to invite the representatives of Afghanistan, Australia, Canada, Germany, India, Iran (Islamic Republic of), Japan, the Netherlands, Pakistan, Sweden and Turkey to participate, without vote, in accordance with rule 37 of its provisional rules of procedure, in the discussion of the item entitled:

"The situation in Afghanistan

> "Report of the Secretary-General on the situation in Afghanistan and its implications for international peace and security (S/2015/422)".

At the same meeting, the Council also decided to extend an invitation, in accordance with rule 39 of its provisional rules of procedure, to Mr. Nicholas Haysom, Special Representative of the Secretary-General for Afghanistan and Head of the United Nations Assistance Mission in Afghanistan.

At the same meeting, the Council further decided to extend an invitation, in accordance with rule 39 of its provisional rules of procedure, to Mr. Thomas Mayr-Harting, Head of the Delegation of the European Union to the United Nations.

RELATIONS BETWEEN CAMEROON AND NIGERIA[141]

Decision

On 12 December 2014, the President of the Security Council addressed the following letter to the Secretary-General:[142]

> I have the honour to inform you that your letter dated 9 December 2014 concerning your intention to continue the activities of the United Nations support team to the Cameroon-Nigeria Mixed Commission, with funding from the regular budget,[143] has been brought to the attention of the members of the Security Council. They take note of the information contained in your letter and the intention expressed therein.

THE SITUATION CONCERNING THE DEMOCRATIC REPUBLIC OF THE CONGO[144]

Decisions

At its 7237th meeting, on 7 August 2014, the Security Council decided to invite the representatives of Angola, the Democratic Republic of the Congo, South Africa and Uganda to participate, without vote, in accordance with rule 37 of its provisional rules of procedure, in the discussion of the item entitled:

"The situation concerning the Democratic Republic of the Congo

> "Report of the Secretary-General on the United Nations Organization Stabilization Mission in the Democratic Republic of the Congo (S/2014/450)".

At the same meeting, the Council also decided to extend invitations, in accordance with rule 39 of its provisional rules of procedure, to Mr. Martin Kobler, Special Representative of the Secretary-General for the Democratic Republic of the Congo and Head of the United Nations Organization Stabilization Mission in the Democratic Republic of the Congo, and Mrs. Mary Robinson, Special Envoy of the Secretary-General for the Great Lakes Region.

At its 7288th meeting, on 27 October 2014, the Council decided to invite the representative of the Democratic Republic of the Congo to participate, without vote, in accordance with rule 37 of its provisional rules of procedure, in the discussion of the item entitled:

"The situation concerning the Democratic Republic of the Congo

> "Report of the Secretary-General on the implementation of the Peace, Security and Cooperation Framework for the Democratic Republic of the Congo and the Region (S/2014/697)
>
> "Report of the Secretary-General on the United Nations Organization Stabilization Mission in the Democratic Republic of the Congo (S/2014/698)".

At the same meeting, the Council also decided to extend invitations, in accordance with rule 39 of its provisional rules of procedure, to Mr. Martin Kobler, Special Representative of the Secretary-General for the Democratic Republic of the Congo and Head of the United Nations Organization Stabilization Mission in the Democratic Republic of the Congo, and Mr. Said Djinnit, Special Envoy of the Secretary-General for the Great Lakes Region.

At its 7296th meeting, on 5 November 2014, the Council considered the item entitled "The situation concerning the Democratic Republic of the Congo".

---

[141] Resolutions or decisions on this question were first adopted by the Security Council in 1996.

[142] S/2014/894.

[143] S/2014/893.

[144] Resolutions or decisions on this question were first adopted by the Security Council in 1997.

At the same meeting, following consultations among members of the Security Council, the President made the following statement on behalf of the Council:[145]

The Security Council expresses its deep concern over the lack of progress of the voluntary disarmament process of the Forces démocratiques de libération du Rwanda, as assessed in the joint International Conference on the Great Lakes Region and Southern African Development Community communiqué of 20 October 2014. The Council recalls its statement to the press of 3 October 2014 and stresses again that there should be no further delay beyond the end date of 2 January 2015 set by the region for the voluntary disarmament process. The Council calls upon the United Nations Organization Stabilization Mission in the Democratic Republic of the Congo and the Government of the Democratic Republic of the Congo to immediately update operational plans for military action that should begin no later than January 2015 against the Forces démocratiques de libération du Rwanda. The Council reiterates once again its call upon the Government, in coordination with the Mission, to immediately undertake military action against those leaders and members of the Forces démocratiques de libération du Rwanda who do not engage in the demobilization process or who continue to carry out human rights abuses.

The Council further recalls that the swift neutralization of the Forces démocratiques de libération du Rwanda is a top priority in bringing stability to and protecting the civilians of the Democratic Republic of the Congo and the Great Lakes region, in line with the wider commitments made in the Peace, Security and Cooperation Framework for the Democratic Republic of the Congo and the Region.[146] The Council recalls that leaders and members of the Forces démocratiques de libération du Rwanda were among the perpetrators of the 1994 genocide against the Tutsi in Rwanda, during which Hutu and others who opposed the genocide were also killed, and recalls that the Forces démocratiques de libération du Rwanda is a group under United Nations sanctions, operating in the Democratic Republic of the Congo, which has continued to promote and commit ethnically based and other killings in Rwanda and in the Democratic Republic of the Congo. The Council reiterates its call upon the region to comply with the commitments under the Peace, Security and Cooperation Framework and to neither tolerate nor provide assistance or support of any kind to armed groups and to neither harbour nor provide protection of any kind to persons accused of violations of international humanitarian law and violations and abuses of human rights, in particular war crimes, crimes against humanity and acts of genocide, or persons falling under the United Nations sanctions regime. The Council further reiterates its readiness to consider targeted sanctions against any individual or entity found to be supporting the Forces démocratiques de libération du Rwanda or any other armed group in the Democratic Republic of the Congo.

The Council strongly condemns the recent attacks by the Allied Democratic Forces in the Beni territory, in which over 100 civilians, mostly women and children, were brutally killed. The Council takes note of the statement by President Kabila to immediately engage further military action to neutralize this group permanently, with the support of the Mission. In accordance with its resolution 2147 (2014), the Council underlines the importance of ensuring the effective protection of civilians. The Council emphasizes that any effort to undermine the ability of the Mission to implement its mandate will not be tolerated and that those responsible for threats or attacks against peacekeepers must be held accountable.

The Council recalls the importance of completing the permanent demobilization of the former 23 March Movement combatants and calls for the acceleration of the implementation of the disarmament, demobilization, repatriation, reintegration and resettlement programme, in coordination with the regional States concerned. The Council stresses the need for all parties to overcome barriers to repatriation at the meeting to be held in Kinshasa on 7 November 2014 and reminds former 23 March Movement combatants of their commitments under the Nairobi declarations.[147]

The Council stresses that the durable return of stability in the Democratic Republic of the Congo and the region also requires the swift fulfilment of implementation of the reforms committed to by the Government of the Democratic Republic of the Congo in the Peace, Security and Cooperation Framework. The Council

---

[145] S/PRST/2014/22.

[146] S/2013/131, annex.

[147] See S/2013/740, annex.

stresses the strategic importance of this agreement and calls upon all signatories to work together in a reinvigorated way in order to ensure delivery of the commitments made under the Framework. The Council expresses concern over the continued slow progress on security sector reform in the Democratic Republic of the Congo, including the establishment of an Armed Forces of the Democratic Republic of the Congo rapid reaction force, and calls upon the Government to consolidate progress on the restoration of State authority and on the wider governance, economic and security sector reforms needed in the Democratic Republic of the Congo.

The Council expresses its full support to the mandate of good offices of the Special Representative of the Secretary-General for the Democratic Republic of the Congo as outlined in its resolution 2147 (2014). The Council also welcomes the engagement of the Special Envoy of the Secretary-General for the Great Lakes Region and calls upon him, in coordination with the Special Representative, to continue to lead, coordinate and assess the implementation of the national and regional commitments under the Peace, Security and Cooperation Framework.

The Council recalls that the Government of the Democratic Republic of the Congo and its national partners bear responsibility for ensuring a transparent and credible electoral process. The Council calls for the publication of a comprehensive electoral calendar and budget and underlines the importance of full and timely planning and preparation for upcoming parliamentary and presidential elections. The Council reiterates the importance of a free, fair, inclusive and peaceful election process that respects the will of the Congolese people, in line with the national commitments of the Democratic Republic of the Congo made under the Peace, Security and Cooperation Framework agreement aimed at furthering the agenda of reconciliation, tolerance and democratization. The Council underlines that successful and credible elections in line with the Constitution of the Democratic Republic of the Congo would be a key element in the continuing work to promote democracy, human rights and the rule of law in the Democratic Republic of the Congo and form a key part of efforts to build long-term peace and stability in the region.

The Council also recalls that logistical support could be provided by the Mission only once the electoral cycle road map and budget have been adopted. The Council also recalls that this support will be continually assessed and reviewed according to the progress made by the Congolese authorities in the steering of the electoral process, in accordance with the criteria set out in paragraph 16 of its resolution 2053 (2012).

The Council recalls the importance of promoting and protecting human rights and fighting impunity. The Council notes with deep concern the persistence of serious human rights abuses and international humanitarian law violations against civilians in the Democratic Republic of the Congo committed by armed groups, including the Forces démocratiques de libération du Rwanda. The Council also expresses deep concern at reports and allegations indicating the persistence of serious human rights and international humanitarian law violations committed by Congolese security and defence forces and reiterates the need to fight against impunity in this regard.

In this context, the Council expresses its grave concern at the decision of the Government of the Democratic Republic of the Congo to expel the head of the United Nations Joint Human Rights Office in the Democratic Republic of the Congo. The Council further expresses concern over recent threats made against other staff members of the Office. The Council recalls that monitoring, reporting and follow-up on human rights violations and abuses and violations of international humanitarian law are fully part of the mandate of the Mission and expresses its full support to the Office, the Mission and the United Nations personnel. The Council recalls the importance of the obligations and commitments of the Government in terms of the promotion and protection of human rights and the fight against impunity, and calls upon the Government to investigate the allegations included in the report. The Council calls for continued cooperation and dialogue between the Mission and the Government. In this regard, the Council takes note of the letter dated 20 October 2014 from the Permanent Representative of the Democratic Republic of the Congo to the President of the Security Council[148] and of the willingness expressed by the Government to continue to work with the Mission, including the Office.

[148] S/2014/753.

The Council reiterates its full support for the Mission and calls upon all parties to cooperate fully with the Mission and to remain committed to the full and objective implementation of the mandate of the Mission. The Council commends the work of the Special Representative of the Secretary-General in the Democratic Republic of the Congo.

At its 7356th meeting, on 8 January 2015, the Council considered the item entitled "The situation concerning the Democratic Republic of the Congo".

At the same meeting, following consultations among members of the Council, the President made the following statement on behalf of the Council:[149]

The Security Council recalls the statement by its President of 5 November 2014[145] and reiterates its deep concern regarding the security and humanitarian crisis in eastern Democratic Republic of Congo due to the ongoing destabilizing activities of foreign and domestic armed groups, and stresses the importance of neutralizing all armed groups, including, among others, the Forces démocratiques de libération du Rwanda.

The Council notes that the deadline of 2 January 2015 set by the International Conference on the Great Lakes Region and the Southern African Development Community has passed, and that the Forces démocratiques de libération du Rwanda has not only failed to unconditionally and fully surrender and demobilize, but has also continued to recruit new fighters in their ranks.

The Council, while noting the surrender of an estimated 300 former rank-and-file members of the Forces démocratiques de libération du Rwanda in 2014, consisting of mainly old and non-essential combatants, stresses that such surrenders alone are insufficient to end the threat posed by the group, and does not come close to representing the full demobilization of the Forces démocratiques de libération du Rwanda as called for by the International Conference on the Great Lakes Region, the Southern African Development Community and the Council.

The Council further recalls that the swift neutralization of the Forces démocratiques de libération du Rwanda is a top priority in bringing stability to and protecting the civilians of the Democratic Republic of the Congo and the Great Lakes region, in line with the wider commitments made in the Peace, Security and Cooperation Framework for the Democratic Republic of the Congo and the Region.[146]

The Council notes the statement by the Government of the Democratic Republic of the Congo of 2 January 2015,[150] in which it stated that military action against the Forces démocratiques de libération du Rwanda is now "inevitable", and that the region, represented by the International Conference on the Great Lakes Region and the Southern African Development Community, has made clear its support for military action by the Democratic Republic of the Congo and the United Nations Organization Stabilization Mission in the Democratic Republic of the Congo, in the absence of the full demobilization of the Forces démocratiques de libération du Rwanda, including its military leadership, with the objective of ending the threat posed by the group.

The Council reiterates the need to put into sustained action the plans of the Armed Forces of the Democratic Republic of the Congo and the Mission, through its Intervention Brigade, in cooperation with the whole of the Mission, in accordance with paragraph 4 (*b*) of Council resolution 2147 (2014), to neutralize the Forces démocratiques de libération du Rwanda by commencing military operations immediately.

To that end, the Council calls upon the authorities of the Democratic Republic of the Congo and, in particular, President Kabila as Commander-in-Chief, to approve swiftly and implement fully the joint directive of the Mission and the Armed Forces of the Democratic Republic of the Congo.

The Council further notes the convening of a summit of the Southern African Development Community and the International Conference on the Great Lakes Region, scheduled for 15 and 16 January 2015 in Luanda.

The Council reiterates its support for the Mission and calls upon all parties, including Intervention Brigade troop-contributing countries, to remain committed to the full and objective implementation of the

[149] S/PRST/2015/1.

[150] S/2015/9, annex.

mandate of the Mission, including military operations to neutralize the Forces démocratiques de libération du Rwanda. The Council stresses that such operations must be done in strict compliance with international law, including international humanitarian law.

The Council further stresses that ending the threat of the Forces démocratiques de libération du Rwanda, including through robust military action by the Armed Forces of the Democratic Republic of the Congo and the Mission, through its Intervention Brigade, in cooperation with the whole of the Mission, in accordance with paragraph 4 (*b*) of resolution 2147 (2014), is a critical and necessary component of civilian protection, and expresses its intention to take into account progress made in ending the threat of the Forces démocratiques de libération du Rwanda in assessing next steps in the Great Lakes region.

The Council reiterates its readiness to consider targeted sanctions against any individual or entity found to be supporting the Forces démocratiques de libération du Rwanda.

The Council further reiterates that Forces démocratiques de libération du Rwanda combatants and their dependants may still, at any point and without any preconditions, choose a peaceful path by entering into the existing disarmament, demobilization and reintegration/repatriation and resettlement programme, which has successfully repatriated a significant number of, and continues to successfully repatriate, former members of the Forces démocratiques de libération du Rwanda to Rwanda.

The Council emphasizes the importance of addressing the root causes of the conflict in eastern Democratic Republic of the Congo and the need for a comprehensive approach to restore peace and stability in the affected areas.

At its 7367th meeting, on 22 January 2015, the Council decided to invite the representative of the Democratic Republic of the Congo to participate, without vote, in accordance with rule 37 of its provisional rules of procedure, in the discussion of the item entitled:

"The situation concerning the Democratic Republic of the Congo

"Report of the Secretary-General on the United Nations Organization Stabilization Mission in the Democratic Republic of the Congo (S/2014/956)

"Report of the Secretary-General on the United Nations Organization Stabilization Mission in the Democratic Republic of the Congo submitted pursuant to paragraph 39 of Security Council resolution 2147 (2014) (S/2014/957)

"Letter dated 12 January 2015 from the Chair of the Security Council Committee established pursuant to resolution 1533 (2004) concerning the Democratic Republic of the Congo addressed to the President of the Security Council (S/2015/19)".

At the same meeting, the Council also decided to extend an invitation, in accordance with rule 39 of its provisional rules of procedure, to Mr. Hervé Ladsous, Under-Secretary-General for Peacekeeping Operations.

At its 7371st meeting, on 29 January 2015, the Council considered the item entitled:

"The situation concerning the Democratic Republic of the Congo

"Letter dated 12 January 2015 from the Chair of the Security Council Committee established pursuant to resolution 1533 (2004) concerning the Democratic Republic of the Congo addressed to the President of the Security Council (S/2015/19)".

Resolution 2198 (2015)
of 29 January 2015

The Security Council,

Recalling its previous resolutions and the statements by its President concerning the Democratic Republic of the Congo,

Reaffirming its strong commitment to the sovereignty, independence, unity and territorial integrity of the Democratic Republic of the Congo as well as all States in the region, and emphasizing the need to respect fully the principles of non-interference, good-neighbourliness and regional cooperation,

Stressing the primary responsibility of the Government of the Democratic Republic of the Congo for ensuring security in its territory and protecting its population, with respect for the rule of law, human rights and international humanitarian law,

Taking note of the interim report[151] and the final report[152] of the Group of Experts on the Democratic Republic of the Congo (the Group of Experts) established pursuant to resolution 1771 (2007) of 10 August 2007, whose mandate was extended pursuant to resolutions 1807 (2008) of 31 March 2008, 1857 (2008) of 22 December 2008, 1896 (2009) of 30 November 2009, 1952 (2010) of 29 November 2010, 2021 (2011) of 29 November 2011, 2078 (2012) of 28 November 2012 and 2136 (2014) of 30 January 2014, and of the recommendations contained therein,

Recalling the strategic importance of the implementation of the Peace, Security and Cooperation Framework for the Democratic Republic of the Congo and the Region,[146] and reiterating its call to all signatories to fulfil promptly, fully and in good faith their respective commitments under this agreement in order to address the root causes of conflict and put an end to recurring cycles of violence,

Reiterating its deep concern regarding the security and humanitarian crisis in eastern Democratic Republic of the Congo due to the ongoing military activities of foreign and domestic armed groups and the smuggling of Congolese natural resources, stressing the importance of neutralizing all armed groups, including the Forces démocratiques de libération du Rwanda, the Allied Democratic Forces, the Lord's Resistance Army, the Forces nationales de libération and all other armed groups in the Democratic Republic of the Congo, in line with resolution 2147 (2014) of 28 March 2014,

Recalling the statement by its President of 8 January 2015,[149] and reiterating that the swift neutralization of the Forces démocratiques de libération du Rwanda is a top priority in bringing stability to and protecting the civilians of the Democratic Republic of the Congo and the Great Lakes region, noting with deep concern repeated reports of collaboration between elements of the Armed Forces of the Democratic Republic of the Congo and the Forces démocratiques de libération du Rwanda at a local level, and recalling that the Forces démocratiques de libération du Rwanda is a group under United Nations sanctions whose leaders and members include perpetrators of the 1994 genocide against the Tutsi in Rwanda, during which Hutu and others who opposed the genocide were also killed, and have continued to promote and commit ethnically based and other killings in Rwanda and in the Democratic Republic of the Congo,

Noting with great concern that the deadline of 2 January 2015 set by the International Conference on the Great Lakes Region and the Southern African Development Community has passed, and that the Forces démocratiques de libération du Rwanda has not only failed to unconditionally and fully surrender and demobilize, but has also continued to recruit new fighters in their ranks,

Condemning the brutal killing of hundreds of civilians in the Beni area in recent months, expressing deep concern regarding the persistence of violence in this region, and stressing the need for a thorough and prompt investigation into these attacks in order to ensure that those responsible are held to account, as well as calling upon the Democratic Republic of the Congo for further military action, in accordance with international law, including international humanitarian law and international human rights law, as applicable, and with the support of the United Nations Organization Stabilization Mission in the Democratic Republic of the Congo, in accordance with its mandate under resolution 2147 (2014), to end the threat posed by the Allied Democratic Forces and all other armed groups operating in the region,

Reaffirming the importance of completing the permanent demobilization of the former 23 March Movement combatants, stressing the importance of ensuring that its ex-combatants do not regroup or join other armed groups, and calling for the acceleration of the implementation of the Nairobi declarations[147] and of the disarmament, demobilization, repatriation, reintegration and resettlement of 23 March Movement ex-combatants, including overcoming obstacles to repatriation, in coordination with the regional States concerned,

Reiterating its strong condemnation of any and all internal or external support to armed groups active in the region, including through financial, logistical and military support,

---

[151] See S/2014/428.

[152] See S/2015/19.

Condemning the illicit flow of weapons within and into the Democratic Republic of the Congo, including their recirculation to and between armed groups, in violation of resolutions 1533 (2004) of 12 March 2004, 1807 (2008), 1857 (2008), 1896 (2009), 1952 (2010), 2021 (2011), 2078 (2012) and 2136 (2014), and declaring its determination to continue to monitor closely the implementation of the arms embargo and other measures set out in its resolutions concerning the Democratic Republic of the Congo,

Acknowledging, in this respect, the important contribution that the Security Council-mandated arms embargo makes to countering the illicit transfer of small arms and light weapons in the Democratic Republic of the Congo and in supporting post-conflict peacebuilding, disarmament, demobilization and reintegration of ex-combatants and security sector reform,

Underlining that the transparent and effective management of its natural resources is critical for the sustainable peace and security of the Democratic Republic of the Congo, and stressing its full respect for the sovereignty of the Government of the Democratic Republic of the Congo over its natural resources and its responsibility to effectively manage these resources in this regard,

Recalling the linkage between the illegal exploitation of natural resources, including poaching and illegal trafficking in wildlife, illicit trade in such resources and the proliferation of and trafficking in arms as one of the major factors fuelling and exacerbating conflicts in the Great Lakes region, encouraging the continuation of the regional efforts of the International Conference on the Great Lakes Region and the Governments involved against the illegal exploitation of natural resources, and stressing in this regard the importance of regional cooperation and deepening economic integration, with special consideration of the exploitation of natural resources,

Noting with concern reports indicating the involvement of elements of the Armed Forces of the Democratic Republic of the Congo, as well as armed groups, in the illegal minerals trade, the illegal production of and trade in charcoal and wood, and wildlife poaching and trafficking,

Noting with great concern the persistence of serious human rights abuses and international humanitarian law violations against civilians in the eastern part of the Democratic Republic of the Congo, including summary executions, sexual and gender-based violence and large-scale recruitment and use of children committed by armed groups,

Noting with deep concern reports and allegations indicating the persistence of serious human rights and international humanitarian law violations committed by some members of the Armed Forces of the Democratic Republic of the Congo and the Congolese National Police, and recalling the importance of fighting against impunity within all ranks of the Armed Forces and the National Police, commending the authorities of the Democratic Republic of the Congo for recent prosecutions and condemnations of two high-ranking officers of the Armed Forces for crimes against humanity and war crimes, and stressing the need for the Government of the Democratic Republic of the Congo to continue to ensure the professionalism of its security forces,

Calling for all those responsible for violations of international humanitarian law and violations or abuses of human rights, including those involving violence or abuses against children and acts of sexual and gender-based violence, to be swiftly apprehended, brought to justice and held accountable,

Recalling all its relevant resolutions on women and peace and security, on children and armed conflict and on the protection of civilians in armed conflict, and recalling the conclusions of the Security Council Working Group on Children and Armed Conflict pertaining to the parties to the armed conflict in the Democratic Republic of the Congo, adopted on 19 September 2014,[153]

Calling upon all parties to cooperate fully with the Mission and to remain committed to the full and objective implementation of the mandate of the Mission, reiterating its condemnation of any attacks against peacekeepers, and emphasizing that those responsible for such attacks must be brought to justice,

Noting the critical importance of effective implementation of the sanctions regime, including the key role that neighbouring States, as well as regional and subregional organizations, can play in this regard, and encouraging efforts to further enhance cooperation,

---

[153] S/AC.51/2014/3.

Underlining the fundamental importance of timely and detailed notifications to the Security Council Committee established pursuant to resolution 1533 (2004) concerning arms, ammunition and training, as set out in section 11 of the guidelines of the Committee,

Determining that the situation in the Democratic Republic of the Congo continues to constitute a threat to international peace and security in the region,

Acting under Chapter VII of the Charter of the United Nations,

Sanctions regime

1. *Decides* to renew until 1 July 2016 the measures on arms imposed by paragraph 1 of resolution 1807 (2008) and reaffirms the provisions of paragraphs 2, 3 and 5 of that resolution, and further decides that the measures on arms imposed by paragraphs 1 and 5 of resolution 1807 (2008) shall not apply to the supply of arms and related materiel, as well as assistance, advice or training, intended solely for the support of or use by the United Nations Organization Stabilization Mission in the Democratic Republic of the Congo or the African Union Regional Task Force;

2. *Also decides* to renew, for the period specified in paragraph 1 above, the measures on transport imposed by paragraphs 6 and 8 of resolution 1807 (2008), and reaffirms the provisions of paragraph 7 of that resolution;

3. *Further decides* to renew, for the period specified in paragraph 1 above, the financial and travel measures imposed by paragraphs 9 and 11 of resolution 1807 (2008), and reaffirms the provisions of paragraphs 10 and 12 of resolution 1807 (2008) in relation to those measures;

4. *Decides* that the measures imposed by paragraph 9 of resolution 1807 (2008) shall not apply, in accordance with the criteria set out in paragraph 10 of resolution 2078 (2012);

5. *Also decides* that the measures referred to in paragraph 3 above shall apply to individuals and entities as designated by the Security Council Committee established pursuant to resolution 1533 (2004) for engaging in or providing support for acts that undermine the peace, stability or security of the Democratic Republic of the Congo, and decides that such acts include:

(*a*) Acting in violation of the measures taken by Member States in accordance with paragraph 1 above;

(*b*) Being political and military leaders of foreign armed groups operating in the Democratic Republic of the Congo who impede the disarmament and the voluntary repatriation or resettlement of combatants belonging to those groups;

(*c*) Being political and military leaders of Congolese militias, including those receiving support from outside the Democratic Republic of the Congo, who impede the participation of their combatants in disarmament, demobilization and reintegration processes;

(*d*) Recruiting or using children in armed conflict in the Democratic Republic of the Congo in violation of applicable international law;

(*e*) Being involved in planning, directing or participating in the targeting of children or women in situations of armed conflict, including killing and maiming, rape and other sexual violence, abduction, forced displacement and attacks on schools and hospitals;

(*f*) Obstructing access to or the distribution of humanitarian assistance in the Democratic Republic of the Congo;

(*g*) Supporting individuals or entities, including armed groups, involved in destabilizing activities in the Democratic Republic of the Congo through illicit trade in natural resources, including gold or wildlife as well as wildlife products;

(*h*) Acting on behalf of or at the direction of a designated individual or entity, or acting on behalf of or at the direction of an entity owned or controlled by a designated individual or entity;

(*i*) Planning, directing, sponsoring or participating in attacks against Mission peacekeepers or United Nations personnel;

(*j*) Providing financial, material or technological support for, or goods or services to, a designated individual or entity;

Group of Experts

6. *Decides* to extend until 1 August 2016 the mandate of the Group of Experts on the Democratic Republic of the Congo established pursuant to resolution 1533 (2004) and renewed by subsequent resolutions, expresses its intention to review the mandate and take appropriate action regarding the further extension no later than 1 July 2016, and requests the Secretary-General to take the necessary administrative measures as expeditiously as possible to re-establish the Group of Experts, in consultation with the Committee, for a period of 18 months from the date of the present resolution, drawing as appropriate upon the expertise of the members of the Group established pursuant to previous resolutions;

7. *Requests* the Group of Experts to fulfil its mandate as consolidated below, with a focus on areas affected by the presence of illegal armed groups, and to provide to the Council, after discussion with the Committee, a midterm report no later than 30 October 2015, and a final report no later than 15 June 2016, as well as submit progress updates to the Committee, especially in situations of urgency, or as the Group deems necessary:

(*a*) Assist the Committee in carrying out its mandate, including through providing the Committee with information relevant to the potential designation of individuals and entities that may be engaging in the activities described in paragraph 5 above;

(*b*) Gather, examine and analyse information regarding the implementation, with a focus on incidents of non-compliance, of the measures decided in the present resolution;

(*c*) Consider and recommend, where appropriate, ways of improving the capabilities of Member States, in particular those in the region, to ensure that the measures imposed by the present resolution are effectively implemented;

(*d*) Gather, examine and analyse information regarding the regional and international support networks of armed groups and criminal networks in the Democratic Republic of the Congo;

(*e*) Gather, examine and analyse information regarding the supply, sale or transfer of arms, related materiel and related military assistance, including through illicit trafficking networks and the transfer of arms and related materiel to armed groups from the security forces of the Democratic Republic of the Congo;

(*f*) Gather, examine and analyse information regarding perpetrators of serious violations of international humanitarian law and human rights violations and abuses, including those within the security forces, in the Democratic Republic of the Congo;

(*g*) Evaluate the impact of minerals traceability referred to in paragraph 22 below and continue collaboration with other forums;

(*h*) Assist the Committee in refining and updating information on the list of individuals and entities subject to the measures imposed by the present resolution, including through the provision of identifying information and additional information for the publicly available narrative summary of reasons for listing;

8. *Expresses its full support* to the Group of Experts, and calls for enhanced cooperation between all States, particularly those in the region, the Mission, relevant United Nations bodies and the Group of Experts, further encourages all parties and all States to ensure cooperation with the Group of Experts by individuals and entities within their jurisdiction or under their control, and reiterates its demand that all parties and all States ensure the safety of the members and support staff of the Group of Experts and that all parties and all States, including the Democratic Republic of the Congo and countries of the region, provide unhindered and immediate access, in particular to persons, documents and sites that the Group of Experts deems relevant to the execution of its mandate;

9. *Calls upon* the Group of Experts to cooperate actively with other panels or groups of experts established by the Security Council, as relevant to the implementation of its mandate;

Armed groups

10. *Strongly condemns* all armed groups operating in the region and their violations of international humanitarian law as well as other applicable international law, and abuses of human rights, including attacks on the civilian population, Mission peacekeepers and humanitarian actors, summary executions, sexual and gender-based violence and large-scale recruitment and use of children, and reiterates that those responsible will be held accountable;

11. *Demands* that the Forces démocratiques de libération du Rwanda, the Allied Democratic Forces, the Lord's Resistance Army and all other armed groups operating in the Democratic Republic of the Congo cease

immediately all forms of violence and other destabilizing activities, including the exploitation of natural resources, and that their members immediately and permanently disband, lay down their arms and liberate and demobilize all children from their ranks;

12. *Calls upon* all States, especially those in the region, to take effective steps to ensure that there is no support, in and from their territories, for armed groups in the Democratic Republic of the Congo, stressing the need to address the networks of support, financing and recruitment of armed groups active in the Democratic Republic of the Congo, as well as the need to address the ongoing collaboration between elements of the Armed Forces of the Democratic Republic of the Congo and armed groups at a local level, and calls upon all States to take steps to hold accountable, where appropriate, leaders and members of the Forces démocratiques de libération du Rwanda and other armed groups residing in their countries;

13. *Demands* that the Government of the Democratic Republic of the Congo, in accordance with its commitments in the Nairobi declarations of 12 December 2013,[147] accelerate the implementation of its disarmament, demobilization and reintegration programme, in coordination with neighbouring countries where former 23 March Movement combatants have found refuge and the United Nations and international organizations, and stresses the importance of overcoming obstacles to the repatriation of these ex-combatants, ensuring that the disarmament, demobilization, reintegration, repatriation and resettlement programme is fully funded and implemented, particularly those programmes necessary to support the successful demobilization and reintegration of former 23 March Movement combatants, that the 23 March Movement does not regroup and resume military activities and that its members do not join or support other armed groups, in line with the Nairobi declarations and relevant Council resolutions;

Commitments of the Government of the Democratic Republic of the Congo

14. *Welcomes* the progress made to date by the Government of the Democratic Republic of the Congo on ending the recruitment and use of children in armed conflict, urges the Government to continue the full implementation and dissemination throughout the military chain of command, including in remote areas, of its commitments made in the action plan signed with the United Nations detailing concrete, time-bound measures to release and reintegrate children associated with the Congolese armed forces and to prevent further recruitment, and for the protection of girls and boys from sexual violence, and further calls upon the Government to ensure that children are not detained on charges related to association with armed groups;

15. *Calls upon* the Government of the Democratic Republic of the Congo to pursue its action plan commitments to end sexual violence and violations committed by its armed forces and to undertake further efforts in that regard, noting that failure to do so may result in the Armed Forces of the Democratic Republic of the Congo being named in the report of the Secretary-General on sexual violence;

16. *Stresses* the importance of the Government of the Democratic Republic of the Congo actively seeking to hold accountable those responsible for war crimes and crimes against humanity in the country and of regional cooperation to this end, including through its ongoing cooperation with the International Criminal Court, encourages the Mission to use its existing authority to assist the Government in this regard, and calls upon all signatories to the Peace, Security and Cooperation Framework agreement[146] to continue to implement their commitments and cooperate fully with one another and the Government, as well as the Mission, to this end;

17. *Recalls* that there should be no impunity for any of those responsible for violations of international humanitarian law and violations and abuses of human rights in the Democratic Republic of the Congo and the region, and in this regard urges the Democratic Republic of the Congo, all countries in the region and other concerned States Members of the United Nations to bring perpetrators to justice and hold them accountable;

18. *Calls upon* the Government of the Democratic Republic of the Congo to enhance stockpile security, accountability and management of arms and ammunition, with the assistance of international partners, to address urgently reports of diversion to armed groups, as necessary and requested, and to urgently implement a national weapons marking programme, in particular for State-owned firearms, in line with the standards established by the Nairobi Protocol for the Prevention, Control and Reduction of Small Arms and Light Weapons in the Great Lakes Region and the Horn of Africa and the Regional Centre on Small Arms and Light Weapons in the Great Lakes Region, the Horn of Africa and Bordering States;

19. *Emphasizes* the primary responsibility of the Government of the Democratic Republic of the Congo to reinforce State authority and governance in eastern Democratic Republic of the Congo, including through effective

security sector reform to allow army, police and justice sector reform, and to end impunity for violations and abuses of human rights and violations of international humanitarian law, and urges the Government to increase efforts in this regard, in accordance with its national commitments under the Peace, Security and Cooperation Framework;

Natural resources

20. *Encourages* the continuation of efforts by the Government of the Democratic Republic of the Congo to address issues of illegal exploitation and smuggling of natural resources, including holding accountable those members of the Armed Forces of the Democratic Republic of the Congo who participate in the illicit trade in natural resources, particularly gold and wildlife products;

21. *Stresses* the need to undertake further efforts to cut off financing for armed groups involved in destabilizing activities through the illicit trade in natural resources, including gold or wildlife products;

22. *Welcomes*, in this regard, the measures taken by the Government of the Democratic Republic of the Congo to implement the due diligence guidelines on the supply chain of minerals,[154] as defined by the Group of Experts and the Organization for Economic Cooperation and Development, recognizes the efforts of the Government to implement minerals traceability schemes, and calls upon all States to assist the Democratic Republic of the Congo, the International Conference on the Great Lakes Region and the countries in the Great Lakes region to develop a responsible minerals trade;

23. *Also welcomes* measures taken by the Governments in the region to implement the Group of Experts due diligence guidelines, including adopting the regional certification mechanism of the International Conference on the Great Lakes Region into their national legislation, in accordance with Organization for Economic Cooperation and Development guidance and international practice, and requests the extension of the certification process to other Member States in the region, and encourages all States, particularly those in the region, to continue to raise awareness of the due diligence guidelines;

24. *Encourages* a swift response by the International Conference on the Great Lakes Region to put in place the necessary technical capacity required to support Member States in their fight against the illegal exploitation of natural resources, and further encourages the International Conference to take immediate action to fully implement the mineral certification process;

25. *Encourages* all States to continue efforts to end the illicit trade in natural resources, in particular in the gold sector, and to hold those complicit in the illicit trade accountable, as part of broader efforts to cut off financing for armed groups and criminal networks, including those with members in the Armed Forces of the Democratic Republic of the Congo;

26. *Reaffirms* the provisions of paragraphs 7 to 9 of resolution 2021 (2011), and calls upon the Democratic Republic of the Congo and States in the Great Lakes region to cooperate at the regional level to investigate and combat regional criminal networks and armed groups involved in the illegal exploitation of natural resources, including wildlife poaching and trafficking, and require their customs authorities to strengthen their control over exports and imports of minerals from the Democratic Republic of the Congo;

Role of the Mission

27. *Recalls* the mandate of the Mission to support the Congolese authorities in the implementation of their national commitments under the Peace, Security and Cooperation Framework agreement, in line with resolution 2147 (2014);

28. *Also recalls* the mandate of the Mission to monitor the implementation of the arms embargo, in cooperation with the Group of Experts, and in particular to observe and report on flows of military personnel, arms or related materiel across the eastern border of the Democratic Republic of the Congo, including by using surveillance capabilities provided by unmanned aerial systems, and to seize, collect and dispose of arms or related materiel brought into the Democratic Republic of the Congo in violation of the measures imposed by paragraph 1 above, in accordance with paragraph 4 (*c*) of resolution 2147 (2014);

---

[154] See S/2011/345, annex I.

29. *Notes* that the Mission has a role to play in encouraging the consolidation of an effective national civilian structure that controls key mining activities and manages in an equitable manner the extraction of and trade in natural resources in eastern Democratic Republic of the Congo, in line with resolution 2147 (2014);

30. *Requests* the Mission to assist the Committee established pursuant to paragraph 8 of resolution 1533 (2004) and the Group of Experts established pursuant to the same resolution, within its capabilities, including by passing information relevant to the implementation of the sanctions measures;

Reporting and review

31. *Calls upon* all States, particularly those in the region and those in which individuals and entities designated pursuant to paragraph 5 of the present resolution are based, to regularly report to the Committee on the actions they have taken to implement the measures imposed by paragraphs 1, 2 and 3 of the present resolution and recommended in paragraph 8 of resolution 1952 (2010);

32. *Emphasizes* the importance of holding regular consultations with concerned Member States, as may be necessary, in order to ensure full implementation of the measures set forth in the present resolution;

33. *Requests* the Special Representative of the Secretary-General for Children and Armed Conflict and the Special Representative of the Secretary-General on Sexual Violence in Conflict to continue to share relevant information with the Committee in accordance with paragraph 7 of resolution 1960 (2010) of 16 December 2010 and paragraph 9 of resolution 1998 (2011) of 12 July 2011;

34. *Decides* that, when appropriate and no later than 1 July 2016, it shall review the measures set forth in the present resolution, with a view to adjusting them, as appropriate, in the light of the security situation in the Democratic Republic of the Congo, in particular progress in security sector reform, including the integration of the armed forces and the reform of the national police, and in disarming, demobilizing, repatriating, resettling and reintegrating, as appropriate, Congolese and foreign armed groups, with a particular focus on children among them;

35. *Also decides* to remain actively seized of the matter.

Adopted unanimously at the 7371st meeting.

Decisions

At its 7410th meeting, on 19 March 2015, the Security Council decided to invite the representative of the Democratic Republic of the Congo to participate, without vote, in accordance with rule 37 of its provisional rules of procedure, in the discussion of the item entitled:

"The situation concerning the Democratic Republic of the Congo

"Report of the Secretary-General on the United Nations Organization Stabilization Mission in the Democratic Republic of the Congo (S/2015/172)

"Report of the Secretary-General on the implementation of the Peace, Security and Cooperation Framework for the Democratic Republic of the Congo and the Region (S/2015/173)".

At the same meeting, the Council also decided to extend invitations, in accordance with rule 39 of its provisional rules of procedure, to Mr. Martin Kobler, Special Representative of the Secretary-General for the Democratic Republic of the Congo and Head of the United Nations Organization Stabilization Mission in the Democratic Republic of the Congo, and Mr. Said Djinnit, Special Envoy of the Secretary-General for the Great Lakes Region.

At its 7415th meeting, on 26 March 2015, the Council decided to invite the representative of the Democratic Republic of the Congo to participate, without vote, in accordance with rule 37 of its provisional rules of procedure, in the discussion of the item entitled:

"The situation concerning the Democratic Republic of the Congo

"Report of the Secretary-General on the United Nations Organization Stabilization Mission in the Democratic Republic of the Congo (S/2015/172)

"Report of the Secretary-General on the implementation of the Peace, Security and Cooperation Framework for the Democratic Republic of the Congo and the Region (S/2015/173)".

Resolution 2211 (2015)
of 26 March 2015

The Security Council,

Recalling its previous resolutions and the statements by its President concerning the Democratic Republic of the Congo, especially its resolutions 2053 (2012) of 27 June 2012, 2076 (2012) of 20 November 2012, 2078 (2012) of 28 November 2012, 2098 (2013) of 28 March 2013, 2136 (2014) of 30 January 2014, 2147 (2014) of 28 March 2014 and 2198 (2015) of 29 January 2015,

Reaffirming the basic principles of peacekeeping, including consent of the parties, impartiality and non-use of force except in self-defence and defence of the mandate, and recognizing that the mandate of each peacekeeping mission is specific to the need and situation of the country concerned,

Reaffirming its strong commitment to the sovereignty, independence, unity and territorial integrity of the Democratic Republic of the Congo as well as all States in the region, and emphasizing the need to respect fully the principles of non-interference, good-neighbourliness and regional cooperation,

Emphasizing that those responsible for violations of international humanitarian law and violations and abuses of human rights must be held accountable and that the Government of the Democratic Republic of the Congo bears the primary responsibility to protect civilians within its territory and subject to its jurisdiction, including protection from crimes against humanity and war crimes,

Noting that eastern Democratic Republic of the Congo has continued to suffer from recurring cycles of conflict and persistent violence by armed groups, both Congolese and foreign, and recalling the strategic importance of the implementation of the Peace, Security and Cooperation Framework for the Democratic Republic of the Congo and the Region,[146] and reiterating its call to all signatories to fulfil promptly, fully and in good faith their respective commitments under this agreement in order to address the root causes of conflict and put an end to recurring cycles of violence, and to promote lasting regional development,

Encouraging the continuation of efforts by the Secretary-General of the United Nations, the International Conference on the Great Lakes Region, the Southern African Development Community and the African Union to restore peace and security in eastern Democratic Republic of the Congo, encouraging the Government of the Democratic Republic of the Congo to ensure continuous close cooperation with these and other international parties, and recognizing the efforts of the Government aiming at the achievement of peace and national development,

Reiterating its deep concern regarding the security and humanitarian crisis in eastern Democratic Republic of the Congo due to ongoing destabilizing activities of foreign and domestic armed groups, stressing the importance of neutralizing the Forces démocratiques de libération du Rwanda, the Allied Democratic Forces, the Lord's Resistance Army, the National Liberation Forces and all other armed groups in the Democratic Republic of the Congo, and recognizing the efforts of the Armed Forces of the Democratic Republic of the Congo against armed groups, especially the Allied Democratic Forces,

Recalling the statement by the President of the Security Council of 8 January 2015,[149] and reiterating that the swift neutralization of the Forces démocratiques de libération du Rwanda is a top priority in bringing stability to and protecting the civilians of the Democratic Republic of the Congo and the Great Lakes region, noting with deep concern repeated reports of collaboration between elements of the Armed Forces of the Democratic Republic of the Congo and elements of the Forces démocratiques de libération du Rwanda at a local level and unfettered regional travel by the Forces démocratiques de libération du Rwanda, and recalling that the Forces démocratiques de libération du Rwanda is a group under United Nations sanctions whose leaders and members include perpetrators of the 1994 genocide against the Tutsi in Rwanda, during which Hutu and others who opposed the genocide were also killed, who have continued to promote and commit ethnically based and other killings in Rwanda and the Democratic Republic of the Congo,

Remaining greatly concerned by the humanitarian situation that continues to severely affect the civilian population, in particular in eastern Democratic Republic of the Congo, expressing deep concern regarding the very high number of internally displaced persons in the Democratic Republic of the Congo, at more than 2.7 million, and the over 490,000 refugees from eastern Democratic Republic of the Congo caused by the various Congolese and foreign armed groups active in the region, and calling upon the Democratic Republic of the Congo and all States in the region to work towards the peaceful environment conducive to the realization of durable solutions for refugees and internally displaced persons, including their eventual voluntary return to and reintegration in the Democratic Republic of the Congo, with the support, as appropriate, of the United Nations country team, supporting the current efforts of the Office of the United Nations High Commissioner for Refugees to complete biometric registration of the Rwandan refugee population in the Democratic Republic of the Congo to help to facilitate the return of these refugees to Rwanda, and calling upon all parties to the conflict to respect the impartiality, independence and neutrality of humanitarian actors,

Remaining deeply concerned by the persistent high levels of violence and violations and abuses of human rights and international law, condemning in particular those involving targeted attacks against civilians, widespread sexual and gender-based violence, systematic recruitment and use of children by certain parties to the conflict, the displacement of significant numbers of civilians, extrajudicial executions and arbitrary arrests, recognizing their deleterious effect on the stabilization, reconstruction and development efforts in the Democratic Republic of the Congo, and calling for all those responsible for all such violations and abuses to be swiftly apprehended, brought to justice and held accountable,

Recalling all its relevant resolutions on women and peace and security, on children and armed conflict and on the protection of civilians in armed conflict, and recalling also the conclusions on children and armed conflict in the Democratic Republic of the Congo adopted on 19 September 2014 by the Security Council Working Group on Children and Armed Conflict, pertaining to the parties to the armed conflict in the Democratic Republic of the Congo,[153]

Welcoming the efforts of the United Nations Organization Stabilization Mission in the Democratic Republic of the Congo and international partners in delivering training in human rights, international humanitarian law, gender mainstreaming, child protection and protection from sexual and gender-based violence for Congolese security institutions and underlining its importance, and welcoming the establishment of the Women's Platform for the Peace, Security and Cooperation Framework in an effort to ensure the full participation of women in the Framework peace process,

Noting the ongoing efforts made by the Government of the Democratic Republic of the Congo to combat sexual violence in conflict, including through its national strategy and the commitments outlined in the joint communiqué between the Government and the United Nations on the fight against sexual violence in conflict, adopted in Kinshasa on 30 March 2013, and strongly encouraging the Government to increase its efforts in this regard,

Acknowledging the adoption of the Framework of Cooperation between the United Nations Office of the Special Representative of the Secretary-General on Sexual Violence in Conflict and the African Union Commission concerning the Prevention and Response to Conflict-related Sexual Violence in Africa, in Addis Ababa on 31 January 2014,

Taking note of the report of the Secretary-General of 13 March 2014,[155] which includes a list of parties responsible for patterns of rape and other forms of sexual violence in situations of armed conflict, being on the Security Council agenda,

Noting with deep concern reports and allegations indicating the persistence of serious human rights and international humanitarian law violations committed by some members of the Armed Forces of the Democratic Republic of the Congo, the Republican Guard and the Congolese National Police, including during the protests in Kinshasa, Goma and Bukavu in January 2015, appealing for calm, urging all parties to refrain from violence, and emphasizing that the response of the Government of the Democratic Republic of the Congo must respect human rights and comply with the principle of proportionality in the use of force,

Recalling the importance of fighting against impunity within all ranks of the Armed Forces of the Democratic Republic of the Congo and the Congolese National Police, commending the authorities of the Democratic Republic of the Congo for recent prosecutions and condemnations of Armed Forces officers for crimes against humanity and war crimes, and stressing the need for the Government of the Democratic Republic of the Congo to continue to ensure the increased professionalism of its security forces,

---

[155] S/2014/181.

Stressing the need for cooperation with the International Criminal Court by the Government of the Democratic Republic of the Congo, welcoming the commitment made by the Government to hold accountable those responsible for serious crimes, in particular war crimes and crimes against humanity, in the country, and stressing the importance of actively seeking to hold accountable those responsible for genocide, war crimes and crimes against humanity in the country,

Reaffirming that the successful protection of civilians is critical to the fulfilment of the mandate of the Mission and the delivery of an improved security environment, and stressing the importance of peaceful means and progress on key reforms to promote the protection of civilians,

Welcoming the report of the Secretary-General on the strategic review of the Mission and the wider United Nations presence, submitted pursuant to paragraph 39 of its resolution 2147 (2014),[156] and further welcoming its recommendations on the Mission's future objectives, activities, exit strategy and effective deployment of resources, bearing in mind the need to continue to increase the effectiveness of the Mission and to respond to changing conditions on the ground,

Taking note of the views expressed by the Government of the Democratic Republic of the Congo regarding its appreciation of the strategic review of the Mission, in particular on the objectives and the reconfiguration of the Mission,

Reaffirming its strong support to the Special Representative of the Secretary-General for the Democratic Republic of the Congo and the Mission in the implementation of their mandate, and strongly encouraging the continuation of their efforts,

Noting that it is important that all Mission contingents, including the contingents of the Intervention Brigade, are properly prepared, effectively equipped and supported to be able to sustain their commitment to carry out their respective tasks,

Reiterating its call upon all parties to cooperate fully with the Mission and to remain committed to the full and objective implementation of the mandate of the Mission, reiterating its condemnation of any and all attacks against peacekeepers, and emphasizing that those responsible for such attacks must be held accountable,

Reiterating its call upon the Secretary-General to take all measures deemed necessary to strengthen United Nations field security arrangements and improve the safety and security of all military contingents, police officers, military observers and, especially, unarmed observers,

Underlining the importance of the Mission deterring any threats to the implementation of its mandate,

Recognizing the contribution of the Mission to a comprehensive strategy for durable peace and security, noting the need for the Mission to strengthen support to the Government of the Democratic Republic of the Congo to enable it to address security challenges and human rights concerns and extend State authority of the Government as expressed in paragraph 5 of the Peace, Security and Cooperation Framework, noting with appreciation the contribution that the Mission makes to early peacebuilding, and emphasizing that the activities of the Mission should be conducted in a manner so as to facilitate post-conflict peacebuilding, prevention of relapse into armed conflict and progress towards sustainable peace and development,

Stressing the crucial importance of the upcoming electoral cycle for stabilization and consolidation of constitutional democracy in the Democratic Republic of the Congo, expressing concern about restrictions of the political space in the Democratic Republic of the Congo, in particular recent arrests of political opposition members and suspension of Internet and social media access, and recalling the need for an open, inclusive and peaceful political dialogue between all stakeholders, while ensuring the protection of fundamental freedoms and human rights, paving the way for peaceful, credible, inclusive, transparent and timely elections in the Democratic Republic of the Congo, particularly presidential and legislative elections, by November 2016, in accordance with the Constitution and the electoral calendar, while respecting the African Charter on Democracy, Elections and Governance,

Determining that the situation in the Democratic Republic of the Congo continues to constitute a threat to international peace and security in the region,

Acting under Chapter VII of the Charter of the United Nations,

---

[156] S/2014/957.

Mandate and strategic review of the United Nations Organization Stabilization Mission in the Democratic Republic of the Congo

1. *Decides* to extend until 31 March 2016 the mandate of the United Nations Organization Stabilization Mission in the Democratic Republic of the Congo, including, on an exceptional basis and without creating a precedent or any prejudice to the agreed principles of peacekeeping, its Intervention Brigade;

2. *Welcomes* the report of the Secretary-General on the strategic review of the Mission and the wider United Nations presence, submitted pursuant to paragraph 39 of its resolution 2147 (2014),[156] fully endorses its recommendations, including on the transformation of the Mission force to become more efficient and effective in implementing its mandate, calls for their effective and rapid implementation, reiterates that multidimensional peacekeeping requires a comprehensive approach, and requests the military, police and civilian components of the Mission to work together in an integrated way;

3. *Endorses* the recommendation of the Secretary-General to reduce the Mission force by 2,000 troops, while maintaining an authorized troop ceiling of 19,815 military personnel, 760 military observers and staff officers, 391 police personnel and 1,050 personnel of formed police units;

4. *Expresses its intention* to make this troop reduction permanent, through a revised troop ceiling, consistent with the report of the Secretary-General on the strategic review of the Mission, once significant progress has been achieved regarding the priorities of the mandate of the Mission, consistent with paragraph 6 below, including the fight against the Forces démocratiques de libération du Rwanda;

5. *Requests* the Mission to continue to maximize force interoperability, flexibility and effectiveness in the implementation of the entirety of the mandate of the Mission, including by deploying rapidly deployable units and continuing to modernize the force, consistent with the recommendations of the strategic review, bearing in mind the safety and security of all military contingents, police officers, military observers and, especially, unarmed observers;

6. *Decides* that future reconfigurations of the Mission and its mandate should be determined in consultation with the Government of the Democratic Republic of the Congo on the basis of the evolution of the situation on the ground and, in the context of implementation by the Government and all other signatories to the Peace, Security and Cooperation Framework for the Democratic Republic of the Congo and the Region,[146] progress towards the following objectives, in line with the three main priorities of protection of civilians, stabilization and support to the implementation of the Framework, including national reforms, as set out in the mission concept:

(*a*) Reduction of the threat posed by Congolese and foreign armed groups, in particular the Forces démocratiques de libération du Rwanda, and violence against civilians, including sexual and gender-based violence and violence against children, to a level that can be effectively managed by the Congolese justice and security institutions;

(*b*) Stabilization through the establishment of functional, professional and accountable State institutions, including security and judicial institutions, in conflict-affected areas, and through strengthened democratic practices that reduce the risk of instability, including adequate political space, promotion and protection of human rights and a credible electoral process;

7. *Stresses* the need for coordination and cooperation between the Government of the Democratic Republic of the Congo and other national authorities, United Nations entities and development actors to stabilize and improve the security situation and assist in the restoration of State authority;

Protection of civilians

8. *Reaffirms* that the protection of civilians must be given priority in decisions about the use of available capacity and resources;

9. *Authorizes* the Mission, in pursuit of the objectives described in paragraph 6 above, to take all measures necessary to perform the following tasks, bearing in mind that these are mutually reinforcing tasks:

(*a*) Ensure, within its area of operations, effective protection of civilians under threat of physical violence, including by deterring, preventing and stopping armed groups from inflicting violence on the population, paying particular attention to civilians gathered in camps for displaced persons and refugee, humanitarian personnel and human rights defenders, in the context of violence emerging from any of the parties engaged in the conflict, and mitigating the risk to civilians before, during and after any military operation;

(*b*) Ensure the protection of United Nations personnel, facilities, installations and equipment and the security and freedom of movement of United Nations and associated personnel;

(*c*) Work with the Government of the Democratic Republic of the Congo to identify threats to civilians and implement existing prevention and response plans and strengthen civil-military cooperation, including joint planning, to ensure the protection of civilians from abuses and violations of human rights and violations of international humanitarian law, including all forms of sexual and gender-based violence and violations and abuses committed against children and persons with disabilities, and requests the Mission to ensure that child protection and gender concerns are integrated into all operations and strategic aspects of the work of the Mission and accelerate the coordinated implementation of monitoring, analysis and reporting arrangements on conflict-related sexual violence and the swift deployment of women's protection advisers as called for in resolutions 1960 (2010) of 16 December 2010 and 2106 (2013) of 24 June 2013, in order to seek commitments on the prevention of and response to conflict-related sexual violence;

(*d*) Support and work with the authorities of the Democratic Republic of the Congo to arrest and bring to justice those allegedly responsible for genocide, war crimes and crimes against humanity and violations of international humanitarian law and violations or abuses of human rights in the country, including leaders of armed groups, including through cooperation with States of the region and the International Criminal Court;

(*e*) *Neutralizing armed groups through the Intervention Brigade*

In support of the authorities of the Democratic Republic of the Congo, on the basis of information collection and analysis, and taking full account of the need to protect civilians and mitigate risk before, during and after any military operation, carry out targeted offensive operations through the Intervention Brigade in cooperation with the whole of the Mission, either unilaterally or jointly with the Armed Forces of the Democratic Republic of the Congo, in a robust, highly mobile and versatile manner and in strict compliance with international law, including international humanitarian law, and in accordance with the standing operating procedures applicable to persons who are captured or who surrender and with the human rights due diligence policy on United Nations support to non-United Nations security forces,[157] prevent the expansion of all armed groups, neutralize these groups and disarm them in order to contribute to the objective of reducing the threat posed by armed groups to State authority and civilian security in eastern Democratic Republic of the Congo and to make space for stabilization activities;

(*f*) *Arms embargo*

Monitor the implementation of the arms embargo as described in paragraph 1 of resolution 2198 (2015) in cooperation with the Group of Experts established pursuant to resolution 1533 (2004) of 12 March 2004 and, in particular, observe and report on flows of military personnel, arms or related materiel across the eastern border of the Democratic Republic of the Congo, including by using, as specified in the letter dated 22 January 2013 from the President of the Security Council to the Secretary-General,[158] surveillance capabilities provided by unmanned aerial systems, seize, collect, record and dispose of arms or related materiel brought into the Democratic Republic of the Congo in violation of the measures imposed by paragraph 1 of resolution 2198 (2015), and share relevant information with the Group of Experts;

Gender issues, child protection and interaction with the civilian population

10. *Requests* the Mission to take fully into account gender considerations as a cross-cutting issue throughout its mandate and to assist the Government of the Democratic Republic of the Congo in ensuring the participation, involvement and representation of women at all levels, including in stabilization activities, security sector reform and disarmament, demobilization and reintegration processes, as well as in the national political dialogue and electoral processes, through, inter alia, the provision of gender advisers, and further requests enhanced reporting by the Mission to the Council on this issue;

11. *Also requests* the Mission to take fully into account child protection as a cross-cutting issue throughout its mandate and to assist the Government of the Democratic Republic of the Congo in ensuring that the protection of

[157] S/2013/110, annex.

[158] S/2013/44.

children's rights is taken into account, inter alia, in disarmament, demobilization and reintegration processes and in security sector reform, as well as during interventions leading to the separation of children from the Armed Forces of the Democratic Republic of the Congo and armed groups in order to end and prevent violations and abuses against children, including those involving detention, including temporary detention, of children by the Armed Forces;

12. *Encourages* the Mission to enhance its interaction with the civilian population to raise awareness and understanding about its mandate and activities through a comprehensive public outreach programme, to identify potential threats against the civilian population and to collect reliable information on violations of international humanitarian law and violations and abuses of human rights perpetrated against civilians;

Stabilization

13. *Authorizes* the Mission, in support of the Congolese authorities and their efforts to stabilize eastern Democratic Republic of the Congo, to contribute to the following tasks, including through the good offices of the Special Representative of the Secretary-General for the Democratic Republic of the Congo:

(*a*) Provide good offices, advice and support to the Government of the Democratic Republic of the Congo to ensure that actions against armed groups are supported by civilian and police components as part of consolidated planning that provides a comprehensive response to area-based stabilization efforts;

(*b*) Provide good offices, advice and support to the Government of the Democratic Republic of the Congo, in close cooperation with other international partners, in the implementation of the revised International Security and Stabilization Support Strategy and related provincial stabilization plans;

(*c*) Provide good offices, advice and support to the Government of the Democratic Republic of the Congo, in close cooperation with other international partners, in the disarmament, demobilization and reintegration of Congolese combatants not suspected of genocide, war crimes, crimes against humanity or abuses of human rights into a peaceful civilian life, in line with a community-based approach that is coordinated under the framework of the International Security and Stabilization Support Strategy, while paying specific attention to the needs of children formerly associated with armed forces and groups;

(*d*) Provide support to the disarmament, demobilization, repatriation, resettlement and reintegration process to return and reintegrate foreign combatants not suspected of genocide, war crimes, crimes against humanity or abuses of human rights and their dependants into a peaceful civilian life in their country of origin, or a receptive third country, while paying specific attention to the needs of children formerly associated with armed forces and groups;

(*e*) Provide good offices, advice and support to the Government of the Democratic Republic of the Congo to promote human rights and political rights and to fight impunity, including through the implementation of the Government's "zero-tolerance policy" with respect to discipline and human rights and international humanitarian law violations committed by elements of the security sector;

(*f*) Continue to collaborate with the Government of the Democratic Republic of the Congo in the swift and vigorous implementation of the action plan to prevent and end the recruitment and use of children and sexual violence against children by the Armed Forces of the Democratic Republic of the Congo, and continue dialogue with all listed parties to obtain further commitments and work towards the development and implementation of action plans to prevent and end violations and abuses against children;

Support to national reform processes

14. *Reiterates* the importance of the implementation of the Peace, Security and Cooperation Framework to the achievement of long-term stability in eastern Democratic Republic of the Congo and the region, urges all signatory States to the Framework to continue to fully and promptly implement their commitments in good faith, including not harbouring war criminals, and calls upon the Government of the Democratic Republic of the Congo, which has the primary responsibility for safeguarding the sovereignty and territorial integrity of the Democratic Republic of the Congo, to make further meaningful progress in implementing its commitments under the Framework;

15. *Authorizes* the Mission, in support of the Congolese authorities and their efforts to deliver the reforms called for in the Peace, Security and Cooperation Framework and stabilization in eastern Democratic Republic of

the Congo, to contribute to the following tasks, in coordination with the United Nations country team and other actors, including through the good offices of the Special Representative of the Secretary-General:

(*a*) Promote peace consolidation and inclusive and transparent political dialogue among all Congolese stakeholders with a view to furthering reconciliation and democratization while ensuring the protection of fundamental freedoms and human rights, paving the way for the holding of elections, consistent with the provisions of paragraph 19 below;

(*b*) Monitor, report and follow up on human rights violations and abuses and violations of international humanitarian law, including in the context of elections, and support the United Nations system in-country to ensure that any support provided by the United Nations shall be consistent with international humanitarian law and human rights law and refugee law, as applicable;

(*c*) Provide good offices, advice and support to the Government of the Democratic Republic of the Congo to encourage and accelerate national ownership of security sector reform by the Government, including through developing a national strategy for the establishment of effective and accountable security institutions, as well as the development of a clear and comprehensive security sector reform implementation road map, including benchmarks and timelines, and play a leading role in coordinating the support for security sector reform provided by international and bilateral partners and the United Nations system;

(*d*) Provide good offices, advice and support to the Government of the Democratic Republic of the Congo, in compliance with the human rights due diligence policy, for army reform that would enhance its accountability, efficiency, self-sustainability and effectiveness, including the support of a vetted, well-trained and adequately equipped "rapid reaction force" within the Armed Forces of the Democratic Republic of the Congo, which should form the nucleus for a professional, accountable, well-sustained and effective national defence force, while noting that any support provided by the United Nations, including in the form of rations and fuel, should be subject to appropriate oversight and scrutiny;

(*e*) Provide good offices, advice and support to the Government of the Democratic Republic of the Congo for the reform of the police, including by contributing, in compliance with the human rights due diligence policy, to the provision of training to units of the Congolese National Police, including human rights training;

(*f*) Provide good offices, advice and support to the Government of the Democratic Republic of the Congo for the development of a national justice strategy and the implementation of justice and prison sector reform in order to develop independent, accountable and functioning justice and security institutions;

(*g*) Encourage the consolidation of an effective national civilian structure that controls key mining activities and manages in an equitable manner the extraction and transport of and trade in natural resources in eastern Democratic Republic of the Congo;

Peace, Security and Cooperation Framework

16. *Urges* the Government of the Democratic Republic of the Congo to remain fully committed to the implementation of the Peace, Security and Cooperation Framework, including through the adoption of a priority action plan, and to protecting the civilian population through the swift establishment of professional, accountable and sustainable security forces, the deployment of an accountable Congolese civil administration, in particular the police, judiciary, prison and territorial administration and the consolidation of the rule of law and the promotion and protection of human rights;

17. *Notes with deep concern* the lack of progress to date in those fields essential for the stabilization of the Democratic Republic of the Congo, and reiterates its call to the Government of the Democratic Republic of the Congo to take immediate steps to uphold its commitment to security sector reform, including the support of an effective and sustainable rapid reaction force, and to implement fully and immediately the national disarmament, demobilization and reintegration programme, all of which will require the allocation of necessary resources and a continued commitment from the Government to prioritize reform;

Special Envoy of the Secretary-General for the Great Lakes Region

18. *Calls upon* the Special Envoy of the Secretary-General for the Great Lakes Region to continue his regional and international engagement in furtherance of peace, stability and economic development in the Democratic Republic of the Congo and the region, including through the promotion of timely, credible and inclusive

national elections and regional dialogue and by continuing, in close coordination with the Special Representative of the Secretary-General for the Democratic Republic of the Congo, to lead, coordinate and assess the implementation of the national and regional commitments under the Peace, Security and Cooperation Framework;

Elections

19. *Calls upon* the Government of the Democratic Republic of the Congo and its national partners to ensure a transparent and credible electoral process, in fulfilment of their primary responsibility to create propitious conditions for the forthcoming elections, including prioritization of those conditions necessary for the presidential and legislative elections scheduled for November 2016 in accordance with the Constitution, and urges the Government as well as all relevant parties to ensure an environment conducive to a free, fair, credible, inclusive, transparent, peaceful and timely electoral process, in accordance with the Congolese Constitution and the electoral calendar, which includes free and constructive political debate, freedom of opinion and expression, freedom of assembly, equitable access to media, including State media, and safety and freedom of movement for all candidates, as well as for election observers and witnesses, journalists, human rights defenders and actors from civil society, including women;

20. *Welcomes* the promulgation of the electoral law and the publication of a comprehensive electoral calendar for the full electoral cycle by the Independent National Electoral Commission, calls upon the Government of the Democratic Republic of the Congo to put swiftly in place an adequate electoral budget and an electoral code of conduct, and to conduct a credible update of the electoral register to ensure the successful and timely holding of elections, in particular presidential and legislative elections in November 2016, in accordance with the Constitution and the electoral calendar, while respecting the African Charter on Democracy, Elections and Governance, and further calls upon all stakeholders to engage into an open political dialogue over the preparations for the upcoming elections, in accordance with the Constitution;

21. *Authorizes* the Mission, only upon notification to the Council by the Secretary-General that the conditions outlined in paragraph 20 above are being met, to provide logistical support, as appropriate and in coordination with Congolese authorities and the United Nations country team, to facilitate the electoral cycle, and decides that this support will be continually assessed and reviewed according to the progress made by the Congolese authorities in the steering of the electoral process, in accordance with paragraphs 19 and 20 above;

Armed groups

22. *Strongly condemns* all armed groups operating in the region and their violations of international humanitarian law as well as other applicable international law, and abuses of human rights, including attacks on the civilian population, Mission peacekeepers and humanitarian actors, summary executions, sexual and gender-based violence and large-scale recruitment and use of children in violation of applicable international law, and reiterates that those responsible must be held accountable;

23. *Demands* that the Forces démocratiques de libération du Rwanda, the Allied Democratic Forces, the Lord's Resistance Army and all other armed groups cease immediately all forms of violence and other destabilizing activities, including the exploitation of natural resources, and that their members immediately and permanently disband, lay down their arms and release children from their ranks;

24. *Takes note* of the commitment of the Government of the Democratic Republic of the Congo in carrying out military operations against the Forces démocratiques de libération du Rwanda, notes the recent launching of initial operations against the Forces démocratiques de libération du Rwanda by the Armed Forces of the Democratic Republic of the Congo, stresses the need to carry out operations in accordance with international law, including international humanitarian law and international human rights law, as applicable, and strongly encourages cooperation between the Government and the Mission on these operations, in accordance with its mandate, to ensure that all efforts possible are being made to neutralize the Forces démocratiques de libération du Rwanda;

25. *Condemns* the brutal killing of hundreds of civilians in the Beni area, expresses deep concern regarding the persistence of violence in this region, stresses the need for a thorough and prompt investigation into these attacks in order to ensure that those responsible are held to account, calls upon the Government of the Democratic Republic of the Congo for further military action, in accordance with international law, including international humanitarian law and international human rights law, as applicable, and with the support of the Mission, in accordance with its mandate, to end the threat posed by the Allied Democratic Forces and all other armed groups operating in the region;

26. *Demands* that the Government of the Democratic Republic of the Congo, in accordance with its commitments in the Nairobi declarations of 12 December 2013,[147] take immediate steps to implement and allocate appropriate funding to its disarmament, demobilization and reintegration plan, with particular focus on the sustainable reintegration of former combatants, in coordination with the United Nations, international organizations and neighbouring countries where former 23 March Movement combatants have found refuge, stresses the importance of overcoming obstacles to the repatriation of these ex-combatants, requests the Governments of the Democratic Republic of the Congo, Uganda and Rwanda to strengthen their collaboration to urgently address the situation of former 23 March Movement combatants located in their territories, consistent with the Nairobi declarations and in line with commitments under the Peace, Security and Cooperation Framework and in cooperation with the United Nations and international organizations, and reiterates the importance of ensuring that all provisions of the signed documents are implemented swiftly and in good faith and, in this regard, that the 23 March Movement does not regroup, join other armed groups or resume military activities, in line with the Nairobi declarations and relevant Council resolutions;

27. *Calls upon* the Government of the Democratic Republic of the Congo to urgently implement and allocate appropriate funding to its disarmament, demobilization and reintegration plan, including with regard to weapons and ammunition management activities, in order to be able to effectively deal with former combatants, including those already under the responsibility of the Armed Forces of the Democratic Republic of the Congo, and acknowledges that the absence of a credible disarmament, demobilization and reintegration process is preventing armed elements from laying down their weapons;

28. *Recognizes* the ongoing contribution of the Mission in the fight against the Lord's Resistance Army, encourages further efforts by the African Union Regional Task Force, and urges greater cooperation, including operational cooperation, and information-sharing between the Mission, other United Nations missions in the Lord's Resistance Army-affected region, the Regional Task Force, regional forces, national Governments, international actors and non-governmental organizations, as appropriate, in tackling the threat of the Lord's Resistance Army;

Human rights/humanitarian issues

29. *Urges* the Government of the Democratic Republic of the Congo to arrest and hold accountable those responsible for violations of international humanitarian law or violations and abuses of human rights, as applicable, in particular those that may amount to war crimes and crimes against humanity, as well as those involving violence or abuses against children and acts of sexual and gender-based violence, stresses the importance to this end of both regional cooperation and cooperation with the International Criminal Court, and urges the Government to undertake the judicial reform necessary to ensure that the Democratic Republic of the Congo effectively addresses impunity;

30. *Calls upon* the Congolese authorities to ensure the prosecution of those responsible for the grave human rights violations and abuses committed in the context of the 28 November 2011 elections;

31. *Encourages* the Government of the Democratic Republic of the Congo to continue its cooperation with the Special Representative of the Secretary-General for Children and Armed Conflict and the Special Representative of the Secretary-General on Sexual Violence in Conflict, and welcomes the appointment by President Kabila of a Presidential Adviser on Sexual Violence and the Recruitment of Children;

32. *Calls upon* the Government of the Democratic Republic of the Congo to pursue the full implementation, with the support of the Mission, as appropriate, of the action plan to prevent and end the recruitment and use of children and sexual violence by the Armed Forces of the Democratic Republic of the Congo and to strengthen its efforts to combat impunity for conflict-related sexual violence, including sexual violence committed by the Armed Forces, noting that failure to do so may result in the Armed Forces being named in the report of the Secretary-General on sexual violence, and to provide all necessary services and protection to survivors and victims;

33. *Requests* the Secretary-General to take the measures necessary to ensure full compliance by the Mission with the United Nations zero-tolerance policy on sexual exploitation and abuse and to keep the Council informed if cases of such conduct occur;

34. *Requests* the Mission to ensure that any support provided to national security forces is in strict compliance with the United Nations human rights due diligence policy, urges the United Nations system in the Democratic Republic of the Congo to adopt a joint and uniform approach regarding implementation of the human rights due diligence policy, and calls upon the Government of the Democratic Republic of the Congo to work with the Mission to support the promotion of Democratic Republic of the Congo security service personnel with reputable human rights records;

35. *Demands* that all parties allow and facilitate the full, safe, immediate and unhindered access of humanitarian personnel, equipment and supplies and the timely delivery of humanitarian assistance to populations in need, in particular to internally displaced persons, throughout the territory of the Democratic Republic of the Congo, respecting the United Nations guiding principles of humanitarian assistance and relevant provisions of international law;

36. *Calls upon* all Member States to generously contribute to the United Nations humanitarian appeal for the Democratic Republic of the Congo to help to ensure that United Nations humanitarian agencies and other international organizations are fully funded and able to address the protection and assistance needs of internally displaced persons, survivors of sexual violence and other vulnerable communities;

Cooperation with the Mission

37. *Demands* that all relevant parties cooperate fully in the deployment, operations and monitoring, verification and reporting functions of the Mission, in particular by guaranteeing the safety, security and unrestricted freedom of movement of United Nations and associated personnel throughout the territory of the Democratic Republic of the Congo;

Support to the Group of Experts

38. *Expresses its full support* to the Group of Experts on the Democratic Republic of the Congo established pursuant to resolution 1533 (2004), and calls for enhanced cooperation between all States, particularly those in the region, the Mission and the Group of Experts, encourages information-sharing between the Mission and the Group of Experts, further encourages all parties and all States to ensure cooperation with the Group of Experts by individuals and entities within their jurisdiction or under their control, and reiterates its demand that all parties and all States ensure the safety of its members and its support staff, and unhindered and immediate access, in particular to persons, documents and sites that the Group of Experts deems relevant to the execution of its mandate;

Exit strategy

39. *Stresses* that the exit of the Mission should be gradual and progressive, tied to specific targets to be jointly developed by the Government of the Democratic Republic of the Congo and the Mission, in consultation with the United Nations country team and other stakeholders;

40. *Encourages* the Government of the Democratic Republic of the Congo to take effective steps to enter into a regular strategic dialogue with the United Nations, building on the joint assessment process initiated in 2010 to jointly develop a road map and exit strategy for the Mission, including its Intervention Brigade;

41. *Notes* the need for a clear exit strategy for the Intervention Brigade, including through sustainable progress in ending the threat of armed groups and the implementation of sustainable security sector reform, which may include the development of a Congolese rapid reaction force, and expresses its intention to review the tasks of the Intervention Brigade on the basis of the evolution of the situation on the ground and the implementation of its tasks in accordance with paragraph 9 of the present resolution;

42. *Requests* the Secretary-General to continue to make recommendations on the transition and reconfiguration of the United Nations presence in the country, based on the comparative advantages of the Mission and the United Nations country team, in order to continue to streamline the tasks assigned to the Mission, urges the international community and donors to support the Mission and the country team, and calls upon the Government of the Democratic Republic of the Congo and neighbouring States to remain engaged in this process;

Reports of the Secretary-General

43. *Requests* the Secretary-General to report to the Council every three months on the implementation of the mandate of the Mission, including its Intervention Brigade, as set out in the present resolution, including on:

(i) The situation on the ground, including updates on operations to neutralize armed groups and any instances where the Mission's protection of civilians obligations are not fully met, as well as sexual violence and the impact of conflict on women and children;

(ii) Progress in the implementation of the recommendations of the strategic review, notably the measures taken to transform the Mission force, including its Intervention Brigade, to become more efficient and effective in implementing its mandate;

(iii) Progress made by the Democratic Republic of the Congo in the implementation of its commitments under the Peace, Security and Cooperation Framework, including through the establishment and implementation of a national security sector reform road map, its provincial stabilization plan, supported by the International Security and Stabilization Support Strategy, and in the implementation of the disarmament, demobilization and reintegration and disarmament, demobilization, repatriation, resettlement and reintegration plans;

(iv) An assessment of the outcomes of the strategic dialogue with the Congolese authorities on the exit strategy of the Mission, including in his September 2015 report recommendations on the reconfiguration and gradual drawdown of the Mission, including its Intervention Brigade, in accordance with paragraphs 4 and 6 above;

(v) Progress made by the Government of the Democratic Republic of the Congo on the electoral process, including on the provisions of paragraphs 19, 20 and 21 above;

(vi) The risks and their implications for the safety and security of United Nations personnel and facilities as a result of possible military operations as well as measures taken to strengthen their security and mitigate risks;

44. *Also requests* the Secretary-General to report to the Council every six months, in coordination with the Special Envoy for the Great Lakes Region and the Special Representative for the Democratic Republic of the Congo, on the implementation of the commitments under the Peace, Security and Cooperation Framework;

45. *Decides* to remain actively seized of the matter.

Adopted unanimously at the 7415th meeting.

Decisions

At its 7484th meeting, on 14 July 2015, the Security Council decided to invite the representative of the Democratic Republic of the Congo to participate, without vote, in accordance with rule 37 of its provisional rules of procedure, in the discussion of the item entitled:

"The situation concerning the Democratic Republic of the Congo

"Report of the Secretary-General on the United Nations Organization Stabilization Mission in the Democratic Republic of the Congo (S/2015/486)".

At the same meeting, the Council also decided to extend an invitation, in accordance with rule 39 of its provisional rules of procedure, to Mr. Martin Kobler, Special Representative of the Secretary-General for the Democratic Republic of the Congo and Head of the United Nations Organization Stabilization Mission in the Democratic Republic of the Congo.

THE SITUATION IN THE CENTRAL AFRICAN REPUBLIC[159]

Decisions

At its 7246th meeting, on 19 August 2014, the Security Council decided to invite the representative of the Central African Republic to participate, without vote, in accordance with rule 37 of its provisional rules of procedure, in the discussion of the item entitled:

"The situation in the Central African Republic

"Report of the Secretary-General on the situation in the Central African Republic (S/2014/562)".

[159] Resolutions or decisions on this question were first adopted by the Security Council in 1997.

At the same meeting, the Council also decided to extend invitations, in accordance with rule 39 of its provisional rules of procedure, to Mr. Babacar Gaye, Special Representative of the Secretary-General for the Central African Republic and Head of the United Nations Multidimensional Integrated Stabilization Mission in the Central African Republic, and Mr. Omar Hilale, Permanent Representative of Morocco to the United Nations, in his capacity as Chair of the Central African Republic configuration of the Peacebuilding Commission.

At its 7280th meeting, on 21 October 2014, the Council considered the item entitled "The situation in the Central African Republic".

Resolution 2181 (2014)
of 21 October 2014

The Security Council,

Recalling its previous resolutions and statements on the Central African Republic, in particular resolutions 2121 (2013) of 10 October 2013, 2127 (2013) of 5 December 2013, 2134 (2014) of 28 January 2014 and 2149 (2014) of 10 April 2014,

Taking note of the letter dated 3 October 2014 from Ms. Catherine Samba-Panza, Central African Republic President of the Transition, to the President of the Security Council,

Taking note also of the letter dated 7 October 2014 from Baroness Ashton, High Representative of the European Union for Foreign Affairs and Security Policy, to the President of the Security Council,

Determining that the situation in the Central African Republic continues to constitute a threat to international peace and security,

Acting under Chapter VII of the Charter of the United Nations,

1. *Decides* to extend the authorization of the European Union operation contained in paragraph 44 of resolution 2134 (2014) until 15 March 2015;

2. *Also decides* to remain seized of the matter.

Adopted unanimously at the 7280th meeting.

Decisions

At its 7329th meeting, on 9 December 2014, the Security Council considered the item entitled:

"The situation in the Central African Republic

"Letter dated 28 October 2014 from the Panel of Experts on the Central African Republic established pursuant to Security Council resolution 2127 (2013) addressed to the President of the Security Council (S/2014/762)

"Report of the Secretary-General on the situation in the Central African Republic (S/2014/857)

"Letter dated 5 December 2014 from the Secretary-General addressed to the President of the Security Council (S/2014/870)".

At the same meeting, the Council decided to extend an invitation, in accordance with rule 39 of its provisional rules of procedure, to Mr. Hervé Ladsous, Under-Secretary-General for Peacekeeping Operations.

At its 7349th meeting, on 18 December 2014, the Council considered the item entitled:

"The situation in the Central African Republic

"Letter dated 28 October 2014 from the Panel of Experts on the Central African Republic established pursuant to Security Council resolution 2127 (2013) addressed to the President of the Security Council (S/2014/762)

"Report of the Secretary-General on the situation in the Central African Republic (S/2014/857)

"Letter dated 5 December 2014 from the Secretary-General addressed to the President of the Security Council (S/2014/870)".

At the same meeting, following consultations among members of the Security Council, the President made the following statement on behalf of the Council:[160]

The Security Council takes note of the final communiqué of the high-level meeting on the Central African Republic held under the auspices of the Secretary-General in New York on 26 September 2014. The Council also takes note of the conclusions of the 6th meeting of the International Contact Group on the Central African Republic, held in Bangui on 11 November 2014, in which the International Mediator in the Central African Republic crisis, the President of the Congo, Mr. Denis Sassou Nguesso, in line with his authority under the Transitional National Charter, was requested to extend the transition by six months, up to August 2015, given that the election date of February 2015 was no longer technically feasible.

The Council recalls that the stabilization of the security situation is first and foremost the responsibility of the Central African Republic stakeholders and reiterates its appeal to all parties and stakeholders, particularly the leaders of the ex-Séléka and anti-balaka groups, as well as all other armed groups, to immediately and permanently lay down their arms, to release all children from their ranks, and to embark upon the path of dialogue as the only viable means towards achieving lasting reconciliation and peace, and an essential condition for the successful implementation of the mandate of the United Nations Multidimensional Integrated Stabilization Mission in the Central African Republic.

The Council reiterates its call upon the transitional authorities to take concrete action, with the full, effective and equal participation of women, towards an inclusive and comprehensive political dialogue and reconciliation process at the local and national levels; preparation for the elections; the fight against impunity; formulation and implementation of a disarmament, demobilization, reintegration and repatriation strategy, including children formerly associated with armed forces and groups; and the rebuilding of effective State institutions, including through security sector reform.

In this regard, the Council urges the transitional authorities to accelerate inclusive preparations for the Bangui Forum on National Reconciliation scheduled for January 2015, with the aim of forging a national-level consensus. The Council welcomes and commends recent efforts by the transitional authorities to gather views of local citizens in advance of the Bangui Forum by dispatching government ministers and officials throughout the Central African Republic.

The Council also urges all actors of the electoral process, including the transitional authorities and the National Electoral Authority, to accelerate preparations in order to hold free, fair, transparent and inclusive presidential and legislative elections that allow for the full, effective and equal participation of women, internally displaced persons and Central African Republic refugees, no later than August 2015, which will mark the end of the transition, and to swiftly implement concrete measures necessary to achieve this objective. To that end, the Council calls upon all international partners of the Central African Republic to provide support to the electoral process, particularly through financing the United Nations Development Programme multi-donor basket fund for elections.

The Council further urges the signatories to the Brazzaville agreement on cessation of hostilities of 23 July 2014 to immediately and fully implement its provisions, in particular articles 4 and 8 thereof, and calls upon the international mediation led by President Denis Sassou Nguesso, the Economic Community of Central African States, the African Union and the United Nations to facilitate the early conclusion of an agreement on the disarmament of the armed groups.

The Council expresses its intent to consider designating additional individuals and entities that engage in or provide support for acts that undermine the peace, stability and security of the Central African Republic, including those that provide support to armed groups through the illicit exploitation of natural resources, for targeted sanctions in accordance with the provisions of Council resolutions 2127 (2014) and 2134 (2014).

The Council further recalls that all Member States must take the measures necessary to prevent the entry into or transit through their territories of individuals designated by the Security Council Committee established pursuant to resolution 2127 (2013).

[160] S/PRST/2014/28.

The Council welcomes the steps towards improving stability in the Central African Republic and commends the African-led International Support Mission in the Central African Republic, Sangaris and the European Union military operation in the Central African Republic for the work done in laying the foundation for increased security ahead of and in support of the deployment of the United Nations Multidimensional Integrated Stabilization Mission in the Central African Republic. The Council notes with concern, however, that, while improving, security in the Central African Republic remains fragile.

The Council strongly condemns the resurgence of violence, which was politically or criminally motivated, that occurred in October 2014 in Bangui, the continuous cycle of provocations and reprisals by armed groups, both inside and outside of Bangui, the threats of violence, human rights violations and abuses and international humanitarian law violations committed by armed elements, which continue to adversely affect the dire humanitarian situation facing the civilian population and to impede humanitarian access to vulnerable populations and encourages the Stabilization Mission, Sangaris and the European Union military operation to use, within their respective mandates, all means necessary to effectively protect civilians and to restore a lasting security.

The Council equally condemns the targeted attacks against the transitional authorities as well as those against troops of the Stabilization Mission, Sangaris and the European Union military operation during the October events in Bangui. The Council underlines that attacks targeting peacekeepers may constitute a war crime and reminds all parties of their obligations under international humanitarian law.

The Council reiterates its grave concern at the threat to peace and security in the Central African Republic arising from the illicit transfer, destabilizing accumulation and misuse of small arms and light weapons.

The Council stresses the important role of the internal security forces (police and gendarmerie) in the restoration of security in the Central African Republic. The Council encourages the Central African Republic authorities to initiate the reform process of the Armed Forces of the Central African Republic, to include appropriate vetting procedures in order to put in place a professional, representative and balanced army, including through the adoption of measures to absorb elements of the armed groups meeting rigorous selection criteria, as well as through the retraining of part of the Armed Forces. The Council reiterates the important role of the Stabilization Mission in providing support for security sector reform and vetting processes, including through the provision of strategic policy advice and coordination of technical assistance and training. The Council encourages the international community, including the European Union, to consider a coordinated and concerted support for reform and capacity-building of the Armed Forces, including through advice, assistance and non-operational training, as appropriate.

The Council commends the work of the Special Representative of the Secretary-General for the Central African Republic, Mr. Babacar Gaye, and takes note of the increased deployment of the military, police and civilian components of the Stabilization Mission, the initial work of the Mission in implementing its mandate, the establishment on 15 September 2014 of the Bangui Task Force and the reconfiguration of the Mission following the violent incidents in Bangui in October.

The Council urges the Secretariat and the Stabilization Mission to accelerate the deployments of its civilian, police and military capabilities in the Central African Republic, including the necessary logistical support and command and control structure, and to speed up recruitment procedures, in order to reach its full operational capacity as soon as possible and enable the Stabilization Mission to effectively discharge its mandate over the entire national territory. To this end, the Council further urges the former troop- and police-contributing countries of the International Support Mission that have been rehatted to the Stabilization Mission to expedite the procurement and deployment of remaining additional contingent-owned equipment. The Council also urges the Stabilization Mission to intensify the implementation of its mandate, in particular in support of the reconciliation, electoral and disarmament, demobilization and reintegration processes, in accordance with priority tasks set out in paragraph 30 of Council resolution 2149 (2014).

The Council recalls the mandate of the Stabilization Mission to protect, without prejudice to the primary responsibility of the Central African Republic authorities, the civilian population from threat of physical violence, within its capabilities and areas of deployment, including through active patrolling.

The Council calls upon partners to pledge or confirm pledges for the lacking capabilities in the Stabilization Mission, in particular the attack helicopter unit, the special forces company and the signals company.

The Council affirms that those responsible for violations of international humanitarian law, human rights violations and abuses and other criminal acts, including those involving killing, maiming, rape and other forms of sexual violence, recruitment and use of children, violations of physical integrity, looting, destruction of properties and restrictions on freedom of movement, as well as attacks against humanitarian personnel, shall be held accountable.

In this regard, the Council notes the opening by the Prosecutor of the International Criminal Court on 24 September 2014 of an investigation on alleged crimes committed since 2012 and welcomes the ongoing cooperation by the transitional authorities of the Central African Republic in this regard.

The Council reiterates the need to strengthen justice institutions and to fight impunity in order to contribute to stabilization and reconciliation, and calls upon the Central African Republic authorities to take concrete steps, without delay, to achieve this objective as a matter of priority. The Council calls upon the transitional authorities to continue their efforts to redeploy State administration in the provinces, including through the effective restoration of the administration of the judiciary and the criminal justice system throughout the country, with the support of the international community.

The Council welcomes the signing on 7 August 2014 of the Memorandum of Understanding on Urgent Temporary Measures, which describes, in particular, the establishment of a national Special Criminal Court in charge of investigating and prosecuting the serious crimes committed in the Central African Republic, and calls for the implementation of the Memorandum of Understanding without delay, in accordance with resolution 2149 (2014) and including through the adoption of the necessary legislation by the transitional authorities.

The Council looks forward to the final report of the International Commission of Inquiry on the Central African Republic established by resolution 2127 (2013).

The Council calls for cooperation between all relevant institutions and mechanisms contributing to investigations and prosecutions of crimes involving violations of international humanitarian law and violations and abuses of human rights.

The Council calls upon all armed groups in the Central African Republic to immediately cease all acts of violence against humanitarian personnel and civilians, and demands that all parties allow the full, safe, immediate, unhindered and timely delivery of humanitarian assistance to populations in need, in particular to internally displaced persons, throughout the territory of the Central African Republic, respecting the United Nations guiding principles of humanitarian assistance and relevant provisions of international law.

The Council notes with appreciation the efforts made by humanitarian personnel, and reiterates its appreciation to the neighbouring countries, which are still hosting approximately 420,000 Central African Republic refugees. The Council calls upon the transitional authorities, humanitarian personnel and all relevant actors to establish favourable conditions for the voluntary and dignified return of internally displaced persons and refugees, and for the finding of a lasting solution for the concerned populations.

The Council urgently appeals to the international community to mobilize additional resources, noting in this regard that a total amount of $321 million is still required to cover the needs identified within the framework of the 2014 Central African Republic Strategic Response Plan and Regional Refugee Response Plan, to alleviate the humanitarian crisis, with an approach linking relief, rehabilitation and development.

The Council stresses that the restoration of lasting peace and stability in the Central African Republic is also contingent upon economic recovery, with concrete prospects for youth employment. In this context, the Council welcomes the pursuit, particularly in Bangui, of employment-generating projects and their extension to other locations, in the country, and calls for the multiplication of projects in the countryside, notably in the east and north-east regions, which have an acute need of development.

The Council calls upon the transitional authorities to continue their efforts to restore sound and transparent public financial management, in line with the recommendations of the recent International Monetary Fund mission to Bangui in November 2014, in particular to mobilize domestic resources, particularly customs revenues, in full respect of financial best practice, in order to meet the expenses related to the functioning of the State; implement early recovery plans; and revitalize the economy. This would create a conducive environment for the restoration of confidence by the economic actors, the mobilization of new private investment and the mobilization of international financial assistance, which is needed to cover 2015 financial needs.

The Council expresses its appreciation for the international mediation led by President Denis Sassou Nguesso of the Congo and comprising Mr. Soumeylou Boubèye Maïga, on behalf of the African Union, and Mr. Abdoulaye Bathily, on behalf of the United Nations, as well as the Secretary-General of the Economic Community of Central African States as rapporteur, and the constructive engagement of the region.

The Council emphasizes that the continued role of the region, including the Secretary-General of the Economic Community of Central African States and its Mediator, as well as of the African Union, together with the United Nations, will be critical for the promotion of lasting peace and stability in the Central African Republic.

The Council calls upon the international community to continue to support the people and the transitional authorities of the Central African Republic and to provide urgent financial contributions to support national dialogue and reconciliation, electoral, disarmament, demobilization and reintegration and security sector reform processes, as well as the restoration of the judicial and penal chains in order to fight against impunity. The Council notes in this respect the role of the Peacebuilding Commission in encouraging and facilitating dialogue, complementarity and coherence among all actors involved, in close collaboration with the United Nations leadership in the field; and in sustaining the attention and commitment of the international community in support of these processes and of the long-term peacebuilding objectives of the country.

At its 7366th meeting, on 22 January 2015, the Council considered the item entitled:

"The situation in the Central African Republic

> "Letter dated 28 October 2014 from the Panel of Experts on the Central African Republic established pursuant to Security Council resolution 2127 (2013) addressed to the President of the Security Council (S/2014/762)".

Resolution 2196 (2015)
of 22 January 2015

The Security Council,

Recalling its previous resolutions and statements on the Central African Republic, in particular resolutions 2121 (2013) of 10 October 2013, 2127 (2013) of 5 December 2013, 2134 (2014) of 28 January 2014, 2149 (2014) of 10 April 2014 and 2181 (2014) of 21 October 2014, as well as the statement by its President of 18 December 2014,[160]

Reaffirming its strong commitment to the sovereignty, independence, unity and territorial integrity of the Central African Republic, and recalling the importance of the principles of non-interference, good-neighbourliness and regional cooperation,

Recalling that the Central African Republic bears the primary responsibility to protect all populations within its territory from genocide, war crimes, ethnic cleansing and crimes against humanity,

Emphasizing that any sustainable solution to the crisis in the Central African Republic should be Central African Republic-owned, including the political process, and should include the restructuring of the Central African Republic security forces,

Reiterating its call upon the transitional authorities to accelerate the transition process, including its action towards an inclusive and comprehensive political dialogue and reconciliation process and towards the holding of free, fair, transparent and inclusive presidential and legislative elections no later than August 2015, with the full, effective and equal participation of women,

Commending the African-led International Support Mission in the Central African Republic, Sangaris and the European Union military operation in the Central African Republic for the work done in laying the foundation for increased security ahead of and in support of the deployment of the United Nations Multidimensional Integrated Stabilization Mission in the Central African Republic, noting also with concern, however, that, while improving, security in the Central African Republic remains fragile,

Welcoming the decision of the European Union to establish a one-year military advice mission based in Bangui, as requested by the transitional authorities of the Central African Republic, in order to contribute to providing them with expert advice on reforming the Armed Forces of the Central African Republic into multi-ethnic, professional and republican armed forces, and underlines the importance of a clear distribution of tasks and close coordination between the international forces or missions in the Central African Republic and the lead role of the Stabilization Mission in this regard, and further requests that this information be included in the regular reporting of the Secretary-General on the Stabilization Mission,

Welcoming also the report of the Secretary-General of 28 November 2014 submitted pursuant to resolution 2149 (2014),[161]

Welcoming further the interim report of 1 July 2014[162] and the final report of 29 October 2014[163] of the Panel of Experts on the Central African Republic established pursuant to resolution 2127 (2013) and expanded and extended pursuant to resolution 2134 (2014),

Taking note of the final report of the International Commission of Inquiry on the Central African Republic of 22 December 2014,[164]

Strongly condemning the resurgence of violence, which was politically or criminally motivated, that occurred in October 2014 in Bangui, the continuous cycle of provocations and reprisals by armed groups, both inside and outside of Bangui, the threats of violence, human rights violations and abuses and international humanitarian law violations, including those involving extrajudicial killings, enforced disappearances, arbitrary arrests and detention, torture, sexual violence against women and children, rape, recruitment and use of children and attacks against civilians, attacks against places of worship and denial of humanitarian access, committed by armed elements, which continue to adversely affect the dire humanitarian situation faced by the civilian population and to impede humanitarian access to vulnerable populations,

Equally condemning the targeted attacks against the transitional authorities as well as those against troops of the Stabilization Mission, Sangaris and the European Union military operation in the Central African Republic during the October events in Bangui, underlining that attacks targeting peacekeepers are among the designation criteria in paragraph 10 of the present resolution and may constitute a war crime, and reminding all parties of their obligations under international humanitarian law,

Reiterating that all perpetrators of such acts must be held accountable and that some of those acts may amount to crimes under the Rome Statute of the International Criminal Court,[165] to which the Central African Republic is a State party, noting in this regard the opening by the Prosecutor of the International Criminal Court on 24 September 2014 of an investigation following the request of the national authorities on alleged crimes committed since 2012, and welcoming the ongoing cooperation by the transitional authorities of the Central African Republic in this regard,

Expressing grave concern at the findings of the Panel of Experts in its final report that armed groups continue to destabilize the Central African Republic and to pose a permanent threat to the peace, security and stability of the country, and further expressing concern that illicit trade, exploitation and smuggling of natural resources, including gold, diamonds and wildlife poaching and trafficking, continues to threaten the peace and stability of the Central African Republic,

Noting with concern the findings of the Panel of Experts in its final report that the Lord's Resistance Army remains active in the Central African Republic and that it has established links to other armed groups,

Stressing the urgent and imperative need to end impunity in the Central African Republic and to bring to justice perpetrators of violations of international humanitarian law and of abuses or violations of human rights, underlining in this regard the need to bolster national accountability mechanisms and to implement without delay the Memorandum of Understanding on Urgent Temporary Measures of 7 August 2014, which describes, in particular, the establishment of a national Special Criminal Court in charge of investigating and prosecuting the serious crimes committed in the Central African Republic, including through the adoption of the necessary legislation by the transitional authorities,

---

[161] S/2014/857.

[162] S/2014/452.

[163] S/2014/762.

[164] S/2014/928.

[165] United Nations, *Treaty Series*, vol. 2187, No. 38544.

Emphasizing the risk of the situation in the Central African Republic providing a conducive environment for transnational criminal activity, such as that involving arms trafficking and the use of mercenaries as well as a potential breeding ground for radical networks,

Acknowledging, in this respect, the important contribution the Security Council-mandated arms embargo can make to countering the illicit transfer of arms and related materiel in the Central African Republic and its region and in supporting post-conflict peacebuilding, disarmament, demobilization and reintegration and security sector reform, recalling its resolutions 2117 (2013) of 26 September 2013 and 2127 (2013), and expressing grave concern at the threat to peace and security in the Central African Republic arising from the illicit transfer, destabilizing accumulation and misuse of small arms and light weapons and the use of such weapons against civilians affected by armed conflict,

Recalling the need for an inclusive and effective disarmament, demobilization and reintegration process, as well as repatriation and resettlement in the case of foreign fighters, including children formerly associated with armed forces and groups, while respecting the need to fight impunity,

Recalling also its decision to establish a sanctions regime pursuant to resolutions 2127 (2013) and 2134 (2014), and emphasizing that the targeted sanctions aim at, inter alia, individuals and entities designated by the Security Council Committee established pursuant to resolution 2127 (2013) and expanded pursuant to resolution 2134 (2014) as engaging in or providing support for acts that undermine the peace, stability or security of the Central African Republic, that impede the political transition process or that fuel violence and at individuals and entities designated by the Committee as involved in planning, directing or committing acts that violate international human rights law or international humanitarian law or that constitute human rights abuses or violations,

Noting the critical importance of effective implementation of the sanctions regime, including the key role that neighbouring States, as well as regional and subregional organizations, can play in this regard, and encouraging efforts to further enhance cooperation,

Determining that the situation in the Central African Republic continues to constitute a threat to international peace and security in the region,

Acting under Chapter VII of the Charter of the United Nations,

Arms embargo

1. *Decides* that, through 29 January 2016, all Member States shall continue to take the measures necessary to prevent the direct or indirect supply, sale or transfer to the Central African Republic, from or through their territories or by their nationals, or using their flag vessels or aircraft, of arms and related materiel of all types, including weapons and ammunition, military vehicles and equipment, paramilitary equipment and spare parts for the aforementioned, and technical assistance, training, financial or other assistance, related to military activities or the provision, maintenance or use of any arms and related materiel, including the provision of armed mercenary personnel, whether or not originating in their territories, and decides further that this measure shall not apply to:

(*a*) Supplies intended solely for the support of or use by the United Nations Multidimensional Integrated Stabilization Mission in the Central African Republic, the African Union Regional Task Force and the European Union missions and French forces deployed in the Central African Republic;

(*b*) The Stabilization Mission, the African Union Regional Task Force, the European Union missions and French forces operating in the Central African Republic to provide organizational advice or non-operational training to the Central African Republic government forces and as relevant to the implementation of their mandates, and requests these forces to report on measures taken in this regard as part of their regular reports to the Security Council;

(*c*) Supplies of non-lethal military equipment intended solely for humanitarian or protective use, and related technical assistance or training, as approved in advance by the Security Council Committee established pursuant to resolution 2127 (2013);

(*d*) Protective clothing, including flak jackets and military helmets, temporarily exported to the Central African Republic by United Nations personnel, representatives of the media and humanitarian and development workers and associated personnel for their personal use only;

(*e*) Supplies of small arms and other related equipment intended solely for use in international patrols providing security in the Sangha River Tri-national Protected Area to defend against poaching, smuggling of ivory and arms and other activities contrary to the national laws of the Central African Republic or its international legal obligations;

(*f*) Supplies of arms and other related lethal equipment to the Central African Republic security forces, intended solely for support of or use in the Central African Republic process of security sector reform, as approved in advance by the Committee; or

(*g*) Other sales or supply of arms and related materiel, or provision of assistance or personnel, as approved in advance by the Committee;

2. *Also decides* to authorize all Member States to, and that all Member States shall, upon discovery of items prohibited by paragraph 1 of the present resolution, seize, register and dispose of (such as through destruction, rendering inoperable, storage or transferring to a State other than the originating or destination States for disposal) items the supply, sale, transfer or export of which is prohibited by paragraph 1 of the present resolution, and decides further that all Member States shall cooperate in such efforts;

3. *Reiterates its call upon* the transitional authorities, with the assistance of the Stabilization Mission and international partners, to address the illicit transfer, destabilizing accumulation and misuse of small arms and light weapons in the Central African Republic and to ensure the safe and effective management, storage and security of their stockpiles of small arms and light weapons and the collection and/or destruction of surplus, seized, unmarked or illicitly held weapons and ammunition, and further stresses the importance of incorporating such elements into security sector reform and disarmament, demobilization, repatriation, resettlement and reintegration programmes;

Travel ban

4. *Decides* that, through 29 January 2016, all Member States shall continue to take the measures necessary to prevent the entry into or transit through their territories of individuals designated by the Committee, provided that nothing in the present paragraph shall oblige a State to refuse its own nationals entry into its territory;

5. *Also decides* that the measures imposed by paragraph 4 above shall not apply:

(*a*) Where the Committee determines on a case-by-case basis that such travel is justified on the grounds of humanitarian need, including religious obligation;

(*b*) Where entry or transit is necessary for the fulfilment of a judicial process;

(*c*) Where the Committee determines on a case-by-case basis that an exemption would further the objectives of peace and national reconciliation in the Central African Republic and stability in the region;

6. *Emphasizes* that violations of the travel ban can undermine the peace, stability or security of the Central African Republic, and observes that individuals who knowingly facilitate the travel of a listed individual in violation of the travel ban may be determined by the Committee to have met the designation criteria provided for in the present resolution;

Asset freeze

7. *Decides* that all Member States shall, through 29 January 2016, continue to freeze without delay all funds, other financial assets and economic resources which are on their territories, which are owned or controlled, directly or indirectly, by the individuals or entities designated by the Committee, or by individuals or entities acting on their behalf or at their direction, or by entities owned or controlled by them, and decides further that all Member States shall continue to ensure that any funds, financial assets or economic resources are prevented from being made available by their nationals or by any individuals or entities within their territories to or for the benefit of the individuals or entities designated by the Committee;

8. *Also decides* that the measures imposed by paragraph 7 above do not apply to funds, other financial assets or economic resources that have been determined by relevant Member States:

(*a*) To be necessary for basic expenses, including payment for foodstuffs, rent or mortgage, medicines and medical treatment, taxes, insurance premiums and public utility charges or exclusively for payment of reasonable professional fees and reimbursement of incurred expenses associated with the provision of legal services in accordance with national laws, or fees or service charges, in accordance with national laws, for routine holding or maintenance of frozen funds, other financial assets and economic resources, after notification by the relevant State to the Committee of the intention to authorize, where appropriate, access to such funds, other financial assets or economic resources and in the absence of a negative decision by the Committee within five working days of such notification;

(*b*) To be necessary for extraordinary expenses, provided that such determination has been notified by the relevant State or Member States to the Committee and has been approved by the Committee; or

(*c*) To be the subject of a judicial, administrative or arbitral lien or judgment, in which case the funds, other financial assets and economic resources may be used to satisfy that lien or judgment provided that the lien or judgment was entered into prior to the date of the present resolution, is not for the benefit of a person or entity designated by the Committee and has been notified by the relevant State or Member States to the Committee;

9. *Further decides* that Member States may permit the addition to the accounts frozen pursuant to the provisions of paragraph 7 above of interest or other earnings due on those accounts or payments due under contracts, agreements or obligations that arose prior to the date on which those accounts became subject to the provisions of the present resolution, provided that any such interest, other earnings and payments continue to be subject to these provisions and are frozen;

10. *Decides* that the measures in paragraph 7 above shall not prevent a designated person or entity from making payment due under a contract entered into prior to the listing of such a person or entity, provided that the relevant States have determined that the payment is not directly or indirectly received by a person or entity designated pursuant to paragraph 7 above, and after notification by the relevant States to the Committee of the intention to make or receive such payments or to authorize, where appropriate, the unfreezing of funds, other financial assets or economic resources for this purpose, 10 working days prior to such authorization;

Designation criteria

11. *Decides* that the measures contained in paragraphs 4 and 7 above shall apply to the individuals and entities designated by the Committee as engaging in or providing support for acts that undermine the peace, stability or security of the Central African Republic, including acts that threaten or violate transitional agreements, or that threaten or impede the political transition process, including a transition toward free and fair democratic elections, or that fuel violence;

12. *Also decides*, in this regard, that the measures contained in paragraphs 4 and 7 above shall also apply to the individuals and entities designated by the Committee as:

(*a*) Acting in violation of the arms embargo established in paragraph 54 of resolution 2127 (2013) and extended by paragraph 1 of the present resolution, or as having directly or indirectly supplied, sold or transferred to armed groups or criminal networks in the Central African Republic, or as having been the recipient of arms or any related materiel, or any technical advice, training or assistance, including financing and financial assistance, related to violent activities of armed groups or criminal networks in the Central African Republic;

(*b*) Involved in planning, directing or committing acts that violate international human rights law or international humanitarian law, as applicable, or that constitute human rights abuses or violations, in the Central African Republic, including acts involving sexual violence, targeting of civilians, ethnic- or religious-based attacks, attacks on schools and hospitals, and abduction and forced displacement;

(*c*) Recruiting or using children in armed conflict in the Central African Republic, in violation of applicable international law;

(*d*) Providing support for armed groups or criminal networks through the illicit exploitation of or trade in natural resources, including diamonds, gold, wildlife as well as wildlife products in or from the Central African Republic;

(*e*) Obstructing the delivery of humanitarian assistance to the Central African Republic, or access to, or distribution of, humanitarian assistance in the Central African Republic;

(*f*) Involved in planning, directing, sponsoring or conducting attacks against United Nations missions or international security presences, including the Stabilization Mission, the European Union missions and French operations supporting them;

(*g*) Being leaders of an entity that the Committee has designated pursuant to paragraphs 36 or 37 of resolution 2134 (2014) or the present resolution, or having provided support to, or acted for or on behalf of, or at the direction of, an individual or an entity that the Committee has designated pursuant to paragraphs 36 or 37 of resolution 2134 (2014) or the present resolution, or an entity owned or controlled by a designated individual or entity;

Sanctions committee

13. *Decides* that the mandate of the Committee established pursuant to paragraph 57 of resolution 2127 (2013) shall apply with respect to the measures imposed in paragraphs 54 and 55 of resolution 2127 (2013) and paragraphs 30 and 32 of resolution 2134 (2014) extended by the present resolution;

14. *Emphasizes* the importance of holding regular consultations with concerned Member States, as may be necessary, in order to ensure full implementation of the measures set forth in the present resolution;

Panel of Experts

15. *Expresses its full support* for the Panel of Experts on the Central African Republic established pursuant to paragraph 59 of resolution 2127 (2013);

16. *Decides* to extend the mandate of the Panel of Experts until 29 February 2016 and expresses its intent to review the mandate and take appropriate action regarding further extension no later than 29 January 2016, and requests the Secretary-General to take the necessary administrative measures as expeditiously as possible to support its action;

17. *Also decides* that the mandate of the Panel of Experts shall include the following tasks:

(*a*) To assist the Committee in carrying out its mandate as specified in the present resolution, including through providing the Committee with information relevant to the potential designation at a later stage of individuals or entities who may be engaging in the activities described in paragraphs 11 and 12 above;

(*b*) To gather, examine and analyse information from States, relevant United Nations bodies, regional organizations and other interested parties regarding the implementation of the measures decided in the present resolution, in particular incidents of non-compliance;

(*c*) To provide to the Committee a midterm update no later than 30 July 2015 and a final report to the Council, after discussion with the Committee, by 31 December 2015 on the implementation of the measures imposed by paragraphs 54 and 55 of resolution 2127 (2013) and paragraphs 30 and 32 of resolution 2134 (2014) renewed by paragraphs 1, 2, 4 and 7 of the present resolution;

(*d*) To submit progress updates to the Committee, especially in situations of urgency, or as the Panel deems necessary;

(*e*) To assist the Committee in refining and updating information on the list of individuals and entities designated by the Committee pursuant to the criteria renewed by paragraphs 11 and 12 above, including through the provision of biometric information and additional information for the publicly available narrative summary of reasons for listing;

(*f*) To assist the Committee by providing information regarding individuals and entities that may meet the designation criteria in paragraphs 11 and 12 above, including by reporting such information to the Committee, as it becomes available, and to include in its formal written reports the names of potential designees, appropriate identifying information and relevant information regarding why the individual or entity may meet the designation criteria in paragraphs 11 and 12 above;

18. *Calls upon* the Panel of Experts to cooperate actively with other panels or groups of experts established by the Council, as relevant to the implementation of their mandate;

19. *Expresses particular concern* about reports of illicit trafficking networks which continue to fund and supply armed groups in the Central African Republic, and encourages the Panel of Experts, in the course of carrying out its mandate, to devote special attention to the analysis of such networks;

20. *Urges* the Central African Republic, its neighbouring States and other States members of the International Conference on the Great Lakes Region to cooperate at the regional level to investigate and combat regional criminal networks and armed groups involved in the illegal exploitation and smuggling of natural resources, including gold, diamonds and wildlife poaching and trafficking;

21. *Urges* all parties and all Member States, as well as international, regional and subregional organizations, to ensure cooperation with the Panel of Experts and the safety of its members;

22. *Further urges* all Member States and all relevant United Nations bodies to ensure unhindered access, in particular to persons, documents and sites in order for the Panel of Experts to execute its mandate;

23. *Requests* the Special Representative of the Secretary-General for Children and Armed Conflict and the Special Representative of the Secretary-General on Sexual Violence in Conflict to continue to share relevant information with the Committee in accordance with paragraph 7 of resolution 1960 (2010) of 16 December 2010 and paragraph 9 of resolution 1998 (2011) of 12 July 2011;

Reporting and review

24. *Calls upon* all States, particularly those in the region and those in which designated individuals and entities designated are based, to regularly report to the Committee on the actions they have taken to implement the measures imposed by paragraphs 54 and 55 of resolution 2127 (2013) and paragraphs 30 and 32 of resolution 2134 (2014) renewed by paragraphs 1, 2, 4 and 7 of the present resolution;

25. *Affirms* that it shall keep the situation in the Central African Republic under continuous review and that it shall be prepared to review the appropriateness of the measures contained in the present resolution, including the strengthening through additional measures, in particular the freezing of assets, modification, suspension or lifting of the measures, as may be needed at any time in the light of the progress achieved in the stabilization of the country and compliance with the present resolution;

26. *Decides* to remain actively seized of the matter.

Adopted unanimously at the 7366th meeting.

Decision

At its 7416th meeting, on 26 March 2015, the Security Council considered the item entitled:

"The situation in the Central African Republic

"Letter dated 29 January 2015 from the Secretary-General addressed to the President of the Security Council (S/2015/85)".

Resolution 2212 (2015)
of 26 March 2015

The Security Council,

Recalling its previous resolutions and statements on the Central African Republic, in particular resolutions 2121 (2013) of 10 October 2013, 2127 (2013) of 5 December 2013, 2134 (2014) of 28 January 2014, 2149 (2014) of 10 April 2014, 2181 (2014) of 21 October 2014 and 2196 (2015) of 22 January 2015 as well as the statement by its President of 18 December 2014,[160]

Taking note of the letter dated 29 January 2015 from the Secretary-General to the President of the Security Council,[166]

Determining that the situation in the Central African Republic continues to constitute a threat to international peace and security,

Acting under Chapter VII of the Charter of the United Nations,

[166] S/2015/85.

1. *Decides* to authorize an increase of 750 military personnel, 280 police personnel and 20 corrections officers for the United Nations Multidimensional Integrated Stabilization Mission in the Central African Republic, in addition to the personnel authorized by paragraph 20 of resolution 2149 (2014);

2. *Requests* that the Secretary-General keep the new levels of military personnel, police personnel and corrections officers in the Stabilization Mission under continuous review;

3. *Decides* to remain actively seized of the matter.

Adopted unanimously at the 7416th meeting.

Decisions

At its 7427th meeting, on 14 April 2015, the Security Council considered the item entitled:

"The situation in the Central African Republic

"Report of the Secretary-General on the situation in the Central African Republic (S/2015/227)

"Letter dated 10 April 2015 from the Secretary-General addressed to the President of the Security Council (S/2015/248)".

At the same meeting, the Council decided to extend an invitation, in accordance with rule 39 of its provisional rules of procedure, to Lieutenant General Babacar Gaye, Special Representative of the Secretary-General for the Central African Republic and Head of the United Nations Multidimensional Integrated Stabilization Mission in the Central African Republic.

At its 7434th meeting, on 28 April 2015, the Council decided to invite the representative of the Central African Republic to participate, without vote, in accordance with rule 37 of its provisional rules of procedure, in the discussion of the item entitled:

"The situation in the Central African Republic

"Report of the Secretary-General on the situation in the Central African Republic (S/2015/227)

"Letter dated 10 April 2015 from the Secretary-General addressed to the President of the Security Council (S/2015/248)".

Resolution 2217 (2015)
of 28 April 2015

The Security Council,

Recalling its previous resolutions and statements on the Central African Republic, in particular resolutions 2121 (2013) of 10 October 2013, 2127 (2013) of 5 December 2013, 2134 (2014) of 28 January 2014, 2149 (2014) of 10 April 2014, 2181 (2014) of 21 October 2014, 2196 (2015) of 22 January 2015 and 2212 (2015) of 26 March 2015,

Reaffirming its strong commitment to the sovereignty, independence, unity and territorial integrity of the Central African Republic, and recalling the importance of the principles of non-interference, good-neighbourliness and regional cooperation,

Reaffirming the basic principles of peacekeeping, including consent of the parties, impartiality and non-use of force except in self-defence and defence of the mandate, and recognizing that the mandate of each peacekeeping mission is specific to the need and situation of the country concerned,

Recalling that the Central African Republic authorities have the primary responsibility to protect all populations in the Central African Republic, in particular from genocide, war crimes, ethnic cleansing and crimes against humanity,

Emphasizing that any sustainable solution to the crisis in the Central African Republic should be Central African Republic-owned, including the political process, and should prioritize reconciliation of the Central African people,

Further emphasizing that the continued role of the region, including the Chair of the Economic Community of Central African States and its Mediator, as well as the African Union and the United Nations as members of the mediation, remains critical for the promotion of lasting peace and stability in the Central African Republic, and reiterates its appreciation for their ongoing efforts in this regard,

Commending the African-led International Support Mission in the Central African Republic, Sangaris and the European Union military operation in the Central African Republic for the work done in laying the foundation for increased security ahead of and in support of the deployment of the United Nations Multidimensional Integrated Stabilization Mission in the Central African Republic, and commending also the transition from the International Support Mission to the Stabilization Mission on 15 September 2014,

Noting with concern, however, that, while improving, the security situation in the Central African Republic remains fragile,

Condemning the multiple violations of international humanitarian law and the widespread human rights violations and abuses, including those involving extrajudicial killings, enforced disappearances, arbitrary arrests and detention, torture, sexual violence against women and children, rape, recruitment and use of children and attacks against civilians, looting and destruction of property and attacks against places of worship, denial of humanitarian access and deliberate attacks against national and international personnel of humanitarian organizations, United Nations personnel and associated personnel and humanitarian assets, including supplies, facilities and transports, committed by both former Séléka elements and militia groups, in particular the "anti-balaka",

Welcoming the submission of the report of the International Commission of Inquiry on the Central African Republic established by resolution 2127 (2013),[164] noting with concern its finding that the main parties to the conflict, including ex-Séléka, the anti-balaka and elements from the Armed Forces of the Central African Republic who collaborated with armed groups committed violations of international humanitarian law and human rights violations and abuses since 1 January 2013 that may amount to war crimes and crimes against humanity, including ethnic cleansing by elements of the anti-balaka militia,

Condemning in the strongest terms all attacks and provocations against Stabilization Mission contingents and other international forces by armed groups, underlining that attacks targeting peacekeepers may constitute war crimes, reminding all parties of their obligations under international humanitarian law, and urging the transitional authorities of the Central African Republic to take all possible measures to ensure the arrest and prosecution of perpetrators,

Stressing the urgent and imperative need to end impunity in the Central African Republic and to bring to justice perpetrators of violations of international humanitarian law and of abuses and violations of human rights, underlining in this regard the need to bolster national accountability mechanisms, and underlining its support for the work of the Independent Expert of the Human Rights Council on human rights in the Central African Republic,

Welcoming, in this regard, the efforts of the transitional authorities, in particular the adoption of the relevant legislation, to establish a Special Criminal Court within the national judicial system, with jurisdiction over serious violations of human rights and of international humanitarian law, consistent with the international humanitarian law and international human rights law obligations of the Central African Republic,

Urging the national authorities to take all appropriate steps to implement the law establishing a national Special Criminal Court, and reiterating the primary responsibility of the national authorities to ensure a conducive environment for the effective and independent investigation, prosecution and adjudication of all cases by the Special Criminal Court and its effective contribution to peace, justice and reconciliation in the country,

Emphasizing the fact that the current security situation in the Central African Republic provides a conducive environment for transnational criminal activity, such as that involving arms trafficking and the use of mercenaries as well as a potential breeding ground for radical networks,

Acknowledging, in this respect, the important contribution the Security Council-mandated arms embargo can make to countering the illicit transfer of arms and related materiel in the Central African Republic and the region and in supporting post-conflict peacebuilding, disarmament, demobilization and reintegration and security sector reform, recalling its resolution 2196 (2015), and expressing grave concern at the threat to peace and security in the Central African Republic arising from the illicit transfer, destabilizing accumulation and misuse of small arms and light weapons and the use of such weapons against civilians affected by armed conflict,

Reiterating that illicit trade, exploitation and smuggling of natural resources, including gold, diamonds and wildlife poaching and trafficking, continues to threaten the peace and stability of the Central African Republic,

Emphasizing that the targeted sanctions renewed by resolution 2196 (2015) aim at, inter alia, individuals and entities designated by the Security Council Committee established pursuant to resolution 2127 (2013) as engaging in or providing support for acts that undermine the peace, stability or security of the Central African Republic, that impede the political transition process or that fuel violence and at individuals and entities designated by the Committee as involved in planning, directing or committing acts that violate international human rights law or international humanitarian law or that constitute human rights abuses or violations,

Expressing concern about reported travel by individuals designated pursuant to resolution 2127 (2013), and noting the critical importance of effective implementation of the sanctions regime, including the key role that neighbouring States, as well as regional and subregional organizations, can play in this regard and encouraging efforts to further enhance cooperation,

Reiterating its serious concern at the dire humanitarian situation in the Central African Republic, and emphasizing in particular the humanitarian needs of the more than 435,000 internally displaced persons, of the thousands of civilians trapped in enclaves and of the more than 450,000 refugees in neighbouring countries, a large number of whom are Muslim, and further expressing concern at the consequences of the flow of refugees on the situation in Chad, Cameroon and the Democratic Republic of the Congo, as well as other countries of the region,

Recalling the responsibility of the transitional authorities to protect and promote the right to freedom of movement of all people in the Central African Republic, including internally displaced persons, without distinction, their freedom to choose where to reside, and to comply with their right to return to their own country or to leave in order to seek asylum in other States,

Urging all parties to take the steps necessary to ensure the safety and security of humanitarian personnel, of United Nations and associated personnel and of United Nations installations, equipment and goods,

Reiterating its appreciation for the efforts of the International Contact Group on the Central African Republic, co-chaired by the African Union and the Congo, taking note of the decision of the International Mediator in the Central African Republic crisis, in accordance with the Transitional National Charter, to extend the transition for six months, until 15 August 2015, welcoming the communiqué issued at its 7th meeting of the Contact Group, held in Brazzaville on 16 March 2015, and encouraging all stakeholders to pursue their efforts,

Welcoming the commitment of the transitional authorities of the Central African Republic to complete the transition process, including on reconciliation aspects, and calling upon the transitional authorities and the National Electoral Authority, in accordance with the Transitional National Charter, to swiftly take the steps necessary to accelerate the preparation of the electoral process with a view to holding as a matter of urgency and as soon as possible the free, fair and credible elections currently scheduled to take place by August 2015,

Welcoming also the holding of, and local participation in, grassroots consultations throughout the country between 21 January and 8 March 2015, which enabled thousands of people in the Central African Republic to express their views on the future of their country,

Recognizing the work of the Preparatory Committee of the Bangui Forum on National Reconciliation, and welcoming the setting of the date for the Bangui Forum, which is a critical step in the political transition process and offers an opportunity to address issues that are of critical importance to the future of the country, including peace and security, justice and reconciliation, governance and economic and social development,

Welcoming the joint action of some domestic religious leaders at the national level in trying to pacify relations and end violence between religious communities, and noting the need to amplify their voices at the local level,

Recalling the need for an inclusive and effective disarmament, demobilization and reintegration process, as well as repatriation in the case of foreign fighters, including children formerly associated with armed forces and groups, while respecting the need to fight against impunity,

Underlining the need to support national, and to coordinate international, efforts towards rebuilding the security sector in the Central African Republic, and stressing the important role of the internal security forces (police and gendarmerie) in the restoration of security in the Central African Republic,

Welcoming, in this regard, the launching by the European Union of a military advice mission based in Bangui, which will support, at their request, the Central African Republic transitional authorities and will work closely with the Stabilization Mission by providing expert advice on reforming the Armed Forces of the Central African Republic into multi-ethnic, professional and republican armed forces,

Recalling its resolutions 1265 (1999) of 17 September 1999, 1296 (2000) of 19 April 2000, 1674 (2006) of 28 April 2006, 1738 (2006) of 23 December 2006 and 1894 (2009) of 11 November 2009 on the protection of civilians in armed conflict, its resolutions 1612 (2005) of 26 July 2005, 1882 (2009) of 4 August 2009, 1998 (2011) of 12 July 2011, 2068 (2012) of 19 September 2012 and 2143 (2014) of 7 March 2014 on children and armed conflict and its resolutions 1325 (2000) of 31 October 2000, 1820 (2008) of 19 June 2008, 1888 (2009) of 30 September 2009, 1889 (2009) of 5 October 2009, 1960 (2010) of 16 December 2010, 2106 (2013) of 24 June 2013 and 2122 (2013) of 18 October 2013 on women and peace and security, and calling upon all parties in the Central African Republic to engage with the Special Representative of the Secretary-General for Children and Armed Conflict and the Special Representative of the Secretary-General on Sexual Violence in Conflict,

Expressing its concern that children have continued to be victims of abuses committed by armed elements of the ex-Séléka and anti-balaka as well as the Lord's Resistance Army, and that women continue to be violently targeted and victims of sexual and gender-based violence in the Central African Republic,

Expressing serious concern about the dire situation of persons with disabilities in the Central African Republic, including abandonment, violence and lack of access to basic services, and emphasizing the need to ensure that the particular needs of persons with disabilities are addressed in the humanitarian response,

Commending the ongoing role and contribution of the African Union to the stabilization of the Central African Republic, and welcoming the deployment of African Union advisers to support the victims of sexual violence in the Central African Republic,

Welcoming the strong engagement of the European Union for the Central African Republic, and further welcoming the contribution of the United States of America and of other Member States to the stabilization of the Central African Republic,

Encouraging the international community to swiftly follow through on pledges to continue providing support in response to the humanitarian situation in the Central African Republic and to prepare for reconstruction with an approach linking relief, rehabilitation and development,

Calling upon international partners to assist the transitional authorities in building the institutional capacity of national police and customs authorities to effectively monitor the borders and points of entry, including to support the implementation of the measures renewed and modified by paragraph 1 of resolution 2196 (2015) and the disarmament and repatriation of foreign armed elements,

Welcoming the World Bank's plan for 2014 presented at the meeting of the Central African Republic configuration of the Peacebuilding Commission held on 19 February 2014, and strongly encouraging international financial institutions to continue to engage with the transitional authorities and to increase their commitments to support the transitional authorities,

Calling upon international partners to urgently provide financial contributions to support national dialogue and reconciliation, the preparation of elections, the extension of State authority, accountability, disarmament, demobilization and reintegration/repatriation and security sector reform processes, as well as the restoration of the judicial and penal chains in order to fight against impunity,

Underlining the role of the Central African Republic configuration of the Peacebuilding Commission in supporting the efforts of the transitional authorities towards national dialogue and reconciliation process, elections and accountability, as well as in addressing challenges facing the country, through mobilizing and sustaining the attention and commitment of partners' efforts as well as the Peacebuilding Fund,

Commending the transitional authorities for the work done to balance the national budget, and calling upon them to continue their effort to strengthen public financial management, transparency and accountability, which will help to create a conducive environment for the international community to increase budget and development support in 2015,

Stressing the need to implement the mandate of the Stabilization Mission, based on the prioritization of tasks, and, when relevant, in a phased manner,

Welcoming the report of the Secretary-General of 1 April 2015,[167]

Taking note of the letter to the Council dated 8 April 2014, by which the President of the Central African Republic conveyed views regarding the mandate of the Stabilization Mission in terms of protection of civilians and urgent temporary measures,

Determining that the situation in the Central African Republic continues to constitute a threat to international peace and security in the region,

Acting under Chapter VII of the Charter of the United Nations,

Political process

1. *Expresses its support* to the transitional authorities under the leadership of Ms. Catherine Samba-Panza as Transitional Head of State, welcomes their commitment to complete the transition process, and reiterates its call upon them to further accelerate its completion;

2. *Reiterates its support* for the Libreville Agreements of 11 January 2013, the N'Djamena Declaration of 18 April 2013, the Constitutional Charter for the Transition of 18 July 2013 as well as the cessation of hostilities agreement signed in Brazzaville on 23 July 2014;

3. *Welcomes* the important role of the region through the active leadership of the Economic Community of Central African States, in particular the mediation by the Congo, and encourages the Economic Community, through its Chairperson and its Mediator, to continue to support the political transition process in the Central African Republic outlined in the above-mentioned Declaration and agreements;

4. *Commends* the initial measures taken by the African Union and the Economic Community of Central African States to restore peace and stability in the Central African Republic;

5. *Demands* that all militias and non-State armed groups lay down their arms, cease all forms of violence and destabilizing activities immediately and release children from their ranks;

6. *Commends* the transitional authorities and Central African Republic stakeholders for the work done in revitalizing the political and reconciliation process in order to lay the ground for a sustainable end to the conflict, welcomes recent efforts by the transitional authorities to gather views of local citizens in advance of the Bangui Forum on National Reconciliation by holding inclusive grassroots-level consultations, underlines the importance of the Bangui Forum to promote peace and stability, in particular through the signing of an agreement on the disarmament of armed groups, and further recalls the crucial role of civil society in the peace and reconciliation process;

7. *Encourages* the submission by Member States of listing requests to the Security Council Committee established pursuant to paragraph 57 of resolution 2127 (2013), including detailed evidentiary support for each request, of individuals and entities engaging in or providing support for acts that undermine the peace, stability or security of the Central African Republic, that impede the transition process or that fuel violence;

8. *Urges* the transitional authorities, as well as the National Electoral Authority, in accordance with the Transitional National Charter, to accelerate the preparations in order to hold as a matter of urgency and as soon as possible the free, fair, transparent and inclusive presidential and legislative elections currently scheduled to take place by August 2015, ensuring the full, effective and equal participation of women, internally displaced persons and Central African Republic refugees, the return of whom should be an important objective;

9. *Calls upon* all actors in the Central African Republic to respect the Constitutional Charter for the Transition, particularly with respect to the preparation and holding of elections, including regarding candidate ineligibility;

10. *Urges* the Central African Republic transitional authorities, with the support of the United Nations Multidimensional Integrated Stabilization Mission in the Central African Republic and the European Union military

[167] S/2015/227.

advice mission in the Central African Republic, to adopt a strategy for a comprehensive reform of the Armed Forces of the Central African Republic and internal security forces (police and gendarmerie) in order to put in place professional, ethnically representative and regionally balanced national defence and internal security forces, including through the adoption of appropriate human rights vetting procedures of all defence and security personnel as well as measures to absorb elements of armed groups meeting rigorous selection and vetting criteria, and requests the Secretary-General to report to the Council on progress made in this regard;

11. *Calls upon* the Central African Republic authorities to take concrete steps, without delay and as a matter of priority, to strengthen justice institutions and to fight impunity in order to contribute to stabilization and reconciliation, and in this regard to swiftly implement the law establishing the Special Criminal Court;

12. *Also calls upon* the transitional authorities to continue their efforts to redeploy State administration in the provinces, including through the effective restoration of the administration of the judiciary and the criminal justice system throughout the country, with the support of the international community;

13. *Calls upon* Member States and international and regional organizations to urgently provide support to the transitional authorities for the conduct of the transition and subsequent reforms, including contributions for the payment of salaries and other needs for the restoration of State authority over the whole territory, as well as for the holding of elections through the United Nations trust fund, for the upcoming disarmament, demobilization and reintegration/repatriation and security sector reform programmes and for the restoration of the judiciary and the criminal justice system, including the Special Criminal Court;

14. *Encourages* the transitional authorities, with the support of the international community, in particular with the international financial institutions leading international efforts, to keep consolidating, based on critical peacebuilding and State-building goals, public financial management and accountability, including revenue collection, expenditure controls, public procurement and concession practices, building on relevant international experiences and in a manner that fosters national ownership and respects the sovereignty of the Central African Republic;

Human rights

15. *Reiterates* the urgent and imperative need to hold accountable all perpetrators of violations of international humanitarian law and human rights violations and abuses, irrespective of their status or political affiliation, and reiterates that some of those acts may amount to crimes under the Rome Statute of the International Criminal Court,[165] to which the Central African Republic is a State party;

16. *Notes* the decision made by the Prosecutor of the International Criminal Court on 24 September 2014 to open, following the request of the national authorities, an investigation into alleged crimes committed since 2012, and welcomes the ongoing cooperation of the transitional authorities in this regard;

17. *Calls upon* all parties to armed conflict in the Central African Republic, including former Séléka elements and anti-balaka elements, to issue clear orders prohibiting all violations and abuses committed against children, in violation of applicable international law, including those involving their recruitment and use, rape and sexual violence, killing and maiming, abductions and attacks on schools and hospitals, and further calls upon the transitional authorities to investigate swiftly alleged violations and abuses in order to hold perpetrators accountable and to ensure that those responsible for such violations and abuses are excluded from the security sector;

18. *Reiterates its demands* that all parties protect and consider as victims those children who have been released or otherwise separated from armed forces and armed groups, and emphasizes the need to pay particular attention to the protection, release and reintegration of all children associated with armed forces and armed groups;

19. *Calls upon* all parties to armed conflict in the Central African Republic, including former Séléka and anti-balaka elements, to issue clear orders against sexual and gender-based violence, and further calls upon the transitional authorities to investigate swiftly alleged abuses in order to hold perpetrators accountable, in line with its resolutions 1960 (2010) and 2106 (2013), to ensure that those responsible for such crimes are excluded from the security sector and prosecuted, and to facilitate immediate access for victims of sexual violence to available services;

Peacekeeping operation

20. *Commends* the transition of authority from the African-led International Support Mission in the Central African Republic to the United Nations Multidimensional Integrated Stabilization Mission in the Central African Republic on 15 September 2014, and welcomes the rehatting of former International Support Mission troops and police under the Stabilization Mission;

21. *Commends* the work of the Special Representative of the Secretary-General for the Central African Republic, Mr. Babacar Gaye, and takes note of the increased deployment of military, police and civilian components of the Stabilization Mission, the initial work of the Mission in implementing its mandate and the establishment of the Bangui Task Force to ensure the stabilization of the capital;

22. *Decides* to extend the mandate of the Stabilization Mission until 30 April 2016;

23. *Also decides* that the Stabilization Mission has an authorized troop ceiling of 10,750 military personnel, including 480 military observers and military staff officers and 2,080 police personnel, including 400 individual police officers and 40 corrections officers, recalls its intention to keep this number under continuous review, in particular for the additional troops authorized by resolution 2212 (2015), calls upon Member States to provide troops and police with adequate capabilities and equipment in order to enhance the capacity of the Mission to operate and discharge its responsibilities effectively, and requests the Secretary-General to accelerate the recruitment of qualified staff who have the competencies, education, work experience and language skills appropriate to the tasks defined under applicable competency areas in paragraphs 32 to 34 below, bearing in mind the need to convey information and provide technical assistance in the most accessible manner to the desired audience;

24. *Requests* the Secretary-General to take all possible steps, including through the full use of existing authorities and, at his discretion, to accelerate the deployments of civilian, police and military capabilities of the Stabilization Mission in the Central African Republic, in order to best respond to the expectations of the Council and the needs of the population of the Central African Republic, and requests the Secretary-General to take the steps necessary to have the Mission reach its full operational capacity and ability to discharge its mandate over the entire territory of the Central African Republic as soon as technically and logistically possible, with no further delay, including to regions in eastern Central African Republic;

25. *Urges*, to this end, the former troop- and police-contributing countries of the International Support Mission that have been rehatted under the Stabilization Mission to expedite the procurement and deployment of remaining additional contingent-owned equipment, in order to comply with United Nations standards for troops and police;

26. *Urges* the Secretariat to continue to explore, on the basis of need, the use of specialized police teams together with specialized required equipment, for police and gendarmerie capacity-building and development and operational support;

27. *Requests* that the Secretary-General and his Special Representative take the steps necessary to reinforce the capacity of the police component of the Stabilization Mission and in particular the Bangui Task Force, within the authorized troop ceiling, including through the strengthening of the chain of command, the acceleration of the deployment across the whole territory and the recruitment and deployment of personnel trained for stabilization tasks in challenging urban environments;

28. *Stresses* the importance of expediting the deployment of the civilian component of the Stabilization Mission in order to support the actions of the police and military components based on the needs of the Mission;

29. *Urges* the Stabilization Mission and all relevant United Nations bodies to ensure unhindered access for the Panel of Experts on the Central African Republic, in particular to persons, documents and sites within their control in order for the Panel to execute its mandate;

30. *Decides* that the mandate of the Stabilization Mission should be implemented based on a prioritization of tasks established in paragraphs 32 to 34 of the present resolution, and, when relevant, in a phased manner, and further requests the Secretary-General to reflect this prioritization in the deployment and in the allocation of resources to the Mission;

31. *Authorizes* the Stabilization Mission to take all means necessary to carry out its mandate within its capabilities and areas of deployment;

32. *Decides* that the mandate of the Stabilization Mission shall include the following immediate priority tasks:

(*a*) *Protection of civilians*

(i) To protect, without prejudice to the primary responsibility of the Central African Republic authorities, the civilian population from the threat of physical violence, within its capabilities and areas of deployment, including through active patrolling, and to mitigate risks to civilians posed by its military operations;

(ii) To provide specific protection for women and children affected by armed conflict, including through the deployment of child protection advisers, women's protection advisers and gender advisers;

(iii) To identify and record threats and attacks against the civilian population, including through regular interaction with the civilian population and working closely with humanitarian and human rights organizations;

(iv) To fully implement and deliver, in close consultation with humanitarian and human rights organizations and other relevant partners, the mission-wide protection strategy;

(*b*) *Support for the implementation of the transition process, the extension of State authority and the preservation of territorial integrity*

(i) To take a leading role in international efforts to assist the transitional authorities working with the Economic Community of Central African States, the African Union, the United Nations Regional Office for Central Africa, relevant stakeholders and the international community to devise, facilitate, coordinate and provide technical assistance to the successful and timely completion of the political transition;

(ii) To provide good offices and political support for the efforts to address root causes of the conflict and establish lasting peace and security in the Central African Republic;

(iii) To provide appropriate support, in coordination with the transitional authorities, and based on the risks on the ground, for the provision of security for key national stakeholders, including members of the Transitional Government;

(iv) To assist the transitional authorities and, subsequently, the elected authorities, in mediation and reconciliation processes at both the national and local levels, working with relevant regional and local bodies and religious leaders, including through inclusive national dialogue, transitional justice and conflict resolution mechanisms, while ensuring the full and effective participation of women;

(v) To devise, coordinate and provide technical, logistical and security assistance to the electoral process and make all necessary preparations, in support of the transitional authorities and working on an urgent basis with the National Electoral Authority, for the holding, in accordance with the Transitional National Charter, as a matter of urgency and as soon as possible, of the free, fair, transparent and inclusive presidential and legislative elections currently scheduled to take place by August 2015, in order to complete the political transition in a timely manner, including the full and effective participation of women at all levels and at an early stage, in all phases of the electoral process, and the participation of internally displaced persons and refugees from the Central African Republic;

(vi) To devise, coordinate and provide technical, logistical and security assistance to the organization and the holding of the constitutional referendum, as appropriate;

(vii) To promote and support the rapid extension of State authority over the entire territory of the Central African Republic, including by supporting the redeployment of the administration;

(viii) To actively seize, confiscate and destroy, as appropriate, the weapons and ammunitions of armed elements, including all militias and non-State armed groups, who refuse or fail to lay down their arms;

(*c*) *Facilitating the immediate, full, safe and unhindered delivery of humanitarian assistance*

To enhance civil-military coordination within the Stabilization Mission and improve coordination with humanitarian actors, to facilitate the creation of a secure environment for the immediate, full, safe and unhindered, civilian-led delivery of humanitarian assistance, in accordance with United Nations guiding humanitarian principles and relevant provisions of international law, and for the voluntary, safe, dignified and sustainable return or local integration or resettlement of internally displaced persons or refugees, in close coordination with humanitarian actors;

(*d*) *Protection of the United Nations*

To protect United Nations personnel, installations, equipment and goods and ensure the security and freedom of movement of United Nations and associated personnel;

(*e*) *Promotion and protection of human rights*

(i) To monitor, help to investigate and report publicly and to the Council on violations of international humanitarian law and on violations and abuses of human rights committed throughout the Central African Republic, in particular by different armed groups, including the former Séléka and the anti-balaka, as well as in connection with the Bangui Forum and the electoral process, and to contribute to efforts to identify and prosecute perpetrators, and to prevent such violations and abuses, including through the deployment of human rights observers;

(ii) To monitor, help to investigate and report on violations and abuses committed against children, women as well as persons with disabilities, including rape and other forms of sexual violence in armed conflict, and to contribute to efforts to identify and prosecute perpetrators, and to prevent such violations and abuses;

(iii) To support the implementation of relevant recommendations of the International Commission of Inquiry on the Central African Republic;

(iv) To assist the Central African Republic authorities in the effort to protect and promote human rights, including through the establishment of a national human rights commission, and to strengthen the capacity of civil society organizations;

(*f*) *Urgent temporary measures*

(i) To continue to adopt, within the limits of its capacities and areas of deployment, at the formal request of the transitional authorities and in areas where national security forces or judicial authorities are not present or operational, urgent temporary measures on an exceptional basis and without creating a precedent and without prejudice to the agreed principles of peacekeeping operations, which are limited in scope, time-bound and consistent with the objectives set out in paragraphs 32 (*a*) to (*e*) above and 33 (*a*) below, to arrest and detain in order to maintain basic law and order and fight impunity;

(ii) Requests the Secretary-General to continue to report to the Council any measures that may be adopted on this basis;

(*g*) *Special Criminal Court*

(i) To assist the transitional authorities and subsequent elected authorities and facilitate other bilateral and multilateral support to the transitional authorities and subsequent elected authorities in the establishment of the national Special Criminal Court consistent with Central African Republic laws and jurisdiction and in line with the international humanitarian law and international human rights law obligations of the Central African Republic with the aim of supporting the extension of State authority;

(ii) To provide technical assistance and capacity-building for the Central African Republic authorities, in order to facilitate the functioning of the Special Criminal Court, in particular in the areas of investigations, arrests, detention, criminal and forensic analysis, evidence collection and storage, recruitment and selection of personnel, and the establishment of a legal aid system, as appropriate, as well as, within existing resources, to provide security for magistrates, and take measures to enhance the security of victims and witnesses as conditions allow, in line with the international human rights obligations of the Central African Republic, including with respect to fair trials and due process;

(*h*) *Disarmament, demobilization, reintegration and repatriation*

(i) To support the transitional authorities and subsequent elected authorities in developing and implementing a revised strategy for the disarmament, demobilization and reintegration and, in the case of foreign elements, repatriation, of former combatants and armed elements to reflect new realities on the ground, while paying specific attention to the needs of children associated with armed forces and groups;

(ii) To support the transitional authorities and subsequent elected authorities in implementing the revised strategy for the reintegration of former combatants in line with the wider security sector reform;

(iii) To support the transitional authorities and subsequent elected authorities in developing and implementing community violence reduction programmes;

(iv) To regroup and canton combatants in accordance with article 4 of the Brazzaville agreement and in cooperation with the transitional authorities and destroy, as appropriate, the weapons and ammunition of disarmed combatants in keeping with its effort to seize and collect arms and related materiel the supply, sale or transfer of which violate the measures imposed by paragraph 1 of resolution 2196 (2015);

33. *Further authorizes* the Stabilization Mission to use its capacities to assist the Central African Republic authorities for, and, where relevant, implement, the following essential tasks:

(*a*) *Support for national and international justice and the rule of law*

(i) To help to build the capacities, including through technical assistance, of the national judicial system and of the national human rights institutions and assist with national reconciliation efforts, coordinating with the Independent Expert of the Human Rights Council on human rights in the Central African Republic as appropriate;

(ii) To provide support and to coordinate international assistance to the policing, justice and correctional institutions to reinstate the criminal justice system, within the framework of the United Nations global focal point on the rule of law, including through assistance in the maintenance of public safety and basic law and order, in a manner that emphasizes civilian oversight, impartiality and the protection of human rights;

(iii) To support the restoration and maintenance of public safety and the rule of law, including through the presence and assistance of United Nations police authorized in paragraph 23 above, including through arresting and handing over to the Central African Republic authorities those responsible for serious human rights violations and abuses and serious violations of international humanitarian law in the country so that they can be brought to justice, and through cooperation with States of the region as well as the International Criminal Court in cases of crimes falling within its jurisdiction;

(*b*) *Security sector reform*

(i) To support the transitional authorities and subsequent elected authorities in devising and implementing the security sector reform and vetting processes, including through the provision of strategic policy advice, in close coordination with the European Union military advice mission;

(ii) To closely coordinate the provision of technical assistance and training between the international partners in the Central African Republic in order to ensure a clear distribution of tasks in the field of security sector reform, for the benefit of both the Armed Forces of the Central African Republic and the Central African Republic internal security forces (police and gendarmerie);

(*c*) *Illicit exploitation of and trafficking in natural resources*

To support the Central African Republic authorities to develop a nationally owned strategy to tackle the illicit exploitation and trafficking networks of natural resources which continue to fund and supply armed groups in the Central African Republic, taking into account, where appropriate, the reports of the Panel of Experts established pursuant to resolution 2127 (2013) and the decisions of the Kimberley Process, with the aim of extending State authority over the entire territory and its resources;

34. *Further authorizes* the Stabilization Mission to carry out within its existing resources the following additional tasks:

(*a*) To coordinate international assistance as appropriate;

(*b*) To assist the Committee established pursuant to paragraph 57 of resolution 2127 (2013) and the Panel of Experts established pursuant to the same resolution, including by passing information relevant to the implementation of the mandate of the Committee and the Panel;

(*c*) To monitor the implementation of the measures renewed and modified by paragraph 1 of resolution 2196 (2015), in cooperation with the Panel of Experts, including by inspecting, as it deems necessary and when appropriate without notice, all arms and related materiel regardless of location, and advise the transitional authorities on efforts to keep armed groups from exploiting natural resources;

(*d*) To seize and collect arms and any related materiel the transfer of which to the Central African Republic violates the measures imposed by paragraph 54 of resolution 2127 (2013) and to record and dispose of such arms and related materiel as appropriate;

(*e*) To provide transport for relevant State authorities in carrying out inspections and monitoring visits in key mining areas and sites as appropriate and on a case-by-case basis and when the situation allows, as a means to promote and support the rapid extension of State authority over the entire territory;

35. *Requests* the Secretary-General to deploy and allocate personnel and expertise within the Stabilization Mission to reflect the priorities identified in paragraphs 32 to 34 of the present resolution, and to continuously adjust this deployment according to the progresses made in the implementation of this mandate;

36. *Requests* the Stabilization Mission to enhance its operational coordination with the African Union Regional Task Force on the Lord's Resistance Army, and requests the Mission to share relevant information with the Regional Task Force and with non-governmental organizations involved in tackling the threat of the Lord's Resistance Army;

37. *Calls upon* the transitional authorities and international partners and relevant United Nations entities, in coordination with the Stabilization Mission and the Mine Action Service of the United Nations, to address the illicit transfer, destabilizing accumulation and misuse of small arms and light weapons in the Central African Republic, and to ensure the safe and effective management, storage and security of stockpiles of small arms and light weapons and the collection and/or destruction of surplus, seized, unmarked or illicitly held weapons and ammunition, and further stresses the importance of incorporating such elements into security sector reform and disarmament, demobilization and reintegration/repatriation programmes;

38. *Urges* the Central African Republic, its neighbouring States and other States members of the International Conference on the Great Lakes Region to cooperate at the regional level to investigate and combat regional criminal networks and armed groups involved in the illegal exploitation and smuggling of natural resources, including gold, diamonds and wildlife poaching and trafficking;

39. *Requests* the Stabilization Mission to take fully into account child protection as a cross-cutting issue throughout its mandate and to assist the transitional authorities in ensuring that the protection of children's rights is taken into account, inter alia, in disarmament, demobilization and reintegration and disarmament, demobilization and reintegration/repatriation processes and in security sector reform in order to end and prevent violations and abuses against children;

40. *Also requests* the Stabilization Mission to take fully into account gender considerations as a cross-cutting issue throughout its mandate and to assist the Government of the Central African Republic in ensuring the full and effective participation, involvement and representation of women in all spheres and at all levels, including in stabilization activities, security sector reform and disarmament, demobilization and reintegration and disarmament, demobilization and reintegration/repatriation processes, as well as in the national political dialogue and electoral processes, through, inter alia, the provision of gender advisers, and further requests enhanced reporting by the Mission to the Council on this issue;

41. *Further requests* the Stabilization Mission, within its existing resources and mandate, to assist the political efforts of the African Union, the Economic Community of Central African States and the United Nations Regional Office for Central Africa to support the transition process;

42. *Reiterates* that the measures imposed by paragraph 1 of resolution 2196 (2015) do not apply to the Stabilization Mission, the African Union Regional Task Force, the European Union missions and the French forces operating in the Central African Republic to provide organizational advice and non-operational training to the Central African Republic government forces and as relevant to the implementation of their mandates, and requests these forces to report on measures taken in this regard as part of their regular reports to the Council;

43. *Requests* the Secretary-General to take the measures necessary to ensure full compliance of the Stabilization Mission with the United Nations zero-tolerance policy on sexual exploitation and abuse and to keep the Council informed if cases of misconduct occur, and notes the relevance of the guidance on contacts with persons who are the subject of arrest warrants or summonses issued by the International Criminal Court;[168]

[168] S/2013/210, annex.

44. *Requests* the Stabilization Mission to ensure that any support provided to non-United Nations security forces is provided in strict compliance with the human rights due diligence policy on United Nations support to non-United Nations security forces,[169] and requests the Secretary-General to include information on any such support in his reports to the Council;

45. *Emphasizes* the need for the Stabilization Mission, the European Union military advice mission and the French forces operating in the Central African Republic, while carrying out their mandate, to act in full respect of the sovereignty, territorial integrity and unity of the Central African Republic and in full compliance with applicable international humanitarian law, human rights law and refugee law, and recalls the importance of training in this regard;

Freedom of movement of the Stabilization Mission

46. *Urges* all parties in the Central African Republic to cooperate fully with the deployment and activities of the Stabilization Mission, in particular by ensuring its safety, security and freedom of movement with unhindered and immediate access throughout the territory of the Central African Republic to enable the Mission to carry out fully its mandate in a complex environment;

47. *Calls upon* Member States, especially those in the region, to ensure the free, unhindered and expeditious movement to and from the Central African Republic of all personnel, as well as equipment, provisions, supplies and other goods, including vehicles and spare parts, which are for the exclusive and official use of the Stabilization Mission;

Humanitarian access

48. *Demands* that all parties allow and facilitate full, safe, immediate and unhindered access for the timely delivery of humanitarian assistance to populations in need, in particular to internally displaced persons, throughout the territory of the Central African Republic, in accordance with the United Nations guiding principles of humanitarian assistance and relevant provisions of international law;

Humanitarian appeal

49. *Welcomes* the humanitarian appeal, regrets its insufficient current funding, and calls upon Member States and international and regional organizations to respond swiftly to this appeal through increased contributions and to ensure that all pledges are honoured in full;

French forces

50. *Authorizes* the French forces, within the limits of their capacities and areas of deployment, from the commencement of the activities of the Stabilization Mission until the end of the mandate of the Mission as authorized in the present resolution, to use all means necessary to provide operational support to elements of the Mission from the date of adoption of the present resolution, at the request of the Secretary-General, and requests France to report to the Council on the implementation of this mandate and to coordinate its reporting with that of the Secretary-General referred to in paragraph 52 of the present resolution;

Review and reporting

51. *Requests* the Secretary-General to review on a regular basis the conditions required for the transition, drawdown and withdrawal of the United Nations operation, in a manner which does not prejudice overall efforts to support long-term objectives for peace and stability, and looks forward to receiving this information as part of this regular reporting to the Council;

52. *Also requests* the Secretary-General to keep the Council regularly informed of the situation in the Central African Republic and the implementation of the mandate of the Stabilization Mission, to report to the Council on 1 August 2015 and then every four months from that date and to include in his reports to the Council

[169] S/2013/110, annex.

updates on and recommendations related to the dynamic implementation of the Mission's mandated tasks, including by providing appropriate financial information, information on the security situation, the priority political elements as defined above on political progress, progress on mechanisms and capacity to advance governance and fiscal management, relevant information on the progress, promotion and protection of human rights and international humanitarian law, as well as a review of the troop and police levels, force and police generation and deployment of all constituent elements of the Mission;

53. *Decides* to remain actively seized of the matter.

Adopted unanimously at the 7434th meeting.

CHILDREN AND ARMED CONFLICT[170]

Decisions

At its 7259th meeting, on 8 September 2014, the Security Council decided to invite the representatives of Afghanistan, Algeria, Austria, Azerbaijan, Belgium, Bosnia and Herzegovina, Botswana, Brazil, Canada, Colombia, the Democratic Republic of the Congo, Estonia, Germany, Guatemala, India, Indonesia, Iran (Islamic Republic of), Iraq, Israel, Italy, Japan, Liechtenstein, Malaysia, Mexico, Montenegro, Morocco, Myanmar, New Zealand, Pakistan, the Philippines, Poland, Portugal, Qatar, Somalia, Spain, the Sudan, Sweden, Switzerland, the Syrian Arab Republic, Thailand, Turkey, Ukraine, Uruguay and Yemen to participate, without vote, in accordance with rule 37 of its provisional rules of procedure, in the discussion of the item entitled:

"Children and armed conflict

"Report of the Secretary-General on children and armed conflict (S/2014/339)".

At the same meeting, the Council also decided to extend invitations, in accordance with rule 39 of its provisional rules of procedure, to Ms. Leila Zerrougui, Special Representative of the Secretary-General for Children and Armed Conflict, Mr. Hervé Ladsous, Under-Secretary-General for Peacekeeping Operations, Ms. Yoka Brandt, Deputy Executive Director of the United Nations Children's Fund, and Mr. Forest Whitaker, Special Envoy for Peace and Reconciliation of the United Nations Educational, Scientific and Cultural Organization.

At the same meeting, the Council further decided to extend an invitation, in accordance with rule 39 of its provisional rules of procedure, to Ms. Sandra Uwiringiyimana.

At the same meeting, the Council decided to extend invitations, in accordance with rule 39 of its provisional rules of procedure, to Mr. Thomas Mayr-Harting, Head of the Delegation of the European Union to the United Nations, and Mr. Ahmed Fathalla, Permanent Observer of the League of Arab States to the United Nations.

At its 7414th meeting, on 25 March 2015, the Council decided to invite the representatives of Afghanistan, Albania, Algeria, Argentina, Australia, Austria, Azerbaijan, Belgium, Benin, Brazil, Burundi, Cambodia, Canada, Colombia, Croatia, the Democratic Republic of the Congo, Egypt, Estonia, Gabon, Germany, Guatemala, Hungary, India, Indonesia, Iraq, Israel, Italy, Japan, Kazakhstan, Liechtenstein, Luxembourg, Mali, Montenegro, Morocco, Myanmar, the Netherlands, Pakistan, the Philippines, Poland, Portugal, Qatar, the Republic of Korea, Slovakia, Slovenia, South Africa, Sri Lanka, the Sudan, Sweden, Switzerland, the Syrian Arab Republic, Thailand, Turkey, Ukraine, Uruguay and Viet Nam to participate, without vote, in accordance with rule 37 of its provisional rules of procedure, in the discussion of the item entitled:

"Children and armed conflict

"Child victims of non-State armed groups

"Letter dated 6 March 2015 from the Permanent Representative of France to the United Nations addressed to the Secretary-General (S/2015/168)".

---

[170] Resolutions or decisions on this question were first adopted by the Security Council in 1998.

At the same meeting, the Council also decided to extend invitations, in accordance with rule 39 of its provisional rules of procedure, to Ms. Leila Zerrougui, Special Representative of the Secretary-General for Children and Armed Conflict and Ms. Yoka Brandt, Deputy Executive Director of the United Nations Children's Fund.

At the same meeting, the Council further decided to extend invitations, in accordance with rule 39 of its provisional rules of procedure, to Ms. Julie Bodin, Child Protection Technical Adviser for Save the Children International in the Central African Republic, and Mr. Junior Nzita, President of Paix pour l'enfance.

At the same meeting, the Council decided to extend invitations, in accordance with rule 39 of its provisional rules of procedure, to Mr. Thomas Mayr-Harting, Head of the Delegation of the European Union to the United Nations, Mr. Stephen Evans, Assistant Secretary-General for Operations of the North Atlantic Treaty Organization, and Mr. Téte António, Permanent Observer of the African Union to the United Nations.

At the same meeting, the Council decided to extend invitations to the Permanent Observer of the Observer State of Palestine to the United Nations, and the Permanent Observer of the Observer State of the Holy See to the United Nations, in accordance with the provisional rules of procedure of the Council and its previous practice in that regard.

At its 7466th meeting, on 18 June 2015, the Council decided to invite the representatives of Albania, Algeria, Andorra, Argentina, Australia, Austria, Azerbaijan, Belgium, Bosnia and Herzegovina, Botswana, Brazil, Bulgaria, Cambodia, Canada, Colombia, Croatia, Cyprus, the Czech Republic, Egypt, Estonia, Finland, Georgia, Germany, Greece, Guatemala, Hungary, Iceland, India, Indonesia, Iran (Islamic Republic of), Iraq, Ireland, Israel, Italy, Japan, Kazakhstan, Kenya, Kuwait, Latvia, Lebanon, Liechtenstein, Luxembourg, Mexico, Monaco, Montenegro, Morocco, Myanmar, the Netherlands, Norway, Pakistan, Palau, Panama, the Philippines, Poland, Portugal, Qatar, the Republic of Korea, the Republic of Moldova, Romania, Slovakia, Slovenia, the Sudan, Sweden, Switzerland, the Syrian Arab Republic, Thailand, Turkey, Ukraine, Uruguay, Viet Nam and Zimbabwe to participate, without vote, in accordance with rule 37 of its provisional rules of procedure, in the discussion of the item entitled:

"Children and armed conflict

> "Letter dated 1 June 2015 from the Permanent Representative of Malaysia to the United Nations addressed to the Secretary-General (S/2015/402)
>
> "Report of the Secretary-General on children and armed conflict (S/2015/409)".

At the same meeting, the Council also decided to extend invitations, in accordance with rule 39 of its provisional rules of procedure, to Ms. Leila Zerrougui, Special Representative of the Secretary-General for Children and Armed Conflict, and Ms. Yoka Brandt, Deputy Executive Director of the United Nations Children's Fund.

At the same meeting, the Council further decided to extend an invitation, in accordance with rule 39 of its provisional rules of procedure, to Ms. Eunice Apio, Director of Facilitation for Peace and Development.

At the same meeting, the Council decided to extend invitations, in accordance with rule 39 of its provisional rules of procedure, to Mr. Thomas Mayr-Harting, Head of the Delegation of the European Union to the United Nations, and Mr. Ahmed Fathalla, Permanent Observer of the League of Arab States to the United Nations.

At the same meeting, the Council also decided to extend invitations to the Permanent Observer of the Observer State of Palestine to the United Nations and the Permanent Observer of the Observer State of the Holy See to the United Nations, in accordance with the provisional rules of procedure of the Council and its previous practice in that regard.

Resolution 2225 (2015) of 18 June 2015

The Security Council,

Reaffirming its resolutions 1261 (1999) of 25 August 1999, 1314 (2000) of 11 August 2000, 1379 (2001) of 20 November 2001, 1460 (2003) of 30 January 2003, 1539 (2004) of 22 April 2004, 1612 (2005) of 26 July 2005, 1882 (2009) of 4 August 2009, 1998 (2011) of 12 July 2011, 2068 (2012) of 19 September 2012 and 2143 (2014) of 7 March 2014, and all relevant statements by its President, which contribute to a comprehensive framework for addressing the protection of children affected by armed conflict,

Reiterating its primary responsibility for the maintenance of international peace and security and, in this connection, its commitment to address the widespread impact of armed conflict on children,

Acknowledging that its resolutions, their implementation and the statements by its President on children and armed conflict as well as the conclusions of the Security Council Working Group on Children and Armed Conflict have generated progress in preventing and responding to violations and abuses committed against children, in particular in the demobilization, rehabilitation and reintegration of thousands of children, the signing of action plans between parties to armed conflict and the delisting of parties to conflict from the annexes to the annual report of the Secretary-General,

Remaining deeply concerned, however, over the lack of progress on the ground in some situations of concern, where parties to conflict continue to violate with impunity the relevant provisions of applicable international law relating to the rights and protection of children in armed conflict,

Recalling that all parties to armed conflict must comply strictly with the obligations applicable to them under international law for the protection of children in armed conflict, including those contained in the Convention on the Rights of the Child[171] and the Optional Protocol thereto on the involvement of children in armed conflict,[172] as well as the Geneva Conventions of 12 August 1949[173] and the Additional Protocols thereto of 1977,[174]

Convinced that the protection of children in armed conflict should be an important aspect of any comprehensive strategy to resolve conflict and build peace, and stressing also the importance of adopting a broad strategy of conflict prevention, which addresses the root causes of armed conflict in a comprehensive manner in order to enhance the protection of children on a long-term basis,

Stressing the primary role of Governments in providing protection and relief to all children affected by armed conflict, and recognizing the importance of strengthening national capacities in this regard,

Reiterating that all action undertaken by United Nations entities within the framework of the monitoring and reporting mechanism must be designed to support and supplement, as appropriate, the protection and rehabilitation roles of national Governments,

Recognizing the important roles that local leaders and civil society networks can play in enhancing community-level protection and rehabilitation, including non-stigmatization, for children affected by armed conflict,

Recalling the responsibility of all Member States to comply with their respective obligations to end impunity and to investigate and prosecute those responsible for genocide, crimes against humanity, war crimes and other egregious crimes perpetrated against children, and noting that the fight against impunity for the most serious crimes of international concern committed against children has been strengthened through the work on and prosecution of these crimes by the International Criminal Court, ad hoc and mixed tribunals and specialized chambers in national tribunals,

Having considered the report of the Secretary-General of 5 June 2015,[175] and stressing that the present resolution does not seek to make any legal determination as to whether situations which are referred to in the report are or are not armed conflicts within the context of the Geneva Conventions and the Additional Protocols thereto, nor does it prejudge the legal status of the non-State parties involved in these situations,

Expressing grave concern over the abduction of children in situations of armed conflict, the majority of which are perpetrated by non-State armed groups, recognizing that abductions occur in a variety of settings, including schools, further recognizing that abduction often precedes or follows other abuses and violations of applicable international law against children, including those involving recruitment and use, killing and maiming, as well as rape and other forms of sexual violence, which may amount to war crimes or crimes against humanity, and calling upon all Member States to hold perpetrators of abductions accountable,

---

[171] United Nations, *Treaty Series*, vol. 1577, No. 27531.

[172] Ibid., vol. 2173, No. 27531.

[173] Ibid., vol. 75, Nos. 970–973.

[174] Ibid., vol. 1125, Nos. 17512 and 17513.

[175] S/2015/409.

Gravely concerned by the human rights abuses and violations of international humanitarian law committed by non-State armed groups, in particular violent extremist groups, including mass abductions, rape and other forms of sexual violence such as sexual slavery, particularly targeting girls, which can cause displacement and affect access to education and health-care services, and emphasizing the importance of accountability for such abuses and violations,

Noting that article 35 of the Convention on the Rights of the Child calls for States parties to take all appropriate national, bilateral and multilateral measures to prevent the abduction of, the sale of or traffic in children for any purpose or in any form,

Gravely concerned by the detrimental effects of the illicit transfer, destabilizing accumulation and misuse of small arms and light weapons on children in armed conflict, in particular owing to recruitment and use of children by parties to armed conflict, as well as their re-recruitment, killing and maiming, rape and other sexual violence, abductions and attacks on schools and hospitals in violation of international law,

Stressing that the best interests of the child as well as the specific needs and vulnerabilities of children should be considered when planning and carrying out actions concerning children in situations of armed conflict,

Recalling the obligations of all parties to armed conflict applicable to them under international humanitarian law and human rights law, emphasizing that no child should be deprived of his or her liberty unlawfully or arbitrarily, and calling upon all parties to conflict to cease unlawful or arbitrary detention as well as torture or other cruel, inhuman or degrading treatment or punishment imposed on children during their detention,

Recognizing the importance of providing timely and appropriate reintegration and rehabilitation assistance to children affected by armed conflict, while ensuring that the specific needs of girls as well as children with disabilities are addressed, including access to health care, psychosocial support and education programmes that contribute to the well-being of children and to sustainable peace and security,

Calling upon all parties to conflict to respect the civilian character of schools as such in accordance with international humanitarian law,

1. *Strongly condemns* all violations of applicable international law involving the recruitment and use of children by parties to armed conflict as well as their re-recruitment, killing and maiming, rape and other forms of sexual violence, abductions, attacks against schools and hospitals as well as denial of humanitarian access by parties to armed conflict and all other violations of international law, including international humanitarian law, human rights law and refugee law, committed against children in situations of armed conflict, and demands that all relevant parties immediately put an end to such practices and take special measures to protect children;

2. *Reaffirms* that the monitoring and reporting mechanism will continue to be implemented in situations listed in annex I and annex II (the annexes) to the reports of the Secretary-General on children and armed conflict, in line with the principles set out in paragraph 2 of its resolution 1612 (2005), and that its establishment and implementation shall not prejudge or imply a decision by the Security Council as to whether or not to include a situation on its agenda;

3. *Recalls* paragraph 16 of its resolution 1379 (2001), and requests the Secretary-General also to include in the annexes to his reports on children and armed conflict those parties to armed conflict that engage, in contravention of applicable international law, in patterns of abduction of children in situations of armed conflict, bearing in mind all other violations and abuses against children, and notes that the present paragraph will apply to situations in accordance with the conditions set out in paragraph 16 of its resolution 1379 (2001);

4. *Calls upon* those parties listed in the annexes to the report of the Secretary-General on children and armed conflict that commit violations and abuses against children in contravention of applicable international law, including abductions of children in situations of armed conflict, to prepare and adopt without delay concrete time-bound action plans to halt those violations and abuses in collaboration with the United Nations;

5. *Urges* the immediate, safe and unconditional release of abducted children by all parties to conflict, and encourages Member States, United Nations entities and regional and subregional organizations to undertake relevant efforts to obtain the safe release of abducted children, including through establishing standard operating procedures on the handover of children to relevant civilian child protection actors, as well as to seek to ensure their family reunification, rehabilitation and reintegration;

6. *Encourages* Member States to consider non-judicial measures as alternatives to prosecution and detention that focus on the rehabilitation and reintegration for children formerly associated with armed forces and armed groups, taking into account that deprivation of liberty of children should be used only as a measure of last resort and for the shortest appropriate period of time, as well as to avoid wherever possible the use of pretrial detention for children;

7. *Expresses deep concern* that the military use of schools in contravention of applicable international law may render schools legitimate targets of attack, thus endangering the safety of children, and in this regard encourages Member States to take concrete measures to deter such use of schools by armed forces and armed groups;

8. *Stresses* the importance of regular and timely consideration of violations and abuses committed against children in armed conflict, in this regard welcomes the sustained activity of its Working Group on Children and Armed Conflict, and invites the Working Group to make full use of tools within its mandate to promote the protection of children affected by armed conflict, including through increasing engagement with concerned Member States, in the light of ongoing discussions on enhancing compliance;

9. *Continues to urge* Member States, United Nations entities, regional and subregional organizations and other parties concerned to ensure that child protection provisions, including those relating to the release and reintegration of children formerly associated with armed forces or armed groups, are integrated into all peace negotiations and ceasefire and peace agreements, and in provisions for ceasefire monitoring;

10. *Welcomes* the progress made under the "Children, Not Soldiers" campaign towards ending and preventing the recruitment and use of children by government armed forces in conflict by 2016, further urges concerned Governments to continue to undertake all efforts in order to ensure that no children are in their ranks in conflict, and calls upon Member States, all relevant United Nations entities, non-governmental organizations and the donor community to support the campaign in their various capacities;

11. *Invites* the Special Representative of the Secretary-General for Children and Armed Conflict to update the Council on the "Children, Not Soldiers" campaign as well as on the progress made in the signing and implementation of action plans or commitments by non-State armed groups, including about the process and progress in delisting concerned parties;

12. *Urges* all parties concerned, including Member States and United Nations entities as well as financial institutions, to support, as appropriate, bearing in mind national ownership, the development and strengthening of the capacities of national institutions and local civil society networks for advocacy, protection and rehabilitation of children affected by armed conflict as well as national accountability mechanisms with timely, sustained and adequate resources and funding;

13. *Urges* concerned Member States, when undertaking security sector reforms, to mainstream child protection, such as the inclusion of child protection in military training and standard operating procedures, including on the handover of children to relevant civilian child protection actors, the establishment of child protection units in national security forces, and the strengthening of effective age assessment mechanisms to prevent underage recruitment, while stressing in the latter regard the importance of ensuring universal birth registration, including late birth registration, which should remain an exception;

14. *Emphasizes* the responsibility of all States to put an end to impunity and to investigate and prosecute those responsible for genocide, crimes against humanity, war crimes and other egregious crimes perpetrated against children, and highlights in this regard the contribution of the International Criminal Court, in accordance with the principle of complementarity to national criminal jurisdictions as set out in the Rome Statute of the Court;[176]

15. *Recognizes* the role of United Nations peacekeeping operations and political missions in the protection of children, particularly the crucial role of child protection advisers in mainstreaming child protection and leading monitoring, prevention and reporting efforts in missions, and in this regard reiterates its decision to continue the inclusion of specific provisions for the protection of children in the mandates of all relevant United Nations

---

[176] United Nations, *Treaty Series*, vol. 2187, No. 38544.

peacekeeping operations and political missions, encourages deployment of child protection advisers to such missions, and calls upon the Secretary-General to ensure that the need for and the number and roles of such advisers are systematically assessed during the preparation and renewal of each United Nations peacekeeping operation and political mission;

16. *Calls for* the continued implementation by United Nations peacekeeping operations of the Secretary-General's zero-tolerance policy on sexual exploitation and abuse and ensuring full compliance of their personnel with the United Nations code of conduct, reiterates its request to the Secretary-General to continue to take all necessary action in this regard and to keep the Council informed, and urges troop-contributing countries to continue taking appropriate preventive action, such as mandatory predeployment child protection training, including on sexual exploitation and abuse, and to ensure full accountability in cases of such conduct involving their personnel;

17. *Further urges* all United Nations entities, including peacekeeping missions, political missions, peacebuilding offices, United Nations offices, agencies, funds and programmes, to give full attention to violations against children in the application of the human rights due diligence policy on United Nations support to non-United Nations security forces;[177]

18. *Reiterates its requests* to the Secretary-General to continue to submit comprehensive annual reports to the Council on the implementation of its resolutions and statements by its President on children and armed conflict and to ensure that, in all his reports on country-specific situations the matter of children and armed conflict, is included as specific aspect of the report;

19. *Decides* to remain actively seized of the matter.

Adopted unanimously at the 7466th meeting.

THE SITUATION IN GUINEA-BISSAU[178]

Decisions

On 15 August 2014, the President of the Security Council addressed the following letter to the Secretary-General:[179]

> I have the honour to inform you that your letter dated 13 August 2014 concerning your reports submitted pursuant to resolution 2048 (2012)[180] has been brought to the attention of the members of the Security Council.
>
> The members of the Council have taken note of the request contained in your letter that your upcoming report be the last one and that further updates be provided every six months in your regular reports on the United Nations Integrated Peacebuilding Office in Guinea-Bissau, while oral briefings to the Council will continue to be provided, as and when required.

At its 7315th meeting, on 18 November 2014, the Council decided to invite the representatives of Ghana, Guinea-Bissau and Timor-Leste to participate, without vote, in accordance with rule 37 of its provisional rules of procedure, in the discussion of the item entitled:

"The situation in Guinea-Bissau

> "Letter dated 11 November 2014 from the Secretary-General addressed to the President of the Security Council (S/2014/805)".

---

[177] S/2013/110, annex.

[178] Resolutions or decisions on this question were first adopted by the Security Council in 1998.

[179] S/2014/601.

[180] S/2014/600.

At the same meeting, the Council also decided to extend invitations, in accordance with rule 39 of its provisional rules of procedure, to Mr. Miguel Trovoada, Special Representative of the Secretary-General for Guinea-Bissau and Head of the United Nations Integrated Peacebuilding Office in Guinea-Bissau, and Mr. Antonio de Aguiar Patriota, Permanent Representative of Brazil to the United Nations, in his capacity as Chair of the Guinea-Bissau configuration of the Peacebuilding Commission.

At its 7321st meeting, on 25 November 2014, the Council considered the item entitled:

"The situation in Guinea-Bissau

"Letter dated 11 November 2014 from the Secretary-General addressed to the President of the Security Council (S/2014/805)".

Resolution 2186 (2014)
of 25 November 2014

The Security Council,

Recalling its previous resolutions, the statements by its President and its statements to the press on the situation in Guinea-Bissau, in particular resolutions 1876 (2009) of 26 June 2009, 2030 (2011) of 21 December 2011, 2048 (2012) of 18 May 2012, 2092 (2013) of 22 February 2013, 2103 (2013) of 22 May 2013 and 2157 (2014) of 29 May 2014,

Taking note of the report of the Secretary-General of 18 August 2014 on Guinea-Bissau[181] and his letter dated 11 November 2014 to the President of the Security Council[182] and the recommendations contained therein, and commending the engagement of the Special Representative of the Secretary-General for Guinea-Bissau and Head of the United Nations Integrated Peacebuilding Office in Guinea-Bissau,

Welcoming the progress made by the Government of Guinea-Bissau in determining its national priorities following the return to constitutional order,

Emphasizing the need for respect of democratic principles, and stressing the importance of inclusive governance, essential for the attainment of lasting peace in Guinea-Bissau,

Stressing that the consolidation of peace and stability in Guinea-Bissau can result only from a consensual, inclusive and nationally owned process, respect for constitutional order, the reforms in the defence, security and justice sectors, the promotion of the rule of law, the protection of human rights, the promotion of socioeconomic development and the fight against impunity and drug trafficking,

Stressing also that all stakeholders in should work to ensure short-, medium- and long-term stability through clear commitment and genuine inclusive political dialogue aimed at creating conditions conducive to finding viable and sustainable solutions to the country's social, economic, political and military problems, which would facilitate the implementation of key reforms and the strengthening of State institutions,

Emphasizing the importance of pursuing a national reconciliation and social cohesion strategy, and underlining the importance of including all Bissau-Guineans in the reconciliation process at the national and local levels, while upholding justice and the rule of law and combating impunity,

Noting efforts of the Government of Guinea-Bissau to gain effective civilian control and oversight over the defence and security forces, as failure to do so could adversely affect the effective functioning of State institutions, as a result of collusion between some political actors and the military leadership,

Commending the efforts of the Economic Community of West African States in helping to sustain peace, security and development and to support the security sector reform process in Guinea-Bissau, namely through the activities of its Mission in Guinea-Bissau,

---

[181] S/2014/603.

[182] S/2014/805.

Taking note of the desire of the new authorities of Guinea-Bissau to maintain the presence of the Mission on the ground to support the implementation of reforms and to build up confidence among international partners,

Reiterating its concern about reports of continuing violations and abuses of human rights, and calling upon the Government of Guinea-Bissau to conduct transparent and credible investigations into all alleged human rights violations and abuses, in accordance with international standards, and to hold those responsible accountable for their actions,

Reiterating its deep concern at the threat that drug trafficking poses to stability, and re-emphasizing the need to tackle the problem of drug trafficking in the countries of origin, transit and final destination through an approach of common and shared responsibility,

Underlining that any lasting solution to instability in Guinea-Bissau should include concrete actions to fight impunity and ensure that those responsible for politically motivated assassinations and other serious crimes such as breaches of constitutional order and drug trafficking-related activities are brought to justice, including through national judicial mechanisms,

Welcoming, in this regard, the efforts of the Government of Guinea-Bissau to update the three-year national plan for combating drug trafficking and organized crime, prepared in June 2011, and to define new priority areas accordingly,

Reiterating the importance of the continued support of the United Nations and international, regional, subregional, and bilateral partners for the long-term security and development of Guinea-Bissau, particularly towards the implementation of security and justice sector reforms, the fight against drug trafficking, organized crime and human trafficking, as well as the creation of an enabling environment for good governance and inclusive and sustainable social and economic development,

Commending the important work of the United Nations Office on Drugs and Crime in collaboration with relevant United Nations entities in the fight against drug trafficking and transnational organized crime in Guinea-Bissau and the subregion, and encouraging enhanced cooperation between the Office and the Integrated Peacebuilding Office,

Stressing the urgent need to maintain in Guinea-Bissau continuous evaluation capacity and to continue to support national, subregional, regional and international institutions in charge of the fight against drug trafficking,

Stressing also the need for increased coherence, coordination and efficiency among relevant partners to enhance their collective efforts toward combating drug trafficking in Guinea-Bissau, in particular through the sharing of information,

Emphasizing the important role of women in the prevention and resolution of conflicts and in peacebuilding, as recognized in resolutions 1325 (2000) of 31 October 2000, 1820 (2008) of 19 June 2008, 1888 (2009) of 30 September 2009, 1889 (2009) of 5 October 2009, 1960 (2010) of 16 December 2010, 2106 (2013) of 24 June 2013 and 2122 (2013) of 18 October 2013, welcoming the mission's work to increase women's participation in Guinea-Bissau, and underlining that a gender perspective must continue to inform the implementation of all relevant aspects of the mandate of the Integrated Peacebuilding Office,

Condemning cases of illegal and unauthorized fishing in Guinea-Bissau's territorial waters and exclusive economic zone, as well as illegal exploitation of natural resources, which undermines prospects for the economic development of the country,

Reaffirming that Guinea-Bissau's partners should continue to actively and closely coordinate their actions to help to bring solutions to the country's political, security and development challenges, and in this regard welcoming the efforts made by the Special Representative of the Secretary-General to convene an international donor conference in close consultation with international, regional and subregional development partners in order to mobilize resources for the country's development priorities, including the Government of Guinea-Bissau's 2014–2018 programme containing immediate and long-term priorities for the country,

Taking note of the statement made by the Chair of the Guinea-Bissau configuration of the Peacebuilding Commission on 18 November 2014,[183] and welcoming the engagement of the Commission with Guinea-Bissau,

Welcoming the reactivation of the International Contact Group on Guinea-Bissau and its 10th meeting, held on 18 November 2014,

Recognizing the need for the Integrated Peacebuilding Office to support national efforts to maintain constitutional order and to promote a multi-layered national dialogue towards peace and reconciliation,

Reaffirming the importance of preparedness by all Member States to detect, prevent, respond to, isolate and mitigate suspected cases of Ebola within and across borders, and recalling the International Health Regulations (2005),[184] which aim to improve the capacity of all countries to detect, assess, notify and respond to public health threats,

Reaffirming its full commitment to the consolidation of peace and stability in Guinea-Bissau,

1. *Decides* to extend the mandate of the United Nations Integrated Peacebuilding Office in Guinea-Bissau for a period of three months beginning on 1 December 2014 until 28 February 2015, to perform the following tasks:

(*a*) Supporting an inclusive political dialogue and national reconciliation process to facilitate democratic governance;

(*b*) Assisting in strengthening democratic institutions and enhancing the capacity of State organs to function effectively and constitutionally;

(*c*) Providing strategic and technical advice and support for the establishment of effective and efficient law enforcement and criminal justice and penitentiary systems, capable of maintaining public security and combating impunity, while respecting human rights and fundamental freedoms;

(*d*) Providing strategic and technical advice and support to national authorities and relevant stakeholders, including in coordination with the Economic Community of West African States and its Mission in Guinea-Bissau, in implementing the national security sector reform and rule of law strategies, as well as developing civilian and military justice systems that are compliant with international standards;

(*e*) Assisting national authorities to combat drug trafficking and transnational organized crime, in close cooperation with the United Nations Office on Drugs and Crime;

(*f*) Assisting national authorities in the promotion and protection of human rights as well as undertaking human rights monitoring and reporting activities;

(*g*) Mainstreaming a gender perspective into peacebuilding, in line with Security Council resolutions 1325 (2000) and 1820 (2008);

(*h*) Working with the Peacebuilding Commission in support of Guinea-Bissau's peacebuilding priorities;

(*i*) Contributing to the mobilization, harmonization and coordination of international assistance, including for the implementation of the national security sector reform and rule of law strategies, and enhancing cooperation with the African Union, the Economic Community of West African States, the Community of Portuguese-speaking Countries, the European Union and other partners in support of the maintenance of constitutional order and the stabilization of Guinea-Bissau;

2. *Reiterates its demand* to the security and defence services to submit themselves fully to civilian control;

3. *Urges* the authorities of Guinea-Bissau to take all measures necessary to protect human rights, put an end to impunity, initiate investigations to identify the perpetrators of human rights violations and abuses and bring them to justice and take action to protect witnesses in order to ensure due process;

[183] See S/PV.7315.

[184] World Health Organization, document WHA58/2005/REC/1, resolution 58.3, annex.

4. *Welcomes* the joint efforts by international partners, in particular the United Nations, the African Union, the Economic Community of West African States, the European Union and the Community of Portuguese-speaking Countries, to enhance cooperation in support of the legitimate democratic Government in Guinea-Bissau, and encourages them to continue to work together towards the stabilization of the country;

5. *Encourages* the efforts in support of security sector reform as a crucial element for long-term stability in Guinea-Bissau, and encourages coordinated action by all relevant subregional, regional and international partners of Guinea-Bissau in this field in order to obtain expeditious and positive results;

6. *Calls upon* the authorities of Guinea-Bissau to review, adopt and implement national legislation and mechanisms to more effectively combat transnational organized crime, in particular drug trafficking and money-laundering, and in this context to provide additional support to the Transnational Crime Unit established under the West Africa Coast Initiative, and urges both the authorities of Guinea-Bissau and its security and defence services to demonstrate full commitment to combating drug trafficking, and calls upon international partners to support their efforts;

7. *Encourages* members of the international community to enhance cooperation with Guinea-Bissau in order to enable it to ensure control of air traffic and surveillance of maritime security within its jurisdiction, in particular to fight drug trafficking and organized crime, as well as illegal fishing in Guinea-Bissau's territorial waters and exclusive economic zone and other cases of illegal exploitation of natural resources;

8. *Requests* the Special Representative of the Secretary-General for Guinea-Bissau to increase efforts to achieve greater coherence, coordination and efficiency among relevant United Nations agencies, funds and programmes in Guinea-Bissau to maximize their collective effectiveness towards combating drug trafficking, in particular through the provision by these agencies, funds and programmes of relevant information to the Special Representative on individuals, groups, undertakings and entities associated with drug trafficking that contribute to creating a threat to the peace, stability and security of Guinea-Bissau and the subregion;

9. *Invites* the Special Representative to share all relevant information with the Security Council Committee established pursuant to resolution 2048 (2012), particularly names of individuals who meet the criteria set forth in paragraph 6 and elaborated upon in paragraph 7 of resolution 2048 (2012);

10. *Stresses* the challenges posed by the fight against drug trafficking in the search for solutions to the overall political and economic crisis in Guinea-Bissau, and requests the Secretary-General to ensure the relevant capacity within the Integrated Peacebuilding Office, by continuing to provide an anti-drug component, including appropriate expertise;

11. *Encourages* international bilateral and multilateral partners to continue their technical support to Guinea-Bissau in strengthening efforts to tackle transnational organized crime, including illicit activities such as money-laundering and drug trafficking, calls upon them to increase their support to the West Africa Coast Initiative and the Transnational Crime Unit to fight transnational organized crime and drug trafficking, which threaten security and stability in Guinea-Bissau and in the subregion, and further encourages them to contribute to support the presence of the United Nations Office on Drugs and Crime in Guinea-Bissau and to the Integrated Peacebuilding Office trust fund for immediate, medium- and longer-term priorities, including for post-election reforms;

12. *Welcomes* the intention of the authorities of Guinea-Bissau to convene an international donor conference in Brussels in February 2015, and encourages participation by Member States;

13. *Urges* Guinea-Bissau to implement relevant temporary recommendations issued under the International Health Regulations (2005)[184] regarding the 2014 Ebola outbreak in West Africa, and to lead the organization, coordination and implementation of national preparedness and response activities, including, as appropriate, in collaboration with international development and humanitarian partners, including the Integrated Peacebuilding Office within its existing mandate;

14. *Looks forward* to the findings and recommendations of the strategic assessment mission to be included in the report of the Secretary-General in January 2015, with a view toward the consideration of such recommendations for appropriate adjustment to the mandate of the Integrated Peacebuilding Office;

15. *Decides* to remain actively seized of the matter.

Adopted unanimously at the 7321st meeting.

Decisions

At its 7376th meeting, on 5 February 2015, the Security Council decided to invite the representatives of Ghana, Guinea-Bissau and Timor-Leste to participate, without vote, in accordance with rule 37 of its provisional rules of procedure, in the discussion of the item entitled:

"The situation in Guinea-Bissau

"Report of the Secretary-General on developments in Guinea-Bissau and the activities of the United Nations Integrated Peacebuilding Office in Guinea-Bissau (S/2015/37)".

At the same meeting, the Council also decided to extend invitations, in accordance with rule 39 of its provisional rules of procedure, to Mr. Miguel Trovoada, Special Representative of the Secretary-General for Guinea-Bissau and Head of the United Nations Integrated Peacebuilding Office in Guinea-Bissau, and Mr. Antonio de Aguiar Patriota, Permanent Representative of Brazil to the United Nations, in his capacity as Chair of the Guinea-Bissau configuration of the Peacebuilding Commission.

At its 7385th meeting, on 18 February 2015, the Council considered the item entitled:

"The situation in Guinea-Bissau

"Report of the Secretary-General on developments in Guinea-Bissau and the activities of the United Nations Integrated Peacebuilding Office in Guinea-Bissau (S/2015/37)".

Resolution 2203 (2015)
of 18 February 2015

The Security Council,

Recalling its previous resolutions, the statements by its President and its statements to the press on the situation in Guinea-Bissau, in particular resolutions 1876 (2009) of 26 June 2009, 2030 (2011) of 21 December 2011, 2048 (2012) of 18 May 2012, 2092 (2013) of 22 February 2013, 2103 (2013) of 22 May 2013, 2157 (2014) of 29 May 2014 and 2186 (2014) of 25 November 2014,

Taking note of the report of the Secretary-General of 19 January 2015 on Guinea-Bissau[185] and the recommendations contained therein, and commending the engagement of the Special Representative of the Secretary-General for Guinea-Bissau and Head of the United Nations Integrated Peacebuilding Office in Guinea-Bissau,

Taking into consideration the recommendation of the Secretary-General to reinforce the role of the Special Representative in assisting the Government of Guinea-Bissau through the use of the good offices and in continuing to coordinate international support,

Welcoming the progress made by Guinea-Bissau, recognizing the concrete steps taken by the Government of Guinea-Bissau towards peace, security and stability in the country by continuing to take steps towards the reform of the security sector, tackling corruption through the reinforcement of the judicial system, and improving public administration and State revenue management, as well as the supply of basic services to the population, and commending its commitment to the implementation of its national priorities,

Welcoming also the establishment of the Peace and Stability Commission by the National Assembly, which constitutes a concrete step towards the establishment of a nationally owned reconciliation process, while recognizing the need for the Integrated Peacebuilding Office to support national efforts to maintain constitutional order and to promote a multi-layered national dialogue towards peace and reconciliation,

Emphasizing the need for respect of democratic principles, stressing the importance of national reconciliation, inclusive dialogue and good governance, essential for the attainment of lasting peace in Guinea-Bissau, further stressing the importance of including all Bissau-Guineans in this process at the national and local levels, while upholding the principles of the separation of powers, the rule of law, justice and combating impunity, and encouraging all stakeholders to engage in the process,

[185] S/2015/37.

Stressing that the consolidation of peace and stability in Guinea-Bissau can result only from a consensual, inclusive and nationally owned process, respect for constitutional order, priority reforms in the defence, security and justice sectors, the promotion of the rule of law, the protection of human rights, the promotion of socioeconomic development and the fight against impunity and drug trafficking,

Underscoring the importance of the Government of Guinea-Bissau, with the support of the Integrated Peacebuilding Office and international partners, continuing to develop national security and rule of law institutions that are transparent, accountable and professional,

Stressing that all stakeholders in Guinea-Bissau should work to ensure short-, medium- and long-term stability through clear commitment and genuine inclusive political dialogue aimed at creating conditions conducive to finding viable and sustainable solutions to the country's social, economic, political and military problems, which would facilitate the implementation of key reforms and the strengthening of State institutions,

Noting efforts of the Government of Guinea-Bissau to gain effective civilian control and oversight over the defence and security forces, as failure to do so could adversely affect the effective functioning of State institutions, as a result of collusion between some political actors and the military leadership,

Commending the efforts of the Economic Community of West African States in helping to sustain peace, security and development and to support the security sector reform process in Guinea-Bissau, namely through the activities of its Mission in Guinea-Bissau,

Welcoming the continued contribution of the Mission in ensuring an environment that enables the implementation of critical reforms in the defence and security sector, and encouraging the international community to support the continuation of such efforts,

Reiterating its call upon the Government of Guinea-Bissau to conduct transparent, independent and credible investigations into all alleged human rights violations and abuses, in accordance with international standards, and to hold those responsible accountable for their actions,

Reiterating its concern at the threat posed by drug trafficking and related transnational organized crime to peace and stability, and in this regard welcoming the efforts of the Government of Guinea-Bissau to update the three-year national plan for combating drug trafficking and organized crime, prepared in June 2011, and to define new priority areas accordingly,

Re-emphasizing the need to tackle the problem of drug trafficking in the countries of origin, transit and final destination on the basis of a common and shared responsibility, to tackle the world drug problem and related criminal activities, and in this regard stressing the need for increased coherence, coordination and efficiency among relevant partners to enhance their collective efforts, in particular through the sharing of information,

Reiterating the importance and urgency of the continued evaluation capacity and support provided by the relevant United Nations entities and international, regional, subregional and bilateral partners for the long-term security and development of Guinea-Bissau, particularly towards the implementation of security and justice sector reforms, the fight against drug trafficking, transnational organized crime and human trafficking, as well as the creation of an enabling environment for good governance and inclusive and sustainable social development, and in this regard commending the important work of the United Nations Office on Drugs and Crime in collaboration with relevant United Nations entities in Guinea-Bissau and the subregion, and encouraging enhanced cooperation between the Office and the Integrated Peacebuilding Office,

Underlining that any lasting solution to instability in Guinea-Bissau should include concrete actions to fight impunity and ensure that those responsible for politically motivated assassinations and other serious crimes such as breaches of constitutional order and drug trafficking-related activities are brought to justice, including through national judicial mechanisms,

Emphasizing the important role of women in the prevention and resolution of conflicts and in peacebuilding, as recognized in resolutions 1325 (2000) of 31 October 2000, 1820 (2008) of 19 June 2008, 1888 (2009) of 30 September 2009, 1889 (2009) of 5 October 2009, 1960 (2010) of 16 December 2010, 2106 (2013) of 24 June 2013 and 2122 (2013) of 18 October 2013, welcoming the cooperation between the Integrated Peacebuilding Office, national authorities and civil society organizations to increase women's participation in Guinea-Bissau, and underlining that a gender perspective must continue to inform the implementation of all relevant aspects of the mandate of the Integrated Peacebuilding Office,

Welcoming the establishment of a national technical commission with a focus on responsible extraction and exploitation of natural resources for inclusive growth and development,

Reaffirming that Guinea-Bissau's partners should continue to actively and closely coordinate their actions in support of the Government of Guinea-Bissau's efforts to address the country's political, security and development challenges, and in this regard welcoming the coordinated support provided by the country's partners, namely those in the United Nations system, the European Union, the World Bank, the African Union, the Economic Community of West African States, the Community of Portuguese-speaking Countries and the African Development Bank, to the Government to organize the international donor conference for Guinea-Bissau on 25 March 2015 in Brussels, and taking note of the final communiqué of 9 February 2015 issued by the preparatory meeting on the Guinea-Bissau international donor conference, held in Accra,

Taking note of the statement made by the Chair of the Guinea-Bissau configuration of the Peacebuilding Commission on 5 February 2015,[186] and welcoming the continued engagement of the Commission with Guinea-Bissau,

Emphasizing the importance of preventing the further spread of the Ebola virus disease, including to Guinea-Bissau, and the need for ongoing preparedness efforts to build domestic capacity to fight further transmission of the disease,

Reaffirming its full commitment to the consolidation of peace and stability in Guinea-Bissau,

1. *Decides* to extend the mandate of the United Nations Integrated Peacebuilding Office in Guinea-Bissau for a period of 12 months beginning on 1 March 2015 until 29 February 2016;

2. *Expresses its strong support* for the key role of the Special Representative of the Secretary-General for Guinea-Bissau, and requests the Integrated Peacebuilding Office, including through the use of the good offices and political support of the Special Representative, to focus, in particular, on the following priorities:

(*a*) Support an inclusive political dialogue and national reconciliation process to strengthen democratic governance and work towards consensus on key political issues, particularly with regard to the implementation of necessary urgent reforms;

(*b*) Provide strategic and technical advice and support to national authorities and relevant stakeholders, including in coordination with the Economic Community of West African States and its Mission in Guinea-Bissau and other international partners, in implementing the national security sector reform and rule of law strategies, as well as developing civilian and military justice systems that are compliant with international standards;

(*c*) Support the Government of Guinea-Bissau towards the mobilization, harmonization and coordination of international assistance, including for the implementation of the national security sector reform and rule of law strategies, and enhance cooperation with the African Union, the Economic Community of West African States, the Community of Portuguese-speaking Countries, the European Union and other partners in support of the maintenance of constitutional order and the stabilization of Guinea-Bissau;

3. *Affirms* that the Integrated Peacebuilding Office and the Special Representative will continue to lead international efforts in the following priority areas:

(*a*) Provide support to the Government of Guinea-Bissau in strengthening democratic institutions and enhancing the capacity of State organs to function effectively and constitutionally;

(*b*) Provide strategic and technical advice and support for the establishment of effective and efficient law enforcement and criminal justice and penitentiary systems, capable of maintaining public security and combating impunity, while respecting human rights and fundamental freedoms;

(*c*) Assist national authorities in the promotion and protection of human rights as well as undertaking human rights monitoring and reporting activities;

(*d*) Provide strategic and technical advice and support to the Government of Guinea-Bissau to combat drug trafficking and transnational organized crime, in close cooperation with the United Nations Office on Drugs and Crime;

[186] See S/PV.7376.

(*e*) Provide support to the Government of Guinea-Bissau to incorporate a gender perspective into peacebuilding, in line with Security Council resolutions 1325 (2000) and 1820 (2008), as well as the implementation of the national action plan on gender in order to ensure the involvement, representation and participation of women at all levels through, inter alia, the provision of gender advisers;

(*f*) Work with the Peacebuilding Commission in support of Guinea-Bissau's peacebuilding priorities;

4. *Calls upon* the authorities of Guinea-Bissau and all stakeholders, including the military, political parties, and civil society, to work together to consolidate the progress made so far and to address the root causes of instability, with particular attention to political-military dynamics, ineffective State institutions and the rule of law, impunity and human rights violations and abuses, poverty and lack of access to basic services;

5. *Reiterates its demand* to the security and defence services to submit themselves fully to civilian control;

6. *Takes note* of the evolving human rights situation in the country, and urges the authorities of Guinea-Bissau to take all measures necessary to protect human rights, put an end to impunity, initiate investigations to identify the perpetrators of human rights violations and abuses, including those against women and children, and bring them to justice and take action to protect witnesses in order to ensure due process;

7. *Welcomes* the joint efforts by international partners, in particular the United Nations, the African Union, the Economic Community of West African States, the European Union and the Community of Portuguese-speaking Countries, to enhance cooperation in support of the Government of Guinea-Bissau, and encourages them to continue to work together towards the stabilization of the country in accordance with the priority structural reforms established by the Government;

8. *Recognizes* the commencement of the implementation of defence and security sector reforms, encourages the continuation of such efforts as a crucial element for long-term stability in Guinea-Bissau, and further encourages coordinated action by all relevant subregional, regional and international partners of Guinea-Bissau in this field in order to obtain expeditious and positive results;

9. *Also recognizes* the important role of the Mission in securing the State institutions and in supporting security sector reform, supports its continuation, in accordance with the expressed will of the authorities of Guinea-Bissau, and encourages the support of the international community to it, as requested by the Heads of State and Government of the Economic Community of West African States at its forty-sixth ordinary summit;

10. *Calls upon* the authorities of Guinea-Bissau to continue to actively reform and strengthen the judicial system, while ensuring the separation of powers and access to justice for all citizens;

11. *Also calls upon* the authorities of Guinea-Bissau to review, adopt and implement national legislation and mechanisms to more effectively combat transnational organized crime, in particular drug trafficking and money-laundering, and in this context to provide additional support to the Transnational Crime Unit established under the West Africa Coast Initiative and the Intergovernmental Action Group against Money Laundering in West Africa, and urges the authorities of Guinea-Bissau to demonstrate full commitment to combating drug trafficking;

12. *Encourages* members of the international community to enhance cooperation with Guinea-Bissau in order to enable it to ensure control of air traffic and surveillance of maritime security within its jurisdiction, in particular to fight drug trafficking and organized crime, as well as illegal fishing in Guinea-Bissau's territorial waters and exclusive economic zone and other cases of illegal exploitation of natural resources;

13. *Encourages* international bilateral and multilateral partners to continue their technical support to Guinea-Bissau in strengthening efforts to tackle transnational organized crime, including illicit activities, such as money-laundering and drug trafficking, calls upon them to increase their support to the West Africa Coast Initiative and the Transnational Crime Unit to fight transnational organized crime and drug trafficking, which threaten security and stability in Guinea-Bissau and in the subregion, and further encourages them to contribute to support the presence of the United Nations Office on Drugs and Crime in Guinea-Bissau and to the Integrated Peacebuilding Office trust fund for immediate, medium- and longer-term priorities, including for post-election reforms;

14. *Stresses* the importance of combating drug trafficking to achieve political and economic stability in Guinea-Bissau, requests the Secretary-General to ensure the relevant capacity within the Integrated Peacebuilding

Office by continuing to provide an anti-drug component, including appropriate expertise, and further requests the Special Representative of the Secretary-General to increase efforts to achieve greater coherence, coordination and efficiency among relevant United Nations agencies, funds and programmes in the country to maximize their collective effectiveness, in particular through provision by these agencies, funds and programmes of relevant information to the Special Representative on individuals, groups, undertakings and entities associated with drug trafficking that contribute to creating a threat to the peace, stability and security of Guinea-Bissau and the subregion;

15. *Commends* the good offices role of the Special Representative of the Secretary-General to support the Government of Guinea-Bissau, and invites the Secretary-General to reinforce the capacities of the Integrated Peacebuilding Office in this regard and to continue to strengthen the coordination of international support;

16. *Welcomes* the convening of an international donor conference in Brussels in March 2015, and strongly encourages the international community to support Guinea-Bissau in mobilizing resources to implement government priorities and start the long-term work of stabilizing the country in order to move it towards sustainable development, and also encourages the Integrated Peacebuilding Office to assist in the coordination of international assistance to the Government of Guinea-Bissau in its fight against poverty;

17. *Also welcomes* steps taken by Guinea-Bissau in building domestic capacity to prevent transmission of the Ebola virus disease, and encourages the continuation of efforts aimed at further developing national capacities and practices for the prevention of and response to the disease;

18. *Requests* the Secretary-General to submit to the Security Council regular reports every six months on the implementation of the present resolution and to submit a report within six months to the Security Council Committee established pursuant to resolution 2048 (2012) on the progress made with regard to the stabilization of the country and the restoration of constitutional order and recommendations on the continuation of the sanctions regime in the post-election environment, in line with paragraph 12 of resolution 2048 (2012);

19. *Decides* to review the sanctions measures established pursuant to resolution 2048 (2012) seven months from the adoption of the present resolution;

20. *Also decides* to remain actively seized of the matter.

Adopted unanimously at the 7385th meeting.

PROTECTION OF CIVILIANS IN ARMED CONFLICT[187]

Decisions

At its 7244th meeting, on 19 August 2014, the Security Council considered the item entitled:

"Protection of civilians in armed conflict

"World Humanitarian Day

"Letter dated 5 August 2014 from the Permanent Representative of the United Kingdom of Great Britain and Northern Ireland to the United Nations addressed to the Secretary-General (S/2014/571)".

At the same meeting, the Council decided to extend an invitation, in accordance with rule 39 of its provisional rules of procedure, to Mr. Peter Maurer, President of the International Committee of the Red Cross.

At the same meeting, the Council also decided to extend an invitation, in accordance with rule 39 of its provisional rules of procedure, to Mr. Masood Karokhail, Director and co-founder of The Liaison Office.

At its 7256th meeting, on 29 August 2014, the Council considered the item entitled "Protection of civilians in armed conflict".

[187] Resolutions or decisions on this question were first adopted by the Security Council in 1999.

Resolution 2175 (2014)
of 29 August 2014

The Security Council,

Reiterating its primary responsibility for the maintenance of international peace and security and, in this context, the need to promote and ensure respect for the principles and rules of international humanitarian law,

Recalling its resolution 1502 (2003) of 26 August 2003 on the protection of humanitarian personnel, its resolutions 1265 (1999) of 17 September 1999, 1296 (2000) of 19 April 2000, 1674 (2006) of 28 April 2006, 1738 (2006) of 23 December 2006 and 1894 (2009) of 11 November 2009 on the protection of civilians in armed conflict, as well as other relevant resolutions and statements by its President on the protection of civilians in armed conflict and on the protection of United Nations personnel, associated personnel and humanitarian personnel in conflict zones,

Recalling also the Geneva Conventions of 1949[188] and the Additional Protocols thereto of 1977,[189] and the obligation of parties to armed conflict to respect and ensure respect for international humanitarian law in all circumstances,

Recalling further the Convention on the Safety of United Nations and Associated Personnel[190] and the Optional Protocol thereto,[191]

Recalling all relevant General Assembly resolutions, including resolutions 68/101, entitled "Safety and security of humanitarian personnel and protection of United Nations personnel", and 68/102, entitled "Strengthening of the coordination of emergency humanitarian assistance of the United Nations", of 13 December 2013,

Reaffirming the need for all parties to armed conflict to respect the humanitarian principles of humanity, neutrality, impartiality and independence in order to ensure the provision of humanitarian assistance, the safety of civilians receiving assistance and the security of humanitarian personnel and United Nations and associated personnel,

Recalling the inclusion of attacks intentionally directed against personnel involved in a humanitarian assistance or peacekeeping mission in accordance with the Charter of the United Nations, as long as they are entitled to the protection given to civilians or civilian objects under the international law of armed conflict, as a war crime in the Rome Statute of the International Criminal Court,[192]

Emphasizing the responsibility of States to comply with their relevant obligations to end impunity and to thoroughly investigate and prosecute persons responsible for genocide, crimes against humanity and war crimes, in order to prevent these crimes, avoid their recurrence and seek sustainable peace, justice, truth and reconciliation, and in this regard reaffirming the need to end impunity for serious violations of international humanitarian law, including those involving attacks against humanitarian personnel,

Stressing that the fight against impunity and to ensure accountability for genocide, crimes against humanity, war crimes and other egregious crimes has been strengthened through the work on and prosecution of these crimes in the international criminal justice system, ad hoc and mixed tribunals as well as specialized chambers in national tribunals; and recognizing in this regard the contribution of the International Criminal Court, in accordance with the principle of complementarity to national criminal jurisdictions as set out in the Rome Statute, towards holding accountable those responsible for such crimes, and reiterating its call on the importance of State cooperation with these courts and tribunals in accordance with the States' respective obligations,

Recalling that the primary responsibility under international law for the security and protection of humanitarian personnel and United Nations and associated personnel lies with the Government hosting a United Nations operation conducted under the Charter or its agreements with relevant organizations,

---

[188] United Nations, *Treaty Series*, vol. 75, Nos. 970–973.

[189] Ibid., vol. 1125, Nos. 17512 and 17513.

[190] Ibid., vol. 2051, No. 35457.

[191] Ibid., vol. 2689, No. 35457.

[192] Ibid., vol. 2187, No. 38544.

Gravely concerned at the growing number of acts of violence in many parts of the world against national and international personnel of humanitarian organizations, United Nations personnel and associated personnel, and humanitarian assets, including humanitarian supplies, facilities and transports, in particular deliberate attacks which are in violation of international humanitarian law, as well as other applicable international law, and the adverse impact of such violence, including on humanitarian access, exacerbated by the presence of armed actors, including non-State armed groups and terrorist and criminal networks, and their activities,

1. *Reaffirms* the obligation of all parties involved in an armed conflict to comply with international humanitarian law, in particular their obligations under the Geneva Conventions of 1949[188] and the obligations applicable to them under the Additional Protocols thereto of 1977,[189] to ensure the respect and protection of all humanitarian personnel and United Nations and associated personnel, as well as with the rules and principles of international human rights law and refugee law;

2. *Strongly condemns* all forms of violence and intimidation, including murder, rape and sexual assault, armed robbery, abduction, hostage-taking, kidnapping, harassment and illegal arrest and detention to which those participating in humanitarian operations are increasingly exposed, as well as attacks on humanitarian convoys and acts of destruction and looting of their assets;

3. *Urges* all parties involved in an armed conflict to allow full unimpeded access by humanitarian personnel to all people in need of assistance and to make available, as far as possible, all necessary facilities for their operations, and to promote the safety, security and freedom of movement of humanitarian personnel and United Nations and associated personnel and their assets;

4. *Urges* States to ensure that crimes against humanitarian personnel do not remain unpunished, affirming the need for States to ensure that perpetrators of attacks committed on their territory against such personnel do not operate with impunity, and that perpetrators of such acts are brought to justice, as provided for by national laws and obligations under international law;

5. *Reaffirms* the obligation of all humanitarian personnel and United Nations and associated personnel to observe and respect the laws of the country in which they are operating, in accordance with international law and the Charter of the United Nations, and underlines the importance for humanitarian organizations to uphold the principles of humanity, neutrality, impartiality and independence in their humanitarian activities;

6. *Expresses its determination* to take appropriate steps in order to ensure the safety and security of humanitarian personnel and United Nations and associated personnel, including by:

(*a*) Ensuring that the mandates of relevant United Nations peacekeeping operations can, where appropriate and on a case-by-case basis, help to contribute to a secure environment to enable the delivery of humanitarian assistance by humanitarian organizations, in accordance with humanitarian principles;

(*b*) Requesting the Secretary-General to seek the inclusion of, and that host countries include, key provisions of the Convention on the Safety of United Nations and Associated Personnel,[190] including those regarding the prevention of attacks against members of United Nations operations, the establishment of such attacks as crimes punishable by law and the prosecution or extradition of offenders, in future as well as, if necessary, in existing status-of-forces, status-of-mission and host country agreements negotiated between the United Nations and those countries, mindful of the importance of the timely conclusion of such agreements;

(*c*) Encouraging the Secretary-General, in accordance with his prerogatives under the Charter, to bring to the attention of the Security Council situations in which humanitarian assistance is unable to reach people in need as a consequence of violence directed against humanitarian personnel and United Nations and associated personnel;

(*d*) Issuing the declaration of exceptional risk for the purposes of article 1 (*c*) (ii) of the Convention, in situations where in its assessment circumstances would support such a declaration, and inviting the Secretary-General to advise the Council, where in his assessment circumstances would support such a declaration;

(*e*) Calling upon all States to consider becoming parties to the Convention and the Optional Protocol thereto,[191] and urging States parties to take steps to enable its effective implementation;

7. *Requests* the Secretary-General to include in all his country-specific situation reports, and other relevant reports which address the protection of civilians, the issue of the safety and security of humanitarian personnel and United Nations and associated personnel, including recording specific acts of violence against such personnel,

remedial actions taken to prevent similar incidents and actions taken to identify and hold accountable those who commit such acts, and to provide the Council with recommendations on measures to prevent similar incidents, ensure accountability and enhance the safety and security of such personnel.

Adopted unanimously at the 7256th meeting.

Decisions

At its 7374th meeting, on 30 January 2015, the Security Council decided to invite the representatives of Afghanistan, Albania, Argentina, Australia, Austria, Azerbaijan, Belgium, Botswana, Brazil, Burundi, Canada, Colombia, Costa Rica, Croatia, Egypt, Germany, Guatemala, India, Indonesia, Iran (Islamic Republic of), Ireland, Israel, Italy, Japan, Kazakhstan, Latvia, Liechtenstein, Luxembourg, Mexico, Morocco, the Netherlands, Pakistan, Poland, the Republic of Korea, Rwanda, Saudi Arabia, Senegal, Slovakia, South Africa, the Sudan, Sweden, Switzerland, the Syrian Arab Republic, Thailand, Turkey, Ukraine, Uruguay and Zimbabwe to participate, without vote, in accordance with rule 37 of its provisional rules of procedure, in the discussion of the item entitled:

"Protection of civilians in armed conflict

"Letter dated 16 January 2015 from the Permanent Representative of Chile to the United Nations addressed to the Secretary-General (S/2015/32)".

At the same meeting, the Council also decided to extend an invitation, in accordance with rule 39 of its provisional rules of procedure, to Ms. Kyung-wha Kang, Assistant Secretary-General for Humanitarian Affairs and Deputy Emergency Relief Coordinator.

At the same meeting, the Council further decided to extend invitations, in accordance with rule 39 of its provisional rules of procedure, to Ms. Helen Durham, Director for International Law and Policy of the International Committee of the Red Cross, and Ms. Ilwad Elman, representative of the NGO Working Group on Women, Peace and Security.

At the same meeting, the Council decided to extend an invitation, in accordance with rule 39 of its provisional rules of procedure, to Mr. Ioannis Vrailas, Deputy Head of the Delegation of the European Union to the United Nations.

At the same meeting, the Council also decided to extend an invitation to the Chargé d'affaires ad interim of the Permanent Observer Mission of the Holy See to the United Nations, in accordance with the provisional rules of procedure of the Council and its previous practice in that regard.

At its 7450th meeting, on 27 May 2015, the Council decided to invite the representatives of Albania, Argentina, Australia, Austria, Azerbaijan, Belgium, Bosnia and Herzegovina, Botswana, Brazil, Bulgaria, Canada, Colombia, Croatia, Cyprus, the Czech Republic, Denmark, Egypt, Estonia, Finland, Georgia, Germany, Greece, Hungary, Iceland, India, Indonesia, Iran (Islamic Republic of), Ireland, Israel, Italy, Japan, Kazakhstan, Kuwait, Latvia, Lebanon, Liechtenstein, Luxembourg, Montenegro, Morocco, the Netherlands, Norway, Pakistan, Palau, Poland, Qatar, the Republic of Moldova, Romania, Serbia, Slovakia, Slovenia, South Africa, Sweden, Switzerland, the Syrian Arab Republic, Thailand, the former Yugoslav Republic of Macedonia, Turkey and Ukraine to participate, without vote, in accordance with rule 37 of its provisional rules of procedure, in the discussion of the item entitled:

"Protection of civilians in armed conflict

"The protection of journalists in conflict situations

"Letter dated 1 May 2015 from the Permanent Representative of Lithuania to the United Nations addressed to the Secretary-General (S/2015/307)".

At the same meeting, the Council also decided to extend an invitation, in accordance with rule 39 of its provisional rules of procedure, to Mr. Christophe Deloire, Director-General of Reporters without Borders, and Ms. Mariane Pearl.

At the same meeting, the Council further decided to extend invitations, in accordance with rule 39 of its provisional rules of procedure, to Mr. Ioannis Vrailas, Deputy Head of the Delegation of the European Union to the United Nations, and Mr. Téte António, Permanent Observer of the African Union to the United Nations.

At the same meeting, the Council decided to extend an invitation to the Permanent Observer of the Observer State of the Holy See to the United Nations, in accordance with the provisional rules of procedure of the Council and its previous practice in that regard.

Resolution 2222 (2015) of 27 May 2015

The Security Council,

Bearing in mind its primary responsibility under the Charter of the United Nations for the maintenance of international peace and security, and underlining the importance of taking measures aimed at conflict prevention and resolution,

Reaffirming its resolutions 1265 (1999) of 17 September 1999, 1296 (2000) of 19 April 2000, 1674 (2006) of 28 April 2006 and 1894 (2009) of 11 November 2009 on the protection of civilians in armed conflict and its resolution 1738 (2006) of 23 December 2006 on the protection of journalists, media professionals and associated personnel in armed conflicts, as well as other relevant resolutions and statements by its President,

Reaffirming its commitment to the purposes of the Charter as set out in Article 1, paragraphs 1 to 4, of the Charter, and to the principles of the Charter as set out in Article 2, paragraphs 1 to 7, of the Charter, including its commitment to the principles of the political independence, sovereign equality and territorial integrity of all States and respect for the sovereignty of all States,

Recalling the Geneva Conventions of 12 August 1949,[188] in particular the Third Geneva Convention on the treatment of prisoners of war, and the Additional Protocols to the Conventions, of 8 June 1977,[189] in particular article 79 of Additional Protocol I regarding the protection of journalists engaged in dangerous professional missions in areas of armed conflict,

Recognizing that the work of journalists, media professionals and associated personnel often puts them at specific risk of intimidation, harassment and violence in situations of armed conflict,

Reaffirming that parties to an armed conflict bear the primary responsibility to take all feasible steps to ensure the protection of affected civilians, including those who exercise their right to freedom of expression by seeking, receiving and disseminating information by different means, online as well as offline, in accordance with article 19 of the International Covenant on Civil and Political Rights,[193]

Recognizing the important role of international humanitarian law, and international human rights law as applicable, in protecting journalists, media professionals and associated personnel in armed conflicts,

Further recognizing that States bear the primary responsibility to respect and ensure the human rights of their citizens, as well as individuals within their territory as provided for by relevant international law,

Recalling the right to freedom of expression reflected in article 19 of the Universal Declaration of Human Rights adopted by the General Assembly in 1948,[194] and recalling also the right to freedom of expression reflected in article 19 of the International Covenant on Civil and Political Rights adopted by the Assembly in 1966, and that any restrictions thereon shall only be such as are provided by law and are necessary on the grounds set out in paragraph 3 of article 19 of the Covenant,

Deeply concerned at the frequency of acts of violence in many parts of the world against journalists, media professionals and associated personnel in armed conflict, in particular deliberate attacks in violation of international humanitarian law,

Emphasizing that there are existing prohibitions under international humanitarian law against attacks intentionally directed against civilians, as such, which in situations of armed conflict constitute war crimes, and recalling the need for States to end impunity for such criminal acts,

---

[193] See General Assembly resolution 2200 A (XXI), annex.

[194] General Assembly resolution 217 A (III).

Bearing in mind that impunity for crimes committed against journalists, media professionals and associated personnel in armed conflict remains a significant challenge to their protection and that ensuring accountability for crimes committed against them is a key element in preventing future attacks,

Recognizing that journalists, media professionals and associated personnel can play an important role in the protection of civilians and conflict prevention by acting as an early warning mechanism in identifying and reporting potential situations that could result in genocide, war crimes, ethnic cleansing and crimes against humanity,

Reaffirming its condemnation of all incitements to violence against civilians in situations of armed conflict, and condemning the use of the media to incite violence, genocide, crimes against humanity and other serious violations of international humanitarian law,

Recalling that States parties to the Geneva Conventions have an obligation to search for persons alleged to have committed or to have ordered to be committed a grave breach of these Conventions, and an obligation to try them before their own courts, regardless of their nationality, or may hand them over for trial to another concerned State, provided that this State has made out a prima facie case against the said persons,

Further recalling the responsibility of all Member States to comply with their respective obligations to end impunity and to investigate and prosecute those responsible for genocide, crimes against humanity, war crimes or other serious violations of international humanitarian law, and noting that the fight against impunity for the most serious crimes of international concern committed against civilians has been strengthened through the work on and prosecution of these crimes by the International Criminal Court, in accordance with the principle of complementarity to national criminal jurisdictions as set out in the Rome Statute of the Court,[192] ad hoc and mixed tribunals and specialized chambers in national tribunals,

Expressing deep concern at the growing threat to the safety of journalists, media professionals and associated personnel posed by terrorist groups, and strongly condemning incidents of killing, kidnapping and hostage-taking committed by terrorist groups for any purpose, including raising funds or gaining political concessions, and expressing its determination to prevent kidnapping and hostage-taking committed by terrorist groups and to secure the safe release of hostages without ransom payments or political concessions, in accordance with applicable international law,

Stressing the contribution that peacekeeping operations and special political missions, where mandated, can make to international efforts to promote and protect human rights and the protection of civilians, including journalists, media professionals and associated personnel, including through monitoring and reporting on violations and abuses as well as providing support for the efforts of national Governments to promote and protect human rights, and in order to strengthen the fight against impunity for crimes committed against civilians, including journalists, media professionals and associated personnel,

Recognizing the importance of a comprehensive, coherent and action-oriented approach, including in early planning, of the protection of civilians in situations of armed conflict, and stressing in this regard the need to adopt a broad strategy of conflict prevention which addresses the root causes of armed conflict in a comprehensive manner in order to enhance the protection of civilians on a long-term basis, including by promoting sustainable development, poverty eradication, national reconciliation, good governance, democracy, the rule of law and respect for and protection of human rights,

Acknowledging the important role that regional and subregional organizations can play in ensuring the protection of journalists, media professionals and associated personnel in armed conflicts and the importance of effective cooperation between the United Nations and those organizations,

Further acknowledging the specific risks faced by women journalists, media professionals and associated personnel in the conduct of their work, and underlining in this context the importance of considering the gender dimension of measures to address their safety in situations of armed conflict,

Recognizing that the consideration of the issue of the protection of journalists in armed conflict by the Security Council is based on the urgency and importance of this issue, and recognizing the valuable role that the Secretary-General can play in providing more information on this issue,

1. *Condemns* all violations and abuses committed against journalists, media professionals and associated personnel in situations of armed conflict, and calls upon all parties to armed conflict to bring an end to such practices;

2. *Affirms* that the work of a free, independent and impartial media constitutes one of the essential foundations of a democratic society and thereby can contribute to the protection of civilians;

3. *Recalls*, in this regard, that journalists, media professionals and associated personnel engaged in dangerous professional missions in areas of armed conflict shall be considered as civilians and shall be respected and protected as such, provided that they take no action adversely affecting their status as civilians; this is without prejudice to the right of war correspondents accredited to the armed forces to the status of prisoners of war provided for in article 4.A, paragraph 4, of the Third Geneva Convention;[195]

4. *Strongly condemns* the prevailing impunity for violations and abuses committed against journalists, media professionals and associated personnel in situations of armed conflict, which in turn may contribute to the recurrence of these acts;

5. *Emphasizes* the responsibility of States to comply with the relevant obligations under international law to end impunity and to prosecute those responsible for serious violations of international humanitarian law;

6. *Urges* Member States to take appropriate steps to ensure accountability for crimes committed against journalists, media professionals and associated personnel in situations of armed conflict through the conduct of impartial, independent and effective investigations within their jurisdiction and to bring perpetrators of such crimes to justice;

7. *Recalls its demand* that all parties to an armed conflict comply fully with the obligations applicable to them under international law related to the protection of civilians in armed conflict, including journalists, media professionals and associated personnel;

8. *Urges* the immediate and unconditional release of journalists, media professionals and associated personnel who have been kidnapped or taken as hostages in situations of armed conflict;

9. *Urges* all parties involved in situations of armed conflict to respect the professional independence and rights of journalists, media professionals and associated personnel as civilians;

10. *Recalls* that media equipment and installations constitute civilian objects, and in this respect shall not be the object of attack or of reprisals, unless they are military objectives;

11. *Recognizes* the important role that education and training in international humanitarian law can play in supporting efforts to halt and prevent attacks against civilians affected by armed conflict, including journalists, media professionals and associated personnel;

12. *Affirms* that United Nations peacekeeping and special political missions, where appropriate, should include in their mandated reporting information on specific acts of violence against journalists, media professionals and associated personnel in situations of armed conflict;

13. *Urges* all parties to armed conflict to do their utmost to prevent violations of international humanitarian law against civilians, including journalists, media professionals and associated personnel;

14. *Calls upon* Member States to create and maintain, in law and in practice, a safe and enabling environment for journalists, media professionals and associated personnel to perform their work independently and without undue interference in situations of armed conflict;

15. *Stresses* the need to ensure better cooperation and coordination at the international level, including among the United Nations and relevant international, regional and subregional organizations, including through technical assistance and capacity-building, with regard to promoting and ensuring the safety of journalists, media professionals and associated personnel in armed conflict;

16. *Encourages* the United Nations and regional and subregional organizations to share expertise on good practices and lessons learned on the protection of journalists, media professionals and associated personnel in armed conflict and, in close cooperation, to enhance the coherent and effective implementation of applicable international humanitarian law and relevant Security Council resolutions, including those on the protection of journalists, media professionals and associated personnel in situations of armed conflict;

---

[195] United Nations, *Treaty Series*, vol. 75, No. 972.

17. *Invites* States that have not yet done so to consider becoming parties to Additional Protocols I and II to the Geneva Conventions, of 8 June 1977[189] at the earliest possible date;

18. *Reaffirms* that it will continue to address the issue of the protection of journalists in armed conflict;

19. *Requests* the Secretary-General to include consistently as a sub-item in his reports on the protection of civilians in armed conflict the issue of the safety and security of journalists, media professionals and associated personnel, including the existence of measures to protect such individuals facing an imminent threat, and to ensure that information on attacks and violence against journalists, media professionals and associated personnel and preventative actions taken to prevent such incidents is included as a specific aspect in relevant country-specific reports.

Adopted unanimously at the 7450th meeting.

SMALL ARMS[196]

Decisions

At its 7442nd meeting, on 13 May 2015, the Security Council decided to invite the representatives of Algeria, Argentina, Armenia, Australia, Austria, Belgium, Benin, Botswana, Brazil, Colombia, Croatia, the Dominican Republic, Egypt, Finland, Germany, Guatemala, India, Indonesia, Iraq, Ireland, Israel, Italy, Japan, Kazakhstan, Kenya, Mexico, Montenegro, Morocco, Mozambique, the Netherlands, Pakistan, Paraguay, the Republic of Korea, the Republic of Moldova, Romania, Serbia, Slovakia, Slovenia, South Africa, Sweden, Switzerland, Thailand, Turkey and Ukraine to participate, without vote, in accordance with rule 37 of its provisional rules of procedure, in the discussion of the item entitled:

"Small arms

"The human cost of the illicit transfer, destabilizing accumulation and misuse of small arms and light weapons

"Report of the Secretary-General on small arms and light weapons (S/2015/289)

"Letter dated 1 May 2015 from the Permanent Representative of Lithuania to the United Nations addressed to the Secretary-General (S/2015/306)".

At the same meeting, the Council also decided to extend an invitation, in accordance with rule 39 of its provisional rules of procedure, to Mr. Zeid Ra'ad Al Hussein, United Nations High Commissioner for Human Rights.

At the same meeting, the Council further decided to extend an invitation, in accordance with rule 39 of its provisional rules of procedure, to Mr. Karamoko Diakité, President of the Côte d'Ivoire chapter of the West African Action Network on Small Arms.

At the same meeting, the Council decided to extend invitations, in accordance with rule 39 of its provisional rules of procedure, to Mr. Téte António, Permanent Observer of the African Union to the United Nations, and Mr. Thomas Mayr-Harting, Head of the Delegation of the European Union to the United Nations.

At its 7447th meeting, on 22 May 2015, the Council decided to invite the representatives of Albania, Australia, Austria, Barbados, Belgium, Bosnia and Herzegovina, Bulgaria, Costa Rica, Côte d'Ivoire, Croatia, Cyprus, the Czech Republic, Denmark, Estonia, Finland, Georgia, Germany, Greece, Guyana, Hungary, Iceland, Ireland, Italy, Jamaica, Japan, Latvia, Liechtenstein, Luxembourg, Malta, Montenegro, Morocco, the Netherlands, Norway, Palau, Paraguay, Poland, Portugal, the Republic of Korea, the Republic of Moldova, Romania, Samoa, Serbia, Seychelles,

---

[196] Resolutions or decisions on this question were first adopted by the Security Council in 1999.

Slovakia, Slovenia, Somalia, Sweden, Switzerland, the former Yugoslav Republic of Macedonia, Trinidad and Tobago and Ukraine to participate, without vote, in accordance with rule 37 of its provisional rules of procedure, in the discussion of the item entitled:

"Small arms

"Report of the Secretary-General on small arms and light weapons (S/2015/289)".

Resolution 2220 (2015)
of 22 May 2015

The Security Council,

Recalling its primary responsibility under the Charter of the United Nations for the maintenance of international peace and security, noting the significance of small arms and light weapons as the most frequently used weapons in the majority of recent armed conflicts, and emphasizing that the excessive accumulation and destabilizing effect of small arms and light weapons have a potential to endanger civilians, including women, children, refugees, internally displaced persons and other vulnerable groups,

Recalling also its resolutions 1196 (1998) of 16 September 1998, 1209 (1998) of 19 November 1998, 1467 (2003) of 18 March 2003 and 2117 (2013) on 26 September 2013, the statements by its President of 24 September 1999,[197] 31 August 2001,[198] 31 October 2002,[199] 19 January 2004,[200] 17 February 2005,[201] 29 June 2007,[202] 14 January 2009,[203] 19 March 2010[204] and 25 April 2012,[205] as well as other relevant resolutions of the Security Council and statements by its President, including on the protection of civilians in armed conflict, women and peace and security and children in armed conflict,

Emphasizing that the right of individual and collective self-defence recognized in Article 51 of the Charter and the legitimate security demands of all countries should be fully taken into account, and recognizing that small arms and light weapons are traded, manufactured and retained by States for legitimate security, sporting and commercial considerations,

Noting that the present resolution focuses on the illicit transfer, destabilizing accumulation and misuse of small arms and light weapons, including in respect of Council-mandated arms embargoes,

Gravely concerned that the illicit transfer, destabilizing accumulation and misuse of small arms and light weapons in many regions of the world continue to pose threats to international peace and security, cause significant loss of life, contribute to instability and insecurity and continue to undermine the effectiveness of the Council in discharging its primary responsibility for the maintenance of international peace and security,

Reiterating its deep regret that civilians continue to account for the vast majority of casualties in situations of armed conflict, and recalling with grave concern that the illicit transfer, destabilizing accumulation and misuse of small arms and light weapons fuel armed conflicts and have a wide range of negative human rights, humanitarian, development and socioeconomic consequences, in particular on the security of civilians in armed conflict, including the disproportionate impact on violence perpetrated against women and girls and exacerbating sexual and gender-based violence,

Gravely concerned by the detrimental effects of the illicit transfer, destabilizing accumulation and misuse of small arms and light weapons on children in armed conflict, in particular due to recruitment and use of children by

---

[197] S/PRST/1999/28.

[198] S/PRST/2001/21.

[199] S/PRST/2002/30.

[200] S/PRST/2004/1.

[201] S/PRST/2005/7.

[202] S/PRST/2007/24.

[203] S/PRST/2009/1.

[204] S/PRST/2010/6.

[205] S/PRST/2012/16.

parties to armed conflict, as well as their rerecruitment, killing and maiming, rape and other sexual violence, abductions, and attacks on schools and hospitals in violation of international law,

Recalling the Geneva Conventions of 1949[206] and the Additional Protocols thereto of 1977[207] and the obligation to respect and ensure respect for international humanitarian law in all circumstances,

Underlining the responsibility of States to prevent threats posed by the illicit transfer, destabilizing accumulation and misuse of small arms and light weapons to international peace and security, and the devastating impact on civilians in armed conflict, and reaffirming that parties to armed conflict bear the primary responsibility to take all feasible steps to ensure the protection of civilians and recalling that States bear the primary responsibility to respect and ensure the human rights of all individuals within their territory and subject to their jurisdiction, as provided for by relevant international law,

Recognizing that the misuse of small arms and light weapons has resulted in grave crimes, expressing its strong opposition to impunity for serious violations of international humanitarian law and serious violations and abuses of human rights, and emphasizing in this context the responsibility of States to comply with their relevant obligations to end impunity and to thoroughly investigate and prosecute persons responsible for war crimes, genocide, crimes against humanity or other serious violations of international humanitarian law, consistent with their obligations under international law,

Reaffirming the relevant provisions of the 2005 World Summit Outcome[208] regarding the protection of civilians in armed conflict, including paragraphs 138 and 139 thereof regarding the responsibility to protect populations from genocide, war crimes, ethnic cleansing and crimes against humanity,

Recognizing that efforts by the United Nations aimed at addressing the illicit transfer, destabilizing accumulation and misuse of small arms and light weapons should be a part of a comprehensive and integrated approach that incorporates and strengthens coherence between political, security, development, human rights and rule of law activities and addresses the root causes of conflict, strengthens community security and mitigates armed violence,

Recognizing also that insecurity resulting from the illicit transfer, destabilizing accumulation and misuse of small arms and light weapons negatively impacts conflict prevention, post-conflict peacebuilding, the consolidation of peace in countries emerging from conflict and their post-conflict development, including education, health and economic opportunity,

Acknowledging the important contribution of Council-mandated arms embargoes in countering the illicit transfer, destabilizing accumulation and misuse of small arms and light weapons, and noting the need to improve information-sharing on possible arms embargo violations between groups of experts, peacekeeping missions within their mandates and other relevant United Nations entities,

Recognizing the desirability of aligning objectives of Council-mandated arms embargoes with the overall objectives of other efforts in the relevant Member State or region by United Nations entities and intergovernmental, regional and subregional organizations, including on disarmament, demobilization and reintegration, improving physical security and stockpile management practices and enhancement of border security,

Reiterating that United Nations peacekeeping operations and other relevant Council-mandated entities located in a Member State or region with a Council-mandated arms embargo may, if deemed necessary by the Council, assist with appropriate expertise and capacity-building for host Governments in the field of weapons collection, disarmament, demobilization and reintegration programmes, enhancing physical security and stockpile management practices, record-keeping and tracing capacities, development of national export and import control systems, enhancement of border security and strengthening judicial institutions and law enforcement capacity,

Recalling with concern the close connection between international terrorism, transnational organized crime, drug trafficking, money-laundering, other illicit financial transactions, illicit brokering in small arms and light

[206] United Nations, *Treaty Series*, vol. 75, Nos. 970–973.

[207] Ibid., vol. 1125, Nos. 17512 and 17513.

[208] General Assembly resolution 60/1.

weapons and arms trafficking, and the link between the illegal exploitation of natural resources, illicit trade in such resources and the proliferation of and trafficking in arms as a major factor fuelling and exacerbating many conflicts,

Emphasizing that the illicit trafficking in small arms and light weapons can aid terrorism and illegal armed groups and facilitate increasing levels of transnational organized crime, and underscoring that such illicit trafficking could harm civilians, including women and children, create instability and long-term governance challenges and complicate conflict resolution,

Stressing the utmost importance of women's full and effective participation in all efforts related to countering the illicit transfer, destabilizing accumulation and misuse of small arms and light weapons, in line with its resolution 1325 (2000) of 31 October 2000,

Expressing concern at the continuing threats posed by the illicit transfer, destabilizing accumulation and misuse of small arms and light weapons to the safety and security of United Nations peacekeepers and their effectiveness in implementing peacekeeping mandates, and to the safety and security of humanitarian workers and their effective provision of humanitarian assistance,

Recognizing the value of effective physical security and management of stockpiles of small arms, light weapons and ammunition as an important means to prevent the illicit transfer, destabilizing accumulation and misuse of small arms and light weapons, in accordance with global and regional standards, including through the application of voluntary guidelines, such as the International Ammunition Technical Guidelines developed under the United Nations Saf*er*Guard programme and the International Small Arms Control Standards in arms and ammunition stockpile management practices,

Noting that the marking and tracing of small arms and light weapons by Member States, particularly countries in conflict and post-conflict situations, can serve to detect violations of applicable arms embargoes and identify weaknesses in stockpile management,

Acknowledging the entry into force of the Arms Trade Treaty[209] on 24 December 2014, taking note of a great number of signatories to the Treaty and the increasing number of States parties, and looking forward to the important contribution it can make to international peace, security and stability, reducing human suffering and promoting cooperation,

Reaffirming the significance and central role of the United Nations Convention against Transnational Organized Crime and the Protocols thereto,[210] including the Protocol against the Illicit Manufacturing of and Trafficking in Firearms, Their Parts and Components and Ammunition, supplementing the United Nations Convention against Transnational Organized Crime, the Programme of Action to Prevent, Combat and Eradicate the Illicit Trade in Small Arms and Light Weapons in All Its Aspects[211] and the International Instrument to Enable States to Identify and Trace, in a Timely and Reliable Manner, Illicit Small Arms and Light Weapons,[212] as crucial instruments in countering the illicit transfer, destabilizing accumulation and misuse of small arms and light weapons,

Noting with appreciation the efforts made by Member States and intergovernmental, regional and subregional organizations in addressing threats to international peace and security posed by the illicit transfer, destabilizing accumulation and misuse of small arms and light weapons, and noting the significant role of civil society in supporting such efforts,

Welcoming the report of the Secretary-General to the Council of 27 April 2015 entitled "Small arms and light weapons",[213]

---

[209] See General Assembly resolution 67/234 B.

[210] United Nations, *Treaty Series*, vols. 2225, 2237, 2241 and 2326, No. 39574.

[211] *Report of the United Nations Conference on the Illicit Trade in Small Arms and Light Weapons in All Its Aspects, New York, 9–20 July 2001* (A/CONF.192/15), chap. IV, para. 24.

[212] See General Assembly decision 60/519 and A/60/88 and Corr.2, annex.

[213] S/2015/289.

Expressing its determination to implement existing and take further practical steps to prevent the illicit transfer, destabilizing accumulation and misuse of small arms and light weapons, including in support of other ongoing processes,

1. *Welcomes* efforts made by Member States and regional and subregional organizations in addressing the illicit transfer, destabilizing accumulation and misuse of small arms and light weapons, and encourages the establishment or strengthening, where appropriate, of subregional and regional cooperation, coordination and information-sharing mechanisms, in particular transborder customs cooperation and networks for information-sharing, with a view to preventing, combating and eradicating the illicit transfer, destabilizing accumulation and misuse of small arms and light weapons;

2. *Reiterates* that the illicit transfer, destabilizing accumulation and misuse of small arms and light weapons fuel conflict and have a devastating impact on the protection of civilians, reiterates its demand that all parties to armed conflict comply strictly with the obligations applicable to them under international humanitarian law, international human rights law and international refugee law, and stresses the need for parties to take all required measures to avoid civilian casualties and respect and protect the civilian population;

3. *Re-emphasizes its call upon* parties to armed conflict, in this regard, to comply with obligations under international humanitarian law to respect and protect humanitarian personnel, facilities and relief consignments, and to take measures to eradicate the negative impact of the illicit transfer, destabilizing accumulation and misuse of small arms and light weapons on humanitarian actors, and to take all required steps to facilitate the safe, rapid and unimpeded passage of relief consignments, equipment and personnel;

4. *Expresses its intention* to continue to take due regard of issues related to the illicit transfer, destabilizing accumulation and misuse of small arms and light weapons when considering or updating mandates of United Nations peacekeeping operations and other Security Council-mandated entities, and in this regard encourages the Secretary-General, where appropriate, to consider identifying capacities of United Nations entities that could contribute to countering the illicit transfer, destabilizing accumulation and misuse of small arms and light weapons at the earliest possible stage, to consider involving these entities in strategic assessments and technical assessment missions and to present options for United Nations engagement in this regard, including through assisting host countries in weapons collection, disarmament, demobilization and reintegration programmes, enhancing physical security and stockpile management practices, record-keeping and tracing capacities, development of national export and import control systems, enhancement of border security and strengthening judicial institutions and law enforcement capacity;

5. *Emphasizes* that Member States, United Nations peacekeeping operations and other Council-mandated entities, where appropriate and mandated, and intergovernmental, regional and subregional organizations may be in a position to assist in capacity-building of Governments upon request to ensure the safe and effective management, storage, security, marking, record-keeping and tracing of stockpiles of small arms and light weapons, and collection and/or destruction of surplus, seized, unmarked or illicitly held weapons and ammunition, and encourages Member States and intergovernmental, regional and subregional organizations in a position to do so to render assistance upon request in implementing these tasks, including through examining technologies that would improve the tracing and detection of illicit transfer in small arms and light weapons, as well as measures to facilitate the transfer of such technologies;

6. *Encourages* the United Nations to gather and share best practices of Member States related to safe storage, marking and destruction of weapons collected as part of weapons collection and disarmament, demobilization and reintegration programmes;

7. *Recognizes* that the effectiveness of weapons collection and disarmament, demobilization and reintegration programmes depends, inter alia, on providing sustainable opportunities to former combatants and on the ability of State institutions to foster an inclusive environment in which people feel safe and secure;

8. *Emphasizes* the importance of security sector reform in improving the ability of the State to extend public security and the rule of law within its boundaries and to train professional, effective and accountable security personnel and assisting States to develop proper procedures for weapon stockpile management, physical security, marking, record-keeping and tracing;

9. *Reaffirms* its responsibility to monitor the implementation of Council-mandated arms embargoes, and reaffirms its intention to take appropriate measures, when needed, to strengthen arms embargo monitoring

mechanisms, including through assigning dedicated staff or monitoring units to relevant United Nations missions to effectively monitor arms embargoes;

10. *Recognizes* the need for Member States to put in place, where they do not exist, adequate laws, regulations and administrative procedures to exercise effective control over the production of small arms and light weapons within their areas of jurisdiction and over the export, import, transit or retransfer of such weapons, in order to prevent illegal manufacture of and illicit trafficking in small arms and light weapons or their diversion to unauthorized recipients;

11. *Urges* Member States, relevant United Nations entities and intergovernmental, regional and subregional organizations in a position to do so, and where appropriate, to cooperate and share information on suspected traffickers and trafficking routes, suspect financial transactions and brokering activities for, or diversions of, small arms or light weapons, and other information relevant to the illicit transfer, destabilizing accumulation or misuse of small arms and light weapons, with potentially affected States and with relevant United Nations entities, including expert groups assisting sanctions committees and peacekeeping operations;

12. *Urges* Member States that have not yet done so to take measures, pursuant to their national laws, to regulate brokering taking place under their jurisdiction for small arms and light weapons, including measures that may require brokers to register or obtain written authorization before engaging in brokering;

13. *Reiterates* that Council-mandated arms embargoes should have clearly established objectives and provisions for regular review of the measures with a view to lifting them when the objectives are met, in accordance with the terms of the applicable Council resolutions, acknowledges that when considering a partial or complete termination, suspension or adjustment of an arms embargo the Council should, where applicable, take into account the capacities by the Member State subject to an arms embargo to, inter alia, apply physical security and stockpile management practices, implement marking, record-keeping and tracing, develop national export and import control systems, enhance border security and strengthen judicial institutions and law enforcement capacity, and welcomes the conduct of assessment missions to evaluate progress by Member States subject to Council-mandated arms embargoes towards meeting the conditions set by the Council for their termination or adjustment and to provide options and recommendations regarding United Nations and other technical assistance to these Member States or their regions;

14. *Notes* that where sanctions committees are mandated to determine if an exemption to the arms embargo is justified, they could benefit from information on the existing holdings, including from the information on small arms and light weapons voluntarily provided to the United Nations Register of Conventional Arms, and self-defence and security needs of arms and related materiel by the Government, quantities of arms and related materiel received on the basis of previously approved exemptions, conditions of their storage, as well as quantities of arms and related materiel destroyed through disarmament, demobilization and reintegration programmes, if applicable, and encourages Member States, expert groups and the Secretary-General to provide such information, if available and upon request by the relevant sanctions committee;

15. *Encourages* sanctions committees to maintain dialogue on implementation of arms embargoes with Member States, in particular those in the region, as well as international, regional and subregional organizations and other stakeholders, including by inviting them to meet with the committee and the holding by the Chair of open briefings for all interested Member States;

16. *Encourages* Member States to better understand the impact of the illicit transfer, destabilizing accumulation and misuse of small arms and light weapons on women and children through, inter alia, strengthening the collection of data disaggregated by sex and age and developing appropriate and effective national risk assessment criteria;

17. *Calls upon* Member States, United Nations entities and intergovernmental, regional and subregional organizations to take into consideration the specific impact of conflict and post-conflict environments on women's security, mobility, economic activity and opportunities, to mitigate the risk of women becoming active players in the illicit transfer of small arms and light weapons;

18. *Urges* Member States, United Nations entities and intergovernmental, regional and subregional organizations to take further measures to facilitate women's full and meaningful participation in all policymaking, planning and implementation processes to combat and eradicate the illicit transfer, destabilizing accumulation and misuse of small arms and light weapons in all its aspects, and in that regard encourages empowering women,

including through capacity-building efforts, as appropriate, to participate in the design and implementation of efforts related to the illicit transfer, destabilizing accumulation and misuse of small arms and light weapons, and calls upon all those involved in the planning for disarmament, demobilization and reintegration and justice and security sector reform efforts to take into account the particular needs of women and children associated with armed forces and armed groups, with the participation of women, and to provide for their full access to these programmes inter alia, through consultation with civil society, including women's organizations, as appropriate;

19. *Reaffirms* its decision that States shall eliminate the supply of weapons, including small arms and light weapons, to terrorists, as well as its calls for States to find ways of intensifying and accelerating the exchange of operational information regarding trafficking in arms, and to enhance coordination of efforts at the national, subregional, regional and international levels;

20. *Recognizes* the importance of preventing the illicit transfers and sales of weapons and ammunition, including small arms and light weapons, to armed groups and criminal networks that target civilians and civilian objects, and underlines that such transfers could exacerbate conflict or facilitate the commitment of serious violations of international humanitarian law and serious violations and abuses of human rights;

21. *Urges* States to consider ratifying or acceding to the Arms Trade Treaty[209] as soon as possible, and encourages States and intergovernmental, regional and subregional organizations that are in a position to do so to render assistance in capacity-building to enable States parties to fulfil and implement the Treaty's obligations;

22. *Recognizes* that improving national implementation of Council-mandated arms embargoes and mandating United Nations peacekeeping operations and other relevant Council-mandated entities to assist in building national and regional capacities by States, in particular related to transfer control systems, physical security and stockpile management, record-keeping and preventing diversion of small arms and light weapons and related materiel to illicit markets, may contribute to a more effective implementation of the Arms Trade Treaty by the States parties;

23. *Notes* that implementation of national reporting provisions of the Arms Trade Treaty by the States parties can contribute to increased transparency of small arms and light weapons transfers and could inform the United Nations activities related to countering the illicit transfer and destabilizing accumulation of small arms and light weapons;

24. *Encourages* all Member States that have not yet done so to consider acceding to and to implement the United Nations Convention against Transnational Organized Crime and the Protocols thereto,[210] including the Protocol against the Illicit Manufacturing of and Trafficking in Firearms, Their Parts and Components and Ammunition, supplementing the United Nations Convention against Transnational Organized Crime;

25. *Stresses* the need for full and effective implementation by States at the national, regional and international levels of the Programme of Action to Prevent, Combat and Eradicate the Illicit Trade in Small Arms and Light Weapons in All Its Aspects[211] and the International Instrument to Enable States to Identify and Trace, in a Timely and Reliable Manner, Illicit Small Arms and Light Weapons,[212] in particular, paying special attention to applying measures contained therein on the prevention of the diversion of small arms and light weapons, in order to make real progress in preventing, combating and eradicating the illicit trade in small arms and light weapons;

26. *Requests* the Secretary-General to include in his reports and briefings to the Council on country-specific situations more comprehensive and detailed information and recommendations relating to the impact of the illicit transfer, destabilizing accumulation and misuse of small arms and light weapons on the protection of civilians in armed conflict, including information specific to such impact on refugees, internally displaced persons, women, children and other vulnerable groups;

27. *Also requests* the Secretary-General to include information and recommendations regarding the impact of the illicit transfer, destabilizing accumulation and misuse of small arms and light weapons on the protection of civilians in armed conflict as a sub-item in his next reports on the protection of civilians in armed conflict;

28. *Reiterates its request* to the Secretary-General to direct any relevant United Nations agencies operating in a State or region in relation to which the Council maintains an arms embargo to provide the utmost assistance to the work of relevant sanctions committees, expert groups and other relevant United Nations entities in the implementation and compliance monitoring of that arms embargo, and requests the Secretary-General to examine and present, in his next report on small arms and light weapons, best practices and arrangements that could be used

by the United Nations peacekeeping operations and other relevant Council-mandated entities to guide the implementation of their mandated tasks on the implementation and compliance monitoring of arms embargoes and the provision of assistance and expertise to host States, sanctions committees and expert groups.

29. *Requests* the Secretary-General to include in his annual reports on children and armed conflict as well as in his country-specific reports on children and armed conflict relevant information and recommendations regarding the impact of the illicit transfer, destabilizing accumulation and misuse of small arms and light weapons on children, to the extent consistent within the existing mandates;

30. *Encourages* the Security Council Committee pursuant to resolutions 1267 (1999) and 1989 (2011) and the Analytical Support and Sanctions Monitoring Team, within their existing mandates and in close cooperation with all relevant United Nations counter-terrorism bodies, to focus on the threats posed by accessibility of weapons used by individuals and entities associated with Al-Qaida and the supply and trafficking of weapons to them, and requests the Monitoring Team to include in its next regular report to the Committee information on such threats and to provide recommendations for actions to enhance the response to such threats;

31. *Encourages* the Counter-Terrorism Committee and the Counter-Terrorism Committee Executive Directorate, within their existing mandates and in close cooperation with all relevant United Nations counter-terrorism bodies, to focus on Member States' capacities and needs to address the threats posed by accessibility of weapons used by terrorists as well as to counter the supply and trafficking of weapons to terrorists, and requests the Executive Directorate to report within the existing reporting framework to the Counter-Terrorism Committee on gaps in such capacities, and to provide concrete plans to facilitate technical assistance for strengthening Member States' capacities and to provide recommendations for actions to enhance response to such threats;

32. *Requests* the Secretary-General to continue to submit to the Council on a biennial basis a report on small arms and light weapons, including on the implementation of the present resolution, and affirms its intention to consider the report in a timely manner;

33. *Decides* to remain seized of the matter.

Adopted at the 7447th meeting
by 9 votes to none, with 6 abstentions
(Angola, Chad, China, Nigeria, Russian Federation
and Venezuela (Bolivarian Republic of)).

GENERAL ISSUES RELATING TO SANCTIONS[214]

Decisions

At its 7323rd meeting, on 25 November 2014, the Security Council considered the item entitled:

"General issues relating to sanctions

"Letter dated 5 November 2014 from the Permanent Representative of Australia to the United Nations addressed to the Secretary-General (S/2014/793)".

At the same meeting, the Council decided to extend an invitation, in accordance with rule 39 of its provisional rules of procedure, to Mr. Jeffrey Feltman, Under-Secretary-General for Political Affairs.

At the same meeting, the Council also decided to extend an invitation, in accordance with rule 39 of its provisional rules of procedure, to Mr. Jürgen Stock, Secretary-General of the International Criminal Police Organization (INTERPOL).

---

[214] Resolutions or decisions on this question were first adopted by the Security Council in 2000.

WOMEN AND PEACE AND SECURITY[214]

Decisions

At its 7289th meeting, on 28 October 2014, the Security Council decided to invite the representatives of Afghanistan, Algeria, Austria, Azerbaijan, Belgium, Bosnia and Herzegovina, Brazil, Burundi, Canada, Colombia, Croatia, Cyprus, the Czech Republic, Egypt, Estonia, Fiji, Germany, Guatemala, India, Indonesia, Iraq, Ireland, Israel, Italy, Jamaica, Japan, Kazakhstan, Liechtenstein, Malaysia, Mexico, Morocco, the Netherlands, New Zealand, Pakistan, Poland, Portugal, Qatar, Slovakia, Spain, the Sudan, Sweden, Switzerland, the Syrian Arab Republic, Thailand, Turkey, Ukraine, the United Arab Emirates, Uruguay, Viet Nam and Zimbabwe to participate, without vote, in accordance with rule 37 of its provisional rules of procedure, in the discussion of the item entitled:

"Women and peace and security

"Displaced women and girls: leaders and survivors

"Report of the Secretary-General on women and peace and security (S/2014/693)

"Letter dated 10 October 2014 from the Permanent Representative of Argentina to the United Nations addressed to the Secretary-General (S/2014/731)".

At the same meeting, the Council also decided to extend invitations, in accordance with rule 39 of its provisional rules of procedure, to Ms. Phumzile Mlambo-Ngcuka, Executive Director of the United Nations Entity for Gender Equality and the Empowerment of Women (UN-Women), Mr. Edmond Mulet, Assistant Secretary-General for Peacekeeping Operations, and Mr. Chaloka Beyani, Special Rapporteur of the Human Rights Council on the human rights of internally displaced persons.

At the same meeting, the Council further decided to extend an invitation, in accordance with rule 39 of its provisional rules of procedure, to Ms. Suaad Allami, representative of the NGO Working Group on Women, Peace and Security.

At the same meeting, the Council decided to extend an invitation, in accordance with rule 39 of its provisional rules of procedure, to Mr. Thomas Mayr-Harting, Head of the Delegation of the European Union to the United Nations.

At the same meeting, the Council also decided to extend invitations, in accordance with rule 39 of its provisional rules of procedure, to Ms. Marriët Schuurman, Special Representative of the Secretary-General of the North Atlantic Treaty Organization for Women, Peace and Security, and Ms. Miroslava Beham, Senior Adviser on Gender Issues of the Organization for Security and Cooperation in Europe.

At the same meeting, following consultations among members of the Security Council, the President made the following statement on behalf of the Council:[215]

The Security Council reaffirms its commitments to the full and effective implementation of resolutions 1325 (2000), 1820 (2008), 1888 (2009), 1889 (2009), 1960 (2010), 2106 (2013) and 2122 (2013) and recalls all statements by its President on women and peace and security as reiterating the Council's commitments.

The Council takes note with appreciation of the report of the Secretary-General on women and peace and security[216] for the purpose of implementation of resolution 1325 (2000), and particularly welcomes its focus on implementation, sustaining progress and the need to translate commitments into improved outcomes.

The Council reaffirms that women's and girls' empowerment and gender equality are critical to efforts to maintain international peace and security, and emphasizes that persistent barriers to full implementation of resolution 1325 (2000) will only be dismantled through dedicated commitment to women's empowerment, participation and human rights, and through concerted leadership, consistent information flows and action, and support, to ensure women's full and equal participation at all levels of decision-making.

The Council welcomes the efforts of Member States to implement resolution 1325 (2000) at the national, regional and local levels, including the development of national action plans and other national,

[215] S/PRST/2014/21.

[216] S/2014/693.

subregional and regional-level strategies and implementation frameworks, and encourages Member States to continue to pursue such implementation. The Council further stresses that United Nations entities should continue to support and supplement, as appropriate, efforts of Member States in the implementation of 1325 (2000). The Council recognizes the critical contributions of civil society, including women's organizations, to conflict prevention, resolution and peacebuilding and in this regard the importance of sustained consultation and dialogue between women and national and international decision makers. The Council encourages the involvement of men in promoting gender equality and ending sexual and gender-based violence.

The Council welcomes the additional steps taken to implement Council resolutions 2106 (2013) and 2122 (2013), and notes the importance of sustained efforts by the United Nations to improve the quality of information and analysis on the impact of armed conflict on women and girls, the role of women in all areas of conflict prevention and resolution, peacemaking and peacebuilding and the gender dimensions of these areas, and to systematically include information and related recommendations on issues of relevance to women and peace and security in their reports and briefings to the Council. The Council reiterates its intention to increase its attention to women and peace and security as a cross-cutting subject in all relevant thematic areas of work on its agenda, including on threats to international peace and security caused by terrorist acts.

The Council recognizes that refugee and internally displaced women and girls are at heightened risk of being subject to various forms of human rights violations and abuses, including sexual and gender-based violence, and discrimination, which can occur during the various stages of the displacement cycle. The Council reaffirms the primary responsibility of Member States in the protection of their populations, including refugee and internally displaced women and girls. The Council stresses the importance of the Secretary-General and relevant United Nations agencies, inter alia, through consultation with women and women-led organizations as appropriate, supporting the development and strengthening of effective mechanisms for preventing and providing protection from violence, including in particular sexual and gender-based violence, to refugee and internally displaced women and girls.

The Council urges Member States to take measures to prevent refugee and internally displaced women and girls from being subject to violence, and to strengthen access to justice for women in such circumstances, including through the prompt investigation, prosecution and punishment of perpetrators of sexual and gender-based violence, as well as reparations for victims as appropriate. The Council stresses that the fight against impunity for the most serious crimes of international concern committed against women and girls has been strengthened through the work of the International Criminal Court, ad hoc and mixed tribunals, as well as specialized chambers in national tribunals.

The Council reiterates with grave concern that the illicit transfer, destabilizing accumulation and misuse of small arms and light weapons fuel armed conflicts and have a disproportionate impact on violence perpetrated against women and girls, and exacerbate sexual and gender-based violence.

The Council urges all parties involved in an armed conflict to allow full and unhindered access by refugee and internally displaced women to humanitarian assistance and protection as well as basic services such as education, health, housing and productive livelihoods, including assets such as land and property, in particular for those refugee and internally displaced women and girls at increased risk of marginalization. The Council recognizes the importance of Member States and United Nations entities seeking to ensure that humanitarian aid and funding includes provision for the full range of medical, legal, psychosocial and livelihood services, and noting the need for access to the full range of sexual and reproductive health services, including regarding pregnancies resulting from rape, without discrimination. The Council further recognizes that refugee and internally displaced women and girls are at increased risk of becoming stateless as a result of discriminatory nationality laws, obstacles to registering and the lack of access to identity documents, and urges States to ensure prompt and equitable provision of all necessary identity documents to such women and girls.

The Council urges Member States, the Secretary-General and relevant United Nations agencies to ensure meaningful participation of refugee and internally displaced women, as well as adolescent girls as appropriate, in the development, implementation, monitoring and evaluation of policies and programmes for refugee and internally displaced women and girls at all stages of the displacement cycle. The Council further calls for the systematic collection, analysis and utilization of sex- and age-disaggregated data that is required to assess the specific needs and capacities of women and to meaningfully measure to what extent recovery programmes are benefiting women, men, girls and boys, by all relevant actors.

The Council expresses its deep concern that violent extremism, which can be conducive to terrorism, often results in increased displacement and is frequently targeted at women and girls, leading to serious human rights violations and abuses committed against them, including murder, abduction, hostage-taking, kidnapping, enslavement, their sale and forced marriage, human trafficking, rape, sexual slavery and other forms of sexual violence. The Council urges all Member States to protect their population, in particular women and girls, affected by violent extremism which can be conducive to terrorism, while respecting all their obligations under international law, in particular international human rights, refugee and international humanitarian law. The Council encourages Member States to engage the participation and leadership of women and women's organizations, including refugee and internally displaced women, in developing strategies to counter violent extremism, and further to address, including by the empowerment of women, the conditions conducive to the spread of violent extremism.

The Council reiterates its intention to convene a high-level review in 2015 to assess progress at the global, regional and national levels in implementing resolution 1325 (2000), renew commitments and address obstacles and constraints that have emerged in the implementation of resolution 1325 (2000). The Council encourages those Member States, regional organizations as appropriate, and United Nations entities that have developed frameworks and plans to support the implementation of resolution 1325 (2000) to start reviewing existing implementation plans and targets, and to accelerate progress and prepare to formulate new targets, in time for the 2015 high-level review.

The Council welcomes the commissioning by the Secretary-General, in preparation for the high-level review, of a global study on the implementation of resolution 1325 (2000), highlighting good practice examples, implementation gaps and challenges, as well as emerging trends and priorities for action. The Council encourages Member States, regional and subregional organizations as appropriate, and United Nations entities to contribute to the study. The Council invites the Secretary-General within his next annual report on the implementation of resolution 1325 (2000) to submit information on the results of the global study and to make this available to all States Members of the United Nations.

At its 7428th meeting, on 15 April 2015, the Council decided to invite the representatives of Afghanistan, Algeria, Argentina, Australia, Azerbaijan, Belgium, Brazil, Canada, Colombia, Costa Rica, Croatia, the Democratic Republic of the Congo, Egypt, El Salvador, Germany, Guatemala, Hungary, India, Indonesia, Iraq, Ireland, Israel, Italy, Japan, Kazakhstan, Kenya, Latvia, Liechtenstein, Luxembourg, Mexico, Morocco, Nepal, the Netherlands, Poland, Portugal, Qatar, the Republic of Korea, Rwanda, Slovenia, the Sudan, Sweden, Switzerland, the Syrian Arab Republic, Thailand, Turkey, Ukraine, the United Arab Emirates, Uruguay, Viet Nam and Zimbabwe to participate, without vote, in accordance with rule 37 of its provisional rules of procedure, in the discussion of the item entitled:

"Women and peace and security

"Report of the Secretary-General on conflict-related sexual violence (S/2015/203)

"Letter dated 9 April 2015 from the Permanent Representative of Jordan to the United Nations addressed to the Secretary-General (S/2015/243)".

At the same meeting, the Council also decided to extend invitations, in accordance with rule 39 of its provisional rules of procedure, to Ms. Zainab Hawa Bangura, Special Representative of the Secretary-General on Sexual Violence in Conflict; and Ms. Hamsatu Allamin, representative of the NGO Working Group on Women, Peace and Security.

At the same meeting, the Council further decided to extend invitations, in accordance with rule 39 of its provisional rules of procedure, to Mr. Thomas Mayr-Harting, Head of the Delegation of the European Union to the United Nations, and Mr. Téte António, Permanent Observer of the African Union to the United Nations.

At the same meeting, the Council decided to extend an invitation to the Permanent Observer of the Observer State of the Holy See to the United Nations, in accordance with the provisional rules of procedure of the Council and its previous practice in that regard.

BRIEFING BY THE PRESIDENT OF THE INTERNATIONAL COURT OF JUSTICE[217]

Decision

At its 7290th meeting, held in private on 29 October 2014, the Security Council decided to authorize its President to issue through the Secretary-General the following communiqué, in accordance with rule 55 of the provisional rules of procedure of the Council:

> At its 7290th meeting, held in private on 29 October 2014, the Security Council considered the item entitled "Briefing by the President of the International Court of Justice".
>
> The President of the Security Council invited Judge Peter Tomka, President of the International Court of Justice, to participate in the meeting in accordance with rule 39 of the provisional rules of procedure of the Council.
>
> The members of the Council heard a briefing by Judge Tomka.
>
> The members of the Council and Judge Tomka had an exchange of views.

BRIEFING BY THE CHAIRPERSON-IN-OFFICE OF THE ORGANIZATION FOR SECURITY AND COOPERATION IN EUROPE[218]

Decisions

At its 7391st meeting, on 24 February 2015, the Security Council considered the item entitled "Briefing by the Chairperson-in-Office of the Organization for Security and Cooperation in Europe".

At the same meeting, the Council decided to extend an invitation, in accordance with rule 39 of its provisional rules of procedure, to Mr. Ivica Dačić, Chairperson-in-Office of the Organization for Security and Cooperation in Europe and First Deputy Prime Minister and Minister for Foreign Affairs of Serbia.

MEETING OF THE SECURITY COUNCIL WITH THE TROOP- AND POLICE-CONTRIBUTING COUNTRIES PURSUANT TO RESOLUTION 1353 (2001), ANNEX II, SECTIONS A AND B[218]

A. United Nations Peacekeeping Force in Cyprus

Decisions

At its 7363rd meeting, held in private on 21 January 2015, the Security Council decided to authorize its President to issue through the Secretary-General the following communiqué, in accordance with rule 55 of the provisional rules of procedure of the Council:

> On 21 January 2015, the Security Council, pursuant to sections A and B of annex II to resolution 1353 (2001) of 13 June 2001, held its 7363rd meeting, in private with the troop- and police-contributing countries to the United Nations Peacekeeping Force in Cyprus.
>
> The President invited Ms. Lisa Buttenheim, Special Representative of the Secretary-General in Cyprus and Head of the United Nations Peacekeeping Force in Cyprus, to participate in the meeting in accordance with rule 39 of the provisional rules of procedure of the Council.
>
> The Council and the troop- and police-contributing countries heard a briefing by Ms. Buttenheim.

---

[217] Resolutions or decisions on this question were first adopted by the Security Council in 2000.

[218] Resolutions or decisions on this question were first adopted by the Security Council in 2001.

At its 7486th meeting, held in private on 16 July 2015, the Council decided to authorize its President to issue through the Secretary-General the following communiqué, in accordance with rule 55 of the provisional rules of procedure of the Council:

On 16 July 2015, the Security Council, pursuant to sections A and B of annex II to resolution 1353 (2001), held its 7486th meeting, in private with the troop- and police-contributing countries to the United Nations Peacekeeping Force in Cyprus.

The President invited Ms. Lisa Buttenheim, Special Representative of the Secretary-General in Cyprus and Head of the United Nations Peacekeeping Force in Cyprus, to participate in the meeting in accordance with rule 39 of the provisional rules of procedure of the Council.

The Council and the troop- and police-contributing countries heard a briefing by Ms. Buttenheim.

B. United Nations Disengagement Observer Force

Decisions

At its 7333rd meeting, held in private on 10 December 2014, the Security Council decided to authorize its President to issue through the Secretary-General the following communiqué, in accordance with rule 55 of the provisional rules of procedure of the Council:

On 10 December 2014, the Security Council, pursuant to sections A and B of annex II to resolution 1353 (2001) of 13 June 2001, held its 7333rd meeting, in private with the troop-contributing countries to the United Nations Disengagement Observer Force.

The President invited Mr. Hervé Ladsous, Under-Secretary-General for Peacekeeping Operations, to participate in the meeting in accordance with rule 39 of the provisional rules of procedure of the Council.

The Council and the troop-contributing countries heard a briefing by Mr. Ladsous.

Members of the Council, Mr. Ladsous and representatives of participating troop-contributing countries had an exchange of views.

At its 7462nd meeting, held in private on 16 June 2015, the Council decided to authorize its President to issue through the Secretary-General the following communiqué, in accordance with rule 55 of the provisional rules of procedure of the Council:

On 16 June 2015, the Security Council, pursuant to sections A and B of annex II to resolution 1353 (2001), held its 7462nd meeting, in private with the troop-contributing countries to the United Nations Disengagement Observer Force.

The President invited Mr. Hervé Ladsous, Under-Secretary-General for Peacekeeping Operations, to participate in the meeting in accordance with rule 39 of the provisional rules of procedure of the Council.

The Council and the troop-contributing countries heard a briefing by Mr. Ladsous.

Members of the Council, Mr. Ladsous and representatives of participating troop-contributing countries had an exchange of views.

C. United Nations Interim Force in Lebanon

Decision

At its 7241st meeting, held in private on 14 August 2014, the Security Council decided to authorize its President to issue through the Secretary-General the following communiqué, in accordance with rule 55 of the provisional rules of procedure of the Council:

On 14 August 2014, the Security Council, pursuant to sections A and B of annex II to resolution 1353 (2001) of 13 June 2001, held its 7241st meeting, in private with the troop-contributing countries to the United Nations Interim Force in Lebanon.

The President invited Mr. Edmond Mulet, Assistant Secretary-General for Peacekeeping Operations, to participate in the meeting in accordance with rule 39 of the provisional rules of procedure of the Council.

The Council and the troop-contributing countries heard a briefing by Mr. Mulet.

Members of the Council, Mr. Mulet and representatives of participating troop-contributing countries had an exchange of views.

D. United Nations Mission for the Referendum in Western Sahara

Decision

At its 7429th meeting, held in private on 16 April 2015, the Security Council decided to authorize its President to issue through the Secretary-General the following communiqué, in accordance with rule 55 of the provisional rules of procedure of the Council:

On 16 April 2015, the Security Council, pursuant to sections A and B of annex II to resolution 1353 (2001) of 13 June 2001, held its 7429th meeting, in private with the troop- and police-contributing countries to the United Nations Mission for the Referendum in Western Sahara.

The President invited Mr. Edmond Mulet, Assistant Secretary-General for Peacekeeping Operations, to participate in the meeting in accordance with rule 39 of the provisional rules of procedure of the Council.

The Council and the troop- and police-contributing countries heard a briefing by Mr. Mulet.

E. United Nations Organization Stabilization Mission in the Democratic Republic of the Congo

Decision

At its 7406th meeting, held in private on 17 March 2015, the Security Council decided to authorize its President to issue through the Secretary-General the following communiqué, in accordance with rule 55 of the provisional rules of procedure of the Council:

On 17 March 2015, the Security Council, pursuant to sections A and B of annex II to resolution 1353 (2001) of 13 June 2001, held its 7406th meeting, in private with the troop- and police-contributing countries to the United Nations Organization Stabilization Mission in the Democratic Republic of the Congo.

The President invited Mr. Martin Kobler, Special Representative of the Secretary-General for the Democratic Republic of the Congo and Head of the United Nations Organization Stabilization Mission in the Democratic Republic of the Congo, to participate in the meeting in accordance with rule 39 of the provisional rules of procedure of the Council.

The Council and the troop- and police-contributing countries heard a briefing by Mr. Kobler.

Members of the Council, Mr. Kobler and representatives of participating troop- and police-contributing countries had an exchange of views.

F. United Nations Mission in Liberia

Decisions

At its 7258th meeting, held in private on 4 September 2014, the Security Council decided to authorize its President to issue through the Secretary-General the following communiqué, in accordance with rule 55 of the provisional rules of procedure of the Council:

On 4 September 2014, the Security Council, pursuant to sections A and B of annex II to resolution 1353 (2001) of 13 June 2001, held its 7258th meeting, in private with the troop- and police-contributing countries to the United Nations Mission in Liberia.

The President invited Mr. Hervé Ladsous, Under-Secretary-General for Peacekeeping Operations, Ms. Karin Landgren, Special Representative of the Secretary-General for Liberia and Head of the United Nations Mission in Liberia, and Mr. Anthony Banbury, Assistant Secretary-General for Field Support, to participate in the meeting in accordance with rule 39 of the provisional rules of procedure of the Council.

The Council and the troop- and police-contributing countries heard briefings by Mr. Ladsous, Ms. Landgren, by video teleconference from Monrovia, and Mr. Banbury.

Members of the Council, Mr. Ladsous, Ms. Landgren, Mr. Banbury and representatives of participating troop- and police-contributing countries had an exchange of views.

At its 7330th meeting, held in private on 9 December 2014, the Council decided to authorize its President to issue through the Secretary-General the following communiqué, in accordance with rule 55 of the provisional rules of procedure of the Council:

On 9 December 2014, the Security Council, pursuant to sections A and B of annex II to resolution 1353 (2001), held its 7330th meeting, in private with the troop- and police-contributing countries to the United Nations Mission in Liberia.

The President invited Mr. Hervé Ladsous, Under-Secretary-General for Peacekeeping Operations, to participate in the meeting in accordance with rule 39 of the provisional rules of procedure of the Council.

The Council and the troop- and police-contributing countries heard a briefing by Mr. Ladsous.

G. United Nations Operation in Côte d'Ivoire

Decision

At its 7454th meeting, held in private on 3 June 2015, the Security Council decided to authorize its President to issue through the Secretary-General the following communiqué, in accordance with rule 55 of the provisional rules of procedure of the Council:

On 3 June 2015, the Security Council, pursuant to sections A and B of annex II to resolution 1353 (2001) of 13 June 2001, held its 7454th meeting, in private with the troop- and police-contributing countries to the United Nations Operation in Côte d'Ivoire.

The President invited Ms. Aïchatou Mindaoudou, Special Representative of the Secretary-General for Côte d'Ivoire and Head of the United Nations Operation in Côte d'Ivoire, to participate in the meeting in accordance with rule 39 of the provisional rules of procedure of the Council.

The Council and the troop- and police-contributing countries heard a briefing by Ms. Mindaoudou, by video teleconference from Abidjan, Côte d'Ivoire.

H. United Nations Stabilization Mission in Haiti

Decisions

At its 7261st meeting, held in private on 10 September 2014, the Security Council decided to authorize its President to issue through the Secretary-General the following communiqué, in accordance with rule 55 of the provisional rules of procedure of the Council:

On 10 September 2014, the Security Council, pursuant to sections A and B of annex II to resolution 1353 (2001) of 13 June 2001, held its 7261st meeting, in private with the troop- and police-contributing countries to the United Nations Stabilization Mission in Haiti.

The President invited Ms. Sandra Honoré, Special Representative of the Secretary-General for Haiti and Head of the United Nations Stabilization Mission in Haiti, to participate in the meeting in accordance with rule 39 of the provisional rules of procedure of the Council.

The Council and the troop- and police-contributing countries heard a briefing by Ms. Honoré.

Members of the Council, Ms. Honoré and representatives of participating troop- and police-contributing countries had an exchange of views.

At its 7404th meeting, held in private on 16 March 2015, the Council decided to authorize its President to issue through the Secretary-General the following communiqué, in accordance with rule 55 of the provisional rules of procedure of the Council:

On 16 March 2015, the Security Council, pursuant to sections A and B of annex II to resolution 1353 (2001), held its 7404th meeting, in private with the troop- and police-contributing countries to the United Nations Stabilization Mission in Haiti.

The President invited Ms. Sandra Honoré, Special Representative of the Secretary-General for Haiti and Head of the United Nations Stabilization Mission in Haiti, to participate in the meeting in accordance with rule 39 of the provisional rules of procedure of the Council.

The Council and the troop- and police-contributing countries heard a briefing by Ms. Honoré.

Members of the Council, Ms. Honoré and representatives of participating troop- and police-contributing countries had an exchange of views.

I. African Union-United Nations Hybrid Operation in Darfur

Decisions

At its 7233rd meeting, held in private on 5 August 2014, the Security Council decided to authorize its President to issue through the Secretary-General the following communiqué, in accordance with rule 55 of the provisional rules of procedure of the Council:

On 5 August 2014, the Security Council, pursuant to sections A and B of annex II to resolution 1353 (2001) of 13 June 2001, held its 7233rd meeting, in private with the troop- and police-contributing countries to the African Union-United Nations Hybrid Operation in Darfur.

The President invited Mr. Mohamed Ibn Chambas, African Union-United Nations Joint Special Representative for Darfur and Head of the African Union-United Nations Hybrid Operation in Darfur, to participate in the meeting in accordance with rule 39 of the provisional rules of procedure of the Council.

The Council and the troop- and police-contributing countries heard a briefing by Mr. Chambas.

Members of the Council, Mr. Chambas and representatives of participating troop- and police-contributing countries had an exchange of views.

At its 7456th meeting, held in private on 4 June 2015, the Council decided to authorize its President to issue through the Secretary-General the following communiqué, in accordance with rule 55 of the provisional rules of procedure of the Council:

On 4 June 2015, the Security Council, pursuant to sections A and B of annex II to resolution 1353 (2001), held its 7456th meeting, in private with the troop- and police-contributing countries to the African Union-United Nations Hybrid Operation in Darfur.

The President invited Ms. Daniela Kroslak, Darfur Integrated Operational Team Leader in the Department of Peacekeeping Operations of the Secretariat, to participate in the meeting in accordance with rule 39 of the provisional rules of procedure of the Council.

The Council and the troop- and police-contributing countries heard a briefing by Ms. Kroslak.

Members of the Council, Ms. Kroslak and representatives of participating troop- and police-contributing countries had an exchange of views.

J. United Nations Mission in South Sudan

Decisions

At its 7305th meeting, held in private on 11 November 2014, the Security Council decided to authorize its President to issue through the Secretary-General the following communiqué, in accordance with rule 55 of the provisional rules of procedure of the Council:

> On 11 November 2014, the Security Council, pursuant to sections A and B of annex II to resolution 1353 (2001) of 13 June 2001, held its 7305th meeting, in private with the troop- and police-contributing countries to the United Nations Mission in South Sudan.
>
> The President invited Mr. Hervé Ladsous, Under-Secretary-General for Peacekeeping Operations, to participate in the meeting in accordance with rule 39 of the provisional rules of procedure of the Council.
>
> The Council and the troop- and police-contributing countries heard a briefing by Mr. Ladsous.
>
> Members of the Council, Mr. Ladsous and representatives of participating troop- and police-contributing countries had an exchange of views.

At its 7437th meeting, held in private on 5 May 2015, the Council decided to authorize its President to issue through the Secretary-General the following communiqué, in accordance with rule 55 of the provisional rules of procedure of the Council:

> On 5 May 2015, the Security Council, pursuant to sections A and B of annex II to resolution 1353 (2001), held its 7437th meeting, in private with the troop- and police-contributing countries to the United Nations Mission in South Sudan.
>
> The President invited Mr. Edmond Mulet, Assistant Secretary-General for Peacekeeping Operations, to participate in the meeting in accordance with rule 39 of the provisional rules of procedure of the Council.
>
> The Council and the troop- and police-contributing countries heard a briefing by Mr. Mulet.
>
> Members of the Council, Mr. Mulet and representatives of participating troop- and police-contributing countries had an exchange of views.

K. United Nations Multidimensional Integrated Stabilization Mission in Mali

Decision

At its 7465th meeting, held in private on 17 June 2015, the Security Council decided to authorize its President to issue through the Secretary-General the following communiqué, in accordance with rule 55 of the provisional rules of procedure of the Council:

> On 17 June 2015, the Security Council, pursuant to sections A and B of annex II to resolution 1353 (2001) of 13 June 2001, held its 7465th meeting, in private with the troop- and police-contributing countries to the United Nations Multidimensional Integrated Stabilization Mission in Mali.
>
> The President invited Mr. Hervé Ladsous, Under-Secretary-General for Peacekeeping Operations, to participate in the meeting in accordance with rule 39 of the provisional rules of procedure of the Council.
>
> The Council and the troop- and police-contributing countries heard a briefing by Mr. Ladsous.
>
> Members of the Council, Mr. Ladsous and representatives of participating troop- and police-contributing countries had an exchange of views.

L. United Nations Multidimensional Integrated Stabilization Mission in the Central African Republic

Decision

At its 7424th meeting, held in private on 8 April 2015, the Security Council decided to authorize its President to issue through the Secretary-General the following communiqué, in accordance with rule 55 of the provisional rules of procedure of the Council:

> On 8 April 2015, the Security Council, pursuant to sections A and B of annex II to resolution 1353 (2001) of 13 June 2001, held its 7424th meeting, in private with the troop- and police-contributing countries to the United Nations Multidimensional Integrated Stabilization Mission in the Central African Republic.
>
> The President invited Lieutenant General Babacar Gaye, Special Representative of the Secretary-General for the Central African Republic and Head of the United Nations Multidimensional Integrated Stabilization Mission in the Central African Republic, to participate in the meeting in accordance with rule 39 of the provisional rules of procedure of the Council.
>
> The Council and the troop- and police-contributing countries heard a briefing by Lieutenant General Gaye, by video teleconference from Bangui.
>
> Members of the Council, Lieutenant General Gaye and representatives of participating troop- and police-contributing countries had an exchange of views.

THREATS TO INTERNATIONAL PEACE AND SECURITY CAUSED BY TERRORIST ACTS[218]

Decision

At its 7242nd meeting, on 15 August 2014, the Security Council decided to invite the representatives of Iraq and the Syrian Arab Republic to participate, without vote, in accordance with rule 37 of its provisional rules of procedure, in the discussion of the item entitled "Threats to international peace and security caused by terrorist acts".

Resolution 2170 (2014) of 15 August 2014

The Security Council,

Reaffirming its resolutions 1267 (1999) of 15 October 1999, 1373 (2001) of 28 September 2001, 1618 (2005) of 4 August 2005, 1624 (2005) of 14 September 2005, 2083 (2012) of 17 December 2012, 2129 (2013) of 17 December 2013, 2133 (2014) of 27 January 2014 and 2161 (2014) of 17 June 2014 and the relevant statements by its President,

Reaffirming also the independence, sovereignty, unity and territorial integrity of Iraq and the Syrian Arab Republic, and reaffirming further the purposes and principles of the Charter of the United Nations,

Reaffirming further that terrorism in all forms and manifestations constitutes one of the most serious threats to international peace and security and that any acts of terrorism are criminal and unjustifiable regardless of their motivations, whenever and by whomsoever committed,

Expressing its gravest concern that territory in parts of Iraq and the Syrian Arab Republic is under the control of Islamic State in Iraq and the Levant and Al-Nusrah Front and about the negative impact of their presence, violent extremist ideology and actions on stability in Iraq, the Syrian Arab Republic and the region, including the devastating humanitarian impact on the civilian populations which has led to the displacement of millions of people, and about their acts of violence that foment sectarian tensions,

Reiterating its condemnation of Islamic State in Iraq and the Levant, Al-Nusrah Front and all other individuals, groups, undertakings and entities associated with Al-Qaida for ongoing and multiple criminal terrorist acts aimed at causing the deaths of civilians and other victims, destruction of property and of cultural and religious sites and greatly undermining stability, and recalling that the asset freeze, travel ban and arms embargo requirements in paragraph 1 of resolution 2161 (2014) apply to Islamic State in Iraq and the Levant, Al-Nusrah Front and all other individuals, groups, undertakings, and entities associated with Al-Qaida,

Reaffirming that terrorism, including the actions of Islamic State in Iraq and the Levant, cannot and should not be associated with any religion, nationality or civilization,

Stressing that terrorism can only be defeated by a sustained and comprehensive approach involving the active participation and collaboration of all States and international and regional organizations to impede, impair, isolate and incapacitate the terrorist threat,

Reaffirming that Member States must ensure that any measures taken to combat terrorism, including while implementing the present resolution, comply with all their obligations under international law, in particular international human rights, refugee and humanitarian law, and underscoring that effective counter-terrorism measures and respect for human rights, fundamental freedoms and the rule of law are complementary and mutually reinforcing, and are an essential part of a successful counter-terrorism effort, and noting the importance of respect for the rule of law so as to effectively prevent and combat terrorism,

Reaffirming also that those who have committed or are otherwise responsible for violations of international humanitarian law or violations or abuses of human rights in Iraq and the Syrian Arab Republic, including persecution of individuals on the basis of their religion or belief, or on political grounds, must be held accountable,

Gravely concerned by the financing of, and financial and other resources obtained by, Islamic State in Iraq and the Levant, Al-Nusrah Front and all other individuals, groups, undertakings and entities associated with Al-Qaida, and underscoring that these resources will support their future terrorist activities,

Strongly condemning incidents of kidnapping and hostage-taking committed by Islamic State in Iraq and the Levant, Al-Nusrah Front and all other individuals, groups, undertakings and entities associated with Al-Qaida for any purpose, including with the aim of raising funds or gaining political concessions, expressing its determination to prevent kidnapping and hostage-taking committed by terrorist groups and to secure the safe release of hostages without ransom payments or political concessions, in accordance with applicable international law, calling upon all Member States to prevent terrorists from benefiting directly or indirectly from ransom payments or from political concessions and to secure the safe release of hostages, and reaffirming the need for all Member States to cooperate closely during incidents of kidnapping and hostage-taking committed by terrorist groups,

Expressing concern at the flow of foreign terrorist fighters to Islamic State in Iraq and the Levant, Al-Nusrah Front and all other individuals, groups, undertakings and entities associated with Al-Qaida, and the scale of this phenomenon,

Expressing concern also at the increased use, in a globalized society, by terrorists and their supporters of new information and communications technologies, in particular the Internet, for the purposes of recruitment and incitement to commit terrorist acts, as well as for the financing, planning and preparation of their activities, and underlining the need for Member States to act cooperatively to prevent terrorists from exploiting technology, communications and resources to incite support for terrorist acts, while respecting human rights and fundamental freedoms and in compliance with other obligations under international law,

Condemning in the strongest terms the incitement of terrorist acts, and repudiating attempts at the justification or glorification (apologie) of terrorist acts that may incite further terrorist acts,

Underlining the primary responsibility of Member States to protect civilian populations on their territories, in accordance with their obligations under international law,

Urging all parties to protect the civilian population, in particular women and children, affected by the violent activities of Islamic State in Iraq and the Levant, Al-Nusrah Front and all other individuals, groups, undertakings and entities associated with Al-Qaida, especially against any form of sexual violence,

Reaffirming the need to combat by all means, in accordance with the Charter and international law, including applicable international human rights, refugee and humanitarian law, threats to international peace and security caused by terrorist acts, stressing in this regard the important role the United Nations plays in leading and coordinating this effort,

Noting with concern the continued threat posed to international peace and security by Islamic State in Iraq and the Levant, Al-Nusrah Front and all other individuals, groups, undertakings and entities associated with Al-Qaida, and reaffirming its resolve to address all aspects of that threat,

Acting under Chapter VII of the Charter,

1. *Deplores and condemns in the strongest terms* the terrorist acts of Islamic State in Iraq and the Levant and its violent extremist ideology, and its continued gross, systematic and widespread abuses of human rights and violations of international humanitarian law;

2. *Strongly condemns* the indiscriminate killing and deliberate targeting of civilians, numerous atrocities, mass executions and extrajudicial killings, including of soldiers, persecution of individuals and entire communities on the basis of their religion or belief, kidnapping of civilians, forced displacement of members of minority groups, killing and maiming of children, recruitment and use of children, rape and other forms of sexual violence, arbitrary detention, attacks on schools and hospitals, destruction of cultural and religious sites and obstructing the exercise of economic, social and cultural rights, including the right to education, especially in the Syrian governorates of Raqqah, Dayr al-Zawr, Aleppo and Idlib, and in northern Iraq, especially in Tamim, Salaheddine and Nineveh provinces;

3. *Recalls* that widespread or systematic attacks directed against any civilian populations because of their ethnic or political background, religion or belief may constitute a crime against humanity, emphasizes the need to ensure that Islamic State in Iraq and the Levant, Al-Nusrah Front and all other individuals, groups, undertakings and entities associated with Al-Qaida are held accountable for abuses of human rights and violations of international humanitarian law, and urges all parties to prevent such violations and abuses;

4. *Demands* that Islamic State in Iraq and the Levant, Al-Nusrah Front and all other individuals, groups, undertakings and entities associated with Al-Qaida cease all violence and terrorist acts and disarm and disband with immediate effect;

5. *Urges* all States, in accordance with their obligations under resolution 1373 (2001), to cooperate in efforts to find and bring to justice individuals, groups, undertakings and entities associated with Al-Qaida, including Islamic State in Iraq and the Levant and Al-Nusrah Front, who perpetrate, organize and sponsor terrorist acts, and in this regard underlines the importance of regional cooperation;

6. *Reiterates its call upon* all States to take all measures as may be necessary and appropriate and in accordance with their obligations under international law to counter incitement of terrorist acts motivated by extremism and intolerance perpetrated by individuals or entities associated with Islamic State in Iraq and the Levant, Al-Nusrah Front and Al-Qaida and to prevent the subversion of educational, cultural and religious institutions by terrorists and their supporters;

Foreign terrorist fighters

7. *Condemns* the recruitment by Islamic State in Iraq and the Levant, Al-Nusrah Front and all other individuals, groups, undertakings and entities associated with Al-Qaida of foreign terrorist fighters, whose presence is exacerbating conflict and contributing to violent radicalization, demands that all foreign terrorist fighters associated with Islamic State in Iraq and the Levant and other terrorist groups withdraw immediately, and expresses its readiness to consider listing those recruiting for or participating in the activities of Islamic State in Iraq and the Levant, Al-Nusrah Front and all other individuals, groups, undertakings and entities associated with Al-Qaida under the Al-Qaida sanctions regime, including through financing or facilitating, for Islamic State in Iraq and the Levant or Al-Nusrah Front, of travel of foreign terrorist fighters;

8. *Calls upon* all Member States to take national measures to suppress the flow of foreign terrorist fighters to, and bring to justice, in accordance with applicable international law, foreign terrorist fighters of, Islamic State in Iraq and the Levant, Al-Nusrah Front and all other individuals, groups, undertakings and entities associated with Al-Qaida, and reiterates further the obligation of Member States to prevent the movement of terrorists or terrorist groups, in accordance with applicable international law, by, inter alia, effective border controls, and in this context to exchange information expeditiously and improve cooperation among competent authorities to prevent the movement of terrorists and terrorist groups to and from their territories, the supply of weapons for terrorists and financing that would support terrorists;

9. *Encourages* all Member States to engage with those within their territories at risk of recruitment and violent radicalization to discourage travel to the Syrian Arab Republic and Iraq for the purposes of supporting or fighting for Islamic State in Iraq and the Levant, Al-Nusrah Front and all other individuals, groups, undertakings and entities associated with Al-Qaida;

10. *Reaffirms* its decision that States shall prevent the direct or indirect supply, sale or transfer to Islamic State in Iraq and the Levant, Al-Nusrah Front and all other individuals, groups, undertakings and entities associated with Al-Qaida from their territories or by their nationals outside their territories, or using their flag vessels or aircraft, of arms and related materiel of all types, including weapons and ammunition, military vehicles and equipment, paramilitary equipment, and spare parts for the aforementioned, and technical advice, assistance or training related to military activities, as well as its calls for States to find ways of intensifying and accelerating the exchange of operational information regarding traffic in arms, and to enhance coordination of efforts at the national, subregional, regional and international levels;

Terrorist financing

11. *Reaffirms* its resolution 1373 (2001) and in particular its decisions that all States shall prevent and suppress the financing of terrorist acts and refrain from providing any form of support, active or passive, to entities or persons involved in terrorist acts, including by suppressing recruitment of members of terrorist groups and eliminating the supply of weapons to terrorists;

12. *Recalls* its decision in resolution 2161 (2014) that all States shall ensure that no funds, financial assets or economic resources are made available, directly or indirectly for the benefit of Islamic State in Iraq and the Levant, Al-Nusrah Front or any other individuals, groups, undertakings and entities associated with Al-Qaida, by their nationals or by persons within their territory, and reaffirms its decision in resolution 1373 (2001) that all States shall prohibit their nationals or any persons and entities within their territories from making any funds, financial assets or economic resources or financial or other related services available, directly or indirectly, for the benefit of persons who commit or attempt to commit or facilitate or participate in the commission of terrorist acts, or for the benefit of entities owned or controlled, directly or indirectly, by such persons and of persons and entities acting on behalf of or at the direction of such persons;

13. *Notes with concern* that oilfields and related infrastructure controlled by Islamic State in Iraq and the Levant, Al-Nusrah Front and all other individuals, groups, undertakings and entities associated with Al-Qaida are generating income which supports their recruitment efforts and strengthens their operational capability to organize and carry out terrorist attacks;

14. *Condemns* any engagement in direct or indirect trade involving Islamic State in Iraq and the Levant, Al-Nusrah Front and all other individuals, groups, undertakings and entities associated with Al-Qaida, and reiterates that such engagement could constitute financial support for entities designated by the Security Council Committee pursuant to resolutions 1267 (1999) and 1989 (2011) (the Committee) and may lead to further listings by the Committee;

15. *Emphasizes* the importance of all Member States complying with their obligation to ensure that their nationals and persons within their territory do not make donations to individuals and entities designated by the Committee or those acting on behalf of or at the direction of designated entities;

16. *Expresses its concern* that aircraft or other transport departing from territory controlled by Islamic State in Iraq and the Levant could be used to transfer gold or other valuable items and economic resources for sale on international markets or to make other arrangements that could result in violations of the asset freeze;

17. *Confirms* that the requirements in paragraph 1 (*a*) of resolution 2161 (2014) shall also apply to the payment of ransoms to individuals, groups, undertakings or entities on the Al-Qaida Sanctions List, regardless of how or by whom the ransom is paid;

Sanctions

18. *Observes* that Islamic State in Iraq and the Levant is a splinter group of Al-Qaida, recalls that Islamic State in Iraq and the Levant and Al-Nusrah Front are included on the Al-Qaida Sanctions List ,and in this regard expresses its readiness to consider listing individuals, groups, undertakings and entities providing support to Islamic State in Iraq and the Levant or to Al-Nusrah Front, including those who are financing, arming, planning or recruiting

for Islamic State in Iraq and the Levant or Al-Nusrah Front and all other individuals, groups, undertakings and entities associated with Al-Qaida through information and communications technologies, including the internet and social media or through any other means;

19. *Decides* that the individuals specified in the annex to the present resolution shall be subject to the measures imposed in paragraph 1 of resolution 2161 (2014) and added to the Al-Qaida Sanctions List;

20. *Directs* the Committee to make accessible on the Committee website the narrative summaries of reasons for listing the individuals specified in the annex to the present resolution as agreed by the Council, and confirms that the provisions of resolution 2161 (2014) and subsequent relevant resolutions shall apply to the names specified in the annex for so long as they remain on the Al-Qaida Sanctions List;

21. *Encourages* the submission of listing requests to the Committee by Member States of individuals and entities supporting Islamic State in Iraq and the Levant, Al-Nusrah Front and all other individuals, groups, undertakings and entities associated with Al-Qaida, and further encourages the Committee to urgently consider additional designations of individuals and entities supporting Islamic State in Iraq and the Levant and Al-Nusrah Front;

Reporting

22. *Directs* the Analytical Support and Sanctions Monitoring Team to submit a report to the Committee within 90 days on the threat, including to the region, posed by Islamic State in Iraq and the Levant and Al-Nusrah Front, their sources of arms, funding, recruitment and demographics, and recommendations for additional action to address the threat, and requests that, after a Committee discussion of this report, the Chair of the Committee brief the Council on its principal findings;

23. *Requests* the United Nations Assistance Mission for Iraq, within its mandate, capabilities and its areas of operation, to assist the Committee and the Monitoring Team established pursuant to resolution 1526 (2004) of 30 January 2004, including by passing information relevant to the implementation of the measures in paragraph 1 of resolution 2161 (2014);

24. *Decides* to remain seized of this matter.

Adopted unanimously at the 7242nd meeting.

Annex

1. Abdelrahman Mouhamad Zafir al Dabidi al Jahani

Abdelrahman Mouhamad Zafir al Dabidi al Jahani is associated with Al-Qaida or any cell, affiliate, splinter group or derivative thereof for "participating in the financing, planning, facilitating, preparing or perpetrating of acts or activities by, in conjunction with, under the name of, on behalf of or in support of" and "recruiting for" Jabhet al-Nusra, an a.k.a. of Al-Nusrah Front for the People of the Levant (QE.A.137.14).

2. Hajjaj bin Fahd al Ajmi

Hajjaj bin Fahd al Ajmi is associated with Al-Qaida or any cell, affiliate, splinter group or derivative thereof for "participating in the financing, planning, facilitating, preparing or perpetrating of acts or activities by, in conjunction with, under the name of, on behalf of or in support of" Al-Nusrah Front for the People of the Levant (QE.A.137.14).

3. Abou Mohamed al Adnani

Abou Mohamed al Adnani is associated with Al-Qaida or any cell, affiliate, splinter group or derivative thereof for "participating in the financing, planning, facilitating, preparing or perpetrating of acts or activities by, in conjunction with, under the name of, on behalf of or in support of" Islamic State in Iraq and the Levant (ISIL), an a.k.a of Al-Qaida in Iraq (QE.J.115.04).

4. Said Arif

Said Arif is associated with Al-Qaida or any cell, affiliate, splinter group or derivative thereof for "participating in the financing, planning, facilitating, preparing or perpetrating of acts or activities by, in conjunction with, under the name of, on behalf of or in support of" and "recruiting for" Jabhet al-Nusra, an a.k.a. of Al-Nusrah Front for the People of the Levant (QE.A.137.14).

5. Abdul Mohsen Abdallah Ibrahim al Charekh

Abdul Mohsen Abdallah Ibrahim al Charekh is associated with Al-Qaida or any cell, affiliate, splinter group or derivative thereof for "participating in the financing, planning, facilitating, preparing or perpetrating of acts or activities by, in conjunction with, under the name of, on behalf of or in support of" Jabhet al-Nusra, listed as an a.k.a. of Al-Nusrah Front for the People of the Levant (QE.A.137.14).

6. Hamid Hamad Hamid al-'Ali

Hamid Hamad Hamid al-'Ali is associated with Al-Qaida or any cell, affiliate, splinter group or derivative thereof for "participating in the financing, planning, facilitating, preparing or perpetrating of acts or activities by, in conjunction with, under the name of, on behalf of or in support of" Islamic State in Iraq and the Levant (ISIL), an a.k.a. of Al-Qaida in Iraq (QE.J.115.04), and Jabhet al-Nusra, an a.k.a. of Al-Nusrah Front for the People of the Levant (QE.A.137.14).

Decisions

At its 7272nd meeting, on 24 September 2014, the Security Council decided to invite the representatives of Afghanistan, Albania, Algeria, Andorra, Armenia, Austria, Azerbaijan, Bahrain, Belgium, Bosnia and Herzegovina, Botswana, Bulgaria, Burkina Faso, Cabo Verde, Canada, Colombia, Côte d'Ivoire, Croatia, Cyprus, the Czech Republic, Denmark, Egypt, Eritrea, Estonia, Finland, Georgia, Germany, Greece, Guinea, Hungary, Iceland, India, Indonesia, Iraq, Ireland, Israel, Italy, Jamaica, Japan, Kazakhstan, Kenya, Kuwait, Latvia, Lebanon, Lesotho, Libya, Liechtenstein, Malaysia, Malta, Mauritania, Micronesia (Federated States of), Monaco, Montenegro, Morocco, Nepal, the Netherlands, New Zealand, Niger, Norway Oman, Pakistan, Palau, Papua New Guinea, Paraguay, the Philippines, Poland, Portugal, Qatar, the Republic of Moldova, Romania, Samoa, San Marino, Saudi Arabia, Senegal, Serbia, Seychelles, Singapore, Slovakia, Slovenia, Somalia, Spain, Sri Lanka, Sweden, Switzerland, the Syrian Arab Republic, the former Yugoslav Republic of Macedonia, Togo, Tonga, Trinidad and Tobago, Turkey, Ukraine, the United Arab Emirates, the United Republic of Tanzania, Uruguay, Vanuatu and Yemen to participate, without vote, in accordance with rule 37 of its provisional rules of procedure, in the discussion of the item entitled:

"Threats to international peace and security caused by terrorist acts

> "Foreign terrorist fighters
>
> "Letter dated 3 September 2014 from the Permanent Representative of the United States of America to the United Nations addressed to the President of the Security Council (S/2014/648)".

At the same meeting, the Council also decided to extend an invitation, in accordance with rule 39 of its provisional rules of procedure, to Mr. Herman Van Rompuy, President of the European Council.

At the same meeting, the Council further decided to extend an invitation, in accordance with rule 39 of its provisional rules of procedure, to Cardinal Pietro Parolin, Secretary of State of the Holy See.

Resolution 2178 (2014)
of 24 September 2014

The Security Council,

Reaffirming that terrorism in all forms and manifestations constitutes one of the most serious threats to international peace and security and that any acts of terrorism are criminal and unjustifiable regardless of their motivations, whenever and by whomsoever committed, and remaining determined to contribute further to enhancing the effectiveness of the overall effort to fight this scourge on a global level,

Noting with concern that the terrorism threat has become more diffuse, with an increase, in various regions of the world, of terrorist acts, including those motivated by intolerance or extremism, and expressing its determination to combat this threat,

Bearing in mind the need to address the conditions conducive to the spread of terrorism, and affirming Member States' determination to continue to do all they can to resolve conflict and to deny terrorist groups the ability to put down roots and establish safe havens to address better the growing threat posed by terrorism,

Emphasizing that terrorism cannot and should not be associated with any religion, nationality or civilization,

Recognizing that international cooperation and any measures taken by Member States to prevent and combat terrorism must comply fully with the Charter of the United Nations,

Reaffirming its respect for the sovereignty, territorial integrity and political independence of all States in accordance with the Charter,

Reaffirming that Member States must ensure that any measures taken to counter terrorism comply with all their obligations under international law, in particular international human rights law, international refugee law and international humanitarian law, underscoring that respect for human rights, fundamental freedoms and the rule of law are complementary and mutually reinforcing with effective counter-terrorism measures, and are an essential part of a successful counter-terrorism effort, noting the importance of respect for the rule of law so as to effectively prevent and combat terrorism, and noting that failure to comply with these and other international obligations, including under the Charter, is one of the factors contributing to increased radicalization and fosters a sense of impunity,

Expressing grave concern over the acute and growing threat posed by foreign terrorist fighters, namely, individuals who travel to a State other than their States of residence or nationality for the purpose of the perpetration, planning or preparation of, or participation in, terrorist acts or providing or receiving terrorist training, including in connection with armed conflict, and resolving to address this threat,

Expressing grave concern also about those who attempt to travel to become foreign terrorist fighters,

Concerned that foreign terrorist fighters increase the intensity, duration and intractability of conflicts, and also may pose a serious threat to their States of origin, the States they transit and the States to which they travel, as well as States neighbouring zones of armed conflict in which foreign terrorist fighters are active and that are affected by serious security burdens, and noting that the threat of foreign terrorist fighters may affect all regions and Member States, even those far from conflict zones, and expressing grave concern that foreign terrorist fighters are using their extremist ideology to promote terrorism,

Expressing concern that international networks have been established by terrorists and terrorist entities among States of origin, transit and destination through which foreign terrorist fighters and the resources to support them have been channelled back and forth,

Expressing particular concern that foreign terrorist fighters are being recruited by and are joining entities such as Islamic State in Iraq and the Levant, Al-Nusrah Front and other cells, affiliates, splinter groups or derivatives of Al-Qaida, as designated by the Security Council Committee pursuant to resolutions 1267 (1999) and 1989 (2011), recognizing that the foreign terrorist fighter threat includes, among others, individuals supporting acts or activities of Al-Qaida and its cells, affiliates, splinter groups and derivative entities, including by recruiting for or otherwise supporting acts or activities of such entities, and stressing the urgent need to address this particular threat,

Recognizing that addressing the threat posed by foreign terrorist fighters requires comprehensively addressing underlying factors, including by preventing radicalization to terrorism, stemming recruitment, inhibiting foreign terrorist fighter travel, disrupting financial support to foreign terrorist fighters, countering violent extremism, which can be conducive to terrorism, countering incitement to terrorist acts motivated by extremism or intolerance, promoting political and religious tolerance, economic development and social cohesion and inclusiveness, ending and resolving armed conflicts, and facilitating reintegration and rehabilitation,

Recognizing also that terrorism will not be defeated by military force, law enforcement measures and intelligence operations alone, and underlining the need to address the conditions conducive to the spread of terrorism, as outlined in pillar I of the United Nations Global Counter-Terrorism Strategy,[219]

Expressing concern over the increased use by terrorists and their supporters of communications technology for the purpose of radicalizing to terrorism, recruiting and inciting others to commit terrorist acts, including through the Internet, and financing and facilitating the travel and subsequent activities of foreign terrorist fighters, and underlining the need for Member States to act cooperatively to prevent terrorists from exploiting technology, communications and resources to incite support for terrorist acts, while respecting human rights and fundamental freedoms and in compliance with other obligations under international law,

[219] General Assembly resolution 60/288.

Noting with appreciation the activities undertaken in the area of capacity-building by United Nations entities, in particular entities of the Counter-Terrorism Implementation Task Force, including the United Nations Office on Drugs and Crime and the United Nations Counter-Terrorism Centre, and also the efforts of the Counter-Terrorism Committee Executive Directorate to facilitate technical assistance, specifically by promoting engagement between providers of capacity-building assistance and recipients, in coordination with other relevant international, regional and subregional organizations, to assist Member States, upon their request, in implementation of the United Nations Global Counter-Terrorism Strategy,

Noting recent developments and initiatives at the international, regional and subregional levels to prevent and suppress international terrorism, and noting the work of the Global Counterterrorism Forum, in particular its recent adoption of a comprehensive set of good practices to address the foreign terrorist fighter phenomenon, and its publication of several other framework documents and good practices, including in the areas of countering violent extremism, criminal justice, prisons, kidnapping for ransom, providing support to victims of terrorism, and community-oriented policing, to assist interested States with the practical implementation of the United Nations counter-terrorism legal and policy framework and to complement the work of the relevant United Nations counter-terrorism entities in these areas,

Noting with appreciation the efforts of the International Criminal Police Organization (INTERPOL) to address the threat posed by foreign terrorist fighters, including through global law enforcement information-sharing enabled by the use of its secure communications network, databases and system of advisory notices, procedures to track stolen, forged identity papers and travel documents, and INTERPOL's counter-terrorism forums and foreign terrorist fighter programme,

Having regard to and highlighting the situation of individuals of more than one nationality who travel to their States of nationality for the purpose of the perpetration, planning, preparation of, or participation in, terrorist acts or the providing or receiving of terrorist training, and urging States to take action, as appropriate, in compliance with their obligations under their domestic law and international law, including international human rights law,

Calling upon States to ensure, in conformity with international law, in particular international human rights law and international refugee law, that refugee status is not abused by the perpetrators, organizers or facilitators of terrorist acts, including by foreign terrorist fighters,

Reaffirming its call upon all States to become party to the international counter-terrorism conventions and protocols as soon as possible, whether or not they are a party to regional conventions on the matter, and to fully implement their obligations under those to which they are a party,

Noting the continued threat to international peace and security posed by terrorism, and affirming the need to combat by all means, in accordance with the Charter, threats to international peace and security caused by terrorist acts, including those perpetrated by foreign terrorist fighters,

Acting under Chapter VII of the Charter,

1. *Condemns* the violent extremism, which can be conducive to terrorism, sectarian violence and the commission of terrorist acts by foreign terrorist fighters, and demands that all foreign terrorist fighters disarm and cease all terrorist acts and participation in armed conflict;

2. *Reaffirms* that all States shall prevent the movement of terrorists or terrorist groups by effective border controls and controls on issuance of identity papers and travel documents, and through measures for preventing counterfeiting, forgery or fraudulent use of identity papers and travel documents, underscores in this regard the importance of addressing, in accordance with their relevant international obligations, the threat posed by foreign terrorist fighters, and encourages Member States to employ evidence-based traveller risk assessment and screening procedures, including collection and analysis of travel data, without resorting to profiling based on stereotypes founded on grounds of discrimination prohibited by international law;

3. *Urges* Member States, in accordance with domestic and international law, to intensify and accelerate the exchange of operational information regarding actions or movements of terrorists or terrorist networks, including foreign terrorist fighters, especially with their States of residence or nationality, through bilateral or multilateral mechanisms, in particular the United Nations;

4. *Calls upon* all Member States, in accordance with their obligations under international law, to cooperate in efforts to address the threat posed by foreign terrorist fighters, including by preventing the radicalization to

terrorism and recruitment of foreign terrorist fighters, including children, preventing foreign terrorist fighters from crossing their borders, disrupting and preventing financial support to foreign terrorist fighters, and developing and implementing prosecution, rehabilitation and reintegration strategies for returning foreign terrorist fighters;

5. *Decides* that Member States shall, consistent with international human rights law, international refugee law and international humanitarian law, prevent and suppress the recruiting, organizing, transporting or equipping of individuals who travel to a State other than their States of residence or nationality for the purpose of the perpetration, planning or preparation of, or participation in, terrorist acts or the providing or receiving of terrorist training, and the financing of their travel and of their activities;

6. *Recalls* its decision, in resolution 1373 (2001) of 28 September 2001, that all Member States shall ensure that any person who participates in the financing, planning, preparation or perpetration of terrorist acts or in supporting terrorist acts is brought to justice, and decides that all States shall ensure that their domestic laws and regulations establish serious criminal offences sufficient to provide the ability to prosecute and to penalize in a manner duly reflecting the seriousness of the offence:

(*a*) Their nationals who travel or attempt to travel to a State other than their States of residence or nationality, and other individuals who travel or attempt to travel from their territories to a State other than their States of residence or nationality, for the purpose of the perpetration, planning or preparation of, or participation in, terrorist acts or the providing or receiving of terrorist training;

(*b*) The wilful provision or collection, by any means, directly or indirectly, of funds by their nationals or in their territories with the intention that the funds should be used, or in the knowledge that they are to be used, in order to finance the travel of individuals who travel to a State other than their States of residence or nationality for the purpose of the perpetration, planning or preparation of, or participation in, terrorist acts or the providing or receiving of terrorist training; and

(*c*) The wilful organization, or other facilitation, including acts of recruitment, by their nationals or in their territories, of the travel of individuals who travel to a State other than their States of residence or nationality for the purpose of the perpetration, planning or preparation of, or participation in, terrorist acts or the providing or receiving of terrorist training;

7. *Expresses its strong determination* to consider listing pursuant to resolution 2161 (2014) of 17 June 2014 individuals, groups, undertakings and entities associated with Al-Qaida who are financing, arming, planning or recruiting for them, or otherwise supporting their acts or activities, including through information and communications technologies, such as the Internet, social media or any other means;

8. *Decides* that, without prejudice to entry or transit necessary in the furtherance of a judicial process, including in furtherance of such a process related to arrest or detention of a foreign terrorist fighter, Member States shall prevent the entry into or transit through their territories of any individual about whom that State has credible information that provides reasonable grounds to believe that he or she is seeking entry into or transit through their territory for the purpose of participating in the acts described in paragraph 6 above, including any acts or activities indicating that an individual, group, undertaking or entity is associated with Al-Qaida, as set out in paragraph 2 of resolution 2161 (2014), provided that nothing in the present paragraph shall oblige any State to deny entry into or require the departure from its territories of its own nationals or permanent residents;

9. *Calls upon* Member States to require that airlines operating in their territories provide advance passenger information to the appropriate national authorities in order to detect the departure from their territories, or attempted entry into or transit through their territories, by means of civil aircraft, of individuals designated by the Security Council Committee pursuant to resolutions 1267 (1999) and 1989 (2011) (the Committee), and further calls upon Member States to report any such departure from their territories, or such attempted entry into or transit through their territories, of such individuals to the Committee, as well as sharing this information with the State of residence or nationality, as appropriate and in accordance with domestic law and international obligations;

10. *Stresses* the urgent need to implement fully and immediately the present resolution with respect to foreign terrorist fighters, underscores the particular and urgent need to implement the present resolution with respect to those foreign terrorist fighters who are associated with Islamic State in Iraq and the Levant, Al-Nusrah Front and other cells, affiliates, splinter groups or derivatives of Al-Qaida, as designated by the Committee, and expresses its readiness to consider designating, under resolution 2161 (2014), individuals associated with Al-Qaida who commit the acts specified in paragraph 6 above;

International cooperation

11. *Calls upon* Member States to improve international, regional and subregional cooperation, if appropriate through bilateral agreements, to prevent the travel of foreign terrorist fighters from or through their territories, including through increased sharing of information for the purpose of identifying foreign terrorist fighters, the sharing and adoption of best practices, and improved understanding of the patterns of travel by foreign terrorist fighters, and for Member States to act cooperatively when taking national measures to prevent terrorists from exploiting technology, communications and resources to incite support for terrorist acts, while respecting human rights and fundamental freedoms and in compliance with other obligations under international law;

12. *Recalls* its decision in resolution 1373 (2001) that Member States shall afford one another the greatest measure of assistance in connection with criminal investigations or proceedings relating to the financing or support of terrorist acts, including assistance in obtaining evidence in their possession necessary for the proceedings, and underlines the importance of fulfilling this obligation with respect to such investigations or proceedings involving foreign terrorist fighters;

13. *Encourages* INTERPOL to intensify its efforts with respect to the foreign terrorist fighter threat and to recommend or put in place additional resources to support and encourage national, regional and international measures to monitor and prevent the transit of foreign terrorist fighters, such as expanding the use of INTERPOL Special Notices to include foreign terrorist fighters;

14. *Calls upon* States to help to build the capacity of States to address the threat posed by foreign terrorist fighters, including to prevent and interdict foreign terrorist fighter travel across land and maritime borders, in particular the States neighbouring zones of armed conflict where there are foreign terrorist fighters, and welcomes and encourages bilateral assistance by Member States to help to build such national capacity;

Countering violent extremism in order to prevent terrorism

15. *Underscores* that countering violent extremism, which can be conducive to terrorism, including preventing radicalization, recruitment and mobilization of individuals into terrorist groups and becoming foreign terrorist fighters, is an essential element of addressing the threat to international peace and security posed by foreign terrorist fighters, and calls upon Member States to enhance efforts to counter this kind of violent extremism;

16. *Encourages* Member States to engage relevant local communities and non-governmental actors in developing strategies to counter the violent extremist narrative that can incite terrorist acts, address the conditions conducive to the spread of violent extremism, which can be conducive to terrorism, including by empowering youth, families, women, religious, cultural and education leaders, and all other concerned groups of civil society and adopt tailored approaches to countering recruitment to this kind of violent extremism and promoting social inclusion and cohesion;

17. *Recalls* its decision in paragraph 14 of resolution 2161 (2014) with respect to improvised explosive devices and individuals, groups, undertakings and entities associated with Al-Qaida, and urges Member States, in this context, to act cooperatively when taking national measures to prevent terrorists from exploiting technology, communications and resources, including audio and video, to incite support for terrorist acts, while respecting human rights and fundamental freedoms and in compliance with other obligations under international law;

18. *Calls upon* Member States to cooperate and consistently support each other's efforts to counter violent extremism, which can be conducive to terrorism, including through capacity-building, coordination of plans and efforts, and sharing lessons learned;

19. *Emphasizes*, in this regard, the importance of Member States' efforts to develop non-violent alternative avenues for conflict prevention and resolution by affected individuals and local communities to decrease the risk of radicalization to terrorism, and of efforts to promote peaceful alternatives to violent narratives espoused by foreign terrorist fighters, and underscores the role education can play in countering terrorist narratives;

United Nations engagement on the foreign terrorist fighter threat

20. *Notes* that foreign terrorist fighters and those who finance or otherwise facilitate their travel and subsequent activities may be eligible for inclusion on the Al-Qaida Sanctions List maintained by the Committee

pursuant to resolutions 1267 (1999) and 1989 (2011) where they participate in the financing, planning, facilitating, preparing or perpetrating of acts or activities by, in conjunction with, under the name of, on behalf of or in support of Al-Qaida, supplying, selling or transferring arms and related materiel to, or recruiting for, or otherwise supporting acts or activities of Al-Qaida or any cell, affiliate, splinter group or derivative thereof, and calls upon States to propose such foreign terrorist fighters and those who facilitate or finance their travel and subsequent activities for possible designation;

21. *Directs* the Committee pursuant to resolutions 1267 (1999) and 1989 (2011) and the Analytical Support and Sanctions Monitoring Team, in close cooperation with all relevant United Nations counter-terrorism bodies, in particular the Counter-Terrorism Committee Executive Directorate, to devote special focus to the threat posed by foreign terrorist fighters recruited by or joining Islamic State in Iraq and the Levant, Al-Nusrah Front and all groups, undertakings and entities associated with Al-Qaida;

22. *Encourages* the Analytical Support and Sanctions Monitoring Team to coordinate its efforts to monitor and respond to the threat posed by foreign terrorist fighters with other United Nations counter-terrorism bodies, in particular the Counter-Terrorism Implementation Task Force;

23. *Requests* the Analytical Support and Sanctions Monitoring Team, in close cooperation with other United Nations counter-terrorism bodies, to report to the Committee pursuant to resolutions 1267 (1999) and 1989 (2011) within 180 days, and provide a preliminary oral update to the Committee within 60 days, on the threat posed by foreign terrorist fighters recruited by or joining Islamic State in Iraq and the Levant, Al -Nusrah Front and all groups, undertakings and entities associated with Al-Qaida, including:

(*a*) A comprehensive assessment of the threat posed by these foreign terrorist fighters, including their facilitators, the most affected regions and trends in radicalization to terrorism, facilitation, recruitment, demographics and financing; and

(*b*) Recommendations for actions that can be taken to enhance the response to the threat posed by these foreign terrorist fighters;

24. *Requests* the Counter-Terrorism Committee, within its existing mandate and with the support of the Counter-Terrorism Committee Executive Directorate, to identify principal gaps in Member States' capacities to implement Council resolutions 1373 (2001) and 1624 (2005) of 14 September 2005 that may hinder States' abilities to stem the flow of foreign terrorist fighters, as well as to identify good practices to stem the flow of foreign terrorist fighters in the implementation of resolutions 1373 (2001) and 1624 (2005), and to facilitate technical assistance, specifically by promoting engagement between providers of capacity-building assistance and recipients, especially those in the most affected regions, including through the development, upon their request, of comprehensive counter-terrorism strategies that encompass countering violent radicalization and the flow of foreign terrorist fighters, recalling the roles of other relevant actors, for example the Global Counterterrorism Forum;

25. *Underlines* that the increasing threat posed by foreign terrorist fighters is part of the emerging issues, trends and developments related to resolutions 1373 (2001) and 1624 (2005) that, in paragraph 5 of resolution 2129 (2013) of 17 December 2013, the Council directed the Counter-Terrorism Committee Executive Directorate to identify, and therefore merits close attention by the Counter-Terrorism Committee, consistent with its mandate;

26. *Requests* the Committee pursuant to resolutions 1267 (1999) and 1989 (2011) and the Counter-Terrorism Committee to update the Council on their respective efforts pursuant to the present resolution;

27. *Decides* to remain seized of the matter.

Adopted unanimously at the 7272nd meeting.

Decisions

At its 7316th meeting, on 19 November 2014, the Security Council decided to invite the representatives of Albania, Algeria, Bahrain, Belgium, Botswana, Brazil, Burundi, Canada, Colombia, Croatia, Cuba, Denmark, Egypt, Ethiopia, Georgia, Germany, Guatemala, Hungary, India, Indonesia, Iran (Islamic Republic of), Iraq, Israel, Italy, Japan, Kazakhstan, Kenya, Kyrgyzstan, Malaysia, Montenegro, Morocco, the Netherlands, New Zealand,

Pakistan, Qatar, Romania, Saudi Arabia, Singapore, Slovenia, South Africa, Spain, Sri Lanka, the Syrian Arab Republic, Turkey, Ukraine and Yemen to participate, without vote, in accordance with rule 37 of its provisional rules of procedure, in the discussion of the item entitled:

"Threats to international peace and security caused by terrorist acts

"International cooperation on combating terrorism and violent extremism

"Letter dated 4 November 2014 from the Permanent Representative of Australia to the United Nations addressed to the Secretary-General (S/2014/787)".

At the same meeting, the Council also decided to extend an invitation, in accordance with rule 39 of its provisional rules of procedure, to Mr. Thomas Mayr-Harting, Head of the Delegation of the European Union to the United Nations.

At the same meeting, following consultations among members of the Security Council, the President made the following statement on behalf of the Council:[220]

The Security Council reaffirms that terrorism in all forms and manifestations constitutes one of the most serious threats to international peace and security and that any acts of terrorism are criminal and unjustifiable regardless of their motivations, whenever and by whomsoever committed.

The Council emphasizes that the threat of terrorism is expanding and intensifying, affecting a greater number of Member States across most regions, owing to, inter alia, global recruitment networks, the spread of violent extremist ideologies that can be conducive to terrorism, ease of movement of terrorists, including foreign terrorist fighters, and access to significant funding streams.

The Council reiterates its grave concern about Islamic State in Iraq and the Levant, Al-Nusrah Front and other terrorist entities associated with Al-Qaida and the negative impact of their presence, violent extremist ideology, and actions on the stability of Iraq, the Syrian Arab Republic and the region, including the devastating humanitarian impact on the civilian populations which has led to the displacement of millions of people, and about their acts of violence that foment sectarian tensions.

The Council further expresses its concern that, according to reports, more than 15,000 foreign terrorist fighters from over 80 countries have travelled to join or fight for terrorist entities associated with Al-Qaida, including in the Syrian Arab Republic, Iraq, Somalia and Yemen, as well as several countries in the Maghreb and Sahel regions.

The Council recalls its resolutions 1267 (1999), 1373 (2001), 1624 (2005), 2161 (2014) 2170 (2014) and 2178 (2014), and underlines the importance of Member States taking urgent action to implement their obligations therein.

The Council reaffirms its respect for the sovereignty, territorial integrity and political independence of all States in accordance with the Charter of the United Nations.

The Council reaffirms that Member States must ensure that any measures taken to counter terrorism comply with the Charter and all their other obligations under international law, in particular international human rights law, international refugee law and international humanitarian law.

The Council recognizes that terrorism will not be defeated by military force, law enforcement measures and intelligence operations alone, and underlines the need to address the conditions conducive to the spread of terrorism, as outlined in pillar I of the United Nations Global Counter-Terrorism Strategy,[219] and reiterates the need to address the factors driving recruitment and radicalization to terrorism, and furthermore recognizes that a comprehensive approach to defeat terrorism is required, involving national, subregional, regional and multilateral action.

The Council recognizes the significant capacity and coordination challenges many Member States face in countering terrorism and violent extremism and preventing terrorist financing, recruitment and all other

[220] S/PRST/2014/23.

forms of support to terrorist organizations; commends work under way by the Counter-Terrorism Committee and its Executive Directorate to identify capacity gaps[221] and to facilitate technical assistance to strengthen the implementation of resolutions 1373 (2001) and 1624 (2005) which supports compliance with 2178 (2014); encourages Member States to continue to cooperate with the Committee and the Executive Directorate on the development of comprehensive and integrated national, subregional and regional counter-terrorism strategies; highlights the important role that Counter-Terrorism Implementation Task Force entities, including the United Nations Counter Terrorism Centre and the United Nations Office on Drugs and Crime, and other providers of capacity-building assistance should play in technical assistance delivery; and in this respect notes the threat posed by foreign terrorist fighters to countries of origin, transit and destination, as well as States neighbouring zones of armed conflict in which foreign terrorist fighters are active.

The Council calls upon Member States to help to build the capacity of other Member States, where necessary and upon request, to address the threat posed by terrorism, and welcomes and encourages bilateral assistance by Member States to help to build such national, subregional or regional capacity.

The Council welcomes recent listings by the Security Council Committee pursuant to resolutions 1267 (1999) and 1989 (2011) of foreign terrorist fighters and recruiters, and urges Member States to identify and propose additional foreign terrorist fighters and those individuals who facilitate or finance their travel and subsequent activities for possible designation by the Committee.

The Council expresses its determination to consider listing pursuant to resolution 2161 (2014) individuals, groups, undertakings and entities associated with Al-Qaida who are financing, arming, planning or recruiting for them, or otherwise supporting their acts or activities, including through information and communications technologies, such as the Internet, social media or any other means.

The Council welcomes recent developments and initiatives at the international, regional and subregional levels to prevent and suppress the foreign terrorist fighter phenomenon, notes the work of the Global Counterterrorism Forum, in particular its recent adoption of a comprehensive set of good practices to address the foreign terrorist fighter phenomenon and the establishment of its Working Group on Foreign Terrorist Fighters, and the work of the Organization for Security and Cooperation in Europe, the European Union, the African Centre for the Study and Research on Terrorism and the Meeting of Heads of Special Services, Security Agencies and Law Enforcement Organizations.

The Council takes note of the communiqué of the African Union Peace and Security Council summit on countering violent extremism and terrorism, held in Nairobi on 2 September 2014, and calls upon United Nations counter-terrorism entities, within existing mandates, and Member States to provide assistance and capacity-building towards Africa's efforts to counter violent extremism and terrorism.

Travel and transit

The Security Council urges Member States to improve bilateral, international, regional and subregional cooperation, to prevent the travel of foreign terrorist fighters from or through their territories, including through increased sharing of information for the purpose of identifying foreign terrorist fighters, understanding patterns of travel by foreign terrorist fighters and sharing practices in evidence-based traveller risk assessment and border screening, noting the need to address the challenges posed by evasive travel routes of foreign terrorist fighters.

The Council reiterates, as called for in resolutions 2161 (2014) and 2178 (2014), its call upon Member States to make use of the International Criminal Police Organization (INTERPOL) databases and to require that airlines under their jurisdiction provide advance passenger information to detect the departure from, entry into or transit through their territories of individuals on the Al-Qaida Sanctions List, and additionally encourages that they provide passenger name records, where appropriate, to the appropriate national authorities, and requests the Counter-Terrorism Committee Executive Directorate to report, within 180 days,

[221] Preliminary analysis of the principal gaps in Member States' capacities to implement Security Council resolutions 1373 (2001) and 1624 (2005) that may hinder their abilities to stem the flow of foreign terrorist fighters pursuant to Security Council resolution 2178 (2014) (S/2014/807, annex).

to the Counter-Terrorism Committee on gaps in the use of advance passenger information and make recommendations to expand the use of advance passenger information, including plans to facilitate the required capacity-building in this regard, working with the Analytical Support and Sanctions Monitoring Team and relevant Counter-Terrorism Implementation Task Force entities, including the International Civil Aviation Organization, as well as industry representatives such as the International Air Transport Association.

The Council reiterates that the increasing threat posed by foreign terrorist fighters is part of the emerging issues, trends and developments related to resolutions 1373 (2001) and 1624 (2005), and encourages the Counter-Terrorism Committee to hold Special Meetings in 2015 with the participation of Member States and relevant international and regional organizations to discuss ways to stem the flow of foreign terrorist fighters and to prevent terrorists from exploiting the Internet and social media to recruit and incite terrorist acts, while respecting human rights and fundamental freedoms and in compliance with other obligations under international law; and in this regard notes the importance of the Committee holding meetings in affected regions on issues related to the mandate of the Committee.

The Council calls upon Member States to ensure, in conformity with international law, in particular international human rights law and international refugee law, that refugee status is not abused by the perpetrators, organizers or facilitators of terrorist acts, including by foreign terrorist fighters.

Countering terrorist narratives and violent extremism

The Council expresses grave concern at the spread of violent extremist ideologies that underpin the terrorist narrative, and that foreign terrorist fighters are using their extremist ideologies to promote terrorism, and reiterates the need to counter violent extremism through effective national responses including by building community resilience, as well as through cooperation at the subregional, regional and international levels, with a strong role for the United Nations in supporting these efforts, and underscores the role education can play in countering terrorist narratives.

The Council highlights the continued need to improve the visibility and effectiveness of the role of the United Nations in countering the spread of violent extremist ideologies that are conducive to terrorism, including through strategic communications, and underscores the need to enhance the efforts of the United Nations and its Member States to tackle this issue more effectively and for further steps in this regard.

The Council encourages the sharing of national and regional experiences in countering violent extremism, and welcomes the efforts of the Counter-Terrorism Committee, with the support of the Counter-Terrorism Committee Executive Directorate, to conduct dialogue with Member States and to hold open briefings on these issues to support efforts to counter incitement and violent extremism, and notes the need for the sharing of experiences to address the threat posed by terrorists and foreign terrorist fighters, including on rehabilitation and reintegration.

The Council notes that terrorism and violent extremism is impacting a growing number of conflict situations, including in States that host United Nations field missions, and in this regard encourages information-sharing, where relevant and appropriate, between Special Representatives of the Secretary General, the Department of Political Affairs and the Department of Peacekeeping Operations of the Secretariat, the Counter-Terrorism Committee Executive Directorate, the Analytical Support and Sanctions Monitoring Team and other relevant Counter-Terrorism Implementation Task Force entities, within existing mandates and resources.

The Council recommends that United Nations regional offices located in regions that face terrorist threats undertake regional information analysis and inter-mission information-sharing on terrorism and violent extremism, within existing mandates and resources.

The Council expresses concern over the increased use by terrorists and their supporters of communications technology for the purpose of radicalizing to terrorism, recruiting and inciting others to commit terrorist acts, including through the Internet, and financing and facilitating the travel and subsequent activities of foreign terrorist fighters.

The Council urges Member States to act cooperatively to prevent terrorists from recruiting, to counter their violent extremist propaganda and incitement on the Internet and social media, including by developing effective counter-narratives, while respecting human rights and fundamental freedoms and in compliance with obligations under international law, stresses the importance of cooperation with civil society and the private sector in this endeavour, and encourages relevant Counter-Terrorism Implementation Task Force entities to support regional initiatives in this regard.

Financing

The Council expresses its deep concern that oilfields and related infrastructure controlled by Islamic State in Iraq and the Levant, Al-Nusrah Front and potentially other individuals, groups, undertakings and entities associated with Al-Qaida are generating a significant portion of the groups' income, which supports their recruitment efforts and strengthens their operational capability to organize and carry out terrorist attacks.

The Council reaffirms that States are required by resolution 2161 (2014) to ensure that their nationals and those in their territory do not make assets or economic resources, directly or indirectly, available to Islamic State in Iraq and the Levant, Al-Nusrah Front and all other individuals, groups, undertakings and entities associated with Al-Qaida, and notes that this obligation applies to the direct and indirect trade in oil and oil products.

The Council encourages Member States to report to the Committee pursuant to resolutions 1267 (1999) and 1989 (2011) seizures or transfers of oil that they have reason to believe originated from territory controlled by Islamic State in Iraq and the Levant and Al-Nusrah Front and seizures of oil refining and related material believed to be for transfer into territory controlled by Islamic State in Iraq and the Levant and Al-Nusrah Front; encourages the Committee to immediately consider designations of individuals and entities engaged in these activities; and expresses its intention to consider additional measures to disrupt this source of terrorism financing, including prohibitions on the transfer of oil, oil products and oil refining and related material to and from territory controlled by Islamic State in Iraq and the Levant, Al-Nusrah Front and all other individuals, groups, undertakings and entities associated with Al-Qaida.

The Council stresses that donations from individuals and entities have played a role in developing and sustaining Islamic State in Iraq and the Levant and Al-Nusrah Front, and that Member States have an obligation to ensure that such support is not made available to those terrorist groups and other individuals, groups, undertakings and entities associated with Al-Qaida by their nationals and persons within their territory, and urges Member States to address this directly through enhanced vigilance of the international financial system and by working with their non-profit and charitable organizations to ensure that financial flows through charitable giving are not diverted to Islamic State in Iraq and the Levant, Al-Nusrah Front or any other individuals, groups, undertakings and entities associated with Al-Qaida.

The Council expresses its concern that aircraft or other transport departing from territory controlled by Islamic State in Iraq and the Levant and Al-Nusrah Front could be used to transfer gold or other valuable items and economic resources for sale on international markets, or to transfer arms and materiel for use by Islamic State in Iraq and the Levant and Al-Nusrah Front, and notes that individuals or entities engaged in such activities may be eligible for listing by the Committee pursuant to resolutions 1267 (1999) and 1989 (2011); expresses its concern regarding reports that items of archaeological, historical, cultural and religious importance are being illegally removed from territory controlled by Islamic State in Iraq and the Levant and Al-Nusrah Front which may be generating income for those groups, and calls upon Member States to take appropriate measures to prevent such illegal trade; and in this regard reminds all States that they are required to ensure that no funds, financial assets or economic resources are made available, directly or indirectly, for the benefit of Islamic State in Iraq and the Levant, Al-Nusrah Front and all other individuals, groups, undertakings and entities associated with Al-Qaida; and looks forward to thorough consideration by the Committee of the relevant recommendations regarding new measures to disrupt such activities contained in the report of the Analytical Support and Sanctions Monitoring Team submitted pursuant to resolution 2170 (2014),[222] with a view to further disrupting the activities of those groups.

[222] See S/2014/815.

The Council strongly condemns incidents of kidnapping and hostage-taking committed by Islamic State in Iraq and the Levant, Al-Nusrah Front and all other individuals, groups, undertakings and entities associated with Al-Qaida for any purpose, including with the aim of raising funds or gaining political concessions, notes with concern that ransoms paid to terrorists are used as one of the sources of funding for their activities, including further kidnappings, expresses its determination to prevent kidnapping and hostage-taking committed by terrorist groups and to secure the safe release of hostages without ransom payments or political concessions, in accordance with applicable international law, calls upon all Member States to prevent terrorists from benefiting directly or indirectly from ransom payments or from political concessions and to secure the safe release of hostages, and reaffirms the need for all Member States to cooperate closely during incidents of kidnapping and hostage-taking committed by terrorist groups.

The Council highlights the relevance of Financial Action Task Force recommendations in support of implementing resolutions 2170 (2014) and 2178 (2014), including its recommendation to States to implement cash declaration/disclosure systems for both incoming and outgoing transportation of currency, and other measures to address the threat that some foreign terrorist fighters and facilitators are acting as cash couriers for terrorist organizations.

The Council expresses its concern regarding the connection, in some cases, between terrorism and transnational organized crime and illicit activities such as drugs, arms and human trafficking, and money-laundering.

The Council reiterates that States are required to prevent the direct or indirect supply, sale or transfer to Islamic State in Iraq and the Levant, Al-Nusrah Front and all other individuals, groups, undertakings and entities associated with Al-Qaida from their territories or by their nationals outside their territories, or using their flag vessels or aircraft, of arms and related materiel of all types, including weapons and ammunition, military vehicles and equipment, paramilitary equipment, and spare parts for the aforementioned, and technical advice, assistance or training related to military activities, as well as its calls for States to find ways of intensifying and accelerating the exchange of operational information regarding traffic in arms, and to enhance coordination of efforts at the national, subregional, regional and international levels.

The Council further reminds all States of their obligation to ensure that any person who participates in the financing, planning, preparation or perpetration of terrorist acts is brought to justice and ensure that such terrorist acts are established as serious criminal offenses in domestic laws and regulations and that the punishment duly reflects the seriousness of such terrorist acts, and encourages the Counter-Terrorism Committee Executive Directorate to provide guidance upon request.

The Council stresses that the intolerance, violence and hatred that Islamic State in Iraq and the Levant, Al-Nusrah Front and other groups associated with Al-Qaida espouse must be countered, and expresses its determination to defeat the threat to international peace and security posed by terrorism.

At its 7362nd meeting, on 19 January 2015, the Council considered the item entitled "Threats to international peace and security caused by terrorist acts".

At the same meeting, following consultations among members of the Security Council, the President made the following statement on behalf of the Council:[223]

The Security Council condemns in the strongest terms the most recent escalation in attacks perpetrated by Boko Haram, in particular the suicide bombings of 10 and 11 January 2015 in Maiduguri, Borno State, and Potiskum, Yobe State, Nigeria, reportedly involving children coerced by Boko Haram to act as suicide bombers, the attacks of 3 to 7 January 2015 in Baga, Borno State, which resulted in the massive destruction of civilian homes and significant civilian casualties, as well as the increasing attacks in the Lake Chad Basin region along Nigeria's borders with Chad and Cameroon and in the northern provinces of Cameroon.

The Council reaffirms that terrorism in all its forms and manifestations is criminal and unjustifiable, regardless of its motivation, wherever, whenever and by whomsoever committed. The Council reaffirms that terrorism cannot and should not be associated with any religion, nationality, civilization or ethnic group.

---

[223] S/PRST/2015/4.

The Council expresses its deep sympathy and condolences to the families of the victims and expresses its sympathy to all those injured in these attacks and to the people and the Government of Nigeria as well as the people and Governments of other affected countries.

The Council strongly condemns and deplores all abuses of human rights and, where applicable, violations of international humanitarian law by the terrorist group Boko Haram, since 2009, including those involving violence against civilian populations, notably women and children, kidnappings, killings, hostage-taking, pillaging, rape, sexual slavery and other sexual violence, recruitment of children and destruction of civilian property. The Council expresses serious concern over the reported violations and abuses of human rights and large-scale displacements of the civilian population, including into Nigeria's neighbouring countries. The Council recalls its decision to place Boko Haram on the Al-Qaida Sanctions List.

The Council demands that Boko Haram immediately and unequivocally cease all hostilities and all abuses of human rights and violations of international humanitarian law and disarm and demobilize. The Council demands the immediate and unconditional release of all those abducted who remain in captivity, including the 276 schoolgirls abducted in Chibok, Borno State, in April 2014. The Council recognizes that some of such acts may amount to crimes against humanity and stresses that those responsible for all abuses and violations of human rights and violations of international humanitarian law must be held accountable. The Council reiterates the primary responsibility of Member States to protect civilian populations on their territories, in accordance with their obligations under international law.

The Council expresses its concern at the scale of the growing humanitarian crisis caused by the activities of Boko Haram, which has resulted in the large-scale displacement of Nigerians within the country and into neighbouring Cameroon, Chad and Niger. The Council, in this regard, commends the support provided to the refugees by the Governments of the said countries, including with the assistance of humanitarian actors and relevant United Nations entities, and calls upon the international community to provide its support in areas which require urgent attention.

The Council expresses deep concern that the activities of Boko Haram are undermining the peace and stability of the West and Central African region.

The Council takes note of the outcome of the Paris summit of 17 May 2014, which underscored the commitment of the countries in the Lake Chad Basin region, including with the support of bilateral and multilateral partners, to enhance information-sharing, coordination and joint operations, to more effectively combat Boko Haram, as well as the outcomes of the follow-up London and Abuja ministerial meetings. The Council also takes note of the communiqué of 7 October 2014 of the extraordinary summit of the Heads of State of the Lake Chad Basin Commission, as well as the communiqué of 25 November 2014 of the African Union Peace and Security Council on the efforts of the Commission member States and Benin to combat Boko Haram.

The Security Council takes note of the decision of the Commission member States and Benin to operationalize the Multinational Joint Task Force, including through the establishment of a joint headquarters and the deployment of national contingents, to conduct military operations against Boko Haram.

The Council welcomes plans for a regional meeting in Niamey on 20 January 2015 to discuss the regional response to the threat posed by Boko Haram. The Council urges the Commission member States and Benin to undertake further planning toward the sustainable, viable and effective operationalization of the Task Force. The Council, in this regard, urges them to identify the means and modalities of the envisaged deployment, especially in the areas of intelligence-sharing and joint operations.

The Council welcomes the assistance to the States in the region already being provided by bilateral and multilateral partners and encourages them to increase support to enhance the operational capacity of the Task Force, including through the provision of financial and logistical assistance, relevant equipment and modalities to increase effective intelligence-sharing to further the region's collective efforts to combat Boko Haram more effectively. The Council underlines that all operations of the Task Force must be conducted in full compliance with international law, including international humanitarian law and human rights law.

The Council takes note of the communiqué of the Government of Chad, issued on 14 January 2015, which pledged active support in the fight against Boko Haram. The Council welcomes the vote by the

National Assembly of Chad on 16 January 2015, which authorized Chadian armed troops and security forces to assist Cameroonian and Nigerian soldiers in the fight against Boko Haram terrorists.

The Council underlines the need to bring perpetrators, organizers, financiers and sponsors of these reprehensible acts of terrorism to justice in accordance with international law and relevant Council resolutions.

At its 7379th meeting, on 12 February 2015, the Council decided to invite the representatives of Armenia, Australia, Austria, Belarus, Belgium, Bulgaria, Cambodia, Croatia, Cyprus, the Czech Republic, Denmark, Egypt, Finland, Germany, Greece, Hungary, Iceland, Iraq, Italy, Japan, Kazakhstan, Lebanon, Luxembourg, Malta, Montenegro, Morocco, the Netherlands, Nicaragua, Norway, the Philippines, Poland, Portugal, the Republic of Korea, Romania, Serbia, Slovakia, Slovenia, Somalia, Sweden, the Syrian Arab Republic, Tunisia and Turkey to participate, without vote, in accordance with rule 37 of its provisional rules of procedure, in the discussion of the item entitled "Threats to international peace and security caused by terrorist acts".

Resolution 2199 (2015)
of 12 February 2015

The Security Council,

Reaffirming its primary responsibility for the maintenance of international peace and security, in accordance with the Charter of the United Nations,

Reaffirming also that terrorism in all forms and manifestations constitutes one of the most serious threats to international peace and security and that any acts of terrorism are criminal and unjustifiable regardless of their motivations, whenever and by whomsoever committed,

Reaffirming further the need to combat by all means, in accordance with the Charter and international law, including applicable international human rights, refugee and humanitarian law, threats to international peace and security caused by terrorist acts, stressing in this regard the important role the United Nations plays in leading and coordinating this effort,

Emphasizing that sanctions are an important tool under the Charter in the maintenance and restoration of international peace and security, including countering terrorism, and underlining the importance of prompt and effective implementation of relevant resolutions, in particular Security Council resolutions 1267 (1999) of 15 October 1999 and 1989 (2011) of 17 June 2011 as key instruments in the fight against terrorism,

Recalling its resolutions 1267 (1999), 1989 (2011), 2161 (2014) of 17 June 2014, 2170 (2014) of 15 August 2014 and 2178 (2014) of 24 September 2014 and the statements by its President of 28 July[224] and 19 November 2014,[220] including its stated intention to consider additional measures to disrupt oil trade by Islamic State in Iraq and the Levant (also known as Da'esh), Al-Nusrah Front and all other individuals, groups, undertakings and entities associated with Al-Qaida, as a source of terrorism financing,

Recognizing the importance of the role that financial sanctions play in disrupting Islamic State in Iraq and the Levant, Al-Nusrah Front and all other individuals, groups, undertakings and entities associated with Al-Qaida, and emphasizing also the need for a comprehensive approach to fully disrupt Islamic State in Iraq and the Levant and Al-Nusrah Front that integrates multilateral strategies with national action by Member States,

Reaffirming the independence, sovereignty, unity and territorial integrity of Iraq and the Syrian Arab Republic, and reaffirming further the purposes and principles of the Charter,

Reaffirming also that terrorism cannot and should not be associated with any religion, nationality or civilization,

Stressing that terrorism can only be defeated by a sustained and comprehensive approach involving the active participation and collaboration of all States and international and regional organizations to impede, impair, isolate and incapacitate the terrorist threat,

---

[224] S/PRST/2014/14.

Expressing in this regard its deep appreciation for League of Arab States resolution 7804 of 7 September 2014,[225] the Paris statement of 15 September 2014, the Financial Action Task Force statement on countering the financing of Islamic State in Iraq and the Levant of 24 October 2014 and the Manama declaration on countering terrorist finance of 9 November 2014,[226]

Reaffirming its resolution 1373 (2001) of 28 September 2001 and in particular its decisions that all States shall prevent and suppress the financing of terrorist acts and refrain from providing any form of support, active or passive, to entities or persons involved in terrorist acts, including by suppressing recruitment of members of terrorist groups and eliminating the supply of weapons to terrorists,

Recognizing the significant need to build capacities of Member States to counter terrorism and terrorist finance,

Reiterating its deep concern that oilfields and their related infrastructure, as well as other infrastructure such as dams and power plants, controlled by Islamic State in Iraq and the Levant, Al-Nusrah Front and potentially other individuals, groups, undertakings and entities associated with Al-Qaida, are generating a significant portion of the groups' income, alongside extortion, private foreign donations, kidnap ransoms and stolen money from the territory they control, which supports their recruitment efforts and strengthens their operational capability to organize and carry out terrorist attacks,

Condemning in the strongest terms abductions of women and children, expressing outrage at their exploitation and abuse, including rape, sexual abuse and forced marriage, committed by Islamic State in Iraq and the Levant, Al-Nusrah Front and other individuals, groups, undertakings and entities associated with Al-Qaida, and encouraging all State and non-State actors with evidence to bring it to the attention of the Council, along with any information that human trafficking may support the perpetrators financially,

Reaffirming the obligation of Member States to freeze without delay funds and other financial assets or economic resources of persons who commit, or attempt to commit, terrorist acts or participate in or facilitate the commission of terrorist acts, of entities owned or controlled directly or indirectly by such persons, and of persons and entities acting on behalf of, or at the direction of such persons and entities, including funds derived or generated from property owned or controlled directly or indirectly by such persons and associated persons and entities,

Expressing its concern that economic resources such as oil, oil products, modular refineries and related material, other natural resources, including precious metals such as gold, silver and copper, diamonds and any other assets are made available to Islamic State in Iraq and the Levant, Al-Nusrah Front and other individuals, groups, undertakings and entities associated with Al-Qaida, and noting that direct or indirect trade with Islamic State in Iraq and the Levant and Al-Nusrah Front in such materials could constitute a violation of the obligations imposed by resolution 2161 (2014),

Reminding all States of their obligation to ensure that any person who participates in the financing, planning, preparation or perpetration of terrorist acts or in supporting terrorist acts is brought to justice,

Reaffirming its decision in resolution 2133 (2014) of 27 January 2014, and noting again that ransom payments to terrorist groups are one of the sources of income which support their recruitment efforts, strengthen their operational capability to organize and carry out terrorist attacks and incentivize future incidents of kidnapping for ransom,

Expressing concern at the increased use, in a globalized society, by terrorists and their supporters, of new information and communications technologies, in particular the Internet, to facilitate terrorist acts, as well as their use to incite, recruit, fund or plan terrorist acts,

Expressing grave concern at the increased incidents of kidnapping and hostage-murdering committed by Islamic State in Iraq and the Levant, and condemning those heinous and cowardly murders which demonstrate that terrorism is a scourge impacting all of humanity and people from all regions and religions or beliefs,

[225] See S/2014/685, annex.

[226] See A/69/602.

Welcoming the report of the Analytical Support and Sanctions Monitoring Team on Al-Nusrah Front and Islamic State in Iraq and the Levant, published on 14 November 2014,[222] and taking note of the recommendations contained therein,

Noting with concern the continued threat posed to international peace and security by Islamic State in Iraq and the Levant, Al-Nusrah Front and all other individuals, groups, undertakings and entities associated with Al-Qaida, and reaffirming its resolve to address all aspects of that threat,

Acting under Chapter VII of the Charter,

Oil trade

1. *Condemns* any engagement in direct or indirect trade, in particular of oil and oil products, and modular refineries and related material, with Islamic State in Iraq and the Levant, Al-Nusrah Front and any other individuals, groups, undertakings and entities designated as associated with Al-Qaida by the Security Council Committee pursuant to resolutions 1267 (1999) and 1989 (2011), and reiterates that such engagement would constitute support for such individuals, groups, undertakings and entities and may lead to further listings by the Committee;

2. *Reaffirms* that States are required by resolution 2161 (2014) to ensure that their nationals and those in their territory do not make assets or economic resources, directly or indirectly, available to Islamic State in Iraq and the Levant, Al-Nusrah Front and all other individuals, groups, undertakings and entities associated with Al-Qaida, and notes that this obligation applies to the direct and indirect trade in oil and refined oil products, modular refineries and related material;

3. *Also reaffirms* that States are required by resolution 2161 (2014) to freeze without delay the funds and other financial assets or economic resources of Islamic State in Iraq and the Levant, Al-Nusrah Front, and other individuals, groups, undertakings and entities associated with Al-Qaida, including funds derived from property owned or controlled directly or indirectly, by them or by persons acting on their behalf or at their direction;

4. *Further reaffirms* that States are required by resolution 2161 (2014) to ensure that no funds, other financial assets or economic resources are made available, directly or indirectly, by their nationals or by persons within their territory for the benefit of Islamic State in Iraq and the Levant, Al-Nusrah Front and other individuals, groups, undertakings and entities associated with Al-Qaida;

5. *Recalls* that funds and other financial assets or economic resources made available to or for the benefit of listed individuals or entities are not always held directly by them, and recalls in addition that, in identifying such funds and benefits, States should be alert to the possibility that property owned or controlled indirectly by the listed party may not be immediately visible;

6. *Confirms* that economic resources include oil, oil products, modular refineries and related material, other natural resources and any other assets which are not funds but which potentially may be used to obtain funds, goods or services;

7. *Emphasizes*, therefore, that States are required by resolution 2161 (2014) to freeze without delay funds, other financial assets and economic resources of Islamic State in Iraq and the Levant, Al-Nusrah Front, and other individuals, groups, undertakings and entities associated with Al-Qaida, including oil, oil products, modular refineries and related material and other natural resources owned or controlled by them, or persons acting on their behalf or at their direction, as well as any funds or negotiable benefit arising from such economic resources;

8. *Recognizes* the need to take measures to prevent and suppress the financing of terrorism, individual terrorists and terrorist organizations, including from the proceeds of organized crime, inter alia, the illicit production of and trafficking in drugs and their chemical precursors, and the importance of continued international cooperation with that aim;

9. *Emphasizes* that States are required to ensure that their nationals and persons in their territory do not make available, directly or indirectly, any funds, other financial assets or economic resources, including oil, oil products, modular refineries and related material and other natural resources that are identified as directed to, collected for, or otherwise for the benefit of Islamic State in Iraq and the Levant, Al-Nusrah Front and other individuals, groups, undertakings and entities associated with Al-Qaida, as well as any funds or negotiable benefit arising from such economic resources;

10. *Expresses concern* that vehicles, including aircraft, cars and trucks and oil tankers, departing from or going to areas of the Syrian Arab Republic and Iraq where Islamic State in Iraq and the Levant, Al-Nusrah Front or any other groups, undertakings and entities associated with Al-Qaida operate, could be used to transfer oil and oil products, modular refineries and related material, cash and other valuable items, including natural resources such as precious metals and minerals like gold, silver, copper and diamonds, as well as grain, livestock, machinery, electronics and cigarettes by or on behalf of such entities for sale on international markets, for barter for arms or for use in other ways that would result in violations of the asset freeze or arms embargo in paragraph 1 of resolution 2161 (2014), and encourages Member States to take appropriate steps in accordance with international law to prevent and disrupt activity that would result in violations of the asset freeze or targeted arms embargo in paragraph 1 of resolution 2161 (2014);

11. *Reaffirms* that all States shall ensure that any person who participates in the financing, planning, preparation or perpetration of terrorist acts or in supporting terrorist acts is brought to justice and ensure that such terrorist acts are established as serious criminal offences in domestic laws and regulations and that the punishment duly reflects the seriousness of such terrorist acts, and emphasizes that such support may be provided through trade in oil and refined oil products, modular refineries and related material with Islamic State in Iraq and the Levant, Al-Nusrah Front and all other individuals, groups, undertakings and entities associated with Al-Qaida;

12. *Decides* that Member States shall inform the Committee within 30 days of the interdiction in their territory of any oil, oil products, modular refineries and related material being transferred to or from Islamic State in Iraq and the Levant or Al-Nusrah Front, and calls upon Member States to report to the Committee the outcome of proceedings brought against individuals and entities as a result of such activity;

13. *Encourages* the submission of listing requests to the Committee by Member States of individuals and entities engaged in oil trade-related activities with Islamic State in Iraq and the Levant, Al-Nusrah Front and all other individuals, groups, undertakings and entities associated with Al-Qaida, and directs the Al-Qaida sanctions Committee to immediately consider designations of individuals and entities engaged in oil trade-related activities with Islamic State in Iraq and the Levant, Al-Nusrah Front and all other individuals, groups, undertakings and entities associated with Al-Qaida;

14. *Calls upon* Member States to improve international, regional and subregional cooperation, including through increased sharing of information for the purpose of identifying smuggling routes used by Islamic State in Iraq and the Levant and Al-Nusrah Front, and for Member States to consider the provision of technical assistance and capacity-building to assist other Member States to counter the smuggling of oil and oil products, and modular refineries and related material, by Islamic State in Iraq and the Levant, Al-Nusrah Front and any other individual, group, undertaking or entity associated with Al-Qaida;

Cultural heritage

15. *Condemns* the destruction of cultural heritage in Iraq and the Syrian Arab Republic, particularly by Islamic State in Iraq and the Levant and Al-Nusrah Front, whether such destruction is incidental or deliberate, including targeted destruction of religious sites and objects;

16. *Notes with concern* that Islamic State in Iraq and the Levant, Al-Nusrah Front and other individuals, groups, undertakings and entities associated with Al-Qaida are generating income from engaging directly or indirectly in the looting and smuggling of cultural heritage items from archaeological sites, museums, libraries, archives and other sites in Iraq and the Syrian Arab Republic, which is being used to support their recruitment efforts and strengthen their operational capability to organize and carry out terrorist attacks;

17. *Reaffirms* its decision in paragraph 7 of resolution 1483 (2003) of 22 May 2003, and decides that all Member States shall take appropriate steps to prevent the trade in Iraqi and Syrian cultural property and other items of archaeological, historical, cultural, rare scientific and religious importance, illegally removed from Iraq since 6 August 1990 and from the Syrian Arab Republic since 15 March 2011, including by prohibiting cross-border trade in such items, thereby allowing for their eventual safe return to the Iraqi and Syrian people, and calls upon the United Nations Educational, Scientific and Cultural Organization, the International Criminal Police Organization (INTERPOL) and other international organizations, as appropriate, to assist in the implementation of the present paragraph;

Kidnapping for ransom and external donations

18. *Reaffirms its condemnation* of incidents of kidnapping and hostage-taking committed by Islamic State in Iraq and the Levant, Al-Nusrah Front and all other individuals, groups, undertakings and entities associated with Al-Qaida for any purpose, including with the aim of raising funds or gaining political concessions, and expresses its determination to prevent kidnapping and hostage-taking committed by terrorist groups and to secure the safe release of hostages without ransom payments or political concessions, in accordance with applicable international law;

19. *Reaffirms* that the requirements of paragraph 1 (*a*) of resolution 2161 (2014) apply to the payment of ransoms to individuals, groups, undertakings or entities on the Al-Qaida Sanctions List, regardless of how or by whom the ransom is paid, emphasizes that this obligation applies to Islamic State in Iraq and the Levant and Al-Nusrah Front, and calls upon all Member States to encourage private sector partners to adopt or to follow relevant guidelines and good practices for preventing and responding to terrorist kidnappings without paying ransom;

20. *Reiterates its call upon* all Member States to prevent terrorists from benefiting directly or indirectly from ransom payments or from political concessions and to secure the safe release of hostages, and reaffirms the need for all Member States to cooperate closely during incidents of kidnapping and hostage-taking committed by terrorist groups;

21. *Expresses its grave concern* about reports that external donations continue to make their way to Islamic State in Iraq and the Levant, Al-Nusrah Front and other individuals, groups, undertakings and entities associated with Al-Qaida, and recalls the importance of all Member States complying with their obligation to ensure that their nationals and persons within their territory do not make donations to individuals and entities designated by the Committee or those acting on behalf of or at the direction of designated entities;

22. *Stresses* that donations from individuals and entities have played a role in developing and sustaining Islamic State in Iraq and the Levant and Al-Nusrah Front and that Member States have an obligation to ensure that such support is not made available to those terrorist groups and other individuals, groups, undertakings and entities associated with Al-Qaida by their nationals and persons within their territory, and urges Member States to address this directly through enhanced vigilance of the international financial system and by working with their non-profit and charitable organizations to ensure that financial flows through charitable giving are not diverted to Islamic State in Iraq and the Levant, Al-Nusrah Front or any other individuals, groups, undertakings and entities associated with Al-Qaida;

Banking

23. *Urges* Member States to take steps to ensure that financial institutions within their territory prevent Islamic State in Iraq and the Levant, Al-Nusrah Front or other individuals, groups, undertakings or entities associated with Al-Qaida from accessing the international financial system;

Arms and related materiel

24. *Reaffirms* its decision that States shall prevent the direct or indirect supply, sale or transfer to Islamic State in Iraq and the Levant, Al-Nusrah Front and all other individuals, groups, undertakings and entities associated with Al-Qaida from their territories or by their nationals outside their territories, or using their flag vessels or aircraft, of arms and related materiel of all types, including weapons and ammunition, military vehicles and equipment, paramilitary equipment, and spare parts for the aforementioned, and technical advice, assistance or training related to military activities, as well as its calls for States to find ways of intensifying and accelerating the exchange of operational information regarding traffic in arms and to enhance coordination of efforts at the national, subregional, regional and international levels;

25. *Expresses concern* at the proliferation of all arms and related materiel of all types, in particular man-portable surface-to-air missiles, to Islamic State in Iraq and the Levant, Al-Nusrah Front and all other individuals, groups, undertakings and entities associated with Al-Qaida, and its potential impact on regional and international peace and security and impeding efforts to combat terrorism in some cases;

26. *Reminds* Member States of their obligation pursuant to paragraph 1 (*c*) of resolution 2161 (2014) to prevent the direct or indirect supply, sale or transfer of arms and related materiel of all types to listed individuals and entities, including Islamic State in Iraq and the Levant and Al-Nusrah Front;

27. *Calls upon* all States to consider appropriate measures to prevent the transfer of all arms and related materiel of all types, in particular man-portable surface-to-air missiles, if there is a reasonable suspicion that such arms and related materiel would be obtained by Islamic State in Iraq and the Levant, Al-Nusrah Front or other individuals, groups, undertakings and entities associated with Al-Qaida;

Asset freeze

28. *Reaffirms* that the requirements in paragraph 1 (*a*) of resolution 2161 (2014) apply to financial and economic resources of every kind, including but not limited to those used for the provision of Internet hosting or related services, used for the support of Al-Qaida and other individuals, groups, undertakings or entities included on the Al-Qaida Sanctions List;

Reporting

29. *Calls upon* Member States to report to the Committee within 120 days on the measures they have taken to comply with the measures imposed in the present resolution;

30. *Requests* the Analytical Support and Sanctions Monitoring Team, in close cooperation with other United Nations counter-terrorism bodies, to conduct an assessment of the impact of these new measures and to report to the Committee within 150 days, and thereafter to incorporate reporting on the impact of these new measures into their reports to the Committee in order to track progress on implementation, identify unintended consequences and unexpected challenges, and to help to facilitate further adjustments as required, and further requests the Committee to update the Council on the implementation of the present resolution as part of its regular oral reports to the Council on the state of the overall work of the Committee and the Monitoring Team;

31. *Decides* to remain actively seized of the matter.

Adopted unanimously at the 7379th meeting.

Decisions

At its 7421st meeting, on 30 March 2015, the Security Council considered the item entitled "Threats to international peace and security caused by terrorist acts".

At the same meeting, the Council decided to extend invitations, in accordance with rule 39 of its provisional rules of procedure, to Mr. Mohammed Ibn Chambas, Special Representative of the Secretary-General for West Africa and Head of the United Nations Office for West Africa, and Ms. Kyung-wha Kang, Assistant Secretary-General for Humanitarian Affairs and Deputy Emergency Relief Coordinator.

At its 7453rd meeting, on 29 May 2015, the Council considered the item entitled:

"Threats to international peace and security caused by terrorist acts

> "Foreign terrorist fighters
>
> "Letter dated 8 May 2015 from the Permanent Representative of Lithuania to the United Nations addressed to the Secretary-General (S/2015/324)
>
> "Letter dated 13 May 2015 from the Chair of the Security Council Committee established pursuant to resolution 1373 (2001) concerning counter-terrorism addressed to the President of the Security Council (S/2015/338)
>
> "Letter dated 19 May 2015 from the Chair of the Security Council Committee pursuant to resolutions 1267 (1999) and 1989 (2011) concerning Al-Qaida and associated individuals and entities addressed to the President of the Security Council (S/2015/358)".

At the same meeting, the Council decided to extend an invitation, in accordance with rule 39 of its provisional rules of procedure, to Mr. Jürgen Stock, Secretary General of the International Criminal Police Organization (INTERPOL).

At the same meeting, following consultations among members of the Security Council, the President made the following statement on behalf of the Council:[227]

The Security Council reaffirms that terrorism in all forms and manifestations constitutes one of the most serious threats to international peace and security and that any acts of terrorism are criminal and unjustifiable regardless of their motivations, whenever and by whomsoever committed.

The Council reaffirms its respect for the sovereignty, territorial integrity and political independence of all States in accordance with the Charter of the United Nations.

The Council emphasizes that terrorism cannot and should not be associated with any religion, nationality or civilization.

The Council reaffirms Member States' determination to continue to do all they can to resolve conflict and to deny terrorist groups the ability to put down roots and establish safe havens to address better the growing threat posed by terrorism.

The Council reiterates its grave concern over the continuing threat posed by foreign terrorist fighters, namely individuals who travel to a State other than their States of residence or nationality for the purpose of the perpetration, planning or preparation of, or participation in, terrorist acts or the providing or receiving of terrorist training, including in connection with armed conflict, and resolves to address this threat.

The Council expresses great concern that foreign terrorist fighters continue to be recruited in significant numbers by, and are joining, entities such as Islamic State in Iraq and the Levant (also known as Da'esh), Al-Nusrah Front and other cells, affiliates, splinter groups or derivatives of Al-Qaida, as designated by the Security Council Committee pursuant to resolutions 1267 (1999) and 1989 (2011), and groups that have pledged allegiance to Islamic State in Iraq and the Levant.

The Council expresses its grave concern that there are now over 25,000 foreign terrorist fighters from over 100 countries who have travelled to join or fight for terrorist entities associated with Al-Qaida, including Islamic State in Iraq and the Levant and Al-Nusrah Front, and notes that the flow is mainly focused on, but not limited to, movement into the Syrian Arab Republic and Iraq, according to the report provided by the Analytical Support and Sanctions Monitoring Team (Monitoring Team).[228]

The Council reiterates its concern that foreign terrorist fighters increase the intensity, duration and intractability of conflicts, and also may pose a serious threat to their States of origin, the States they transit and the States to which they travel, as well as States neighbouring zones of armed conflict in which foreign terrorist fighters are active and that are affected by serious security burdens, notes that the threat of foreign terrorist fighters may affect all regions and Member States, even those far from conflict zones, and expresses grave concern that foreign terrorist fighters are using their extremist ideology to promote terrorism.

The Council recognizes that addressing the threat posed by foreign terrorist fighters requires comprehensively addressing underlying factors, including by preventing radicalization to terrorism, stemming recruitment, inhibiting foreign terrorist fighter travel, disrupting financial support to foreign terrorist fighters, countering violent extremism, which can be conducive to terrorism, countering incitement to terrorist acts motivated by extremism or intolerance, promoting political and religious tolerance, economic development and social cohesion and inclusiveness, ending and resolving armed conflicts, and facilitating reintegration and rehabilitation.

The Council reaffirms that Member States must ensure that any measures taken to counter terrorism comply with all their obligations under international law, in particular international human rights law, international refugee law and international humanitarian law, underscores that respect for human rights, fundamental freedoms and the rule of law are complementary and mutually reinforcing with effective counter-terrorism measures, and are an essential part of a successful counter-terrorism effort, notes the importance of respect for the rule of law so as to effectively prevent and combat terrorism, and notes that failure to comply

---

[227] S/PRST/2015/11.

[228] See S/2015/358.

with these and other international obligations, including under the Charter, is one of the factors contributing to increased radicalization and fosters a sense of impunity.

The Council welcomes the extraordinary efforts undertaken to date to implement resolution 2178 (2014) on foreign terrorist fighters since its adoption on 24 September 2014, and the statement by its President adopted on 19 November 2014,[220] as well as other relevant resolutions, including resolutions 1373 (2001) and 1624 (2005). The Council expresses concern that large numbers of individuals continue to become radicalized to terrorism and travel as foreign terrorist fighters to conflict zones and pose a dire threat and that Member States need to improve prevention, interdiction and enforcement efforts through greater international information-sharing and timely coordination to prevent the flow of foreign terrorist fighters. The Council underscores the need for Member States to intensify these efforts and to identify and undertake priority actions, particularly those mentioned in the present statement, with assistance from others where needed, as expeditiously as possible. The Council further underscores the need to implement all aspects of resolution 2178 (2014), including countering violent extremism and managing foreign terrorist fighter returnees.

The Council underscores the critical importance of Member States implementing fully their international obligations, including those relevant to counter-terrorism and described in paragraph 6 of resolution 2178 (2014) to ensure that their domestic laws and regulations establish serious criminal offences sufficient to provide the ability to prosecute and to penalize in a matter duly reflecting the seriousness of the offences. To this effect, the Council commends the many Member States that have reviewed and, if needed, revised their domestic legislation in the recent past to address foreign terrorist fighters but notes that many other Member States have not yet done so sufficiently and calls upon Member States to fully implement their obligations found in paragraph 6 of resolution 2178 (2014) as expeditiously as possible. Recalling the international obligation in paragraph 5 of resolution 2178 (2014) to prevent and suppress the recruiting, organizing, transporting or equipping of foreign terrorist fighters, the Council calls upon Member States to implement these obligations through enforcement of relevant laws, including by prosecuting and penalizing foreign terrorist fighters to suppress and deter their flow.

The Council expresses great concern that many Member States still have not required airlines operating in their territories to provide to appropriate national authorities advance passenger information of travellers in order to detect the departure from their territories, or attempted entry into or transit through their territories, by means of civil aircraft, of individuals designated by the Committee pursuant to resolutions 1267 (1999) and 1989 (2011), as is called for in paragraph 9 of resolution 2178 (2014).

The Council notes that only 51 Member States to date are reported to be using advance passenger information to support evidence-based traveller risk assessment and screening procedures, according to the report provided by the Counter-Terrorism Committee Executive Directorate,[229] and strongly encourages Member States to urgently begin using advance passenger information to support evidence-based traveller risk assessment and screening procedures, including collection and analysis of travel data, without resorting to profiling based on stereotypes founded on grounds of discrimination prohibited by international law, as is encouraged in paragraph 2 of resolution 2178 (2014), and further encourages Member States to consider utilizing passenger name record data to enhance traveller screening. The Council notes that such actions can be particularly effective at reducing the ability of foreign terrorist fighters to evade detection at their borders.

The Council underscores the critical need for Member States to significantly increase their border management efforts in order to implement resolution 2178 (2014), including through strengthened border control measures and greater law enforcement cooperation as well as greater collection and sharing of terrorist identities for screening purposes among relevant national, regional and local authorities. The Council underscores in this regard, particularly for air and land travel, the importance of international collaboration amongst States' border security and customs officials and providing them with the tools and authorities necessary to effectively monitor and prevent the travel of foreign terrorist fighters.

The Council reiterates its call upon Member States to improve international, regional and subregional cooperation to prevent the travel of foreign terrorist fighters from or through their territories. Recognizing that transit countries face enormous difficulties in terms of disrupting access to conflict zones in the absence of

[229] See S/2015/377.

reliable intelligence, the Council calls upon Member States to increase and improve intraregional and interregional information-sharing between origin and transit States in a timely manner. The Council also encourages greater coordination between Member States and with private sector stakeholders such as airlines and travel agents to more effectively counter the flow of foreign terrorist fighters. The Council further notes the important contributions that public-private partnerships and civil society actors can make in efforts to prevent and combat terrorism.

The Council notes with continuing appreciation the efforts of the International Criminal Police Organization (INTERPOL) to address the threat posed by foreign terrorist fighters. The Council expresses concern, however, that INTERPOL's foreign terrorist fighter database still only contains a portion of basic identifying information of known foreign terrorist fighters, notes that global utilization could be significantly increased, and calls upon Member States to increase exchanging information with, and use of, INTERPOL's foreign terrorist fighter database to help identify, monitor or prevent the transit of foreign terrorist fighters, to enhance and complement bilateral, regional and other international information-sharing arrangements and databases for countering foreign terrorist fighters. Such reporting may include providing additional basic identifying information on known foreign terrorist fighters contained in the database, as well as systematic reporting of stolen and lost travel documents to INTERPOL and broad use of INTERPOL's I-24/7 network at ports of entry. The Council encourages INTERPOL to continue to intensify its efforts with respect to the foreign terrorist fighter threat, and calls upon the international community to strengthen INTERPOL's capabilities to support Member States' efforts in this regard, and develop capacity-building assistance for Member States to facilitate broader use of INTERPOL's I-24/7 network and reporting to INTERPOL's stolen and lost travel documents database.

The Council notes with concern that terrorist recruitment efforts, in particular by Islamic State in Iraq and the Levant, appear to be increasingly targeting women and youth and stresses the need for Member States to more effectively identify and work with relevant local communities and civil society leaders to develop comprehensive solutions to the threat of recruitment and radicalization to violence, notably through programmes at schools and in prisons and recognizing the role that victims of terrorism can play in countering radicalization, and develop robust social media campaigns and counter-messaging efforts to blunt terrorist narratives and online recruitment attempts.

The Council expresses concern over the increased use by terrorists and their supporters of communications technology for the purpose of radicalizing to terrorism, recruiting and inciting others to commit terrorist acts, including through the Internet, and financing and facilitating the travel and subsequent activities of foreign terrorist fighters, and underlines again the need for Member States to act cooperatively to prevent terrorists from exploiting technology, communications and resources to incite support for terrorist acts, while respecting human rights and fundamental freedoms and in compliance with other obligations under international law.

The Council further expresses its concern that facilitation networks continue to operate and enable the regular flow of foreign terrorist fighters coming from many parts of the world into the Syrian Arab Republic and Iraq, which must be shut down as soon as possible. The Council reaffirms that Member States shall prevent and suppress the financing of the travel and of the activities of foreign terrorist fighters in accordance with paragraph 6 of resolution 2178 (2014), recalls its decision in resolution 1373 (2001) that all Member States shall ensure that any person who participates in the financing of terrorist acts or in supporting terrorist acts is brought to justice, and stresses the need to disrupt and dismantle facilitation networks, consistent with international human rights law, international refugee law and international humanitarian law.

The Council recognizes the need to assess global progress in the implementation of international obligations under resolution 2178 (2014) that can enable the international community to target its attention and resources on one of the most significant challenges and obstacles faced by Member States today, especially those in the most affected regions. The Council therefore requests the Monitoring Team and the Counter-Terrorism Committee Executive Directorate to provide in a joint presentation to a joint meeting of the Al-Qaida sanctions Committee and the Counter-Terrorism Committee an impact assessment of Member States' implementation-related actions for resolution 2178 (2014) to date that includes quantitative and qualitative evaluations of the foreign terrorist fighter threat, its trends and metrics, Member States' actions to stem the flow of foreign terrorist fighters that could include interdictions and prosecutions, and other relevant outcome-related information on Member States' recent actions gathered through the use of the Monitoring

Team and Executive Directorate's regular assessment tools and country visits conducted for the most affected countries. The Council requests the two committees, in continuation of the request found in paragraph 26 of resolution 2178 (2014), to hold such a meeting in preparation for a Council meeting after the one-year anniversary of the adoption of resolution 2178 (2014).

The Council further requests that the Al-Qaida sanctions Committee and the Counter-Terrorism Committee continue to pay due attention to concrete steps taken by Member States to implement resolution 2178 (2014), including the creation of new or enhancement of existing laws, law enforcement authorities and tools, national and multilateral information collection and sharing initiatives, border management programmes and capabilities, and capacity-building assistance to those Member States most affected by the foreign terrorist fighter phenomenon, while properly balancing the need to fulfil other tasks within their mandates.

The Council welcomes the report provided by the Monitoring Team through the Al-Qaida sanctions Committee[228] and the reports provided by the Counter-Terrorism Committee Executive Directorate through the Counter-Terrorism Committee on foreign terrorist fighters.[230] The Council strongly recommends that the Counter-Terrorism Implementation Task Force Office, in close consultation with the Executive Directorate and based on its Counter-Terrorism Committee-approved analyses and reports and taking into account the Al-Qaida sanctions Committee-approved analytical reports produced by the Monitoring Team, develop a United Nations capacity-building implementation plan for countering the flow of foreign terrorist fighters through the Counter-Terrorism Implementation Task Force Working Group on Foreign Terrorist Fighters. The Council also strongly recommends that the Task Force Office include in this plan its priority recommendations for capacity-building assistance needs of the most affected Member States and set out a prioritized list of capacity-building and technical assistance programmes to be implemented by Task Force entities and the United Nations Counter-Terrorism Centre over the next 24 months.

The Council underscores the importance of the Counter-Terrorism Implementation Task Force undertaking such delivery of capacity-building programmes in consultation and cooperation with the Counter-Terrorism Committee Executive Directorate, the United Nations Office on Drugs and Crime, INTERPOL, the International Civil Aviation Organization, the World Customs Organization, the International Organization for Migration and other relevant and appropriate institutions capable of providing the needed technical advice, including the International Air Transport Association, the Global Counterterrorism Forum and the International Institute for Justice and the Rule of Law, and encourages Member States to provide needed financial and other assistance to the Task Force and the United Nations Counter-Terrorism Centre.

The Council strongly urges Member States, if they are able, to assist in the delivery of impactful capacity-building and other technical assistance needed by the most affected States, especially those burdened with the need to commit extraordinary resources to counter the foreign terrorist fighter phenomenon, including States neighbouring zones of armed conflict in which foreign terrorist fighters are active, including by promoting the sharing of lessons learned and adopting best practices, on the range of measures required by resolutions 2178 (2014) and 1373 (2001) to counter the flow of foreign terrorist fighters. The Council encourages Member States to coordinate with the Counter-Terrorism Implementation Task Force, when appropriate, in order to ensure more efficient and effective delivery of technical assistance.

At its 7492nd meeting, on 28 July 2015, the Council considered the item entitled "Threats to international peace and security caused by terrorist acts".

At the same meeting, following consultations among members of the Security Council, the President made the following statement on behalf of the Council:[231]

The Security Council recalls its primary responsibility for the maintenance of international peace and security.

The Council reaffirms Member States' determination to continue to do all they can to resolve conflict and to deny terrorist groups the ability to put down roots and establish safe havens to address better the growing threat posed by terrorism.

---

[230] S/2015/338 and S/2015/377.

[231] S/PRST/2015/14.

The Council stresses that terrorism can only be defeated by a sustained and comprehensive approach involving the active participation and collaboration of all States and international, regional and subregional organizations to counter the terrorist threat.

The Council affirms that terrorism in all its forms and manifestations constitutes one of the most serious threats to international peace and security, and that any acts of terrorism are criminal and unjustifiable, regardless of their motivation, wherever, whenever and by whosoever committed. The Council expresses its concern at the continued threat posed to international peace and security by Jama'atu Ahlis Sunna Lidda'Awati Wal-Jihad (also known as "Boko Haram" and hereinafter referred to as such) and all other individuals, groups, undertakings and entities associated with Al-Qaida, reaffirms its resolve to address all aspects of that threat, and reaffirms that terrorism, including the actions of the Boko Haram terrorist group, cannot and should not be associated with any religion, nationality or civilization.

The Council reiterates its strong condemnation of all the terrorist attacks, abuses of human rights and violations of international humanitarian law by Boko Haram in the Lake Chad Basin region, recognizes that women and girls are particularly targeted by Boko Haram, expresses its deep sympathy and condolences to the families of the victims as well as to the peoples and Governments of Nigeria, Niger, Cameroon and Chad and wishes a speedy recovery to those injured.

The Council recalls that those responsible for abuses and violations of human rights and violations of international humanitarian law must be held accountable and brought to justice.

The Council takes note of the communiqué of the African Union Peace and Security Council of 25 November 2014 on the threat posed by Boko Haram and the efforts of the States members of the Lake Chad Basin Commission (Cameroon, Chad, Niger and Nigeria) and Benin to combat Boko Haram. The Security Council further takes note of the letter sent by the Chairperson of the African Union Commission to the Secretary-General on 6 March 2015, forwarding the communiqués adopted by the Peace and Security Council on 29 January and 3 March 2015, as well as the Multinational Joint Task Force strategic concept of operations to fight against Boko Haram.[232]

The Security Council, while acknowledging the progress made on the ground following joint regional military efforts in recent months, condemns strongly the continued deadly attacks perpetrated by the Boko Haram terrorist group, particularly against civilians, and encourages increased regional cooperation.

The Council commends the States members of the Lake Chad Basin Commission and Benin for their continued efforts to fully operationalize the Multinational Joint Task Force in order to collectively enhance regional military cooperation and coordination to more effectively combat the threat posed by the Boko Haram terrorist group to the Lake Chad Basin region. In this respect, the Council notes the establishment of the operational headquarters in N'Djamena, in accordance with the conclusions of the 5th Meeting of Ministers for Foreign Affairs and Defence of the Commission member States, of 20 January 2015, and also notes the inauguration of the said operational headquarters in N'Djamena on 25 May 2015, in which the following participated: the African Union Commissioner for Peace and Security, Mr. Smaïl Chergui; the Special Representative of the Secretary-General for West Africa and Head of the United Nations Office for West Africa, Mr. Mohammed Ibn Chambas; the Special Representative of the Secretary-General for Central Africa and Head of the United Nations Regional Office for Central Africa, Mr. Abdoulaye Bathily; the Executive Secretary of the Commission, Mr. Sanusi Imran Abdullahi; and the Minister delegate at the Presidency of the Republic in charge of National Defence and Veterans Affairs of Chad, Mr. Benaindo Tatola.

The Council takes note of the final communiqué adopted by the extraordinary summit of the Heads of State and Government of the States members of the Lake Chad Basin Commission and Benin, held in Abuja on 11 June 2015, including the decisions to approve the strategic and operational concepts of operations and other related documents for the Multinational Joint Task Force; the deployment of national contingents to the Task Force under the operational command of the Task Force Commander by 30 July 2015; the designation of the Executive Secretary of the Commission as the Head of Mission; and the nomination of the Force Commander, Deputy Force Commander and Chief of Staff of the Task Force.

[232] S/2015/198, annex.

The Council reaffirms that Member States must ensure that any measures taken to counter terrorism comply with all their obligations under international law, in particular international human rights law, international refugee law and international humanitarian law.

The Council encourages the Economic Community of Central African States and the Economic Community of West African States, in coordination with the African Union Commission, to accelerate joint efforts to adopt a comprehensive strategy to more effectively and urgently combat the threat posed by Boko Haram, and in this regard welcomes plans to convene a summit in August 2015 and urges the two subregional organizations to adopt a common strategy and develop active cooperation and coordination.

The Council acknowledges the economic burden borne by the Boko Haram-affected countries and welcomes the continuing commitment of Member States and international partners participating in support of the Multinational Joint Task Force in combating the Boko Haram terrorist group.

The Council notes the steps being taken by the African Union Commission to provide the support necessary for the full operationalization of the Multinational Joint Task Force in line with the relevant provisions of the Task Force strategic concept of operations to fight against Boko Haram.

The Council calls upon the international community and donors to support the Multinational Joint Task Force, particularly its operational capability, and welcomes in this regard the plans of the African Union Commission to organize a donors' conference in support of the efforts of the States members of the Lake Chad Basin Commission and Benin. The Council invites the Secretary-General to support the plans of the African Union Commission for a donors' conference, calls upon Member States to contribute generously to the African Union trust fund and requests the Secretary-General to advocate strongly with the international community and donors in support of this effort.

The Council stresses the need to complement the joint regional military and security operations against the Boko Haram terrorist group by sustained national and regional efforts, with international support, to improve livelihoods, provide humanitarian assistance to internally displaced persons, refugees and other conflict-affected populations, promote education and job creation, facilitate stabilization efforts and economic recovery, prevent illicit trafficking in weapons to armed groups and criminal networks as well as ensure the protection of human rights, particularly those of women and children. In this respect, it notes the adoption by the extraordinary summit of the States members of the Lake Chad Basin Commission and Benin, held on 11 June 2015, of the Emergency Plan for Development in the Lake Chad Basin and commends efforts by Member States and international organizations to extend all the necessary support to address the development challenges in the Lake Chad Basin region, and invites the United Nations, its Secretariat, and particularly its relevant agencies, funds and programmes, to work with the African Union Commission to identify practical steps through which it could contribute to these efforts.

The Council is concerned with the deteriorating humanitarian situation in the Lake Chad Basin countries, with close to 1.9 million people forcibly displaced in the region. The Council takes note of the efforts of the Governments of affected countries in responding to the regional humanitarian needs generated by the actions of Boko Haram. The Council reaffirms the need for all parties to armed conflict to respect the humanitarian principles of humanity, neutrality, impartiality and independence in order to ensure the provision of humanitarian assistance, the safety of civilians receiving assistance and the security of humanitarian personnel and United Nations and associated personnel. It recalls that States bear the primary responsibility to respect and ensure the human rights of their citizens, as well as all individuals within their territory as provided for by relevant international law. It calls upon the Member States contributing to the Multinational Joint Task Force to create a secure environment conducive for the civilian-led delivery of humanitarian assistance and the voluntary, safe and sustainable return, resettlement or local integration of internally displaced persons and refugees. The Council encourages all actors involved in the response to support recovery programmes and the provision of the necessary protection measures for civilians, and to pay particular attention to the release and reintegration of children abducted by Boko Haram or formerly associated with this terrorist group.

The Council recalls that Boko Haram has been designated as associated with Al-Qaida by the Security Council Committee pursuant to resolutions 1267 (1999) and 1989 (2011) and in this regard expresses its readiness to consider listing individuals, groups, undertakings and entities providing support to Boko Haram, including those who are financing, arming, planning or recruiting for Boko Haram and all other individuals, groups, undertakings and entities associated with Al-Qaida through information and communications technologies, including the Internet and social media or through any other means.

BRIEFINGS BY CHAIRS OF SUBSIDIARY BODIES OF THE SECURITY COUNCIL[233]

Decisions

At its 7331st meeting, on 9 December 2014, the Security Council considered the item entitled "Briefings by Chairmen of subsidiary bodies of the Security Council".

At its 7463rd meeting, on 16 June 2015, the Council considered the item entitled "Briefings by Chairs of subsidiary bodies of the Security Council".[*]

THE SITUATION IN CÔTE D'IVOIRE[233]

Decisions

At its 7292nd meeting, on 29 October 2014, the Security Council considered the item entitled:

"The situation in Côte d'Ivoire

> "Letter dated 10 October 2014 from the Chair of the Security Council Committee established pursuant to resolution 1572 (2004) concerning Côte d'Ivoire addressed to the President of the Security Council (S/2014/729)".

At its 7358th meeting, on 13 January 2015, the Council decided to invite the representative of Côte d'Ivoire to participate, without vote, in accordance with rule 37 of its provisional rules of procedure, in the discussion of the item entitled:

"The situation in Côte d'Ivoire

> "Thirty-fifth progress report of the Secretary-General on the United Nations Operation in Côte d'Ivoire (S/2014/892)".

At the same meeting, the Council also decided to extend an invitation, in accordance with rule 39 of its provisional rules of procedure, to Ms. Aïchatou Mindaoudou Souleymane, Special Representative of the Secretary-General for Côte d'Ivoire and Head of the United Nations Operation in Côte d'Ivoire.

At its 7431st meeting, on 22 April 2015, the Council decided to invite the representative of Côte d'Ivoire to participate, without vote, in accordance with rule 37 of its provisional rules of procedure, in the discussion of the item entitled:

"The situation in Côte d'Ivoire

> "Letter dated 13 April 2015 from the Chair of the Security Council Committee established pursuant to resolution 1572 (2004) concerning Côte d'Ivoire addressed to the President of the Security Council (S/2015/252)".

[233] Resolutions or decisions on this question were first adopted by the Security Council in 2002.

[*] As from the 7463rd meeting, held on 16 June 2015, the wording of the item "Briefings by Chairmen of subsidiary bodies of the Security Council" was revised to read "Briefings by Chairs of subsidiary bodies of the Security Council".

At its 7436th meeting, on 28 April 2015, the Council decided to invite the representative of Côte d'Ivoire to participate, without vote, in accordance with rule 37 of its provisional rules of procedure, in the discussion of the item entitled:

"The situation in Côte d'Ivoire

"Letter dated 13 April 2015 from the Chair of the Security Council Committee established pursuant to resolution 1572 (2004) concerning Côte d'Ivoire addressed to the President of the Security Council (S/2015/252)".

Resolution 2219 (2015) of 28 April 2015

The Security Council,

Recalling its previous resolutions and the statements by its President relating to the situation in Côte d'Ivoire, in particular resolutions 1880 (2009) of 30 July 2009, 1893 (2009) of 29 October 2009, 1911 (2010) of 28 January 2010, 1933 (2010) of 30 June 2010, 1946 (2010) of 15 October 2010, 1962 (2010) of 20 December 2010, 1975 (2011) of 30 March 2011, 1980 (2011) of 28 April 2011, 2000 (2011) of 27 July 2011, 2045 (2012) of 26 April 2012, 2062 (2012) of 26 July 2012, 2101 (2013) of 25 April 2013, 2112 (2013) of 30 July 2013, 2153 (2014) of 29 April 2014 and 2162 (2014) of 25 June 2014,

Reaffirming its strong commitment to the sovereignty, independence, territorial integrity and unity of Côte d'Ivoire, and recalling the importance of the principles of good-neighbourliness, non-interference and regional cooperation,

Welcoming the special report of the Secretary-General of 12 December 2014,[234] and noting the midterm report of 9 September 2014[235] and the final report of 6 March 2015[236] of the Group of Experts on Côte d'Ivoire,

Welcoming also the overall progress towards restoring security, peace and stability in Côte d'Ivoire, commending the continued efforts of the President and Government of Côte d'Ivoire to stabilize the security situation and promote economic recovery in Côte d'Ivoire and strengthen international and regional cooperation, and notably the continued cooperation with the Governments of Ghana and Liberia, and calling upon all national stakeholders to work together to consolidate the significant progress made so far and to address the underlying causes of tension and conflict,

Recognizing the continued contribution to the stability of Côte d'Ivoire of the measures imposed by resolutions 1572 (2004) of 15 November 2004, 1643 (2005) of 15 December 2005, 1975 (2011) and 1980 (2011), as modified by later resolutions, including resolution 2153 (2014), including by countering the illicit transfer of small arms and light weapons in Côte d'Ivoire, as well as in supporting post-conflict peacebuilding, disarmament, demobilization and reintegration and security sector reform, stressing that these measures aim at supporting the peace process in Côte d'Ivoire with a view to possibly further modifying or lifting all or part of the remaining measures, in accordance with progress achieved in relation to disarmament, demobilization and reintegration and security sector reform, national reconciliation and the fight against impunity, and underlining the significance of a peaceful, credible and transparent presidential election in this regard and the effective management of arms and related materiel,

Noting the upcoming presidential election in October 2015, welcoming in this regard the reforms adopted to prepare for this election, including the amendments to the electoral code, as well as the work undertaken by the Independent Electoral Commission, including through the establishment of its local branches, and encouraging it to continue to engage all political stakeholders in preparation for this election, further welcoming the steps taken by the Government of Côte d'Ivoire to foster political dialogue and reconciliation, and encouraging the Government and the opposition to continue to work positively and collaboratively to ensure that the political space remains open and transparent,

Welcoming the political commitment of the Ivorian authorities to the security sector reform process and the efforts made towards its implementation, including through the elaboration of the legal framework for security

[234] S/2014/892.

[235] See S/2014/729.

[236] See S/2015/252.

sector reform, the defining of the national strategy for security sector reform as well as the national security strategy, enhanced cooperation between the National Security Council and the line ministries and the international community, as well as the efforts towards the decentralization of the security sector reform process, the reinforcement of the democratic governance of this sector and efforts towards improving the gender balance within the security forces, while expressing concern about the delays in the adoption of certain laws and regulations relevant to security sector reform and the insufficient cohesion within the army, and urging an acceleration of efforts to reform the security sector, including by putting in place an effective chain of command, a system of military justice and appropriate budgetary allocations,

Welcoming also the progress made in the overall security situation and efforts to address security challenges as well as the significant achievements of the disarmament, demobilization and reintegration of former combatants, while expressing concern at delays in its implementation, re-emphasizing that the Government of Côte d'Ivoire must provide sufficient financial resources and develop viable reintegration opportunities for former combatants in order to complete the disarmament, demobilization and reintegration process before the presidential election of 2015, in accordance with the objective announced by the President of Côte d'Ivoire, and stressing the necessity for continued efforts to target unregistered combatants and to follow up on disarmament, demobilization and reintegration efforts after June 2015 in order to ensure their sustainability,

Welcoming further efforts towards better monitoring and management of weapons through the National Commission to Fight against the Proliferation and Illicit Traffic of Small Arms and Light Weapons, with the support of the United Nations Operation in Côte d'Ivoire, including through the marking of arms and related lethal materiel and efforts in the rehabilitation and improvement of armouries, and emphasizing the importance of continued efforts in this area, taking note in this regard of the signature and ratification of the Arms Trade Treaty[237] by Côte d'Ivoire, and encouraging States and intergovernmental, regional and subregional organizations that are in a position to do so to support Côte d'Ivoire to fulfil and implement its relevant obligations,

Reiterating the urgent need for the Government of Côte d'Ivoire to continue to train and equip its security forces, especially the police and gendarmerie, with standard policing weapons and ammunition, and stressing the primary role of the police and the gendarmerie in maintaining law and order, including to secure the upcoming electoral process,

Re-emphasizing the importance of the Government of Côte d'Ivoire being able to respond proportionately to threats to the security of all citizens in Côte d'Ivoire, and calling upon the Government to ensure that its security forces remain committed to upholding human rights and applicable international law,

Recognizing the efforts made by the Government of Côte d'Ivoire to notably improve its cooperation with the Group of Experts on Côte d'Ivoire, originally established pursuant to paragraph 7 of resolution 1584 (2005) of 1 February 2005, and encouraging further close cooperation between the Government and the Group of Experts,

Welcoming the ongoing efforts made by the Secretariat to expand and improve the roster of experts for the Security Council Subsidiary Organs Branch, bearing in mind the guidance provided in the note by the President of the Security Council of 22 December 2006,[238]

Welcoming also the progress made by the Ivorian authorities in combating illegal taxation systems, acknowledging the efforts undertaken to reduce the number of illegal checkpoints and incidents of racketeering, stressing the need to continue such efforts, including through developing a national border management strategy, and encouraging implementation of the 2015–2016 action plan on customs administration, while noting the need for capacity-building and the allocation of resources in order to control borders, in particular in the western part of the country,

Recalling its decision to terminate, through resolution 2153 (2014), the measures preventing the importation by any State of all rough diamonds from Côte d'Ivoire, imposed by paragraph 6 of resolution 1643 (2005), in the light of progress made towards implementation of the Kimberley Process Certification Scheme[239] and better governance of the sector,

---

[237] See General Assembly resolution 67/234 B.

[238] S/2006/997.

[239] See A/57/489.

Noting that the Kimberley Process, in its final communiqué of 22 November 2013,[240] recognized that Côte d'Ivoire had fulfilled the minimum requirements of the Kimberley Process Certification Scheme, encouraging full implementation by Côte d'Ivoire of its action plan to develop its diamond sector in line with Kimberley Process standards, including participation in the Kimberley Process regional approach for the Mano River Union countries, welcoming the Kimberley Process review visit that took place in March 2015, and commending efforts made by the Property Rights and Artisanal Diamond Development II project in cooperation with the Friends of Côte d'Ivoire to build alternate livelihoods within mining communities,

Recalling all its relevant resolutions on women and peace and security, on children and armed conflict and on the protection of civilians in armed conflict,

Reiterating its firm condemnation of all violations of human rights and international humanitarian law in Côte d'Ivoire, condemning all violence committed against civilians, including women, children, internally displaced persons and foreign nationals, and other violations and abuses of human rights, stressing that the perpetrators on all sides must be brought to justice, whether in domestic or international courts, and encouraging the Government of Côte d'Ivoire to further continue its close cooperation with the International Criminal Court,

Welcoming, in this regard, national and international efforts to bring to justice alleged perpetrators from all sides of violations and abuses of human rights and of violations of international humanitarian law,

Stressing the importance for the Group of Experts to be provided with sufficient resources for the implementation of its mandate,

Determining that the situation in Côte d'Ivoire continues to pose a threat to international peace and security in the region,

Acting under Chapter VII of the Charter of the United Nations,

1. *Decides* that, for a period ending on 30 April 2016, all States shall take the measures necessary to prevent the direct or indirect supply, sale or transfer to Côte d'Ivoire, from their territories or by their nationals, or using their flag vessels or aircraft, of arms and any related lethal materiel, whether or not originating in their territories;

2. *Also decides* that supplies of non-lethal equipment and the provision of any technical assistance, training or financial assistance, intended to enable the Ivorian security forces to use only appropriate and proportionate force while maintaining public order, shall not require notification to the Security Council Committee established pursuant to paragraph 14 of resolution 1572 (2004);

3. *Notes* that the measures on arms and related lethal materiel in paragraph 1 above do not apply to the provision of training, advice, technical or financial assistance and expertise related to security and military activities, or to non-lethal materiel, including supplies of civilian vehicles to the Ivorian security forces;

4. *Decides* that the measures imposed by paragraph 1 above shall not apply to:

(*a*) Supplies intended solely for the support of or use by the United Nations Operation in Côte d'Ivoire and the French forces supporting it and supplies transiting through Côte d'Ivoire intended for the support of or to be used by United Nations peacekeeping operations;

(*b*) Supplies temporarily exported to Côte d'Ivoire to the forces of a State which is taking action, in accordance with international law, solely and directly to facilitate the evacuation of its nationals and those for whom it has consular responsibility in Côte d'Ivoire, as notified in advance to the Committee;

(*c*) Supplies of arms and related lethal materiel to the Ivorian security forces intended solely for the support of or use in the Ivorian process of security sector reform, as notified in advance to the Committee, except for those arms and related lethal materiel which are set out in the annex to the present resolution, which require the advance approval of the Committee;

[240] A/68/649, enclosure.

5. *Also decides* that the Committee shall add, remove or clarify items on the list of arms and related lethal materiel specified in the annex to the present resolution, as appropriate;

6. *Further decides* that, for the period referred to in paragraph 1 above, the Ivorian authorities shall notify or request approval in advance, as appropriate, from the Committee for any shipments of items referred to in paragraph 4 (*c*) above, and further decides that the Member State delivering assistance may, in the alternative, make this notification or approval request pursuant to paragraph 4 (*c*) after informing the Government of Côte d'Ivoire that it intends to do so;

7. *Requests* the Government of Côte d'Ivoire to ensure that notifications and approval requests sent to the Committee contain all relevant information, including the purpose of the use and the end user, including the intended destination unit in the Ivorian security forces or the intended place of storage, the technical specifications, the quantity of the equipment to be shipped, the details of the manufacturer and supplier of the equipment, the proposed date of delivery, the mode of transportation and the itinerary of the shipments, further stresses the importance of a specific focus on detailed explanations for how the requested equipment will support security sector reform, and emphasizes that such notifications and approval requests should include information about any intended modification of non-lethal equipment into lethal equipment;

8. *Decides* that the Ivorian authorities shall submit biannual reports to the Committee by 15 September 2015 and by 30 March 2016 on progress achieved in relation to disarmament, demobilization and reintegration and security sector reform;

9. *Encourages* the Ivorian authorities to consult with the United Nations Operation in Côte d'Ivoire, within its existing mandate and resources, to ensure that notifications and authorization requests contain the required information;

10. *Urges* the Government of Côte d'Ivoire to allow the Group of Experts on Côte d'Ivoire and the United Nations Operation in Côte d'Ivoire access to the exempted arms and lethal materiel at the time of import and before the transfer to the end user takes place, welcomes the efforts of the National Commission to Fight against the Proliferation and Illicit Traffic of Small Arms and Light Weapons to mark the arms and related lethal materiel when received in the territory of Côte d'Ivoire and encourages it to continue such efforts, and urges the Government to maintain a registry of all arms and materiel present in the country, with specific attention to small arms and light weapons, including any private arms caches, with a clear process delineated for how the Government intends to track the movement of weapons;

11. *Decides* to review by the end of the period mentioned in paragraph 1 above the measures decided in the paragraphs above, with a view to possibly further modifying or lifting all or part of the remaining measures, in the light of the progress achieved in the stabilization of Côte d'Ivoire, in accordance with progress achieved in relation to disarmament, demobilization and reintegration and security sector reform, national reconciliation and the fight against impunity, bearing in mind in this regard the significance of a peaceful, credible and transparent election process and the effective management of arms and related materiel as described in paragraph 10 above;

12. *Also decides* to renew until 30 April 2016 the financial and travel measures imposed by paragraphs 9 to 12 of resolution 1572 (2004) and paragraph 12 of resolution 1975 (2011), and stresses its intention to review the continued listing of individuals subject to such measures provided that they engage in actions that further the objective of national reconciliation;

13. *Requests* the Government of Côte d'Ivoire to continue to update the Security Council, through the Committee, on its progress in implementing its action plan for diamonds, including on any enforcement activities involving illegal smuggling, the development of its customs regime, including the creation of a risk profile for customs and law enforcement officials, and the reporting of financial flows from diamonds;

14. *Welcomes* the steps taken by the Government of Côte d'Ivoire to start implementing the recommendations outlined in the report of the Kimberley Process review visit of October 2013, expresses concern that the smuggling of rough diamonds from Cote d'Ivoire continues, and urges the Government to continue its efforts to fully and quickly implement all of these recommendations in order to support the development of a legitimate supply chain for the export of rough diamonds;

15. *Encourages* Côte d'Ivoire and other adjacent countries to continue participation in the Kimberley Process regional cooperation and law enforcement activities, such as the regional approach for the countries of the Mano River Union;

16. *Invites* the Kimberley Process Certification Scheme, in particular its Working Groups on Monitoring, on Statistics and of Diamond Experts, to communicate information, as appropriate, regarding compliance by Côte d'Ivoire with the Certification Scheme to the Council, through the Committee and, when possible, for review by the Group of Experts, and encourages donors to support the efforts of Côte d'Ivoire by sharing related information and providing technical assistance;

17. *Calls upon* the Government of Côte d'Ivoire to take the steps necessary to enforce the measures imposed by paragraph 1 above, including by incorporating relevant provisions in its national legal framework;

18. *Calls upon* all Member States, in particular those in the subregion, to fully implement the measures mentioned in paragraphs 1 and 6 above;

19. *Expresses its continued concern* about the instability in western Côte d'Ivoire, and welcomes and further encourages the coordinated action by authorities from neighbouring countries to address this issue, particularly with respect to the border area, including through continuing monitoring, information-sharing and conducting coordinated actions, and in developing and implementing a shared border strategy to, inter alia, support the disarmament and repatriation of foreign armed elements on both sides of the border;

20. *Encourages* the United Nations Operation in Côte d'Ivoire and the United Nations Mission in Liberia, within their respective mandates, capabilities and areas of deployment, to continue to coordinate closely in assisting respectively the Governments of Côte d'Ivoire and Liberia in monitoring their border, and welcomes continued cooperation between the Group of Experts and the Panel of Experts on Liberia appointed pursuant to paragraph 5 of resolution 2188 (2014) of 9 December 2014;

21. *Urges* all illegal Ivorian armed combatants, including in neighbouring countries, to lay down their arms immediately, encourages the United Nations Operation in Côte d'Ivoire, within its mandate and the limits of its capabilities and its areas of deployment, to continue to assist the Government of Côte d'Ivoire in collecting and storing those arms and registering all relevant information related to those arms, and further calls upon the Government, including the National Commission to Fight against the Proliferation and Illicit Traffic of Small Arms and Light Weapons, to ensure that those arms are neutralized or are not illegally disseminated, in accordance with the Economic Community of West African States Convention on Small Arms and Light Weapons, Their Ammunition and Other Related Materials;

22. *Recalls* that the United Nations Operation in Côte d'Ivoire is mandated, within the monitoring of the arms embargo, to collect, as appropriate, arms and any related materiel brought into Côte d'Ivoire in violation of the measures imposed by paragraph 1 of the present resolution and to dispose of such arms and related materiel as appropriate;

23. *Reiterates* the necessity for the Ivorian authorities to provide unhindered access to the Group of Experts, as well as the United Nations Operation in Côte d'Ivoire and the French forces supporting it, to equipment, sites and installations referred to in paragraph 2 (*a*) of resolution 1584 (2005), and to all weapons, ammunition and related materiel of all armed security forces, regardless of location, including the arms issued from the collection referred to in paragraph 10 or 11 above, when appropriate and without notice, as set out in its resolutions 1739 (2007) of 10 January 2007, 1880 (2009), 1933 (2010), 1962 (2010), 1980 (2011), 2062 (2012), 2112 (2013) and 2153 (2014);

24. *Requests* all States concerned, in particular those in the subregion, to cooperate fully with the Committee, and authorizes the Committee to request whatever further information it may consider necessary;

25. *Decides* to extend the mandate of the Group of Experts, as set out in paragraph 7 of resolution 1727 (2006) of 15 December 2006, until 30 May 2016, expresses its intent to consider the renewal of this mandate no later than 30 April 2016, and requests the Secretary-General to take the measures necessary to support its action;

26. *Reiterates* that paragraph 7 (*b*) of resolution 1727 (2006) includes a mandate for the Group of Experts to gather and analyse all relevant information on sources of financing, including from the exploitation of natural resources in Côte d'Ivoire, for the purchase of arms and related materiel and activities, and notes that, pursuant to

paragraph 12 (*a*) of resolution 1727 (2006), those who are determined to be a threat to the peace and national reconciliation process in Côte d'Ivoire through illicit trafficking in natural resources, including diamonds and gold, may be designated by the Committee;

27. *Requests* the Group of Experts to submit an interim update on its work to the Committee by 15 September 2015 and to submit a final report to the Council by 8 April 2016, after discussion with the Committee, on the implementation of the measures imposed by paragraph 1 above, paragraphs 9 and 11 of resolution 1572 (2004), paragraph 12 of resolution 1975 (2011) and paragraph 10 of resolution 1980 (2011), with recommendations in this regard, as well as to submit progress updates to the Committee, especially in situations of urgency, or as the Group deems necessary;

28. *Decides* that the update and the report of the Group of Experts, as referred to in paragraph 27 above, may include, as appropriate, any information and recommendations relevant to the possible additional designation by the Committee of the individuals and entities described in paragraphs 9 and 11 of resolution 1572 (2004) and paragraph 10 of resolution 1980 (2011) and recalls the report of the Informal Working Group of the Security Council on General Issues of Sanctions on best practices and methods,[238] including paragraphs 21, 22 and 23 thereof, which discuss possible steps for clarifying methodological standards for monitoring mechanisms;

29. *Also decides* that the Group of Experts will also report on the activities of sanctioned individuals as well as on any continued threat to peace and security in Côte d'Ivoire posed by those individuals or others, consistent with paragraph 28 above;

30. *Requests* the Secretary-General to communicate, as appropriate, to the Council, through the Committee, information gathered by the United Nations Operation in Côte d'Ivoire and, where possible, reviewed by the Group of Experts, concerning the supply of arms and related materiel to Côte d'Ivoire;

31. *Requests* the Government of France to communicate, as appropriate, to the Council, through the Committee, information gathered by the French forces and, where possible, reviewed by the Group of Experts, concerning the supply of arms and related materiel to Côte d'Ivoire;

32. *Welcomes* the efforts of the Government of Côte d'Ivoire to participate in the Organization for Economic Cooperation and Development-hosted implementation programme with regard to the Due Diligence Guidance for Responsible Supply Chains of Minerals from Conflict-Affected and High-Risk Areas, and urges the Government to reach out to international organizations, with a view to taking advantage of lessons learned from other initiatives and countries that have and are confronting similar issues, and calls upon all States to take appropriate steps to raise awareness of the guidelines referred to above and to urge importers, processing industries and consumers of Ivorian mineral products to exercise due diligence by applying the aforementioned guidelines, with special attention to gold;

33. *Calls upon* the Ivorian authorities to continue to take the measures necessary to dismantle the illegal taxation networks, including by undertaking relevant and thorough investigations, further reduce the number of checkpoints and prevent incidents of racketeering throughout the country, and increase control and oversight over the areas where natural resources, particularly gold, are illegally exploited, and further calls upon the authorities to continue to take the steps necessary to continue to re-establish and reinforce relevant institutions and to accelerate the deployment of customs and border control officials in the north, west and east of the country;

34. *Asks* the Group of Experts to assess the effectiveness of these border measures and controls in the region, encourages all neighbouring States to be aware of Ivorian efforts in that regard, and encourages the United Nations Operation in Côte d'Ivoire, within its mandate, to continue its assistance to the Ivorian authorities in the re-establishment of normal customs and border control operations;

35. *Urges* all States, relevant United Nations bodies and other organizations and interested parties to cooperate fully with the Committee, the Group of Experts, the United Nations Operation in Côte d'Ivoire and the French forces, in particular by supplying any information at their disposal on possible violations of the measures imposed by paragraphs 1 to 3 above, paragraphs 9 and 11 of resolution 1572 (2004), paragraph 6 of resolution 1643 (2005) and paragraph 12 of resolution 1975 (2011), and further requests the Group of Experts to coordinate its activities, as appropriate, with all political actors and to implement its mandate in accordance with the report of the Informal Working Group of the Security Council on General Issues of Sanctions;

36. *Requests* the Special Representative of the Secretary-General for Children and Armed Conflict and the Special Representative of the Secretary-General on Sexual Violence in Conflict to continue to share relevant

information with the Committee, in accordance with paragraph 7 of resolution 1960 (2010) of 16 December 2010 and paragraph 9 of resolution 1998 (2011) of 12 July 2011;

37. *Urges*, in this context, that all Ivorian parties and all States, particularly those in the region, ensure:

– The safety of the members of the Group of Experts;

– Unhindered access by the Group of Experts, in particular to persons, documents and sites, in order for the Group of Experts to execute its mandate;

38. *Decides* to remain actively seized of the matter.

Adopted unanimously at the 7436th meeting

Annex

1. Weapons, direct and indirect fire artillery, and guns with a calibre bigger than 12.7 mm, their ammunition and components;
2. Rocket-propelled grenades, rockets, light anti-tank weapons, rifle grenades and grenade launchers;
3. Surface-to-air missiles, including man-portable air-defence systems (MANPADS); surface-to-surface missiles; and air-to-surface missiles;
4. Mortars with a calibre bigger than 82 mm;
5. Guided anti-tank weapons, especially guided anti-tank missiles, their ammunition and components;
6. Armed aircraft, including rotary wing or fixed wing;
7. Military armed vehicles or military vehicles equipped with weapon mounts;
8. Explosive charges and devices containing explosive materials, designed for military purposes, mines and related material;
9. Night observation and night shooting devices.

Decisions

On 5 June 2015, the President of the Security Council addressed the following letter to the Secretary-General:[241]

> I have the honour to inform you that your letter dated 3 June 2015 concerning your intention to appoint Major General Didier L'Hôte, of France, as Force Commander of the United Nations Operation in Côte d'Ivoire[242] has been brought to the attention of the members of the Security Council. They take note of the intention expressed in your letter.

At its 7459th meeting, on 9 June 2015, the Council decided to invite the representative of Côte d'Ivoire to participate, without vote, in accordance with rule 37 of its provisional rules of procedure, in the discussion of the item entitled:

"The situation in Côte d'Ivoire

"Thirty-sixth progress report of the Secretary-General on the United Nations Operation in Côte d'Ivoire (S/2015/320)".

At the same meeting, the Council also decided to extend an invitation, in accordance with rule 39 of its provisional rules of procedure, to Ms. Aïchatou Mindaoudou Souleymane, Special Representative of the Secretary-General for Côte d'Ivoire and Head of the United Nations Operation in Côte d'Ivoire.

---

[241] S/2015/412.

[242] S/2015/411.

At its 7471st meeting, on 25 June 2015, the Council decided to invite the representative of Côte d'Ivoire to participate, without vote, in accordance with rule 37 of its provisional rules of procedure, in the discussion of the item entitled:

"The situation in Côte d'Ivoire

"Thirty-sixth progress report of the Secretary-General on the United Nations Operation in Côte d'Ivoire (S/2015/320)".

Resolution 2226 (2015) of 25 June 2015

The Security Council,

Recalling its previous resolutions, in particular resolutions 2162 (2014) of 25 June 2014 and 2219 (2015) of 28 April 2015, and the statements by its President relating to the situation in Côte d'Ivoire, resolutions 2188 (2014) of 9 December 2014, 2190 (2014) of 15 December 2014 and 2215 (2015) of 2 April 2015 on the situation in Liberia and resolution 2164 (2014) of 25 June 2014 on the situation in Mali,

Reaffirming its strong commitment to the sovereignty, independence, territorial integrity and unity of Côte d'Ivoire, and recalling the principles of good-neighbourliness, non-interference and regional cooperation,

Recalling that the Government of Côte d'Ivoire bears primary responsibility for ensuring peace, stability and the protection of civilians in Côte d'Ivoire,

Taking note of the report of the Secretary-General of 7 May 2015,[243]

Welcoming the progress being made in Côte d'Ivoire on the path of reconciliation, stability and economic recovery, and commending the leadership of the President of Côte d'Ivoire in this regard,

Welcoming also the continued improvement in the security situation in Côte d'Ivoire, including in the western part of the country and along the border with Liberia, while condemning the attacks of 10 and 16 January 2015, acknowledging the need to address remaining challenges, and noting the continued cooperation between the United Nations Operation in Côte d'Ivoire and the United Nations Mission in Liberia, as well as the Governments of Côte d'Ivoire and Liberia and countries in the subregion, in coordinating activities, including on security, in the border areas in the subregion,

Calling upon all Ivorian stakeholders, including political parties, civil society and the media, to work together to consolidate the progress made so far and to address the underlying causes of tension and conflict, including with respect to land and nationality, encouraging the Government of Côte d'Ivoire to further strengthen the rule of law, welcoming the steps taken by the Government to organize and finance the 2015 presidential election process, including reforms of the legal framework for elections through the adoption of amendments to this framework, welcoming the work undertaken by the Independent Electoral Commission and welcoming also the steps taken by the Government to facilitate an environment conducive to fair, credible and transparent elections, while underlining the necessity to continue and intensify efforts in this field,

Welcoming the ongoing political dialogue among the political parties, including extra-parliamentary parties, welcoming also the decision by the Government of Côte d'Ivoire, on an exceptional basis, to finance political parties ahead of the election, commending the engagement of the Special Representative of the Secretary-General for Côte d'Ivoire through her good offices mandate, especially in support of the dialogue between the Government and opposition political parties, and expressing its appreciation for the work of the United Nations Operation in Côte d'Ivoire and its overall contribution to the maintenance of peace and security in Côte d'Ivoire,

Taking note of the letter dated 18 June 2014 from the Government of Côte d'Ivoire to the Secretary-General requesting the possible provision of electoral assistance for the 2015 presidential election,

Welcoming the continued improvement of the humanitarian situation, including with regard to the situation of internally displaced persons, and urging the resumption of the voluntary, safe and durable return of refugees to their places of origin in Côte d'Ivoire,

---

[243] S/2015/320.

Taking note of the final framework on disarmament, demobilization and reintegration adopted by the Authority on Disarmament, Demobilization and Reintegration and the successful disarmament and demobilization of more than 50,000 former combatants, welcoming the initiative to enrol all former combatants in the disarmament and demobilization programme by 30 June 2015 and underlining the need to continue efforts to include former combatants associated with the previous Government, taking note of the continuing work of the Authority, with the support of the United Nations Operation in Côte d'Ivoire, in this regard, and emphasizing the need to implement post-June 2015 reinsertion activities in a coordinated manner, including through the designation by the Government of Côte d'Ivoire of a lead institution to achieve this objective,

Commending the efforts of the Government of Côte d'Ivoire to restructure and professionalize its defence and security sector, including through the implementation of the national security strategy, underlining the need for the Government to continue prioritizing efforts to implement completely its security sector reform strategy, with special attention to the training and equipment of the police and gendarmerie as well as the streamlining of security structures, and underlining the importance of measures to rebuild confidence within and between the security forces and the population, including ahead of the 2015 presidential election,

Emphasizing the importance of pursuing a national reconciliation and social cohesion strategy, welcoming in this regard efforts to take forward intercommunal dialogue, encouraging the publication by the Government of Côte d'Ivoire of the final report and recommendations provided by the Dialogue, Truth and Reconciliation Commission, welcoming the establishment of the National Commission for Reconciliation and Compensation of Victims and encouraging the full implementation of its mandate, and underlining the importance of including all Ivorians in the reconciliation process at the national and local levels,

Reiterating the vital role of women in conflict resolution and peacebuilding, the importance of their equal participation and full involvement in all efforts for the maintenance and promotion of peace and security and their key role in re-establishing the fabric of societies recovering from conflict, and further reaffirming the importance of implementing the Côte d'Ivoire national action plan, adopted in 2008, for the implementation of resolution 1325 (2000) of 31 October 2000,

Welcoming the efforts to improve the human rights situation, which have led to progress in this field, including through the inauguration of the first national mechanism aimed at enhancing gender balance in all institutions, further welcoming the recent reform of the criminal code and the criminal procedure code, consistent with Côte d'Ivoire's international commitments, while expressing its concern about the continued reports, including those reported by the Secretary-General, in his report of 7 May 2015, of human rights violations and abuses and violations of international humanitarian law, including against women and children, in particular sexual violence, and stressing the importance of investigating and prosecuting such alleged violations and abuses, including those that occurred throughout the post-election crisis, committed by all parties, irrespective of their status or political affiliation,

Welcoming also national and international efforts to bring to justice alleged perpetrators of violations and abuses of human rights and of violations of international humanitarian law in Côte d'Ivoire, urging the Government of Côte d'Ivoire to increase and expedite its efforts to combat impunity and ensure equitable and independent justice without discrimination, and encouraging in this regard the Government to continue its close cooperation with the International Criminal Court,

Expressing concern at reports about difficult conditions in detention, calling upon the Government of Côte d'Ivoire to ensure that the conditions of detention are in line with international obligations and to take all steps necessary to prevent and investigate violations and abuses of human rights in the context of detention, and welcoming the support provided by the European Union and France in this regard,

Commending the contribution of troop- and police-contributing countries and donors to the United Nations Operation in Côte d'Ivoire, and underlining the importance of providing military troops and police officers qualified with appropriate specialized and linguistic skills,

Recognizing the continued contribution of the arms embargo, as defined by resolution 2219 (2015), to the stability of Côte d'Ivoire, including by countering the illicit transfer, destabilizing accumulation and misuse of small arms and light weapons,

Commending the African Union and the Economic Community of West African States for their efforts to consolidate peace and stability in Côte d'Ivoire, and encouraging them to continue to support the Ivorian authorities in addressing key challenges, especially the underlying causes of recent conflict and insecurity in the border area, including the movement of armed elements and weapons, and promoting justice and national reconciliation,

Welcoming the ratification by Côte d'Ivoire of the 1954 Convention relating to the Status of Stateless Persons[244] and the 1961 Convention on the Reduction of Statelessness[245] and the steps being taken to revise its nationality laws, welcoming the important steps being taken by States members of the Economic Community of West African States to address statelessness, including through the ministerial-level regional conference held in Abidjan, from 23 to 25 February 2015, and recalling the decision of the Secretary-General on durable solutions and expressing support for the implementation of the national durable solution strategy for internally displaced persons,

Determining that the situation in Côte d'Ivoire continues to pose a threat to international peace and security in the region,

Acting under Chapter VII of the Charter of the United Nations,

National reconciliation and social cohesion

1. *Welcomes* the resumption of the dialogue between the Government of Côte d'Ivoire and the political opposition in December 2014 and January and May 2015, and calls upon all political parties to play a constructive role and contribute towards reconciliation;

2. *Commends* the Special Representative of the Secretary-General for Côte d'Ivoire for her good offices efforts and political support, and requests that such important efforts and support continue, in particular with a view to the October 2015 presidential election, in line with paragraph 19 (*b*) of the present resolution;

3. *Emphasizes* the importance of the Government of Côte d'Ivoire continuing to pursue a national reconciliation and social cohesion strategy, particularly ahead of the October 2015 presidential election, through concrete measures to promote justice and reconciliation at all levels and involving all stakeholders, and calls for a direct, open and constructive dialogue between the Government and all political parties, including the opposition, to expedite further progress on crucial reforms on nationality and land;

4. *Welcomes* the work undertaken by the Independent Electoral Commission, urges the Government of Côte d'Ivoire to continue to take all steps necessary to implement, in accordance with the existing time frame, the legal framework for the October 2015 presidential election, including the updating of the voters list and the allocation of adequate budgetary resources, as well as to continue its efforts to strengthen national logistical capacities to enable the organization and conduct of the election across the country, calls upon all national stakeholders to facilitate the creation of an environment conducive to the holding of free, fair, transparent and inclusive presidential elections, as well as to refrain from acts that could incite violence, including hate speech, particularly through the media, and affirms its intention to pay close attention to such acts;

5. *Affirms its intention* to review the listing of individuals subject to the financial and travel measures imposed by paragraphs 9 to 12 of resolution 1572 (2004) of 15 November 2004 and paragraph 12 of resolution 1975 (2011) of 30 March 2011, provided that they engage in actions that further the objective of national reconciliation;

Disarmament, demobilization and reintegration

6. *Calls upon* the Government of Côte d'Ivoire to complete the disarmament, demobilization and reintegration process before the presidential election of 2015 in accordance with the objective announced by the President of Côte d'Ivoire, requests the United Nations Operation in Côte d'Ivoire to facilitate the implementation of this process, including by continuing its technical support to the Authority on Disarmament, Demobilization and Reintegration and relevant institutions and swiftly disbursing support to the Ivorian disarmament, demobilization and reintegration programme, and further calls upon Member States and regional and international organizations to provide financial contributions to meet the needs of the programme;

[244] United Nations, *Treaty Series*, vol. 360, No. 5158.

[245] Ibid., vol. 989, No. 14458.

7. *Encourages* the United Nations country team to facilitate the planning and implementation of programmes which support this process, in consultation with the United Nations Operation in Côte d'Ivoire and international partners;

8. *Urges* the Government of Côte d'Ivoire to provide for a transparent and inclusive disarmament, demobilization and reintegration process that includes unregistered former combatants, encourages further efforts by the Authority on Disarmament, Demobilization and Reintegration and relevant institutions to enhance the collection and disposal of weapons and ammunition as part of the disarmament, demobilization and reintegration process, and reiterates the need for the Government to develop and implement long-term solutions to address the residual caseload of former combatants and for the sustained social and economic integration of former combatants, including former female combatants;

Security sector reform

9. *Calls upon* the Government of Côte d'Ivoire to accelerate the implementation of the national security sector reform strategy, adopted in September 2012 and updated in 2014, with a view to setting up inclusive and accountable security forces that include an effective chain of command, a system of military justice and adequate and sustainable budgetary allocations;

10. *Underscores*, in this regard, the importance of accelerating the deployment of the police and gendarmerie to take over public order tasks currently performed by the Republican Forces of Côte d'Ivoire and other groups, including by equipping the police and gendarmerie with standard policing weapons and ammunition following the partial lifting of the arms embargo pursuant to its resolution 2153 (2014) and reaffirmed in resolution 2219 (2015);

11. *Reiterates its call* to the Government of Côte d'Ivoire and all international partners, including private companies, involved in assisting the Government in the security sector reform process, to comply with the provisions of resolution 2219 (2015) and to coordinate their efforts with a view to promoting transparency and a clear division of labour between all international partners;

Human rights

12. *Strongly urges* the Government of Côte d'Ivoire to ensure in the shortest possible time frame that, irrespective of their status or political affiliation, all those responsible for serious violations and abuses of human rights and violations of international humanitarian law, including those committed during and after the post-electoral crisis in Côte d'Ivoire, are brought to justice in accordance with its international obligations and that all detainees receive clarity about their status in a transparent manner, and urges the Government to continue its cooperation with the International Criminal Court;

13. *Emphasizes*, in this regard, the importance of the work conducted by the National Commission of Inquiry and the Dialogue, Truth and Reconciliation Commission to lasting reconciliation in Côte d'Ivoire, encourages the Government of Côte d'Ivoire to publish the final report and recommendations of the Dialogue, Truth and Reconciliation Commission to contribute to such reconciliation, calls for the implementation and conclusion of related investigations, further calls upon the Government to create the enabling environment to ensure that the work of the Ivorian judicial system is impartial, credible, transparent and consistent with internationally agreed standards, and in this regard welcomes the renewal of the Special Investigation and Examination Cell, and encourages the Government to continue to provide the Cell with the support that it needs to conduct its investigations;

14. *Urges* the Government of Côte d'Ivoire to take concrete and discernible steps to prevent and mitigate violence, including intercommunal tensions, by seeking a broad national consensus on addressing effectively identity and land tenure issues;

15. *Welcomes* the work of the National Human Rights Commission, underscores the importance of its independence and its compliance with the principles relating to the status of national institutions for the promotion and protection of human rights (the Paris Principles),[246] and calls upon the United Nations Operation in Côte d'Ivoire to continue to support the Ivorian authorities and institutions in ensuring the human rights of all persons;

[246] General Assembly resolution 48/134, annex.

16. *Calls upon* those responsible to cease committing acts of sexual and gender-based violence immediately, and further calls upon the United Nations Operation in Côte d'Ivoire, where consistent with its authorities and responsibilities, to continue to support national and international efforts to bring to justice perpetrators of serious violations and abuses of human rights and violations of international humanitarian law in Côte d'Ivoire, irrespective of their status or political affiliation;

17. *Welcomes* the continued cooperation between, and the conduct of coordinated activities by, the United Nations Operation in Côte d'Ivoire and the defence and security forces, including the Republican Forces of Côte d'Ivoire, and calls for strict adherence by the defence and security forces, including the Republican Forces, to international humanitarian, human rights and refugee law, and in this context recalls the importance of training in human rights, child protection and sexual and gender-based violence for security and law enforcement agencies;

Mandate of the United Nations Operation in Côte d'Ivoire

18. *Decides* to extend the mandate of the United Nations Operation in Côte d'Ivoire until 30 June 2016;

19. *Also decides* that the mandate of the United Nations Operation in Côte d'Ivoire shall be the following:

(*a*) *Protection of civilians*

– To protect, without prejudice to the primary responsibility of the Ivorian authorities, the civilian population from threat of physical violence, within its capabilities and areas of deployment, and welcomes steps taken by the United Nations Operation in Côte d'Ivoire to move to a more preventive and pre-emptive posture in pursuit of its priorities and in active defence of its mandate, while underlining the need to continue such an effort, without prejudice to the agreed basic principles of peacekeeping;

– To implement the comprehensive strategy for the protection of civilians in coordination with the United Nations country team;

– To work closely with humanitarian agencies, particularly in relation to areas of tension and with respect to the return of displaced persons, to collect information on and identify potential threats against the civilian population and bring them to the attention of the Ivorian authorities, as appropriate;

(*b*) *Political support*

– To provide, through the Special Representative of the Secretary-General, good offices and political support for the efforts of the Ivorian authorities to address the root causes of the conflict and establish lasting peace and security in Côte d'Ivoire, including in the priority areas of security sector reform, disarmament, demobilization and reintegration and reconciliation processes at both the national and local levels;

– To provide, through the Special Representative of the Secretary-General, good offices support to the Ivorian authorities for and throughout the 2015 electoral period, including by facilitating dialogue between all political stakeholders, inclusive of representatives of civil society and political parties;

– To assist the Government of Côte d'Ivoire with the 2015 presidential election process by providing limited logistical support, particularly to access remote areas, within existing resources and capabilities, at the request of the Government, while bearing in mind the primary responsibility of the Government in this regard;

(*c*) *Addressing remaining security threats and border-related challenges*

– To support, within its existing authorities, capabilities and areas of deployment, the national authorities in stabilizing the security situation in the country, with special attention to providing support for the provision of security through the 2015 presidential electoral period;

– To monitor and deter the activities of militias, mercenaries and other illegal armed groups and to support the Government of Côte d'Ivoire in addressing border security challenges consistent with its existing mandate to protect civilians, including cross-border security and other challenges in the border areas, notably with Liberia, and, to this end, to coordinate closely with the United Nations Mission in Liberia in order to further inter-mission cooperation, such as through undertaking coordinated patrols and contingency planning, where appropriate and within their existing mandates and capabilities;

– To liaise with the Republican Forces of Côte d'Ivoire in order to promote mutual trust among all elements composing the Republican Forces;

(*d*) *Disarmament, demobilization and reintegration programme and collection of weapons*

– To assist the Government of Côte d'Ivoire, in close coordination with other bilateral and international partners, in implementing, at the national and local levels, the national programme for the disarmament, demobilization and reintegration of former combatants and the dismantling of militias and self-defence groups, taking into account the rights and needs of the distinct categories of persons to be disarmed, demobilized and reintegrated, including children and women;

– To support the registration and screening of former combatants and assist in assessing and verifying the reliability of the listings of former combatants;

– To support the disarmament and repatriation of foreign armed elements, where relevant, in cooperation with the United Nations Mission in Liberia and United Nations country teams in the region;

– To assist the national authorities, including the National Commission to Fight against the Proliferation and Illicit Traffic of Small Arms and Light Weapons, in collecting, registering, securing and disposing of weapons and in clearing explosive remnants of war, as appropriate, in accordance with resolution 2219 (2015);

– To coordinate with the Government of Côte d'Ivoire in ensuring that the collected weapons are not disseminated or reutilized outside a comprehensive national security strategy, as referred to in point (*e*) below;

(*e*) *Reconstitution and reform of security institutions*

– To assist the Government of Côte d'Ivoire in implementing, without delay and in close coordination with other international partners, its comprehensive national security strategy;

– To support the Government of Côte d'Ivoire in providing effective, transparent and harmonized coordination of assistance, including the promotion of a clear division of tasks and responsibilities, by international partners to the security sector reform process;

– To advise the Government of Côte d'Ivoire, as appropriate, on security sector reform and the organization of the future national army, to facilitate the provision, within its current resources and as requested by the Government and in close coordination with other international partners, of training in human rights, child protection and protection from sexual and gender-based violence to the security and law enforcement institutions, as well as capacity-building support by providing technical assistance, co-location and mentoring programmes for the police and gendarmerie and to contribute to restoring their presence throughout Côte d'Ivoire and to promote trust and confidence within and between the security and law enforcement agencies, and to offer support to the development of a sustainable vetting mechanism for personnel that will be absorbed into security sector institutions;

(*f*) *Monitoring of the arms embargo*

– To monitor the implementation of the measures imposed by paragraph 7 of resolution 1572 (2004), in cooperation with the Group of Experts on Côte d'Ivoire established pursuant to resolution 1584 (2005) of 1 February 2005, including by inspecting, as they deem it necessary and, when appropriate, without notice, all weapons, ammunition and related materiel regardless of location, consistent with resolution 2219 (2015);

– To collect, as appropriate, arms and any related materiel brought into Côte d'Ivoire in violation of the measures imposed by paragraph 7 of resolution 1572 (2004) and to dispose of such arms and related materiel as appropriate;

– To assist the Government of Côte d'Ivoire, upon its request, and within its existing resources, to ensure the Government's notification and approval requests contain the required information identified in paragraph 7 of resolution 2219 (2015), consistent with paragraph 9 of resolution 2219 (2015);

(*g*) *Support for compliance with international humanitarian and human rights law*

– To contribute to the promotion and protection of human rights in Côte d'Ivoire, with special attention to grave violations and abuses committed against children and women, notably sexual and gender-based violence, in close coordination with the Independent Expert established pursuant to Human Rights Council resolution 17/21 of 17 June 2011;[247]

– To monitor, help to investigate and report to the Security Council abuses and violations of human rights and violations of international humanitarian law, including those against children, in line with resolutions 1612 (2005) of 26 July 2005, 1882 (2009) of 4 August 2009, 1998 (2011) of 12 July 2011, 2068 (2012) of 19 September 2012 and 2143 (2014) of 7 March 2014, in order to prevent such abuses and violations and to end impunity;

– To bring to the attention of the Security Council all individuals identified as perpetrators of serious human rights violations and to keep the Security Council Committee established pursuant to resolution 1572 (2004) informed of any significant developments in this regard, when appropriate;

– To support the efforts of the Government of Côte d'Ivoire in combating sexual and gender-based violence, including through contributing to the implementation of a nationally owned multisectoral strategy in cooperation with United Nations Action against Sexual Violence in Conflict entities;

– To provide specific protection for women affected by armed conflict to ensure gender expertise and training, as appropriate and within existing resources, in accordance with resolutions 1888 (2009) of 30 September 2009, 1889 (2009) of 5 October 2009, 1960 (2010) of 16 December 2010 and 2106 (2013) of 24 June 2013;

(*h*) *Support for humanitarian assistance*

– To facilitate, as necessary, unhindered humanitarian access and to help to strengthen the delivery of humanitarian assistance to conflict-affected and vulnerable populations, notably by contributing to enhancing security for its delivery;

– To support the Ivorian authorities in preparing for the voluntary, safe and sustainable return of refugees and internally displaced persons, in cooperation with relevant humanitarian organizations, and in creating the security conditions conducive to it;

(*i*) *Public information*

– To continue to use the broadcasting capacity of the United Nations Operation in Côte d'Ivoire, through ONUCI FM, to contribute to the overall effort to create a peaceful environment through the 2015 presidential electoral period;

– To monitor any public incidents of incitement to hatred, intolerance and violence and bring to the attention of the Security Council all individuals identified as instigators of political violence and to keep the Committee established pursuant to resolution 1572 (2004) informed of any significant developments in this regard, when appropriate;

(*j*) *Protection of United Nations personnel*

– To protect United Nations personnel, installations and equipment and ensure the security and freedom of movement of United Nations personnel;

20. *Authorizes* the United Nations Operation in Côte d'Ivoire to use all means necessary to carry out its mandate, within its capabilities and its areas of deployment;

21. *Decides* that the protection of civilians shall remain the priority of the United Nations Operation in Côte d'Ivoire, in accordance with paragraph 19 (*a*) above, and further decides that the Operation shall continue to focus on supporting the Government of Côte d'Ivoire in disarmament, demobilization and reintegration, the collection of weapons and security sector reform, in accordance with paragraphs 19 (*d*) and (*e*) of the present resolution, with the objective of transitioning security responsibilities from the Operation to the Government;

[247] See *Official Records of the General Assembly, Sixty-sixth Session, Supplement No. 53* (A/66/53), chap. I.

22. *Requests* the United Nations Operation in Côte d'Ivoire to ensure that any support provided to non-United Nations security forces is provided in strict compliance with the human rights due diligence policy on United Nations support to non-United Nations security forces;[248]

Force structure

23. *Decides* that the authorized ceiling of the military component of the United Nations Operation in Côte d'Ivoire shall remain at 5,437 military personnel, comprising 5,245 troops and staff officers and 192 military observers;

24. *Also decides* that the authorized ceiling of the police component of the United Nations Operation in Côte d'Ivoire shall remain at 1,500 personnel, and further decides to maintain the 8 customs officers previously authorized;

25. *Reaffirms its intention* to consider further downsizing the United Nations Operation in Côte d'Ivoire, reviewing its mandate and its possible termination after the October 2015 presidential election based on security conditions on the ground and the capacity of the Government of Côte d'Ivoire to take over the security role of the Operation;

26. *Acknowledges* the importance of the reconfiguration of the military presence and resources of the United Nations Operation in Côte d'Ivoire to high-risk areas, expresses support for the mobile concept of operations of the military component of the Operation, and requests the Operation to continue to update its configuration in this regard, with a view to focusing on the west and other high-risk areas, as appropriate, while continuing its shift to a more mobile posture and enhancing its situational awareness and early warning capabilities;

27. *Requests* the United Nations Operation in Côte d'Ivoire to focus and continue to streamline its activities across its military, police and civilian components in order to achieve progress on the tasks outlined in paragraph 19 above;

French forces

28. *Decides* to extend until 30 June 2016 the authorization that the Council provided to the French forces in order to support the United Nations Operation in Côte d'Ivoire, within the limits of their deployment and their capabilities;

29. *Urges* all parties to cooperate fully with the operations of the United Nations Operation in Côte d'Ivoire and of the French forces supporting it, in particular by ensuring their safety, security and freedom of movement with unhindered and immediate access throughout the territory of Côte d'Ivoire to enable them to fully carry out their mandates;

Regional and inter-mission cooperation

30. *Calls upon* the Governments of Côte d'Ivoire and Liberia to continue reinforcing their cooperation, particularly with respect to the border area, including through increased monitoring, information-sharing and coordinated actions, and to implement the shared border strategy to, inter alia, support the disarmament and repatriation of foreign armed elements on both sides of the border and the voluntary and safe repatriation of refugees as well as to address the root causes of conflict and tension;

31. *Affirms* the importance of inter-mission cooperation arrangements as the United Nations Mission in Liberia and the United Nations Operation in Côte d'Ivoire downsize, reaffirms the inter-mission cooperation framework set out in its resolution 1609 (2005) of 24 June 2005, and further recalls its endorsement in its resolution 2062 (2012) of 26 July 2012 of the recommendation of the Secretary-General to transfer three armed helicopters from the Mission to the Operation to be used in both Côte d'Ivoire and Liberia along and across their border, and reaffirms its decision in its resolution 2162 (2014) that all military utility helicopters of the Operation and the Mission shall be utilized in both Côte d'Ivoire and Liberia in order to facilitate rapid response and mobility, while not affecting the area of responsibility of either mission;

32. *Welcomes* the full operationalization of the quick reaction force established pursuant to resolution 2162 (2014) to implement the mandate of the United Nations Operation in Côte d'Ivoire, as defined in paragraph 19 of

[248] S/2013/110, annex.

the present resolution, and to support the United Nations Mission in Liberia, as defined in paragraph 33 of the present resolution, while recognizing that this unit will remain primarily an asset of the Operation, and requests the Secretary-General, in the context of inter-mission cooperation arrangements between the Mission and the Operation, to continue to maintain such a unit for a period of one year and within the authorized military strength of the Operation;

33. *Authorizes* the Secretary-General to deploy this unit to Liberia, subject to the consent of the troop-contributing countries concerned and the Government of Liberia, in the event of a serious deterioration of the security situation on the ground, in order to temporarily reinforce the United Nations Mission in Liberia, with the sole purpose of implementing its mandate, and stresses that this unit should prioritize implementation of the United Nations Operation in Côte d'Ivoire mandate in Côte d'Ivoire;

34. *Requests* the Secretary-General to inform the Council immediately of any deployment of this unit to Liberia and to obtain Council authorization for any such deployment for a period that exceeds 90 days;

35. *Calls upon* all United Nations entities in Côte d'Ivoire and Liberia, including all relevant components of the United Nations Operation in Côte d'Ivoire and the United Nations Mission in Liberia, within their respective mandates, capabilities and areas of deployment, to enhance their support for the stabilization of the border area, including through increased inter-mission cooperation and the development of a shared, strategic vision and plan, in support of the Ivorian and Liberian authorities and support for implementing regional security strategies, including those of the Mano River Union and the Economic Community of West African States;

36. *Commends* inter-mission cooperation between the United Nations Operation in Côte d'Ivoire and the United Nations Multidimensional Integrated Stabilization Mission in Mali, and encourages both United Nations missions to continue in this direction, as authorized by paragraph 25 of its resolution 2164 (2014);

Reporting

37. *Requests* the Secretary-General to keep the Council regularly informed of the situation in Côte d'Ivoire and the implementation of the mandate of the United Nations Operation in Côte d'Ivoire and to provide to the Council no later than 15 December 2015 a midterm report on the situation on the ground and the implementation of the present resolution that includes options for implementing by 31 March 2016 the elements contained in paragraph 65 of his report of 15 May 2014,[249] and affirms its intention to consider these options pursuant to the successful conduct of the 2015 presidential election process, and requests the Secretary-General to provide to the Council no later than 31 March 2016 a report containing recommendations consistent with paragraph 25 above, with a view to possible termination, to be considered by the Council, taking into account the situation in Côte d'Ivoire;

38. *Decides* to remain seized of the matter.

Adopted unanimously at the 7471st meeting.

SECURITY COUNCIL MISSION[250]

Decisions

On 8 August 2014, the President of the Security Council addressed the following letter to the Secretary-General:[251]

> I have the honour to inform you that the members of the Security Council have agreed to send a mission to Europe and Africa from 8 to 14 August 2014. The mission plans to visit Belgium, the Netherlands, South Sudan, Somalia and Kenya. The members of the Council have agreed on the terms of reference of the mission, which are annexed hereto.

[249] S/2014/342.

[250] Resolutions or decisions on this question were first adopted by the Security Council in 2003.

[251] S/2014/579.

Several members will co-lead the different legs of the mission. In Belgium, I will be co-leading the mission with Mr. Michael Bliss. In the Netherlands, Ambassador Cristián Barros Melet and Mr. Olivier Maes will be co-leading. In South Sudan, Ambassador Samantha Power and Ambassador Eugène-Richard Gasana will be co-leading the mission and in Somalia I will be co-leading the mission with Ambassador Usman Sarki.

Following consultations with the members, it has been agreed that the composition of the mission is as follows:

Argentina (Mr. Mario Oyarzábal)

Australia (Mr. Michael Bliss)

Chad (Ambassador Mahamat Zene Cherif)

Chile (Ambassador Cristián Barros Melet)

China (Mr. Zhao Yong)

France (Mr. Alexis Lamek)

Jordan (Ambassador Dina Kawar)

Lithuania (Ambassador Raimonda Murmokaitė)

Luxembourg (Mr. Olivier Maes)

Nigeria (Ambassador Usman Sarki)

Republic of Korea (Ambassador Oh Joon)

Russian Federation (Mr. Alexander Pankin)

Rwanda (Ambassador Eugène-Richard Gasana)

United Kingdom of Great Britain and Northern Ireland (Ambassador Mark Lyall Grant)

United States of America (Ambassador Samantha Power)

I should be grateful if you could have the present letter and its annex circulated as a document of the Security Council.

Annex

Security Council mission to Europe and Africa: terms of reference

Belgium

Co-leads: Australia and United Kingdom of Great Britain and Northern Ireland

To commemorate the centenary of the First World War. To pay tribute to the sacrifices of all those who served their country during that war.

To draw lessons from the First World War to assist the Security Council in discharging its mandate in maintaining international peace and security. To engage in discussions with representatives of civil society and academic institutions on the tools that the Council could deploy to better prevent conflict and loss of civilian life in situations of conflict.

To engage with the Government of Belgium on matters of mutual interest.

The Netherlands

Co-leads: Chile and Luxembourg

To underline the commitment of the Security Council to the international courts and tribunals located in The Hague in the light of the common objective of settling international disputes peacefully and establishing accountability for serious international crimes.

To express the support of the Council for the work of the International Court of Justice, the principal judicial organ of the United Nations, to visit the premises of the Court and to receive an update regarding its caseload and other developments.

To reaffirm the relationship between the Council and the International Criminal Court, to receive an update on the work of the Court and to discuss the interaction between the Court and the Council.

To reaffirm the relationship between the Council and the international criminal courts and tribunals located in The Hague and mandated by, or established with the support of, the Council (the International Tribunal for the Former Yugoslavia, the International Criminal Tribunal for Rwanda, the Special Tribunal for Lebanon and the Residual Special Court for Sierra Leone) and to get first-hand updates on their activities and other developments.

To express gratitude to the Organization for the Prohibition of Chemical Weapons for its close collaboration with the United Nations, including through the Organization for the Prohibition of Chemical Weapons-United Nations Joint Mission, established to implement Council resolution 2118 (2013) and eliminate the chemical weapons programme of the Syrian Arab Republic.

To receive an update on progress in eliminating the chemical weapons programme of the Syrian Arab Republic.

To engage on matters of mutual interest with the Government of the Netherlands.

South Sudan

Co-leads: United States of America and Rwanda

To convey its deep alarm regarding the deteriorating political, security and humanitarian crisis in South Sudan resulting from the internal Sudan People's Liberation Movement political dispute and the subsequent violence caused by the country's political and military leaders, and to condemn actions that perpetuate the crisis.

To demand that all armed groups immediately cease all forms of violence, including sexual violence, renounce force as a means of resolving political grievances, comply with the cessation of hostilities agreement of 23 January 2014 and allow full access for the monitoring and verification teams of the Intergovernmental Authority on Development.

To engage directly with all parties in the Intergovernmental Authority on Development-led multi-stakeholder political negotiations and to urge engagement in an open and fully inclusive national dialogue seeking to establish lasting peace, reconciliation and good governance through a transitional agenda and a government of national unity, including through the full and effective participation of youth, women, diverse communities, faith groups, civil society and formerly detained leaders of the Sudanese People's Liberation Movement.

To reiterate the serious concerns of the Security Council about the protection of civilians, including foreign nationals, and to emphasize the need to protect civilians under threat of physical violence, irrespective of the source of such violence.

To reaffirm the support of the Council to the United Nations Mission in South Sudan and to receive a briefing on the implementation of Council resolution 2155 (2014), in particular as regards the reconfiguration of the Mission in response to a more focused peacekeeping mandate.

To assess the situation of the more than 1 million internally displaced persons, including those seeking refuge in Mission compounds, to underscore the seriousness of the humanitarian crisis, which may soon reach the threshold of famine, and to advocate for the creation of the conditions necessary for the delivery of humanitarian assistance, including the security and freedom of movement of United Nations, humanitarian and associated personnel.

To express serious concern at persistent restrictions placed upon and obstructions to the movement and operations of the Mission, to strongly condemn the attacks by government and opposition forces and other groups on United Nations personnel and facilities and to call upon the Government of South Sudan to complete its investigations of these attacks in a swift and thorough manner and hold those responsible to account.

To emphasize that dismantling barriers to the full implementation of Council resolution 1325 (2000) will be achieved only through a dedicated commitment to women's empowerment, participation and human rights, and to emphasize the importance of the full and effective participation of women at all levels, including through providing support to women's civil society organizations, incorporating gender expertise in peace talks and increasing the deployment of women in the military, police and civilian components of the Mission.

To demand that all parties follow up on the commitments they recently made to the Special Representative of the Secretary-General for Children and Armed Conflict.

Somalia

Co-leads: Nigeria and United Kingdom

To recall the commitment of the Security Council to the sovereignty, territorial integrity and political unity of Somalia.

To underline the support of the Council to the peace and reconciliation process in Somalia. To emphasize the support of the Council to the United Nations Assistance Mission in Somalia. To get an update from the Mission on the implementation of its mandate, as set out in Council resolution 2158 (2014). To get an update on stabilization efforts in areas recovered from Al-Shabaab control.

To express its gratitude to the African Union Mission in Somalia. To receive an update on the implementation of Council resolution 2124 (2013), in particular on progress in the African Union Mission and Somali National Army's military campaign against Al-Shabaab. To receive progress reports on the efforts of the African Union Mission towards reducing civilian casualties, including the establishment of a Civilian Casualty Tracking, Analysis and Response Cell.

To receive an update from the Federal Government of Somalia on the implementation of its requirements under the terms of the partial suspension of the arms embargo, as set out in Council resolution 2142 (2014). To reiterate to the Federal Government that any decision on the continuation of the partial suspension of the arms embargo shall be taken in view of its efforts to comply with the relevant Council resolutions.

To reiterate to the Federal Government of Somalia the urgent need for progress in the development of a federal system, the review and implementation of the Somali Provisional Federal Constitution and a clear plan for elections in 2016.

To reaffirm the important role of women in the prevention and resolution of conflicts and in peacebuilding. To get an update on the impact of the efforts of the Federal Government of Somalia to promote increased representation of women at all decision-making levels in Somali institutions.

To underscore the concern of the Council at the ongoing incidence of sexual violence in Somalia. To highlight the support of the Council for, and get an update on, the action plan of the Federal Government of Somalia to end sexual violence, as well as the plan for implementing the joint communiqué of the Federal Government and the United Nations on the prevention of sexual violence. To get an update on the work done by the United Nations to assist in preventing and responding to sexual and gender-based violence, including the strengthening of the justice and security sectors.

To reaffirm the importance of the swift and full implementation of the action plan of the Federal Government of Somalia to end and prevent the recruitment and use of children by the Somali national armed forces as well as the action plan to end the killing and maiming of children, both signed in 2012.

To reiterate its deep concern at the humanitarian situation in Somalia. To get a better understanding of some of the challenges in delivering humanitarian assistance and ways in which the international community can assist.

To underline the enduring support of the Council for greater peace and stability in Somalia, and to all actors working on the ground to this end.

Kenya

To engage on matters of mutual interest with the Government of Kenya.

At its 7245th meeting, on 19 August 2014, the Council considered the item entitled:

"Security Council mission

"Briefing by Security Council mission to Europe and Africa (8 to 14 August 2014)".

On 19 January 2015, the President of the Security Council addressed the following letter to the Secretary-General:[252]

Further to my letter of 2 January 2015, I have the honour to confirm that the members of the Security Council have agreed to send a mission to Haiti from 23 to 25 January 2015. The members of the Council have agreed on the terms of reference of the mission, which are annexed hereto.

I will be co-leading the mission together with Ambassador Samantha Power.

Following consultations with the members, it has been agreed that the composition of the mission is as follows:

Angola (Ambassador Ismael Abraão Gaspar Martins)

Chad (Mr. Bante Mangaral)

Chile (Ambassador Cristián Barros Melet)

China (Ambassador Liu Jieyi)

France (Mr. Alexis Lamek)

Jordan (Ambassador Ms. Dina Kawar)

Lithuania (Mr. Dainius Baublys)

Malaysia (Ambassador Hussein Haniff)

New Zealand (Ambassador Jim McLay)

Nigeria (Ambassador Usman Sarki)

Russian Federation (Mr. Petr Iliichev)

Spain (Ambassador Román Oyarzun Marchesi)

United Kingdom of Great Britain and Northern Ireland (Ambassador Peter Wilson)

United States of America (Ambassador Samantha Power)

Venezuela (Bolivarian Republic of) (Ambassador Rafael Darío Ramírez Carreño)

I should be grateful if you would have the present letter and its annex circulated as a document of the Security Council.

Annex

Security Council mission to Haiti: terms of reference

Co-leads: Chile and United States of America

To underscore the importance of inclusiveness and constructiveness to political stability, democratic governance and development, all of which promote conflict prevention.

To reaffirm the continued support of the Security Council for the Government and people of Haiti and their efforts to consolidate peace, democracy and stability and promote recovery and sustainable development.

[252] S/2015/40.

To urge Haiti's political actors to work cooperatively and without further delays to ensure the urgent holding of free, fair, inclusive and transparent legislative, partial senatorial, municipal and local elections, including those that are long overdue, in accordance with the Constitution of Haiti.

To assess the ongoing strengthening of the Haitian National Police and the increasing exercise by national authorities of the responsibility of the Haitian State for the maintenance of stability and security in the country, examine efforts by the United Nations Stabilization Mission in Haiti to increase coordination with the National Police and to strengthen their capacity in order for them to take full responsibility for security needs, underscore the importance of adequate funding for the National Police, encourage the Government of Haiti to take advantage of the support being provided by the international community to guarantee the provision of adequate security for the Haitian people, and assess the full range of the rule of law, security and security-related structures of the country.

To assess the implementation of relevant Council resolutions, in particular resolution 2180 (2014), taking into account the importance of maintaining a secure and stable environment, including for elections expected in 2015, and the impact of social and political realities on Haiti's stability and security; the increasing development of Haitian State capabilities, in particular the ongoing strengthening of the Haitian National Police; and the increasing exercise by the national authorities of the responsibility of the Haitian State for the maintenance of stability and security in the country.

To express strong support for the Mission and the Special Representative of the Secretary-General for Haiti and their efforts to improve stability and governance in Haiti, as well as create conditions conducive to the security, reconstruction and development of Haiti.

To reiterate the importance of immediate, medium- and long-term sustained efforts to consolidate democracy, peace and stability, ensure the protection of human rights and promote sustainable development, while bearing in mind the ownership and primary responsibility of the Government and people of Haiti and recognizing the importance of civil society organizations in this regard.

At its 7372nd meeting, on 29 January 2015, the Council considered the item entitled:

"Security Council mission

"Briefing by Security Council mission to Haiti (23 to 25 January 2015)".

On 5 March 2015, the President of the Security Council addressed the following letter to the Secretary-General:[253]

Further to the letter dated 3 February 2015 from the Permanent Representative of China to the United Nations, Mr. Liu Jieyi, I have the honour to inform you that the members of the Security Council have decided to send a mission to Africa from 9 to 13 March 2015. The mission plans to visit the Central African Republic, Ethiopia and Burundi. The members of the Council have agreed on the terms of reference of the mission, which are contained in the annex to the present letter.

I will co-lead the mission with Ambassador Ismael Abraão Gaspar Martins. We will be joined by a third co-lead, Ambassador Samantha Power, during the Council's visit to Burundi.

Following consultations with the members, it has been agreed that the composition of the mission is as follows:

Angola (Ambassador Ismael Abraão Gaspar Martins)

Chad (Ambassador Mahamat Zene Cherif)

Chile (Ambassador Carlos Olguín Cigarroa)

[253] S/2015/162.

China (Mr. Zhao Yong)

France (Ambassador François Delattre)

Jordan (Ambassador Dina Kawar)

Lithuania (Ambassador Raimonda Murmokaitė)

Malaysia (Mrs. Siti Hajjar Adnin)

New Zealand (Ambassador Jim McLay)

Nigeria (Ambassador Usman Sarki)

Russian Federation (Mr. Petr Iliichev)

Spain (Ambassador Juan Manuel González de Linares Palou)

United Kingdom of Great Britain and Northern Ireland (Ambassador Peter Wilson)

United States of America (Ambassador Samantha Power)

Venezuela (Bolivarian Republic of) (Ambassador Rafael Darío Ramírez Carreño)

I should be grateful if you would have the present letter and its annex circulated as a document of the Security Council.

Annex

Security Council mission to Africa: Central African Republic, African Union and Burundi

Terms of reference

Central African Republic

1. To recall that the Central African Republic authorities bear the primary responsibility to protect all populations within their territory from genocide, war crimes, ethnic cleansing and crimes against humanity and to emphasize that any sustainable solution to the crisis in the Central African Republic should be owned by that country.

2. To commend the African-led International Support Mission in the Central African Republic, Operation Sangaris and the European Union military operation in the Central African Republic for the work done in laying the foundation for increased security ahead of and in support of the deployment of the United Nations Multidimensional Integrated Stabilization Mission in the Central African Republic.

3. To express grave concern that armed groups continue to destabilize the Central African Republic and pose a permanent threat to the peace, security and stability of the country, and to further express concern at the recent increase in kidnappings and attacks against humanitarian workers in the Central African Republic, which impedes humanitarian access to vulnerable populations.

4. To reiterate the appeal to all parties and stakeholders, particularly the leaders of the ex-Séléka and anti-balaka groups, as well as all other armed groups, to immediately cease all forms of violence, including sexual violence, to permanently lay down their arms, to release all children from their ranks and to embark upon the path of dialogue as the only viable means towards achieving lasting reconciliation and peace.

5. To remind all parties of their obligations under international humanitarian and human rights law to ensure the immediate, full, safe and unhindered civilian-led delivery of humanitarian assistance and the principle of safe, dignified and sustainable return of internally displaced persons and refugees.

6. To commend efforts by the transitional authorities to gather views of local citizens in advance of the Bangui Forum on National Reconciliation by dispatching government ministers and officials throughout the Central African Republic and to welcome the holding of the Bangui Forum as an important milestone for a comprehensive political dialogue and reconciliation process at the local and national levels.

7. To reiterate the call upon the transitional authorities to accelerate the transition process and to take concrete action, with the full, effective and equal participation of women, for the holding of free, fair, transparent and inclusive presidential and legislative elections that allow for the full, effective and equal participation of internally displaced persons and Central African Republic refugees, no later than August 2015; the fight against impunity, including for crimes of sexual and gender-based violence; the formulation and implementation of a disarmament, demobilization, reintegration and repatriation strategy; and the rebuilding of effective State institutions, including through security sector reform.

8. To reinforce the need for an inclusive and effective disarmament, demobilization and reintegration process, as well as repatriation and resettlement, in the case of foreign fighters, including women and children formerly associated with armed forces and groups, while respecting the need to fight impunity.

9. To stress the important role of the internal security forces (police and gendarmerie) in the restoration of security in the Central African Republic and encourage the Central African Republic authorities to initiate the reform process of the Central African Republic armed forces, to include appropriate vetting procedures in order to put in place a professional, representative and balanced army, including through the adoption of measures to absorb elements of the armed groups meeting rigorous selection criteria, building the capacity of the security forces to address sexual and gender-based violence and retraining part of the Central African Republic armed forces.

10. To welcome in this regard the decision of the European Union to establish a one-year military advice mission based in Bangui (European Union Military Advisory Mission in the Central African Republic), as requested by the transitional authorities of the Central African Republic, in order to contribute to providing them with expert advice on reforming the Central African Republic armed forces, and to underline the importance of a clear distribution of tasks and close coordination between the international forces or missions in the Central African Republic and the lead role of the United Nations Multidimensional Integrated Stabilization Mission in the Central African Republic in this regard.

11. To assess the deployment of the military, police and civilian components of the Stabilization Mission, the initial work of the Mission in implementing its mandate, the establishment of the Bangui task force and the reconfiguration of the Mission following the violent incidents in Bangui in October 2014.

12. To urge the Stabilization Mission to accelerate the deployments of its civilian, police and military capabilities, including gender advisers and women's protection advisers, in the Central African Republic in order to reach its full operational capacity as soon as possible and enable the Mission to effectively discharge its mandate over the entire national territory.

13. To assess the security situation and the ability of the Stabilization Mission to intensify the implementation of its mandate, in particular to protect civilians under threat of physical violence; prevent and report on all forms of violence, including sexual violence; support the implementation of the transition process, in particular the reconciliation and electoral processes, with the full and effective participation of women; facilitate the civilian-led delivery of humanitarian assistance; support the promotion and protection of human rights; support national and international justice and the rule of law and support the disarmament, demobilization, reintegration and repatriation and security sector reform processes, in accordance with the priority tasks set out in paragraph 30 of Security Council resolution 2149 (2014).

14. To assess the plight of vulnerable populations in the Central African Republic, including those located in enclaves in Bangui and around the country.

15. To urge the former troop- and police-contributing countries of the African-led International Support Mission in the Central African Republic that have been rehatted to the Stabilization Mission to expedite the procurement and deployment of remaining additional contingent-owned equipment.

16. To call upon all international partners of the Central African Republic to provide urgent financial contributions to support national dialogue and reconciliation, disarmament, demobilization and reintegration and security sector reform processes and the restoration of the judicial and penal chains in order to fight against impunity.

17. To further call upon all international partners to provide support to the electoral process as a matter of urgency, particularly through financing the United Nations Development Programme multi-donor basket fund for elections.

18. To express grave concern at the threat to peace and security in the Central African Republic arising from the illicit transfer, destabilizing accumulation and misuse of small arms and light weapons and the use of such weapons against civilians affected by armed conflict, and to recall in this regard the important contribution that the Council-mandated arms embargo can make to countering the illicit transfer of arms and related materiel in the Central African Republic and its region and to supporting post-conflict peacebuilding, disarmament, demobilization and reintegration and security sector reform.

19. To stress the urgent and imperative need to end impunity in the Central African Republic and to bring to justice perpetrators of violations of international humanitarian law and of abuses or violations of human rights, including sexual violence, underlining in this regard the need to bolster national accountability mechanisms and to implement without delay the Memorandum of Understanding on Urgent Temporary Measures of 7 August 2014, which describes, in particular, the establishment of a national special penal court in charge of investigating and prosecuting the serious crimes committed in the Central African Republic.

20. To welcome the ongoing cooperation of the transitional authorities of the Central African Republic with the Prosecutor of the International Criminal Court, who opened an investigation on 24 September 2014, following the request of the national authorities, into alleged crimes committed since 2012.

21. To exchange views with members of civil society, including local women and women's organizations in the field, in accordance with paragraph 6 of Council resolution 2122 (2013).

22. To express concern that illicit trade, exploitation and smuggling of natural resources, including gold, diamonds and wildlife poaching and trafficking, continue to threaten the peace and stability of the Central African Republic.

23. To note the critical importance of effective implementation of the sanctions regime, including the key role that neighbouring States and regional and subregional organizations can play in this regard, and to encourage efforts to further enhance cooperation.

24. To call upon the transitional authorities to continue their efforts to restore sound and transparent public financial management, in line with the recommendations of the recent International Monetary Fund mission in Bangui (November 2014), in particular to mobilize domestic resources, particularly customs revenues, in full respect of financial best practice, in order to meet the expenses related to the functioning of the State; implement early recovery plans; and revitalize the economy.

25. To express its appreciation for the international mediation led by the President of the Congo, Mr. Denis Sassou Nguesso, and comprising Mr. Soumeylou Boubèye Maïga, on behalf of the African Union, and Mr. Abdoulaye Bathily, on behalf of the United Nations, as well as the Secretary-General of the Economic Community of Central African States as rapporteur, in view of the Bangui Forum on National Reconciliation and the upcoming legislative and presidential elections, and the constructive engagement of the region in this regard.

African Union

26. To strengthen partnership and enhance cooperation between the African Union and the United Nations through an exchange of views on issues of interest to both the United Nations Security Council and the African Union Peace and Security Council, in accordance with Security Council resolution 2033 (2012).

27. To exchange views and explore ways of reinforcing and supporting the African Union conflict prevention tools.

28. To exchange views on situations of interest to both the United Nations Security Council and the African Union Peace and Security Council, on the basis of an agenda to be agreed by both Councils.

Burundi

29. To take note of the significant progress made by Burundi since the adoption of the Arusha Agreement in 2000, notably in the restoration of security and stability in the country, and to welcome Burundi's contribution to and active participation in United Nations and African Union peacekeeping operations, especially in Somalia and the Central African Republic.

30. To stress the crucial need for a free, transparent, credible, inclusive and peaceful electoral process in 2015, with the effective participation of women as observers, voters, candidates and mediators, in order to ensure that the significant progress achieved is not reversed.

31. To encourage the Government of Burundi and the Independent National Electoral Commission as well as all stakeholders in the electoral process, including the opposition, to continue to implement the code of conduct for political parties and political actors and the road map towards the elections and to make further efforts to ensure a space for all political parties and to improve dialogue between all political actors, with a view to ensuring a conducive, free and open environment for the run-up to the 2015 elections.

32. To stress that it is critical that the Independent National Electoral Commission continue to take effective measures to strengthen the public's confidence in the electoral process and also to encourage the opposition to play its part and remain engaged throughout the electoral process and to use peaceful and democratic means to address any electoral dispute.

33. To recall that the Security Council pays sustained attention to the electoral process in Burundi and to recall the mandate of the United Nations Electoral Observer Mission in Burundi to follow and report on the electoral process before, during and after the elections, in accordance with resolution 2137 (2014), and to call upon the Government of Burundi, the Independent National Electoral Commission and all relevant electoral stakeholders to ensure close cooperation with the Observer Mission in this regard.

34. To assess the efforts made by the Government of Burundi to improve the human rights situation in the country and to call for further efforts to address concerns about restrictions on freedom of expression and opinion, peaceful assembly and association, continued threats against journalists and representatives of civil society, including those who work on human rights, and reports of intimidation, harassment, political violence, arbitrary arrest and detention.

35. To express concern about the insufficient progress on the fight against impunity and call for the Government of Burundi to deploy greater efforts to ensure that all human rights violations and abuses are seriously investigated and that perpetrators are held accountable.

36. To stress the utmost importance of fighting against poverty and to emphasize the need for the United Nations system and the international community to maintain their support for peace consolidation and long-term development in Burundi, to call upon the Government of Burundi and international and regional partners to fully implement the mutual commitments made in the joint communiqué of the round-table meeting held in Bujumbura in December 2014, and to welcome the continued engagement of the Burundi configuration of the Peacebuilding Commission.

37. To reiterate its call upon the United Nations country team and its component United Nations agencies to scale up their activities and to emphasize the need to address the implications of the departure of the United Nations Office in Burundi as identified in the Joint Transition Plan, in particular in the areas of political dialogue, high-level facilitation and advocacy, and human rights; and to ensure that women, peace and security functions and overall efforts towards inclusion are properly embedded and resourced within the United Nations country team and are part of the political dialogue with the Government of Burundi and the United Nations Electoral Observer Mission in Burundi.

At its 7407th meeting, on 18 March 2015, the Council considered the item entitled:

"Security Council mission

"Briefing by Security Council mission to Africa (9 to 13 March 2015)".

CENTRAL AFRICAN REGION[254]

Decisions

At its 7334th meeting, on 10 December 2014, the Security Council considered the item entitled:

"Central African region

"Report of the Secretary-General on the activities of the United Nations Regional Office for Central Africa and on the Lord's Resistance Army-affected areas (S/2014/812)".

At the same meeting, the Council decided to extend invitations, in accordance with rule 39 of its provisional rules of procedure, to Mr. Abdoulaye Bathily, Special Representative of the Secretary-General for Central Africa and Head of the United Nations Regional Office for Central Africa, and Mr. Jackson Kiprono Tuwei, African Union Special Envoy on the Lord's Resistance Army Issue.

At the same meeting, following consultations among members of the Security Council, the President made the following statement on behalf of the Council:[255]

The Security Council expresses its concern at the grave security situation in parts of Central Africa within the remit of the United Nations Regional Office for Central Africa, in particular the ongoing crisis in the Central African Republic and its regional impact, the continuing threat of the Lord's Resistance Army, and the expansion of Boko Haram terrorist activities into countries in the subregion. The Council also expresses its continuing concern regarding maritime insecurity in the Gulf of Guinea, the illegal wildlife trade and transnational organized crime. The Council welcomes the local and parliamentary elections held in the subregion and stresses the need for upcoming elections in the region to be held in a timely, transparent and inclusive manner according to their constitutions, and encourages the Regional Office to continue to support States in this regard, including through the promotion of women's political participation.

The Council reiterates its strong condemnation of the appalling attacks, war crimes and crimes against humanity carried out by the Lord's Resistance Army and its violations of international humanitarian law and abuses of human rights, including the Lord's Resistance Army's recruitment and use of children in armed conflict, killing and maiming, rape, sexual slavery and other sexual violence, and abductions. The Council demands an immediate end to all attacks by the Lord's Resistance Army and urges the Lord's Resistance Army to release all those abducted and to disarm and demobilize. The Council welcomes the progress made with regard to ending Lord's Resistance Army war crimes and crimes against humanity in Central Africa and reiterates its resolve to maintain the current momentum until a permanent end to the threat posed by the Lord's Resistance Army has been achieved.

The Council pays tribute to the efforts of the Special Representative of the Secretary-General for Central Africa and Head of the United Nations Regional Office for Central Africa, Mr. Abdoulaye Bathily, and the outgoing African Union Special Envoy on the Lord's Resistance Army Issue, Mr. Francisco Madeira, to strengthen regional cooperation and facilitate continued operations of the African Union Regional Task Force in the region. The Council commends Mr. Madeira for his leadership and welcomes the recent appointment of Lieutenant General (retired) Jackson Kiprono Tuwei as the new African Union Special Envoy on the Lord's Resistance Army Issue. The Council urges the Regional Office, in its coordination role, as well as the United Nations political and peacekeeping missions in the region and other relevant United Nations presences to enhance their efforts in support of the implementation of the United Nations regional strategy to address the threat and impact of the activities of the Lord's Resistance Army (the United Nations strategy),[256] as appropriate and within the limits of their mandates and capacities. The Council encourages the Secretary-General to optimize the efforts of the Regional Office in this regard, including through the use of staff and the provision of support to counter-Lord's Resistance Army efforts.

[254] Resolutions or decisions on this question were first adopted by the Security Council in 2003.

[255] S/PRST/2014/25.

[256] S/2012/481, annex.

The Council reiterates its strong support for the African Union Regional Cooperation Initiative for the Elimination of the Lord's Resistance Army, and strongly encourages Lord's Resistance Army-affected and neighbouring States to cooperate with the African Union Regional Task Force, in order to end the Lord's Resistance Army threat. The Council commends the significant progress made by the Task Force and its troop-contributing countries, and pays tribute to the important role played by the Uganda People's Defence Forces in tackling the Lord's Resistance Army threat. The Council urges all regional Governments to fulfil their commitments under the Initiative. The Council notes the importance of continued international support for the operations, logistics and headquarters of the Task Force. In this regard, the Council welcomes the continued advisory and logistical support provided by the United States of America as well as funding provided by the European Union. The Council underlines the need for all military action against the Lord's Resistance Army to be conducted in compliance with international law, including international humanitarian law, human rights law and refugee law, as applicable, and to minimize the risk of harm to civilians in all areas of operation and to take into account the association of children with the Lord's Resistance Army. The Council also reiterates its encouragement to deploy child protection advisers within the Task Force.

The Council expresses concern about the statements in the report of the Secretary-General on the United Nations Regional Office for Central Africa and the Lord's Resistance Army[257] that the bulk of the Lord's Resistance Army has moved from the Central African Republic to the northeast of the Democratic Republic of the Congo, but continues to carry out attacks against communities in the east of the Central African Republic. The Council calls upon the affected States to ensure that the Lord's Resistance Army does not find safe haven in their territory, in accordance with international law. The Council takes note that the presence of some senior Lord's Resistance Army leaders in the disputed Kafia Kingi enclave, on the border between the Central African Republic, South Sudan and the Sudan continues to be reported. The Council takes note that the Government of the Sudan has denied this. The Council welcomes the invitation extended to the African Union to verify reports of the presence of the Lord's Resistance Army in Kafia Kingi, and encourages the African Union Commission and the African Union Peace and Security Council to verify the allegations. The Security Council expresses its continued concern at the gravity of the national crisis in the Central African Republic and strongly condemns the Lord's Resistance Army's opportunistic cooperation in the Central African Republic with other armed groups including some ex-Séléka combatants.

The Council notes the overall decline in the number, intensity and violence of the Lord's Resistance Army attacks, killings and abductions and the decrease in the estimate by the Office for the Coordination of Humanitarian Affairs of the Secretariat of the number of people displaced by the Lord's Resistance Army threat, from 159,927 in March 2014 to 131,090 in September 2014. The Council commends efforts by international donors to provide humanitarian assistance to Lord's Resistance Army-affected populations in the Central African Republic, the Democratic Republic of the Congo and South Sudan but notes with concern that renewed efforts are urgently needed to provide humanitarian assistance to Lord's Resistance Army-affected populations. The Council reaffirms its call for all parties to allow safe and unhindered humanitarian access, consistent with the relevant provisions of international humanitarian law and the United Nations guiding principles of humanitarian assistance.

The Council welcomes the steps taken to deliver an enhanced, comprehensive and more regional approach to the humanitarian situation, including assistance to victims of sexual violence and other attacks, and urges further progress in this regard.

The Council underlines the primary responsibility of States in the Lord's Resistance Army-affected region to protect civilians.

The Council urges the United Nations Multidimensional Integrated Stabilization Mission in the Central African Republic, the United Nations Organization Stabilization Mission in the Democratic Republic of the Congo and the African Union-United Nations Hybrid Operation in Darfur, as relevant and in accordance with their mandates, to cooperate and share information related to the regional threat of the Lord's Resistance Army in a timely manner, and to share relevant information with regional Governments, with non-governmental organizations and with relevant partners, to enhance cross-border cooperation in order to better anticipate and

[257] S/2014/812.

respond to Lord's Resistance Army movements. The Council emphasizes the need for operational coordination and information-sharing between the African Union Regional Task Force and all relevant United Nations and African Union missions, in the context of their protection of civilians activities, human rights monitoring, implementation of disarmament, demobilization, repatriation, reintegration and resettlement programmes and counter-Lord's Resistance Army operations, as appropriate and in accordance with their mandates.

The Council strongly reiterates its calls for the United Nations, the African Union and the Economic Community of Central African States to continue to work together, including through joint field assessments, to further develop and maintain a common operating picture of the Lord's Resistance Army's current capabilities and areas of operation, as well as to investigate the Lord's Resistance Army's logistical networks and possible sources of military support and illicit financing, including alleged involvement in wildlife poaching and related illicit smuggling. The Council expresses its concern at the link between illicit trafficking in wildlife and financing of armed groups in the subregion, including the Lord's Resistance Army, and in this regard encourages the United Nations Regional Office for Central Africa to continue to support the development of a coherent and concerted subregional approach to address this disturbing phenomenon.

The Council urges the United Nations Organization Stabilization Mission in the Democratic Republic of the Congo and the United Nations Multidimensional Integrated Stabilization Mission in the Central African Republic and other United Nations actors in the Lord's Resistance Army-affected region to continue to work with regional forces, national Governments, international actors and non-governmental organizations, as appropriate, to develop a common approach to the promotion of defections and support for disarmament, demobilization, repatriation, reintegration and resettlement efforts across the Lord's Resistance Army-affected area. The Council highlights the importance of programmes in encouraging defections and in support of the release, return and successful reintegration of men, women and children abducted by the Lord's Resistance Army, in particular those that target community acceptance of such individuals, in particular children.

The Council encourages donors to increase funding for early recovery projects to help affected communities to restore stability and rebuild their livelihoods as the Lord's Resistance Army threat begins to recede. The Council requests that the United Nations Regional Office for Central Africa work with the African Union, the World Bank, the United Nations Development Programme, the United Nations Children's Fund and other international experts to develop a development framework for international efforts to promote the long-term stabilization of areas in South Sudan, the Democratic Republic of the Congo and the Central African Republic formerly affected by the Lord's Resistance Army, including through early recovery projects and programmes to strengthen community cohesion.

The Council reiterates its call for the swift and full implementation of the conclusions of its Working Group on Children and Armed Conflict concerning the situation of children and armed conflict affected by the Lord's Resistance Army.[258] In this regard, the Council encourages those countries affected by the Lord's Resistance Army which have not yet done so to establish standard operating procedures for the reception and handover of Lord's Resistance Army children to civilian child protection actors.

The Council recalls that the arrest warrants issued by the International Criminal Court for Lord's Resistance Army leaders, including Mr. Joseph Kony, on charges of war crimes and crimes against humanity, including murder, rape, cruel treatment, intentionally directing attacks against a civilian population and the forced enlistment of children, have yet to be executed, and calls upon all States to cooperate with relevant national Governments and the Court, in accordance with their respective obligations, in order to execute those warrants and to bring to justice those responsible.

The Council commends the role of the Heads of States of the Economic Community of Central African States in the Economic Community-led international mediation process in the Central African Republic and welcomes the designation by the Secretary-General of his Special Representative for Central Africa, Mr. Bathily, to support the process. The Council commends Mr. Bathily for his diplomatic efforts, in collaboration with the Economic Community mediator, the President of the Congo, Mr. Denis Sassou

[258] S/AC.51/2013/1.

Nguesso, the African Union Special Envoy for the Central African Republic, Mr. Soumeylou Boubèye Maïga, as well as the Special Representative of the Secretary-General for the Central African Republic, Lieutenant General (retired) Babacar Gaye. In particular, the Council welcomes the signing of the Brazzaville Agreement on 23 July 2014. The Council encourages Mr. Bathily and his Office to continue supporting these efforts and to support the United Nations Multidimensional Integrated Stabilization Mission in the Central African Republic, and the transition process in the Central African Republic through the international mediation process.

The Council expresses deep concern at the terrorist attacks conducted by Boko Haram since 2009, which have caused large-scale and devastating loss of life and represent a threat to the stability and peace of West and Central Africa. In particular, the Council strongly condemns the continued increase in attacks perpetrated by the terrorist group in Nigeria, along the Nigeria-Cameroon border, in the northern provinces of Cameroon and near the Nigeria-Chad border. The Council expresses concern that the activities of Boko Haram continue to have an adverse humanitarian impact on West and Central Africa, including the displacement of an estimated 80,000 Nigerians into neighbouring Cameroon, Chad and Niger. The Council commends the initiative of the Heads of States of the Lake Chad Basin region and Benin to enhance cooperation, in line with the outcomes of the Paris summit, the follow-up London and Abuja summits and the meeting held in Niamey, in order to tackle the threat posed by Boko Haram to the region. The Council calls upon the United Nations Regional Office for Central Africa to continue its collaboration with the United Nations Office for West Africa in order to continue to support, as appropriate, the States of the Lake Chad Basin region to address the impact of the threat on peace and security, including the political, socioeconomic and humanitarian situation in the subregion. The Council underlines the need for all actions to counter Boko Haram to be conducted in compliance with international law, including international humanitarian law, human rights law and refugee law.

The Council commends the support of the United Nations Regional Office for Central Africa for regional anti-piracy efforts, in cooperation with the United Nations Office for West Africa, to address maritime insecurity in the Gulf of Guinea that continues to affect States of Central and West Africa. The Council encourages the Regional Office to continue to assist the region in implementing the decisions of the Yaoundé summit and in the establishment of a regional information-sharing architecture.

The Council requests that the Secretary-General keep it informed on the activities of the United Nations Regional Office for Central Africa, progress made in conducting assessments of the Lord's Resistance Army's evolving area of operations and logistical and support networks, and the efforts being undertaken respectively by missions in the region and relevant United Nations agencies to implement the United Nations strategy, including through a single report on the situation in Central Africa and the activities of the Regional Office, to be submitted before 15 May 2015.

At its 7461st meeting, on 11 June 2015, the Council considered the item entitled:

"Central African region

"Report of the Secretary-General on the situation in Central Africa and the activities of the United Nations Regional Office for Central Africa (S/2015/339)".

At the same meeting, the Council decided to extend an invitation, in accordance with rule 39 of its provisional rules of procedure, to Mr. Abdoulaye Bathily, Special Representative of the Secretary-General for Central Africa and Head of the United Nations Regional Office for Central Africa.

At the same meeting, following consultations among members of the Security Council, the President made the following statement on behalf of the Council:[259]

The Security Council expresses its concern at the grave security situation in parts of Central Africa within the remit of the United Nations Regional Office for Central Africa, in particular the ongoing crisis in the Central African Republic and its regional impact, the continuing threat of the Lord's Resistance Army, and the continued terrorist activities perpetrated by Boko Haram in countries in the subregion. The Council also expresses its continuing concern regarding maritime insecurity in the Gulf of Guinea, the illegal wildlife trade

[259] S/PRST/2015/12.

and transnational organized crime. The Council welcomes the local, parliamentary and presidential elections held in the subregion and stresses the need for upcoming elections in the region to be held in a timely, transparent and inclusive manner according to their constitutions, and encourages the Regional Office to continue to support States in this regard, including through the promotion of women's political participation.

The Council commends the role of the Heads of States of the Economic Community of Central African States in the Economic Community-led international mediation process in the Central African Republic and welcomes the leadership of the Special Representative of the Secretary-General for Central Africa, Mr. Abdoulaye Bathily, in the process. The Council commends Mr. Bathily for his diplomatic efforts, in collaboration with the Economic Community mediator, the President of the Congo, Mr. Denis Sassou Nguesso, the African Union Special Envoy for the Central African Republic, Mr. Soumeylou Boubèye Maïga, as well as the Special Representative of the Secretary-General for the Central African Republic, Lieutenant General (retired) Babacar Gaye. In particular, the Council welcomes the holding of the Bangui Forum on National Reconciliation from 4 to 11 May 2015, chaired by Mr. Bathily, and welcomes the outcomes of the meeting. The Council encourages Mr. Bathily and his Office to continue supporting these efforts and to support the United Nations Multidimensional Integrated Stabilization Mission in the Central African Republic and the transition process in the Central African Republic through the international mediation process. The Council also stresses the critical importance of effective implementation of the sanctions regime established pursuant to resolution 2127 (2013), and the key role that regional States, as well as regional and subregional organizations, can play in this regard.

The Council condemns in the strongest terms the terrorist attacks conducted by Boko Haram since 2009, which have caused large-scale and devastating loss of life and represent a threat to the stability and peace of West and Central Africa. In particular, the Council strongly condemns the continued increase in attacks perpetrated by the terrorist group in Nigeria, along the Nigeria-Cameroon border, in the northern provinces of Cameroon and near the Nigeria-Chad border. The Council expresses concern that the activities of Boko Haram continue to have an adverse humanitarian impact on West and Central Africa, including the displacement of an estimated 74,000 Nigerians into neighbouring Cameroon, 96,000 internally displaced persons within Cameroon and, in Chad, almost 20,000 Nigerian refugees, 8,500 returnees and 14,500 internally displaced persons.

The Council welcomes the recent gains made by States in the region against Boko Haram and commends the bravery of the troops involved. The Council underlines the continuing threat presented by Boko Haram to peace and stability in the region. It urges States in the region to further enhance regional military cooperation and coordination to more effectively and immediately combat Boko Haram, in accordance with international law. In this regard, it welcomes efforts by the region to set up a multinational joint task force, and strongly encourages the ongoing coordination efforts of the Economic Community of Central African States, and the Economic Community of West African States to counter Boko Haram. The Council stresses the need to adopt a comprehensive approach in order to successfully tackle the threat presented by Boko Haram to the region. The Council encourages partners to increase security assistance to Lake Chad Basin Commission countries and Benin and humanitarian support across the region for those affected by Boko Haram activities. The Council calls upon the United Nations Regional Office for Central Africa to continue its collaboration with the United Nations Office for West Africa in order to continue to support, as appropriate, the States of the Lake Chad Basin region to address the impact of the threat on peace and security, including the political, socioeconomic and humanitarian situation in the subregion. The Council underlines the need for all actions to counter Boko Haram to be conducted in compliance with international law, including international humanitarian law, human rights law and refugee law, as applicable.

The Council reiterates its strong condemnation of the appalling attacks, including those that may amount to war crimes and crimes against humanity, carried out by the Lord's Resistance Army and other violations of international humanitarian law and abuses of human rights, including the Lord's Resistance Army's recruitment and use of children in armed conflict, killing and maiming, rape, sexual slavery and other sexual violence, and abductions. The Council demands an immediate end to all attacks by the Lord's Resistance Army and urges the Lord's Resistance Army to release all those abducted and to disarm and demobilize. The Council welcomes the progress made with regard to ending crimes under international law in Central Africa and reiterates its resolve to maintain the current momentum until a permanent end to the threat posed by the Lord's Resistance Army has been achieved.

The Council pays tribute to the efforts of the Special Representative of the Secretary-General for Central Africa and Head of the United Nations Regional Office for Central Africa, Mr. Abdoulaye Bathily, and the African Union Special Envoy on the Lord's Resistance Army Issue, Lieutenant General (retired) Jackson Kiprono Tuwei, to strengthen regional cooperation and facilitate continued operations of the African Union Regional Task Force in the region. The Council urges the Regional Office, in its coordination role, as well as the United Nations political and peacekeeping missions in the region and other relevant United Nations presences to enhance their efforts in support of the implementation of the United Nations regional strategy to address the threat and impact of the activities of the Lord's Resistance Army (the United Nations strategy),[256] as appropriate and within the limits of their mandates and capacities. The Council encourages the Secretary-General to optimize the efforts of the Regional Office in this regard, including through the use of staff and the provision of support to counter-Lord's Resistance Army efforts.

The Council urges the United Nations Multidimensional Integrated Stabilization Mission in the Central African Republic, the United Nations Organization Stabilization Mission in the in the Democratic Republic of the Congo and the African Union-United Nations Hybrid Operation in Darfur, as relevant and in accordance with their mandates, to cooperate, coordinate and share information related to the regional threat of the Lord's Resistance Army in a timely manner, and to share relevant information with Governments of States of the region, with non-governmental organizations and with relevant partners, to enhance cross-border cooperation in order to better anticipate and respond to Lord's Resistance Army movements. The Council emphasizes the need for operational coordination and information-sharing between the African Union Regional Task Force and all relevant United Nations and African Union missions, in the context of their protection of civilians activities, human rights monitoring, implementation of disarmament, demobilization, repatriation, reintegration and resettlement programmes and counter-Lord's Resistance Army operations, as appropriate and in accordance with their mandates.

The Council urges the United Nations Organization Stabilization Mission in the Democratic Republic of the Congo and the United Nations Multidimensional Integrated Stabilization Mission in the Central African Republic and other United Nations actors in the Lord's Resistance Army-affected region to continue to work with regional forces, national Governments, international actors and non-governmental organizations, as appropriate, to develop a common approach to the promotion of defections and support for disarmament, demobilization, repatriation, reintegration and resettlement efforts across the Lord's Resistance Army-affected area. The Council highlights the importance of programmes in encouraging defections and in support of the release, return and successful reintegration of women, children and men abducted by the Lord's Resistance Army, in particular those that target community acceptance of such individuals, in particular children.

The Council commends the significant progress made by the African Union Regional Task Force and its troop-contributing countries, and pays tribute to the important role played by the Uganda People's Defence Forces in tackling the Lord's Resistance Army threat. The Council notes the importance of continued regional and international support for the operations, logistics and headquarters of the Task Force. In this regard, the Council welcomes the continued advisory and logistical support provided by the United States of America as well as funding provided by the European Union. The Council underlines the primary responsibility of States in the Lord's Resistance Army-affected region to protect civilians. The Council underlines the need for all military action against the Lord's Resistance Army to be conducted in compliance with international law, including international humanitarian law, human rights law and refugee law, as applicable, and to minimize the risk of harm to civilians in all areas of operation and to take into account the association of children with the Lord's Resistance Army. The Council also reiterates its encouragement to deploy child protection advisers within the Task Force.

The Council expresses concern that the Lord's Resistance Army continues to pose a regional security threat, particularly in the Central African Republic and the Democratic Republic of the Congo. The Council calls upon the affected States to ensure that the Lord's Resistance Army does not find safe haven in their territory, in accordance with international law. The Council takes note that the presence of some senior Lord's Resistance Army leaders in the disputed Kafia Kingi enclave, on the border between the Central African Republic, South Sudan and the Sudan continues to be reported. The Council takes note that the Government of the Sudan has denied this. The Council welcomes the invitation extended to the African Union to verify reports of the presence of the Lord's Resistance Army in Kafia Kingi, and urges the African Union Commission and the African Union Peace and Security Council to verify the allegations. The Security Council expresses its continued concern at the gravity of the national crisis in the Central African Republic and strongly condemns the Lord's Resistance Army's opportunistic cooperation in the Central African Republic with other armed groups including some ex-Séléka combatants.

The Council notes that the number of deaths for which the Lord's Resistance Army was responsible decreased from 76 civilian deaths in 2013 to 36 deaths in 2014, but that the number of abductions in the Central African Republic and eastern Democratic Republic of the Congo significantly increased to several hundreds. The Council expresses its concern at the increase in the estimate by the Office for the Coordination of Humanitarian Affairs of the Secretariat of the number of people displaced by the Lord's Resistance Army threat, from 131,090 in September 2014 to 180,000 in December 2014. The Council commends efforts by international donors to provide humanitarian assistance to Lord's Resistance Army-affected populations in the Central African Republic, the Democratic Republic of the Congo and South Sudan but notes with concern that renewed efforts are urgently needed to provide humanitarian assistance to Lord's Resistance Army-affected populations. The Council reaffirms its call for all parties to allow safe and unhindered humanitarian access, consistent with the relevant provisions of international law and the United Nations guiding principles of humanitarian assistance.

The Council welcomes the steps taken to deliver an enhanced, comprehensive and more regional approach to the humanitarian situation, including assistance to victims of sexual violence and other attacks, and urges further progress in this regard.

The Council reiterates its call for the swift and full implementation of the conclusions of its Working Group on Children and Armed Conflict concerning the situation of children and armed conflict affected by the Lord's Resistance Army.[258] In this regard, the Council encourages those countries affected by the Lord's Resistance Army which have not yet done so to establish standard operating procedures for the reception and handover of Lord's Resistance Army children to civilian child protection actors.

The Council encourages donors to increase funding for early recovery projects to help affected communities to restore stability and rebuild their livelihoods as the Lord's Resistance Army threat begins to recede. The Council requests that the United Nations Regional Office for Central Africa work with the African Union, the World Bank, the United Nations Development Programme, the United Nations Children's Fund and other international experts to develop a development framework for international efforts to promote the long-term stabilization of areas in South Sudan, the Democratic Republic of the Congo and the Central African Republic formerly affected by the Lord's Resistance Army, including through early recovery projects and programmes to strengthen community cohesion.

The Council welcomes the transfer of Mr. Dominic Ongwen to the International Criminal Court in The Hague in January 2015. The Council expresses its appreciation to all those who cooperated in this effort, notably the Governments of Uganda, the Central African Republic and the United States, as well as the African Union, the United Nations Multidimensional Integrated Stabilization Mission in the Central African Republic and the Court. The Council recalls that the arrest warrants issued by the Court have yet to be executed for other Lord's Resistance Army leaders, including Mr. Joseph Kony, on charges of war crimes and crimes against humanity, including murder, rape, cruel treatment, intentionally directing attacks against a civilian population and forced enlistment of children, and calls upon all States to cooperate with relevant national Governments and the Court, in accordance with their respective obligations, in order to execute those warrants and to bring to justice those responsible.

The Council expresses its concern at the link between illicit trafficking in wildlife and natural resources and financing of armed groups in the subregion, including the Lord's Resistance Army, and in this regard encourages the United Nations Regional Office for Central Africa to continue to support the development of a coherent and concerted subregional approach to address this disturbing phenomenon.

The Council commends the support of the United Nations Regional Office for Central Africa for regional anti-piracy efforts, in cooperation with the United Nations Office for West Africa, to address maritime insecurity in the Gulf of Guinea that continues to affect States of Central and West Africa. The Council encourages the Regional Office to continue to assist the region in implementing the decisions of the Yaoundé summit and in the establishment of a regional information-sharing architecture.

The Council welcomes the recommendations of the strategic assessment review conducted in March 2015. In particular, the Council notes the recommendation that the United Nations Regional Office for Central Africa focus on areas of work in which the Office has recognized strengths and a comparative advantage, including in the four areas of good offices, preventive diplomacy and mediation; supporting United Nations, regional and subregional initiatives on peace and security; enhancing United Nations coherence and coordination in the subregion; and advising the Secretary-General and United Nations entities in the region on significant peace and security developments in Central Africa.

The Council requests that the Secretary-General keep it informed through a report on the situation in Central Africa and the activities of the United Nations Regional Office for Central Africa, to be submitted before 30 November 2015, and every six months thereafter, on the activities of the Regional Office, progress made in conducting assessments of the Lord's Resistance Army's evolving area of operations and logistical and support networks, and the efforts being undertaken respectively by missions in the region and relevant United Nations agencies to implement the United Nations strategy.

On 21 July 2015, the President of the Security Council addressed the following letter to the Secretary-General:[260]

I have the honour to inform you that your letter dated 16 July 2015 concerning your recommendation to extend the mandate of the United Nations Regional Office for Central Africa for a period of three years, from 31 August 2015 until 31 August 2018,[261] has been brought to the attention of the members of the Security Council. They take note of the information contained in your letter and the recommendation expressed therein.

NON-PROLIFERATION OF WEAPONS OF MASS DESTRUCTION[262]

Decision

At its 7319th meeting, on 24 November 2014, the Security Council considered the item entitled:

"Non-proliferation of weapons of mass destruction

"Briefing by the Chair of the Security Council Committee established pursuant to resolution 1540 (2004)".

REPORTS OF THE SECRETARY-GENERAL ON THE SUDAN AND SOUTH SUDAN[262]

Decisions

At its 7235th meeting, on 6 August 2014, the Security Council decided to invite the representative of South Sudan to participate, without vote, in accordance with rule 37 of its provisional rules of procedure, in the discussion of the item entitled:

"Reports of the Secretary-General on the Sudan and South Sudan

"Report of the Secretary-General on South Sudan (S/2014/537)".

At the same meeting, the Council also decided to extend an invitation, in accordance with rule 39 of its provisional rules of procedure, to Mr. Edmond Mulet, Assistant Secretary-General for Peacekeeping Operations.

---

[260] S/2015/555.

[261] S/2015/554.

[262] Resolutions or decisions on this question were first adopted by the Security Council in 2004.

At its 7238th meeting, on 7 August 2014, the Council decided to invite the representative of the Sudan to participate, without vote, in accordance with rule 37 of its provisional rules of procedure, in the discussion of the item entitled:

"Reports of the Secretary-General on the Sudan and South Sudan

"Report of the Secretary-General on the African Union-United Nations Hybrid Operation in Darfur (S/2014/515)".

At the same meeting, the Council also decided to extend an invitation, in accordance with rule 39 of its provisional rules of procedure, to Mr. Mohamed Ibn Chambas, Joint African Union-United Nations Special Representative for Darfur and Head of the African Union-United Nations Hybrid Operation in Darfur.

At its 7240th meeting, on 8 August 2014, the Council considered the item entitled "Reports of the Secretary-General on the Sudan and South Sudan".

At the same meeting, following consultations among members of the Security Council, the President made the following statement on behalf of the Council:[263]

The Security Council expresses grave alarm and concern regarding the substantial deterioration of the political and security situation and developing humanitarian catastrophe in South Sudan resulting from the internal Sudan People's Liberation Movement political dispute and unrelenting violence, including against civilians, caused by the country's political and military leaders since 15 December 2013.

The Council strongly condemns the repeated violations of the cessation of hostilities agreement accepted and signed by South Sudan and the Sudan People's Liberation Movement/Army (in Opposition) on 23 January 2014, and emphasizes that the actions of President Salva Kiir and former Vice President Riek Machar in continuing to pursue a military solution to this conflict are unacceptable.

The Council urgently calls upon President Salva Kiir, former Vice-President Riek Machar and all parties to implement the Agreement to Resolve the Crisis in South Sudan signed on 9 May 2014 by South Sudan and the Sudan People's Liberation Movement/Army (in Opposition), to engage fully and inclusively in ongoing peace talks in Addis Ababa, and to uphold their commitment to establish a Transitional Government of National Unity, for which the deadline was set as 10 August 2014, and in this regard strongly appeals to the parties to finalize appropriate arrangements without further delay, and expresses its readiness to consider, in consultation with relevant partners, including the Intergovernmental Authority on Development and the African Union, all appropriate measures, including targeted sanctions, against those who take action that undermines the peace, stability and security of South Sudan, including those who prevent the implementation of these agreements.

The Council strongly condemns reported and ongoing human rights violations and abuses and violations of international humanitarian law, including those involving extrajudicial killings, ethnically targeted violence, sexual and gender-based violence, rape, recruitment and use of children, enforced disappearances, arbitrary arrests and detention, violence aimed at spreading terror among the civilian population, and attacks on schools and hospitals as well as United Nations peacekeeping personnel, by all parties, including armed groups and national security forces. The Council recalls that some of these acts may amount to war crimes or crimes against humanity under international law.

The Council emphasizes the need to ensure accountability for serious violations and abuses of human rights and serious violations of international humanitarian law. In that regard, the Council underscores the importance of the ongoing work of the African Union Commission of Inquiry on South Sudan and looks forward to its findings and recommendations, and welcomes the efforts of the United Nations Mission in South Sudan to continue to monitor, investigate and publicly report on human rights violations and abuses in pursuit of justice and an end to impunity, as set out in resolution 2155 (2014).

The Council underscores its grave concern about the catastrophic food insecurity situation in South Sudan that may soon reach the threshold of famine as a result of continued conflict, civilian targeting, and

[263] S/PRST/2014/16.

displacement, stresses the responsibility borne by all parties to the conflict for the suffering of the people of South Sudan and the necessity of ensuring that the basic needs of the population are met, underscores the urgent need to increase funding for humanitarian operations in South Sudan, and encourages States Members of the United Nations to contribute funds critically needed now to provide life-saving assistance.

The Council condemns all attacks against humanitarian personnel and facilities, commends United Nations humanitarian agencies and partners for their efforts to provide urgent and coordinated support to the population, and calls upon all parties to the conflict to allow and facilitate, in accordance with relevant provisions of international law and United Nations guiding principles of humanitarian assistance, the full, safe and unhindered access of relief personnel, equipment and supplies to all those in need and timely delivery of humanitarian assistance, in particular to internally displaced persons and refugees.

The Council renews its deep appreciation for the actions taken by Mission personnel and troop- and police-contributing countries to protect tens of thousands of civilians under threat of physical violence and to stabilize the security situation.

The Council commends the Intergovernmental Authority on Development, as supported by the United Nations and African Union, for its relentless work in establishing a forum for political and security dialogue, establishing and operationalizing the Monitoring and Verification Mechanism for the cessation of hostilities agreement, and leading multi-stakeholder political negotiations to establish a Transitional Government of National Unity.

On 21 August 2014, the President of the Security Council issued the following note:[264]

Following consultations among the members of the Security Council, it has been agreed to amend the reporting period established in paragraph 6 of resolution 2046 (2012) and subsequently amended in a note by the President of the Security Council[265] to three-month intervals.

At its 7250th meeting, on 27 August 2014, the Council decided to invite the representative of the Sudan to participate, without vote, in accordance with rule 37 of its provisional rules of procedure, in the discussion of the item entitled:

"Reports of the Secretary-General on the Sudan and South Sudan

"Report of the Secretary-General on the African Union-United Nations Hybrid Operation in Darfur (S/2014/515)".

Resolution 2173 (2014) of 27 August 2014

The Security Council,

Reaffirming all its previous resolutions and the statements by its President concerning the situation in the Sudan, and underlining the importance of full compliance with these,

Reaffirming also its strong commitment to the sovereignty, unity, independence and territorial integrity of the Sudan and its determination to work with the Government of the Sudan, in full respect of its sovereignty, to assist in tackling the various challenges in the Sudan,

Recalling the importance of the principles of the peaceful settlement of international disputes, good-neighbourliness, non-interference and cooperation in the relations among States in the region,

Reaffirming the basic principles of peacekeeping, including consent of the parties, impartiality and non-use of force except in self-defence and defence of the mandate, and recognizing that the mandate of each peacekeeping mission is specific to the country concerned,

Reaffirming also its resolutions 1265 (1999) of 17 September 1999, 1296 (2000) of 19 April 2000, 1674 (2006) of 28 April 2006, 1738 (2006) of 23 December 2006 and 1894 (2009) of 11 November 2009 on the

[264] S/2014/613.

[265] S/2013/657.

protection of civilians in armed conflict and resolution 1502 (2003) of 26 August 2003 on the protection of humanitarian and United Nations personnel; resolutions 1612 (2005) of 26 July 2005, 1882 (2009) of 4 August 2009, 1998 (2011) of 12 July 2011, 2068 (2012) of 19 September 2012 and 2143 (2014) of 7 March 2014 on children and armed conflict; resolutions 1325 (2000) of 31 October 2000, 1820 (2008) of 19 June 2008, 1888 (2009) of 30 September 2009, 1889 (2009) of 5 October 2009, 1960 (2010) of 16 December 2010, 2106 (2013) of 24 June 2013 and 2122 (2013) of 18 October 2013 on women and peace and security, and resolution 2086 (2013) of 21 January 2013 on United Nations peacekeeping operations,

Expressing deep concern at the serious deterioration in the security situation overall so far in 2014, and the profound negative impact of this on civilians, in particular women and children, including through continued clashes between government forces and rebel armed groups, an escalation of inter-tribal fighting and other local clashes, including with the involvement of paramilitary units and tribal militias, and an increase in criminality and banditry, further expressing deep concern that such clashes, including attacks by rebel groups and government forces and aerial bombardment by the Government of the Sudan, inter-tribal fighting, banditry and criminality continue to threaten civilians, while welcoming a slight improvement in the security situation since May, and reiterating its demand that all parties to the conflict in Darfur immediately end violence, including attacks on civilians, peacekeepers and humanitarian personnel,

Recalling its resolution 2117 (2013) of 26 September 2013, and expressing concern at the threat to peace and security in Darfur arising from the illicit transfer, destabilizing accumulation and misuse of small arms and light weapons, and the continued threats to civilians posed by unexploded ordnance,

Expressing deep concern at the significant increase in population displacements in 2014 and the consequent increase in humanitarian assistance and protection needs, with an estimated 359,000 persons newly displaced since January 2014, about 260,000 of whom have been unable to return to their homes, alongside more than 2 million long-term internally displaced persons,

Recalling the commitments made by the Government of the Sudan and other signatories to the Doha Document for Peace in Darfur[266] to ensure the unimpeded access of humanitarian assistance to the population in need and the protection of humanitarian workers and their operations in areas under their control, as well as to guarantee the African Union-United Nations Hybrid Operation in Darfur unimpeded freedom of movement in all areas and at all times in Darfur in the exercise of its mandate,

Expressing concern that the suspension of operations or the withdrawal of some international humanitarian actors has left significant gaps in the delivery of humanitarian assistance, calling upon the Government of the Sudan to ensure that humanitarian actors can operate in support of addressing basic needs, and calling upon donors, the Darfur Regional Authority and the Government of the Sudan to provide the financial resources necessary to reach those in need,

Reiterating that there can be no military solution to the conflict in Darfur and that an inclusive political settlement is essential to re-establishing peace, and underscoring the importance of fully addressing the root causes of the conflict in the search for a sustainable peace, which should rapidly deliver real benefits for the Darfuri people, in this regard reiterating its support for the Doha Document for Peace in Darfur as a viable framework for the Darfur peace process, and for its accelerated implementation, and noting that this process and the national initiative for dialogue in the Sudan could be complementary and mutually reinforcing processes,

Welcoming, in this regard, the announcement by President Bashir on 27 January 2014 of a national dialogue, noting that the modalities of such a dialogue should provide an opportunity to address the legitimate grievances of the people of Darfur, that the national dialogue has the potential to offer an opportunity to pave the way for lasting peace throughout the Sudan, building on existing peace processes, including the Doha Document for Peace in Darfur, noting the stated commitment of the Government of the Sudan to an inclusive national dialogue, and calling for an enabling environment conducive to the national dialogue, which would constitute a key step towards achieving a credible, transparent, inclusive, nationally owned and Sudanese-led process; further calling upon all parties to engage constructively with this process, urging all parties to refrain from any attempt to obstruct it, and looking forward to further developments towards the implementation of an inclusive dialogue process,

---

[266] S/2011/449, enclosure 2.

Deploring the fact that some armed groups have refused to join the peace process and are impeding the implementation of the Doha Document for Peace in Darfur, reiterating its demand for the release of members of the former movement of Mohamed Bashar, taken captive in May 2013 by Justice and Equality Movement-Gibril Ibrahim forces, and condemning any actions by any armed group aimed at forced overthrow of the Government of the Sudan,

Noting, in this regard, that the ability of the African Union-United Nations Hybrid Operation in Darfur to facilitate progress in the implementation of the Doha Document for Peace in Darfur is hampered by delays by the signatory parties and the absence of an inclusive political settlement between the Government of the Sudan and non-signatory movements, urging the signatory parties to take the remaining steps necessary to implement the Doha Document fully, expressing concern that the humanitarian and security situation, as well as the lack of capacity of the Darfur Regional Authority, hinder the transition from relief to stabilization and development activities, urging donors and the Government of the Sudan to honour their pledges and fulfil their obligations in a timely manner, including those commitments made at the conference held in Doha in April 2013, welcoming the confirmation by the Government of Qatar of its pledge of 88.5 million United States dollars and the transfer of 10 million dollars of this amount to the United Nations Darfur Fund in April 2014, and affirming that development can support a lasting peace in Darfur,

Noting also that local dispute resolution mechanisms play an important role in preventing and resolving intercommunal conflict, including conflict over natural resources, and urging an intensification of effective efforts to prevent local disputes leading to violence, with its corresponding impact on the local civilian populations, acknowledging the efforts of Sudanese authorities and local mediators to mediate in inter-tribal fighting, with support from the African Union-United Nations Hybrid Operation in Darfur and the United Nations country team, and urging their continued work,

Welcoming regional and other initiatives, undertaken in close interaction with the Government of the Sudan, to address the root causes of the conflict in Darfur and to promote a sustainable peace, including the convening by the President of Chad, Mr. Idriss Déby Itno, of a second mediation forum in Um Jaras from 26 to 29 March 2014, and encouraging the full coordination of such initiatives with the efforts of the African Union-United Nations Joint Special Representative for Darfur,

Underlining, without prejudice to the primary responsibility of the Security Council for the maintenance of international peace and security, the importance of the partnership between the United Nations and the African Union, consistent with Chapter VIII of the Charter of the United Nations, with regard to the maintenance of peace and security in Africa, particularly in the Sudan,

Calling upon all parties to comply with their obligations under international human rights law and international humanitarian law, stressing the importance that the Council attaches to ending impunity, including through ensuring accountability and bringing to justice the perpetrators of crimes committed by all parties in Darfur, urging the Government of the Sudan to comply with its obligations in this respect, welcoming the ongoing investigations by the Special Prosecutor for Darfur appointed by the Government and stressing the need for further progress in this regard, calling for swift progress on the draft memorandum of understanding providing for observation by the African Union-United Nations Hybrid Operation in Darfur and the African Union of the proceedings of the Special Court for Darfur, and calling upon the Government swiftly to investigate attacks against the Operation and to bring the perpetrators to justice,

Reaffirming its concern over the negative effect of ongoing violence in Darfur on the stability of the Sudan as a whole as well as the region, welcoming the ongoing good relations between the Sudan and Chad, including on border control, and encouraging the Sudan, Chad and the Central African Republic to continue to cooperate in order to achieve peace and stability in Darfur and the wider region,

Commending the efforts of the African Union-United Nations Hybrid Operation in Darfur towards promoting peace and stability in Darfur, and reiterating its full support for the Operation,

Welcoming the report of the Secretary-General of 22 July 2014 on the African Union-United Nations Hybrid Operation in Darfur,[267]

---

[267] S/2014/515.

Welcoming also the announcement by the Secretary-General on 2 July 2014 of a review, following recent serious allegations against the African Union-United Nations Hybrid Operation in Darfur, looking forward to the swift and thorough implementation of this review, and stressing the importance of prompt and effective action on the results of that review, if necessary,

Determining that the situation in the Sudan constitutes a threat to international peace and security,

1. *Decides* to extend the mandate of the African Union-United Nations Hybrid Operation in Darfur, as set out in resolution 1769 (2007) of 31 July 2007, for a further 10 months, until 30 June 2015, in order to align the renewal cycle with the decision of the African Union Peace and Security Council of 9 July 2014, reiterates its endorsement of the revised strategic priorities of the Operation as set out in paragraph 4 of resolution 2148 (2014) of 3 April 2014, and requests that the Operation continue to align all its activity and direct the use of its resources to the achievement of these priorities;

2. *Notes* that certain elements of the mandate and tasks of the African Union-United Nations Hybrid Operation in Darfur, as authorized in resolution 1769 (2007), in which it was decided that the mandate of the Operation shall be as set out in paragraphs 54 and 55 of the report of the Secretary-General and the Chairperson of the African Union Commission of 5 June 2007,[268] are no longer relevant, namely those enumerated in paragraphs 54 (*h*), 55 (*a*) (v), and 55 (*b*) (ii), (iii) and (v) of that report;

3. *Commends* the efforts of the African Union-United Nations Joint Special Representative for Darfur to revitalize the peace process and to increase its inclusiveness, guided by the framework for African Union and United Nations facilitation of the Darfur peace process,[269] including through renewed engagement of the non-signatory movements, and emphasizes the importance of the Joint Special Representative's strengthened coordination with the African Union High-level Implementation Panel and the Special Envoy of the Secretary-General for the Sudan and South Sudan in synchronizing their mediation efforts while taking into account ongoing transformation at the national level;

4. *Decides* that the African Union-United Nations Hybrid Operation in Darfur shall consist of up to 15,845 military personnel, 1,583 police personnel and 13 formed police units of up to 140 personnel each;

5. *Welcomes* the steps taken so far by the African Union-United Nations Hybrid Operation in Darfur to implement the review of the Operation conducted pursuant to resolution 2113 (2014) of 30 July 2013; requests continued swift and full implementation of the review, including the streamlining of all components of the Operation and aligning of activities to support achievement of its strategic priorities, and the discontinuing of all other tasks not aligned to the mission's strategic priorities; stresses the importance of the appropriate distribution of tasks and coordination between the Operation and the United Nations country team in order to implement the review of the Operation; and requests a detailed update on the streamlining of the civilian component by 15 September 2014;

6. *Urges* the Secretary-General and the African Union to expedite the appointment of personnel for leadership vacancies in the African Union-United Nations Hybrid Operation in Darfur;

7. *Requests* the Secretary-General, in close consultation with the African Union, and seeking perspectives from all relevant parties, to conduct an analysis of the implementation of the review of the African Union-United Nations Hybrid Operation in Darfur, including specific achievements reached under the revised strategic priorities, progress in addressing the challenges facing the mission, as identified by the review, any significant developments in the situation in Darfur and their impact on the mandate and tasks of the Operation, and an analysis of those tasks that remain relevant and on the fulfilment of which the United Nations country team has comparative advantage, with a road map to transfer those tasks to the fullest extent possible to the country team, taking into account the contributions of donors and other relevant actors; requests that he present this analysis, together with recommendations for the future mandate, composition, configuration and exit strategy of the Operation, as well as for its relationship with other United Nations actors in Darfur and the Sudan, by 28 February 2015; and expresses its intention to take decisions accordingly on the future of the Operation and to make necessary changes fully and promptly following presentation of the analysis and recommendations of the Secretary-General;

---

[268] S/2007/307/Rev.1.

[269] See S/2012/166.

8. *Underlines* that the African Union-United Nations Hybrid Operation in Darfur should continue to give priority in decisions about the use of available capacity and resources to (*a*) the protection of civilians across Darfur, including women and children, through, and without prejudice to the agreed basic principles of peacekeeping, inter alia, continuing to move to a more preventive and pre-emptive posture in pursuit of its priorities and in active defence of its mandate; enhanced early warning; proactive military deployment and active and effective patrolling in areas of high risk of conflict and high concentration of internally displaced persons; more prompt and effective responses to threats of violence against civilians, including through regular reviews of the geographic deployment of the Operation force; and securing camps for internally displaced persons, adjacent areas and areas of return, including development and training of community policing; and (*b*) ensuring safe, timely and unhindered humanitarian access and the safety and security of humanitarian personnel and activities, in accordance with relevant provisions of international law and the United Nations guiding principles of humanitarian assistance; and requests the Operation to maximize the use of its capabilities, in cooperation with the United Nations country team and other international and non-governmental actors, in the implementation of its mission-wide comprehensive strategy for the achievement of these objectives;

9. *Emphasizes* the Chapter VII mandate of the African Union-United Nations Hybrid Operation in Darfur, as defined in resolution 1769 (2007), to deliver its core tasks to protect civilians without prejudice to the primary responsibility of the Government of the Sudan and to ensure the freedom of movement and security of the Operation's own personnel and humanitarian workers; recalls that the Operation is authorized to take all the necessary action in fulfilment of this mandate; and urges the Operation to deter any threats against itself and its mandate;

10. *Welcomes* that some progress has been made in the implementation of some elements of the Doha Document for Peace in Darfur,[266] including steps towards the verification and integration of Liberation and Justice Movement and Justice and Equality Movement-Sudan combatants under the Doha Document security arrangements, but deplores continuing serious delays in overall implementation of the Doha Document; urges the signatory parties to implement the Doha Document in full, including by ensuring that the institutions established under it are resourced and empowered to carry out their mandates; welcomes in this regard the inauguration on 15 June 2014 of the Justice, Truth and Reconciliation Commission, and stresses the importance of its effective work; demands that the non-signatory armed groups refrain from impeding the implementation of the Doha Document; and encourages the African Union-United Nations Hybrid Operation in Darfur, in accordance with its revised strategic priorities, and the United Nations country team to continue to engage fully in support of the implementation of the Doha Document;

11. *Demands* that all parties to the conflict in Darfur, including in particular all the non-signatory armed groups, and other groups immediately cease all acts of violence and commit themselves to a sustained and permanent ceasefire, in order to bring a stable and durable peace to the region;

12. *Reaffirms its support* for a Darfur-based internal dialogue that takes place in an environment of full respect for the civil and political rights of participants, including the full and effective participation of women; welcomes the launch of the Implementation Committee of the Darfur Internal Dialogue and Consultation on 26 May 2014; expresses concern that prevailing insecurity, lack of adequate funding, and intimidation of participants could undermine effective implementation of the Dialogue and Consultation; calls upon the Government of the Sudan and the armed groups to ensure the necessary enabling environment; and requests the African Union-United Nations Hybrid Operation in Darfur to continue to support, monitor and report on the development of the Dialogue and Consultation and the overall environment for it;

13. *Calls for* an urgent end to inter-tribal clashes, criminality and banditry that affect civilians, and further calls for reconciliation and dialogue; expresses deep concern over the proliferation of arms, in particular small arms and light weapons; requests the African Union-United Nations Hybrid Operation in Darfur to continue to support local conflict resolution mechanisms, including with civil society mechanisms, and to continue to cooperate in this context with the Panel of Experts on the Sudan established pursuant to resolution 1591 (2005) of 29 March 2005 in order to facilitate its work;

14. *Commends* the troop- and police-contributing countries of the African Union-United Nations Hybrid Operation in Darfur; welcomes that some progress has been made in addressing contingent-owned equipment and self-sustainment shortfalls, but expresses concern that significant shortfalls remain; and calls for continued efforts by the Operation, the Secretariat and troop- and police-contributing countries to address such shortfalls, including by

providing appropriate training and resources to fulfil priority protection functions, especially in areas necessary for contingents' temporary deployment capability and ability to conduct long-range patrols;

15. *Strongly condemns* all attacks on the African Union-United Nations Hybrid Operation in Darfur, while noting the significant decline in fatal attacks on the Operation since August 2013; underlines that any attack or threat of attack on the Operation is unacceptable; demands that there be no recurrence of such attacks and that those responsible be held to account following prompt and thorough investigation; urges the Operation to take all measures necessary within its rules of engagement to protect United Nations personnel and equipment; condemns the ongoing impunity for those who attack peacekeepers, and in this regard urges the Government of the Sudan to do its utmost to bring all perpetrators of any such crimes to justice and to cooperate with the Operation to this end;

16. *Welcomes* the improved cooperation between the African Union-United Nations Hybrid Operation in Darfur and the Government of the Sudan and a sustained and more effective approach by the Operation, which have resulted in improvements in mandate implementation, including through the more timely issuance of visas and a considerable recent reduction of movement restrictions on the Operation; reiterates its deep concern that hindrances nevertheless remain to the Operation in the implementation of its mandate, including movement and access restrictions, caused by insecurity, acts of criminality and movement restrictions by government forces, armed movements and militia groups; calls upon all parties in Darfur to remove all obstacles to the full and proper discharge by the Operation of its mandate, including by ensuring its security and freedom of movement; and in this regard demands that the Government comply with the status-of-forces agreement fully and without delay, particularly provisions relevant to the movement of patrols in conflict-affected areas and flight clearances, building on the recent improvement in these areas, as well as those provisions relevant to the removal of obstacles to the use of aerial assets of the Operation and the timely processing of Operation equipment at the port of entry to the Sudan;

17. *Demands* that all parties in Darfur immediately end attacks targeting civilians, peacekeepers and humanitarian personnel and comply with their obligations under international human rights and humanitarian law; and affirms the Security Council's condemnation of all violations of international humanitarian law and violations and abuses of human rights;

18. *Expresses serious concern* at the deteriorating humanitarian situation in Darfur and at the threats to and attacks on humanitarian personnel and facilities; welcomes that, despite multiple challenges, humanitarian access improved in the months of April and May compared to the first quarter of 2014, including progress in accessing part of the Jebel Marra area through the recent inter-agency mission to Guldo; expresses concern that access to some conflict areas where vulnerable populations reside remains restricted and that some conflict areas are inaccessible, including in North and Central Darfur and eastern Jebel Marra, owing to insecurity, acts of criminality and movement restrictions by government forces, armed movements and militia groups; welcomes that humanitarian organizations are able to deliver some aid to most people in need of assistance in Darfur; deplores the continued restrictions on humanitarian access in Darfur resulting from increased insecurity, attacks against humanitarian workers, denial of access by the parties to the conflict and bureaucratic impediments imposed by the Government of the Sudan; further expresses concern over the insufficient availability of funding for humanitarian actors; stresses the need for the timely issuance of visas and travel permits for humanitarian organizations; and demands that the Government, all militias, armed groups and all other stakeholders ensure the safe, timely and unhindered access of humanitarian organizations and relief personnel and the delivery of humanitarian assistance to populations in need, in accordance with the relevant provisions of international law and United Nations guiding principles of humanitarian assistance, including humanity, impartiality, neutrality and independence;

19. *Condemns* increased human rights violations and abuses in, and relating to, Darfur, including those involving extrajudicial killings, the excessive use of force, abduction of civilians, acts of sexual and gender-based violence, violations and abuses against children and arbitrary arrests and detentions; expresses deep concern about the situation of all those so detained, including civil society members and internally displaced persons; emphasizes the importance of ensuring, within its current mandate, the ability of the African Union-United Nations Hybrid Operation in Darfur and other relevant organizations to monitor such cases; and in this regard urges the Government of the Sudan to extend even greater cooperation with the Operation towards the fulfilment of this goal and to provide accountability and access to justice for victims; and calls upon the Government fully to respect its obligations, including by fulfilling its commitment to lift the state of emergency in Darfur, releasing all political prisoners and allowing free expression;

20. *Requests* the African Union-United Nations Hybrid Operation in Darfur to continue to implement the United Nations human rights due diligence policy,[270] and to monitor, verify and draw to the attention of the authorities abuses and violations of human rights, including those committed against women and children, and violations of international humanitarian law, and further requests enhanced, detailed, full and public reporting by the Secretary-General to the Council on this issue, as part of his regular 90-day reports;

21. *Urges* close coordination among United Nations missions in the region, including the African Union-United Nations Hybrid Operation in Darfur, the United Nations Interim Security Force for Abyei and the United Nations Mission in South Sudan, and requests the Secretary-General to ensure effective inter-mission cooperation;

22. *Emphasizes* the importance of cooperation and information-sharing between the African Union-United Nations Hybrid Operation in Darfur, the United Nations Mission in South Sudan, the United Nations Organization Stabilization Mission in the Democratic Republic of the Congo, the United Nations Multidimensional Integrated Stabilization Mission in the Central African Republic and relevant regional and international partners in addressing the regional threat, including of the Lord's Resistance Army, and recalls its encouragement to the Operation, within existing capacities and consistent with its mandate, to cooperate and share information in this regard;

23. *Stresses* the importance of achieving dignified and durable solutions for refugees and internally displaced persons and of ensuring their full participation in the planning and management of these solutions; demands that all parties to the conflict in Darfur create the conditions conducive to allowing the voluntary, informed, safe, dignified and sustainable return of refugees and internally displaced persons or, where appropriate, their local integration; calls in this regard for the reactivation of the Joint Verification Mechanism in order to verify the extent to which these returns are voluntary and informed in nature, and underlines the importance of addressing land issues for the realization of durable solutions in Darfur;

24. *Demands* that the parties to the conflict immediately cease all acts of sexual and gender-based violence; further demands that the parties to the conflict make and implement specific and time-bound commitments to combat sexual violence, in accordance with resolution 2106 (2013); requests the African Union-United Nations Hybrid Operation in Darfur to report on sexual and gender-based violence and actions taken to combat it, including through the timely appointment of women's protection advisers; and requests the Secretary-General to ensure that the relevant provisions of resolution 1325 (2000) and subsequent resolutions on women and peace and security are implemented, including supporting the full and effective participation of women during all stages of peace processes, particularly in conflict resolution, post-conflict planning and peacebuilding, including women's civil society organizations, and to include information on this in his reporting to the Council;

25. *Also demands* that the parties to the conflict immediately cease all violations and abuses against children and develop and implement concrete and time-bound action plans to end and prevent the recruitment and use of children in violation of applicable international law, and requests the Secretary-General to ensure (*a*) continued monitoring and reporting of the situation of children in Darfur; and (*b*) continued dialogue with the parties to the conflict towards the development and implementation of the aforementioned action plans, in accordance with resolution 1612 (2005) and subsequent resolutions on children and armed conflict;

26. *Requests* the Secretary-General to report to the Council every 90 days following the adoption of the present resolution on the African Union-United Nations Hybrid Operation in Darfur, including information on the political, humanitarian and security situation in Darfur, including detailed reporting on incidents of violence and attacks against civilians, by whomsoever perpetrated; information on violations of the status-of-forces agreement, as well as violations of international humanitarian law perpetrated by any party to the conflict; developments and progress towards achievement of the Operation's strategic priorities and benchmarks; and developments and progress in addressing the challenges facing the Operation as identified in the review of the Operation; and on the implementation of the present resolution;

27. *Decides* to remain seized of the matter.

Adopted unanimously at the 7250th meeting.

[270] S/2013/110, annex.

Decision

At its 7276th meeting, on 14 October 2014, the Security Council decided to invite the representatives of South Sudan and the Sudan to participate, without vote, in accordance with rule 37 of its provisional rules of procedure, in the discussion of the item entitled:

"Reports of the Secretary-General on the Sudan and South Sudan

"Report of the Secretary-General on the situation in Abyei (S/2014/709)".

Resolution 2179 (2014) of 14 October 2014

The Security Council,

Recalling its previous resolutions and the statements by its President on the situation in the Sudan and South Sudan, in particular resolutions 1990 (2011) of 27 June 2011, 2024 (2011) of 14 December 2011, 2032 (2011) of 22 December 2011, 2046 (2012) of 2 May 2012, 2047 (2012) of 17 May 2012, 2075 (2012) of 16 November 2012, 2104 (2013) of 29 May 2013, 2126 (2013) of 25 November 2013 and 2156 (2014) of 29 May 2014, as well as the statements by its President of 31 August 2012[271] and 23 August 2013[272] and its statements to the press of 18 June, 21 and 28 September 2012, 6 May and 14 June 2013 and 14 February and 17 March 2014,

Reaffirming its strong commitment to the sovereignty, independence, unity and territorial integrity of the Sudan and South Sudan and to the purposes and principles of the Charter of the United Nations, and recalling the importance of the principles of good-neighbourliness, non-interference and regional cooperation,

Reiterating that the territorial boundaries of States shall not be altered by force and that any territorial disputes shall be settled exclusively by peaceful means,

Affirming the priority it attaches to the full and urgent implementation of all outstanding issues from the Comprehensive Peace Agreement of 9 January 2005,[273]

Reaffirming its previous resolutions 1265 (1999) of 17 September 1999, 1296 (2000) of 19 April 2000, 1674 (2006) of 28 April 2006, 1738 (2006) of 23 December 2006 and 1894 (2009) of 11 November 2009 on the protection of civilians in armed conflict; its resolutions 1612 (2005) of 26 July 2005, 1882 (2009) of 4 August 2009, 1998 (2011) of 12 July 2011, 2068 (2012) of 19 September 2012 and 2143 (2014) of 7 March 2014 on children and armed conflict; its resolution 1502 (2003) of 26 August 2003 on the protection of humanitarian and United Nations personnel; and its resolutions 1325 (2000) of 31 October 2000, 1820 (2008) of 19 June 2008, 1888 (2009) of 30 September 2009, 1889 (2009) of 5 October 2009, 1960 (2010) of 16 December 2010, 2106 (2013) of 24 June 2013 and 2122 (2013) of 18 October 2013 on women and peace and security,

Recalling the commitments made by the Government of the Sudan and the Government of South Sudan in the Agreement between the Government of the Sudan and the Sudan People's Liberation Movement on Temporary Arrangements for the Administration and Security of the Abyei Area of 20 June 2011,[274] the Agreement between the Government of the Sudan and the Government of Southern Sudan on Border Security and the Joint Political and Security Mechanism of 29 June 2011 and the Agreement on the Border Monitoring Support Mission between the Government of the Sudan and the Government of South Sudan of 30 July 2011,[275] as well as the agreements on cooperation and security arrangements of 27 September 2012,[276] the decision of the Joint Political and Security Mechanism of 8 March 2013 and the implementation matrix of 12 March 2013,[277] reached by the Government of the Sudan and the Government of South Sudan in Addis Ababa under the auspices of the African Union High-level Implementation Panel,

---

[271] S/PRST/2012/19.

[272] S/PRST/2013/14.

[273] S/2005/78, annex.

[274] See S/2011/384, annex.

[275] S/2011/510, annex.

[276] See S/2012/733, annex, and S/2012/753, annex.

[277] S/2013/168, annex.

Emphasizing the importance of the full participation of women in the implementation of agreements and in the prevention and resolution of conflict and peacebuilding more broadly,

Expressing its full support for the efforts of the African Union on the situation between the Sudan and South Sudan, in order to ease the current tension and facilitate the resumption of negotiations on post-secession relations and the normalization of their relations, recalling in this regard the African Union Peace and Security Council communiqués of 24 April[278] and 24 October 2012, 25 January, 7 May, 29 July, 23 September, 26 October and 12 November 2013 and 12 September 2014, the Peace and Security Council press statement of 6 November 2013 and the statement made by the Chairperson of the African Union Commission on 28 October 2013,

Noting with concern the stalled efforts by the Government of the Sudan and the Government of South Sudan to demilitarize the Safe Demilitarized Border Zone, including the "14-mile area", and to fully implement the Joint Border Verification and Monitoring Mechanism, in accordance with Security Council resolution 2046 (2012) and the Peace and Security Council road map of 24 April 2012,[278] as a result of South Sudan's continued disagreement with the location of the centreline of the Zone,

Underlining the importance of fully establishing and maintaining effective monitoring by the Joint Border Verification and Monitoring Mechanism of the Safe Demilitarized Border Zone, including the 14-mile area,

Stressing that both countries will have much to gain if they show restraint and choose the path of dialogue instead of resorting to violence or provocations,

Welcoming further regular meetings between President Bashir and President Kiir for continuing dialogue, recalling the decision in resolution 2046 (2012) that the parties must resume immediately negotiations to reach agreement on the final status of Abyei under the auspices of the African Union High-level Implementation Panel, calling upon all parties to engage constructively in the process mediated by the Implementation Panel towards final agreement on the final status of the Abyei Area, and stressing that the parties must immediately implement pending aspects of the Agreement of 20 June 2011, in particular to resolve the dispute over the Abyei Area Council and immediately establish the Abyei Area Administration and Abyei Police Service,

Commending the continued assistance provided to the parties by the African Union High-level Implementation Panel, including its Chairperson, President Thabo Mbeki, and former Presidents Abdulsalami Abubakar and Pierre Buyoya, the Chairperson of the Intergovernmental Authority on Development, Prime Minister Hailemariam Dessalegn of Ethiopia, the Special Envoy of the Secretary-General for the Sudan and South Sudan, Mr. Haile Menkerios, and the United Nations Interim Security Force for Abyei,

Commending also the efforts of the Force in effectively carrying out its mandate, including by its ongoing facilitation of peaceful migration throughout the Abyei Area, conflict prevention, mediation and deterrence, and expressing its deep appreciation for the work of the troop-contributing countries,

Noting with concern the fragility of the security situation in the Abyei Area, acknowledging the contribution of the Force to enhanced peace and stability since its deployment, and determined to prevent the recurrence of violence against or displacements of civilians and to avert intercommunal conflict,

Expressing its determination that the future status of Abyei shall be resolved by negotiations between the parties in a manner consistent with the Comprehensive Peace Agreement and not by the unilateral actions of either party,

Deeply concerned by the public administration and rule of law vacuum in the Abyei Area, due to continued delays in the establishment of the Abyei Area Administration, Council and Police Service, including a special unit to deal with particular issues related to nomadic migration, which are essential to maintain law and order and prevent intercommunal conflict in Abyei,

Noting with concern the continued threat of intercommunal violence in the Abyei Area, including the ongoing tensions that prevent Sudanese staff of the Force and other agencies from returning to Abyei,

Noting that the continued delay in establishing the temporary institutions and resolving the final status of Abyei contributes to tension in the region, urging all parties to refrain from any unilateral action to aggravate

[278] See S/2012/298, enclosure 3.

intercommunal relations within the Abyei Area, and expressing concern over the continued implications of what the Peace and Security Council described in its press statement of 6 November 2013 as "the decision by the Ngok Dinka to conduct a unilateral referendum",

Taking note of the announcement on 7 September 2014 by the Sudan National Election Commission to include the Abyei Area as a geographical constituency in the 2015 elections, which, according to the report of the Secretary-General of 30 September 2014,[279] "can pose a serious risk to the stability of Abyei",

Bearing in mind the importance of coherence of United Nations assistance in the region,

Welcoming and encouraging efforts by the United Nations to sensitize peacekeeping personnel in the prevention and control of HIV/AIDS and other communicable diseases in all its peacekeeping operations,

Stressing the need for effective human rights monitoring, including of any sexual and gender-based violence and violations and abuses committed against children, taking note that there have been no developments with regard to the operationalization of human rights monitoring in the Abyei Area, and reiterating its concern at the lack of cooperation by the parties with the Secretary-General to this end,

Stressing also the urgency of facilitating the delivery of humanitarian assistance to all affected communities in the Abyei Area,

Affirming the importance of voluntary, safe, orderly return and sustainable reintegration of displaced persons, and of peaceful and orderly migration cycles respecting the traditional migratory routes from the Sudan to South Sudan through Abyei, and urging the Force to take measures as necessary to ensure security in the Abyei Area in accordance with its mandate,

Recalling its resolution 2117 (2013) of 26 September 2013, and expressing grave concern at the threat to peace and security in Abyei arising from the illicit transfer, destabilizing accumulation and misuse of small arms and light weapons,

Expressing concern about the residual threat of landmines and explosive remnants of war in the Abyei Area, which hinders the safe return of displaced persons to their homes and safe migration,

Taking note of the report of the Secretary-General of 30 September 2014, including the assessment that the political and security situation on the ground is relatively calm, but can easily escalate into open conflict, with a commensurate risk of deterioration of bilateral relations between the Sudan and South Sudan, and the recommendations contained therein,

Recognizing that the current situation in Abyei and along the border between the Sudan and South Sudan continues to constitute a serious threat to international peace and security,

1. *Decides* to extend until 28 February 2015 the mandate of the United Nations Interim Security Force for Abyei as set out in paragraph 2 of resolution 1990 (2011) and modified by resolution 2024 (2011) and paragraph 1 of resolution 2075 (2012), and, acting under Chapter VII of the Charter of the United Nations, further decides to extend until 28 February 2015 the mandate of the Force as set out in paragraph 3 of resolution 1990 (2011), and determines that, for the purposes of paragraph 1 of resolution 2024 (2011), support to the operational activities of the Joint Border Verification and Monitoring Mechanism shall include support to the Ad Hoc Committees, as appropriate when so requested by consensual decisions of these mechanisms, within the operational area and existing capabilities of the Force;

2. *Takes note* of the recommendations in the report of the Secretary-General of 30 September 2014,[279] and welcomes the initiatives of the Force to support resumption of community dialogue and administration by the communities under the supervision of the Abyei Joint Oversight Committee; in this regard calls upon the communities and the Governments of the Sudan and South Sudan to take concrete steps towards that goal; and further welcomes the current and future support in these efforts from the United Nations, the African Union and the Government of Ethiopia;

---

[279] S/2014/709.

3. *Reiterates its demand* that the Sudan and South Sudan immediately resume the work of the Abyei Joint Oversight Committee, and calls upon the Government of South Sudan to name immediately an Oversight Committee Co-Chair to ensure steady progress on the implementation of the Agreement on Temporary Arrangements for the Administration and Security of the Abyei Area of 20 June 2011,[274] including the implementation of the decisions of the Oversight Committee, and requests the Secretary-General to provide an assessment of progress on these issues in his regular reports, including on his recommendations resulting from the strategic review of the Force in May 2014;[280]

4. *Further reiterates its demand* that the Sudan and South Sudan urgently commence the establishment of the Abyei Area Administration and Council, including by resolving the deadlock over the composition of the Council, and constitute the Abyei Police Service, to enable it to take over policing functions throughout the Abyei Area, including the protection of oil infrastructure, in accordance with their commitments in the Agreement of 20 June 2011;

5. *Decides* to maintain the troops authorized by resolution 2104 (2013) already deployed, and that the remaining authorized forces shall continue to be deployed consistent with the progressive reactivation of the Joint Border Verification and Monitoring Mechanism, to enable the Force to provide required force protection to the Mechanism and to enable the Force to fully support the Mechanism to conduct extended operations into the Safe Demilitarized Border Zone as soon as possible, and requests the Secretary-General to keep the Security Council fully updated on the status of deployment as part of his regular reporting cycle;

6. *Expresses concern* regarding the stalled efforts to fully operationalize the Joint Border Verification and Monitoring Mechanism, as a result of South Sudan's continued disagreement with the location of the centreline of the Safe Demilitarized Border Zone, and calls upon the Government of the Sudan and the Government of South Sudan to make timely and effective use of the Joint Border Verification and Monitoring Mechanism, the Joint Political and Security Mechanism and other agreed joint mechanisms to ensure the security and transparency of the Zone, including the 14-mile area;

7. *Urges* renewed efforts to determine conclusively the centreline of the Safe Demilitarized Border Zone on the ground, and reiterates that the centreline of the Zone in no way prejudices the current or future legal status of the border, ongoing negotiations on the disputed and claimed areas, and demarcation of the borders;

8. *Underscores* that the protection of civilians mandate of the Force as set out in paragraph 3 of resolution 1990 (2011) includes taking the actions necessary to protect civilians under imminent threat of physical violence, irrespective of the source of such violence;

9. *Condemns* the presence of South Sudan security service personnel and Diffra oil police units deployed in the Abyei Area, as well as the repeated entry of Misseriya militias into the territory, and reiterates its demands that immediately and without preconditions the Government of South Sudan fully redeploy its security service personnel from the Abyei Area and that the Government of the Sudan also redeploy the oil police in Diffra from the Abyei Area, and further reiterates, in accordance with relevant resolutions, in particular resolutions 1990 (2011) and 2046 (2012), that the Abyei Area shall be demilitarized from any forces, as well as armed elements of the local communities, other than the Force and the Abyei Police Service;

10. *Supports* the decision of the Abyei Joint Oversight Committee of 3 May 2013 on Abyei's status as a weapons-free area, underscores the concern expressed by the African Union Peace and Security Council in its communiqué of 7 May 2013 over reports that various communities living in Abyei are heavily armed, recalls that in the Agreement of 20 June 2011 it is stipulated that Abyei should be a weapons-free area and that only the Force is authorized to carry weapons inside the Area, and in this regard urges the two Governments to take all steps necessary to ensure that Abyei is effectively demilitarized, including through disarmament programmes as necessary;

11. *Requests* that the Force, consistent with its mandate and within its existing capabilities, observe, document and report on the movement of weapons into Abyei and the presence of weapons within Abyei as part of the Secretary-General's regular reporting cycle;

---

[280] See S/2014/336.

12. *Urges* the two Governments immediately to take steps to implement confidence-building measures among the respective communities in the Abyei Area, including through reconciliation processes at the grass-roots level and supporting the Force in convening a peace conference between the Ngok Dinka and Misseriya traditional chiefs, and strongly urges all Abyei communities to exercise maximum restraint in all their engagements and to desist from inflammatory acts or statements that may lead to violent clashes, or any further unilateral activities;

13. *Requests* the Force to continue its dialogue with the Abyei Joint Oversight Committee and with the Misseriya and Ngok Dinka communities on effective strategies and oversight mechanisms for ensuring full compliance by all relevant parties with Abyei's status as a weapons-free area, with a particular priority placed on the urgent elimination of heavy or crew-served weapons, as well as rocket-propelled grenades, and calls upon the Governments of the Sudan and South Sudan, the Oversight Committee and the Misseriya and Ngok Dinka communities to extend full cooperation to the Force in this regard;

14. *Calls upon* all parties to cooperate fully with the findings and recommendations following the investigation by the Abyei Area Joint Investigation and Inquiry Committee into the killing of a Force peacekeeper and the Ngok Dinka Paramount Chief;

15. *Expresses its intention* to review, as appropriate, the mandate of the Force for possible reconfiguration of the mission in the light of the compliance by the Sudan and South Sudan with the decisions set forth in resolution 2046 (2012) and their commitments as set forth in the Agreements of 20 and 29 June and 30 July 2011[275] and 27 September 2012,[276] including the redeployment of all forces from the Safe Demilitarized Border Zone, achieving full operational capability for the Joint Border Verification and Monitoring Mechanism and the Ad Hoc Committees, as well as completing the full demilitarization of the Abyei Area;

16. *Calls upon* all Member States, in particular the Sudan and South Sudan, to ensure the free, unhindered and expeditious movement to and from Abyei and throughout the Safe Demilitarized Border Zone of all personnel, as well as equipment, provisions, supplies and other goods, including vehicles, aircraft and spare parts, which are for the exclusive and official use of the Force;

17. *Renews its call upon* the Governments of the Sudan and South Sudan to provide full support to the United Nations, including by promptly issuing visas to military, police and civilian United Nations personnel, including humanitarian personnel, without prejudice to their nationality, facilitating basing arrangements and flight clearances, and providing logistical support, and calls upon all parties to fully adhere to their obligations under the status-of-forces agreements;

18. *Recognizes* the absence of critical infrastructure projects affecting peacekeeping personnel of the Force, notes the action being taken to address this situation, and urges the Secretary-General to continue to take the measures available to him to remediate this situation and better enable the Force to implement its mandate;

19. *Demands* that the Government of the Sudan and the Government of South Sudan continue to facilitate the deployment of the Mine Action Service of the United Nations to ensure the freedom of movement of the Joint Border Verification and Monitoring Mechanism as well as the identification and clearance of mines in the Abyei Area and the Safe Demilitarized Border Zone;

20. *Also demands* that all parties involved provide humanitarian personnel with full, safe and unhindered access to civilians in need of assistance and all facilities necessary for their operations, in accordance with international law, including applicable international humanitarian law, and United Nations guiding principles of humanitarian assistance;

21. *Requests* the Secretary-General to ensure that effective human rights monitoring is carried out and the results included in his reports to the Security Council, and reiterates its call upon the Government of the Sudan and the Government of South Sudan to extend their full cooperation to the Secretary-General to this end, including by issuing visas to the concerned United Nations personnel;

22. *Also requests* the Secretary-General to take the measures necessary to ensure full compliance of the Force with the United Nations zero-tolerance policy on sexual exploitation and abuse and to keep the Security Council informed if cases of such conduct occur;

23. *Stresses* that continued cooperation between the Government of the Sudan and the Government of South Sudan is also critical for peace, security and stability and future relations between them;

24. *Requests* the Secretary-General, with support from the African Union Commission and the Government of Ethiopia, to explore options in the context of the Peace and Security Council communiqué of 12 September 2014, in which the parties are urged to use creative provisions based on mutual understanding to expedite implementation of the outstanding administrative and security elements of the Agreement of 20 June 2011, as appropriate, and to include their findings in the consolidated recommendations on the Force to be presented to the Security Council in the next report of the Secretary-General;

25. *Also requests* the Secretary-General to continue to inform the Security Council of progress in implementing the mandate of the Force in two written reports, no later than 1 December 2014 and 2 February 2015 respectively, and to continue to bring to the Council's immediate attention any serious violations of the above-referenced agreements;

26. *Notes* the efforts of the Secretary-General to ensure close cooperation among United Nations missions in the region, including the Force, the United Nations Mission in South Sudan and the African Union-United Nations Hybrid Operation in Darfur, as well as his Special Envoy for the Sudan and South Sudan, and requests him to continue this practice;

27. *Decides* to remain actively seized of the matter.

Adopted unanimously at the 7276th meeting.

Decisions

At its 7282nd meeting, on 22 October 2014, the Security Council decided to invite the representative of South Sudan to participate, without vote, in accordance with rule 37 of its provisional rules of procedure, in the discussion of the item entitled:

"Reports of the Secretary-General on the Sudan and South Sudan

"Report of the Secretary-General on South Sudan (S/2014/708)".

At the same meeting, the Council also decided to extend invitations, in accordance with rule 39 of its provisional rules of procedure, to Ms. Ellen Margrethe Løj, Special Representative of the Secretary-General for South Sudan and Head of the United Nations Mission in South Sudan, and Ms. Zainab Hawa Bangura, Special Representative of the Secretary-General on Sexual Violence in Conflict.

On 20 November 2014, the President of the Security Council addressed the following letter to the Secretary-General:[281]

> I have the honour to inform you that your letter dated 18 November 2014 concerning your intention to appoint Major General Birhanu Jula Gelalcha, of Ethiopia, as Force Commander of the United Nations Interim Security Force for Abyei[282] has been brought to the attention of the members of the Security Council. They take note of the intention expressed in your letter.

At its 7320th meeting, on 24 November 2014, the Council considered the item entitled:

"Reports of the Secretary-General on the Sudan and South Sudan

"Briefing by the Chair of the Security Council Committee established pursuant to resolution 1591 (2005) concerning the Sudan".

At its 7322nd meeting, on 25 November 2014, the Council decided to invite the representative of South Sudan to participate, without vote, in accordance with rule 37 of its provisional rules of procedure, in the discussion of the item entitled:

"Reports of the Secretary-General on the Sudan and South Sudan

"Report of the Secretary-General on South Sudan (S/2014/821)".

---

[281] S/2014/836.

[282] S/2014/835.

Resolution 2187 (2014)
of 25 November 2014

The Security Council,

Recalling its previous resolutions 1996 (2011) of 8 July 2011, 2046 (2012) of 2 May 2012, 2057 (2012) of 5 July 2012, 2109 (2013) of 11 July 2013, 2132 (2013) of 24 December 2013 and 2155 (2014) of 27 May 2014,

Reaffirming its strong commitment to the sovereignty, independence, territorial integrity and national unity of South Sudan, and recalling the importance of the principles of non-interference, good-neighbourliness and regional cooperation,

Recalling its resolution 2086 (2013) of 21 January 2013 and reaffirming the basic principles of peacekeeping, including consent of the parties, impartiality and non-use of force except in self-defence and defence of the mandate, and recognizing that the mandate of each peacekeeping mission is specific to the need and situation of the country concerned,

Expressing grave alarm and concern regarding the further deteriorating political, security and humanitarian crisis in South Sudan resulting from the internal Sudan People's Liberation Movement political dispute and subsequent violence caused by the country's political and military leaders,

Strongly condemning reported and ongoing human rights violations and abuses and violations of international humanitarian law, including those involving extrajudicial killings, ethnically targeted violence, rape and other forms of sexual and gender-based violence, recruitment and use of children, enforced disappearances, arbitrary arrests and detention, violence aimed at spreading terror among the civilian population, and attacks on schools, places of worship, hospitals and United Nations and associated peacekeeping personnel, by all parties, including armed groups and national security forces, as well as the incitement to commit such abuses and violations, further condemning harassment and targeting of civil society, humanitarian personnel and journalists, and emphasizing that those responsible for violations of international humanitarian law and violations and abuses of human rights must be held accountable and that the Government of South Sudan bears the primary responsibility to protect civilians within its territory and subject to its jurisdiction, including from potential crimes against humanity and war crimes,

Expressing deep concern over the large-scale displacement of persons and deepening humanitarian crisis, stressing the responsibility borne by all parties to the conflict for the suffering of the people of South Sudan, and the necessity of ensuring that the basic needs of the population are met, commending United Nations humanitarian agencies and partners for their efforts to provide urgent and coordinated support to the population, calling upon all parties to the conflict to allow and facilitate, in accordance with relevant provisions of international law and United Nations guiding principles of humanitarian assistance, the full, safe and unhindered access of relief personnel, equipment and supplies to all those in need and timely delivery of humanitarian assistance, in particular to internally displaced persons and refugees, condemning all attacks against humanitarian personnel and facilities, and recalling that attacks against humanitarian personnel and depriving civilians of objects indispensable to their survival may amount to violations of international humanitarian law,

Commending the Intergovernmental Authority on Development initiative, as supported by the United Nations and the African Union, in establishing a forum for political and security dialogue, and expecting all parties to participate in this process and respect the decisions reached by successive Assemblies of Heads of State and Government of the Intergovernmental Authority,

Welcoming the cessation of hostilities and status of detainees agreements of 23 January 2014 mediated by the Intergovernmental Authority on Development, consensus on the declaration of principles between the parties, the establishment of the ceasefire Monitoring and Verification Mechanism, the Agreement to Resolve the Crisis in South Sudan of 9 May 2014 and the rededication and implementation modalities for the cessation of hostilities agreement, of 9 November 2014, while strongly condemning repeated and continuing violations of the cessation of hostilities agreement by all parties, which undermine peace efforts,

Acknowledging with appreciation the Intergovernmental Authority on Development Assembly of Heads of State and Government communiqués of 10 June, 25 August and 7 November 2014, highlighting commitments in the areas of inclusive governance, security, economic and financial management, justice, humanitarian action and constitutional process, and the African Union Peace and Security Council communiqués of 12 June and 17 September 2014,

Expressing its deep appreciation for the actions taken by United Nations Mission in South Sudan peacekeepers and troop- and police-contributing countries to protect civilians, including foreign nationals, under threat of physical violence and to stabilize the security situation within and beyond Mission sites, expressing appreciation for the efforts of the Mission to support internally displaced persons seeking protection on its sites, while underlining the necessity to find sustainable solutions for the internally displaced population, including in alternative safe and secure locations, and in keeping with the Guiding Principles on Internal Displacement,[283] and further expressing appreciation for those Member States that have deployed troops and police after the adoption of resolution 2155 (2014),

Taking note with interest of the United Nations Mission in South Sudan interim human rights report, of 21 February 2014, and its report entitled "Conflict in South Sudan: A Human Rights Report", of 8 May 2014,

Expressing grave concern that, according to the report of 8 May 2014, there are reasonable grounds to believe that war crimes and crimes against humanity, including extrajudicial killings, rape and other acts of sexual violence, enforced disappearances and arbitrary arrests and detention have been committed by both government and opposition forces,

Stressing the increasingly urgent and imperative need to end impunity in South Sudan and to bring to justice perpetrators of such crimes,

Welcoming the work of the African Union Commission of Inquiry on South Sudan in independent and public human rights monitoring, investigation and reporting, and the interim report of the Commission of Inquiry, of 27 June 2014, and anticipating with interest its findings and recommendations,

Strongly condemning the use of radio to broadcast hate speech and transmit messages instigating sexual violence against a particular ethnic group, which has the potential to play a significant role in promoting mass violence and exacerbating conflict, calling upon the Government of South Sudan to take the appropriate measures in order to deter such activity, and further urging all parties to desist from these actions and instead to contribute to promoting peace and reconciliation among the communities,

Emphasizing that persistent barriers to full implementation of resolution 1325 (2000) of 31 October 2000 will only be dismantled through dedicated commitment to women's empowerment, participation and human rights, and through concerted leadership, consistent information and action, and support, to build women's engagement in all levels of decision-making,

Expressing deep concern at persistent restrictions placed upon the movement and operations of the Mission, strongly condemning the attacks by government and opposition forces and other groups on United Nations and Intergovernmental Authority on Development personnel and facilities, including the December 2012 downing of a United Nations helicopter by the Sudan People's Liberation Army, the April 2013 attack on a United Nations convoy, the December 2013 attack on the Mission camp in Akobo, the August 2014 shooting down of a United Nations helicopter by unidentified armed groups, the August 2014 arrest and detention of an Intergovernmental Authority monitoring and verification team, the detentions and kidnappings of United Nations and associated personnel and the 2014 attacks on the Mission camps in Bor and Bentiu, and calling upon the Government of South Sudan to complete its investigations of these attacks in a swift and thorough manner and to hold those responsible to account,

Reiterating its request that the Mission take additional measures, as appropriate, to ensure the security of its air operations in South Sudan, and report thereon to the Security Council,

Stressing the importance of effective engagement and liaison with local communities, both within and outside the protection of civilians sites, in order to fulfil the protection of civilians mandate of the Mission,

Expressing grave concern regarding the threats made to oil installations, petroleum companies and their employees, and urging all parties to ensure the security of economic infrastructure,

---

[283] E/CN.4/1998/53/Add.2, annex.

Recalling its resolution 2117 (2013) of 26 September 2013, and expressing grave concern at the threat to peace and security in South Sudan arising from the illicit transfer, destabilizing accumulation and misuse of small arms and light weapons,

Noting with serious concern reports of the indiscriminate use of cluster munitions, made by the Mine Action Service of the United Nations in Jonglei State in February 2014, and urging all parties to refrain from similar such use in the future,

Welcoming the deployment by the Intergovernmental Authority on Development of the Monitoring and Verification Mechanism, calling for the redeployment and/or progressive withdrawal of armed groups and allied forces invited by either side, consistent with the cessation of hostilities agreement of 23 January 2014, and warning of the serious consequences that could result from any regionalization of the conflict,

Welcoming also the appointment by the Secretary-General of Ms. Ellen Margrethe Løj as his Special Representative for South Sudan and Head of the Mission and Lieutenant General Yohannes Gebremeskel Tesfamariam as the Force Commander of the Mission,

Reaffirming its resolutions 1265 (1999) of 17 September 1999, 1296 (2000) of 19 April 2000, 1674 (2006) of 28 April 2006, 1738 (2006) of 23 December 2006 and 1894 (2009) of 11 November 2009 on the protection of civilians in armed conflict, and resolution 1502 (2003) of 26 August 2003 on the protection of humanitarian and United Nations personnel; resolutions 1612 (2005) of 26 July 2005, 1882 (2009) of 4 August 2009, 1998 (2011) of 12 July 2011, 2068 (2012) of 19 September 2012 and 2143 (2014) of 7 March 2014 on children and armed conflict; and resolutions 1325 (2000) of 31 October 2000, 1820 (2008) of 19 June 2008, 1888 (2009) of 30 September 2009, 1889 (2009) of 5 October 2009, 1960 (2010) of 16 December 2010, 2106 (2013) of 24 June 2013 and 2122 (2013) of 18 October 2013 on women and peace, and security; resolution 2150 (2014) of 16 April 2014 on the prevention of and fight against genocide; resolution 2151 (2014) of 28 April 2014 on security sector reform; and resolution 2171 (2014) of 21 August 2014 on conflict prevention,

Taking note of the reports of the Secretary-General of 30 September[284] and 18 November 2014[285] and the recommendations contained therein,

Determining that the situation in South Sudan continues to constitute a threat to international peace and security in the region,

Acting under Chapter VII of the Charter of the United Nations,

1. *Reiterates its endorsement* of the cessation of hostilities agreement accepted and signed by the Government of South Sudan and the Sudan People's Liberation Movement/Army (in Opposition) on 23 January 2014, further reiterates its endorsement of the Agreement to Resolve the Crisis in South Sudan signed on 9 May 2014 by the Government of South Sudan and the Sudan People's Liberation Movement/Army (in Opposition); endorses the rededication and implementation modalities for the cessation of hostilities agreement, of 9 November 2014; calls for immediate and full implementation of the agreements by both parties, and expresses its intention to consider all appropriate measures, in consultation with relevant partners, including the Intergovernmental Authority on Development and the African Union, against those who take action that undermines the peace, stability and security of South Sudan, including those who prevent the implementation of these agreements;

2. *Urges* all parties to engage in an open and fully inclusive national dialogue seeking to establish lasting peace, reconciliation and good governance, including through the full and effective participation of youth, women, diverse communities, faith groups, civil society and the formerly detained Sudan People's Liberation Movement leaders, encourages the efforts of the Intergovernmental Authority on Development and the United Nations to reach a peace agreement between the parties, and further urges them to ensure that child protection provisions are integrated into all peace negotiations and peace agreements;

3. *Decides* to extend the mandate of the United Nations Mission in South Sudan until 30 May 2015;

---

[284] S/2014/708.

[285] S/2014/821.

4. *Also decides* that the mandate of the Mission shall be as follows, and authorizes the Mission to use all means necessary to perform the following tasks:

(*a*) *Protection of civilians*:

(i) To protect civilians under threat of physical violence, irrespective of the source of such violence, within its capacity and areas of deployment, with specific protection for women and children, including through the continued use of the Mission's child protection and women's protection advisers;

(ii) To deter violence against civilians, including foreign nationals, especially through proactive deployment, active patrolling with particular attention to displaced civilians, including those in protection sites and refugee camps, humanitarian personnel and human rights defenders, and identification of threats and attacks against the civilian population, including through regular interaction with the civilian population and closely with humanitarian, human rights and development organizations, in areas at high risk of conflict, including, as appropriate, schools, places of worship, hospitals and the oil installations, in particular when the Government of South Sudan is unable or failing to provide such security;

(iii) To implement a Mission-wide early warning strategy, including a coordinated approach to information-gathering, monitoring, verification, early warning and dissemination, and response mechanisms, including response mechanisms to prepare for further potential attacks on United Nations personnel and facilities;

(iv) To maintain public safety and security within and of the Mission's protection of civilians sites;

(v) To exercise good offices, confidence-building and facilitation in support of the Mission's protection strategy, especially in regard to women and children, including to facilitate intercommunal reconciliation in areas at high risk of conflict as an essential part of long-term State-building activity;

(vi) To foster a secure environment for the eventual safe and voluntary return of internally displaced persons and refugees, including, where compatible and in strict compliance with the United Nations human rights due diligence policy,[270] through monitoring of, ensuring the maintenance of international human rights standards by, and specific operational coordination with the police services in relevant and protection-focused tasks, in order to strengthen the protection of civilians;

(*b*) *Monitoring and investigating human rights*:

(i) To monitor, investigate, verify and report publicly and regularly on abuses and violations of human rights and violations of international humanitarian law, including those that may amount to war crimes or crimes against humanity;

(ii) To monitor, investigate, verify and report specifically and publicly on violations and abuses committed against children and women, including all forms of sexual and gender-based violence in armed conflict by accelerating the implementation of monitoring, analysis and reporting arrangements on conflict-related sexual violence and by strengthening the monitoring and reporting mechanism for grave violations against children;

(iii) To coordinate with, and offer technical support to, where appropriate, the African Union Commission of Inquiry on South Sudan;

(*c*) *Creating the conditions for the delivery of humanitarian assistance*:

(i) To contribute to the creation of the conditions for the delivery of humanitarian assistance, including by helping to establish the necessary security conditions and by exercising its good offices, confidence-building and facilitation, so as to allow, in accordance with relevant provisions of international law and United Nations guiding principles of humanitarian assistance, the full, safe and unhindered access of relief personnel to all those in need in South Sudan and timely delivery of humanitarian assistance, in particular to internally displaced persons and refugees;

(ii) To ensure the security and freedom of movement of United Nations and associated personnel where appropriate, and to ensure the security of installations and equipment necessary for the implementation of mandated tasks;

(*d*) *Supporting the implementation of the cessation of hostilities agreement*:

(i) To ensure proper coordination with the Joint Technical Committee, the Monitoring and Verification Mechanism and monitoring and verification teams, as appropriate;

(ii) To provide mobile and dedicated fixed site security to the Monitoring and Verification Mechanism of the Intergovernmental Authority on Development, as established in line with the decisions taken by the Assembly of Heads of State and Government of the Intergovernmental Authority at its meetings held on 31 January and 13 March 2014;

(iii) To provide support to the work of the Monitoring and Verification Mechanism as described in the cessation of hostilities agreement;

5. *Emphasizes* that the protection of civilians, as described in paragraph 4 (*a*) above, must be given priority in decisions about the use of available capacity and resources within the Mission;

6. *Requests* the Secretary-General, through his Special Representative for South Sudan, to continue to direct the operations of an integrated Mission, coordinate all activities of the United Nations system in South Sudan and support a coherent international approach to achieving peace in South Sudan;

7. *Endorses* the recommendation made by the Secretary-General in his report of 18 November 2014[285] to maintain the overall force levels of the Mission to support its mandate as defined in paragraph 4 of the present resolution;

8. *Decides* that the Mission shall consist of a military component of up to 12,500 troops of all ranks and of a police component, including appropriate formed police units, of up to 1,323 personnel; and that the civilian component shall continue to be reduced according to tasks outlined in paragraph 4 above; requests that the Secretary-General provide detailed information on force generation, restructuring of the Mission force, logistical support and enablers, including as part of his regular reports; and requests the Secretary-General to review needs on the ground and provide an updated assessment of the force's operations, deployment and future requirements in his regular reports to the Security Council;

9. *Requests* the Mission to continue to focus and streamline its activities across its military, police and civilian components in order to achieve progress on the tasks outlined in paragraph 4 above, and recognizes that certain Mission tasks will therefore be ceased;

10. *Expresses its intention* to keep the requirements and composition of Mission components under active review, and to review this mandate and make any necessary adjustments, at an appropriate stage in the implementation of a credible peace agreement between the parties;

11. *Authorizes* the Secretary-General to take the steps necessary, in accordance with paragraph 8 above, to expedite force and asset generation;

12. *Requests* the Mission to increase its presence and active patrolling in areas of high risk of conflict, high concentrations of internally displaced persons, including as guided by its early warning strategy, in both government- and opposition-held areas, and key routes for population movement, and to conduct regular reviews of its geographic deployment to ensure that its forces are best placed to protect civilians, and requests the Secretary-General to provide updates on these reviews as part of his regular reports;

13. *Further requests* that the Mission continue to ensure full compliance with the United Nations zero-tolerance policy on sexual exploitation and abuse and to keep the Council fully informed about the progress of the Mission in this regard, and urges troop-contributing countries to take appropriate preventive action, including predeployment awareness training, and to ensure full accountability in cases of such conduct involving their personnel;

14. *Encourages* the Mission to fully implement the human rights due diligence policy, and requests the Secretary-General to include progress made in implementing the policy in his reports to the Council;

15. *Condemns in the strongest terms* attacks on and threats made to Mission personnel and United Nations facilities, as well as those of the Intergovernmental Authority on Development, such as the August 2014 shooting down of a United Nations helicopter by unidentified armed groups, the August 2014 arrest and detention of an Intergovernmental Authority monitoring and verification team, the detentions and kidnappings of United Nations and associated personnel, and the 2014 attacks on the Mission camps in Bor and Bentiu, stresses that such attacks may constitute violations of the status-of-forces agreement and/or war crimes, demands that all parties respect the inviolability of United Nations premises and immediately desist and refrain from any violence against those gathered at United Nations facilities, further demands the immediate and safe release of detained and kidnapped

United Nations and associated personnel, and stresses that efforts to undermine the ability of the Mission to implement its mandate and attacks on United Nations personnel will not be tolerated;

16. *Reiterates its request* that the Mission take additional measures, as appropriate, to ensure the security of its air operations in South Sudan and report thereon to the Council;

17. *Demands* that the Government of South Sudan and all relevant parties cooperate fully in the deployment, operations and monitoring, verification and reporting functions of the Mission, in particular by guaranteeing the safety, security and unrestricted freedom of movement of United Nations and associated personnel throughout the territory of South Sudan, and further calls upon the Government to ensure freedom of movement for internally displaced persons, including those leaving and entering protection of civilians sites, and to continue to support the Mission by the allocation of land for protection of civilians sites;

18. *Also demands* that all parties allow, in accordance with relevant provisions of international law and United Nations guiding principles of humanitarian assistance, the full, safe and unhindered access of relief personnel, equipment and supplies to all those in need and timely delivery of humanitarian assistance, in particular to internally displaced persons and refugees, and stresses that any returns of internally displaced persons or refugees must be undertaken on a voluntary and informed basis in conditions of dignity and safety;

19. *Further demands* that all parties immediately cease all forms of violence, human rights violations and abuses, violations of international humanitarian law, including rape and other forms of sexual and gender-based violence, and violations and abuses against children in violation of applicable international law such as those involving their recruitment and use, killing and maiming, abduction and attacks against schools and hospitals, strongly urges the Government of South Sudan to fully and immediately implement its revised action plan to end and prevent the recruitment and use of children, as recommitted to on 24 June 2014, and its military order of 14 August 2013 prohibiting the Sudan People's Liberation Movement to attack, occupy or use for any purposes schools, school buildings or property, takes note of the national launch on 29 October 2014 of the "Children, Not Soldiers" campaign by the Government, and further strongly urges the opposition forces to fully and immediately implement their commitment to end grave violations against children, signed on 10 May 2014;

20. *Expresses grave concern* at the findings of the Special Representative of the Secretary-General on Sexual Violence in Conflict of rampant sexual violence, and welcomes the joint communiqué of South Sudan and the United Nations on the prevention of conflict-related sexual violence of 11 October 2014,[286] urges the Government of South Sudan to implement without delay the commitments made in accordance with resolutions 1960 (2010) and 2106 (2013), calls upon the Sudan People's Liberation Movement/Army (in Opposition) to sign and implement such a communiqué, and further calls for specific and time-bound commitments to combat sexual violence in accordance with resolutions 1960 (2010) and 2106 (2013);

21. *Calls upon* the Government of South Sudan to move forward expeditiously and transparently to complete the investigations of allegations of human rights violations and abuses consistent with international standards, to hold to account all those responsible for violations and abuses of human rights and violations of international humanitarian law and to ensure that all victims of sexual violence have equal protection under the law and equal access to justice, and to safeguard equal respect for the rights of women and girls in these processes;

22. *Emphasizes* the importance of the full and effective participation of women at all levels in the implementation of agreements and in the prevention and resolution of conflict and peacebuilding more broadly, calls upon all parties to take measures to ensure women's full and effective representation and leadership in all conflict resolution and peacebuilding efforts, including through support to women's civil society organizations and incorporating gender expertise in peace talks, encourages troop- and police-contributing countries to take measures to increase the deployment of women in the military, police and civilian components of the Mission, and reaffirms the importance of appropriate gender expertise and training in all missions mandated by the Council;

23. *Condemns* attacks on oil installations, petroleum companies and their employees, and the continued fighting around these facilities, and urges all parties to ensure the security of economic infrastructure;

---

[286] S/2014/796, annex.

24. *Requests* that the Secretary-General report to the Council on the implementation of the mandate of the Mission in two written reports, no later than 16 February 2015 and 30 April 2015 respectively, which could include the issues of accountability in South Sudan;

25. *Decides* to remain actively seized of the matter.

Adopted unanimously at the 7322nd meeting.

Decisions

At its 7326th meeting, on 4 December 2014, the Security Council decided to invite the representative of the Sudan to participate, without vote, in accordance with rule 37 of its provisional rules of procedure, in the discussion of the item entitled:

"Reports of the Secretary-General on the Sudan and South Sudan

"Report of the Secretary-General on the African Union-United Nations Hybrid Operation in Darfur (S/2014/852)".

At the same meeting, the Council also decided to extend an invitation, in accordance with rule 39 of its provisional rules of procedure, to Mr. Hervé Ladsous, Under-Secretary-General for Peacekeeping Operations.

At its 7337th meeting, on 12 December 2014, the Council considered the item entitled "Reports of the Secretary-General on the Sudan and South Sudan".

At the same meeting, the Council decided to extend an invitation, in accordance with rule 39 of its provisional rules of procedure, to Ms. Fatou Bensouda, Prosecutor of the International Criminal Court.

At its 7341st meeting, on 15 December 2014, the Council considered the item entitled "Reports of the Secretary-General on the Sudan and South Sudan".

At the same meeting, following consultations among members of the Security Council, the President made the following statement on behalf of the Council:[287]

The Security Council recalls the great hope and optimism felt by the South Sudanese people at the establishment of the Republic of South Sudan in July 2011 and the prospect of the end of decades of civil war. On the one-year mark of the outbreak of the current conflict it expresses its profound disappointment that their aspirations have not been met, and that instead the actions of their leaders have led to yet more fighting and division.

The Council recalls with deep alarm the escalation of the internal Sudan People's Liberation Movement political dispute that erupted into conflict on 15 December 2013 and the subsequent violence caused by the country's political and military leaders that has plunged this young nation into a man-made political, security and humanitarian catastrophe over this past year.

The Council underscores its strong condemnation of the serious human rights violations and abuses that have caused the death of tens of thousands of civilians, the displacement of nearly 2 million people in just 12 months, and the attacks upon, and deaths of, United Nations peacekeepers and humanitarian personnel. In this regard, it places full responsibility for these tragic events with South Sudan's leaders, those in government as well as with the opposition, and looks to President Salva Kiir Mayardit and former Vice-President Riek Machar Teny to make the necessary compromises for peace.

The Council commends the work of the Intergovernmental Authority on Development in leading the mediation since the onset of the crisis, the initiatives by the African Union, including to establish a mechanism for seeking accountability and reconciliation through its Commission of Inquiry on South Sudan, the overwhelming humanitarian assistance offered by the international community to help to mitigate the consequences of the conflict, including staving off famine in 2014, and the hosting by South Sudan's neighbours of nearly 500,000 refugees from South Sudan.

[287] S/PRST/2014/26.

The Council renews its deep appreciation for the courageous actions taken and ongoing by United Nations Mission in South Sudan personnel and troop- and police-contributing countries to protect tens of thousands of civilians under threat of physical violence and to stabilize the security situation, and pays tribute to those peacekeepers who have tragically been killed in this endeavour, and expresses condolences to their families.

The Council expresses its grave concern that, given the continued disregard of the cessation of hostilities agreement of 23 January 2014 and the Agreement to Resolve the Crisis in South Sudan of 9 May 2014, and the absence of the establishment and implementation of a credible peace agreement, the risks of famine, State failure and regionalization of the conflict persist.

In this regard, the Council urgently demands that President Salva Kiir Mayardit, former Vice-President Riek Machar Teny and all parties refrain from further violence, implement the Agreement to Resolve the Crisis in South Sudan signed on 9 May 2014 by South Sudan and the Sudan People's Liberation Movement/Army (in Opposition), engage fully and inclusively in ongoing peace talks in Addis Ababa, uphold their commitment to establish a Transitional Government of National Unity, and allow and facilitate, in accordance with relevant provisions of international law and United Nations guiding principles of humanitarian assistance, the full, safe and unhindered access of relief personnel, equipment and supplies to all those in need and timely delivery of humanitarian assistance.

The Council reiterates its intention to commence consideration, in consultation with relevant partners, including the Intergovernmental Authority on Development and the African Union, on all appropriate measures, including targeted sanctions, against those impeding the peace process. The Council underscores the significant importance of fighting impunity and ensuring accountability for serious violations and abuses of human rights and serious violations of international humanitarian law in South Sudan, and of continued delivery of life-saving and other humanitarian assistance to the South Sudanese people.

On 26 January 2015, the President of the Security Council addressed the following letter to the Secretary-General:[288]

I have the honour to inform you that your letter dated 21 January 2015 concerning your intention to appoint Mr. Haile Tilahun Gebremariam, of Ethiopia, as Head of Mission for the United Nations Interim Security Force for Abyei[289] has been brought to the attention of the members of the Security Council. They take note of the intention expressed in your letter.

At its 7380th meeting, on 12 February 2015, the Council decided to invite the representative of the Sudan to participate, without vote, in accordance with rule 37 of its provisional rules of procedure, in the discussion of the item entitled:

"Reports of the Secretary-General on the Sudan and South Sudan

"Letter dated 16 January 2015 from the Vice-Chair of the Security Council Committee established pursuant to resolution 1591 (2005) concerning the Sudan addressed to the President of the Security Council (S/2015/31)".

Resolution 2200 (2015) of 12 February 2015

The Security Council,

Recalling its previous resolutions and the statements by its President concerning the Sudan,

Reaffirming its commitment to the cause of peace throughout the Sudan, to the sovereignty, independence, unity and territorial integrity of the Sudan and to the full and timely implementation of resolution 1591 (2005) of 29 March 2005, recalling the importance of the principles of good-neighbourliness, non-interference and

[288] S/2015/53.

[289] S/2015/52.

cooperation in the relations among States in the region, and recalling that the Government of the Sudan bears the primary responsibility for protecting all populations within its territory, with respect for the rule of law, international human rights law and international humanitarian law,

Reiterating the need for an end to the violence and continued abuses in Darfur, underscoring the importance of fully addressing the root causes of the conflict in the search for a sustainable peace, and recognizing that the Darfur conflict cannot be resolved militarily and that a durable solution can only be obtained through an inclusive political process,

Noting the importance of the work of the African Union High-Level Implementation Panel, the aims of the Doha Document for Peace in Darfur[266] and the stated commitment of the Government of the Sudan to an inclusive national dialogue building on the Implementation Panel's ongoing peace efforts, and calling for an environment conducive to that national dialogue,

Expressing deep concern at the increased violence and insecurity in Darfur in recent months, including fighting between the Government of the Sudan and armed groups and intercommunal fighting, expressing deep concern that such violence has had an adverse effect on the security situation, has contributed to the significant increase in the number of internally displaced persons observed in 2014, and continues to restrict humanitarian access to conflict areas where vulnerable civilian populations reside, and reaffirming the crucial need to address the urgent humanitarian crisis faced by the people of Darfur, including by facilitating safe, timely and unhindered humanitarian access to all areas by humanitarian agencies and personnel, consistent with the United Nations guiding principles of humanitarian assistance, including humanity, impartiality, neutrality and independence, and the relevant provisions of international law,

Emphasizing the imperative for all armed actors to refrain from all acts of violence against civilians, in particular members of vulnerable groups such as women and children, and to end all violations and abuses of human rights and violations of international humanitarian law, and further emphasizing that some of these acts may amount to war crimes or crimes against humanity under international law,

Expressing concern about the external links, in particular military, between non-signatory armed groups in Darfur and groups outside Darfur, and demanding that direct or indirect military support for such armed groups in Darfur cease, and condemning actions by any armed group aimed at the forced overthrow of the Government of the Sudan, noting there is no military solution to the conflict in the Sudan,

Demanding that the parties to the conflict exercise restraint and cease military action of all kind, including aerial bombardments,

Recalling its resolution 2117 (2013) of 26 September 2013 and expressing concern at the threat to peace and security in Darfur arising from the illicit transfer, destabilizing accumulation and misuse of small arms and light weapons and the use of such weapons against civilians affected by armed conflict, and the continued threats to civilians posed by unexploded ordnance,

Deploring the continued violations of resolution 1591 (2005) by the Government of the Sudan, including its Rapid Support Forces, and government-affiliated armed groups involving the routine movement of weapons and ammunition into Darfur, without prior authorization of the Security Council Committee established pursuant to paragraph 3 (*a*) of resolution 1591 (2005) (hereinafter "the Committee"),

Demanding an immediate and complete cessation by all parties to the armed conflict of all acts of sexual violence against civilians, recruitment and use of children in violation of applicable international law, other violations and abuses against children and indiscriminate attacks on civilians, in line with all relevant resolutions on these issues,

Reaffirming its concern over the negative effect of ongoing violence in Darfur on the stability of the Sudan as a whole, as well as the region, welcoming the ongoing good relations between the Sudan and Chad, and encouraging the Sudan and the countries of the region to continue to cooperate in order to achieve peace and stability in Darfur and the wider region,

Deploring the violations of international humanitarian law and human rights violations and abuses committed by the Government of the Sudan security forces, their proxies, and armed groups, including those opposing the Government, especially at the Khor Abeche internally displaced persons camp and at Taweisha, North Darfur, as reported by the Panel of Experts on the Sudan,

Expressing concern at the continued obstacles imposed by the Government of the Sudan on the work of the Panel of Experts during the course of its mandate, including restrictions to the freedom of movement of the Panel and limitations on access to areas of armed conflict and areas of reported violations and abuses of human rights and violations of international humanitarian law,

Welcoming improved cooperation between the Government of the Sudan and the Panel of Experts, encouraging increased cooperation by the Government to accede to requests from the Panel for access to areas of armed conflict and for information, and reiterating its call upon all parties in Darfur to cooperate fully with the mission, including by ensuring its free and unfettered access,

Recalling the report of the Panel of Experts of 12 December 2014,[290] and expressing its intent to further study, through the Committee, the recommendations of the Panel and to consider appropriate next steps,

Emphasizing the need to respect the provisions of the Charter of the United Nations concerning privileges and immunities and the Convention on the Privileges and Immunities of the United Nations,[291] as applicable to United Nations operations and persons engaged in such operations,

Noting the critical importance of effective implementation of the sanctions regime, including the key role that neighbouring States, as well as regional and subregional organizations, can play in this regard, and encouraging efforts to further enhance cooperation,

Reminding all States, particularly States in the region, including the Government of the Sudan, of the obligations contained in resolutions 1556 (2004) of 30 July 2004, 1591 (2005), and 1945 (2010) of 14 October 2010, in particular those obligations relating to arms and related materiel,

Calling upon the Government of the Sudan to fulfil all its commitments, including lifting the state of emergency in Darfur, allowing free expression and undertaking effective efforts to ensure accountability for violations and abuses of human rights and violations of international humanitarian law, by whomsoever perpetrated,

Noting that acts of hostility, violence or intimidation against the civilian population, including internally displaced persons, in Darfur endanger or undermine the commitment by the parties to a complete and durable cessation of hostilities and would be inconsistent with the aims of the Doha Document for Peace in Darfur,

Determining that the situation in the Sudan continues to constitute a threat to international peace and security in the region,

Acting under Chapter VII of the Charter,

1. *Decides* to extend the mandate of the Panel of Experts on the Sudan originally appointed pursuant to resolution 1591 (2005), previously extended by resolutions 1651 (2005) of 21 December 2005, 1665 (2006) of 29 March 2006,, 1713 (2006) of 29 September 2006, 1779 (2007) of 28 September 2007, 1841 (2008) of 15 October 2008, 1891 (2009) of 13 October 2009, 1945 (2010), 1982 (2011) of 17 May 2011, 2035 (2012) of 17 February 2012, 2091 (2013) of 14 February 2013 and 2138 (2014) of 13 February 2014, until 12 March 2016, expresses its intent to review the mandate and take appropriate action regarding further extension no later than 12 February 2016, and requests the Secretary-General to take the necessary administrative measures, including basing arrangements, as expeditiously as possible;

2. *Requests* the Panel of Experts to provide, no later than 12 August 2015, a midterm update on its work to the Committee and a final report to the Security Council no later than 15 January 2016, with its findings and recommendations;

3. *Also requests* the Panel of Experts to provide updates every three months to the Committee regarding its activities, including travel by the Panel, and requests that any obstacles encountered to the fulfilment of its mandate, as well as violations of any part of the sanctions regime be reported immediately;

4. *Further requests* the Panel of Experts to report, in the time frame identified in paragraph 3 above, on the implementation and effectiveness of paragraph 10 of resolution 1945 (2010);

---

[290] See S/2015/31.

[291] General Assembly resolution 22 A (I).

5. *Reiterates its support* for the efforts of the African Union-United Nations Hybrid Operation in Darfur , the United Nations Secretary-General, the African Union High-level Implementation Panel, the African Union-United Nations Joint Special Representative for Darfur and the leaders of the region to promote peace and stability in Darfur;

Arms embargo

6. *Expresses its concern* that the direct or indirect supply, sale or transfer to the Sudan of technical assistance and support, including training, financial or other assistance and the provision of spare parts, weapons systems and related materiel, could be used by the Government of the Sudan to support military aircraft being used in violation of resolutions 1556 (2004) and 1591 (2005), including those aircraft identified by the Panel of Experts, and urges all States to be mindful of this risk in the light of the measures contained in resolution 1591 (2005);

7. *Recalls* the obligations of the Government of the Sudan under resolution 1591 (2005), including the requirement to request advance approval from the Committee for the movement of military equipment and supplies into the Darfur region;

8. *Calls upon* the Government of the Sudan to address the illicit transfer, destabilizing accumulation and misuse of small arms and light weapons in Darfur, which also contributes to instability in the region, and further to ensure the safe and effective management, storage and security of its stockpiles of small arms and light weapons and the collection and/or destruction of surplus, seized, unmarked or illicitly held weapons and ammunition;

9. *Expresses its concern* that certain items continue to be converted for military purposes and transferred to Darfur, and urges all States to be mindful of this risk in the light of the measures contained in resolution 1591 (2005);

Implementation

10. *Condemns* the continued violations of the measures contained in paragraphs 7 and 8 of resolution 1556 (2004) and paragraph 7 of resolution 1591 (2005), as updated in paragraph 9 of resolution 1945 (2010) and paragraph 4 of resolution 2035 (2012), and directs the Committee, in line with its mandate and guidelines, to consult as soon as possible with any Member State about which the Committee deems there is credible information that provides reasonable grounds to believe the State is facilitating such violations or any other acts of non-compliance with these measures;

11. *Expresses its concern* that the travel ban and asset freeze on designated individuals is not being implemented by all Member States, requests the Panel of Experts to share with the Committee any information regarding possible non-compliance with the travel ban and asset freeze as soon as possible, and directs the Committee to respond effectively to any reports of non-compliance by Member States with paragraph 3 of resolution 1591 (2005) and resolution 1672 (2006) of 25 April 2006, including by engaging immediately with all relevant parties;

12. *Reiterates* that all States, particularly those in the region, shall take the measures necessary to prevent entry into or transit through their territories of all persons as designated by the Committee, in accordance with paragraph 3 of resolution 1591 (2005), and calls upon the Government of the Sudan to enhance cooperation and information-sharing with other States in this regard;

13. *Urges* all States, in particular those in the region, to report to the Committee on the actions they have taken to implement measures imposed by resolutions 1556 (2004) and 1591 (2005), including the imposition of targeted measures;

14. *Expresses its intention*, following the midterm update, to review the state of implementation, including obstacles to full and effective implementation of the measures, imposed in resolutions 1591 (2005) and 1945 (2010), with a view to ensuring full compliance;

15. *Regrets* that some individuals of the Government of the Sudan and armed groups in Darfur continue to commit violence against civilians, impede the peace process and disregard the demands of the Council, expresses its intention to impose targeted sanctions against individuals and entities that meet the listing criteria in paragraph 3 (*c*) of resolution 1591 (2005), and encourages the Panel of Experts, in coordination with the joint African Union-United Nations mediation, to provide to the Committee, when appropriate, the names of any individuals, groups or entities that may meet the listing criteria;

16. *Deplores* the attacks against the African Union-United Nations Hybrid Operation in Darfur, and calls upon the Government of the Sudan to swiftly investigate and bring the perpetrators to justice, taking into account the findings of the 2014 final report of the Panel of Experts,[290] and reaffirms its deep condolences to the Governments and families of those killed;

17. *Condemns* the use of civilian establishments, in particular the camps for internally displaced persons, by the armed groups, including those opposing the Government of the Sudan, to gain a military advantage in a manner that places the civilians and civilian objects at risk from the dangers arising from armed conflict;

18. *Requests* the Panel of Experts to continue to investigate the financing and role of armed, military and political groups in attacks against personnel of the African Union-United Nations Hybrid Operation in Darfur;

19. *Recalls* that individuals and entities that plan, sponsor or participate in such attacks constitute a threat to stability in Darfur and may therefore meet the designation criteria provided for in paragraph 3 (*c*) of resolution 1591 (2005), and expresses its intention to impose targeted sanctions on individuals and entities that plan, sponsor or participate in such attacks;

Cooperation

20. *Insists* that the Government of the Sudan remove all restrictions, limitations and bureaucratic impediments imposed on the work of the Panel of Experts, including by issuing timely multiple-entry visas to all members of the Panel for the duration of its mandate, and by waiving the requirement of Darfur travel permits for said Panel members, and enhance its cooperation and information-sharing with the Panel and allow the Panel free and unfettered access to all of Darfur;

21. *Urges* the Government of the Sudan to respond to the Committee's requests on measures put in place to protect civilians in various parts of Darfur, including those affected by new displacements; investigations conducted and accountability measures undertaken for unlawful killings of civilians and other human rights violations and abuses and violations of international humanitarian law, including investigations conducted and accountability measures undertaken for attacks against peacekeepers and humanitarian personnel; and the situation of civilian populations in areas such as eastern Jebel Marra and especially those areas in North Darfur where the Panel of Experts, the African Union-United Nations Hybrid Operation in Darfur and humanitarian agencies and personnel have been denied access, and measures taken to allow timely, safe and unhindered access for humanitarian relief to these areas, in accordance with international law, including international humanitarian law, and the United Nations guiding principles of humanitarian assistance, including humanity, impartiality, neutrality and independence;

22. *Welcomes* the work of the Committee, which has drawn on the reports of the Panel of Experts and taken advantage of the work done in other forums, and urges all States, relevant United Nations bodies, the African Union and other interested parties to cooperate fully with the Committee and the Panel, in particular by supplying any information at their disposal on implementation of the measures imposed by resolutions 1591 (2005), 1556 (2004) and 1945 (2010) and to provide timely responses to information requests;

23. *Requests* the Panel of Experts to continue to coordinate its activities, as appropriate, with the operations of the African Union-United Nations Hybrid Operation in Darfur, with international efforts to promote a political process in Darfur, and with other panels or groups of experts established by the Council, as relevant to the implementation of its mandate;

24. *Also requests* the Panel of Experts to assess in its midterm update and its final report progress towards reducing violations by all parties of the measures imposed by paragraphs 7 and 8 of resolution 1556 (2004), paragraph 7 of resolution 1591 (2005) and paragraph 10 of resolution 1945 (2010) and progress towards removing impediments to the political process, threats to stability in Darfur and the region; violations of international humanitarian law or violations or abuses of human rights, including those that involve attacks on the civilian population, sexual and gender-based violence and violations and abuses against children, and other violations of the above-mentioned resolutions, and to provide the Committee with information on the individuals and entities that meet the listing criteria in paragraph 3 (*c*) of resolution 1591 (2005);

Sanctions committee

25. *Reaffirms* the mandate of the Committee to encourage dialogue with interested Member States, in particular those in the region, including by inviting representatives of such States to meet with the Committee to

discuss implementation of the measures, and further encourages the Committee to continue its dialogue with the African Union-United Nations Hybrid Operation in Darfur;

26. *Emphasizes* the importance of holding regular consultations with concerned Member States, as may be necessary, in order to ensure full implementation of the measures set forth in the present resolution;

27. *Decides* to remain actively seized of the matter.

Adopted unanimously at the 7380th meeting.

Decisions

At its 7392nd meeting, on 24 February 2015, the Security Council decided to invite the representative of South Sudan to participate, without vote, in accordance with rule 37 of its provisional rules of procedure, in the discussion of the item entitled:

"Reports of the Secretary-General on the Sudan and South Sudan

"Report of the Secretary-General on South Sudan (S/2015/118)".

At the same meeting, the Council also decided to extend invitations, in accordance with rule 39 of its provisional rules of procedure, to Mr. Hervé Ladsous, Under-Secretary-General for Peacekeeping Operations, and Mr. Ivan Šimonović, Assistant Secretary-General for Human Rights.

At its 7393rd meeting, on 26 February 2015, the Council decided to invite the representatives of South Sudan and the Sudan to participate, without vote, in accordance with rule 37 of its provisional rules of procedure, in the discussion of the item entitled:

"Reports of the Secretary-General on the Sudan and South Sudan

"Report of the Secretary-General on the situation in Abyei (S/2015/77)".

Resolution 2205 (2015) of 26 February 2015

The Security Council,

Recalling its previous resolutions and the statements by its President on the situation in the Sudan and South Sudan, in particular resolutions 1990 (2011) of 27 June 2011, 2024 (2011) of 14 December 2011, 2032 (2011) of 22 December 2011, 2046 (2012) of 2 May 2012, 2047 (2012)) of 17 May 2012, 2075 (2012) of 16 November 2012, 2104 (2013) of 29 May 2013, 2126 (2013) of 25 November 2013, 2156 (2014) of 29 May 2014 and 2179 (2014) of 14 October 2014, as well as the statements by its President of 31 August 2012[271] and 23 August 2013[272] and its statements to the press of 18 June, 21 and 28 September 2012, 6 May and 14 June 2013 and 14 February, 17 March and 11 December 2014,

Reaffirming its strong commitment to the sovereignty, independence, unity and territorial integrity of the Sudan and South Sudan and to the purposes and principles of the Charter of the United Nations, and recalling the importance of the principles of good-neighbourliness, non-interference and regional cooperation,

Reiterating that the territorial boundaries of States shall not be altered by force and that any territorial disputes shall be settled exclusively by peaceful means, affirming the priority it attaches to the full and urgent implementation of all outstanding issues from the Comprehensive Peace Agreement of 9 January 2005,[273] and underscoring that the future status of Abyei shall be resolved by negotiations between the parties in a manner consistent with the Agreement and not by the unilateral actions of either party,

Recalling the commitments made by the Government of the Sudan and the Government of South Sudan in the Agreement between the Government of the Sudan and the Sudan People's Liberation Movement on Temporary Arrangements for the Administration and Security of the Abyei Area of 20 June 2011,[274] the Agreement between the Government of the Sudan and the Government of Southern Sudan on Border Security and the Joint Political and Security Mechanism of 29 June 2011 and the Agreement on the Border Monitoring Support Mission between the Government of the Sudan and the Government of South Sudan of 30 July 2011,[275] as well as the agreements on cooperation and security arrangements of 27 September 2012,[276] the decision of the Joint Political and Security

Mechanism of 8 March 2013 and the implementation matrix of 12 March 2013,[277] reached by the Government of the Sudan and the Government of South Sudan in Addis Ababa under the auspices of the African Union High-level Implementation Panel,

Expressing its full support for the efforts of the African Union on the situation between the Sudan and South Sudan, in order to ease the current tension and facilitate the resumption of negotiations on post-secession relations and the normalization of their relations, recalling in this regard the African Union Peace and Security Council communiqués of 24 April[278] and 24 October 2012, 25 January, 7 May, 29 July, 23 September, 26 October and 12 November 2013 and 12 September 2014, its press statement of 6 November 2013 and the statement made by the Chairperson of the African Union Commission on 28 October 2013,

Reaffirming its previous resolutions 1265 (1999) of 17 September 1999, 1296 (2000) of 19 April 2000, 1674 (2006) of 28 April 2006, 1738 (2006) of 23 December 2006, 1894 (2009) of 11 November 2009 and 2175 (2014) of 29 August 2014 on the protection of civilians in armed conflict; its resolutions 1612 (2005) of 26 July 2005, 1882 (2009) of 4 August 2009, 1998 (2011) of 12 July 2011, 2068 (2012) of 19 September 2012 and 2143 (2014) of 7 March 2014 on children and armed conflict; its resolution 1502 (2003) of 26 August 2003 on the protection of humanitarian and United Nations personnel; and its resolutions 1325 (2000) of 31 October 2000, 1820 (2008) of 19 June 2008, 1888 (2009) of 30 September 2009, 1889 (2009) of 5 October 2009, 1960 (2010) of 16 December 2010, 2106 (2013) of 24 June 2013 and 2122 (2013) of 18 October 2013 on women and peace and security,

Stressing the need for effective human rights monitoring, including of any sexual and gender-based violence and violations and abuses committed against women and children, taking note that there have been no developments with regard to the operationalization of human rights monitoring in the Abyei Area, and reiterating its concern at the lack of cooperation by the parties with the Secretary-General to this end,

Recalling that in its resolution 2086 (2013) of 21 January 2013 it reiterated the importance, when establishing and renewing the mandates of United Nations missions, of including provisions on the promotion of gender equality and the empowerment of women in post-conflict situations and on children and armed conflict, and emphasizing that persistent barriers to full implementation of resolution 1325 (2000) will only be dismantled through dedicated commitment to women's empowerment, participation and human rights, and through concerted leadership, consistent information and action, and support, to build women's engagement in all levels of decision-making,

Noting with concern the minimum attention the parties have given to the management of the Abyei Area as well as the stalled efforts by the Government of the Sudan and the Government of South Sudan to demilitarize the Safe Demilitarized Border Zone, including the "14-mile area", and to fully implement the Joint Border Verification and Monitoring Mechanism, in accordance with Security Council resolution 2046 (2012) and the African Union Peace and Security Council road map of 24 April 2012,[278] including as a result of South Sudan's continued disagreement with the location of the centreline of the Zone, the temporary unavailability of aircraft, the denial of security clearances and the tense security situation in the vicinity of Kadugli,

Underlining the importance of fully establishing and maintaining effective monitoring by the Joint Border Verification and Monitoring Mechanism of the Safe Demilitarized Border Zone, including the 14-mile area,

Welcoming further regular meetings between President Bashir and President Kiir for continuing dialogue, recalling the decision in resolution 2046 (2012) that the parties must resume immediately negotiations to reach agreement on the final status of Abyei under the auspices of the African Union High-level Implementation Panel, calling upon all parties to engage constructively in the process mediated by the Implementation Panel towards final agreement on the final status of the Abyei Area, and stressing that the parties must immediately implement pending aspects of the Agreement of 20 June 2011, in particular to resolve the dispute over the Abyei Area Council and immediately establish the Abyei Area Administration and Abyei Police Service,

Stressing that both countries will have much to gain if they show restraint and choose the path of dialogue instead of resorting to violence or provocations,

Commending the continued assistance provided to the parties by the African Union High-level Implementation Panel, the Intergovernmental Authority on Development, Ethiopia, the Special Envoy of the Secretary-General for the Sudan and South Sudan and the United Nations Interim Security Force for Abyei,

Further commending the efforts of the Force in effectively carrying out its mandate, including by its ongoing facilitation of peaceful migration throughout the Abyei Area, conflict prevention, mediation and deterrence, expressing its deep appreciation for the work of the troop-contributing countries, strongly condemning the attacks on United Nations personnel, and calling for investigations of these attacks in a swift and thorough manner and to hold those responsible to account,

Underscoring concern for the fragility of the security situation in the Abyei Area, acknowledging the contribution of the Force to enhanced peace and stability since its deployment, and expressing its determination to prevent the recurrence of violence against or displacements of civilians and to avert intercommunal conflict,

Reiterating its deep concern regarding the public administration and rule of law vacuum in the Abyei Area, due to continued delays in the establishment of the Abyei Area Administration, Council and Police Service, including a special unit to deal with particular issues related to nomadic migration, which are essential to maintain law and order and prevent intercommunal conflict in Abyei,

Noting with concern the continued delay in establishing the temporary institutions and resolving the final status of Abyei and that the continued threat of intercommunal violence contributes to heightened tensions in the Abyei Area, including those ongoing tensions that prevent Sudanese staff of the Force and other agencies from returning to Abyei,

Urging all parties to refrain from any unilateral action that could aggravate intercommunal relations within the Abyei Area, expressing concern over the continued implications of what the Peace and Security Council described in its press statement of 6 November 2013 as "the decision by the Ngok Dinka to conduct a unilateral referendum", and also in this context taking note that, according to the report of the Secretary-General of 30 January 2015[292] the Government of the Sudan is proceeding with the preparations for the organization of its national elections in Abyei,

Bearing in mind the current humanitarian situation, in which humanitarian actors continue to provide assistance to approximately 81,000 people in the Abyei Area, and the importance of coherence of United Nations assistance in the region, and further stressing the urgency of facilitating the delivery of humanitarian assistance to all affected populations,

Affirming the importance of voluntary, safe, orderly return and sustainable reintegration of displaced persons, and of peaceful and orderly migration cycles respecting the traditional migratory routes from the Sudan to South Sudan through Abyei, and urging the Force to continue to take measures as necessary to ensure security in the Abyei Area in accordance with its mandate,

Recalling its resolution 2117 (2013) of 26 September 2013, and expressing grave concern at the threat to peace and security in Abyei arising from the illicit transfer, destabilizing accumulation and misuse of small arms and light weapons,

Expressing concern about the residual threat of landmines and explosive remnants of war in the Abyei Area, which hinders the safe return of displaced persons to their homes and safe migration,

Taking note of the report of the Secretary-General of 30 January 2015, including the assessment that the political and security situation on the ground is increasingly tense and requires dialogue and cooperation to prevent it becoming more contentious, divisive and destabilizing in the coming months, and the recommendations contained therein,

Recognizing that the current situation in Abyei and along the border between the Sudan and South Sudan continues to constitute a serious threat to international peace and security,

1. *Decides* to extend until 15 July 2015 the mandate of the United Nations Interim Security Force for Abyei as set out in paragraph 2 of resolution 1990 (2011) and modified by resolution 2024 (2011) and paragraph 1 of resolution 2075 (2012), and, acting under Chapter VII of the Charter of the United Nations, further decides to extend until 15 July 2015 the tasks of the Force as set out in paragraph 3 of resolution 1990 (2011), and determines that, for the purposes of paragraph 1 of resolution 2024 (2011), support to the operational activities of the Joint Border Verification and Monitoring Mechanism shall include support to the Ad Hoc Committees, as appropriate when so requested by consensual decisions of these mechanisms, within the operational area and existing capabilities of the Force;

---

[292] S/2015/77.

2. *Takes note* of the recommendations in the report of the Secretary-General of 30 January 2015,[292] and welcomes the initiatives of the Force to support resumption of community dialogue and administration by the communities under the supervision of the Abyei Joint Oversight Committee; in this regard calls upon the communities and the Governments of the Sudan and South Sudan to take concrete steps towards those goals; and further welcomes the current and future support in these efforts from the United Nations, the African Union and the Government of Ethiopia;

3. *Underscores* that continued cooperation between the Government of the Sudan and the Government of South Sudan is also critical for peace, security and stability and the future relations between them;

4. *Reiterates its demand* that the Sudan and South Sudan immediately resume the work of the Abyei Joint Oversight Committee, without preconditions, welcomes the Government of South Sudan's decision on 4 December 2014 to name an Oversight Committee Co-Chair to ensure steady progress on the implementation of the Agreement on Temporary Arrangements for the Administration and Security of the Abyei Area of 20 June 2011,[274] including the implementation of the decisions of the Oversight Committee, welcomes African Union initiatives to support this goal and encourages its continued engagement, and requests the Secretary-General to provide an assessment of progress on these issues in his regular reports;

5. *Further reiterates its demand* that the Sudan and South Sudan urgently commence the establishment of the Abyei Area Administration and Council, including by resolving the deadlock over the composition of the Council, and constitute the Abyei Police Service, to enable it to take over policing functions throughout the Abyei Area, including the protection of oil infrastructure, in accordance with their commitments in the Agreement of 20 June 2011;

6. *Decides* to maintain the troops authorized by resolution 2104 (2013) already deployed, and that the remaining authorized forces shall continue to be deployed consistent with the evolution of the Joint Border Verification and Monitoring Mechanism, to enable the Force to provide required force protection to the Mechanism and to enable the Force to fully support the Mechanism to conduct extended operations into the Safe Demilitarized Border Zone as soon as possible, and requests the Secretary-General to keep the Security Council fully updated on the status of deployment as part of his regular reporting cycle;

7. *Expresses concern* regarding the stalled efforts to fully operationalize the Joint Border Verification and Monitoring Mechanism, welcomes the forthcoming detailed assessment of the Secretary-General and expresses its intention to consider the recommendations regarding operations of the Mechanism, and calls upon the Government of the Sudan and the Government of South Sudan to make timely and effective use of the Joint Border Verification and Monitoring Mechanism, the Joint Political and Security Mechanism and other agreed joint mechanisms to ensure the security and transparency of the Safe Demilitarized Border Zone, including the 14-mile area;

8. *Urges* renewed efforts to determine conclusively the centreline of the Safe Demilitarized Border Zone on the ground, and reiterates that the centreline of the Zone in no way prejudices the current or future legal status of the border, ongoing negotiations on the disputed and claimed areas, and demarcation of the borders;

9. *Underscores* that the protection of civilians mandate of the Force as set out in paragraph 3 of resolution 1990 (2011), includes taking the actions necessary to protect civilians under imminent threat of physical violence, irrespective of the source of such violence;

10. *Condemns* the presence of Diffra oil police units deployed in the Abyei Area, as well as the repeated entry of armed militias into the territory, and reiterates its demands that immediately and without preconditions the Government of the Sudan redeploy the oil police in Diffra from the Abyei Area, and further reiterates, in accordance with relevant resolutions, in particular resolutions 1990 (2011) and 2046 (2012), that the Abyei Area shall be demilitarized from any forces, as well as armed elements of the local communities, other than the Force and the Abyei Police Service;

11. *Supports* the decision of the Abyei Joint Oversight Committee of 3 May 2013 on Abyei's status as a weapons-free area, underscores the concern expressed by the African Union Peace and Security Council in its communiqué of 7 May 2013 over reports that various communities living in Abyei are heavily armed, recalls that in the Agreement of 20 June 2011 it is stipulated that Abyei should be a weapons-free area and that only the Force is authorized to carry weapons inside the Area, and in this regard urges the two Governments to take all steps necessary to ensure that Abyei is effectively demilitarized, including through disarmament programmes as necessary;

12. *Affirms* that the Force may undertake weapons confiscation and destruction in the Abyei Area as authorized under resolution 1990 (2011), consistent with its mandate and within its existing capabilities, in coordination with the signatories of the Agreement of 20 June 2011, the Abyei Joint Oversight Committee and the Misseriya and Ngok Dinka communities and consistent with the previous decision of the Oversight Committee to establish the Area as a "weapons-free area", and reiterates its request that the Force observe, document and report on the movement of weapons into Abyei and the presence, destruction and confiscation of weapons within Abyei as part of the Secretary-General's regular reporting cycle;

13. *Requests* the Force to continue its dialogue with the Abyei Joint Oversight Committee and with the Misseriya and Ngok Dinka communities on effective strategies and oversight mechanisms for ensuring full compliance by all relevant parties with Abyei's status as a weapons-free area, with a particular priority placed on the urgent elimination of heavy or crew-served weapons, as well as rocket-propelled grenades, and calls upon the Governments of the Sudan and South Sudan, the Oversight Committee and the Misseriya and Ngok Dinka communities to extend full cooperation to the Force in this regard;

14. *Urges* the two Governments immediately to take steps to implement confidence-building measures among the respective communities in the Abyei Area, including through reconciliation processes at the grass-roots level and supporting the Force in promoting community dialogue and in convening a peace conference between the Ngok Dinka and Misseriya traditional chiefs, and strongly urges all Abyei communities to exercise maximum restraint in all their engagements and to desist from inflammatory acts or statements that may lead to violent clashes, or any further unilateral activities;

15. *Requests* the Force, within its existing capabilities and resources and in close coordination with the Misseriya and Ngok Dinka communities, to strengthen the capacities of community protection committees in order to assist with the management of law and order processes in Abyei;

16. *Calls upon* all parties to cooperate fully with the findings and recommendations following the investigation by the Abyei Area Joint Investigation and Inquiry Committee into the killing of a Force peacekeeper and the Ngok Dinka Paramount Chief, and reiterates the need to enable the two communities find closure on the assassination of the Ngok Dinka Paramount Chief;

17. *Expresses its intention* to review, as appropriate, the mandate of the Force for possible reconfiguration of the mission in the light of the compliance by the Sudan and South Sudan with the decisions set forth in resolution 2046 (2012) and their commitments as set forth in the Agreements of 20 and 29 June and 30 July 2011[275] and 27 September 2012,[276] including the redeployment of all forces from the Safe Demilitarized Border Zone, achieving full operational capability for the Joint Border Verification and Monitoring Mechanism and the Ad Hoc Committees, as well as completing the full demilitarization of the Abyei Area;

18. *Calls upon* all Member States, in particular the Sudan and South Sudan, to ensure the free, unhindered and expeditious movement to and from Abyei and throughout the Safe Demilitarized Border Zone of all personnel, as well as equipment, provisions, supplies and other goods, including vehicles, aircraft and spare parts, which are for the exclusive and official use of the Force;

19. *Renews its call upon* the Governments of the Sudan and South Sudan to provide full support to the United Nations, including by promptly issuing visas to military, police and civilian United Nations personnel, including humanitarian personnel, without prejudice to their nationality, for entry into the Sudan and South Sudan, facilitating basing arrangements and flight clearances, and providing logistical support, calls upon the Governments of the Sudan and South Sudan to facilitate travel from within the Sudan and South Sudan to and from Abyei, and further calls upon all parties to fully adhere to their obligations under the status-of-forces agreements;

20. *Recognizes* that the absence of development projects and the inability to deliver basic government services has had an adverse effect on Abyei populations, and calls upon the Government of the Sudan and the Government of South Sudan, as well as donors, to support reconstruction and capacity-building;

21. *Demands* that the Government of the Sudan and the Government of South Sudan continue to facilitate the deployment of the Mine Action Service of the United Nations to ensure the freedom of movement of the Joint Border Verification and Monitoring Mechanism as well as the identification and clearance of mines in the Abyei Area and the Safe Demilitarized Border Zone;

22. *Also demands* that all parties involved allow and facilitate all humanitarian personnel with full, safe and unhindered access to civilians in need of assistance and all facilities necessary for their operations, in accordance with international law, including applicable international humanitarian law, and United Nations guiding principles of humanitarian assistance;

23. *Strongly urges* that all parties cease all forms of violence, human rights violations and abuses, violations of international humanitarian law and violations and abuses against children in violation of applicable international law;

24. *Requests* the Secretary-General to ensure that effective human rights monitoring is carried out and the results included in his reports to the Security Council, and reiterates its call upon the Government of the Sudan and the Government of South Sudan to extend their full cooperation to the Secretary-General to this end, including by issuing visas to the concerned United Nations personnel;

25. *Also requests* the Secretary-General to take the measures necessary to ensure full compliance of the Force with the United Nations zero-tolerance policy on sexual exploitation and abuse and to keep the Council informed if cases of such conduct occur;

26. *Welcomes* the appointment of the civilian Head of Mission for the Force, and encourages close communication and coordination with the Force Commander, United Nations country teams and diplomatic communities of Khartoum and Juba, as well as civil society, the African Union and the Government of Ethiopia;

27. *Requests* the Secretary-General to continue to inform the Council of progress in implementing the mandate of the Force in two written reports, no later than 1 May 2015 and 15 June 2015 respectively, and continue to bring to the Council's immediate attention any serious violations of the above-referenced agreements;

28. *Notes* the efforts of the Secretary-General to ensure close cooperation among United Nations missions in the region, including the Force, the United Nations Mission in South Sudan and the African Union-United Nations Hybrid Operation in Darfur, as well as his Special Envoy for the Sudan and South Sudan, and requests that he continue this practice;

29. *Decides* to remain actively seized of this matter.

Adopted unanimously at the 7393rd meeting.

Decision

At its 7396th meeting, on 3 March 2015, the Security Council decided to invite the representatives of Australia, Luxembourg, Norway and South Sudan to participate, without vote, in accordance with rule 37 of its provisional rules of procedure, in the discussion of the item entitled "Reports of the Secretary-General on the Sudan and South Sudan".

Resolution 2206 (2015)
of 3 March 2015

The Security Council,

Recalling its previous resolutions and statements on South Sudan, in particular resolutions 2057 (2012) of 5 July 2012, 2109 (2013) of 11 July 2013, 2132 (2013) of 24 December 2013, 2155 (2014) of 27 May 2014 and 2187 (2014) of 25 November 2014,

Expressing grave alarm and concern regarding the conflict between the Government of South Sudan and opposition forces since December 2013 which emanated from internal political disputes among the country's political and military leaders,

Deeply concerned that the conflict has resulted in great human suffering, including significant loss of life, displacement of 2 million people and the loss of property, further impoverishing and disadvantaging the people of South Sudan,

Strongly condemning past and ongoing human rights violations and abuses and violations of international humanitarian law, including those involving targeted killings of civilians, ethnically targeted violence, extrajudicial killings, rape and other forms of sexual and gender-based violence, recruitment and use of children in armed conflict, abductions, enforced disappearances, arbitrary arrests and detention, violence aimed at spreading terror among the civilian population, and attacks on schools, places of worship and hospitals, as well as United Nations and associated peacekeeping personnel and objects, by all parties, including armed groups and national security forces, as well as the incitement to commit such abuses and violations, further condemning harassment and targeting of civil society, humanitarian personnel and journalists, and emphasizing that those responsible for violations of international humanitarian law and violations and abuses of human rights must be held accountable and that the Government of South Sudan bears the primary responsibility to protect its population from genocide, war crimes, ethnic cleansing and crimes against humanity,

Expressing deep concern over the large-scale displacement of persons and deepening humanitarian crisis, stressing the responsibility borne by all parties to the conflict for the suffering of the people of South Sudan, and the necessity of ensuring that the basic needs of the population are met, commending United Nations humanitarian agencies and partners for their efforts to provide urgent and coordinated support to the population, calling upon all parties to the conflict to allow and facilitate, in accordance with relevant provisions of international law and United Nations guiding principles of humanitarian assistance, the full, safe and unhindered access of relief personnel, equipment and supplies to all those in need and the timely delivery of humanitarian assistance, in particular to internally displaced persons and refugees, condemning all attacks against humanitarian personnel and facilities, and recalling that attacks against humanitarian personnel and depriving civilians of objects indispensable to their survival may amount to violations of international humanitarian law,

Commending the Intergovernmental Authority on Development Ministerial Group initiative, as supported by the United Nations and the African Union, in establishing a forum for political and security dialogue, and expecting all parties to participate in this process and respect the decisions reached by the Assembly of Heads of State and Government of the Intergovernmental Authority on 13 March 2014,

Welcoming the Intergovernmental Authority on Development-mediated commitments made to resolve the crisis in South Sudan, namely the cessation of hostilities agreement of 23 January 2014, the Agreement to Resolve the Crisis in South Sudan of 9 May 2014 and the Areas of Agreement on the Establishment of the Transitional Government of National Unity in the Republic of South Sudan of 1 February 2015,

Welcoming also the resolve indicated in the communiqués of the Assembly of Heads of State and Government of the Intergovernmental Authority on Development of 10 June and 25 August 2014 that States members of the Intergovernmental Authority would take further collective action, including through the imposition of punitive measures, to pressure any party that fails to honour its commitments to date or acts contrary to the communiqués of that Assembly,

Welcoming further the communiqué of the African Union Peace and Security Council of 12 June 2014, which, inter alia, reiterated the readiness of that Council, upon recommendation by the Intergovernmental Authority on Development, to immediately pursue targeted sanctions and other measures against any party that continues to undermine the search for a solution to the conflict and fails to honour its commitments,

Welcoming the communiqué of the African Union Peace and Security Council of 17 September 2014, which, inter alia, reiterated its determination, in coordination with the Intergovernmental Authority on Development, to take the necessary measures against any party that fails to honour its commitments and continues to undermine the search for a negotiated solution to the current crisis,

Strongly condemning the Government of South Sudan and the Sudan People's Liberation Movement (in Opposition) for failing to reach agreement to form a transitional government within the 60-day period outlined in the communiqué of the twenty-sixth extraordinary session of the Assembly of Heads of State and Government of the Intergovernmental Authority on Development, held in Addis Ababa on 10 June 2014,

Taking note of the communiqué of the twenty-seventh extraordinary session of the Assembly of Heads of State and Government of the Intergovernmental Authority on Development, held in Addis Ababa on 25 August 2014, which, inter alia, deplored the numerous violations of the agreements signed by the parties to date, reiterated the need for an inclusive and broad-based approach to negotiations; expressed serious concerns over the worsening humanitarian situation in South Sudan, and called upon the stakeholders to negotiate and complete the agreement on a Transitional Government of National Unity within 45 days,

Taking note also of the communiqué of the twenty-eighth extraordinary session of the Assembly of Heads of State and Government of the Intergovernmental Authority on Development, held in Addis Ababa on

7 November 2014, which, inter alia, resolved that the Government of South Sudan and opposition forces commit to an unconditional, complete and immediate end to all hostilities; invited collective action by the States of the Intergovernmental Authority region to enact asset freezes and travel bans within the region, and denied the supply of arms and ammunition and any other materiel that could be used in war if the Government of South Sudan and opposition forces commit any violation of the cessation of hostilities; and called upon the African Union Peace and Security Council, the United Nations Security Council and the international community to render all possible assistance in the implementation of these measures, should it be necessary to implement these measures,

Taking note further of the Agreement on the Reunification of the Sudan People's Liberation Movement of 21 January 2015, agreed under the aegis of the Government of the United Republic of Tanzania, and the communiqué of 16 February 2015 of the Meeting of the Sudan People's Liberation Movement Tripartite Committee on the Implementation of Phase I of the Arusha Sudan People's Liberation Movement Reunification Agreement,

Taking note of the communiqués of the African Union Peace and Security Council of 5 December 2014 and 29 January 2015, which, inter alia, stressed that sanctions would be imposed against all parties that continue to obstruct the political process and undermine the cessation of hostilities agreement of 23 January 2014,

Welcoming the China-mediated "Five-Point Plan" agreed upon by the representatives of the Government of South Sudan and the Sudan People's Liberation Movement/Army (in Opposition) during the special consultation in support of the Intergovernmental Authority on Development-led South Sudan peace process, convened on 12 January 2015 in Khartoum, namely (i) earnestly commit to the full implementation of all signed agreements; (ii) speed up the pace of negotiations towards the formation of a transitional government at an early date; (iii) take concrete steps to relieve the humanitarian situation in conflict-affected areas and facilitate access of international humanitarian assistance; (iv) ensure the safety of all personnel and assets of all countries and international entities operating in South Sudan; and (v) provide strong support for and take active part in the Intergovernmental Authority on Development-led mediation efforts, and in this regard strongly urging both parties to immediately implement the Five-Point Plan,

Expressing its deep appreciation for the actions taken by the United Nations Mission in South Sudan peacekeepers and troop- and police-contributing countries to protect civilians, including foreign nationals, under threat of physical violence and to stabilize the security situation,

Recognizing the importance of independent and public human rights monitoring, investigation and reporting for its useful role in laying the groundwork for justice, accountability, reconciliation and healing among all South Sudanese communities,

Taking note with interest of the United Nations Mission in South Sudan interim human rights report of 21 February 2014, its report of 8 May 2014 entitled "Conflict in South Sudan: a human rights report", its report of 19 December 2014 entitled "Special report: attack on Bentiu, Unity State, 29 October 2014" and its report of 9 January 2015 entitled "Attacks on civilians in Bentiu and Bor, April 2014",

Expressing grave concern that, according to the report of the Mission of 8 May 2014, there are reasonable grounds to believe that crimes against humanity, including extrajudicial killings, rape and other acts of sexual violence, enforced disappearances and arbitrary detention, have been committed by both government and opposition forces, and that war crimes have been committed, and stressing the urgent and imperative need to end impunity in South Sudan and to bring to justice perpetrators of such crimes,

Stressing the importance of accountability, reconciliation and healing as prominent elements of a transitional agenda, while taking note of the important role that international investigations and, where appropriate, prosecutions can play with respect to holding to account those responsible for war crimes and crimes against humanity,

Recognizing the work of the African Union Commission of Inquiry on South Sudan in investigating and documenting violations as well as abuses of international human rights law and international humanitarian law in South Sudan, anticipating with interest its findings and recommendations, encouraging the public release of its final report as soon as possible, and welcoming the further engagement of the African Union to ensure justice and accountability, as well as healing and reconciliation for South Sudan,

Strongly condemning the use of media to broadcast hate speech and transmit messages instigating sexual violence against a particular ethnic group, which has the potential to play a significant role in promoting mass violence and exacerbating conflict, calling upon the Government of South Sudan to take appropriate measures to address such activity, and further urging all parties to desist from these actions and instead to contribute to promoting peace and reconciliation among the communities,

Recognizing the important role played by civil society organizations, faith leaders, women and youth in South Sudan, underscoring the importance of their participation – along with the former Sudan People's Liberation Movement detainees and other political parties – to finding a sustainable solution to the crisis in the country, and concerned by efforts by the Government of South Sudan to limit such participation, including by preventing individuals from travelling to join the talks and by increased restrictions of freedom of expression,

Reaffirming all its relevant resolutions on women and peace and security, on children and armed conflict and on the protection of civilians in armed conflict, as well as resolution 1502 (2003) of 26 August 2003 on the protection of humanitarian and United Nations personnel, resolution 2150 (2014) of 16 April 2014 on the prevention of and fight against genocide and resolution 2151 (2014) of 28 April 2014 on security sector reform,

Recalling resolutions 1209 (1998) of 19 November 1998 and 2117 (2013) of 26 September 2013, and expressing grave concern at the threat to peace and security in South Sudan arising from the illicit transfer, destabilizing accumulation and misuse of small arms and light weapons, and emphasizing the importance of strengthening efforts to combat the illicit circulation of such weapons,

Expressing deep concern at persistent restrictions placed upon the movement and operations of the United Nations Mission in South Sudan, strongly condemning the attacks by Government and opposition forces and other groups on United Nations and Intergovernmental Authority on Development personnel and facilities, and the detentions and kidnappings of United Nations and associated personnel, and calling upon the Government of South Sudan to complete its investigations of these attacks in a swift and thorough manner and to hold those responsible to account,

Determining that the situation in South Sudan continues to constitute a threat to international peace and security in the region,

Acting under Article 41 of Chapter VII of the Charter of the United Nations,

1. *Endorses* the cessation of hostilities agreements accepted and signed by the Government of South Sudan and the Sudan People's Liberation Movement (in Opposition) on 23 January and 6 and 9 May 2014;

2. *Expresses deep concern* at the failure of both parties to honour their commitments to date, to engage the peace process meaningfully toward political resolution of the crisis and to bring an end to the violence, and, in particular, condemns the continued and flagrant violations of the cessation of hostilities agreements as documented by the Intergovernmental Authority on Development Monitoring and Verification Mechanism;

3. *Demands* that the parties respect all aspects of the cessation of hostilities agreements and immediately implement the necessary modalities in accordance with the agreement of 9 May 2014 and other relevant agreements, including the progressive withdrawal of foreign forces deployed in South Sudan since 15 December 2013, calls upon all parties to armed conflict in South Sudan to issue clear orders prohibiting all violations of international humanitarian law and human rights violations and abuses, and underscores the necessity for all parties to ensure immediate access to humanitarian agencies and further demands that the parties commit to finding a comprehensive agreement without further delay;

4. *Reiterates* that there is no military solution to the conflict;

Sanctions designation criteria

5. *Underscores its willingness* to impose targeted sanctions in order to support the search for an inclusive and sustainable peace in South Sudan;

6. *Decides* that the provisions of paragraph 9 below shall apply to individuals and that the provisions of paragraph 12 below shall apply to individuals and entities, as designated for such measures by the Security Council Committee established pursuant to paragraph 16 of the present resolution (the Committee) pursuant to paragraphs 16 (*c*) and (*d*), respectively, as responsible for or complicit in, or having engaged in, directly or indirectly, actions or policies that threaten the peace, security or stability of South Sudan;

7. *Underscores* that such actions or policies as described in paragraph 6 above may include, but are not limited to:

(*a*) Actions or policies that have the purpose or effect of expanding or extending the conflict in South Sudan or obstructing reconciliation or peace talks or processes, including breaches of the cessation of hostilities agreement;

(*b*) Actions or policies that threaten transitional agreements or undermine the political process in South Sudan;

(*c*) Planning, directing or committing acts that violate applicable international human rights law or international humanitarian law, or acts that constitute human rights abuses, in South Sudan;

(*d*) The targeting of civilians, including women and children, through the commission of acts of violence (including killing, maiming, torture, or rape or other sexual violence), abduction, enforced disappearance, forced displacement or attacks on schools, hospitals, religious sites or locations where civilians are seeking refuge, or through conduct that would constitute a serious abuse or violation of human rights or a violation of international humanitarian law;

(*e*) The use or recruitment of children by armed groups or armed forces in the context of the armed conflict in South Sudan;

(*f*) The obstruction of the activities of international peacekeeping, diplomatic or humanitarian missions in South Sudan, including the Intergovernmental Authority on Development Monitoring and Verification Mechanism, or of the delivery or distribution of, or access to, humanitarian assistance;

(*g*) Attacks against United Nations missions, international security presences or other peacekeeping operations, or humanitarian personnel; or

(*h*) Acting for or on behalf of, directly or indirectly, an individual or entity designated by the Committee;

8. *Decides* that the provisions of paragraphs 9 and 12 of the present resolution shall apply to individuals, as designated for such measures by the Committee, who are leaders of any entity, including any Government of South Sudan, opposition, militia or other group that has, or whose members have, engaged in any of the activities described in paragraphs 6 and 7 above;

Travel ban

9. *Decides* that, for an initial period of one year from the date of adoption of the present resolution, all Member States shall take the measures necessary to prevent the entry into or transit through their territories of any individuals who may be designated by the Committee, provided that nothing in the present paragraph shall oblige a State to refuse its own nationals entry into its territory;

10. *Notes* that designated individuals may have multiple nationalities or passports, expresses its concern that travel between the two States of which a designated individual has nationality or a passport may undermine the objectives of the travel ban imposed in paragraph 9 above, and requests that the Panel of Experts on South Sudan established in paragraph 18 of the present resolution (the Panel of Experts) report to the Committee information about such travel;

11. *Decides* that the measures imposed by paragraph 9 above shall not apply:

(*a*) Where the Committee determines on a case-by-case basis that such travel is justified on the grounds of humanitarian need, including religious obligation;

(*b*) Where entry or transit is necessary for the fulfilment of a judicial process;

(*c*) Where the Committee determines on a case-by-case basis that an exemption would further the objectives of peace and national reconciliation in South Sudan and stability in the region;

Asset freeze

12. *Decides* that, for an initial period of one year from the date of adoption of the present resolution, all Member States shall freeze without delay all funds, other financial assets and economic resources which are on their territories, which are owned or controlled, directly or indirectly, by any individuals or entities that may be designated

by the Committee, or by any individuals or entities acting on their behalf or at their direction, or by entities owned or controlled by them, and decides further that all Member States shall for this initial period ensure that neither these nor any other funds, financial assets or economic resources are made available, directly or indirectly, for the benefit of such persons, by their nationals or by persons within their territory;

13. *Also decides* that the measures imposed by paragraph 12 above do not apply to funds, other financial assets or economic resources that have been determined by relevant Member States:

(*a*) To be necessary for basic expenses, including payment for foodstuffs, rent or mortgage, medicines and medical treatment, taxes, insurance premiums and public utility charges or exclusively for payment of reasonable professional fees and reimbursement of incurred expenses associated with the provision of legal services in accordance with national laws, or fees or service charges, in accordance with national laws, for routine holding or maintenance of frozen funds, other financial assets and economic resources, after notification by the relevant State to the Committee of the intention to authorize, where appropriate, access to such funds, other financial assets or economic resources and in the absence of a negative decision by the Committee within five working days of such notification;

(*b*) To be necessary for extraordinary expenses, provided that such determination has been notified by the relevant State or Member States to the Committee and has been approved by the Committee;

(*c*) To be the subject of a judicial, administrative or arbitral lien or judgment, in which case the funds, other financial assets and economic resources may be used to satisfy that lien or judgment, provided that the lien or judgment was entered into prior to the date of the present resolution, is not for the benefit of a person designated by the Committee and has been notified by the relevant State or Member States to the Committee;

14. *Further decides* that Member States may permit the addition to the accounts frozen pursuant to the provisions of paragraph 12 above of interest or other earnings due on those accounts or payments due under contracts, agreements or obligations that arose prior to the date on which those accounts became subject to the provisions of the present resolution, provided that any such interest, other earnings and payments continue to be subject to these provisions and are frozen;

15. *Decides* that the measures in paragraph 12 above shall not prevent a designated person from making payment due under a contract entered into prior to the listing of such a person, provided that the relevant States have determined that the payment is not directly or indirectly received by a person designated pursuant to paragraph 12 above, and after notification by the relevant States to the Committee of the intention to make or receive such payments or to authorize, where appropriate, the unfreezing of funds, other financial assets or economic resources for this purpose, 10 working days prior to such authorization;

Sanctions committee/Panel of Experts

16. *Decides* to establish, in accordance with rule 28 of its provisional rules of procedure, a Committee of the Security Council consisting of all the members of the Council (herein "the Committee"), to undertake the following tasks:

(*a*) To monitor implementation of the measures imposed by paragraphs 9 and 12 of the present resolution with a view to strengthening, facilitating and improving implementation of these measures by Member States;

(*b*) To seek and review information regarding those individuals and entities that may be engaging in the acts described in paragraphs 6 and 7 above;

(*c*) To designate individuals subject to the measures imposed by paragraph 9 above and to consider requests for exemptions in accordance with paragraph 11 above;

(*d*) To designate individuals and entities subject to the measures imposed by paragraph 12 above and to consider requests for exemptions in paragraph 13 above;

(*e*) To establish such guidelines as may be necessary to facilitate the implementation of the measures imposed above;

(*f*) To report within 60 days to the Council on its work and thereafter to report as deemed necessary by the Committee;

(*g*) To encourage a dialogue between the Committee and interested Member States, in particular those in the region, including by inviting representatives of such States to meet with the Committee to discuss implementation of the measures;

(*h*) To seek from all States whatever information it may consider useful regarding the actions taken by them to implement effectively the measures imposed;

(*i*) To examine and take appropriate action on information regarding alleged violations or non-compliance with the measures contained in the present resolution;

17. *Calls upon* all Member States to report to the Committee 90 days from the adoption of the present resolution on the steps they have taken to implement effectively paragraphs 9 and 12 of the present resolution;

18. *Requests* the Secretary-General to create for an initial period, 13 months from the adoption of the present resolution, in consultation with the Committee, a group of up to five experts (the Panel of Experts), under the direction of the Committee, and to make the necessary financial and security arrangements to support the work of the Panel, expresses its intent to consider the renewal of this mandate no later than 2 March 2016, and decides that the Panel shall carry out the following tasks:

(*a*) Assist the Committee in carrying out its mandate as specified in the present resolution, including through providing the Committee with information relevant to the potential designation of individuals and entities that may be engaging in the activities described in paragraphs 6 and 7 above;

(*b*) Gather, examine and analyse information regarding the implementation of the measures decided in the present resolution, in particular incidents of non-compliance, with particular focus on the benchmarks outlined in paragraphs 21 and 22 below;

(*c*) Gather, examine and analyse information regarding the supply, sale or transfer of arms and related materiel and related military or other assistance, including through illicit trafficking networks, to individuals and entities undermining political processes to reach a final peace agreement or participating in acts that violate international human rights law or international humanitarian law, as applicable;

(*d*) Provide to the Council, after discussion with the Committee, an interim report by 1 September 2015, a final report by 1 February 2016, and, except in the months when these reports are due, updates each month;

(*e*) Assist the Committee in refining and updating information on the list of individuals and entities subject to the measures imposed by the present resolution, including through the provision of identifying information and additional information for the publicly available narrative summary of reasons for listing;

19. *Urges* all parties and all Member States, as well as international, regional and subregional organizations, to ensure cooperation with the Panel of Experts, and further urges all Member States involved to ensure the safety of the members of the Panel and unhindered access, in particular to persons, documents and sites, in order for the Panel to execute its mandate;

20. *Requests* the Special Representative of the Secretary-General for Children and Armed Conflict and the Special Representative of the Secretary-General on Sexual Violence in Conflict to share relevant information with the Committee in accordance with paragraph 7 of resolution 1960 (2010) of 16 December 2010 and paragraph 9 of resolution 1998 (2011) of 12 July 2011;

Review

21. *Expresses its intent* to review the situation after the Intergovernmental Authority on Development-agreed deadline of 5 March 2015, and again after the envisioned start of the Pre-Transition Period on 1 April 2015, and at 60-day intervals thereafter or more frequently, as needed, and also expresses its intent to impose any sanctions that may then be appropriate to respond to the situation, which may include an arms embargo and the designation of senior individuals responsible for actions or policies that threaten the peace, security or stability of South Sudan, so as to encourage the Government of South Sudan and opposition forces to form a Transitional Government of National Unity, take effective and comprehensive steps to cause forces under direct or indirect control to cease military operations, acts of violence, as well as violations of human rights, and enable full access for humanitarian assistance;

22. *Affirms* that it shall be prepared to adjust the measures contained in the present resolution, including by strengthening through additional measures, as well as modification, suspension or lifting of the measures, as may be needed at any time in the light of the progress achieved in the peace, accountability and reconciliation process, and in the light of the implementation of the parties' commitments, including the cessation of hostilities agreement and other commitments specified in the preamble of the present resolution, and compliance with the present resolution;

23. *Decides* to remain seized of the matter.

Adopted unanimously at the 7396th meeting.

Decisions

At its 7405th meeting, on 17 March 2015, the Security Council decided to invite the representative of the Sudan to participate, without vote, in accordance with rule 37 of its provisional rules of procedure, in the discussion of the item entitled:

"Reports of the Secretary-General on the Sudan and South Sudan

"Report of the Secretary-General on the African Union-United Nations Hybrid Operation in Darfur (S/2015/141)

"Special report of the Secretary-General on the African Union-United Nations Hybrid Operation in Darfur (S/2015/163)".

At the same meeting, the Council also decided to extend an invitation, in accordance with rule 39 of its provisional rules of procedure, to Mr. Hervé Ladsous, Under-Secretary-General for Peacekeeping Operations.

At its 7413th meeting, on 24 March 2015, the Council decided to invite the representative of South Sudan to participate, without vote, in accordance with rule 37 of its provisional rules of procedure, in the discussion of the item entitled "Reports of the Secretary-General on the Sudan and South Sudan".

At the same meeting, following consultations among members of the Security Council, the President made the following statement on behalf of the Council:[293]

The Security Council underscores the seriousness and urgency of the situation in South Sudan, as demonstrated by its unanimous adoption on 3 March 2015 of resolution 2206 (2015) establishing a United Nations sanctions regime for those undermining the peace, security or stability of South Sudan, with initial dates for the Council's review of 5 March and 1 April 2015, demanding that the parties commit to finding a comprehensive agreement and calling upon all parties to armed conflict in South Sudan to issue clear orders prohibiting all violations of international humanitarian law and human rights violations and abuses without further delay.

In this regard, the Council expresses its profound disappointment that President Salva Kiir, former Vice-President Riek Machar and all parties have failed to conclude an agreement on the transitional arrangements outlined in the Areas of Agreement on the Establishment of the Transitional Government of National Unity in the Republic of South Sudan of 1 February 2015 signed by South Sudan and the Sudan People's Liberation Movement/Army (in Opposition) by the deadline of 5 March 2015 set by the Intergovernmental Authority on Development. In this context the Council reiterates its willingness to impose sanctions against those who threaten the peace, security or stability of South Sudan.

The Council reiterates its strong condemnation of the repeated violations of the cessation of hostilities agreement accepted and signed by South Sudan and the Sudan People's Liberation Movement/Army (in Opposition) on 23 January 2014, and emphasizes that the actions of President Salva Kiir and former Vice-President Riek Machar in continuing to pursue a military solution to this conflict are in breach of their obligations under the cessation of hostilities agreement.

The Council commends the Intergovernmental Authority on Development, as supported by the United Nations and the African Union, for its relentless work in establishing a forum for political and security

[293] S/PRST/2015/9.

dialogue, establishing and operationalizing the Monitoring and Verification Mechanism for the cessation of hostilities agreement, and leading multi-stakeholder political negotiations to establish a Transitional Government of National Unity.

The Council takes note of the message of 6 March 2015 from the Prime Minister of Ethiopia and Chairperson of the Intergovernmental Authority on Development, Mr. Hailemariam Dessalegn, to the people of South Sudan explaining that the peace talks did not produce the necessary breakthrough.

The Council welcomes the intention of the Intergovernmental Authority on Development, joined by the friends of South Sudan from Africa and abroad, including the United Nations, to implement a common plan and to table a reasonable and comprehensive solution to end the crisis in South Sudan and urges all parties to engage meaningfully in the peace process so to bring about a political resolution of the crisis and an end to the violence.

The Council reiterates its intent to impose any sanctions that may be appropriate to respond to the situation, which may include an arms embargo and the designation of senior individuals responsible for actions or policies that threaten the peace, security or stability of South Sudan, so as to encourage the Government of South Sudan and opposition forces to form a Transitional Government of National Unity, take effective and comprehensive steps to cause forces under direct or indirect control to cease military operations, acts of violence, as well as violations of human rights, and enable full access for humanitarian assistance.

The Council renews its deep appreciation for the courageous actions taken and ongoing by United Nations Mission in South Sudan personnel and troop- and police-contributing countries for the protection of civilians and the stabilization of the security situation, and reiterates its support for the Mission.

The Council reaffirms its deep concern that the conflict has resulted in great human suffering, including significant loss of life, displacement of 2 million people and the loss of property, further impoverishing and disadvantaging the people of South Sudan.

The Council further underscores the significant importance of fighting impunity and ensuring accountability for serious violations and abuses of human rights and violations of international humanitarian law in South Sudan, including those that may amount to war crimes and crimes against humanity.

The Council renews its calls for parties to the conflict to allow and facilitate, in accordance with relevant provisions of international law and United Nations guiding principles of humanitarian assistance, the full, safe and unhindered access of humanitarian personnel, equipment and supplies to all those in need and timely delivery of humanitarian assistance.

The Council recognizes the work of the African Union Commission of Inquiry on South Sudan in investigating and documenting violations as well as abuses of international human rights law and international humanitarian law, anticipates with interest its findings and recommendations, encourages the public release of the final report as soon as possible, and welcomes the further engagement of the African Union to ensure justice and accountability, as well as healing and reconciliation.

The Council looks forward to the rapid establishment of the Panel of Experts on South Sudan, which will play a central role in assisting the South Sudan sanctions committee established in resolution 2206 (2015), including by providing it with information relevant to the potential designation of individuals and entities that may be engaging in the activities described in paragraphs 6 and 7 of resolution 2206 (2015).

The Council reaffirms that it shall be prepared to adjust the measures contained in resolution 2206 (2015), including by strengthening through additional measures, as well as modification, suspension or lifting of the measures, as may be needed at any time in the light of the progress achieved in the peace, accountability, and reconciliation process, and in the light of the implementation of the parties' commitments, including the cessation of hostilities agreement and other obligations specified in the preamble of said resolution, and compliance with it.

The Council further reaffirms its support for the people of South Sudan, renews its steadfast commitment to the peace and security of South Sudan and the region, including through its full implementation of resolution 2206 (2015), and echoes the statement made by the Chairperson of the Intergovernmental Authority on Development on 6 March 2015 that the world stands with the people and peace will be achieved.

At its 7444th meeting, on 14 May 2015, the Council decided to invite the representative of South Sudan to participate, without vote, in accordance with rule 37 of its provisional rules of procedure, in the discussion of the item entitled:

"Reports of the Secretary-General on the Sudan and South Sudan

"Report of the Secretary-General on South Sudan (S/2015/296)".

At the same meeting, the Council also decided to extend an invitation, in accordance with rule 39 of its provisional rules of procedure, to Ms. Ellen Margrethe Løj, Special Representative of the Secretary-General for South Sudan and Head of the United Nations Mission in South Sudan.

At its 7451st meeting, on 28 May 2015, the Council considered the item entitled:

"Reports of the Secretary-General on the Sudan and South Sudan

"Report of the Secretary-General on South Sudan (S/2015/296)".

Resolution 2223 (2015)
of 28 May 2015

The Security Council,

Recalling its previous resolutions 1996 (2011) of 8 July 2011, 2046 (2012) of 2 May 2012, 2057 (2012) of 5 July 2012, 2109 (2013) of 11 July 2013, 2132 (2013) of 24 December 2013, 2155 (2014) of 27 May 2014, 2187 (2014) of 25 November 2014 and 2206 (2015) of 3 March 2015 and the statements by the President of the Security Council of 8 August 2014,[263] 15 December 2014[287] and 24 March 2015,[293]

Reaffirming its strong commitment to the sovereignty, independence, territorial integrity and national unity of South Sudan, and recalling the importance of the principles of non-interference, good-neighbourliness and regional cooperation,

Recalling its resolution 2086 (2013) of 21 January 2013 and reaffirming the basic principles of peacekeeping, including consent of the parties, impartiality and non-use of force except in self-defence and defence of the mandate, and recognizing that the mandate of each peacekeeping mission is specific to the need and situation of the country concerned,

Underscoring its grave alarm and concern regarding the worsening political, security and humanitarian crisis in South Sudan resulting from the internal Sudan People's Liberation Movement political dispute and subsequent violence caused by the country's political and military leaders,

Strongly condemning reported and ongoing human rights violations and abuses and violations of international humanitarian law, including those involving extrajudicial killings, ethnically targeted violence, rape and other forms of sexual and gender-based violence, recruitment and use of children, enforced disappearances, arbitrary arrests and detention, violence aimed at spreading terror among the civilian population, and attacks on schools, places of worship, hospitals and United Nations and associated peacekeeping personnel, by all parties, including armed groups and national security forces, as well as the incitement to commit such abuses and violations,

Further condemning harassment and targeting of civil society, humanitarian personnel and journalists, and emphasizing that those responsible for violations of international humanitarian law and violations and abuses of human rights must be held accountable and that the Government of South Sudan bears the primary responsibility to protect civilians within its territory and subject to its jurisdiction, including from potential crimes against humanity and war crimes,

Expressing serious and urgent concern over the more than 2 million displaced persons and deepening humanitarian crisis, stressing the responsibility borne by all parties to the conflict for the suffering of the people of South Sudan, and the necessity of ensuring that the basic needs of the population are met, and commending United Nations humanitarian agencies, partners and donors for their efforts to provide urgent and coordinated support to the population,

Recalling the need for all parties to the conflict to allow and facilitate, in accordance with relevant provisions of international law and United Nations guiding principles of humanitarian assistance, the full, safe and unhindered access of relief personnel, equipment and supplies to all those in need and timely delivery of humanitarian assistance, in particular to internally displaced persons and refugees,

Condemning all attacks against humanitarian personnel and facilities, and recalling that attacks against humanitarian personnel and depriving civilians of objects indispensable to their survival may amount to violations of international humanitarian law,

Commending the Intergovernmental Authority on Development initiative, as supported by the United Nations and the African Union, for its relentless work in establishing a forum for political and security dialogue, establishing and operationalizing the Monitoring and Verification Mechanism for the cessation of hostilities agreement, and leading multi-stakeholder political negotiations to establish a Transitional Government of National Unity,

Strongly condemning repeated and continuing violations of the cessation of hostilities agreement by all parties which undermine peace efforts, while stressing the continued importance of the cessation of hostilities and status of detainees agreements of 23 January 2014 mediated by the Intergovernmental Authority on Development, consensus on the declaration of principles between the parties, the establishment of the ceasefire Monitoring and Verification Mechanism, the Agreement to Resolve the Crisis in South Sudan of 9 May 2014, the rededication and implementation modalities for the cessation of hostilities agreement, of 9 November 2014, and the Areas of Agreement on the Establishment of the Transitional Government of National Unity in the Republic of South Sudan of 1 February 2015,

Taking note of the message of 6 March 2015 from the Prime Minister of Ethiopia and Chairperson of the Intergovernmental Authority on Development, Mr. Hailemariam Dessalegn, to the people of South Sudan, and expressing its profound disappointment that the parties have failed to reach an agreement on the arrangements outlined in the Areas of Agreement on the Establishment of the Transitional Government of National Unity in the Republic of South Sudan of 1 February 2015,

Looking forward to the renewed efforts by the Intergovernmental Authority on Development, joined by the friends of South Sudan from Africa and abroad, including the United Nations, to implement a common plan and to table a reasonable and comprehensive solution to end the crisis in South Sudan, and urges all parties to engage meaningfully in the peace process so as to bring about a political resolution of the crisis and an end to the violence, and in this regard further welcoming the decision of 24 March 2015 by the African Union Peace and Security Council forming the African Union High-level Ad Hoc Committee for South Sudan, and encouraging continued close cooperation between the United Nations, the Intergovernmental Authority and the African Union in mediation efforts and peace negotiations,

Expressing its deep appreciation for the actions taken by United Nations Mission in South Sudan peacekeepers and troop- and police-contributing countries to protect civilians, including foreign nationals, under threat of physical violence and to stabilize the security situation within and beyond Mission sites, and expressing appreciation for the efforts of the Mission to support internally displaced persons seeking protection on its sites, while underlining the necessity to find sustainable solutions for the internally displaced population, including in alternative safe and secure locations, and in keeping with the Guiding Principles on Internal Displacement,[283]

Taking note with interest of the reports on the human rights situation in South Sudan, including the report of the Secretary-General of 11 December 2014 on the situation of children in armed conflict in South Sudan,[294] and the reports of the United Nations Mission in South Sudan entitled "Special report: attack on Bentiu, Unity State, 29 October 2014", released on 19 December 2014, and "Attacks on civilians in Bentiu and Bor, April 2014", of 9 January 2015, in addition to its interim human rights report of 21 February 2014 and its report of 8 May 2014 entitled "Conflict in South Sudan: a human rights report",

Expressing grave concern that according to these reports there are reasonable grounds to believe that war crimes and crimes against humanity, including extrajudicial killings, rape and other acts of sexual violence, enforced disappearances, the use of children in armed conflict and arbitrary arrests and detention have been committed by both government and opposition forces, and noting that such crimes constitute actions that threaten the peace, security and stability of South Sudan,

[294] S/2014/884.

Stressing the increasingly urgent and imperative need to end impunity in South Sudan and to bring to justice perpetrators of such crimes, and further stressing the importance of accountability, reconciliation and healing in ending impunity and ensuring a sustainable peace,

Emphasizing that individuals or entities responsible for or complicit in, or having engaged in, directly or indirectly, actions or policies that threaten the peace, security or stability of South Sudan may be designated for targeted sanctions pursuant to resolution 2206 (2015), recalling its willingness to impose targeted sanctions, and noting with interest the press statement of 22 May 2015 by the African Union Peace and Security Council calling for urgent steps to designate individuals and entities under resolution 2206 (2015),

Recognizing the work of the African Union Commission of Inquiry on South Sudan in independent and public human rights monitoring, investigation and reporting, and the interim report the Commission of Inquiry, of 27 June 2014, anticipating with interest its findings and recommendations, and encouraging the public release of the final report on South Sudan as soon as possible,

Strongly condemning the use of media to broadcast hate speech and transmit messages instigating violence against a particular ethnic group, which has the potential to play a significant role in promoting mass violence and exacerbating conflict, calling upon the Government of South Sudan to take the appropriate measures in order to deter such activity, and further urging all parties to desist from these actions and instead to contribute to promoting peace and reconciliation among the communities,

Recognizing the important role played by civil society organizations, faith leaders, women and youth in South Sudan, underscoring the importance of their participation – along with the former Sudan People's Liberation Movement detainees and other political parties – to finding a sustainable solution to the crisis in the country, and concerned by efforts by all parties to limit such participation, including by preventing individuals from travelling to join the talks and by increased restrictions of freedom of expression,

Emphasizing that persistent barriers to full implementation of resolution 1325 (2000) of 31 October 2000 will only be dismantled through dedicated commitment to women's empowerment, participation and human rights, and through concerted leadership, consistent information and action, and support, to build women's engagement in all levels of decision-making,

Expressing deep concern at persistent restrictions placed upon the movement and operations of the Mission, including through repeated violations of the status-of-forces agreement and blocking the deployment of essential assets and enablers, and underscoring the importance of close cooperation and communication between the Mission and the Government of South Sudan in addressing these issues,

Strongly condemning the attacks by Government and opposition forces and other groups on United Nations and Intergovernmental Authority on Development personnel and facilities, including the December 2012 downing of a United Nations helicopter by the Sudan People's Liberation Army, the April 2013 attack on a United Nations convoy, the December 2013 attack on the Mission camp in Akobo, the August 2014 shooting down of a United Nations helicopter by unidentified armed groups, the August 2014 arrest and detention of an Intergovernmental Authority monitoring and verification team, the detentions and kidnappings of United Nations and associated personnel, the repeated attacks on the Mission camps in Bor, Bentiu, Malakal and Melut, and the disappearance, purportedly caused by Sudan People's Liberation Army forces, of two United Nations-affiliated national staff and one national contractor in Upper Nile State, and calling upon the Government of South Sudan to complete its investigations of these attacks in a swift and thorough manner and to hold those responsible to account,

Reiterating its request that the Mission take additional measures, as appropriate, to ensure the security of its air operations in South Sudan, and report thereon to the Security Council,

Stressing the importance of effective engagement and liaison with local communities, both within and outside the protection of civilians sites, in order to fulfil the protection of civilians mandate of the Mission,

Expressing grave concern regarding the threats made to oil installations, petroleum companies and their employees, and urging all parties to ensure the security of economic infrastructure,

Recalling its resolution 2117 (2013) of 26 September 2013, and expressing grave concern at the threat to peace and security in South Sudan arising from the illicit transfer, destabilizing accumulation and misuse of small arms and light weapons,

Noting with serious concern reports made by the Mine Action Service of the United Nations in Jonglei State in February 2014 of the indiscriminate use of cluster munitions and urging all parties to refrain from similar such use in the future, and further expressing serious concerns about the increased level of unexploded ordnance,

Welcoming the continued operations of the Monitoring and Verification Mechanism of the Intergovernmental Authority on Development, reiterating its call for the redeployment and/or progressive withdrawal of armed groups and allied forces invited by either side, consistent with the cessation of hostilities agreement of 23 January 2014, and warning of the serious consequences that could result from any regionalization of the conflict,

Reaffirming its resolutions 1265 (1999) of 17 September 1999, 1296 (2000) of 19 April 2000, 1674 (2006) of 28 April 2006, 1738 (2006) of 23 December 2006 and 1894 (2009) of 11 November 2009 on the protection of civilians in armed conflict, and resolutions 1502 (2003) of 26 August 2003 and 2175 (2014) of 29 August 2014 on the protection of humanitarian and United Nations personnel; resolutions 1612 (2005) of 26 July 2005, 1882 (2009) of 4 August 2009, 1998 (2011) of 12 July 2011, 2068 (2012) of 19 September 2012 and 2143 (2014) of 7 March 2014 on children and armed conflict; resolutions 1325 (2000) of 31 October 2000, 1820 (2008) of 19 June 2008, 1888 (2009) of 30 September 2009, 1889 (2009) of 5 October 2009, 1960 (2010) of 16 December 2010, 2106 (2013) of 24 June 2013 and 2122 (2013) of 18 October 2013 on women and peace and security; resolution 2150 (2014) of 16 April 2014 on the prevention of and fight against genocide; resolution 2151 (2014) of 28 April 2014 on security sector reform; and resolution 2171 (2014) of 21 August 2014 on conflict prevention,

Taking note of the reports of the Secretary-General of 17 February[295] and 29 April 2015[296] and the recommendations contained therein,

Determining that the situation in South Sudan continues to constitute a threat to international peace and security in the region,

Acting under Chapter VII of the Charter of the United Nations,

1. *Reiterates its endorsement* of the cessation of hostilities agreement accepted and signed by the Government of South Sudan and the Sudan People's Liberation Movement/Army (in Opposition) on 23 January 2014, further reiterates its endorsement of the Agreement to Resolve the Crisis in South Sudan signed on 9 May 2014 by the Government of South Sudan and the Sudan People's Liberation Movement/Army (in Opposition); endorses the rededication and implementation modalities for the cessation of hostilities agreement, of 9 November 2014; calls for immediate and full implementation of the agreements by both parties, and expresses its intention to consider all appropriate measures, as demonstrated by its unanimous adoption on 3 March 2015 of resolution 2206 (2015), against those who take action that undermines the peace, stability and security of South Sudan, including those who prevent the implementation of these agreements;

2. *Urges* all parties to engage in an open and fully inclusive national dialogue seeking to establish lasting peace, reconciliation and good governance, including through the full and effective participation of youth, women, diverse communities, faith groups, civil society and the formerly detained Sudan People's Liberation Movement leaders, encourages the efforts of the Intergovernmental Authority on Development and the United Nations to reach a peace agreement between the parties, and further urges them to ensure that child protection provisions are integrated into all peace negotiations and peace agreements;

3. *Decides* to extend the mandate of the United Nations Mission in South Sudan until 30 November 2015;

4. *Also decides* that the mandate of the Mission shall be as follows, and authorizes the Mission to use all means necessary to perform the following tasks:

(*a*) *Protection of civilians*:

(i) To protect civilians under threat of physical violence, irrespective of the source of such violence, within its capacity and areas of deployment, with specific protection for women and children, including through the continued use of the Mission's child protection and women's protection advisers;

---

[295] S/2015/118.

[296] S/2015/296.

(ii) To deter violence against civilians, including foreign nationals, especially through proactive deployment, active patrolling with particular attention to displaced civilians, including but not limited to those in protection sites and refugee camps, humanitarian personnel and human rights defenders, and identification of threats and attacks against the civilian population, including through regular interaction with the civilian population and closely with humanitarian, human rights and development organizations, in areas at high risk of conflict, including, as appropriate, schools, places of worship, hospitals and the oil installations, in particular when the Government of South Sudan is unable or failing to provide such security;

(iii) To implement a Mission-wide early warning strategy, including a coordinated approach to information-gathering, monitoring, verification, early warning and dissemination, and response mechanisms, including response mechanisms to prepare for further potential attacks on United Nations personnel and facilities;

(iv) To maintain public safety and security of and within the Mission's protection of civilians sites;

(v) To exercise good offices, confidence-building and facilitation in support of the Mission's protection strategy, especially in regard to women and children, including to facilitate the prevention, mitigation and resolution of intercommunal conflict in order to foster sustainable local and national reconciliation as an essential part of preventing violence and of long-term State-building activity;

(vi) To foster a secure environment for the eventual safe and voluntary return of internally displaced persons and refugees, including through monitoring of, ensuring respect for human rights by, and, where compatible and in strict compliance with the United Nations human rights due diligence policy,[270] coordination with police services and civil society actors in relevant and protection-focused activities, such as sensitization to issues of sexual and gender-based violence, in order to strengthen the protection of civilians;

(*b*) *Monitoring and investigating human rights*:

(i) To monitor, investigate, verify and report publicly and regularly on abuses and violations of human rights and violations of international humanitarian law, including those that may amount to war crimes or crimes against humanity;

(ii) To monitor, investigate, verify and report specifically and publicly on violations and abuses committed against children and women, including all forms of sexual and gender-based violence in armed conflict by accelerating the implementation of monitoring, analysis and reporting arrangements on conflict-related sexual violence and by strengthening the monitoring and reporting mechanism for grave violations against children;

(iii) To coordinate with, and offer technical support to, where appropriate, the African Union Commission of Inquiry on South Sudan;

(*c*) *Creating the conditions conducive to the delivery of humanitarian assistance*:

(i) To contribute, in close coordination with humanitarian actors, to the creation of security conditions conducive to the delivery of humanitarian assistance, confidence-building and facilitation, so as to allow, in accordance with relevant provisions of international law and United Nations guiding principles of humanitarian assistance, the rapid, safe and unhindered access of relief personnel to all those in need in South Sudan and timely delivery of humanitarian assistance, in particular to internally displaced persons and refugees;

(ii) To ensure the security and freedom of movement of United Nations and associated personnel where appropriate, and to ensure the security of installations and equipment necessary for the implementation of mandated tasks;

(*d*) *Supporting the implementation of the cessation of hostilities agreement*:

(i) To ensure proper coordination with the Joint Technical Committee, the Monitoring and Verification Mechanism and monitoring and verification teams, as appropriate;

(ii) To provide mobile and dedicated fixed site security to the Monitoring and Verification Mechanism of the Intergovernmental Authority on Development, as established in line with the decisions taken by the Assembly of Heads of State and Government of the Intergovernmental Authority at its meetings held on 31 January and 13 March 2014;

(iii) To provide support to the work of the Monitoring and Verification Mechanism as described in the cessation of hostilities agreement;

5. *Emphasizes* that the protection of civilians, as described in paragraph 4 (*a*) above, must be given priority in decisions about the use of available capacity and resources within the Mission;

6. *Requests* the Secretary-General, through his Special Representative for South Sudan, to continue to direct the operations of an integrated Mission, coordinate all activities of the United Nations system in South Sudan and support a coherent international approach to achieving peace in South Sudan, and expresses support for the use of United Nations good offices to engage with the parties and other stakeholders;

7. *Endorses* the recommendation made by the Secretary-General in his report of 29 April 2015[296] to maintain the overall force levels of the Mission to support its mandate as defined in paragraph 4 of the present resolution;

8. *Decides* that the Mission shall consist of a military component of up to 12,500 troops of all ranks and of a police component, including appropriate formed police units, of up to 1,323 personnel; and that the civilian component shall continue to be reduced according to tasks outlined in paragraph 4 above; requests that the Secretary-General provide detailed information on force generation, restructuring of the Mission force, logistical support and enablers, including as part of his regular reports; and requests the Secretary-General to review needs on the ground and provide an updated assessment of the force's operations, deployment and future requirements in his regular reports to the Security Council;

9. *Requests* the Mission to continue to focus and streamline its activities across its military, police and civilian components in order to achieve progress on the tasks outlined in paragraph 4 above, and recognizes that certain Mission tasks will therefore be ceased;

10. *Expresses its intention* to keep the requirements and composition of Mission components under active review, and to review this mandate and make any necessary adjustments, at an appropriate stage in the implementation of a credible peace agreement between the parties;

11. *Authorizes* the Secretary-General to take the steps necessary, in accordance with paragraph 8 above, to continue to expedite force and asset generation;

12. *Requests* the Mission to further intensify its presence and active patrolling in areas of high risk of conflict, high concentrations of internally displaced persons, including as guided by its early warning strategy, in both government- and opposition-held areas, and key routes for population movement, and to conduct regular reviews of its geographic deployment to ensure that its forces are best placed to protect civilians, and requests the Secretary-General to provide an update to the Council on how the Mission is working towards meeting its protection of civilian obligations, including but not limited to new patrol areas and proactive deployment, and on the measures to be taken to transform the Mission to become more efficient and effective in implementing its mandate, in his next report in August 2015, as well as further updates on these reviews as part of his regular reports;

13. *Further requests* that the Mission continue to ensure full compliance with the United Nations zero-tolerance policy on sexual exploitation and abuse and keep the Council fully informed about the progress of the Mission in this regard, and urges troop- and police-contributing countries to take appropriate preventive action, including predeployment awareness training, and to ensure full accountability in cases of such conduct involving their personnel;

14. *Encourages* the Mission to fully implement the human rights due diligence policy, and requests the Secretary-General to include progress made in implementing the policy in his reports to the Council;

15. *Requests* the Mission, within existing resources, to assist the Security Council Committee established pursuant to paragraph 16 of resolution 2206 (2015) and the Panel of Experts on South Sudan established pursuant to the same resolution; further urges all parties and Member States, as well as international, regional and subregional organizations, to ensure cooperation with the Panel, and further urges all Member States involved to ensure the safety of the members of the Panel and unhindered access, in particular to persons, documents and sites in order for the Panel to execute its mandate;

16. *Condemns in the strongest terms* attacks on and threats made to Mission personnel and United Nations facilities, as well as those of the Intergovernmental Authority on Development, such as the August 2014 shooting down of a United Nations helicopter by unidentified armed groups, the August 2014 arrest and detention of an Intergovernmental Authority monitoring and verification team, the detentions and kidnappings of United Nations and associated personnel, and the repeated attacks on the Mission camps in Bor, Bentiu, Malakal and Melut, stresses

that such attacks may constitute violations of the status-of-forces agreement and/or war crimes, demands that all parties respect the inviolability of United Nations premises and immediately desist and refrain from any violence against those gathered at United Nations facilities, and further demands the immediate and safe release of detained and kidnapped United Nations and associated personnel;

17. *Recalls* the designation criteria detailed in paragraph 7 of resolution 2206 (2015), stresses the sanctity of United Nations protection sites, and specifically underscores that individuals or entities that are responsible or complicit in, or have engaged in, directly or indirectly, attacks against United Nations missions, international security presences or other peacekeeping operations, or humanitarian personnel, threaten the peace, security and stability of South Sudan and therefore may meet the designation criteria;

18. *Reiterates its request* that the Mission take additional measures, as appropriate, to ensure the security of its air operations in South Sudan and report thereon to the Council;

19. *Demands* that the Government of South Sudan and all relevant parties cooperate fully in the deployment, operations and monitoring, verification and reporting functions of the Mission, in particular by guaranteeing the safety, security and unrestricted freedom of movement of United Nations and associated personnel throughout the territory of South Sudan, and further calls upon the Government to ensure freedom of movement for internally displaced persons, including those leaving and entering protection of civilians sites, and to continue to support the Mission by the allocation of land for protection of civilians sites;

20. *Also demands* that all parties allow, in accordance with relevant provisions of international law and United Nations guiding principles of humanitarian assistance, the rapid, safe and unhindered access of relief personnel, equipment and supplies to all those in need and timely delivery of humanitarian assistance, in particular to internally displaced persons and refugees, and stresses that any returns or other durable solutions for internally displaced persons or refugees must be undertaken on a voluntary and informed basis in conditions of dignity and safety;

21. *Further demands* that all parties immediately cease all forms of violence, human rights violations and abuses and violations of international humanitarian law, including rape and other forms of sexual and gender-based violence;

22. *Condemns* all violations of applicable international law, including international humanitarian law, and violations and abuses of international human rights committed by all parties to the conflict, in particular against children, such as those involving their recruitment and use, killing and maiming, and abduction, as well as attacks against schools and hospitals, urges all parties to the conflict to implement the conclusions on children and armed conflict in South Sudan adopted by the Security Council Working Group on Children and Armed Conflict on 12 May 2015,[297] strongly urges the Government of South Sudan to fully and immediately implement its revised action plan to end and prevent violations committed against children, and further strongly urges the Sudan People's Liberation Movement/Army (in Opposition) to fully and immediately implement its commitment to end violations and abuses against children signed on 10 May 2014, takes note of the national launch on 29 October 2014 of the "Children, Not Soldiers" campaign by the Government, and welcomes the release of children by the South Sudan Democratic Movement/Army (Cobra faction);

23. *Expresses grave concern* at the findings of the Special Representative of the Secretary-General on Sexual Violence in Conflict of rampant sexual violence, and welcomes the joint communiqué of South Sudan and the United Nations on the prevention of conflict-related sexual violence of 11 October 2014,[286] the unilateral communiqué issued on 18 December 2014 by the Sudan People's Liberation Movement/Army (in Opposition) on preventing conflict-related sexual violence, the appointment by the Government of South Sudan of a high-level focal point to address conflict-related sexual violence and the establishment and work of the Joint Technical Working Group, calls upon both parties as a matter of urgency to finalize action plans to implement the commitments made under their respective communiqués, urges the Government to implement without delay the commitments made in accordance with resolutions 1960 (2010) and 2106 (2013), and further calls for specific and time-bound commitments by both parties to combat sexual violence in accordance with resolutions 1960 (2010) and 2106 (2013);

[297] S/AC.51/2015/1.

24. *Calls upon* the Government of South Sudan to move forward expeditiously and transparently to complete the investigations of allegations of human rights violations and abuses consistent with international standards, and encourages it to release the reports of those investigations;

25. *Also calls upon* the Government of South Sudan to hold to account all those responsible for violations and abuses of human rights and violations of international humanitarian law and to ensure that all victims of sexual violence have equal protection under the law and equal access to justice, and to safeguard equal respect for the rights of women and girls in these processes;

26. *Emphasizes* the importance of the full and effective participation of women at all levels in the implementation of agreements and in the prevention and resolution of conflict and peacebuilding more broadly, calls upon all parties to ensure women's full and effective representation and leadership in all conflict resolution and peacebuilding efforts, including in the resumption of peace talks, and through support to women's civil society organizations; welcomes the identification by the Intergovernmental Authority on Development of a gender adviser, encourages their swift deployment and the full integration of gender concerns in future peace agreements, and encourages troop- and police-contributing countries to take measures to increase the deployment of women in the military, police and civilian components of the Mission, and reaffirms the importance of appropriate gender expertise and training in all missions mandated by the Council;

27. *Condemns* attacks on oil installations, petroleum companies and their employees, and the continued fighting around these facilities, and urges all parties to ensure the security of economic infrastructure;

28. *Requests* that the Secretary-General report to the Council on the implementation of the mandate of the Mission in two written reports, no later than 17 August 2015 and 30 October 2015 respectively;

29. *Decides* to remain actively seized of the matter.

Adopted unanimously at the 7451st meeting.

Decisions

At its 7460th meeting, on 10 June 2015, the Security Council decided to invite the representative of the Sudan to participate, without vote, in accordance with rule 37 of its provisional rules of procedure, in the discussion of the item entitled:

"Reports of the Secretary-General on the Sudan and South Sudan

"Report of the Secretary-General on the African Union-United Nations Hybrid Operation in Darfur (S/2015/378)".

At the same meeting, the Council also decided to extend an invitation, in accordance with rule 39 of its provisional rules of procedure, to Mr. Edmond Mulet, Assistant Secretary-General for Peacekeeping Operations.

At its 7475th meeting, on 29 June 2015, the Council decided to invite the representative of the Sudan to participate, without vote, in accordance with rule 37 of its provisional rules of procedure, in the discussion of the item entitled:

"Reports of the Secretary-General on the Sudan and South Sudan

"Report of the Secretary-General on the African Union-United Nations Hybrid Operation in Darfur (S/2015/378)".

Resolution 2228 (2015)
of 29 June 2015

The Security Council,

Reaffirming all its previous resolutions and the statements by its President concerning the situation in the Sudan, and underlining the importance of full compliance with these,

Reaffirming also its strong commitment to the sovereignty, unity, independence and territorial integrity of the Sudan and its determination to work with the Government of the Sudan, in full respect of its sovereignty, to assist in tackling the various challenges in the Sudan,

Recalling the importance of the principles of the peaceful settlement of international disputes, good-neighbourliness, non-interference and cooperation in the relations among States in the region,

Reaffirming the basic principles of peacekeeping, including consent of the parties, impartiality and non-use of force except in self-defence and defence of the mandate, and recognizing that the mandate of each peacekeeping mission is specific to the country concerned,

Recalling all its relevant resolutions on women and peace and security, on children and armed conflict, on the protection of humanitarian and United Nations personnel and on the protection of civilians in armed conflict,

Expressing deep concern at the serious deterioration in the security situation in Darfur overall so far in 2015, and the profound negative impact of this on civilians, in particular women and children, in particular through a marked escalation of hostilities between government forces and rebel armed groups, as well as an escalation of intercommunal conflicts over land, access to resources, migration issues and tribal rivalries, including with the involvement of paramilitary units and tribal militias, and a rise in criminality and banditry targeting the local population; further expressing deep concern that the deteriorating security situation, as characterized by attacks by rebel groups and government forces, aerial bombardment by the Government of the Sudan, inter-tribal fighting, banditry and criminality, continues to threaten civilians; and reiterating its demand that all parties to the conflict in Darfur immediately end violence, including attacks on civilians, peacekeepers and humanitarian personnel,

In this regard, *expressing concern* at evidence, collected by the African Union-United Nations Hybrid Operation in Darfur, of two air-delivered cluster bombs near Kirigiyati, North Darfur, taking note that the Operation disposed of them safely, and reiterating the Secretary-General's call upon the Government of the Sudan to immediately investigate the use of cluster munitions,

Emphasizing that those responsible for violations of international humanitarian law and violations and abuses of human rights must be held accountable and that the Government of the Sudan bears the primary responsibility to protect civilians within its territory and subject to its jurisdiction, including protection from crimes against humanity and war crimes,

Recalling its resolution 2117 (2013) of 26 September 2013, and expressing concern at the threat to peace and security in Darfur arising from the illicit transfer, destabilizing accumulation and misuse of small arms and light weapons, and the continued threats to civilians posed by unexploded ordnance,

Expressing deep concern at the significant increase in population displacements in 2014 and so far in 2015 and the consequent increase in humanitarian assistance and protection needs, with 430,000 persons newly displaced in 2014, about 300,000 of whom have been unable to return to their homes, a total number of long-term internally displaced persons of 2.5 million and a total number of people in need of humanitarian assistance of 4.4 million,

Recalling the commitments made by the Government of the Sudan and other signatories to the Doha Document for Peace in Darfur[266] to ensure the unimpeded access of humanitarian assistance to the population in need and the protection of humanitarian workers and their operations in areas under their control, as well as to guarantee the African Union-United Nations Hybrid Operation in Darfur unimpeded freedom of movement in all areas and at all times in Darfur in the exercise of its mandate, and further recalling the role of the Implementation Follow-up Commission in assessing the implementation of the Doha Document,

Expressing concern that the continued denial of access and restrictions imposed on humanitarian actors have left significant gaps in the delivery of humanitarian assistance, and calling upon the Government of the Sudan to ensure that humanitarian actors can operate in support of addressing basic needs,

Calling upon donors, the Darfur Regional Authority and the Government of the Sudan to provide the financial resources necessary to reach those in need,

Reiterating that there can be no military solution to the conflict in Darfur and that an inclusive political settlement is essential to re-establishing peace, underscoring the importance of fully addressing the root causes of the conflict in the search for a sustainable peace, which should rapidly deliver real benefits for the Darfuri people, and in this regard reiterating its support for the Doha Document for Peace in Darfur as a viable framework for the peace process in Darfur, and for its accelerated implementation, as well as the peace talks mediated by the African Union High-level Implementation Panel and any credible moves to lay the groundwork for an inclusive, comprehensive and nationally owned national dialogue in the Sudan,

Deploring the fact that some armed groups are impeding the peace process and have continued to resort to violence, reiterating its demand for the release of members of the former movement of Mohamed Bashar, taken captive in May 2013 by Justice and Equality Movement-Gibril Ibrahim forces, and condemning any actions by any armed group aimed at the forced overthrow of the Government of the Sudan,

Noting that the ability of the African Union-United Nations Hybrid Operation in Darfur to facilitate progress in the implementation of the Doha Document for Peace in Darfur is hampered by delays and the absence of an inclusive political settlement between the Government of the Sudan and non-signatory movements, urging the signatory parties to take the remaining steps necessary to implement the Doha Document fully, expressing concern that the humanitarian and security situation, as well as the lack of capacity of the Darfur Regional Authority, hinder the transition from relief to stabilization and development activities, urging donors and the Government to honour their pledges and fulfil their obligations in a timely manner, including those commitments made at the conference held in Doha in April 2013, and affirming that development can support a lasting peace in Darfur,

Noting also that local dispute resolution mechanisms play an important role in preventing and resolving intercommunal conflict, including conflict over natural resources, urging an intensification of effective efforts to prevent local disputes leading to violence, with its corresponding impact on the local civilian populations, acknowledging the efforts of Sudanese authorities and local mediators to mediate in inter-tribal fighting, with support from the African Union-United Nations Hybrid Operation in Darfur and the United Nations country team, and urging their continued work,

Welcoming regional and other initiatives, undertaken in close interaction with the Government of the Sudan, to address the root causes of the conflict in Darfur and to promote a sustainable peace, including the convening by the President of Chad, Mr. Idriss Déby Itno, of two mediation forums, encouraging the full coordination of such initiatives with the efforts of the African Union-United Nations Joint Special Representative for Darfur, and commending the efforts of the Joint Special Representative to secure peace, stability and security in Darfur, including through support to international, regional and national efforts to revitalize the peace process and increase its inclusiveness,

Underlining, without prejudice to the primary responsibility of the Security Council for the maintenance of international peace and security, the importance of the partnership between the United Nations and the African Union, consistent with Chapter VIII of the Charter of the United Nations, with regard to the maintenance of peace and security in Africa, particularly in the Sudan,

Calling upon all parties to comply with their obligations under international human rights law and international humanitarian law, stressing the importance that the Council attaches to ending impunity, including through ensuring accountability and bringing to justice the perpetrators of crimes committed by all parties in Darfur, urging the Government of the Sudan to comply with its obligations in this respect, welcoming the ongoing investigations by the Special Prosecutor for Darfur appointed by the Government and stressing the need for further progress in this regard, reiterating the call for swift progress on the draft memorandum of understanding providing for observation by the African Union-United Nations Hybrid Operation in Darfur and the African Union of the proceedings of the Special Court for Darfur, and calling upon the Government swiftly to investigate attacks against the Operation and to bring the perpetrators to justice,

Reaffirming its concern over the negative effect of ongoing violence in Darfur on the stability of the Sudan as a whole as well as the region, welcoming the ongoing good relations between the Sudan and Chad, including on border control, and encouraging the Sudan, Chad and the Central African Republic to continue to cooperate in order to achieve peace and stability in Darfur and the wider region,

Commending the efforts of the African Union-United Nations Hybrid Operation in Darfur towards promoting peace and stability in Darfur, and reiterating its full support for the Operation,

Welcoming the report of the Secretary-General of 26 May 2015 on the African Union-United Nations Hybrid Operation in Darfur,[298] as well as his special report of 6 March 2015,[299]

[298] S/2015/378.

[299] S/2015/163.

Taking note of the completion of the review commissioned by the Secretary-General on 2 July 2014 of the issue of under-reporting, and allegations of manipulation of reporting, by the African Union-United Nations Hybrid Operation in Darfur, and welcoming the recommendations and conclusions contained in the review[300] and the continued implementation of measures to address this issue,

Determining that the situation in the Sudan constitutes a threat to international peace and security,

1. *Decides* to extend the mandate of the African Union-United Nations Hybrid Operation in Darfur, as set out in resolution 1769 (2007) of 31 July 2007, until 30 June 2016, and further decides that the Operation shall consist of up to 15,845 military personnel, 1,583 police personnel and 13 formed police units of up to 140 personnel each;

2. *Reiterates*, in the context of the lack of progress on the benchmarks and the significant deterioration of the security situation, its endorsement of the revised strategic priorities of the African Union-United Nations Hybrid Operation in Darfur as set out in paragraph 4 of resolution 2148 (2014) of 3 April 2014, namely the protection of civilians, the facilitation of the delivery of humanitarian assistance and the safety and security of humanitarian personnel; mediation between the Government of the Sudan and non-signatory armed movements on the basis of the Doha Document for Peace in Darfur,[266] while taking into account ongoing democratic transformation at the national level; and support to the mediation of community conflict, including through measures to address its root causes, in conjunction with the United Nations country team; welcomes the steps taken so far by the Operation to implement the review of the Operation conducted pursuant to resolution 2113 (2013) of 30 July 2013, and requests that the Operation continue to align all its activity and direct the use of its resources to the achievement of these priorities, discontinue all other tasks not aligned to these priorities and continue to streamline the mission accordingly, and stresses the importance of the appropriate distribution of tasks and coordination between the Operation and the United Nations country team in order to implement the review of the Operation;

3. *Notes* that certain elements of the mandate and tasks of the African Union-United Nations Hybrid Operation in Darfur, as authorized in resolution 1769 (2007), in which it was decided that the mandate of the Operation shall be as set out in paragraphs 54 and 55 of the report of the Secretary-General and the Chairperson of the African Union Commission of 5 June 2007,[268] are no longer relevant, or are either being undertaken by or will soon transition to other entities with comparative advantage, namely those enumerated in paragraphs 54 (*g*) and (*h*), 55 (*a*) (v), 55 (*b*) (ii),(iii), (v) and (x), and 55 (*c*) (iii) and (iv) of that report;

4. *Underlines* that the African Union-United Nations Hybrid Operation in Darfur must continue to give priority in decisions about the use of available capacity and resources to (*a*) the protection of civilians across Darfur, including women and children, through, and without prejudice to the basic principles of peacekeeping, inter alia, continuing to move to a more preventive and pre-emptive posture in pursuit of its priorities and in active defence of its mandate; enhanced early warning; proactive military deployment and active and effective patrolling in areas of high risk of conflict and high concentration of internally displaced persons; more prompt and effective responses to threats of violence against civilians, including through regular reviews of the geographic deployment of the Operation force; and securing camps for internally displaced persons, adjacent areas and areas of return, including development and training of community policing; and (*b*) ensuring safe, timely and unhindered humanitarian access and the safety and security of humanitarian personnel and activities, in accordance with relevant provisions of international law and the United Nations guiding principles on humanitarian assistance; and requests the Operation to maximize the use of its capabilities, in cooperation with the United Nations country team and other international and non-governmental actors, in the implementation of its mission-wide comprehensive strategy for the achievement of these objectives;

5. *Emphasizes* the Chapter VII mandate of the African Union-United Nations Hybrid Operation in Darfur, as defined in resolution 1769 (2007), to deliver its core tasks to protect civilians without prejudice to the primary responsibility of the Government of the Sudan and to ensure the freedom of movement and security of Operation personnel and humanitarian workers; recalls that the Operation is authorized to take all the necessary action in fulfilment of this mandate; and urges the Operation to deter any threats against itself and its mandate;

6. *Stresses* that, in the context of the evolving security situation, any refinement of the mission should be based on progress against the benchmarks and the conditions on the ground, and implemented in a gradual, phased, flexible and reversible manner;

[300] See S/2014/771.

7. *Commends* the efforts of the Joint Special Representative to revitalize the peace process and to increase its inclusiveness, guided by the framework for African Union and United Nations facilitation of the Darfur peace process,[269] including through renewed engagement of the non-signatory movements; emphasizes the importance of the strengthened coordination of the Joint Special Representative with the African Union High-level Implementation Panel and the United Nations Special Envoy for the Sudan and South Sudan in synchronizing their mediation efforts and in generating progress on direct negotiations between the Government of the Sudan and the Darfur armed movements;

8. *Welcomes* that progress has been made in implementation of some elements of the Doha Document for Peace in Darfur, including the completion of security arrangements for Liberation and Justice Movement and Justice and Equality Movement-Sudan combatants and the conversion of the Liberation and Justice Movement into two political parties, the integration of former rebels into power structures of the Sudan but deplores continuing serious delays in overall implementation of the Doha Document; urges the signatory parties to implement the Doha Document in full, including by ensuring that the institutions established under it are resourced and empowered to carry out their mandates; demands that the non-signatory armed groups refrain from impeding the implementation of the Doha Document; and encourages the African Union-United Nations Hybrid Operation in Darfur, in accordance with its revised strategic priorities, and the United Nations country team to continue to engage fully in support of implementation of the Doha Document;

9. *Demands* that all parties to the conflict in Darfur, including in particular all the non-signatory armed groups, and other groups immediately cease all acts of violence and commit themselves to a sustained and permanent ceasefire, in order to bring a stable and durable peace to the region;

10. *Reaffirms its support* for a Darfur-based internal dialogue that takes place in an inclusive environment with full respect for the civil and political rights of participants, including the full and effective participation of women and internally displaced persons; welcomes the successful completion of the first phase of the Darfur Internal Dialogue and Consultation on 26 May 2015; further welcomes the release of 2.5 million United States dollars by the Government of the Sudan as part of its contribution to the funding of the Dialogue and Consultation; expresses concern that prevailing insecurity, and lack of adequate funding, could undermine effective implementation of future phases of the Dialogue and Consultation; calls upon the Government and the armed groups to ensure the necessary enabling environment; and requests the African Union-United Nations Hybrid Operation in Darfur to continue to support, monitor and report on the development of the Dialogue and Consultation and the overall environment for it;

11. *Calls for* an urgent end to inter-tribal clashes, criminality and banditry that affect civilians; further calls for reconciliation and dialogue; and requests the African Union-United Nations Hybrid Operation in Darfur to continue to support local conflict resolution mechanisms, including with civil society mechanisms;

12. *Expresses deep concern* over the proliferation of arms, in particular small arms and light weapons, and requests the African Union-United Nations Hybrid Operation in Darfur to continue to cooperate in this context with the Panel of Experts on the Sudan established pursuant to resolution 1591 (2005) of 29 March 2005 in order to facilitate its work;

13. *Commends* the troop- and police-contributing countries of the African Union-United Nations Hybrid Operation in Darfur; welcomes that some progress has been made in addressing contingent-owned equipment and self-sustainment shortfalls, but expresses concern that shortfalls remain; and calls for continued efforts by the Operation, the Secretariat and troop- and police-contributing countries to address such shortfalls, including by providing appropriate training and resources to fulfil priority protection functions, especially in areas necessary for contingents' temporary deployment capability and ability to conduct long-range patrols;

14. *Strongly condemns* all attacks on the African Union-United Nations Hybrid Operation in Darfur; underlines that any attack or threat of attack on the Operation is unacceptable; demands that there be no recurrence of such attacks and that those responsible be held to account following prompt and thorough investigation; urges the Operation to take all measures necessary within its rules of engagement to protect United Nations personnel and equipment; condemns the ongoing impunity for those who attack peacekeepers, and in this regard urges the Government of the Sudan to do its utmost to bring all perpetrators of any such crimes to justice and to cooperate with the Operation to this end;

15. *Reiterates its deep concern* that hindrances remain to the African Union-United Nations Hybrid Operation in Darfur in the implementation of its mandate, including movement and access restrictions, caused by

insecurity, acts of criminality and significant movement restrictions by government forces, armed movements and militia groups; calls upon all parties in Darfur to remove all obstacles to the full and proper discharge by the Operation of its mandate, including by ensuring its security and freedom of movement; and in this regard demands that the Government of the Sudan comply with the status-of-forces agreement fully and without delay, particularly provisions relevant to the movement of patrols in conflict-affected areas and flight clearances, as well as those provisions relevant to the removal of obstacles to the use of aerial assets of the Operation and the timely processing of Operation equipment at the port of entry to the Sudan;

16. *Demands* that all parties in Darfur immediately end attacks targeting civilians, peacekeepers and humanitarian personnel and comply with their obligations under international human rights and humanitarian law; and affirms the Security Council's condemnation of all violations of international humanitarian law and violations and abuses of human rights;

17. *Expresses serious concern* at the deteriorating humanitarian situation in Darfur and at the threats to and attacks on humanitarian personnel and facilities; expresses concern that access to some conflict areas where vulnerable populations reside remains restricted and that some conflict areas are inaccessible, including in North and Central Darfur and eastern Jebel Marra, owing to insecurity, acts of criminality and movement restrictions by government forces, armed movements and militia groups; welcomes that humanitarian organizations are able to deliver some aid to most people in need of assistance in Darfur; deplores the continued restrictions on humanitarian access in Darfur resulting from increased insecurity, attacks against humanitarian workers, denial of access by the parties to the conflict and bureaucratic impediments imposed by the Government of the Sudan; further expresses concern over the insufficient availability of funding for humanitarian actors; stresses the need for the timely issuance of visas and travel permits for humanitarian organizations; and demands that the Government, all militias, armed groups and all other stakeholders ensure the safe, timely and unhindered access of humanitarian organizations and relief personnel and the delivery of humanitarian assistance to populations in need, in accordance with the relevant provisions of international law and United Nations guiding principles of humanitarian assistance, including humanity, impartiality, neutrality and independence;

18. *Condemns* increased human rights violations and abuses in, and relating to, Darfur, including those involving extrajudicial killings, the excessive use of force, abduction of civilians, acts of sexual and gender-based violence, violations and abuses against children and arbitrary arrests and detentions; calls upon the Government of the Sudan to investigate allegations of such violations and abuses and bring those responsible to justice; expresses deep concern about the situation of all those so detained, including civil society members and internally displaced persons; emphasizes the importance of ensuring, within its current mandate, the ability of the African Union-United Nations Hybrid Operation in Darfur and other relevant organizations to monitor such cases; and in this regard urges the Government to extend even greater cooperation with the Operation towards the fulfilment of this goal and to provide accountability and access to justice for victims; and calls upon the Government fully to respect its obligations, including by fulfilling its commitment to lift the state of emergency in Darfur, releasing all political prisoners and allowing free expression;

19. *Requests* the African Union-United Nations Hybrid Operation in Darfur to monitor, verify and draw to the attention of the authorities abuses and violations of human rights, including those committed against women and children, and violations of international humanitarian law, and further requests enhanced, detailed, full and public reporting by the Secretary-General to the Council on this issue, as part of his regular 90-day reports;

20. *Also requests* the African Union-United Nations Hybrid Operation in Darfur to ensure that any support provided to non-United Nations security forces is provided in strict compliance with the human rights due diligence policy on United Nations support to non-United Nations security forces,[270] and requests the Secretary-General to include progress made in implementing the policy in his reports to the Council;

21. *Urges* close coordination among United Nations missions in the region, including the African Union-United Nations Hybrid Operation in Darfur, the United Nations Interim Security Force for Abyei and the United Nations Mission in South Sudan, and requests the Secretary-General to ensure effective inter-mission cooperation;

22. *Emphasizes* the importance of cooperation and information-sharing between the African Union-United Nations Hybrid Operation in Darfur, the United Nations Mission in South Sudan, the United Nations Organization Stabilization Mission in the Democratic Republic of the Congo, the United Nations Multidimensional Integrated Stabilization Mission in the Central African Republic and relevant regional and international partners in addressing

the regional threat, including of the Lord's Resistance Army, and recalls its encouragement to the Operation, within existing capacities and consistent with its mandate, to cooperate and share information in this regard;

23. *Stresses* the importance of achieving dignified and durable solutions for refugees and internally displaced persons and of ensuring their full participation in the planning and management of these solutions; demands that all parties to the conflict in Darfur create the conditions conducive to allowing the voluntary, informed, safe, dignified and sustainable return of refugees and internally displaced persons or, where appropriate, their local integration; in this regard stresses the need for the establishment of a mechanism in order to verify the extent to which these returns are voluntary and informed in nature, and underlines the importance of addressing land issues for the realization of durable solutions in Darfur;

24. *Demands* that the parties to the conflict immediately cease all acts of sexual and gender-based violence and make and implement specific and time-bound commitments to combat sexual violence, in accordance with resolution 2106 (2013) of 24 June 2013; urges the Government of the Sudan, with the support of the United Nations and the African Union, to develop a structured framework through which conflict-related sexual violence will be comprehensively addressed and to allow access for service provision for sexual violence survivors; requests the African Union-United Nations Hybrid Operation in Darfur to strengthen its reporting on sexual and gender-based violence and actions taken to combat it, including through the swift deployment of women's protection advisers; requests the Secretary-General to ensure that the relevant provisions of resolution 1325 (2000) of 31 October 2000 and subsequent resolutions on women and peace and security are implemented, including supporting the full and effective participation of women during all stages of peace processes, particularly in conflict resolution, post-conflict planning and peacebuilding, including women's civil society organizations, and to include information on this in his reporting to the Council; and further requests the Operation to monitor and assess the implementation of these tasks and requests the Secretary-General to include information on this in his reporting to the Council;

25. *Also demands* that the parties to the conflict immediately cease all violations and abuses against children and develop and implement concrete and time-bound action plans to end and prevent the recruitment and use of children in violation of applicable international law, and requests the Secretary-General to ensure:

(*a*) Continued monitoring and reporting of the situation of children in Darfur;

(*b*) Continued dialogue with the parties to the conflict towards the development and implementation of the aforementioned action plans, in accordance with resolution 1612 (2005) of 26 July 2005 and subsequent resolutions on children and armed conflict;

26. *Underscores* the importance of regular review by the Council of each United Nations peacekeeping mission's progress in implementing its mandate, and recalls its request to the Secretary-General, in close consultation with the African Union, and seeking perspectives from all relevant parties, to conduct an analysis of the implementation of the review of the African Union-United Nations Hybrid Operation in Darfur; in this regard takes note of the efforts of the Secretary-General to make recommendations on the future of the Operation, including its exit strategy, as requested by the Council in paragraph 7 of resolution 2173 (2014) of 27 August 2014; concurs that the long-term planning of the Operation should be based upon progress towards the mission's benchmarks as set out in the report of the Secretary-General of 16 October 2012[301] and subsequently refined in his reports of 25 February[302] and 15 April 2014[303] (annex A); and notes that the Secretary-General, in his report of 26 May 2015,[298] emphasizes that a political settlement in Darfur and direct talks between the Government of the Sudan and the non-signatory armed movements, starting with a cessation of hostilities in Darfur, is essential to re-establishing peace in Darfur and is primary to the achievement of these benchmarks;

27. *Takes note* of the consultations between the United Nations, the African Union and the Government of the Sudan, notably in the framework of the joint working group to develop an exit strategy in accordance with the mission's benchmarks and in response to paragraph 7 of resolution 2173 (2014); calls for early resumption of consultations between the African Union, the United Nations and the Government in this regard; looks forward to

[301] S/2012/771.

[302] S/2014/138.

[303] S/2014/279.

the recommendations of the Secretary-General, including by building on any agreed recommendations of the joint working group; and undertakes to consider the recommendations of the Secretary-General in due course;

28. *Requests* the Secretary-General to report to the Council every 90 days following the adoption of the present resolution on the African Union-United Nations Hybrid Operation in Darfur, including:

(i) Information on the political, humanitarian and security situation in Darfur, including detailed reporting on incidents of violence and attacks against civilians, by whomsoever perpetrated;

(ii) Information on violations of the status-of-forces agreement, including those involving attacks or threats of attack on the Operation, as well as violations of international humanitarian law perpetrated by any party to the conflict;

(iii) Developments and progress towards achievement of the Operation's strategic priorities and benchmarks;

(iv) Developments and progress in addressing the challenges facing the Operation as identified in the review of the Operation;

(v) Implementation of the present resolution;

29. *Decides* to remain seized of the matter.

Adopted unanimously at the 7475th meeting.

Annex A

African Union-United Nations Hybrid Operation in Darfur benchmarks as set out in annex 1 to the report of the Secretary-General of 15 April 2014[303]

Benchmark 1: inclusive peace process through mediation between the Government and non-signatory armed movements on the basis of the Doha Document for Peace in Darfur[266]

Requirements for progress would include a commitment on the part of the Government of the Sudan and non-signatory movements to reach a comprehensive negotiated political settlement to the conflict and adhere to its full and timely implementation; and credible Darfur-based internal dialogue and consultations that seek to reflect the views of the civilian population, including women, on Darfur in the peace process.

Indicators

High-level mediation:

- The Government and the non-signatory movements enter into direct negotiations brokered by the Joint African Union-United Nations Chief Mediator for Darfur over an all-inclusive comprehensive settlement to the Darfur conflict within the context of the Doha Document for Peace in Darfur.
- The signatory parties, with the support of international partners, implement the provisions of the Doha Document for Peace in Darfur, which remain essential in addressing the root causes of conflict in Darfur.
- The Government and the non-signatory movements conclude and observe a comprehensive and inclusive cessation of hostilities.
- The outcomes of the Darfur peace process are reflected in a national constitutional process supported by the African Union High-level Implementation Panel for the Sudan, as provided for in the framework for African Union and United Nations facilitation of the Darfur peace process.[269]

Darfur-based internal dialogue and consultations:

- Darfur-based internal dialogue and consultations take place in an inclusive and transparent environment that ensures the proportional representation of Darfuris and respect for the human rights of participants, as monitored by the African Union-United Nations Hybrid Operation in Darfur (UNAMID).
- The outcomes of the Darfur-based internal dialogue and consultations are widely disseminated and implemented in a manner that promotes and consolidates peace and stability in Darfur.

- A functioning Darfur Regional Authority that oversees the implementation of the Doha Document for Peace in Darfur, in conjunction with the Government of the Sudan.

Benchmark 2: protection of civilians and unhindered humanitarian access and the safety and security of humanitarian personnel

Requirements for progress would include the demonstrated commitment of the parties to the conflict, including government forces, non-signatory movements and other armed groups, to cease hostilities and respect and implement ceasefire and security arrangements; the demonstrated commitment of the parties to the conflict to implement measures to protect civilians (or promote/respect human rights); the demonstrated commitment of the parties to the conflict to allow unrestricted humanitarian access; the willingness of local actors to facilitate the safe, voluntary and sustainable return, reintegration or resettlement of internally displaced persons and refugees; improvement of troop- and police-contributing countries' performance and equipment; support by the international donor community for humanitarian activities and, where appropriate, early recovery and rehabilitation; the improved coordination between UNAMID and humanitarian actors with regard to the facilitation of the delivery of humanitarian assistance and the safety and security of humanitarian personnel; and the commitment of the Government of the Sudan at the national and local levels to improve the capacity of its security, judicial and penal institutions to promote and protect human rights.

Indicators

Protection of civilians from imminent threats of physical violence:

- Civilians facing imminent threats of physical violence are protected by UNAMID.
- Civilians at risk of physical attack, in particular women and children, carry out livelihood activities safely and securely under UNAMID protection.
- Civilians receive emergency medical assistance from UNAMID, including through evacuation to medical facilities, in extreme circumstances (i.e., when humanitarian actors are unable to assist).

Protective environment:

- Security and stability (as indicated by an absence of serious crime or violent conflict) for civilians within camps for internally displaced persons and temporary settlements.
- Security and stability (as indicated by an absence of serious crime or violent conflict) for civilians in areas outside of camps for internally displaced persons and temporary settlements, including in particular in areas adjacent to camps.
- Reduction in the number of violent crimes against civilians.
- Reduction in human rights violations, including incidents of sexual and gender-based violence, as recorded by UNAMID.
- Reduction in the recruitment of child soldiers by the parties to the conflict.
- Improved environment for the protection of civil and political rights, including through the development of sustainable foundations for professional, democratic policing and law enforcement.
- Trials monitored by UNAMID are fair and in accordance with international legal standards and practices.
- The prevalence of arms and armed actors is reduced through the disarmament, demobilization and reintegration of combatants in accordance with the provisions of the Doha Document for Peace in Darfur.
- Threats to civilians posed by unexploded ordnance are addressed through, inter alia, the safe disposal of such materials and through risk-awareness training.

Safe, timely and unhindered humanitarian access and safety and security for humanitarian personnel:

- Humanitarian actors requesting UNAMID protection and other support are able to conduct operations (e.g., inter alia, aid delivery and distribution and needs assessments) in a safe, timely and unhindered manner.

- Humanitarian actors and their property are safe and secure, in particular when UNAMID protection is provided.
- Parties to the conflict honour their commitments and international obligations to combat all acts of sexual violence against women, men and children and put an end to the recruitment and use of child soldiers.

Benchmark 3: prevention or mitigation of community conflict through mediation and, in conjunction with the United Nations country team, measures to address its root causes

Requirements for progress would include willingness on the part of the authorities and traditional community leaders to play a constructive role in resolving intercommunal conflict peacefully; the provision of access to UNAMID to facilitate mediation efforts; strengthened traditional conflict resolution mechanisms and greater respect thereof; the inclusion of measures in reconciliation agreements to address the root causes of intercommunal conflict; a willingness on the part of the authorities and other parties to the conflict to fulfil their responsibilities in regard to preventing or resolving intercommunal clashes; and the provision of access to the United Nations country team to enable measures that address root causes related to natural resources, recovery and reconstruction.

Indicators

- Dialogue between pastoralist and agriculturalist communities over peaceful coexistence and shared access to natural resources, in particular prior to and during the migration season.
- Interventions by the authorities and traditional community mediators, facilitated by UNAMID, that prevent or resolve violent intercommunal conflict.
- Dialogue between conflicting parties over local settlements to violent intercommunal conflict.
- Conflicting parties enter into and adhere to local agreements that settle violent intercommunal conflict.
- Reduction in the number of incidents of and new displacement resulting from intercommunal conflict.
- Transitional justice mechanisms, including the National Human Rights Commission, the Special Court for Darfur and the Truth and Reconciliation Commission, are established and operating in accordance with international human rights standards and best practice.
- Improved access to justice through the adoption of measures aimed at enhancing victims' rights to truth, justice and remedy.

Decisions

At its 7478th meeting, on 29 June 2015, the Security Council decided to invite the representative of the Sudan to participate, without vote, in accordance with rule 37 of its provisional rules of procedure, in the discussion of the item entitled "Reports of the Secretary-General on the Sudan and South Sudan".

At the same meeting, the Council also decided to extend an invitation, in accordance with rule 39 of its provisional rules of procedure, to Ms. Fatou Bensouda, Prosecutor of the International Criminal Court.

At its 7483rd meeting, on 14 July 2015, the Council decided to invite the representatives of South Sudan and the Sudan to participate, without vote, in accordance with rule 37 of its provisional rules of procedure, in the discussion of the item entitled:

"Reports of the Secretary-General on the Sudan and South Sudan

"Report of the Secretary-General on the situation in Abyei (S/2015/439)".

Resolution 2230 (2015) of 14 July 2015

The Security Council,

Recalling its previous resolutions and the statements by its President on the situation in the Sudan and South Sudan, in particular resolutions 1990 (2011) of 27 June 2011, 2024 (2011) of 14 December 2011, 2032 (2011) of 22 December 2011, 2046 (2012) of 2 May 2012, 2047 (2012) of 17 May 2012, 2075 (2012) of 16 November 2012,

2104 (2013) of 29 May 2013, 2126 (2013) of 25 November 2013, 2156 (2014) of 29 May 2014, 2179 (2014) of 14 October 2014 and 2205 (2015) of 26 February 2015, as well as the statements by its President of 31 August 2012[271] and 23 August 2013[272] and its statements to the press of 18 June, 21 and 28 September 2012, 6 May and 14 June 2013 and 14 February, 17 March and 11 December 2014,

Reaffirming its strong commitment to the sovereignty, independence, unity and territorial integrity of the Sudan and South Sudan and to the purposes and principles of the Charter of the United Nations, and recalling the importance of the principles of good-neighbourliness, non-interference and regional cooperation,

Reiterating that the territorial boundaries of States shall not be altered by force and that any territorial disputes shall be settled exclusively by peaceful means, affirming the priority it attaches to the full and urgent implementation of all outstanding issues from the Comprehensive Peace Agreement of 9 January 2005,[273] and underscoring that the future status of Abyei shall be resolved by negotiations between the parties in a manner consistent with the Agreement and not by the unilateral actions of either party,

Recalling the commitments made by the Government of the Sudan and the Government of South Sudan in the Agreement between the Government of the Sudan and the Sudan People's Liberation Movement on Temporary Arrangements for the Administration and Security of the Abyei Area of 20 June 2011,[274] the Agreement between the Government of the Sudan and the Government of Southern Sudan on Border Security and the Joint Political and Security Mechanism of 29 June 2011 and the Agreement on the Border Monitoring Support Mission between the Government of the Sudan and the Government of South Sudan of 30 July 2011,[275] as well as the agreements on cooperation and security arrangements of 27 September 2012,[276] the decision of the Joint Political and Security Mechanism of 8 March 2013 and the implementation matrix of 12 March 2013,[277] reached by the Government of the Sudan and the Government of South Sudan in Addis Ababa under the auspices of the African Union High-level Implementation Panel,

Expressing its full support for the efforts of the African Union on the situation between the Sudan and South Sudan, in order to ease the current tension and facilitate the resumption of negotiations on post-secession relations and the normalization of their relations, recalling in this regard the African Union Peace and Security Council communiqués of 24 April[278] and 24 October 2012, 25 January, 7 May, 29 July, 23 September, 26 October and 12 November 2013 and 12 September 2014; the Peace and Security Council press statements of 6 November 2013 and 24 March 2015; and the statement made by the Chairperson of the African Union Commission on 28 October 2013 and the statement by the Commission of 24 June 2015,

Reaffirming its previous resolutions 1265 (1999) of 17 September 1999, 1296 (2000) of 19 April 2000, 1674 (2006) of 28 April 2006, 1738 (2006) of 23 December 2006, 1894 (2009) of 11 November 2009, 2175 (2014) of 29 August 2014 and 2222 (2015) of 27 May 2015 on the protection of civilians in armed conflict; its resolutions 1612 (2005) of 26 July 2005, 1882 (2009) of 4 August 2009, 1998 (2011) of 12 July 2011, 2068 (2012) of 19 September 2012, 2143 (2014) of 7 March 2014 and 2225 (2015) of 18 June 2015 on children and armed conflict; its resolution 1502 (2003) of 26 August 2003 on the protection of humanitarian and United Nations personnel and its resolutions 1325 (2000) of 31 October 2000, 1820 (2008) of 19 June 2008, 1888 (2009) of 30 September 2009, 1889 (2009) of 5 October 2009, 1960 (2010) of 16 December 2010, 2106 (2013) of 24 June 2013 and 2122 (2013) of 18 October 2013 on women and peace and security,

Stressing the need for effective human rights monitoring, including of any sexual and gender-based violence and violations and abuses committed against women and children, taking note that there have been no developments with regard to the operationalization of human rights monitoring in the Abyei Area, and reiterating its concern at the lack of cooperation by the parties with the Secretary-General to this end,

Recalling that in its resolution 2086 (2013) of 21 January 2013 it reiterated the importance, when establishing and renewing the mandates of United Nations Missions, of including provisions on the promotion of gender equality and the empowerment of women in post-conflict situations and on children and armed conflict, and emphasizing that persistent barriers to full implementation of resolution 1325 (2000) will only be dismantled through dedicated commitment to women's empowerment, participation and human rights, and through concerted leadership, consistent information and action, and support, to build women's engagement in all levels of decision-making,

Noting with concern the minimum attention the parties have given to the management of the Abyei Area as well as the stalled efforts by the Government of the Sudan and the Government of South Sudan to delineate or agree on the coordinates of and demilitarize the Safe Demilitarized Border Zone, including the "14-mile area", and to fully implement the Joint Border Verification and Monitoring Mechanism, in accordance with Security Council resolution 2046 (2012) and the African Union Peace and Security Council road map of 24 April 2012,[278] including as a result of the temporary unavailability of aircraft, South Sudan's continued disagreement with the location of the centreline of the Zone and the denial of flight clearances,

Underlining the importance of fully establishing and maintaining effective monitoring by the Joint Border Verification and Monitoring Mechanism of the Safe Demilitarized Border Zone, including the 14-mile area,

Recognizing the importance of regular meetings between President Bashir and President Kiir for continuing dialogue, recalling the decision in resolution 2046 (2012) that the parties must resume immediately negotiations to reach agreement on the final status of Abyei under the auspices of the African Union High-level Implementation Panel, calling upon all parties to engage constructively in the process mediated by the Implementation Panel towards final agreement on the final status of the Abyei Area, and stressing that the parties must immediately implement pending aspects of the Agreement of 20 June 2011, in particular to resolve the dispute over the Abyei Area agreement, and to resolve the dispute over the Abyei Area Council and immediately establish the Abyei Area Administration and Abyei Police Service,

Stressing that both countries and communities will have much to gain if they show restraint and choose the path of dialogue instead of resorting to violence or provocations,

Commending the continued assistance provided to the parties by the African Union High-level Implementation Panel, the Intergovernmental Authority on Development, Ethiopia, the Special Envoy of the Secretary-General for the Sudan and South Sudan and the United Nations Interim Security Force for Abyei,

Further commending the efforts of the Force in effectively carrying out its mandate, including by its ongoing facilitation of peaceful migration throughout the Abyei Area, conflict prevention, mediation and deterrence, expressing its deep appreciation for the work of the troop-contributing countries, strongly condemning the attacks on United Nations personnel, and calling for investigations of these attacks in a swift and thorough manner and to hold those responsible to account,

Underscoring concern for the fragility of the security situation in the Abyei Area, acknowledging the contribution of the Force to enhanced peace and stability since its deployment, and expressing its determination to prevent the recurrence of violence against or displacements of civilians and to avert intercommunal conflict,

Reiterating its deep concern regarding the public administration and rule of law vacuum in the Abyei Area, due to continued delays in the establishment of the Abyei Area Administration, Council and Police Service, including a special unit to deal with particular issues related to nomadic migration, which are essential to maintain law and order and prevent intercommunal conflict in Abyei, and in this regard welcoming the efforts of the Force to support and strengthen community protection committees,

Noting with concern the continued delay in establishing the temporary institutions and resolving the final status of Abyei and that the continued threat of intercommunal violence contributes to heightened tensions in the Abyei Area, including those ongoing tensions that prevent Sudanese staff of the Force and other agencies from returning to Abyei,

Urging all parties to refrain from any unilateral action that could aggravate intercommunal relations within the Abyei Area, expressing concern over the continued implications of what the African Union Peace and Security Council described in its press statement of 6 November 2013 as "the decision by the Ngok Dinka to conduct a unilateral referendum", and also in this context taking note that the Government of the Sudan proceeded with its April 2015 national elections in Abyei,

Bearing in mind the current humanitarian situation in which humanitarian actors continue to provide assistance to approximately 81,000 people in the Abyei Area and the importance of coherence of United Nations assistance in the region, and further stressing the urgency of facilitating the delivery of humanitarian assistance to all affected populations,

Affirming the importance of voluntary, safe, dignified return and sustainable reintegration of displaced persons, and of peaceful and orderly migration cycles respecting the traditional migratory routes from the Sudan to South Sudan through Abyei, and urging the Force to continue to take measures as necessary to ensure security in the Abyei Area in accordance with its mandate,

Recalling its resolution 2117 (2013) of 26 September 2013, and expressing grave concern at the threat to peace and security in Abyei arising from the illicit transfer, destabilizing accumulation and misuse of small arms and light weapons, and in this regard welcoming the progress of the Force on improving infrastructure and systems for weapons confiscation, storage and destruction,

Expressing concern about the residual threat of landmines and explosive remnants of war in the Abyei Area, which hinders the safe return of displaced persons to their homes and safe migration,

Taking note of the reports of the Secretary-General of 29 April[304] and 16 June 2015,[305] including the assessment that the political and security situation on the ground is relatively calm but unpredictable, and requires dialogue and cooperation to prevent it becoming more contentious, divisive and destabilizing in the coming months, and the recommendations contained therein,

Recognizing that the current situation in Abyei and along the border between the Sudan and South Sudan continues to constitute a serious threat to international peace and security,

1. *Decides* to extend until 15 December 2015 the mandate of the United Nations Interim Security Force for Abyei as set out in paragraph 2 of resolution 1990 (2011) and modified by resolution 2024 (2011) and paragraph 1 of resolution 2075 (2012), and, acting under Chapter VII of the Charter of the United Nations, further decides to extend until 15 December 2015 the tasks of the Force as set out in paragraph 3 of resolution 1990 (2011), and determines that, for the purposes of paragraph 1 of resolution 2024 (2011), support to the operational activities of the Joint Border Verification and Monitoring Mechanism shall include support to the Ad Hoc Committees, as appropriate when so requested by consensual decisions of these mechanisms, within the operational area and existing capabilities of the Force;

2. *Takes note* of the recommendations in the report of the Secretary-General of 16 June 2015,[305] and welcomes the initiatives of the Force to support community dialogue and administration by the communities under the supervision of the Abyei Joint Oversight Committee; in this regard calls upon the communities and the Governments of the Sudan and South Sudan to take concrete steps towards those goals; and further welcomes the current and future support in these efforts from the United Nations, the African Union and the Government of Ethiopia;

3. *Underscores* that continued cooperation between the Government of the Sudan and the Government of South Sudan is also critical for peace, security and stability and the future relations between them;

4. *Welcomes* the resumption of the work of the Abyei Joint Oversight Committee by the Sudan and South Sudan in March 2015, and urges the resumption of regular meetings to ensure steady progress on the implementation of the Agreement on Temporary Arrangements for the Administration and Security of the Abyei Area of 20 June 2011,[274] including the implementation of the decisions of the Oversight Committee, welcomes African Union initiatives to support this goal and encourages its continued engagement, and requests the Secretary-General to provide an assessment of progress on these issues in his regular reports;

5. *Further reiterates its demand* that the Sudan and South Sudan urgently commence the establishment of the Abyei Area Administration and Council, including by resolving the deadlock over the composition of the Council, and constitute the Abyei Police Service, to enable it to take over policing functions throughout the Abyei Area, including the protection of oil infrastructure, in accordance with their commitments in the Agreement of 20 June 2011;

6. *Decides* to maintain the troops authorized by resolution 2104 (2013) already deployed, and that the remaining authorized forces shall continue to be deployed consistent with the evolution of the Joint Border Verification and Monitoring Mechanism, to enable the Force to provide required force protection to the Mechanism and to enable the Force to fully support the Mechanism to conduct extended operations into the Safe Demilitarized Border Zone as soon as possible, and requests the Secretary-General to keep the Security Council fully updated on the status of deployment as part of his regular reporting cycle;

---

[304] S/2015/302.

[305] S/2015/439.

7. *Takes note* of the establishment of the initial operating capability of the Joint Border Verification and Monitoring Mechanism, expresses renewed concern regarding the stalled efforts to fully operationalize the Mechanism, welcomes the Secretary-General's technical assessment of the Mechanism in May 2015, takes note of the recommendations of the Secretary-General that continued investment in achieving full operational capability of the Mechanism should be based on a set of conditions, including resolution of the dispute over the Safe Demilitarized Border Zone, resumption of border demarcation discussions, occurrence of regular meetings of the Joint Political and Security Mechanism, and granting of full freedom of movement, and expresses its intention to consider the final recommendations of the Secretary-General regarding operations of the Joint Border Verification and Monitoring Mechanism, to be presented in his next report;

8. *Calls upon* the Government of the Sudan and the Government of South Sudan to make timely and effective use of the Joint Border Verification and Monitoring Mechanism, the Joint Political and Security Mechanism and other agreed joint mechanisms to ensure the security and transparency of the Safe Demilitarized Border Zone, including the 14-mile area;

9. *Urges* renewed efforts to determine conclusively the centreline of the Safe Demilitarized Border Zone on the ground, and reiterates that the centreline of the Zone in no way prejudices the current or future legal status of the border, ongoing negotiations on the disputed and claimed areas, and demarcation of the borders;

10. *Underscores* that the protection of civilians mandate of the Force as set out in paragraph 3 of resolution 1990 (2011) includes taking the actions necessary to protect civilians under imminent threat of physical violence, irrespective of the source of such violence;

11. *Condemns* the intermittent presence of South Sudan security service personnel and the deployment of Diffra oil police units in the Abyei Area, as well as the repeated entry of armed militias into the territory, and reiterates its demands that immediately and without preconditions the Government of South Sudan fully redeploy its security service personnel from the Abyei Area and that the Government of the Sudan redeploy the oil police in Diffra from the Abyei Area, and further reiterates, in accordance with relevant resolutions, in particular resolutions 1990 (2011) and 2046 (2012), that the Abyei Area shall be demilitarized from any forces, as well as armed elements of the local communities, other than the Force and the Abyei Police Service;

12. *Supports* the decisions of the Abyei Joint Oversight Committee of 3 May 2013 and 30 March 2015 on Abyei's status as a weapons-free area, underscores the concern expressed by the African Union Peace and Security Council in its communiqué of 7 May 2013 over reports that various communities living in Abyei are heavily armed, recalls that in the Agreement of 20 June 2011it is stipulated that Abyei should be a weapons-free area and that only the Force is authorized to carry weapons inside the Area, and in this regard urges the two Governments to take all steps necessary to ensure that Abyei is effectively demilitarized, including through disarmament programmes as necessary;

13. *Reaffirms* that the Force may undertake weapons confiscation and destruction in the Abyei Area as authorized under resolution 1990 (2011), consistent with its mandate and within its existing capabilities, in coordination with the signatories to the Agreement of 20 June 2011, the Abyei Joint Oversight Committee and the Misseriya and Ngok Dinka communities and consistent with the previous Oversight Committee decision to establish the Area as a "weapons free area", and reiterates its request that the Force observe, document and report on the movement of weapons into Abyei and the presence, destruction and confiscation of weapons within Abyei as part of the Secretary-General's regular reporting cycle;

14. *Requests* the Force to continue its dialogue with the Abyei Joint Oversight Committee and with the Misseriya and Ngok Dinka communities on effective strategies and oversight mechanisms for ensuring full compliance by all relevant parties with Abyei's status as a weapons-free area, with a particular priority placed on the urgent elimination of heavy or crew-served weapons, as well as rocket-propelled grenades, and calls upon the Governments of the Sudan and South Sudan, the Oversight Committee and the Misseriya and Ngok Dinka communities to extend full cooperation to the Force in this regard;

15. *Urges* the two Governments immediately to take steps to implement confidence-building measures among the respective communities in the Abyei Area, including through reconciliation processes at the grass-roots level and supporting the Force in promoting community dialogue, urges the planned convening of a meeting between the Ngok Dinka and Misseriya traditional leaders, and strongly urges all Abyei communities to exercise maximum restraint in all their engagements and to desist from inflammatory acts or statements that may lead to violent clashes, or any further unilateral activities;

16. *Requests* the Force, within its existing capabilities and resources and in close coordination with the Misseriya and Ngok Dinka communities, to intensify efforts to strengthen the capacities of community protection committees in order to assist with the management of law and order processes in Abyei;

17. *Calls upon* all parties to cooperate fully with the findings and recommendations following the investigation by the Abyei Area Joint Investigation and Inquiry Committee into the killing of a Force peacekeeper and the Ngok Dinka Paramount Chief, welcomes the press statement by the African Union Peace and Security Council of 24 March 2015 requesting the African Union Commission to engage the parties on the findings and recommendations, and reiterates the need to enable the two communities to find closure on the assassination of the Ngok Dinka Paramount Chief, bearing in mind the need to promote stability and reconciliation in the Abyei Area;

18. *Expresses its intention* to review, as appropriate, the mandate of the Force for possible reconfiguration of the Force in the light of the compliance by the Sudan and South Sudan with the decisions set forth in resolution 2046 (2012) and their commitments as set forth in the Agreements of 20 and 29 June and 30 July 2011[275] and 27 September 2012,[276] including the redeployment of all forces from the Safe Demilitarized Border Zone, achieving full operational capability for the Joint Border Verification and Monitoring Mechanism and the Ad Hoc Committees, as well as completing the full demilitarization of the Abyei Area;

19. *Calls upon* all Member States, in particular the Sudan and South Sudan, to ensure the free, unhindered and expeditious movement to and from Abyei and throughout the Safe Demilitarized Border Zone of all personnel, as well as equipment, provisions, supplies and other goods, including vehicles, aircraft and spare parts, which are for the exclusive and official use of the Force;

20. *Renews its call upon* the Governments of the Sudan and South Sudan to provide full support to the United Nations, including by promptly issuing visas to military, police and civilian United Nations personnel, including humanitarian personnel, without prejudice to their nationality, for entry into the Sudan and South Sudan, facilitating basing arrangements, infrastructure construction in the mission area and flight clearances, and providing logistical support, calls upon the Governments of the Sudan and South Sudan to facilitate travel from within the Sudan and South Sudan to and from Abyei, and further calls upon all parties to fully adhere to their obligations under the status-of-forces agreements;

21. *Recognizes* that the absence of development projects and the inability to deliver basic government services has had an adverse effect on Abyei populations, and calls upon the Government of the Sudan and the Government of South Sudan, as well as donors, to support reconstruction and capacity-building;

22. *Demands* that the Government of the Sudan and the Government of South Sudan continue to facilitate the deployment of the Mine Action Service of the United Nations to ensure the freedom of movement of the Joint Border Verification and Monitoring Mechanism as well as the identification and clearance of mines in the Abyei Area and the Safe Demilitarized Border Zone;

23. *Also demands* that all parties involved allow all humanitarian personnel full, safe and unhindered access to civilians in need of assistance and all facilities necessary for their operations, in accordance with international law, including applicable international humanitarian law, and United Nations guiding principles of humanitarian assistance;

24. *Strongly urges* that all parties cease all forms of violence, human rights violations and abuses, violations of international humanitarian law and violations and abuses against children in violation of applicable international law;

25. *Requests* the Secretary-General to ensure that effective human rights monitoring is carried out and the results included in his reports to the Security Council, and reiterates its call upon the Government of the Sudan and the Government of South Sudan to extend their full cooperation to the Secretary-General to this end, including by issuing visas to the concerned United Nations personnel;

26. *Also requests* the Secretary-General to take the measures necessary to ensure full compliance of the Force with the United Nations zero-tolerance policy on sexual exploitation and abuse and to keep the Council informed if cases of such conduct occur;

27. *Further requests* the Secretary-General to continue to inform the Council of progress in implementing the mandate of the Force in two written reports, no later than 15 September 2015 and 15 November 2015 respectively, and to continue to bring to the Council's immediate attention any serious violations of the above-referenced agreements, including on fulfilment of the conditions set out in paragraph 7 of the present resolution regarding the Joint Border Verification and Monitoring Mechanism;

28. *Notes* the efforts of the Secretary-General to ensure close cooperation among United Nations missions in the region, including the Force, the United Nations Mission in South Sudan and the African Union-United Nations Hybrid Operation in Darfur, as well as his Special Envoy for the Sudan and South Sudan, and requests that he continue this practice;

29. *Decides* to remain actively seized of the matter.

Adopted unanimously at the 7483rd meeting.

POST-CONFLICT PEACEBUILDING[306]

Decisions

On 9 January 2015, the President of the Security Council addressed the following letter to the Secretary-General:[307]

> I have the honour to refer to Security Council resolution 1646 (2005), in which the Council, in keeping with its resolution 1645 (2005), decided that the permanent members listed in Article 23, paragraph 1, of the Charter of the United Nations should be members of the Organizational Committee of the Peacebuilding Commission and that, in addition, the Council should annually select two of its elected members to participate in the Organizational Committee.
>
> I therefore have the honour to inform you that, following informal consultations, the members of the Council agreed on the selection of Chad and Chile as the two elected members of the Council to participate in the Organizational Committee for a term of one year, until the end of 2015.

At its 7359th meeting, on 14 January 2015, the Council considered the item entitled:

"Post-conflict peacebuilding

"Report of the Secretary-General on peacebuilding in the aftermath of conflict (S/2014/694)".

At the same meeting, the Council decided to extend an invitation, in accordance with rule 39 of its provisional rules of procedure, to Mr. Antonio de Aguiar Patriota, Permanent Representative of Brazil to the United Nations, in his capacity as Chair of the Peacebuilding Commission.

At the same meeting, following consultations among members of the Security Council, the President made the following statement on behalf of the Council:[308]

> The Security Council recalls its resolutions and the statements by its President on post-conflict peacebuilding, in particular the statements of 22 July 2009,[309] 13 October 2010,[310] 21 January 2011,[311] 11 February 2011[312] and 20 December 2012,[313] and reaffirms the critical importance of peacebuilding as the foundation for sustainable peace and development in the aftermath of conflict.
>
> The Council takes note with appreciation of the report of the Secretary-General on peacebuilding in the aftermath of conflict[314] and the country-specific evidence of impacts and lessons learned it contains.

---

[306] Resolutions or decisions on this question were first adopted by the Security Council in 2005.

[307] S/2015/15.

[308] S/PRST/2015/2.

[309] S/PRST/2009/23.

[310] S/PRST/2010/20.

[311] S/PRST/2011/2.

[312] S/PRST/2011/4.

[313] S/PRST/2012/29.

[314] S/2014/694.

The Council recognizes that peacebuilding is an important element of the United Nations efforts in countries emerging from conflict; and reaffirms that sustainable peace and security requires an integrated sustained approach based on coherence among political, security and development approaches which are essential for effectively improving respect for human rights, advancing gender equality, strengthening the rule of law and advancing economic development in countries emerging from conflict, recognizing the specific needs and situation of the country concerned.

The Council underlines that the primary responsibility for successful peacebuilding lies with national Governments and relevant local actors, including civil society, in countries emerging from conflict.

The Council emphasizes the importance of inclusivity in advancing national peacebuilding processes and objectives in order to ensure that the needs of all segments of society are taken into account.

The Council reaffirms that national ownership and leadership is key to establishing sustainable peace and reaffirms also the primary responsibility of national authorities in identifying their priorities and strategies for post-conflict peacebuilding.

The Council underscores that peacebuilding, in particular institution-building, the extension of State authority and the re-establishment of core public administration functions, requires sustained international and national attention, and financial and technical support in order to effectively build and sustain peace in countries emerging from conflict. The Council recognizes that the gaps in the provision of rapid and sustained financial support continue to hamper peacebuilding efforts. The Council welcomes the role played by the United Nations Peacebuilding Fund in filling these gaps and urges Member States to contribute to the Fund and other relevant multi-donor trust funds that support countries emerging from conflict in order to replenish them.

The Council recognizes recent successes in collective peacebuilding efforts of the United Nations and the wider international community and also acknowledges the setbacks and the challenges that the United Nations system, including the Council and the wider international community, have faced in preventing or reducing the risks of relapse into conflict. The Council expresses its determination to continue to take into consideration the underlying causes of relapse into conflict.

The Council looks forward to the outcome of the 2015 review of the peacebuilding architecture and to the consideration of its recommendations in order to improve the peacebuilding capacity of the United Nations system, inter alia, by strengthening the performance and impact of the peacebuilding architecture with a view to realizing its full potential in line with the agreed terms of reference.

The Council underlines the need for the review of the peacebuilding architecture to be undertaken in conjunction and synergy with the upcoming Secretary-General's review of peace operations.

The Council recognizes the continuing need to increase women's participation and the consideration of gender-related issues in all discussions pertinent to the prevention and resolution of armed conflict, the maintenance of peace and security and post-conflict peacebuilding.

The Council recalls its resolution 1645 (2005) and acknowledges the important role of the Peacebuilding Commission in the peacebuilding architecture, and stresses its willingness to strengthen its links with the Commission by, inter alia, making greater use of its advisory role. The Council calls upon the Commission to make further efforts in promoting improved coherence and alignment of partners' policies around national peacebuilding strategies and priorities, and ensure regional and international support and effective response through engagement and establishing partnerships with international financial institutions, neighbouring countries and regional and subregional organizations. The Council underscores the importance of the regional aspect of peacebuilding and the need for engaging and collaborating with regional actors in policy related and country-specific issues in the advice made by the Commission.

The Council notes that the Commission's advisory role to the Council is particularly appreciated in view of its contribution to the implementation of the Council's mandates on the ground in countries on its agenda.

The Council requests the Secretary-General to brief the Council by December 2015 and to submit to the Council no later than December 2016 a report on further United Nations peacebuilding efforts in the aftermath of conflict, including progress towards increasing the participation of women in peacebuilding, taking into consideration the views of the Commission.

At its 7472nd meeting, on 25 June 2015, the Council considered the item entitled:

"Post-conflict peacebuilding

"Report of the Peacebuilding Commission on its eighth session (S/2015/174)".

At the same meeting, the Council decided to extend invitations, in accordance with rule 39 of its provisional rules of procedure, to Mr. Antonio de Aguiar Patriota, Permanent Representative of Brazil to the United Nations, in his capacity as former Chair of the Peacebuilding Commission, and Mr. Olof Skoog, Permanent Representative of Sweden to the United Nations, in his capacity as Chair of the Peacebuilding Commission.

THE SITUATION CONCERNING IRAQ[315]

Decisions

At its 7271st meeting, on 19 September 2014, the Security Council decided to invite the representatives of Albania, Bahrain, Belgium, Canada, Denmark, Egypt, Finland, Georgia, Germany, Iran (Islamic Republic of), Iraq, Italy, Japan, Lebanon, the Netherlands, New Zealand, Norway, Oman, Poland, Qatar, Saudi Arabia, Spain, the Syrian Arab Republic, Turkey and the United Arab Emirates to participate, without vote, in accordance with rule 37 of its provisional rules of procedure, in the discussion of the item entitled "The situation concerning Iraq".

At the same meeting, the Council also decided to extend an invitation, in accordance with rule 39 of its provisional rules of procedure, to Mr. Nickolay Mladenov, Special Representative of the Secretary-General for Iraq and Head of the United Nations Assistance Mission for Iraq.

At the same meeting, following consultations among members of the Security Council, the President made the following statement on behalf of the Council:[316]

> The Security Council welcomes the newly formed Government of Iraq and calls upon the international community to support its efforts to strengthen further democratic institutions, to maintain security and combat terrorism and to create a safe, stable and prosperous future for the people of Iraq. The Council reaffirms its support for the independence, sovereignty, unity and territorial integrity of Iraq and reaffirms further the purposes and principles of the Charter of the United Nations.
>
> The Council underscores the need for all segments of the Iraqi population to participate in the political process and engage in political dialogue. The Council is encouraged by the Government of Iraq's commitment to resolve longstanding issues through an inclusive political process and consistent with the Iraqi Constitution and looks forward to implementation of this commitment through its new national agenda. The Council encourages Iraq's leaders to accelerate implementation of this agenda and national reconciliation to address the needs of Iraq's diverse communities.
>
> The Council also urges Member States to work closely with the Government of Iraq to identify how best the international community can aid implementation of the new Iraqi agenda. The Council reaffirms its full support for the United Nations Assistance Mission for Iraq in advising and assisting the Iraqi people and the Government of Iraq in strengthening democratic institutions and advancing inclusive political dialogue.
>
> The Council strongly condemns attacks by terrorist organizations, including the terrorist organization operating under the name "Islamic State in Iraq and the Levant" and associated armed groups, in Iraq, the Syrian Arab Republic and Lebanon and emphasizes that this large-scale offensive poses a major threat to the region. The Council expresses again its deep outrage about all Iraqis as well as nationals of other States who have been killed, kidnapped, raped or tortured by Islamic State in Iraq and the Levant, as well as its

---

[315] Resolutions or decisions on this question were first adopted by the Security Council in 2005.

[316] S/PRST/2014/20.

recruitment and use of children. The Council stresses the need that those who have committed or are otherwise responsible for violations of international humanitarian law or violations or abuses of human rights in Iraq must be held accountable, noting that some of these acts may constitute war crimes and crimes against humanity. The Council stresses the need for those responsible for such violations of international humanitarian law or violations or abuses of human rights to be held to account, and calls upon the Government of Iraq and the international community to work towards ensuring that all perpetrators are brought to justice.

The Council welcomes the Government of Iraq's efforts, in association with local and regional authorities, to combat the terrorist threat facing all Iraqis, including members of its ethnic and religious minorities, notably Yezidis and Christians, and women from all communities who have been particularly targeted by Islamic State in Iraq and the Levant.

The Council reaffirms that all parties, including Islamic State in Iraq and the Levant, associated armed groups and other militias, must respect the human rights of the Iraqi people and abide by all applicable obligations under international humanitarian law, including those protecting the civilian population, by which both official Iraqi forces and Member States that assist them must also abide.

The Council also recognizes the steps taken to address the urgent humanitarian needs of those displaced by the current conflict. The Council calls for an intensification of these efforts by all parties and urges all Member States to continue to fund the United Nations humanitarian appeals.

The Council urges the international community, in accordance with international law, to further strengthen and expand support for the Government of Iraq as it fights Islamic State in Iraq and the Levant and associated armed groups. The Council welcomes the International Conference on Peace and Security in Iraq that took place in Paris on 15 September 2014 and the summit-level meeting of the Council responding to the global threat posed by foreign terrorist fighters that is scheduled for 24 September 2014.

The Council stresses that terrorism can only be defeated by a sustained and comprehensive approach involving the active participation and collaboration of all States, as well as international and regional organizations, to impede, impair, isolate and incapacitate the terrorist threat.

The Council reiterates the urgent need to stop any direct or indirect trade in oil from Iraq involving Islamic State in Iraq and the Levant with the aim of putting an end to financing terrorism.

The Council supports Iraq's further economic, social, political and diplomatic integration into the region and the international community and calls upon regional States to engage more actively to facilitate this process. The Council recognizes that the situation that now exists in Iraq is significantly different from that which existed at the time of the adoption of resolution 661 (1990), and further recognizes the importance of Iraq achieving international standing equal to that which it held prior to the adoption of resolution 661 (1990).

The Council reiterates that no terrorist act can reverse the path toward peace, democracy and reconstruction in Iraq, which is supported by the people and the Government of Iraq and by the international community.

At its 7314th meeting, on 18 November 2014, the Council decided to invite the representative of Iraq to participate, without vote, in accordance with rule 37 of its provisional rules of procedure, in the discussion of the item entitled:

"The situation concerning Iraq

"First report of the Secretary-General pursuant to paragraph 6 of resolution 2169 (2014) (S/2014/774)

"Fourth report of the Secretary-General pursuant to paragraph 4 of Security Council resolution 2107 (2013) (S/2014/776)".

At the same meeting, the Council also decided to extend invitations, in accordance with rule 39 of its provisional rules of procedure, to Mr. Nickolay Mladenov, Special Representative of the Secretary-General for Iraq and Head of the United Nations Assistance Mission for Iraq, Mr. Zeid Ra'ad Al-Hussein, United Nations High Commissioner for Human Rights, and Ms. Valerie Amos, Under-Secretary-General for Humanitarian Affairs and Emergency Relief Coordinator.

At its 7383rd meeting, on 17 February 2015, the Council decided to invite the representative of Iraq to participate, without vote, in accordance with rule 37 of its provisional rules of procedure, in the discussion of the item entitled:

"The situation concerning Iraq

"Fifth report of the Secretary-General pursuant to paragraph 4 of Security Council resolution 2107 (2013) (S/2015/70)

"Second report of the Secretary-General pursuant to paragraph 6 of resolution 2169 (2014) (S/2015/82)".

At the same meeting, the Council also decided to extend an invitation, in accordance with rule 39 of its provisional rules of procedure, to Mr. Nickolay Mladenov, Special Representative of the Secretary-General for Iraq and Head of the United Nations Assistance Mission for Iraq.

On 23 February 2015, the President of the Security Council addressed the following letter to the Secretary-General:[317]

I have the honour to inform you that your letter dated 19 February 2015 concerning your intention to appoint Mr. Ján Kubiš, of Slovakia, as your Special Representative for Iraq and Head of the United Nations Assistance Mission for Iraq[318] has been brought to the attention of the members of the Security Council. They take note of the intention expressed in your letter.

At its 7443rd meeting, on 14 May 2015, the Council decided to invite the representative of Iraq to participate, without vote, in accordance with rule 37 of its provisional rules of procedure, in the discussion of the item entitled:

"The situation concerning Iraq

"Sixth report of the Secretary-General pursuant to paragraph 4 of Security Council resolution 2107 (2013) (S/2015/298)

"Third report of the Secretary-General pursuant to paragraph 6 of resolution 2169 (2014) (S/2015/305)".

At the same meeting, the Council also decided to extend invitations, in accordance with rule 39 of its provisional rules of procedure, to Mr. Ján Kubiš, Special Representative of the Secretary-General for Iraq and Head of the United Nations Assistance Mission for Iraq, and Ms. Valerie Amos, Under-Secretary-General for Humanitarian Affairs and Emergency Relief Coordinator.

At its 7489th meeting, on 22 July 2015, the Council decided to invite the representative of Iraq to participate, without vote, in accordance with rule 37 of its provisional rules of procedure, in the discussion of the item entitled:

"The situation concerning Iraq

"Seventh report of the Secretary-General pursuant to paragraph 4 of Security Council resolution 2107 (2013) (S/2015/518)

"Fourth report of the Secretary-General pursuant to paragraph 6 of resolution 2169 (2014) (S/2015/530)".

At the same meeting, the Council also decided to extend an invitation, in accordance with rule 39 of its provisional rules of procedure, to Mr. Ján Kubiš, Special Representative of the Secretary-General for Iraq and Head of the United Nations Assistance Mission for Iraq.

At its 7495th meeting, on 29 July 2015, the Council considered the item entitled:

"The situation concerning Iraq

"Seventh report of the Secretary-General pursuant to paragraph 4 of Security Council resolution 2107 (2013) (S/2015/518)

"Fourth report of the Secretary-General pursuant to paragraph 6 of resolution 2169 (2014) (S/2015/530)".

[317] S/2015/130.

[318] S/2015/129.

Resolution 2233 (2015)
of 29 July 2015

The Security Council,

Recalling all its previous relevant resolutions on Iraq, in particular resolutions 1500 (2003) of 14 August 2003, 1546 (2004) of 8 June 2004, 1557 (2004) of 12 August 2004, 1619 (2005) of 11 August 2005, 1700 (2006) of 10 August 2006, 1770 (2007) of 10 August 2007, 1830 (2008) of 7 August 2008, 1883 (2009) of 7 August 2009, 1936 (2010) of 5 August 2010, 2001 (2011) of 28 July 2011, 2061 (2012) of 25 July 2012, 2110 (2013) of 24 July 2013 and 2169 (2014) of 30 July 2014, and resolution 2107 (2013) of 27 June 2013 on the situation between Iraq and Kuwait,

Reaffirming the independence, sovereignty, unity and territorial integrity of Iraq,

Emphasizing the importance of the stability and security of Iraq for the people of Iraq, the region and the international community,

Expressing grave concern at the current security situation in Iraq as a result of a large-scale offensive carried out by terrorist groups, in particular Islamic State in Iraq and the Levant (also known as Da'esh) and associated armed groups, involving violations of international humanitarian law, heavy civilian casualties, including women and children, the displacement of more than three million Iraqi civilians, use of sexual violence against and the sexual enslavement of women and girls, threats against all religious and ethnic groups, and the threat to the safety of journalists, media professionals and associated personnel; condemning the attacks perpetrated by these terrorist groups and associated armed groups against the people of Iraq in an attempt to destabilize the country and region, and reiterating its commitment to the security and territorial integrity of Iraq,

Noting that the presence of Islamic State in Iraq and the Levant on the sovereign territory of Iraq is a major threat to the future of Iraq, underscoring that the only way to address this threat is for all Iraqis to work together by addressing needs in the security as well as the political realm, stressing that the long-term solution to the instability will require the political leadership of Iraq to make decisions that will unite the country, and emphasizing the importance of the international community supporting Iraq in this regard,

Calling upon all political entities to overcome divisions and work together in an inclusive and timely political process aimed at strengthening the national unity, sovereignty and independence of Iraq, and for Iraq's leaders to engage in dialogue that would contribute to finding a viable and sustainable solution to the country's current challenges; and reaffirming its belief that through its democratic institutions, in cooperation with Iraqi society, Iraq can work to address the challenges facing the country for the benefit of all Iraqis,

Underscoring the need for all segments of the Iraqi population to participate in the political process, in an inclusive political dialogue and in the economic and social life of Iraq, to refrain from statements and actions which could aggravate tensions, to reach a comprehensive solution on the fair distribution of resources, and to promote stability, develop a just and fair solution for the nation's disputed internal boundaries and work to strengthen national unity, and stressing the importance of a comprehensive and inclusive Iraqi-led political process to support dialogue for all those who renounce violence, have no links to international terrorist organizations including Islamic State in Iraq and the Levant, and respect the Constitution,

Encouraging the Government of Iraq to continue strengthening governance, promoting human rights and the rule of law, improving the situation of women and girls, especially those impacted by Islamic State in Iraq and the Levant, improving security and public order, and combating terrorism and sectarian violence and reiterating its support to the people and the Government of Iraq in their efforts to build a secure, stable, federal, united and democratic nation, based on the rule of law and respect for human rights,

Expressing grave concern for the more than three million individuals seeking refuge in other areas of Iraq, reiterating its gratitude to the host communities, underscoring that host communities should provide access to safe areas for internally displaced persons, emphasizing the urgency of addressing humanitarian issues confronting the Iraqi people, stressing the need to continue to plan and implement a coordinated response and to provide adequate resources to address these issues, calling for an intensification of these efforts by all parties and urging all Member States to continue to fund the United Nations humanitarian appeals, encouraging Member States to support the United Nations humanitarian response in Iraq, working with the Government of Iraq, to assist all Iraqi individuals affected by the ongoing conflict, and commending the efforts of Member States that have contributed to the humanitarian effort,

Emphasizing the need to continue efforts to promote international and regional cooperation aimed at supporting Iraq both in its reconciliation and political dialogue and in its fight against Islamic State in Iraq and the Levant, and to prevent terrorist groups included on the sanctions list established by the Security Council Committee pursuant to resolutions 1267 (1999) and 1989 (2011), in particular Islamic State in Iraq and the Levant, from using the territories of Iraq and neighbouring States to carry out violence or other illicit acts to destabilize Iraq and the region, expressing its readiness to sanction further individuals, groups, undertakings and entities that are supporting Islamic State in Iraq and the Levant, expressing grave concern over reports of access to and seizure of oilfields and pipelines in Iraq by terrorist groups listed by the Committee, strongly condemning any engagement in direct or indirect trade in oil and refined oil products, modular refineries and related material, other natural resources and antiquities from Iraq involving these terrorist groups, consistent with Council resolution 2199 (2015) of 12 February 2015, and emphasizing that such engagement constitutes financial support for such terrorists and may lead to further sanctions listings by the Committee,

Reaffirming the importance of the United Nations, in particular the United Nations Assistance Mission for Iraq, in advising, supporting and assisting the Iraqi people, including civil society, and the Government of Iraq to strengthen democratic institutions, advance inclusive political dialogue and national reconciliation according to the Constitution, facilitate regional dialogue, develop processes acceptable to the Government to resolve disputed internal boundaries, aid youth and vulnerable groups, including refugees and internally displaced persons, and promote the protection of human rights, gender equality, children and youth and vulnerable groups, and emphasizing the importance of the United Nations, in particular the Mission, prioritizing advice, support and assistance to the Iraqi people, including civil society, and the Government to achieve these goals,

Further expressing grave concern that the violent extremism and terrorism perpetrated by Islamic State in Iraq and the Levant in Iraq has frequently targeted women and girls, and that Islamic State in Iraq and the Levant has committed serious human rights abuses and violations of international humanitarian law against women and children, including those involving murder, kidnapping, hostage-taking, enslavement, their sale into or otherwise forced marriage, human trafficking, rape, sexual slavery and other forms of sexual violence, and expressing grave concern at the recruitment and use of children by Islamic State in Iraq and the Levant and other armed groups in violation of international law,

Encouraging the Government of Iraq to continue in its efforts to promote and protect the rights of women, and reaffirming its resolutions 1325 (2000) of 31 October 2000, 1820 (2008) of 19 June 2008, 1888 (2009) of 30 September 2009, 1889 (2009) of 5 October 2009, 1960 (2010) of 16 December 2010, 2106 (2013) of 24 June 2013, and 2122 (2013) of 18 October 2013 on women and peace, and security, and reiterating the need for the full, equal and effective participation of women; reaffirming the key role women can play in re-establishing the fabric of society and stressing the need for their full political participation, including in peace processes, political decision-making and the development of national strategies, in order to take into account their perspectives, and looking forward to the full implementation, including funding, of Iraq's national action plan on Security Council resolution 1325 (2000),

Reaffirming that all parties should continue to take all feasible steps to ensure the protection of affected civilians, including children, women and members of religious and ethnic minority groups, and should create conditions conducive to the voluntary, safe, dignified and sustainable return of refugees and internally displaced persons or local integration of internally displaced persons, particularly in areas newly liberated from Islamic State in Iraq and the Levant, and to promote stabilization activities and long-term sustainable development, welcoming commitments and encouraging continued efforts of the Government of Iraq for the relief of internally displaced persons, refugees and returnees, noting the important role of the Office of the United Nations High Commissioner for Refugees, based on its mandate, in providing continued advice and support to the Government, in coordination with the Mission, on these issues, and encouraging the Government to continue to work with the Mission and humanitarian agencies to ensure the delivery of humanitarian relief to those in need,

Urging the Government of Iraq to continue to promote and protect human rights and also to consider additional steps to support the Independent High Commission for Human Rights in carrying out its mandate, and reaffirming that all parties, including Islamic State in Iraq and the Levant, associated armed groups and militias, must respect human rights and abide by all applicable obligations under international humanitarian law, including those protecting the civilian population, by which both official Iraqi forces and Member States that assist them must also abide,

Reaffirming that all States shall ensure that any person who participates in the financing, planning, preparation or perpetration of terrorist acts or in supporting terrorist acts is brought to justice,

Urging all those concerned to allow full unimpeded access by humanitarian personnel to all people in need of assistance and to make available, as far as possible, all facilities necessary for their operations, and to promote the safety, security and freedom of movement of humanitarian personnel and United Nations staff, associated personnel and their assets, and also to respect and protect health-care workers and medical transport and facilities,

Condemning the destruction of cultural heritage in Iraq, particularly by Islamic State in Iraq and the Levant, including targeted destruction of religious sites and objects, and noting with concern that Islamic State in Iraq and the Levant and other individuals, groups, undertakings and entities associated with Al-Qaida are generating income from engaging directly or indirectly in the looting and smuggling of cultural heritage items from archaeological sites, museums, libraries, archives and other sites in Iraq, which is being used to support their recruitment efforts and strengthen their operational capability to organize and carry out terrorist attacks,

Recognizing that the situation that now exists in Iraq is significantly different from that which existed at the time of the adoption of resolution 661 (1990) on 6 August 1990, and further recognizing the importance of Iraq achieving international standing equal to that which it held prior to the adoption of resolution 661 (1990),

Expressing deep gratitude to all the United Nations staff in Iraq for their courageous and tireless efforts, and commending the leadership and good offices role of the Special Representative of the Secretary-General for Iraq, Mr. Ján Kubiš,

1. *Decides* to extend the mandate of the United Nations Assistance Mission for Iraq until 31 July 2016;

2. *Also decides* that the Special Representative of the Secretary-General for Iraq and the Mission, at the request of the Government of Iraq, and taking into account the letter dated 8 July 2015 from the Minister for Foreign Affairs of Iraq to the Secretary-General,[319] shall continue to pursue their mandate as stipulated in resolution 2169 (2014), and recalls the provisions of resolution 2107 (2013);

3. *Welcomes* the recommendation of the Secretary-General, in his latest report,[320] to revise and prioritize the tasks of the Mission, requests the Secretary-General, in full consultation with the Government of Iraq, to report back in further detail about such recommendation to the Security Council within the next 90 days;

4. *Recognizes* that security of United Nations personnel is essential for the Mission to carry out its work for the benefit of the people of Iraq, and calls upon the Government of Iraq to continue to provide security and logistical support to the United Nations presence in Iraq;

5. *Welcomes* the contributions of Member States in providing the Mission with the financial, logistical and security resources and support that it needs to fulfil its mission, and calls upon Member States to continue to provide the Mission with sufficient resources and support;

6. *Expresses its intention* to review the mandate of the Mission in 12 months or sooner, if requested by the Government of Iraq;

7. *Requests* the Secretary-General to report to the Council every three months on the progress made towards the fulfilment of all the responsibilities of the Mission;

8. *Decides* to remain seized of the matter.

Adopted unanimously at the 7495th meeting.

[319] S/2015/520, annex.

[320] S/2015/530.

THREATS TO INTERNATIONAL PEACE AND SECURITY[321]

Decisions

At its 7351st meeting, on 19 December 2014, the Security Council decided to invite the representatives of Algeria, Bangladesh, Brazil, Colombia, Egypt, Ethiopia, Germany, Guatemala, India, Iran (Islamic Republic of), Iraq, Israel, Italy, Japan, Kazakhstan, Libya, Malaysia, Mali, Morocco, the Netherlands, New Zealand, Niger, Pakistan, Senegal, Spain, Sweden, the Syrian Arab Republic, Tunisia, Turkey, Uganda and Ukraine to participate in the meeting, without vote, in accordance with rule 37 of its provisional rules of procedure, in the discussion of the item entitled:

"Threats to international peace and security

> "Terrorism and cross-border crime
>
> "Report of the Secretary-General on the work of the United Nations to help States and subregional and regional entities in Africa in fighting terrorism (S/2014/9)
>
> "Letter dated 4 December 2014 from the Permanent Representative of Chad to the United Nations addressed to the Secretary-General (S/2014/869)".

At the same meeting, the Council also decided to extend an invitation, in accordance with rule 39 of its provisional rules of procedure, to Mr. Jeffrey Feltman, Under-Secretary-General for Political Affairs.

At the same meeting, the Council further decided to extend invitations, in accordance with rule 39 of its provisional rules of procedure, to Mr. Téte António, Permanent Observer of the African Union to the United Nations, and Ms. Mara Marinaki, Managing Director for Global and Multilateral Issues of the European External Action Service of the European Union.

Resolution 2195 (2014) of 19 December 2014

The Security Council,

Reaffirming its primary responsibility for the maintenance of international peace and security,

Reaffirming also that terrorism in all its forms and manifestations constitutes one of the most serious threats to international peace and security and that any acts of terrorism are criminal and unjustifiable regardless of their motivations, whenever and by whomsoever committed,

Reaffirming further that terrorism cannot and should not be associated with any religion, nationality or civilization,

Stressing that terrorism can only be defeated by a sustained and comprehensive approach involving the active participation and collaboration of all States and international and regional organizations to impede, impair, isolate and incapacitate the terrorist threat,

Gravely concerned by the financing of and financial and other resources obtained by terrorists, and underscoring that these resources will support their future terrorist activities,

Reaffirming the need to prevent and suppress the financing of terrorist acts,

Expressing concern that terrorists benefit from transnational organized crime in some regions, including from the trafficking in arms, persons, drugs and artefacts and from the illicit trade in natural resources, including gold and other precious metals and stones, minerals, wildlife, charcoal and oil, as well as from kidnapping for ransom and other crimes, including extortion and bank robbery,

Stressing that the development and maintenance of fair and effective criminal justice systems should be a fundamental basis of any strategy to counter terrorism and transnational organized crime,

[321] Resolutions or decisions on this question were first adopted by the Security Council in 2005.

Noting the communiqué of the African Union Peace and Security Council summit on countering violent extremism and terrorism, held in Nairobi on 2 September 2014, and calling upon United Nations counter-terrorism entities, within existing mandates, and Member States to provide assistance and capacity-building towards Africa's efforts to counter violent extremism and terrorism,

Gravely concerned that in some cases individuals, groups, undertakings and entities associated with Al-Qaida continue to profit from involvement in transnational organized crime, and stressing in this regard the need for robust implementation of the measures in paragraph 1 of resolution 2161 (2014) of 17 June 2014 as a significant tool in combating terrorist activity,

Urging, in this respect, all Member States to participate actively in maintaining and updating the list created pursuant to resolutions 1267 (1999) of 15 October 1999, 1333 (2000) of 19 December 2000 and 1989 (2011) of 17 June 2011 (the Al-Qaida Sanctions List) by contributing additional information pertinent to current listings, submitting delisting requests when appropriate, and by identifying and nominating for listing additional individuals, groups, undertakings and entities which should be subject to the measures referred to in paragraph 1 of resolution 2161 (2014),

Recalling its recent condemnation in resolution 2170 (2014) of 15 August 2014 of any engagement in direct or indirect trade involving Islamic State in Iraq and the Levant, Al-Nusrah Front and all other individuals, groups, undertakings and entities associated with Al-Qaida, and its reiteration that such engagement could constitute financial support for entities designated by the Security Council Committee pursuant to resolutions 1267 (1999) and 1989 (2011) (the Committee) and may lead to further listings by the Committee,

Deeply concerned that terrorist groups benefiting from transnational organized crime may contribute to undermining affected States, specifically their security, stability, governance and social and economic development,

Reaffirming the need to increase attention to women and peace and security issues in all relevant thematic areas of work on its agenda, including in threats to international peace and security caused by terrorist acts, and noting the importance of incorporating the participation of women and youth in developing strategies to counter terrorism and violent extremism,

Emphasizing the need to address conditions conducive to the spread of terrorism,

Emphasizing also that the combined presence of terrorism, violent extremism and transnational organized crime may exacerbate conflicts in affected regions, including in Africa, and noting that terrorist groups benefiting from transnational organized crime can, in some cases and in some regions, complicate conflict prevention and resolution efforts,

Seriously concerned, in this regard, by recent examples of terrorist groups, including those benefiting from transnational organized crime, attacking United Nations personnel,

Recalling its resolution 2133 (2014) of 27 January 2014 and strongly condemning incidents of kidnapping and hostage-taking committed by terrorist groups for any purpose, including raising funds or gaining political concessions, and expressing its determination to prevent kidnapping and hostage-taking committed by terrorist groups and to secure the safe release of hostages without ransom payments or political concessions, in accordance with applicable international law,

Noting recent developments and initiatives at the international, regional and subregional levels to prevent and suppress international terrorism, noting the work of the Global Counterterrorism Forum, in particular its recent adoption of a comprehensive set of good practices to address the foreign terrorist fighter phenomenon, and its publication of several other framework documents and good practices, including in the areas of countering violent extremism, criminal justice, prisons, kidnapping for ransom, providing support to victims of terrorism, and community-oriented policing, to assist interested States with the practical implementation of the United Nations counter-terrorism legal and policy framework and to complement the work of the relevant United Nations counter-terrorism entities in these areas,

Reaffirming the need to combat by all means, in accordance with the Charter of the United Nations and international law, including applicable international human rights, refugee and humanitarian law, threats to international peace and security caused by terrorist acts, stressing in this regard the important role the United Nations plays in leading and coordinating this effort,

Recognizing that a comprehensive approach to defeat terrorism is required, involving national, subregional, regional and multilateral action,

Noting the important contribution that public-private partnerships can make in efforts to prevent and combat criminal activities, such as transnational organized crime, corruption and terrorism,

Reaffirming its respect for the sovereignty, territorial integrity and political independence of all States in accordance with the Charter,

Reiterating the obligation of Member States to prevent the movement of terrorists or terrorist groups, in accordance with applicable international law, by, inter alia, effective border controls,

1. *Stresses* the need to work collectively to prevent and combat terrorism in all its forms and manifestations, including terrorism benefiting from transnational organized crime;

2. *Calls upon* Member States to strengthen border management to effectively prevent the movement of terrorists and terrorist groups, including those benefiting from transnational organized crime;

3. *Urges*, as a matter of priority, that Member States ratify, accede to and implement the relevant international conventions, such as the Single Convention on Narcotic Drugs of 1961 as amended by the 1972 Protocol,[322] the Convention on Psychotropic Substances of 1971,[323] the United Nations Convention against Illicit Traffic in Narcotic Drugs and Psychotropic Substances of 1988,[324] the United Nations Convention against Transnational Organized Crime of 2000 and the Protocols thereto[325] and the United Nations Convention against Corruption of 2003,[326] and the international counter-terrorism conventions and protocols;

4. *Requests* the relevant United Nations entities to assist Member States, upon their request, and within existing mandates and resources, to implement the relevant international legal instruments relating to terrorism and to develop their capacity to effectively respond to, prevent, investigate and prosecute terrorist acts;

5. *Stresses* the importance of good governance and the need to fight against corruption, money-laundering and illicit financial flows, in particular through the implementation of the United Nations Convention against Corruption and the comprehensive international standards set forth in the Financial Action Task Force revised Forty Recommendations on Combating Money Laundering and the Financing of Terrorism and Proliferation, including by adopting and effectively implementing legislative and regulatory measures, to enable the competent domestic authorities to freeze or seize, confiscate and manage criminal assets, in order to combat illicit financial activity, including terrorist financing and money-laundering, and encourages the States of the African region to further their engagement within the Financial Action Task Force-style regional bodies, such as the Inter-Governmental Action Group against Money Laundering in West Africa, the Eastern and Southern Africa Anti-Money Laundering Group and the Middle East and North Africa Financial Action Task Force, in promoting capacity and cooperation;

6. *Recalls* the obligations referred to in paragraph 2 (*e*) of resolution 1373 (2001) of 28 September 2001, and recalls them in particular with regard to terrorist attacks against United Nations staff, peacekeepers and installations;

International and regional cooperation

7. *Further stresses* the importance of strengthening transregional and international cooperation on a basis of a common and shared responsibility to counter the world drug problem and related criminal activities, and underlines that it must be addressed in a comprehensive, balanced and multidisciplinary manner;

8. *Encourages* Member States and relevant organizations, as appropriate, to enhance cooperation and strategies to prevent terrorists from benefiting from transnational organized crime, and to build the capacity to secure their borders against and investigate and prosecute such terrorists and transnational organized criminals

---

322 United Nations, *Treaty Series*, vol. 976, No. 14152.

323 Ibid., vol. 1019, No. 14956.

324 Ibid., vol. 1582, No. 27627.

325 Ibid., vols. 2225, 2237, 2241 and 2326, No. 39574.

326 Ibid., vol. 2349, No. 42146.

working with them, including through the strengthening of national, regional and global systems to collect, analyse and exchange information, including law enforcement and intelligence information;

9. *Commends*, in this regard, the regional cooperative mechanisms in Africa, notably, the Sahel Fusion and Liaison Unit, the Nouakchott Process on the Enhancement of Security Cooperation and the Operationalization of the African Peace and Security Architecture in the Sahel-Saharan Region, the African Union-led Regional Cooperation Initiative for the Elimination of the Lord's Resistance Army and the Lake Chad Basin Commission Multinational Joint Task Force and its Regional Intelligence Fusion Unit, as well as the Economic Community of West African States;

10. *Also commends* the initiatives to strengthen security and border control in the region of North Africa and the Sahel-Saharan region, with the adoption of the action plan on border security during the first Regional Ministerial Conference on Border Security, held in Tripoli on 11 and 12 March 2012, and the creation of a regional training centre to enhance border security, during the second Regional Ministerial Conference, held in Rabat on 14 November 2013, as well as other subregional initiatives supported by the United Nations;

11. *Urges* all Member States, notably Sahel and Maghreb States, to coordinate their efforts to prevent the serious threat posed to international and regional security by terrorist groups crossing borders and seeking safe havens in the Sahel region, to enhance cooperation and coordination in order to develop inclusive and effective strategies to combat in a comprehensive and integrated manner the activities of terrorist groups, and to prevent the expansion of those groups as well as to limit the proliferation of all arms and transnational organized crime;

12. *Welcomes and supports* the establishment of the African Police Cooperation Organization (AFRIPOL), and takes note of the elaboration of an African arrest warrant for persons charged with or convicted of terrorist acts;

13. *Calls upon* Member States in Africa to support the implementation of the African Union Plan of Action on Drug Control (2013–2017);

Capacity-building and the United Nations coordination

14. *Calls upon* Member States to help build the capacity of other Member States where necessary and appropriate and upon request, to address the threat posed by terrorism benefiting from transnational organized crime, and welcomes and encourages bilateral assistance by Member States to help build such national, subregional or regional capacity;

15. *Recognizes* the significant capacity and coordination challenges many Member States face in countering terrorism and violent extremism, and preventing terrorist financing, recruitment and all other forms of support to terrorist organizations, including terrorists benefiting from transnational organized crime, commends work under way by the Counter-Terrorism Committee and its Executive Directorate to identify capacity gaps and to facilitate technical assistance to strengthen the implementation of resolutions 1373 (2001) and 1624 (2005) of 14 September 2005, encourages Member States to continue to cooperate with the Committee and its Executive Directorate on the development of comprehensive and integrated national, subregional and regional counter-terrorism strategies, highlights the important role that Counter-Terrorism Implementation Task Force entities, in particular the United Nations Office on Drugs and Crime, as well as the United Nations Counter-Terrorism Centre, and other providers of capacity-building assistance should play in technical assistance delivery, and requests the relevant entities of the United Nations, whenever appropriate and within existing resources, to take into account in their technical assistance to counter terrorism the elements necessary for addressing terrorism benefiting from transnational organized crime;

16. *Calls upon* relevant entities of the United Nations and other relevant international and regional organizations to support the development and strengthening of the capacities of national and regional institutions to address terrorism benefiting from transnational organized crime, in particular law enforcement and counter-terrorism agencies, and in this regard notes the advisory role of the Peacebuilding Commission, in accordance with its mandate;

17. *Encourages* the Counter-Terrorism Implementation Task Force to consider expanding its Integrated Assistance for Countering Terrorism Initiative to the countries of the Group of Five for the Sahel and Central Africa, upon their request;

18. *Reiterates* that United Nations peacekeeping and special political missions, may, if mandated by the Security Council, assist in capacity-building for host Governments, as requested, to implement commitments under

existing global and regional instruments and to address the illicit trafficking in small arms and light weapons, including through weapons collection, disarmament, demobilization and reintegration programmes, enhancing physical security and stockpile management practices, record-keeping and tracing capacities, development of national export and import control systems, enhancement of border security, and strengthening judicial institutions, policing and other law enforcement capacities;

19. *Encourages* information-sharing, where relevant and appropriate, between Special Representatives of the Secretary-General, the Department of Peacekeeping Operations and the Department of Political Affairs of the Secretariat, the Counter-Terrorism Committee Executive Directorate, the United Nations Office on Drugs and Crime, the Counter-Terrorism Implementation Task Force and the United Nations Development Programme, within existing mandates and resources, when considering means to address, in a comprehensive and integrated manner, transnational organized crime, terrorism and violent extremism which can be conducive to terrorism;

Reporting

20. *Requests* the Secretary-General to submit to the Council a report on the efforts of the United Nations entities to address the threat of terrorists benefiting from transnational organized crime in affected regions, including Africa, with respect to matters of which the Council is seized, with input from the relevant entities of the United Nations system, including the United Nations Office on Drugs and Crime, the Counter-Terrorism Committee Executive Directorate, the Analytical Support and Sanctions Monitoring Team and other relevant Counter-Terrorism Implementation Task Force entities;

21. *Also requests* that the report include recommendations of concrete options for strengthening Member States' capabilities, including financing such proposed United Nations projects and activities to build capacity with existing resources and contributions in the United Nations system, as well as United Nations activities to reduce the negative impacts of terrorists benefiting from transnational organized crime, including those relevant to its conflict resolution efforts with a focus on border security, counter-terrorist financing and anti-money-laundering, and that the report be submitted to the Council no later than six months from the adoption of the present resolution;

22. *Recalls* the request, in resolution 2178 (2014) of 24 September 2014, to the Analytical Support and Sanctions Monitoring Team, in close cooperation with all relevant United Nations counter-terrorism bodies, to report to the Committee pursuant to resolutions 1267 (1999) and 1989 (2011) within 180 days on the threat posed by foreign terrorist fighters recruited by or joining Islamic State in Iraq and the Levant, Al-Nusrah Front and all groups, undertakings and entities associated with Al-Qaida, and reiterates that this report should also focus on trends related to foreign terrorist fighters joining and working with all terrorist groups listed on the Al-Qaida Sanctions List, and should include an oral briefing to the Committee and a Committee brief to the Council at the next regular briefing on counter-terrorism on those operating in Africa.

Adopted unanimously at the 7351st meeting.

NON-PROLIFERATION[327]

Decisions

At its 7265th meeting, on 15 September 2014, the Security Council considered the item entitled:

"Non-proliferation

"Briefing by the Chair of the Security Council Committee established pursuant to resolution 1737 (2006)".

At its 7350th meeting, on 18 December 2014, the Council considered the item discussed at the 7265th meeting.

[327] Resolutions or decisions on this question were first adopted by the Security Council in 2006.

At its 7412th meeting, on 24 March 2015, the Council also considered the item discussed at the 7265th meeting.

At its 7458th meeting, on 9 June 2015, the Council considered the item entitled:

"Non-proliferation

"Note by the President of the Security Council (S/2015/401)".

Resolution 2224 (2015) of 9 June 2015

The Security Council,

Recalling its previous relevant resolutions, including resolutions 1696 (2006) of 31 July 2006, 1737 (2006) of 23 December 2006, 1747 (2007) of 24 March 2007, 1803 (2008) of 3 March 2008, 1835 (2008) of 27 September 2008, 1887 (2009) of 24 September 2009, 1929 (2010) of 9 June 2010, 1984 (2011) of 9 June 2011, 2049 (2012) of 7 June 2012, 2105 (2013) of 5 June 2013 and 2159 (2014) of 9 June 2014, as well as the statement by its President of 29 March 2006,[328] and reaffirming their provisions,

Recalling also the creation, pursuant to paragraph 29 of resolution 1929 (2010), of the Panel of Experts on the Islamic Republic of Iran, under the direction of the Security Council Committee established pursuant to resolution 1737 (2006), to carry out the tasks provided for in that paragraph,

Recalling further the interim report of 7 November 2014 of the Panel of Experts appointed by the Secretary-General pursuant to paragraph 29 of resolution 1929 (2010) and the final report[329] of the Panel, of 1 June 2015,

Recalling the methodological standards for reports of sanctions monitoring mechanisms contained in the report of the Informal Working Group of the Security Council on General Issues of Sanctions,[330]

Welcoming the efforts made by the Secretariat to expand and improve the roster of experts for the Security Council Subsidiary Organs Branch, bearing in mind the guidance provided in the note by the President of 22 December 2006,[330]

Emphasizing, in that regard, the importance of credible, fact-based, independent assessments, analysis and recommendations, in accordance with the mandate of the Panel of Experts, as specified in paragraph 29 of resolution 1929 (2010),

Determining that the proliferation of weapons of mass destruction, as well as their means of delivery, continues to constitute a threat to international peace and security,

Acting under Article 41 of Chapter VII of the Charter of the United Nations,

1. *Decides* to extend until 9 July 2016 the mandate of the Panel of Experts on the Islamic Republic of Iran, as specified in paragraph 29 of resolution 1929 (2010), expresses its intent to review the mandate and take appropriate action regarding further extension no later than 9 June 2016, and requests the Secretary-General to take the necessary administrative measures to this effect;

2. *Requests* the Panel of Experts to provide to the Security Council Committee established pursuant to resolution 1737 (2006), no later than 9 November 2015, a midterm report on its work, and further requests that, after a discussion with the Committee, the Panel submit to the Council its midterm report by 9 December 2015, and also requests a final report to the Committee by 9 May 2016 with its findings and recommendations, and further requests that, after a discussion with the Committee, the Panel submit to the Council its final report by 9 June 2016;

3. *Also requests* the Panel of Experts to provide to the Committee a planned programme of work no later than 30 days after the reappointment of the Panel, encourages the Committee to engage in regular discussions about this programme of work and to engage regularly with the Panel about its work, and further requests the Panel to provide to the Committee any updates to this programme of work;

---

[328] S/PRST/2006/15.

[329] See S/2015/401.

[330] See S/2006/997.

4. *Expresses its intent* to continue to follow the work of the Panel of Experts;

5. *Urges* all States, relevant United Nations bodies and other interested parties to cooperate fully with the Committee and with the Panel of Experts, in particular by supplying any information at their disposal on the implementation of the measures imposed by resolutions 1737 (2006), 1747 (2007), 1803 (2008) and 1929 (2010);

6. *Decides* to remain actively seized of the matter.

Adopted unanimously at the 7458th meeting.

Decisions

At its 7469th meeting, on 23 June 2015, the Security Council considered the item entitled:

"Non-proliferation

"Briefing by the Chair of the Security Council Committee established pursuant to resolution 1737 (2006)".

At its 7488th meeting, on 20 July 2015, the Council decided to invite the representatives of Germany and Iran (Islamic Republic of) to participate, without vote, in accordance with rule 37 of its provisional rules of procedure, in the discussion of the item entitled "Non-proliferation".

At the same meeting, the Council also decided to extend an invitation, in accordance with rule 39 of its provisional rules of procedure, to Mr. Thomas Mayr-Harting, Head of the Delegation of the European Union to the United Nations.

Resolution 2231 (2015)
of 20 July 2015

The Security Council,

Recalling the statement by its President of 29 March 2006[328] and its resolutions 1696 (2006) of 31 July 2006, 1737 (2006) of 23 December 2006, 1747 (2007) of 24 March 2007, 1803 (2008) of 3 March 2008, 1835 (2008) of 27 September 2008 and 1929 (2010) of 9 June 2010,

Reaffirming its commitment to the Treaty on the Non-Proliferation of Nuclear Weapons[331] and the need for all States party to that Treaty to comply fully with their obligations, and recalling the right of States party, in conformity with articles I and II of that Treaty, to develop research, production and use of nuclear energy for peaceful purposes without discrimination,

Emphasizing the importance of political and diplomatic efforts to find a negotiated solution guaranteeing that the Islamic Republic of Iran's nuclear programme is exclusively for peaceful purposes, and noting that such a solution would benefit nuclear non-proliferation,

Welcoming diplomatic efforts by China, France, Germany, the Russian Federation, the United Kingdom of Great Britain and Northern Ireland, the United States of America, the High Representative of the European Union for Foreign Affairs and Security Policy and the Islamic Republic of Iran to reach a comprehensive, long-term and proper solution to the Iranian nuclear issue, culminating in the Joint Comprehensive Plan of Action (JCPOA) concluded on 14 July 2015, as contained in annex A to the present resolution, and the establishment of the Joint Commission,

Welcoming also the Islamic Republic of Iran's reaffirmation in the JCPOA that it will under no circumstances ever seek, develop or acquire any nuclear weapons,

Noting the statement of 14 July 2015 from China, France, Germany, the Russian Federation, the United Kingdom, the United States and the European Union aimed at promoting transparency and creating an atmosphere conducive to the full implementation of the JCPOA, as contained in annex B to the present resolution,

[331] United Nations, *Treaty Series*, vol. 729, No. 10485.

Affirming that conclusion of the JCPOA marks a fundamental shift in its consideration of this issue, and expressing its desire to build a new relationship with the Islamic Republic of Iran strengthened by the implementation of the JCPOA and to bring to a satisfactory conclusion its consideration of this matter,

Affirming also that full implementation of the JCPOA will contribute to building confidence in the exclusively peaceful nature of the Islamic Republic of Iran's nuclear programme,

Strongly supporting the essential and independent role of the International Atomic Energy Agency in verifying compliance with safeguards agreements, including the non-diversion of declared nuclear material to undeclared purposes and the absence of undeclared nuclear material and undeclared nuclear activities, and, in this context, in ensuring the exclusively peaceful nature of the Islamic Republic of Iran's nuclear programme, including through the implementation of the Framework for Cooperation agreed between the Islamic Republic of Iran and the Agency on 11 November 2013 and the Road map for the Clarification of Past and Present Outstanding Issues, and recognizing the important role of the Agency in supporting full implementation of the JCPOA,

Affirming that International Atomic Energy Agency safeguards are a fundamental component of nuclear non-proliferation, promote greater confidence among States, inter alia, by providing assurance that States are complying with their obligations under relevant safeguards agreements, contribute to strengthening their collective security and help to create an environment conducive to nuclear cooperation, and further recognizing that effective and efficient safeguards implementation requires a cooperative effort between the Agency and States, that the secretariat of the Agency will continue to engage in open dialogue on safeguards matters with States to increase transparency and build confidence and to interact with them on the implementation of safeguards, and in this case, avoid hampering the economic and technological development of the Islamic Republic of Iran or international cooperation in the field of peaceful nuclear activities; respect health, safety, physical protection and other security provisions in force and the rights of individuals; and take every precaution to protect commercial, technological and industrial secrets as well as other confidential information coming to its knowledge,

Encouraging Member States to cooperate, including through International Atomic Energy Agency involvement, with the Islamic Republic of Iran in the framework of the JCPOA in the field of peaceful uses of nuclear energy and to engage in mutually determined civil nuclear cooperation projects, in accordance with annex III to the JCPOA,

Noting the termination of provisions of previous resolutions and other measures foreseen in the present resolution, and inviting Member States to give due regard to these changes,

Emphasizing that the JCPOA is conducive to promoting and facilitating the development of normal economic and trade contacts and cooperation with the Islamic Republic of Iran, and having regard to States' rights and obligations relating to international trade,

Underscoring that Member States are obligated under Article 25 of the Charter of the United Nations to accept and carry out the decisions of the Security Council,

1. *Endorses* the JCPOA, and urges its full implementation on the timetable established in the JCPOA;

2. *Calls upon* all Member States, regional organizations and international organizations to take such actions as may be appropriate to support the implementation of the JCPOA, including by taking actions commensurate with the implementation plan set out in the JCPOA and the present resolution and by refraining from actions that undermine implementation of commitments under the JCPOA;

3. *Requests* the Director General of the International Atomic Energy Agency to undertake the necessary verification and monitoring of the Islamic Republic of Iran's nuclear-related commitments for the full duration of those commitments under the JCPOA, and reaffirms that the Islamic Republic of Iran shall cooperate fully as the Agency requests to be able to resolve all outstanding issues, as identified in reports of the Agency;

4. *Also requests* the Director General of the International Atomic Energy Agency to provide regular updates to the Board of Governors of the Agency and, as appropriate, in parallel to the Security Council on the Islamic Republic of Iran's implementation of its commitments under the JCPOA and also to report to the Board of Governors and in parallel to the Council at any time if the Director General has reasonable grounds to believe there is an issue of concern directly affecting fulfilment of JCPOA commitments;

Terminations

5. *Requests* that, as soon as the International Atomic Energy Agency has verified that the Islamic Republic of Iran has taken the actions specified in paragraphs 15.1 to 15.11 of annex V to the JCPOA, the Director General of the Agency submit a report confirming this fact to the Board of Governors of the Agency and in parallel to the Security Council;

6. *Requests*, further, that, as soon as the International Atomic Energy Agency has reached the Broader Conclusion that all nuclear material in the Islamic Republic of Iran remains in peaceful activities, the Director General of the Agency submit a report confirming this conclusion to the Board of Governors of the Agency and in parallel to the Security Council;

7. *Decides*, acting under Article 41 of the Charter of the United Nations, that, upon receipt by the Security Council of the report from the International Atomic Energy Agency described in paragraph 5:

(*a*) The provisions of resolutions 1696 (2006), 1737 (2006), 1747 (2007), 1803 (2008), 1835 (2008), 1929 (2010) and 2224 (2015) of 9 June 2015 shall be terminated;

(*b*) All States shall comply with paragraphs 1, 2, 4 and 5 and the provisions in subparagraphs (a) to (f) of paragraph 6 of annex B for the duration specified in each paragraph or subparagraph, and are called upon to comply with paragraphs 3 and 7 of annex B;

8. *Also decides*, acting under Article 41 of the Charter of the United Nations, that on the date 10 years after the JCPOA Adoption Day, as defined in the JCPOA, all the provisions of the present resolution shall be terminated, and none of the previous resolutions described in paragraph 7 (*a*) shall be applied, the Security Council will have concluded its consideration of the Iranian nuclear issue, and the item "Non-proliferation" will be removed from the list of matters of which the Council is seized;

9. *Further decides*, acting under Article 41 of the Charter of the United Nations, that the terminations described in annex B and paragraph 8 of the present resolution shall not occur if the provisions of previous resolutions have been applied pursuant to paragraph 12;

Application of provisions of previous resolutions

10. *Encourages* China, France, Germany, the Russian Federation, the United Kingdom of Great Britain and Northern Ireland, the United States of America, the European Union and the Islamic Republic of Iran (the JCPOA participants) to resolve any issues arising with respect to implementation of JCPOA commitments through the procedures specified in the JCPOA, and expresses its intention to address possible complaints by JCPOA participants about significant non-performance by another JCPOA participant;

11. *Decides*, acting under Article 41 of the Charter of the United Nations, that, within 30 days of receiving a notification by a JCPOA participant State of an issue that the JCPOA participant State believes constitutes significant non-performance of commitments under the JCPOA, it shall vote on a draft resolution to continue in effect the terminations in paragraph 7 (*a*) of the present resolution, decides further that if, within 10 days of the notification referred to above, no member of the Security Council has submitted such a draft resolution for a vote, then the President of the Security Council shall submit such a draft resolution and put it to a vote within 30 days of the notification referred to above, and expresses its intention to take into account the views of the States involved in the issue and any opinion on the issue by the Advisory Board established in the JCPOA;

12. *Also decides*, acting under Article 41 of the Charter of the United Nations, that, if the Security Council does not adopt a resolution under paragraph 11 to continue in effect the terminations in paragraph 7 (*a*), then effective midnight Greenwich Mean Time after the thirtieth day after the notification to the Security Council described in paragraph 11, all of the provisions of resolutions 1696 (2006), 1737 (2006), 1747 (2007), 1803 (2008), 1835 (2008) and 1929 (2010) that have been terminated pursuant to paragraph 7 (*a*) shall apply in the same manner as they applied before the adoption of the present resolution, and the measures contained in paragraphs 7, 8 and 16 to 20 of the present resolution shall be terminated, unless the Security Council decides otherwise;

13. *Underscores* that, in the event of a notification to the Security Council described in paragraph 11, the Islamic Republic of Iran and the other JCPOA participants should strive to resolve the issue giving rise to the notification, expresses its intention to prevent the reapplication of the provisions if the issue giving rise to the

notification is resolved, decides, acting under Article 41 of the Charter of the United Nations, that if the notifying JCPOA participant State informs the Security Council that such an issue has been resolved before the end of the 30-day period specified in paragraph 12 above, then the provisions of the present resolution, including the terminations in paragraph 7 (*a*), shall remain in effect notwithstanding paragraph 12 above, and notes the Islamic Republic of Iran's statement that if the provisions of previous resolutions are applied pursuant to paragraph 12 in whole or in part, the Islamic Republic of Iran will treat this as grounds to cease performing its commitments under the JCPOA;

14. *Affirms* that the application of the provisions of previous resolutions pursuant to paragraph 12 does not apply with retroactive effect to contracts signed between any party and the Islamic Republic of Iran or Iranian individuals and entities prior to the date of application, provided that the activities contemplated under and execution of such contracts are consistent with the JCPOA, the present resolution and the previous resolutions;

15. *Also affirms* that any application of the provisions of previous resolutions pursuant to paragraph 12 is not intended to harm individuals and entities that, prior to that application of those provisions, engaged in business with the Islamic Republic of Iran or Iranian individuals and entities that is consistent with the JCPOA and the present resolution, encourages Member States to consult with each other with regard to such harm, and to take action to mitigate such unintended harm for these individuals and entities, and decides if the provisions of previous resolutions are applied pursuant to paragraph 12 not to impose measures with retroactive effect on individuals and entities for business activities with the Islamic Republic of Iran that were consistent with the JCPOA, the present resolution and the previous resolutions prior to the application of these provisions;

JCPOA implementation

16. *Decides*, acting under Article 41 of the Charter of the United Nations, to review recommendations of the Joint Commission regarding proposals by States to participate in or permit nuclear-related activities set forth in paragraph 2 of annex B, and that such recommendations shall be deemed to be approved unless the Security Council adopts a resolution to reject a Joint Commission recommendation within five working days of receiving it;

17. *Requests* Member States seeking to participate in or permit activities set forth in paragraph 2 of annex B to submit proposals to the Security Council, expresses its intention to share such proposals with the Joint Commission established in the JCPOA for its review, invites any member of the Security Council to provide relevant information and opinions about these proposals, encourages the Joint Commission to give due consideration to any such information and opinions, and requests the Joint Commission to provide its recommendations on these proposals to the Security Council within 20 working days (or, if extended, within 30 working days);

18. *Requests* the Secretary-General, in order to support JCPOA implementation, to take the necessary administrative measures to facilitate communications with Member States and between the Security Council and the Joint Commission through agreed practical arrangements;

19. *Requests* the International Atomic Energy Agency and the Joint Commission to consult and exchange information, where appropriate, as specified in the JCPOA, and requests further that the exporting States cooperate with the Joint Commission in accordance with annex IV to the JCPOA;

20. *Requests* the Joint Commission to review proposals for transfers and activities described in paragraph 2 of annex B with a view to recommending approval where consistent with the present resolution and the provisions and objectives of the JCPOA so as to provide for the transfer of items, materials, equipment, goods and technology required for the Islamic Republic of Iran's nuclear activities under the JCPOA, and encourages the Joint Commission to establish procedures to ensure detailed and thorough review of all such proposals;

Exemptions

21. *Decides*, acting under Article 41 of the Charter of the United Nations, that the measures imposed in resolutions 1696 (2006), 1737 (2006), 1747 (2007), 1803 (2008), 1835 (2008) and 1929 (2010) shall not apply to the supply, sale or transfer of items, materials, equipment, goods and technology, and the provision of any related technical assistance, training, financial assistance, investment, brokering or other services, by JCPOA participant States or Member States acting in coordination with them, that is directly related to (*a*) the modification of two cascades at the Fordow facility for stable isotope production; (*b*) the export of the Islamic Republic of Iran's

enriched uranium in excess of 300 kilograms in return for natural uranium; and (*c*) the modernization of the Arak reactor based on the agreed conceptual design and, subsequently, on the agreed final design of such reactor;

22. *Also decides*, acting under Article 41 of the Charter of the United Nations, that Member States engaging in the activities permitted in paragraph 21 shall ensure that (*a*) all such activities are undertaken strictly in accordance with the JCPOA; (*b*) they notify the Security Council Committee established pursuant to resolution 1737 (2006) and, when constituted, the Joint Commission 10 days in advance of such activities; (*c*) the requirements, as appropriate, of the Guidelines as set out in the relevant INFCIRC referenced in resolution 1737 (2006), as updated, have been met; (*d*) they have obtained and are in a position to exercise effectively a right to verify the end-use and end-use location of any supplied item; and (*e*) in case of supplied items, materials, equipment, goods and technology listed in the INFCIRCs referenced in resolution 1737 (2006), as updated, they also notify the International Atomic Energy Agency within 10 days of the supply, sale or transfer;

23. *Further decides*, acting under Article 41 of the Charter of the United Nations, that the measures imposed in resolutions 1696 (2006), 1737 (2006), 1747 (2007), 1803 (2008), 1835 (2008) and 1929 (2010) shall not apply to the extent necessary to carry out transfers and activities, as approved on a case-by-case basis in advance by the Committee established pursuant to resolution 1737 (2006), that are:

(*a*) Directly related to implementation of the nuclear-related actions specified in paragraphs 15.1 to 15.11 of annex V of the JCPOA;

(*b*) Required for preparation for the implementation of the JCPOA; or

(*c*) Determined by the Committee to be consistent with the objectives of the present resolution;

24. *Notes* that the provisions of paragraphs 21, 22, 23 and 27 continue in effect if the provisions of previous resolutions are applied pursuant to paragraph 12;

Other matters

25. *Decides* to make the necessary practical arrangements to undertake directly tasks related to the implementation of the present resolution, including those tasks specified in annex B and the release of guidance;

26. *Urges* all States, relevant United Nations bodies and other interested parties to cooperate fully with the Security Council in its exercise of the tasks related to the present resolution, in particular by supplying any information at their disposal on the implementation of the measures in the present resolution;

27. *Decides* that all provisions contained in the JCPOA are only for the purposes of its implementation between the E3/EU+3 and the Islamic Republic of Iran and should not be considered as setting precedents for any other State or for principles of international law and the rights and obligations under the Treaty on the Non-Proliferation of Nuclear Weapons[331] and other relevant instruments, as well as for internationally recognized principles and practices;

28. *Recalls* that the measures imposed by paragraph 12 of resolution 1737 (2006) shall not prevent a designated person or entity from making payment due under a contract entered into prior to the listing of such a person or entity, provided that the conditions specified in paragraph 15 of that resolution are met, and underscores that if the provisions of previous resolutions are reapplied pursuant to paragraph 12 of the present resolution, then this provision will apply;

29. *Emphasizes* the importance of all States taking the necessary measures to ensure that no claim shall lie at the instance of the Government of the Islamic Republic of Iran, or any person or entity in the Islamic Republic of Iran, or of persons or entities designated pursuant to resolution 1737 (2006) and related resolutions, or any person claiming through or for the benefit of any such person or entity, in connection with any contract or other transaction where its performance was prevented by reason of the application of the provisions of resolutions 1737 (2006), 1747 (2007), 1803 (2008), 1929 (2010) and the present resolution;

30. *Decides* to remain seized of the matter until the termination of the provisions of the present resolution in accordance with paragraph 8.

Adopted unanimously at the 7488th meeting.

Annex A: Joint Comprehensive Plan of Action (JCPOA), Vienna, 14 July 2015[332]

PREFACE

The E3/EU+3 (China, France, Germany, the Russian Federation, the United Kingdom and the United States, with the High Representative of the European Union for Foreign Affairs and Security Policy) and the Islamic Republic of Iran welcome this historic Joint Comprehensive Plan of Action (JCPOA), which will ensure that Iran's nuclear programme will be exclusively peaceful, and mark a fundamental shift in their approach to this issue. They anticipate that full implementation of this JCPOA will positively contribute to regional and international peace and security. Iran reaffirms that under no circumstances will Iran ever seek, develop or acquire any nuclear weapons.

Iran envisions that this JCPOA will allow it to move forward with an exclusively peaceful, indigenous nuclear programme, in line with scientific and economic considerations, in accordance with the JCPOA, and with a view to building confidence and encouraging international cooperation. In this context, the initial mutually determined limitations described in this JCPOA will be followed by a gradual evolution, at a reasonable pace, of Iran's peaceful nuclear programme, including its enrichment activities, to a commercial programme for exclusively peaceful purposes, consistent with international non-proliferation norms.

The E3/EU+3 envision that the implementation of this JCPOA will progressively allow them to gain confidence in the exclusively peaceful nature of Iran's programme. The JCPOA reflects mutually determined parameters, consistent with practical needs, with agreed limits on the scope of Iran's nuclear programme, including enrichment activities and R&D. The JCPOA addresses the E3/EU+3's concerns, including through comprehensive measures providing for transparency and verification.

The JCPOA will produce the comprehensive lifting of all UN Security Council sanctions as well as multilateral and national sanctions related to Iran's nuclear programme, including steps on access in areas of trade, technology, finance, and energy.

PREAMBLE AND GENERAL PROVISIONS

i. The Islamic Republic of Iran and the E3/EU+3 (China, France, Germany, the Russian Federation, the United Kingdom and the United States, with the High Representative of the European Union for Foreign Affairs and Security Policy) have decided upon this long-term Joint Comprehensive Plan of Action (JCPOA). This JCPOA, reflecting a step-by-step approach, includes the reciprocal commitments as laid down in this document and the annexes hereto and is to be endorsed by the United Nations (UN) Security Council.

ii. The full implementation of this JCPOA will ensure the exclusively peaceful nature of Iran's nuclear programme.

iii. Iran reaffirms that under no circumstances will Iran ever seek, develop or acquire any nuclear weapons.

iv. Successful implementation of this JCPOA will enable Iran to fully enjoy its right to nuclear energy for peaceful purposes under the relevant articles of the nuclear Non-Proliferation Treaty (NPT) in line with its obligations therein, and the Iranian nuclear programme will be treated in the same manner as that of any other non-nuclear-weapon state party to the NPT.

v. This JCPOA will produce the comprehensive lifting of all UN Security Council sanctions as well as multilateral and national sanctions related to Iran's nuclear programme, including steps on access in areas of trade, technology, finance and energy.

vi. The E3/EU+3 and Iran reaffirm their commitment to the purposes and principles of the United Nations as set out in the UN Charter.

vii. The E3/EU+3 and Iran acknowledge that the NPT remains the cornerstone of the nuclear non-proliferation regime and the essential foundation for the pursuit of nuclear disarmament and for the peaceful uses of nuclear energy.

[332] Circulated under the symbol S/2015/544.

viii. The E3/EU+3 and Iran commit to implement this JCPOA in good faith and in a constructive atmosphere, based on mutual respect, and to refrain from any action inconsistent with the letter, spirit and intent of this JCPOA that would undermine its successful implementation. The E3/EU+3 will refrain from imposing discriminatory regulatory and procedural requirements in lieu of the sanctions and restrictive measures covered by this JCPOA. This JCPOA builds on the implementation of the Joint Plan of Action (JPOA) agreed in Geneva on 24 November 2013.

ix. A Joint Commission consisting of the E3/EU+3 and Iran will be established to monitor the implementation of this JCPOA and will carry out the functions provided for in this JCPOA. This Joint Commission will address issues arising from the implementation of this JCPOA and will operate in accordance with the provisions as detailed in the relevant annex.

x. The International Atomic Energy Agency (IAEA) will be requested to monitor and verify the voluntary nuclear-related measures as detailed in this JCPOA. The IAEA will be requested to provide regular updates to the Board of Governors, and as provided for in this JCPOA, to the UN Security Council. All relevant rules and regulations of the IAEA with regard to the protection of information will be fully observed by all parties involved.

xi. All provisions and measures contained in this JCPOA are only for the purpose of its implementation between E3/EU+3 and Iran and should not be considered as setting precedents for any other state or for fundamental principles of international law and the rights and obligations under the NPT and other relevant instruments, as well as for internationally recognised principles and practices.

xii. Technical details of the implementation of this JCPOA are dealt with in the annexes to this document.

xiii. The EU and E3+3 countries and Iran, in the framework of the JCPOA, will cooperate, as appropriate, in the field of peaceful uses of nuclear energy and engage in mutually determined civil nuclear cooperation projects as detailed in Annex III, including through IAEA involvement.

xiv. The E3+3 will submit a draft resolution to the UN Security Council endorsing this JCPOA affirming that conclusion of this JCPOA marks a fundamental shift in its consideration of this issue and expressing its desire to build a new relationship with Iran. This UN Security Council resolution will also provide for the termination on Implementation Day of provisions imposed under previous resolutions; establishment of specific restrictions; and conclusion of consideration of the Iran nuclear issue by the UN Security Council 10 years after the Adoption Day.

xv. The provisions stipulated in this JCPOA will be implemented for their respective durations as set forth below and detailed in the annexes.

xvi. The E3/EU+3 and Iran will meet at the ministerial level every 2 years, or earlier if needed, in order to review and assess progress and to adopt appropriate decisions by consensus.

Iran and E3/EU+3 will take the following voluntary measures within the timeframe as detailed in this JCPOA and its Annexes

NUCLEAR

A. ENRICHMENT, ENRICHMENT R&D, STOCKPILES

1. Iran's long term plan includes certain agreed limitations on all uranium enrichment and uranium enrichment-related activities including certain limitations on specific research and development (R&D) activities for the first 8 years, to be followed by gradual evolution, at a reasonable pace, to the next stage of its enrichment activities for exclusively peaceful purposes, as described in Annex I. Iran will abide by its voluntary commitments, as expressed in its own long-term enrichment and enrichment R&D plan to be submitted as part of the initial declaration for the Additional Protocol to Iran's Safeguards Agreement.

2. Iran will begin phasing out its IR-1 centrifuges in 10 years. During this period, Iran will keep its enrichment capacity at Natanz at up to a total installed uranium enrichment capacity of 5060 IR-1 centrifuges. Excess centrifuges and enrichment-related infrastructure at Natanz will be stored under IAEA continuous monitoring, as specified in Annex I.

3. Iran will continue to conduct enrichment R&D in a manner that does not accumulate enriched uranium. Iran's enrichment R&D with uranium for 10 years will only include IR-4, IR-5, IR-6 and IR-8 centrifuges as laid out in Annex I, and Iran will not engage in other isotope separation technologies for enrichment of uranium as specified in Annex I. Iran will continue testing IR-6 and IR-8 centrifuges, and will commence testing of up to 30 IR-6 and IR-8 centrifuges after eight and a half years, as detailed in Annex I.

4. As Iran will be phasing out its IR-1 centrifuges, it will not manufacture or assemble other centrifuges, except as provided for in Annex I, and will replace failed centrifuges with centrifuges of the same type. Iran will manufacture advanced centrifuge machines only for the purposes specified in this JCPOA. From the end of the eighth year, and as described in Annex I, Iran will start to manufacture agreed numbers of IR-6 and IR-8 centrifuge machines without rotors and will store all of the manufactured machines at Natanz, under IAEA continuous monitoring until they are needed under Iran's long-term enrichment and enrichment R&D plan.

5. Based on its own long-term plan, for 15 years, Iran will carry out its uranium enrichment-related activities, including safeguarded R&D exclusively in the Natanz Enrichment facility, keep its level of uranium enrichment at up to 3.67%, and, at Fordow, refrain from any uranium enrichment and uranium enrichment R&D and from keeping any nuclear material.

6. Iran will convert the Fordow facility into a nuclear, physics and technology centre. International collaboration including in the form of scientific joint partnerships will be established in agreed areas of research. 1044 IR-1 centrifuges in six cascades will remain in one wing at Fordow. Two of these cascades will spin without uranium and will be transitioned, including through appropriate infrastructure modification, for stable isotope production. The other four cascades with all associated infrastructure will remain idle. All other centrifuges and enrichment-related infrastructure will be removed and stored under IAEA continuous monitoring as specified in Annex I.

7. During the 15 year period, and as Iran gradually moves to meet international qualification standards for nuclear fuel produced in Iran, it will keep its uranium stockpile under 300 kg of up to 3.67% enriched uranium hexafluoride (UF6) or the equivalent in other chemical forms. The excess quantities are to be sold based on international prices and delivered to the international buyer in return for natural uranium delivered to Iran, or are to be down-blended to natural uranium level. Enriched uranium in fabricated fuel assemblies from Russia or other sources for use in Iran's nuclear reactors will not be counted against the above stated 300 kg UF6 stockpile, if the criteria set out in Annex I are met with regard to other sources. The Joint Commission will support assistance to Iran, including through IAEA technical cooperation as appropriate, in meeting international qualification standards for nuclear fuel produced in Iran. All remaining uranium oxide enriched to between 5% and 20% will be fabricated into fuel for the Tehran Research Reactor (TRR). Any additional fuel needed for the TRR will be made available to Iran at international market prices.

B. ARAK, HEAVY WATER, REPROCESSING

8. Iran will redesign and rebuild a modernised heavy water research reactor in Arak, based on an agreed conceptual design, using fuel enriched up to 3.67 %, in a form of an international partnership which will certify the final design. The reactor will support peaceful nuclear research and radioisotope production for medical and industrial purposes. The redesigned and rebuilt Arak reactor will not produce weapons grade plutonium. Except for the first core load, all of the activities for redesigning and manufacturing of the fuel assemblies for the redesigned reactor will be carried out in Iran. All spent fuel from Arak will be shipped out of Iran for the lifetime of the reactor. This international partnership will include participating E3/EU+3 parties, Iran and such other countries as may be mutually determined. Iran will take the leadership role as the owner and as the project manager and the E3/EU+3 and Iran will, before Implementation Day, conclude an official document which would define the responsibilities assumed by the E3/EU+3 participants.

9. Iran plans to keep pace with the trend of international technological advancement in relying on light water for its future power and research reactors with enhanced international cooperation, including assurance of supply of necessary fuel.

10. There will be no additional heavy water reactors or accumulation of heavy water in Iran for 15 years. All excess heavy water will be made available for export to the international market.

11. Iran intends to ship out all spent fuel for all future and present power and research nuclear reactors, for further treatment or disposition as provided for in relevant contracts to be duly concluded with the recipient party.

12. For 15 years Iran will not, and does not intend to thereafter, engage in any spent fuel reprocessing or construction of a facility capable of spent fuel reprocessing, or reprocessing R&D activities leading to a spent fuel reprocessing capability, with the sole exception of separation activities aimed exclusively at the production of medical and industrial radio-isotopes from irradiated enriched uranium targets.

C. TRANSPARENCY AND CONFIDENCE BUILDING MEASURES

13. Consistent with the respective roles of the President and Majlis (Parliament), Iran will provisionally apply the Additional Protocol to its Comprehensive Safeguards Agreement in accordance with Article 17(b) of the Additional Protocol, proceed with its ratification within the timeframe as detailed in Annex V and fully implement the modified Code 3.1 of the Subsidiary Arrangements to its Safeguards Agreement.

14. Iran will fully implement the "Roadmap for Clarification of Past and Present Outstanding Issues" agreed with the IAEA, containing arrangements to address past and present issues of concern relating to its nuclear programme as raised in the annex to the IAEA report of 8 November 2011 (GOV/2011/65). Full implementation of activities undertaken under the Roadmap by Iran will be completed by 15 October 2015, and subsequently the Director General will provide by 15 December 2015 the final assessment on the resolution of all past and present outstanding issues to the Board of Governors, and the E3+3, in their capacity as members of the Board of Governors, will submit a resolution to the Board of Governors for taking necessary action, with a view to closing the issue, without prejudice to the competence of the Board of Governors.

15. Iran will allow the IAEA to monitor the implementation of the voluntary measures for their respective durations, as well as to implement transparency measures, as set out in this JCPOA and its Annexes. These measures include: a long-term IAEA presence in Iran; IAEA monitoring of uranium ore concentrate produced by Iran from all uranium ore concentrate plants for 25 years; containment and surveillance of centrifuge rotors and bellows for 20 years; use of IAEA approved and certified modern technologies including on-line enrichment measurement and electronic seals; and a reliable mechanism to ensure speedy resolution of IAEA access concerns for 15 years, as defined in Annex I.

16. Iran will not engage in activities, including at the R&D level, that could contribute to the development of a nuclear explosive device, including uranium or plutonium metallurgy activities, as specified in Annex I.

17. Iran will cooperate and act in accordance with the procurement channel in this JCPOA, as detailed in Annex IV, endorsed by the UN Security Council resolution.

SANCTIONS

18. The UN Security Council resolution endorsing this JCPOA will terminate all provisions of previous UN Security Council resolutions on the Iranian nuclear issue – 1696 (2006), 1737 (2006), 1747 (2007), 1803 (2008), 1835 (2008), 1929 (2010) and 2224 (2015) – simultaneously with the IAEA-verified implementation of agreed nuclear-related measures by Iran and will establish specific restrictions, as specified in Annex V.[333]

19. The EU will terminate all provisions of the EU Regulation, as subsequently amended, implementing all nuclear-related economic and financial sanctions, including related designations, simultaneously with the IAEA-verified implementation of agreed nuclear-related measures by Iran as specified in Annex V, which cover all sanctions and restrictive measures in the following areas, as described in Annex II:

    i. Transfers of funds between EU persons and entities, including financial institutions, and Iranian persons and entities, including financial institutions;

    ii. Banking activities, including the establishment of new correspondent banking relationships and the opening of new branches and subsidiaries of Iranian banks in the territories of EU Member States;

    iii. Provision of insurance and reinsurance;

[333] The provisions of this Resolution do not constitute provisions of this JCPOA.

iv. Supply of specialised financial messaging services, including SWIFT, for persons and entities set out in Attachment 1 to Annex II, including the Central Bank of Iran and Iranian financial institutions;

v. Financial support for trade with Iran (export credit, guarantees or insurance);

vi. Commitments for grants, financial assistance and concessional loans to the Government of Iran;

vii. Transactions in public or public-guaranteed bonds;

viii. Import and transport of Iranian oil, petroleum products, gas and petrochemical products;

ix. Export of key equipment or technology for the oil, gas and petrochemical sectors;

x. Investment in the oil, gas and petrochemical sectors;

xi. Export of key naval equipment and technology;

xii. Design and construction of cargo vessels and oil tankers;

xiii. Provision of flagging and classification services;

xiv. Access to EU airports of Iranian cargo flights;

xv. Export of gold, precious metals and diamonds;

xvi. Delivery of Iranian banknotes and coinage;

xvii. Export of graphite, raw or semi-finished metals such as aluminum and steel, and export or software for integrating industrial processes;

xviii. Designation of persons, entities and bodies (asset freeze and visa ban) set out in Attachment 1 to Annex II; and

xix. Associated services for each of the categories above.

20. The EU will terminate all provisions of the EU Regulation implementing all EU proliferation-related sanctions, including related designations, 8 years after Adoption Day or when the IAEA has reached the Broader Conclusion that all nuclear material in Iran remains in peaceful activities, whichever is earlier.

21. The United States will cease the application, and will continue to do so, in accordance with this JCPOA of the sanctions specified in Annex II to take effect simultaneously with the IAEA-verified implementation of the agreed nuclear-related measures by Iran as specified in Annex V. Such sanctions cover the following areas as described in Annex II:

i. Financial and banking transactions with Iranian banks and financial institutions as specified in Annex II, including the Central Bank of Iran and specified individuals and entities identified as Government of Iran by the Office of Foreign Assets Control on the Specially Designated Nationals and Blocked Persons List (SDN List), as set out in Attachment 3 to Annex II (including the opening and maintenance of correspondent and payable through-accounts at non-U.S. financial institutions, investments, foreign exchange transactions and letters of credit);

ii. Transactions in Iranian Rial;

iii. Provision of U.S. banknotes to the Government of Iran;

iv. Bilateral trade limitations on Iranian revenues abroad, including limitations on their transfer;

v. Purchase, subscription to, or facilitation of the issuance of Iranian sovereign debt, including governmental bonds;

vi. Financial messaging services to the Central Bank of Iran and Iranian financial institutions set out in Attachment 3 to Annex II;

vii. Underwriting services, insurance, or reinsurance;

viii. Efforts to reduce Iran's crude oil sales;

ix. Investment, including participation in joint ventures, goods, services, information, technology and technical expertise and support for Iran's oil, gas and petrochemical sectors;

x. Purchase, acquisition, sale, transportation or marketing of petroleum, petrochemical products and natural gas from Iran;

xi. Export, sale or provision of refined petroleum products and petrochemical products to Iran;

xii. Transactions with Iran's energy sector;

xiii. Transactions with Iran's shipping and shipbuilding sectors and port operators;

xiv. Trade in gold and other precious metals;

xv. Trade with Iran in graphite, raw or semi-finished metals such as aluminum and steel, coal, and software for integrating industrial processes;

xvi. Sale, supply or transfer of goods and services used in connection with Iran's automotive sector;

xvii. Sanctions on associated services for each of the categories above;

xviii. Remove individuals and entities set out in Attachment 3 to Annex II from the SDN List, the Foreign Sanctions Evaders List, and/or the Non-SDN Iran Sanctions Act List; and

xix. Terminate Executive Orders 13574, 13590, 13622, and 13645, and Sections 5 – 7 and 15 of Executive Order 13628.

22. The United States will, as specified in Annex II and in accordance with Annex V, allow for the sale of commercial passenger aircraft and related parts and services to Iran; license non-U.S. persons that are owned or controlled by a U.S. person to engage in activities with Iran consistent with this JCPOA; and license the importation into the United States of Iranian-origin carpets and foodstuffs.

23. Eight years after Adoption Day or when the IAEA has reached the Broader Conclusion that all nuclear material in Iran remains in peaceful activities, whichever is earlier, the United States will seek such legislative action as may be appropriate to terminate, or modify to effectuate the termination of, the sanctions specified in Annex II on the acquisition of nuclear-related commodities and services for nuclear activities contemplated in this JCPOA, to be consistent with the U.S. approach to other non-nuclear-weapon states under the NPT.

24. The E3/EU and the United States specify in Annex II a full and complete list of all nuclear-related sanctions or restrictive measures and will lift them in accordance with Annex V. Annex II also specifies the effects of the lifting of sanctions beginning on "Implementation Day". If at any time following the Implementation Day, Iran believes that any other nuclear-related sanction or restrictive measure of the E3/EU+3 is preventing the full implementation of the sanctions lifting as specified in this JCPOA, the JCPOA participant in question will consult with Iran with a view to resolving the issue and, if they concur that lifting of this sanction or restrictive measure is appropriate, the JCPOA participant in question will take appropriate action. If they are not able to resolve the issue, Iran or any member of the E3/EU+3 may refer the issue to the Joint Commission.

25. If a law at the state or local level in the United States is preventing the implementation of the sanctions lifting as specified in this JCPOA, the United States will take appropriate steps, taking into account all available authorities, with a view to achieving such implementation. The United States will actively encourage officials at the state or local level to take into account the changes in the U.S. policy reflected in the lifting of sanctions under this JCPOA and to refrain from actions inconsistent with this change in policy.

26. The EU will refrain from re-introducing or re-imposing the sanctions that it has terminated implementing under this JCPOA, without prejudice to the dispute resolution process provided for under this JCPOA. There will be no new nuclear-related UN Security Council sanctions and no new EU nuclear-related sanctions or restrictive measures. The United States will make best efforts in good faith to sustain this JCPOA and to prevent interference with the realisation of the full benefit by Iran of the sanctions lifting specified in Annex II. The U.S. Administration, acting consistent with the respective roles of the President and the Congress, will refrain from re-introducing or re-imposing the sanctions specified in Annex II that it has ceased applying under this JCPOA, without prejudice to the dispute resolution process provided for under this JCPOA. The U.S. Administration, acting consistent with the respective roles of the President and the Congress, will refrain from imposing new nuclear-related sanctions. Iran has stated that it will treat such a re-introduction or re-imposition of the sanctions specified in Annex II, or such an imposition of new nuclear-related sanctions, as grounds to cease performing its commitments under this JCPOA in whole or in part.

27. The E3/EU+3 will take adequate administrative and regulatory measures to ensure clarity and effectiveness with respect to the lifting of sanctions under this JCPOA. The EU and its Member States as well as the United States will issue relevant guidelines and make publicly accessible statements on the details of sanctions or restrictive measures which have been lifted under this JCPOA. The EU and its Member States and the United States commit to consult with Iran regarding the content of such guidelines and statements, on a regular basis and whenever appropriate.

28. The E3/EU+3 and Iran commit to implement this JCPOA in good faith and in a constructive atmosphere, based on mutual respect, and to refrain from any action inconsistent with the letter, spirit and intent of this JCPOA that would undermine its successful implementation. Senior Government officials of the E3/EU+3 and Iran will make every effort to support the successful implementation of this JCPOA including in their public statements.[334] The E3/EU+3 will take all measures required to lift sanctions and will refrain from imposing exceptional or discriminatory regulatory and procedural requirements in lieu of the sanctions and restrictive measures covered by the JCPOA.

29. The EU and its Member States and the United States, consistent with their respective laws, will refrain from any policy specifically intended to directly and adversely affect the normalisation of trade and economic relations with Iran inconsistent with their commitments not to undermine the successful implementation of this JCPOA.

30. The E3/EU+3 will not apply sanctions or restrictive measures to persons or entities for engaging in activities covered by the lifting of sanctions provided for in this JCPOA, provided that such activities are otherwise consistent with E3/EU+3 laws and regulations in effect. Following the lifting of sanctions under this JCPOA as specified in Annex II, ongoing investigations on possible infringements of such sanctions may be reviewed in accordance with applicable national laws.

31. Consistent with the timing specified in Annex V, the EU and its Member States will terminate the implementation of the measures applicable to designated entities and individuals, including the Central Bank of Iran and other Iranian banks and financial institutions, as detailed in Annex II and the attachments thereto. Consistent with the timing specified in Annex V, the United States will remove designation of certain entities and individuals on the Specially Designated Nationals and Blocked Persons List, and entities and individuals listed on the Foreign Sanctions Evaders List, as detailed in Annex II and the attachments thereto.

32. EU and E3+3 countries and international participants will engage in joint projects with Iran, including through IAEA technical cooperation projects, in the field of peaceful nuclear technology, including nuclear power plants, research reactors, fuel fabrication, agreed joint advanced R&D such as fusion, establishment of a state-of-the-art regional nuclear medical centre, personnel training, nuclear safety and security, and environmental protection, as detailed in Annex III. They will take necessary measures, as appropriate, for the implementation of these projects.

33. The E3/EU+3 and Iran will agree on steps to ensure Iran's access in areas of trade, technology, finance and energy. The EU will further explore possible areas for cooperation between the EU, its Member States and Iran, and in this context consider the use of available instruments such as export credits to facilitate trade, project financing and investment in Iran.

IMPLEMENTATION PLAN

34. Iran and the E3/EU+3 will implement their JCPOA commitments according to the sequence specified in Annex V. The milestones for implementation are as follows:

    i. Finalisation Day is the date on which negotiations of this JCPOA are concluded among the E3/EU+3 and Iran, to be followed promptly by submission of the resolution endorsing this JCPOA to the UN Security Council for adoption without delay.

    ii. Adoption Day is the date 90 days after the endorsement of this JCPOA by the UN Security Council, or such earlier date as may be determined by mutual consent of the JCPOA participants, at which time this

[334] 'Government officials' for the U.S. means senior officials of the U.S. Administration.

JCPOA and the commitments in this JCPOA come into effect. Beginning on that date, JCPOA participants will make necessary arrangements and preparations for the implementation of their JCPOA commitments.

iii. Implementation Day is the date on which, simultaneously with the IAEA report verifying implementation by Iran of the nuclear-related measures described in Sections 15.1. to 15.11 of Annex V, the EU and the United States take the actions described in Sections 16 and 17 of Annex V respectively and in accordance with the UN Security Council resolution, the actions described in Section 18 of Annex V occur at the UN level.

iv. Transition Day is the date 8 years after Adoption Day or the date on which the Director General of the IAEA submits a report stating that the IAEA has reached the Broader Conclusion that all nuclear material in Iran remains in peaceful activities, whichever is earlier. On that date, the EU and the United States will take the actions described in Sections 20 and 21 of Annex V respectively and Iran will seek, consistent with the Constitutional roles of the President and Parliament, ratification of the Additional Protocol.

v. UN Security Council resolution Termination Day is the date on which the UN Security Council resolution endorsing this JCPOA terminates according to its terms, which is to be 10 years from Adoption Day, provided that the provisions of previous resolutions have not been reinstated. On that date, the EU will take the actions described in Section 25 of Annex V.

35. The sequence and milestones set forth above and in Annex V are without prejudice to the duration of JCPOA commitments stated in this JCPOA.

DISPUTE RESOLUTION MECHANISM

36. If Iran believed that any or all of the E3/EU+3 were not meeting their commitments under this JCPOA, Iran could refer the issue to the Joint Commission for resolution; similarly, if any of the E3/EU+3 believed that Iran was not meeting its commitments under this JCPOA, any of the E3/EU+3 could do the same. The Joint Commission would have 15 days to resolve the issue, unless the time period was extended by consensus. After Joint Commission consideration, any participant could refer the issue to Ministers of Foreign Affairs, if it believed the compliance issue had not been resolved. Ministers would have 15 days to resolve the issue, unless the time period was extended by consensus. After Joint Commission consideration – in parallel with (or in lieu of) review at the Ministerial level - either the complaining participant or the participant whose performance is in question could request that the issue be considered by an Advisory Board, which would consist of three members (one each appointed by the participants in the dispute and a third independent member). The Advisory Board should provide a non-binding opinion on the compliance issue within 15 days. If, after this 30-day process the issue is not resolved, the Joint Commission would consider the opinion of the Advisory Board for no more than 5 days in order to resolve the issue. If the issue still has not been resolved to the satisfaction of the complaining participant, and if the complaining participant deems the issue to constitute significant non-performance, then that participant could treat the unresolved issue as grounds to cease performing its commitments under this JCPOA in whole or in part and/or notify the UN Security Council that it believes the issue constitutes significant non-performance.

37. Upon receipt of the notification from the complaining participant, as described above, including a description of the good-faith efforts the participant made to exhaust the dispute resolution process specified in this JCPOA, the UN Security Council, in accordance with its procedures, shall vote on a resolution to continue the sanctions lifting. If the resolution described above has not been adopted within 30 days of the notification, then the provisions of the old UN Security Council resolutions would be re-imposed, unless the UN Security Council decides otherwise. In such event, these provisions would not apply with retroactive effect to contracts signed between any party and Iran or Iranian individuals and entities prior to the date of application, provided that the activities contemplated under and execution of such contracts are consistent with this JCPOA and the previous and current UN Security Council resolutions. The UN Security Council, expressing its intention to prevent the reapplication of the provisions if the issue giving rise to the notification is resolved within this period, intends to take into account the views of the States involved in the issue and any opinion on the issue of the Advisory Board. Iran has stated that if sanctions are reinstated in whole or in part, Iran will treat that as grounds to cease performing its commitments under this JCPOA in whole or in part.

JCPOA Annex I – Nuclear-related measures

A. GENERAL

1. The sequence of implementation of the commitments detailed in this Annex is specified in Annex V to the Joint Comprehensive Plan of Action (JCPOA). Unless otherwise specified, the durations of the commitments in this Annex are from Implementation Day.

B. ARAK HEAVY WATER RESEARCH REACTOR

2. Iran will modernise the Arak heavy water research reactor to support peaceful nuclear research and radioisotopes production for medical and industrial purposes. Iran will redesign and rebuild the reactor, based on the agreed conceptual design (as attached to this Annex) to support its peaceful nuclear research and production needs and purposes, including testing of fuel pins and assembly prototypes and structural materials. The design will be such as to minimise the production of plutonium and not to produce weapon-grade plutonium in normal operation. The power of the redesigned reactor will not exceed 20 MWth. The E3/EU+3 and Iran share the understanding that the parameters in the conceptual design are subject to possible and necessary adjustments in developing the final design while fully preserving the above-mentioned purposes and principles of modernisation.

3. Iran will not pursue construction at the existing unfinished reactor based on its original design and will remove the existing calandria and retain it in Iran. The calandria will be made inoperable by filling any openings in the calandria with concrete such that the IAEA can verify that it will not be usable for a future nuclear application. In redesigning and reconstructing of the modernized Arak heavy water research reactor, Iran will maximise the use of existing infrastructure already installed at the current Arak research reactor.

4. Iran will take the leadership role as the owner and as the project manager, and have responsibility for overall implementation of the Arak modernisation project, with E3/EU+3 participants assuming responsibilities regarding the modernisation of the Arak reactor as described in this Annex. A Working Group composed of E3/EU+3 participants will be established to facilitate the redesigning and rebuilding of the reactor. An international partnership composed of Iran and the Working Group would implement the Arak modernisation project. The Working Group could be enlarged to include other countries by consensus of the participants of the Working Group and Iran. E3/EU+3 participants and Iran will conclude an official document expressing their strong commitments to the Arak modernisation project in advance of Implementation Day which would provide an assured path forward to modernise the reactor and would define the responsibilities assumed by the E3/EU+3 participants, and subsequently contracts would be concluded. The participants of the Working Group will provide assistance needed by Iran for redesigning and rebuilding the reactor, consistent with their respective national laws, in such a manner as to enable the safe and timely construction and commissioning of the modernised reactor.

5. Iran and the Working Group will cooperate to develop the final design of the modernised reactor and the design of the subsidiary laboratories to be carried out by Iran, and review conformity with international safety standards, such that the reactor can be licensed by the relevant Iranian regulatory authority for commissioning and operation. The final design of the modernised reactor and the design of the subsidiary laboratories will be submitted to the Joint Commission. The Joint Commission will aim to complete its review and endorsement within three months after the submission of the final design. If the Joint Commission does not complete its review and endorsement within three months, Iran could raise the issue through the dispute resolution mechanism envisaged by this JCPOA.

6. The IAEA will monitor the construction and report to the Working Group for confirmation that the construction of the modernised reactor is consistent with the approved final design.

7. As the project manager, Iran will take responsibility for the construction efforts. E3/EU+3 parties will, consistent with their national laws, take appropriate administrative, legal, technical, and regulatory measures to support co-operation.

   E3/EU+3 parties will support the purchase by Iran, the transfer and supply of necessary materials, equipment, instrumentation and control systems and technologies required for the construction of the redesigned reactor, through the mechanism established by this JCPOA, as well as through exploration of relevant funding contributions.

8. E3/EU+3 parties will also support and facilitate the timely and safe construction of the modernized Arak reactor and its subsidiary laboratories, upon request by Iran, through IAEA technical cooperation if appropriate, including but not limited to technical and financial assistance, supply of required materials and equipment, state-of-the-art instrumentation and control systems and equipment and support for licensing and authorization.

9. The redesigned reactor will use up to 3.67 percent enriched uranium in the form of UO2 with a mass of approximately 350 kg of UO2 in a full core load, with a fuel design to be reviewed and approved by the Joint Commission. The international partnership with the participation of Iran will fabricate the initial fuel core load for the reactor outside Iran. The international partnership will cooperate with Iran, including through technical assistance, to fabricate, test and license fuel fabrication capabilities in Iran for subsequent fuel core reloads for future use with this reactor. Destructive and non-destructive testing of this fuel including Post-Irradiation-Examination (PIE) will take place in one of the participating countries outside of Iran and that country will work with Iran to license the subsequent fuel fabricated in Iran for the use in the redesigned reactor under IAEA monitoring.

10. Iran will not produce or test natural uranium pellets, fuel pins or fuel assemblies, which are specifically designed for the support of the originally designed Arak reactor, designated by the IAEA as IR-40. Iran will store under IAEA continuous monitoring all existing natural uranium pellets and IR-40 fuel assemblies until the modernised Arak reactor becomes operational, at which point these natural uranium pellets and IR-40 fuel assemblies will be converted to UNH, or exchanged with an equivalent quantity of natural uranium. Iran will make the necessary technical modifications to the natural uranium fuel production process line that was intended to supply fuel for the IR-40 reactor design, such that it can be used for the fabrication of the fuel reloads for the modernised Arak reactor.

11. All spent fuel from the redesigned Arak reactor, regardless of its origin, for the lifetime of the reactor, will be shipped out of Iran to a mutually determined location in E3/EU+3 countries or third countries, for further treatment or disposition as provided for in relevant contracts to be concluded, consistent with national laws, with the recipient party, within one year from the unloading from the reactor or whenever deemed to be safe for transfer by the recipient country.

12. Iran will submit the DIQ of the redesigned reactor to the IAEA which will include information on the planned radio-isotope production and reactor operation programme. The reactor will be operated under IAEA monitoring.

13. Iran will operate the Fuel Manufacturing Plant only to produce fuel assemblies for light water reactors and reloads for the modernized Arak reactor.

C. HEAVY WATER PRODUCTION PLANT

14. All excess heavy water which is beyond Iran's needs for the modernised Arak research reactor, the Zero power heavy water reactor, quantities needed for medical research and production of deuterate solutions and chemical compounds including, where appropriate, contingency stocks, will be made available for export to the international market based on international prices and delivered to the international buyer for 15 years. Iran's needs, consistent with the parameters above, are estimated to be 130 metric tonnes of nuclear grade heavy water or its equivalent in different enrichments prior to commissioning of the modernised Arak research reactor, and 90 metric tonnes after the commissioning, including the amount contained in the reactor.

15. Iran will inform the IAEA about the inventory and the production of the HWPP and will allow the IAEA to monitor the quantities of the heavy water stocks and the amount of heavy water produced, including through IAEA visits, as requested, to the HWPP.

D. OTHER REACTORS

16. Consistent with its plan, Iran will keep pace with the trend of international technological advancement in relying only on light water for its future nuclear power and research reactors with enhanced international cooperation including assurances of supply of necessary fuel.

17. Iran intends to ship out all spent fuel for all future and present nuclear power and research reactors, for further treatment or disposition as provided for in relevant contracts to be concluded consistent with national laws with the recipient party.

E. SPENT FUEL REPROCESSING ACTIVITIES

18. For 15 years Iran will not, and does not intend to thereafter, engage in any spent fuel reprocessing or spent fuel reprocessing R&D activities. For the purpose of this annex, spent fuel includes all types of irradiated fuel.

19. For 15 years Iran will not, and does not intend to thereafter, reprocess spent fuel except for irradiated enriched uranium targets for production of radio-isotopes for medical and peaceful industrial purposes.

20. For 15 years Iran will not, and does not intend to thereafter, develop, acquire or build facilities capable of separation of plutonium, uranium or neptunium from spent fuel or from fertile targets, other than for production of radio-isotopes for medical and peaceful industrial purposes.

21. For 15 years, Iran will only develop, acquire, build, or operate hot cells (containing a cell or interconnected cells), shielded cells or shielded glove boxes with dimensions less than 6 cubic meters in volume compatible with the specifications set out in Annex I of the Additional Protocol. These will be co-located with the modernised Arak research reactor, the Tehran Research Reactor, and radio-medicine production complexes, and only capable of the separation and processing of industrial or medical isotopes and non-destructive PIE. The needed equipment will be acquired through the procurement mechanism established by this JCPOA. For 15 years, Iran will develop, acquire, build, or operate hot cells (containing a cell or interconnected cells), shielded cells or shielded glove boxes with dimensions beyond 6 cubic meters in volume and specifications set out in Annex I of the Additional Protocol, only after approval by the Joint Commission.

22. The E3/EU+3 are ready to facilitate all of the destructive and non-destructive examinations on fuel elements and/or fuel assembly prototypes including PIE for all fuel fabricated in or outside Iran and irradiated in Iran, using their existing facilities outside Iran. Except for the Arak research reactor complex, Iran will not develop, build, acquire or operate hot cells capable of performing PIE or seek to acquire equipment to build/develop such a capability, for 15 years.

23. For 15 years, in addition to continuing current fuel testing activities at the TRR, Iran will undertake non-destructive post irradiation examination (PIE) of fuel pins, fuel assembly prototypes and structural materials. These examinations will be exclusively at the Arak research reactor complex. However, the E3/EU+3 will make available their facilities to conduct destructive testing with Iranian specialists, as agreed. The hot cells at the Arak research reactor in which non-destructive PIE are performed will not be physically interconnected to cells that process or handle materials for the production of medical or industrial radioisotopes.

24. For 15 years, Iran will not engage in producing or acquiring plutonium or uranium metals or their alloys, or conducting R&D on plutonium or uranium (or their alloys) metallurgy, or casting, forming, or machining plutonium or uranium metal.

25. Iran will not produce, seek, or acquire separated plutonium, highly enriched uranium (defined as 20% or greater uranium-235), or uranium-233, or neptunium-237 (except for use as laboratory standards or in instruments using neptunium-237) for 15 years.

26. If Iran seeks to initiate R&D on uranium metal based TRR fuel in small agreed quantities after 10 years and before 15 years, Iran will present its plan to, and seek approval by, the Joint Commission.

F. ENRICHMENT CAPACITY

27. Iran will keep its enrichment capacity at no more than 5060 IR-1 centrifuge machines in no more than 30 cascades in their current configurations in currently operating units at the Natanz Fuel Enrichment Plant (FEP) for 10 years.

28. Iran will keep its level of uranium enrichment at up to 3.67 percent for 15 years.

29. Iran will remove the following excess centrifuges and infrastructure not associated with 5060 IR-1 centrifuges in FEP, which will be stored at Natanz in Hall B of FEP under IAEA continuous monitoring:

    29.1. All excess centrifuge machines, including IR-2m centrifuges. Excess IR-1 centrifuges will be used for the replacement of failed or damaged centrifuges of the same type on a one-for-one basis.

    29.2. UF6 pipework including sub headers, valves and pressure transducers at cascade level, and frequency inverters, and UF6 withdrawal equipment from one of the withdrawal stations, which is currently not in service, including its vacuum pumps and chemical traps.

30. For the purpose of this Annex, the IAEA will confirm through the established practice the failed or damaged status of centrifuge machines before removal.

31. For 15 years, Iran will install gas centrifuge machines, or enrichment-related infrastructure, whether suitable for uranium enrichment, research and development, or stable isotope enrichment, exclusively at the locations and for the activities specified under this JCPOA.

G. CENTRIFUGES RESEARCH AND DEVELOPMENT

32. Iran will continue to conduct enrichment R&D in a manner that does not accumulate enriched uranium. For 10 years and consistent with its enrichment R&D plan, Iran's enrichment R&D with uranium will only include IR-4, IR-5, IR-6 and IR-8 centrifuges. Mechanical testing on up to two single centrifuges for each type will be carried out only on the IR-2m, IR-4, IR-5, IR-6, IR-6s, IR-7 and IR-8. Iran will build or test, with or without uranium, only those gas centrifuges specified in this JCPOA.

33. Consistent with its plan, Iran will continue working with the 164-machine IR-2m cascade at PFEP in order to complete the necessary tests until 30 November 2015 or the day of implementation of this JCPOA, whichever comes later, and after that it will take these machines out of the PFEP and store them under IAEA continuous monitoring at Natanz in Hall B of FEP.

34. Consistent with its plan, Iran will continue working with the 164-machine IR-4 cascade at PFEP in order to complete the necessary tests until 30 November 2015 or the day of implementation of this JCPOA, whichever comes later, and after that it will take these machines out of the PFEP and store them under IAEA continuous monitoring at Natanz in Hall B of FEP.

35. Iran will continue the testing of a single IR-4 centrifuge machine and IR-4 centrifuge cascade of up to 10 centrifuge machines for 10 years.

36. Iran will test a single IR-5 centrifuge machine for 10 years.

37. Iran will continue testing of the IR-6 on single centrifuge machines and its intermediate cascades and will commence testing of up to 30 centrifuge machines from one and a half years before the end of year 10. Iran will proceed from single centrifuge machines and small cascades to intermediate cascades in a logical sequence.

38. Iran will commence, upon start of implementation of the JCPOA, testing of the IR-8 on single centrifuge machines and its intermediate cascades and will commence the testing of up to 30 centrifuges machines from one and a half years before the end of year 10. Iran will proceed from single centrifuges to small cascades to intermediate cascades in a logical sequence.

39. For 10 years, Iran, consistent with the established practice, will recombine the enriched and depleted streams from the IR-6 and IR-8 cascades through the use of welded pipework on withdrawal main headers in a manner that precludes the withdrawal of enriched and depleted uranium materials and verified by the IAEA.

40. For 15 years, Iran will conduct all testing of centrifuges with uranium only at the PFEP. Iran will conduct all mechanical testing of centrifuges only at the PFEP and the Tehran Research Centre.

41. For the purpose of adapting PFEP to the R&D activities in the enrichment and enrichment R&D plan, Iran will remove all centrifuges except those needed for testing as described in the relevant paragraphs above, except for the IR-1 cascade (No. 1) as described below. For the full IR-1 cascade (No. 6), Iran will modify associated infrastructure by removing UF6 pipework, including sub-headers, valves and pressure transducers at cascade level, and frequency inverters. The IR-1 cascade (No. 1) centrifuges will be kept but made inoperable, as verified by the IAEA, through the removal of centrifuge rotors and the injection of epoxy resin into the sub headers, feeding, product, and tails pipework, and the removal of controls and electrical systems for vacuum, power and cooling. Excess centrifuges and infrastructure will be stored at Natanz in Hall B of FEP under IAEA continuous monitoring. The R&D space in line No. 6 will be left empty until Iran needs to use it for its R&D programme.

42. Consistent with the activities in the enrichment and enrichment R&D plan, Iran will maintain the cascade infrastructure for testing of single centrifuges and small and intermediate cascades in two R&D lines (No. 2

and No. 3) and will adapt two other lines (No. 4 and No. 5) with infrastructure similar to that for lines No. 2 and No. 3 in order to enable future R&D activities as specified in this JCPOA. Adaptation will include modification of all UF6 pipework (including removal of all sub headers except as agreed as needed for the R&D programme) and associated instrumentation to be compatible with single centrifuges and small and intermediate cascade testing instead of full scale testing.

43. Consistent with its plan and internationally established practices, Iran intends to continue R&D on new types of centrifuges through computer modelling and simulations, including at universities. For any such project to proceed to a prototype stage for mechanical testing within 10 years, a full presentation to, and approval by, the Joint Commission is needed.

H. FORDOW FUEL ENRICHMENT PLANT

44. The Fordow Fuel Enrichment Plant (FFEP) will be converted into a nuclear, physics, and technology centre and international collaboration will be encouraged in agreed areas of research. The Joint Commission will be informed in advance of the specific projects that will be undertaken at Fordow.

45. Iran will not conduct any uranium enrichment or any uranium enrichment related R&D and will have no nuclear material at the Fordow Fuel Enrichment Plant (FFEP) for 15 years.

46. For 15 years, Iran will maintain no more than 1044 IR-1 centrifuge machines at one wing of the FFEP of which:

46.1. Two cascades that have not experienced UF6 before will be modified for the production of stable isotopes. The transition to stable isotope production of these cascades at FFEP will be conducted in joint partnership between the Russian Federation and Iran on the basis of arrangements to be mutually agreed upon. To prepare these two cascades for installation of a new cascade architecture appropriate for stable isotope production by the joint partnership, Iran will remove the connection to the UF6 feed main header, and move cascade UF6 pipework (except for the dump line in order to maintain vacuum) to storage in Fordow under IAEA continuous monitoring. The Joint Commission will be informed about the conceptual framework of stable isotope production at FFEP.

46.2. For four cascades with all associated infrastructure remaining except for pipework that enables crossover tandem connections, two will be placed in an idle state, not spinning. The other two cascades will continue to spin until the transition to stable isotope production described in the previous subparagraph has been completed. Upon completion of the transition to stable isotope production described in the previous subparagraph, these two spinning cascades will be placed in an idle state, not spinning.

47. Iran will:

47.1. remove the other 2 cascades of IR-1 centrifuges from this wing, by removing all centrifuges and cascade UF6 pipework, including sub-headers, valves and pressure transducers at cascade level, and frequency inverters.

47.2. also subsequently remove cascade electrical cabling, individual cascade control cabinets and vacuum pumps. All these excess centrifuges and infrastructure will be stored at Natanz in Hall B of FEP under IAEA continuous monitoring.

48. Iran will:

48.1. remove all excess centrifuges and uranium enrichment related infrastructure from the other wing of the FFEP. This will include removal of all centrifuges and UF6 pipework, including sub headers, valves and pressure gauges and transducers, and frequency inverters and converters, and UF6 feed and withdrawal stations.

48.2. also subsequently remove cascade electrical cabling, individual cascade control cabinets, vacuum pumps and centrifuge mounting blocks. All these excess centrifuges and infrastructure will be stored at Natanz in Hall B of FEP under IAEA continuous monitoring.

49. Centrifuges from the four idle cascades may be used for the replacement of failed or damaged centrifuges in stable isotope production at Fordow.

50. Iran will limit its stable isotope production activities with gas centrifuges to the FFEP for 15 years and will use no more than 348 IR-1 centrifuges for these activities at the FFEP. The associated R&D activities in Iran will occur at the FFEP and at Iran's declared and monitored centrifuge manufacturing facilities for testing, modification and balancing these IR-1 centrifuges.

51. The IAEA will establish a baseline for the amount of uranium legacy from past enrichment operations that will remain in Fordow. Iran will permit the IAEA regular access, including daily as requested by the IAEA, access to the FFEP in order to monitor Iran's production of stable isotopes and the absence of undeclared nuclear material and activities at the FFEP for 15 years.

I. OTHER ASPECTS OF ENRICHMENT

52. Iran will abide by its voluntary commitments as expressed in its own long term enrichment and enrichment R&D plan to be submitted as part of the initial declaration described in Article 2 of the Additional Protocol.[335] The IAEA will confirm on an annual basis, for the duration of the plan that the nature and scope and scale of Iran's enrichment and enrichment R&D activities are in line with this plan.

53. Iran will start to install necessary infrastructure for the IR-8 at Natanz in Hall B of FEP after year 10.

54. An agreed template for describing different centrifuge types (IR-1, IR-2m, IR-4, IR-5, IR-6, IR-6s, IR-7, IR-8) and the associated definitions need to be accomplished by implementation day.

55. An agreed procedure for measuring IR-1, IR-2m and IR-4 centrifuge performance data needs to be accomplished by implementation day.

J. URANIUM STOCKS AND FUELS

56. Iran will maintain a total enriched uranium stockpile of no more than 300 kg of up to 3.67% enriched uranium hexafluoride (or the equivalent in different chemical forms) for 15 years.

57. All enriched uranium hexafluoride in excess of 300 kg of up to 3.67% enriched UF6 (or the equivalent in different chemical forms) will be down blended to natural uranium level or be sold on the international market and delivered to the international buyer in return for natural uranium delivered to Iran. Iran will enter into a commercial contract with an entity outside Iran for the purchase and transfer of its enriched uranium stockpile in excess of 300 kg UF6 in return for natural uranium delivered to Iran. The E3/EU+3 will facilitate, where applicable, the conclusion and implementation of this contract. Iran may choose to seek to sell excess enriched uranium to the IAEA fuel bank in Kazakhstan when the fuel bank becomes operational.

58. All uranium oxide enriched to between 5% and 20% will be fabricated into fuel plates for the Tehran Research Reactor or transferred, based on a commercial transaction, outside of Iran or diluted to an enrichment level of 3.67% or less. Scrap oxide and other forms not in plates that cannot be fabricated into TRR fuel plates will be transferred, based on a commercial transaction, outside of Iran or diluted to an enrichment level of 3.67% or less. In case of future supply of 19.75% enriched uranium oxide (U3O8) for TRR fuel plates fabrication, all scrap oxide and other forms not in plates that cannot be fabricated into TRR fuel plates, containing uranium enriched to between 5% and 20%, will be transferred, based on a commercial transaction, outside of Iran or diluted to an enrichment level of 3.67% or less within 6 months of its production. Scrap plates will be transferred, based on a commercial transaction, outside Iran. The commercial transactions should be structured to return an equivalent amount of natural uranium to Iran. For 15 years, Iran will not build or operate facilities for converting fuel plates or scrap back to UF6.

59. Russian designed, fabricated and licensed fuel assemblies for use in Russian-supplied reactors in Iran do not count against the 300 kg UF6 stockpile limit. Enriched uranium in fabricated fuel assemblies from other sources outside of Iran for use in Iran's nuclear research and power reactors, including those which will be

[335] Iran will permit the IAEA to share the content of the enrichment and enrichment R&D plan, as submitted as part of the initial declaration, with the Joint Commission participants.

fabricated outside of Iran for the initial fuel load of the modernised Arak research reactor, which are certified by the fuel supplier and the appropriate Iranian authority to meet international standards, will not count against the 300 kg UF6 stockpile limit. The Joint Commission will establish a Technical Working Group with the goal of enabling fuel to be fabricated in Iran while adhering to the agreed stockpile parameters (300 kg of up to 3.67 % enriched UF6 or the equivalent in different chemical forms). This Technical Working Group will also, within one year, work to develop objective technical criteria for assessing whether fabricated fuel and its intermediate products can be readily converted to UF6. Enriched uranium in fabricated fuel assemblies and its intermediate products manufactured in Iran and certified to meet international standards, including those for the modernised Arak research reactor, will not count against the 300 kg UF6 stockpile limit provided the Technical Working Group of the Joint Commission approves that such fuel assemblies and their intermediate products cannot be readily reconverted into UF6. This could for instance be achieved through impurities (e.g. burnable poisons or otherwise) contained in fuels or through the fuel being in a chemical form such that direct conversion back to UF6 would be technically difficult without dissolution and purification. The objective technical criteria will guide the approval process of the Technical Working Group. The IAEA will monitor the fuel fabrication process for any fuel produced in Iran to verify that the fuel and intermediate products comport with the fuel fabrication process that was approved by the Technical Working Group. The Joint Commission will also support assistance to Iran including through IAEA technical cooperation as appropriate, in meeting international qualification standards for nuclear fuel produced by Iran.

60. Iran will seek to enter into a commercial contract with entities outside Iran for the purchase of fuel for the TRR and enriched uranium targets. The E3/EU+3 will facilitate, as needed, the conclusion and implementation of this contract. In the case of lack of conclusion of a contract with a fuel supplier, E3/EU+3 will supply a quantity of 19.75% enriched uranium oxide (U3O8) and deliver to Iran, exclusively for the purpose of fabrication in Iran of fuel for the TRR and enriched uranium targets for the lifetime of the reactor. This 19.75% enriched uranium oxide (U3O8) will be supplied in increments no greater than approximately 5 kg and each new increment will be provided only when the previous increment of this material has been verified by the IAEA to have been mixed with aluminum to make fuel for the TRR or fabricated into enriched uranium targets. Iran will notify the E3/EU+3 within 2 years before the contingency of TRR fuel will be exhausted in order to have the uranium oxide available 6 months before the end of the 2 year period.

K. CENTRIFUGE MANUFACTURING

61. Consistent with its enrichment and enrichment R&D plan, Iran will only engage in production of centrifuges, including centrifuge rotors suitable for isotope separation or any other centrifuge components, to meet the enrichment and enrichment R&D requirements of this Annex.

62. Consistent with its plan, Iran will use the stock of IR-1 centrifuge machines in storage, which are in excess of the remaining 5060 IR-1 centrifuges in Natanz and the IR-1 centrifuges installed at Fordow, for the replacement of failed or damaged machines. Whenever during the 10 year period from the start of the implementation of the JCPOA, the level of stock of IR-1 machines falls to 500 or below, Iran may maintain this level of stock by resuming production of IR-1 machines at a rate up to the average monthly crash rate without exceeding the stock of 500.

63. Consistent with its plan, at the end of year 8, Iran will commence manufacturing of IR-6 and IR-8 centrifuges without rotors through year 10 at a rate of up to 200 centrifuges per year for each type. After year 10, Iran will produce complete centrifuges with the same rate to meet its enrichment and enrichment R&D needs. Iran will store them at Natanz in an above ground location, under IAEA continuous monitoring, until they are needed for final assembly according to the enrichment and enrichment R&D plan.

L. ADDITIONAL PROTOCOL AND MODIFIED CODE 3.1

64. Iran will notify the IAEA of provisional application of the Additional Protocol to its Safeguards Agreement in accordance with Article 17(b) of the Additional Protocol pending its entry into force, and subsequently seek ratification and entry into force, consistent with the respective roles of the President and the Majlis (Parliament).

65. Iran will notify the IAEA that it will fully implement the Modified Code 3.1 of the Subsidiary Arrangement to Iran's Safeguards Agreement as long as the Safeguards Agreement remains in force.

M. PAST AND PRESENT ISSUES OF CONCERN

66. Iran will complete all activities as set out in paragraphs 2, 4, 5, and 6 of the "Roadmap for Clarification of Past and Present Outstanding Issues", as verified by the IAEA in its regular updates by the Director General of the IAEA on the implementation of this Roadmap.

N. MODERN TECHNOLOGIES AND LONG TERM PRESENCE OF IAEA

67. For the purpose of increasing the efficiency of monitoring for this JCPOA, for 15 years or longer, for the specified verification measures:

    67.1. Iran will permit the IAEA the use of on-line enrichment measurement and electronic seals which communicate their status within nuclear sites to IAEA inspectors, as well as other IAEA approved and certified modern technologies in line with internationally accepted IAEA practice. Iran will facilitate automated collection of IAEA measurement recordings registered by installed measurement devices and sending to IAEA working space in individual nuclear sites.

    67.2. Iran will make the necessary arrangements to allow for a long-term IAEA presence, including issuing long-term visas, as well as providing proper working space at nuclear sites and, with best efforts, at locations near nuclear sites in Iran for the designated IAEA inspectors for working and keeping necessary equipment.

    67.3. Iran will increase the number of designated IAEA inspectors to the range of 130–150 within 9 months from the date of the implementation of the JCPOA, and will generally allow the designation of inspectors from nations that have diplomatic relations with Iran, consistent with its laws and regulations.

O. TRANSPARENCY RELATED TO URANIUM ORE CONCENTRATE (UOC)

68. Iran will permit the IAEA to monitor, through agreed measures that will include containment and surveillance measures, for 25 years, that all uranium ore concentrate produced in Iran or obtained from any other source, is transferred to the uranium conversion facility (UCF) in Esfahan or to any other future uranium conversion facility which Iran might decide to build in Iran within this period.

69. Iran will provide the IAEA with all necessary information such that the IAEA will be able to verify the production of the uranium ore concentrate and the inventory of uranium ore concentrate produced in Iran or obtained from any other source for 25 years.

P. TRANSPARENCY RELATED TO ENRICHMENT

70. For 15 years, Iran will permit the IAEA to implement continuous monitoring, including through containment and surveillance measures, as necessary, to verify that stored centrifuges and infrastructure remain in storage, and are only used to replace failed or damaged centrifuges, as specified in this Annex.

71. Iran will permit the IAEA regular access, including daily access as requested by the IAEA, to relevant buildings at Natanz, including all parts of the FEP and PFEP, for 15 years.

72. For 15 years, the Natanz enrichment site will be the sole location for all of Iran's uranium enrichment related activities including safeguarded R&D.

73. Iran intends to apply nuclear export policies and practices in line with the internationally established standards for the export of nuclear material, equipment and technology. For 15 years, Iran will only engage, including through export of any enrichment or enrichment related equipment and technology, with any other country, or with any foreign entity in enrichment or enrichment related activities, including related research and development activities, following approval by the Joint Commission.

Q. ACCESS

74. Requests for access pursuant to provisions of this JCPOA will be made in good faith, with due observance of the sovereign rights of Iran, and kept to the minimum necessary to effectively implement the verification responsibilities under this JCPOA. In line with normal international safeguards practice, such requests will not be aimed at interfering with Iranian military or other national security activities, but will be exclusively for

resolving concerns regarding fulfilment of the JCPOA commitments and Iran's other non-proliferation and safeguards obligations. The following procedures are for the purpose of JCPOA implementation between the E3/EU+3 and Iran and are without prejudice to the safeguards agreement and the Additional Protocol thereto. In implementing this procedure as well as other transparency measures, the IAEA will be requested to take every precaution to protect commercial, technological and industrial secrets as well as other confidential information coming to its knowledge.

75. In furtherance of implementation of the JCPOA, if the IAEA has concerns regarding undeclared nuclear materials or activities, or activities inconsistent with the JCPOA, at locations that have not been declared under the comprehensive safeguards agreement or Additional Protocol, the IAEA will provide Iran the basis for such concerns and request clarification.

76. If Iran's explanations do not resolve the IAEA's concerns, the Agency may request access to such locations for the sole reason to verify the absence of undeclared nuclear materials and activities or activities inconsistent with the JCPOA at such locations. The IAEA will provide Iran the reasons for access in writing and will make available relevant information.

77. Iran may propose to the IAEA alternative means of resolving the IAEA's concerns that enable the IAEA to verify the absence of undeclared nuclear materials and activities or activities inconsistent with the JCPOA at the location in question, which should be given due and prompt consideration.

78. If the absence of undeclared nuclear materials and activities or activities inconsistent with the JCPOA cannot be verified after the implementation of the alternative arrangements agreed by Iran and the IAEA, or if the two sides are unable to reach satisfactory arrangements to verify the absence of undeclared nuclear materials and activities or activities inconsistent with the JCPOA at the specified locations within 14 days of the IAEA's original request for access, Iran, in consultation with the members of the Joint Commission, would resolve the IAEA's concerns through necessary means agreed between Iran and the IAEA. In the absence of an agreement, the members of the Joint Commission, by consensus or by a vote of 5 or more of its 8 members, would advise on the necessary means to resolve the IAEA's concerns. The process of consultation with, and any action by, the members of the Joint Commission would not exceed 7 days, and Iran would implement the necessary means within 3 additional days.

R. CENTRIFUGE COMPONENT MANUFACTURING TRANSPARENCY

79. Iran and the IAEA will take the necessary steps for containment and surveillance on centrifuge rotor tubes and bellows for 20 years.

80. In this context:

    80.1. Iran will provide the IAEA with an initial inventory of all existing centrifuge rotor tubes and bellows and subsequent reports on changes in such inventory and will permit the IAEA to verify the inventory by item counting and numbering, and through containment and surveillance, of all rotor tubes and bellows, including in all existing and newly produced centrifuges.

    80.2. Iran will declare all locations and equipment, namely flow-forming machines, filament-winding machines and mandrels that are used for production of centrifuge rotor tubes or bellows, and will permit the IAEA to implement continuous monitoring, including through containment and surveillance on this equipment, to verify that this equipment is being used to manufacture centrifuges only for the activities specified in this JCPOA.

S. OTHER URANIUM ISOTOPE SEPARATION ACTIVITIES

81. For 10 years, Iran's uranium isotope separation-related research and development or production activities will be exclusively based on gaseous centrifuge technology.[336] Iran will permit IAEA access to verify that uranium isotope separation production and R&D activities are consistent with this Annex.

[336] For the purpose of this Annex, non-gaseous centrifuge uranium isotope separation-related research and development or production will include laser isotope separation systems, electromagnetic isotope separation systems, chemical exchange systems, gaseous diffusion systems, vortex and aerodynamic systems, and other such processes that separate uranium isotopes.

T. ACTIVITIES WHICH COULD CONTRIBUTE TO THE DESIGN AND DEVELOPMENT OF A NUCLEAR EXPLOSIVE DEVICE

82. Iran will not engage in the following activities which could contribute to the development of a nuclear explosive device:

    82.1. Designing, developing, acquiring, or using computer models to simulate nuclear explosive devices.

    82.2. Designing, developing, fabricating, acquiring, or using multi-point explosive detonation systems suitable for a nuclear explosive device, unless approved by the Joint Commission for non-nuclear purposes and subject to monitoring.

    82.3. Designing, developing, fabricating, acquiring, or using explosive diagnostic systems (streak cameras, framing cameras and flash x-ray cameras) suitable for the development of a nuclear explosive device, unless approved by the Joint Commission for non-nuclear purposes and subject to monitoring.

    82.4. Designing, developing, fabricating, acquiring, or using explosively driven neutron sources or specialized materials for explosively driven neutron sources.

Attachment: Arak conceptual design

Fundamental Principles:

- Maximize use of the current infrastructure of original design of Arak research reactor, designated by the IAEA as IR-40, according to their respective ratings.
- Modernizing of the original design in order to be a multi-purpose research reactor comprising radio-isotope production, structural materials and fuel (pins and assembly prototypes) testing and able to conduct other neutronic experiments which demand high neutron fluxes (more than 10^{14}).
- Using heavy water as coolant, moderator and reflector. Light water would be utilized as an annular ring around the compact new core for safety reasons if necessary.
- Around 78 fuel assemblies in a tight hexagonal grid spacing with the following preliminary characteristics will be loaded.
- Up to 3.67 percent enriched UO_2, in the improved assembly design, will be used as fuel.
- Power will not exceed to 20 MWth.
- Adding different types of beam tubes to the existing beam tubes which being extended to the edge of the new compact core.
- Having one central channel in the center of the new core with passive cooling system for the purpose of structural materials and fuel pins and assembly prototypes testing with neutron flux beyond $2 \cdot 10^{14}$, twelve in-core irradiation channels (IIC) inside the core and twelve lateral irradiation chennals (LIC) just next to the outer ring of fuel assemblies.
- The location of the in-core and lateral irradiation channels should be designed and fixed to meet the best anticipated performances.
- Consistent with relevant Section of Annex 1, subsidiary laboratories are part of the modernization project of the Arak Research Reactor. In Addition, Annex III reinforce design and construction of subsidiary laboratories.
- The highest tolerable pressure for the first and second loop is 0.33 Mpa (at the entrance of the reactor pit).
- The highest possible flow rate for coolant is 610 kg/s at the pressure of 0.33 MPa in the main piping system and 42 Kg/sec for Moderator with the same conditions.

Preliminary Characteristics:

Core Parameters	Values
Power (MW)	20
Number of fuel assemblies	~ 78
Active length (cm)	~ 110
Lattice configuration	Hexagonal
Fuel pellets Material	UO_2
Fuel enrichment level	Up to 3.67 %
Clad material	Zr Alloys
Burnable poison	Yes, if necessary
Lattice pitch (cm)	~ 11
Coolant medium	D_2O
Moderator medium	D_2O
Reflector medium	D_2O
Reflector thickness (cm)	~ 50
Purity of D2O	~ 99.8%
Mass of D2O (mtons)	~ 60–70
Yearly makeup	Yes
K_{eff}	< 1.25
Core Excess reactivity (pcm)	< 20000
Cycle length (days) $_{approximately}$	~ 250
^{239}Pu at EoC (g)	~ 850
^{239}Pu purity at EoC	~ 78%
^{235}U consumption	~ 60%
Maximum Thermal Flux, E<0.625ev	~ $3 \cdot 10^{14}$
Maximum Fast Flux, E>0.625ev	~ $1 \cdot 10^{14}$
Minimum Thermal Flux, E<0.625ev	~ $1 \cdot 10^{14}$
Minimum Fast Flux, E>0.625ev	~ $1 \cdot 10^{14}$
Fluid velocity in channels (m/s)	~ 3.8
Channel mass flow rate (kg/s)	~ 2.4
Working pressure (MPa)	0.33
Fluid inlet temperature (°C)	~ 47
Fluid outlet temperature (°C)	~ 78
Core material	Mainly S.S. 304
Core wall Thickness (mm)	~ 30
Fuel Pellet Diameter (cm)	~ 0.65
Inner Clad Diameter (cm)	~ 0.67
Outer Clad Diameter (cm)	~ 0.8
Number of pins per assembly	12
Mass of UO2 in full core load (Kg)	~ 350
Core diameter (cm)	~ 240

JCPOA Annex II – Sanctions-related commitments

The sequence of implementation of the commitments detailed in this Annex is specified in Annex V (Implementation Plan) to this Joint Comprehensive Plan of Action (JCPOA).

A. European Union[337]

1. The EU and EU Member States commit to terminate all provisions of Council Regulation (EU) No 267/2012 (as subsequently amended) implementing all nuclear-related sanctions or restrictive measures as specified in Sections 1.1–1.10 below, to terminate all provisions of Council Decision 2010/413/CFSP (as subsequently amended), as specified in Sections 1.1–1.10 below, and to terminate or amend national implementing legislation as required, in accordance with Annex V:

1.1. Financial, banking and insurance measures[338]

1.1.1 Prohibition and authorisation regimes on financial transfers to and from Iran (Article 10 of Council Decision 2010/413/CFSP; Articles 30, 30a, 30b and 31 of Council Regulation (EU) No 267/2012);

1.1.2. Sanctions on banking activities (Article 11 of Council Decision 2010/413/CFSP; Article 33 of Council Regulation (EU) No 267/2012);

1.1.3. Sanctions on insurance (Article 12 of Council Decision 2010/413/CFSP; Article 35 of Council Regulation (EU) No 267/2012);

1.1.4. Sanctions on financial messaging services (Article 20(12) of Council Decision 2010/413/CFSP; Article 23(4) of Council Regulation (EU) No 267/2012);

1.1.5. Sanctions on financial support for trade with Iran (Article 8 of Council Decision 2010/413/CFSP);

1.1.6. Sanctions on grants, financial assistance and concessional loans (Article 9 of Council Decision 2010/413/CFSP);

1.1.7. Sanctions on Government of Iran public-guaranteed bonds (Article 13 of Council Decision 2010/413/CFSP; Article 34 of Council Regulation (EU) No 267/2012); and

1.1.8. Sanctions on associated services[339] for each of the categories above (see the references above).

1.2. Oil, gas and petrochemical sectors

1.2.1. Sanctions on the import of oil and gas from Iran (Articles 3a, 3c and 3e of Council Decision 2010/413/CFSP; Articles 11, 12 and 14a, and Annexes IV and IVA of Council Regulation (EU) No 267/2012);

1.2.2. Sanctions on the import of Iranian petrochemical products (Articles 3b and 3d of Council Decision 2010/413/CFSP; Articles 13 and 14, and Annex V of Council Regulation (EU) No 267/2012);

1.2.3. Sanctions on the export of key equipment for the oil, gas and petrochemical sectors (Articles 4, 4a and 4b of Council Decision 2010/413/CFSP; Articles 8, 9 and 10, and Annexes VI and VIA of Council Regulation (EU) No 267/2012);

---

[337] For the purposes of EU legislation, "Iranian person, entity or body" means:

(i) the State of Iran or any public authority thereof;

(ii) any natural person in, or resident in, Iran;

(iii) any legal person, entity or body having its registered office in Iran;

(iv) any legal person, entity or body, inside or outside Iran, owned or controlled directly or indirectly by one or more of the above mentioned persons or bodies.

[338] The headings and subheadings in this Annex are for descriptive purposes only.

[339] For the purposes of this Annex, the term "associated services" means any service – including technical assistance, training, insurance, re-insurance, brokering, transportation or financial service – necessary and ordinarily incident to the underlying activity for which sanctions have been lifted pursuant to this JCPOA.

1.2.4. Sanctions on investment in the oil, gas and petrochemical sectors (Articles 6, 6a and 7 of Council Decision 2010/413/CFSP; Articles 17(1), 17(2)(b) and (c), 17(3), 17(4), 17(5), 20 and 21 of Council Regulation (EU) No 267/2012); and

1.2.5. Sanctions on associated services for each of the categories above (see the references above).

1.3. Shipping, shipbuilding and transport sectors

1.3.1. Sanctions related to shipping and shipbuilding (Articles 4g, 4h, 8a, 18a and 18b of Council Decision 2010/413/CFSP; Articles 10a, 10b, 10c, 37a, and 37b, and Annex VIB of Council Regulation (EU) No 267/2012);

1.3.2. Sanctions related to the transport sector (Articles 15, 16, 17 and 18 of Council Decision 2010/413/CFSP; Articles 36 and 37 of Council Regulation (EU) No 267/2012); and

1.3.3. Sanctions on associated services for each of the categories above (see the references above).

1.4. Gold, other precious metals, banknotes and coinage

1.4.1. Sanctions on gold, precious metals and diamonds, banknotes and coinage (Articles 4c and 4d of Council Decision 2010/413/CFSP; Articles 15 and 16, and Annex VII of Council Regulation (EU) No 267/2012); and

1.4.2. Sanctions on associated services for each of the categories above (see the references above).

1.5. Nuclear proliferation-related measures

1.5.1. Sanctions related to proliferation-sensitive nuclear activities (goods and technology, investment and specialised training) (Articles 1(1) (a), (b), (d), (e), (2), (3) and (4), 2, 3, 5, 14 and 21 of Council Decision 2010/413/CFSP; Articles 2, 3, 4, 5, 6,7, 17(1) and (2)(a), 18, 19 and 22, and Annexes I, II and III of Council Regulation (EU) No 267/2012); and

1.5.2. Sanctions on associated services for the category above (see the references above).

1.6. Metals

1.6.1. Sanctions on metals (Articles 4e and 4f of Council Decision 2010/413/CFSP; Articles 15a, 15b and 15c, and Annex VIIB of Council Regulation (EU) No 267/2012); and

1.6.2. Sanctions on associated services for the category above (see the references above).

1.7. Software

1.7.1. Sanctions on software (Articles 4i and 4j of Council Decision 2010/413/CFSP; Articles 10d, 10e and 10f, and Annex VIIA of Council Regulation (EU) No 267/2012); and

1.7.2. Sanctions on associated services for the category above (see the references above).

1.8. Arms

1.8.1. Sanctions on arms (Articles 1(1)(c), (3) and (4), and 3 of Council Decision 2010/413/CFSP; Articles 5(1)(a) and (c), 17(1) and (2)(a), and 19 of Council Regulation (EU) No 267/2012); and

1.8.2. Sanctions on associated services for the category above (see the references above).

1.9. Listing of persons, entities and bodies (asset freeze and visa ban)

1.9.1. Asset freeze and visa ban measures applicable to:

1.9.1.1. listed Iranian banks and financial institutions, including the Central Bank of Iran;

1.9.1.2. listed persons, entities and bodies related to the oil, gas and petrochemical sectors;

1.9.1.3. listed persons, entities and bodies related to shipping, shipbuilding and transport;

1.9.1.4. other listed persons, entities and bodies not related to proliferation-sensitive nuclear-, arms- and ballistic missile-related activities;

1.9.1.5. listed persons, entities and bodies related to proliferation-sensitive nuclear-, arms- and ballistic missile-related activities; and

1.9.1.6. entities and individuals listed by the UN Security Council, as set out in Attachment 1, part I to this Annex for categories 1.9.1.1–1.9.1.4, Attachment 2, part I to this Annex for category 1.9.1.5, and Parts II of Attachments 1 and 2 to this Annex for category 1.9.1.6 (Articles 19 and 20, and Annexes I and II to Council Decision 2010/413/CFSP; Articles 23, 24, 25, 26, 27, 28, 28a, 28b and 29, and Annexes VIII and IX to Council Regulation (EU) No 267/2012).

1.10. Other provisions

1.10.1. The commitment in Section 1 covers all remaining provisions of Council Decision 2010/413/CFSP and Council Regulation (EU) No 267/2012 not specified above.

1.10.1.1. Definitions (Article 1 of Council Regulation (EU) No 267/2012); and

1.10.1.2. General and final provisions (Articles 22, 23, 24, 25, 26, 26a, 27 and 28 of Council Decision 2010/413/CFSP; Articles 38, 39, 40, 41, 42, 43, 43a, 44, 45, 46, 47, 48, 49, 50 and 51, and Annex X of Council Regulation (EU) No 267/2012).

2. The EU represents that the provisions listed in Section 1 above constitute the full and complete list of all EU nuclear-related sanctions or restrictive measures. These sanctions or restrictive measures will be lifted in accordance with Annex V.

3. Effects of the lifting of EU economic and financial sanctions

3.1. As a result of the lifting of sanctions specified in Section 1 above, the following activities, including associated services, will be allowed, beginning on implementation day, in accordance with this JCPOA and provided that such activities are otherwise consistent with EU and EU Member States' laws and regulations in effect:[340]

3.2. Financial, banking and insurance measures (See Sections 1.1.1 to 1.1.8)

3.2.1. Transfers of funds between EU persons, entities or bodies, including EU financial and credit institutions, and Iranian persons, entities or bodies, including Iranian financial and credit institutions, without the requirement for authorisation or notification;

3.2.2. Opening of new branches, subsidiaries or representative offices of Iranian banks in the territories of EU Member States; and the establishment of new joint ventures, or the taking of an ownership interest or the establishment of new correspondent banking relationships by Iranian banks with EU banks; and opening by EU persons, including EU financial and credit institutions, of representative offices, subsidiaries, joint ventures or bank accounts in Iran;

3.2.3. Provision of insurance or reinsurance to Iran or the Government of Iran, an Iranian legal person, entity or body, or a natural person or a legal person, entity or body acting on their behalf or at their direction;

3.2.4. Supply of specialised financial messaging services to any Iranian natural or legal persons, entities or bodies, including those listed in Attachment 1 to this Annex;

3.2.5. Entering into commitments by EU Member States to provide financial support for trade with Iran, including the granting of export credits, guarantees or insurance; and into commitments for grants, financial assistance and concessional loans to the Government of Iran; and

[340] Unless specifically provided otherwise, the sanctions lifting described in this Section does not apply to transactions that involve persons still subject to restrictive measures and is without prejudice to sanctions that may apply under legal provisions other than those referred to in Section 1. Nothing in this JCPOA reflects a change in Iran's position on EU sanctions.

3.2.6. Sale or purchase of public or public-guaranteed bonds to and from Iran, the Government of Iran, the Central Bank of Iran, or Iranian banks and financial institutions or persons acting on their behalf.

3.3. Oil, gas and petrochemical sectors (See Sections 1.2.1 to 1.2.5)

3.3.1. Import, purchase, swap or transport of Iranian crude oil and petroleum products, natural gas or petrochemical products and related financing;

3.3.2. Sale, supply, transfer or export of equipment or technology, technical assistance, including training, used in the sectors of the oil, gas and petrochemical industries in Iran covering exploration, production and refining of oil and natural gas, including liquefaction of natural gas, to any Iranian person, in or outside Iran, or for use in Iran; and

3.3.3. Granting of any financial loan or credit to, the acquisition or extension of a participation in, and the creation of any joint venture with, any Iranian person that is engaged in the oil, gas and petrochemical sectors in Iran or outside Iran.

3.4. Shipping, shipbuilding and transport sectors (See Sections 1.3.1 to 1.3.3)

3.4.1. Sale, supply, transfer or export of naval equipment and technology for ship building, maintenance or refit, to Iran or to any Iranian persons engaged in this sector; the design, construction or the participation in the design or construction of cargo vessels and oil tankers for Iran or for Iranian persons; the provision of vessels designed or used for the transport or storage of oil and petrochemical products to Iranian persons, entities or bodies; and the provision of flagging and classification services, including those pertaining to technical specification, registration and identification numbers of any kind, to Iranian oil tankers and cargo vessels;

3.4.2. Access to the airports under the jurisdiction of EU Member States of all cargo flights operated by Iranian carriers or originating from Iran;

3.4.3. Cessation of inspection, seizure and disposal by EU Member States of cargoes to and from Iran in their territories with regard to items which are no longer prohibited; and

3.4.4. Provision of bunkering or ship supply services, or any other servicing of vessels, to Iranian-owned or Iranian-contracted vessels not carrying prohibited items; and the provision of fuel, engineering and maintenance services to Iranian cargo aircraft not carrying prohibited items.

3.5. Gold, other precious metals, banknotes and coinage (See Sections 1.4.1 to 1.4.2)

3.5.1. Sale, supply, purchase, export, transfer or transport of gold and precious metals as well as diamonds, and provision of related brokering, financing and security services, to, from or for the Government of Iran, its public bodies, corporations and agencies, or the Central Bank of Iran; and

3.5.2. Delivery of newly printed or minted or unissued Iranian denominated banknotes and coinage to, or for the benefit of the Central Bank of Iran.

3.6. Metals (See Sections 1.6.1 to 1.6.2)

3.6.1. Sale, supply, transfer or export of graphite and raw or semi-finished metals, such as aluminum and steel to any Iranian person, entity or body or for use in Iran, in connection with activities consistent with this JCPOA.

3.7. Software (See Sections 1.7.1 to 1.7.2)

3.7.1. Sale, supply, transfer or export of software for integrating industrial processes, including updates, to any Iranian person, entity or body, or for use in Iran, in connection with activities consistent with this JCPOA,

3.8. Listing of persons, entities and bodies (asset freeze and visa ban) (See Section 1.9.1)

3.8.1. As a result of delisting as specified in this Annex, releasing of all funds and economic resources which belong to, and making available funds or economic resources to, the persons, entities and bodies, including Iranian banks and financial institutions, the Central Bank of Iran, listed in Attachment 1 to this Annex; and

3.8.2. As a result of delisting as specified in this Annex, entry into, or transit through the territories of EU Member States of individuals listed in Attachment 1 to this Annex.

B. United States[341]

4. The United States commits to cease the application of, and to seek such legislative action as may be appropriate to terminate, or modify to effectuate the termination of, all nuclear-related sanctions[342] as specified in Sections 4.1–4.9 below, and to terminate Executive Orders 13574, 13590, 13622 and 13645, and Sections 5–7 and 15 of Executive Order 13628, in accordance with Annex V.[343]

4.1. Financial and banking measures

4.1.1. Sanctions on transactions with individuals and entities set out in Attachment 3 to this Annex, including: the Central Bank of Iran (CBI) and other specified Iranian financial institutions; the National Iranian Oil Company (NIOC),[344] Naftiran Intertrade Company (NICO), National Iranian Tanker Company (NITC) and other specified individuals and entities identified as Government of Iran by the Office of Foreign Assets Control; and certain designated individuals and entities on the Specially Designated Nationals and Blocked Persons List (SDN List) (Comprehensive Iran Sanctions, Accountability, and Divestment Act of 2010 (CISADA) Section 104(c)(2)(E)(ii)(I); National Defense Authorization Act for Fiscal Year 2012 (NDAA) Sections 1245(d)(1) and (3); Iran Freedom and Counter-Proliferation Act of 2012 (IFCA) Sections 1244(c)(1) and (d), 1245(a)(1)(A), (a)(1)(C)(i)(II) and (c), 1246(a) and 1247(a); Sections 1(a)(i) and 5(a) of Executive Order (E.O.) 13622 and Sections 2(a)(i) and 3(a)(i) of E.O. 13645);

4.1.2. Sanctions on the Iranian Rial (NDAA Sections 1245(d)(1) and (3); IFCA Sections 1244(c)(1), 1246(a) and 1247(a); Section 5(a) of E.O. 13622 and Sections 1(a), 2(a)(i) and 3(a)(i) of E.O. 13645);

4.1.3. Sanctions on the provision of U.S. banknotes to the Government of Iran (NDAA Sections 1245(d)(1) and (3); IFCA Sections 1244(c)(1) and (d), 1246(a) and 1247(a); Section 5(a) of E.O. 13622 and Sections 2(a)(i) and 3(a)(i) of E.O. 13645);

4.1.4. Bilateral trade limitations on Iranian revenues held abroad, including limitations on their transfer (NDAA Sections 1245(d)(1) and (3); IFCA Sections 1244(c)(1), (d) and (h)(2), 1246(a) and 1247(a); Sections 1(a)(i)-(ii), 2(a)(i) and 5(a) of E.O. 13622 and Sections 2(a)(i) and 3(a)(i) of E.O. 13645);

---

[341] For the purposes of U.S. legislation, "Iranian person" means (A) an individual who is a citizen or national of Iran; and (B) an entity organised under the laws of Iran or otherwise subject to the jurisdiction of the Government of Iran.

[342] The sanctions that the United States will cease to apply, and subsequently terminate, or modify to effectuate the termination of, pursuant to its commitment under Section 4 are those directed towards non-U.S. persons. For the purposes of Sections 4 and 6–7 of this JCPOA, the term "non-U.S. person" means any individual or entity, excluding (i) any United States citizen, permanent resident alien, entity organised under the laws of the United States or any jurisdiction within the United States (including foreign branches), or any person in the United States, and (ii) any entity owned or controlled by a U.S. person. For the purposes of (ii) of the preceding sentence, an entity is "owned or controlled" by a U.S. person if the U.S. person: (i) holds a 50 percent or greater equity interest by vote or value in the entity; (ii) holds a majority of seats on the board of directors of the entity; or (iii) otherwise controls the actions, policies, or personnel decisions of the entity. U.S. persons and U.S.-owned or -controlled foreign entities will continue to be generally prohibited from conducting transactions of the type permitted pursuant to this JCPOA, unless authorised to do so by the U.S. Department of the Treasury's Office of Foreign Assets Control (OFAC).

[343] All citations to statutes and Executive orders included in this JCPOA refer to the statute or Executive order as amended as of the conclusion date of this JCPOA, including: the Iran Sanctions Act of 1996 (ISA), as amended by Section 102 of the Comprehensive Iran Sanctions, Accountability, and Divestment Act of 2010 (CISADA) and Sections 201–207 and 311 of the Iran Threat Reduction and Syria Human Rights Act of 2012 (TRA); CISADA, as amended by Sections 214–216, 222, 224, 311–312, 402–403 and 605 of TRA and Section 1249 of the Iran Freedom and Counter-Proliferation Act of 2012 (IFCA); the National Defense Authorization Act for Fiscal Year 2012 (NDAA), as amended by Sections 503–504 of TRA and Section 1250 of IFCA; Executive Order (E.O.) 13622, as amended by Section 15 of E.O. 13628 and Section 16 of E.O. 13645. The citations listed in Section 4 include authorities under which secondary sanctions will no longer apply as a result of actions described in Section 4.8.1.

[344] Removal of NIOC from the SDN List, as provided for in Section 4.8.1, will include resolution of related designations and determinations.

4.1.5. Sanctions on the purchase, subscription to, or facilitation of the issuance of Iranian sovereign debt, including governmental bonds (NDAA Sections 1245(d)(1) and (3); Iran Threat Reduction and Syria Human Rights Act of 2012 (TRA) Section 213(a); IFCA Sections 1244(c)(1) and (d), 1246(a) and 1247(a); Sections 1(a)(i) and 5(a) of E.O. 13622 and Sections 2(a)(i) and 3(a)(i) of E.O. 13645);

4.1.6. Sanctions on financial messaging services to the CBI and Iranian financial institutions set out in Attachment 3 to this Annex (NDAA Sections 1245(d)(1) and (3); TRA Section 220; IFCA Sections 1244(c)(1) and (d), 1246(a) and 1247(a); Section 5(a) of E.O. 13622 and Sections 2(a)(i) and 3(a)(i) of E.O. 13645); and

4.1.7. Sanctions on associated services[345] for each of the categories above (see individual citation references above).

4.2. Insurance measures

4.2.1. Sanctions on the provision of underwriting services, insurance, or re-insurance in connection with activities consistent with this JCPOA, including activities with individuals and entities set forth in Attachment 3 to this Annex (Iran Sanctions Act of 1996 (ISA) Section 5(a)(7); NDAA Sections 1245(d)(1) and (3); TRA Sections 211(a) and 212(a); IFCA Sections 1244(c)(1) and (d), 1246(a) and 1247(a); Section 5(a) of E.O. 13622 and Sections 2(a)(i) and 3(a)(i) of E.O. 13645).

4.3. Energy and petrochemical sectors

4.3.1. Efforts to reduce Iran's crude oil sales, including limitations on the quantities of Iranian crude oil sold and the nations that can purchase Iranian crude oil (ISA Section 5(a)(7); NDAA Sections 1245(d)(1) and (3); TRA Section 212(a); IFCA Sections 1244(c)(1) and (d), 1246(a) and 1247(a); Section 1 of E.O. 13574, Sections 1(a)(i)-(ii), 2(a)(i) and 5(a) of E.O. 13622, Section 5 of E.O. 13628, and Sections 2(a)(i) and 3(a)(i) of E.O. 13645);

4.3.2. Sanctions on investment, including participation in joint ventures, goods, services, information, technology and technical expertise and support for Iran's oil, gas, and petrochemical sectors (ISA Sections 5(a)(1)-(2) and (4)-(8); TRA Section 212(a); IFCA Sections 1244(c)(1), (d) and (h)(2), 1245(a)(1)(B), (a)(1)(C)(i)(I)-(II), (a)(1)(C)(ii)(I)-(II) and (c), 1246(a) and 1247(a); Section 1 of E.O. 13574, Section 1 of E.O. 13590, Sections 1(a)(i)-(ii), 2(a)(i)-(iii) and 5(a) of E.O. 13622, and Sections 2(a)(i) and 3(a)(i) of E.O. 13645);

4.3.3. Sanctions on the purchase, acquisition, sale, transportation, or marketing of petroleum, petrochemical products and natural gas from Iran (NDAA Sections 1245(d)(1) and (3); TRA Section 212(a); IFCA Sections 1244(c)(1), (d) and (h)(2), 1246(a) and 1247(a); Sections 1(a)(i)-(iii), 2(a)(i)-(ii) and 5(a) of E.O. 13622, and Sections 2(a)(i) and 3(a)(i) of E.O. 13645);

4.3.4. Sanctions on the export, sale or provision of refined petroleum products and petrochemical products to Iran (ISA Section 5(a)(3); NDAA Sections 1245(d)(1) and (3); TRA Section 212(a); IFCA Sections 1244(c)(1) and (d), 1246(a) and 1247(a); Section 1 of E.O. 13574, Sections 1(a)(i) and 5(a) of E.O. 13622, Section 5 of E.O. 13628, and Sections 2(a)(i) and 3(a)(i) of E.O. 13645);

4.3.5. Sanctions on transactions with Iran's energy sector including with NIOC, NICO and NITC (NDAA Sections 1245(d)(1) and (3); IFCA Sections 1244(c)(1), (d) and (h)(2), 1246(a) and 1247(a); TRA Section 212(a); Sections 1(a)(i)-(iii), 2(a)(i)-(ii) and 5(a) of E.O. 13622, and Sections 2(a)(i) and 3(a)(i) of E.O. 13645); and

4.3.6. Sanctions on associated services for each of the categories above (see individual citation references above).

[345] See footnote 339 for the meaning of "associated services".

4.4. Shipping, shipbuilding and port sectors

4.4.1. Sanctions on transactions with Iran's shipping and shipbuilding sectors and port operators including IRISL, South Shipping Line, and NITC, and the port operator(s) of Bandar Abbas[346] (TRA Sections 211(a) and 212(a); IFCA Sections 1244(c)(1) and (d); 1245(a)(1)(B), (a)(1)(C)(i)(I)-(II), (a)(1)(C)(ii)(I)-(II) and (c), 1246(a) and 1247(a); Section 5(a) of E.O. 13622 and Sections 2(a)(i) and 3(a)(i) of E.O. 13645); and

4.4.2. Sanctions on associated services for each of the categories above (see individual citation references above).

4.5. Gold and other precious metals

4.5.1. Sanctions on Iran's trade in gold and other precious metals (NDAA Sections 1245(d)(1) and (3); IFCA Sections 1244(c)(1), 1245(a)(1)(A) and (c), 1246(a) and 1247(a); Section 5(a) of E.O. 13622 and Sections 2(a)(i) and 3(a)(i) of E.O. 13645); and

4.5.2. Sanctions on associated services for each of the categories above (see individual citation references above).

4.6. Software and metals

4.6.1. Sanctions on trade with Iran in graphite, raw or semi-finished metals such as aluminum and steel, coal, and software for integrating industrial processes, in connection with activities consistent with this JCPOA, including trade with individuals and entities set forth in Attachments 3 and 4 to this Annex (NDAA Sections 1245(d)(1) and (3); IFCA Sections 1244(c)(1), 1245(a)(1)(B)-(C) and (c), 1246(a) and 1247(a); Section 5(a) of E.O. 13622 and Sections 2(a)(i) and 3(a)(i) of E.O. 13645); and

4.6.2. Sanctions on associated services for each of the categories above (see individual citation references above).

4.7. Automotive sector

4.7.1. Sanctions on the sale, supply or transfer of goods and services used in connection with Iran's automotive sector (NDAA Sections 1245(d)(1) and (3); IFCA Sections 1244(c)(1), 1245(a)(1)(B), (a)(1)(C)(i)(II), (a)(1)(C)(ii)(II) and (c), 1246(a) and 1247(a); Section 5(a) of E.O. 13622 and Sections 2(a)(i), 3(a)(i)-(ii), 5 and 6 of E.O. 13645); and

4.7.2. Sanctions on associated services for each of the categories above (see individual citation references above).

4.8. Designations and other sanctions listings

4.8.1. Removal of individuals and entities set out in Attachments 3 and 4 to this Annex from the Specially Designated Nationals and Blocked Persons List (SDN List), the Foreign Sanctions Evaders List, and/or the Non-SDN Iran Sanctions Act List (Removal of designations and/or sanctions imposed under ISA Section 5(a), IFCA Section 1244(d)(1) and TRA Section 212; and removals pursuant to the International Emergency Economic Powers Act of certain persons listed pursuant to E.O. 13382, E.O. 13608, E.O. 13622, and E.O. 13645).

4.9. Nuclear proliferation-related measures

4.9.1. Sanctions under the Iran, North Korea and Syria Nonproliferation Act on the acquisition of nuclear-related commodities and services for nuclear activities contemplated in the JCPOA, to be consistent with the U.S. approach to other non-nuclear-weapon states under the NPT;

4.9.2. Sanctions on joint ventures relating to the mining, production, or transportation of uranium (ISA Section 5(b)(2)); and

4.9.3. Exclusion of Iranian citizens from higher education coursework related to careers in nuclear science, nuclear engineering or the energy sector (TRA Section 501).

---

[346] This commitment in Section 4.4.1 is based on the port operator(s) of Bandar Abbas no longer being controlled by a person on the SDN List.

5. Other trade measures

5.1. The United States commits to:[347]

5.1.1. Allow for the sale of commercial passenger aircraft and related parts and services to Iran by licensing the (i) export, re-export, sale, lease or transfer to Iran of commercial passenger aircraft for exclusively civil aviation end-use, (ii) export, re-export, sale, lease or transfer to Iran of spare parts and components for commercial passenger aircraft, and (iii) provision of associated serviced, including warranty, maintenance, and repair services and safety-related inspections, for all the foregoing, provided that licensed items and services are used exclusively for commercial passenger aviation;[348]

5.1.2. License non-U.S. entities that are owned or controlled by a U.S. person[349] to engage in activities with Iran that are consistent with this JCPOA; and

5.1.3. License the importation into the United States of Iranian-origin carpets and foodstuffs, including pistachios and caviar.

6. The United States represents that the provisions listed in Section 4 above constitute the full and complete list of all U.S. nuclear-related sanctions. These sanctions will be lifted in accordance with Annex V.

7. Effects of the lifting of U.S. economic and financial sanctions:

7.1. As a result of the lifting of sanctions specified in Section 4 above, beginning on implementation day such sanctions, including associated services, would not apply to non-U.S. persons who carry out the following or that:[350]

7.2. Financial and banking measures[351] (See Sections 4.1.1 to 4.1.7)

Engage in activities, including financial and banking transactions, with the Government of Iran, the Central Bank of Iran, Iranian financial institutions and other Iranian persons specified in Attachment 3 to this Annex, including the provision of loans, transfers, accounts (including the opening and maintenance of correspondent and payable through accounts at non-U.S. financial institutions), investments, securities, guarantees, foreign exchange (including Rial related transactions), letters of credit and commodity futures or options, the provision of specialised financial messaging services and facilitation of direct or indirect access thereto, the purchase or acquisition by the Government of Iran of U.S. bank notes, and the purchase, subscription to, or facilitation of the issuance of Iranian sovereign debt.[352]

---

[347] To give effect to the measures described in this Section 5.1, the United States will license activities that do not involve any person on the SDN List and are otherwise consistent with applicable U.S. laws and regulations, including but not limited to the Export Administration Act, the Federal Food, Drug and Cosmetic Act and the Iran-Iraq Arms Nonproliferation Act.

[348] Licenses issued in furtherance of Section 5.1.1 will include appropriate conditions to ensure that licensed activities do not involve, and no licensed aircraft, goods, or services are re-sold or re-transferred to, any person on the SDN list. Should the United States determine that licensed aircraft, goods, or services have been used for purposes other than exclusively civil aviation end-use, or have been re-sold or re-transferred to persons on the SDN List, the United States would view this as grounds to cease performing its commitments under Section 5.1.1 in whole or in part.

[349] For the purposes of Section 5.1.2 of this JCPOA, a non-U.S. entity is owned or controlled by a U.S. person if the U.S. person: (i) holds a 50 per cent or greater equity interest by vote or value in the entity; (ii) holds a majority of seats on the board of directors of the entity; or (iii) otherwise controls the actions, policies, or personnel decisions of the entity.

[350] Unless specifically provided otherwise, the sanctions lifting described in this Section does not apply to transactions that involve persons on the SDN List and is without prejudice to sanctions that may apply under legal provisions other than those cited in Section 4. Nothing in this JCPOA reflects a change in Iran's position on U.S. sanctions.

[351] For the purposes of the cessation of application of the provisions set out in Sections 4.1.1–4.1.7, the effects described for non-U.S. financial institutions extend to the activities outside of U.S. jurisdiction of international financial institutions.

[352] Non-U.S., non-Iranian financial institutions engaging in transactions with Iranian financial institutions (including the Central Bank of Iran) not appearing on the SDN List will not be exposed to sanctions as a result of those Iranian financial institutions engaging in transactions or banking relationships involving Iranian individuals and entities, including financial institutions, on the SDN List, provided that the non-U.S., non-Iranian financial institution does not conduct or facilitate, and is not otherwise involved in, those specific transactions or banking relationships with the Iranian individuals and entities, including financial institutions, on the SDN List.

7.3. Insurance measures (See Section 4.2.1)

Provide underwriting services, insurance, or re-insurance in connection with activities consistent with this JCPOA, including activities with individuals and entities set forth in Attachment 3 to this Annex, including underwriting services, insurance, or re-insurance in connection with activities in the energy, shipping, and shipbuilding sectors of Iran, for the National Iranian Oil Company (NIOC) or the National Iranian Tanker Company (NITC), or for vessels that transport crude oil, natural gas, liquefied natural gas, petroleum and petrochemical products to or from Iran.

7.4. Energy and petrochemical sectors (See Sections 4.3.1 to 4.3.6)

Are part of the energy sector of Iran; purchase, acquire, sell, transport or market petroleum, petroleum products (including refined petroleum products), petrochemical products or natural gas (including liquefied natural gas) to or from Iran; provide to Iran support, investment (including through joint ventures), goods, services (including financial services) and technology that can be used in connection with Iran's energy sector, the development of its petroleum resources, its domestic production of refined petroleum products and petrochemical products; or engage in activities with Iran's energy sector, including NIOC, NITC, and NICO).

7.5. Shipping, shipbuilding and port sectors (See Sections 4.4.1 to 4.4.2)

Are part of the shipping or shipbuilding sectors of Iran; own, operate, control or insure a vessel used to transport crude oil, petroleum products (including refined petroleum products), petrochemical products or natural gas (including liquefied natural gas) to or from Iran; operate a port in Iran, engage in activities with, or provide financial services and other goods and services used in connection with, the shipping and shipbuilding sectors of Iran or a port operator in Iran (including the port operator(s) of Bandar Abbas[353]), including port services, such as bunkering and inspection, classification, and financing, and the sale, leasing, and provision of vessels to Iran, including to the Islamic Republic of Iran Shipping Lines (IRISL), NITC, and South Shipping Line Iran or their affiliates.

7.6. Gold and other precious metals (See Sections 4.5.1 to 4.5.2)

Sell, supply, export or transfer, directly or indirectly, to or from Iran, gold and other precious metals, or conduct or facilitate a financial transaction or provide services for the foregoing including security, insurance and transportation.

7.7. Software and metals (See Sections 4.6.1 to 4.6.2)

Sell, supply, or transfer, directly or indirectly, graphite, raw or semi-finished metals such as aluminum and steel, coal, and software for integrating industrial processes, to or from Iran in connection with activities consistent with this JCPOA, including trade with individuals and entities set forth in Attachment 3 to this Annex, and the sale, supply, or transfer of such materials to the energy, petrochemical, shipping and shipbuilding sectors of Iran, and Iranian ports, or conduct or facilitate a financial transaction or provide services for the foregoing, including insurance and transportation.

7.8. Automotive sector (See Sections 4.7.1 to 4.7.2)

Conduct or facilitate financial or other transactions for the sale, supply or transfer to Iran of goods and services used in connection with the automotive sector of Iran.

7.9. Designations and other sanctions listings (See Section 4.8.1)

The removal of designations and/or sanctions as described in Section 4.8.1, ceasing the application of secondary sanctions for transactions with individuals and entities set out in Attachment 3 to this Annex; and unblocking of property and interests in property within U.S. jurisdiction for individuals and entities set out in Attachment 3 to this Annex.

[353] The effects described in Section 7.5 with respect to the port operator(s) of Bandar Abbas are based on the port operator(s) of Bandar Abbas no longer being controlled by a person on the SDN List.

ATTACHMENT 1 - PART I

LIST OF PERSONS, ENTITIES AND BODIES SET OUT IN ANNEX II TO COUNCIL DECISION 2010/413/CFSP AND ANNEX IX TO COUNCIL REGULATION (EU) NO 267/2012

ACENA SHIPPING COMPANY LIMITED
ADVANCE NOVEL
AGHAJARI OIL & GAS PRODUCTION COMPANY
AGHAZADEH, Reza
AHMADIAN, Mohammad
AKHAVAN-FARD, Massoud
ALPHA EFFORT LTD
ALPHA KARA NAVIGATION LIMITED
ALPHA NARI NAVIGATION LIMITED
ARIAN BANK
ARVANDAN OIL & GAS COMPANY
ASHTEAD SHIPPING COMPANY LTD
ASPASIS MARINE CORPORATION
ASSA CORPORATION
ASSA CORPORATION LTD
ATLANTIC INTERMODAL
AVRASYA CONTAINER SHIPPING LINES
AZARAB INDUSTRIES
AZORES SHIPPING COMPANY ALIAS AZORES SHIPPING FZE LLC
BANCO INTERNACIONAL DE DESARROLLO CA
BANK KARGOSHAE
BANK MELLAT
BANK MELLI IRAN INVESTMENT COMPANY
BANK MELLI IRAN ZAO
BANK MELLI PRINTING AND PUBLISHING COMPANY
BANK MELLI,
BANK OF INDUSTRY AND MINE
BANK REFAH KARGARAN
BANK TEJARAT
BATENI, Naser
BEST PRECISE LTD
BETA KARA NAVIGATION LTD
BIIS MARITIME LIMITED
BIS MARITIME LIMITED
BONAB RESEARCH CENTER
BRAIT HOLDING SA
BRIGHT JYOTI SHIPPING
BRIGHT SHIP FZC
BUSHEHR SHIPPING COMPANY LIMITED
BYFLEET SHIPPING COMPANY LTD
CEMENT INVESTMENT AND DEVELOPMENT COMPANY
CENTRAL BANK OF IRAN
CHAPLET SHIPPING LIMITED

COBHAM SHIPPING COMPANY LTD
CONCEPT GIANT LTD
COOPERATIVE DEVELOPMENT BANK
CRYSTAL SHIPPING FZE
DAJMAR, Mohammad Hossein
DAMALIS MARINE CORPORATION
DARYA CAPITAL ADMINISTRATION GMBH
DARYA DELALAN SEFID KHAZAR SHIPPING COMPANY
DELTA KARA NAVIGATION LTD
DELTA NARI NAVIGATION LTD
DIAMOND SHIPPING SERVICES
DORKING SHIPPING COMPANY LTD
EAST OIL & GAS PRODUCTION COMPANY
EDBI EXCHANGE COMPANY
EDBI STOCK BROKERAGE COMPANY
EFFINGHAM SHIPPING COMPANY LTD
EIGHTH OCEAN ADMINISTRATION GMBH
EIGHTH OCEAN GMBH & CO. KG
ELBRUS LTD
ELCHO HOLDING LTD
ELEGANT TARGET DEVELOPMENT LIMITED
ELEVENTH OCEAN ADMINISTRATION GMBH
ELEVENTH OCEAN GMBH & CO. KG
EMKA COMPANY
EPSILON NARI NAVIGATION LTD
E-SAIL A.K.A.E-SAIL SHIPPING COMPANY
ETA NARI NAVIGATION LTD
ETERNAL EXPERT LTD.
EUROPÄISCH-IRANISCHE HANDELSBANK
EXPORT DEVELOPMENT BANK OF IRAN
FAIRWAY SHIPPING
FAQIHIAN, Dr Hoseyn
FARNHAM SHIPPING COMPANY LTD
FASIRUS MARINE CORPORATION
FATSA
FIFTEENTH OCEAN ADMINISTRATION GMBH
FIFTEENTH OCEAN GMBH & CO. KG
FIFTH OCEAN ADMINISTRATION GMBH
FIFTH OCEAN GMBH & CO. KG
FIRST ISLAMIC INVESTMENT BANK
FIRST OCEAN ADMINISTRATION GMBH
FIRST OCEAN GMBH & CO. KG
FIRST PERSIAN EQUITY FUND
FOURTEENTH OCEAN ADMINISTRATION GMBH
FOURTEENTH OCEAN GMBH & CO. KG
FOURTH OCEAN ADMINISTRATION GMBH
FOURTH OCEAN GMBH & CO. KG

FUTURE BANK BSC
GACHSARAN OIL & GAS COMPANY
GALLIOT MARITIME INCORPORATION
GAMMA KARA NAVIGATION LTD
GIANT KING LIMITED
GOLDEN CHARTER DEVELOPMENT LTD.
GOLDEN SUMMIT INVESTMENTS LTD.
GOLDEN WAGON DEVELOPMENT LTD.
GOLPARVAR, Gholam Hossein
GOMSHALL SHIPPING COMPANY LTD
GOOD LUCK SHIPPING COMPANY LLC
GRAND TRINITY LTD.
GREAT EQUITY INVESTMENTS LTD.
GREAT METHOD LTD
GREAT PROSPECT INTERNATIONAL LTD.
HAFIZ DARYA SHIPPING LINES
HANSEATIC TRADE TRUST & SHIPPING GMBH
HARVEST SUPREME LTD.
HARZARU SHIPPING
HELIOTROPE SHIPPING LIMITED
HELIX SHIPPING LIMITED
HK INTERTRADE COMPANY LTD
HONG TU LOGISTICS PRIVATE LIMITED
HORSHAM SHIPPING COMPANY LTD
IFOLD SHIPPING COMPANY LIMITED
INDUS MARITIME INCORPORATION
INDUSTRIAL DEVELOPMENT & RENOVATION ORGANIZATION
INSIGHT WORLD LTD
INTERNATIONAL SAFE OIL
IOTA NARI NAVIGATION LIMITED
IRAN ALUMINIUM COMPANY
IRAN FUEL CONSERVATION ORGANIZATION
IRAN INSURANCE COMPANY
IRAN LIQUEFIED NATURAL GAS CO.
IRANIAN OFFSHORE ENGINEERING & CONSTRUCTION CO
IRANIAN OIL COMPANY LIMITED
IRANIAN OIL PIPELINES AND TELECOMMUNICATIONS COMPANY (IOPTC)
IRANIAN OIL TERMINALS COMPANY
IRANO MISR SHIPPING COMPANY
IRINVESTSHIP LTD
IRISL (MALTA) LTD
IRISL EUROPE GMBH
IRISL MARINE SERVICES AND ENGINEERING COMPANY
IRISL MARITIME TRAINING INSTITUTE
IRITAL SHIPPING SRL
ISI MARITIME LIMITED
ISIM AMIN LIMITED

ISIM ATR LIMITED
ISIM OLIVE LIMITED
ISIM SAT LIMITED
ISIM SEA CHARIOT LTD
ISIM SEA CRESCENT LTD
ISIM SININ LIMITED
ISIM TAJ MAHAL LTD
ISIM TOUR COMPANY LIMITED
ISLAMIC REPUBLIC OF IRAN SHIPPING LINES
JACKMAN SHIPPING COMPANY
KALA NAFT
KALAN KISH SHIPPING COMPANY LTD
KAPPA NARI NAVIGATION LTD
KARA SHIPPING AND CHARTERING GMBH
KAROON OIL & GAS PRODUCTION COMPANY
KAVERI MARITIME INCORPORATION
KAVERI SHIPPING LLC
KEY CHARTER DEVELOPMENT LTD.
KHALILIPOUR, Said Esmail
KHANCHI, Ali Reza
KHAZAR EXPL & PROD CO
KHAZAR SHIPPING LINES
KHEIBAR COMPANY
KING PROSPER INVESTMENTS LTD.
KINGDOM NEW LTD
KINGSWOOD SHIPPING COMPANY LIMITED
KISH SHIPPING LINE MANNING COMPANY
LAMBDA NARI NAVIGATION LIMITED
LANCING SHIPPING COMPANY LIMITED
LOGISTIC SMART LTD
LOWESWATER LTD
MACHINE SAZI ARAK
MAGNA CARTA LIMITED
MALSHIP SHIPPING AGENCY
MARBLE SHIPPING LIMITED
MAROUN OIL & GAS COMPANY
MASJED-SOLEYMAN OIL & GAS COMPANY
MASTER SUPREME INTERNATIONAL LTD.
MAZANDARAN CEMENT COMPANY
MEHR CAYMAN LTD.
MELLAT BANK SB CJSC
MELLI AGROCHEMICAL COMPANY PJS
MELLI BANK PLC
MELLI INVESTMENT HOLDING INTERNATIONAL
MELODIOUS MARITIME INCORPORATION
METRO SUPREME INTERNATIONAL LTD.
MIDHURST SHIPPING COMPANY LIMITED (MALTA)

MILL DENE LTD
MINISTRY OF ENERGY
MINISTRY OF PETROLEUM
MODALITY LTD
MODERN ELEGANT DEVELOPMENT LTD.
MOUNT EVEREST MARITIME INCORPORATION
NAFTIRAN INTERTRADE COMPANY
NAFTIRAN INTERTRADE COMPANY SRL
NAMJOO, Majid
NARI SHIPPING AND CHARTERING GMBH & CO. KG
NARMADA SHIPPING
NATIONAL IRANIAN DRILLING COMPANY
NATIONAL IRANIAN GAS COMPANY
NATIONAL IRANIAN OIL COMPANY
NATIONAL IRANIAN OIL COMPANY NEDERLAND (A.K.A.: NIOC NETHERLANDS REPRESENTATION OFFICE)
NATIONAL IRANIAN OIL COMPANY PTE LTD
NATIONAL IRANIAN OIL COMPANY, INTERNATIONAL AFFAIRS LIMITED
NATIONAL IRANIAN OIL ENGINEERING AND CONSTRUCTION COMPANY (NIOEC)
NATIONAL IRANIAN OIL PRODUCTS DISTRIBUTION COMPANY (NIOPDC)
NATIONAL IRANIAN OIL REFINING AND DISTRIBUTION COMPANY
NATIONAL IRANIAN TANKER COMPANY
NEUMAN LTD
NEW DESIRE LTD
NEW SYNERGY
NEWHAVEN SHIPPING COMPANY LIMITED
NINTH OCEAN ADMINISTRATION GMBH
NINTH OCEAN GMBH & CO. KG
NOOR AFZA GOSTAR
NORTH DRILLING COMPANY
NUCLEAR FUEL PRODUCTION AND PROCUREMENT COMPANY
OCEAN CAPITAL ADMINISTRATION GMBH
OCEAN EXPRESS AGENCIES PRIVATE LIMITED
ONERBANK ZAO
OXTED SHIPPING COMPANY LIMITED
PACIFIC SHIPPING
PARS SPECIAL ECONOMIC ENERGY ZONE
PARTNER CENTURY LTD
PEARL ENERGY COMPANY LTD
PEARL ENERGY SERVICES, SA
PERSIA INTERNATIONAL BANK PLC
PETRO SUISSE
PETROIRAN DEVELOPMENT COMPANY LTD
PETROLEUM ENGINEERING & DEVELOPMENT COMPANY
PETROPARS INTERNATIONAL FZE
PETROPARS IRAN COMPANY
PETROPARS LTD.
PETROPARS OILFIELD SERVICES COMPANY

PETROPARS OPERATION & MANAGEMENT COMPANY
PETROPARS RESOURCES ENGINEERING LTD
PETROPARS UK LIMITED
PETWORTH SHIPPING COMPANY LIMITED
POST BANK OF IRAN
POWER PLANTS' EQUIPMENT MANUFACTURING COMPANY (SAAKHTE TAJHIZATE NIROOGAHI)
PROSPER METRO INVESTMENTS LTD.
RASTKHAH, Engineer Naser
REIGATE SHIPPING COMPANY LIMITED
RESEARCH INSTITUTE OF NUCLEAR SCIENCE & TECHNOLOGY
REZVANIANZADEH, Mohammad Reza
RISHI MARITIME INCORPORATION
SACKVILLE HOLDINGS LTD
SAFIRAN PAYAM DARYA SHIPPING COMPANY
SALEHI, Ali Akbar
SANFORD GROUP
SANTEXLINES
SECOND OCEAN ADMINISTRATION GMBH
SECOND OCEAN GMBH & CO. KG
SEIBOW LOGISTICS LIMITED
SEVENTH OCEAN ADMINISTRATION GMBH
SEVENTH OCEAN GMBH & CO. KG
SHALLON LTD
SHEMAL CEMENT COMPANY
SHINE STAR LIMITED
SHIPPING COMPUTER SERVICES COMPANY
SILVER UNIVERSE INTERNATIONAL LTD.
SINA BANK
SINO ACCESS HOLDINGS
SINOSE MARITIME
SISCO SHIPPING COMPANY LTD
SIXTEENTH OCEAN ADMINISTRATION GMBH
SIXTEENTH OCEAN GMBH & CO. KG
SIXTH OCEAN ADMINISTRATION GMBH
SIXTH OCEAN GMBH & CO. KG
SMART DAY HOLDINGS LTD
SOLTANI, Behzad
SORINET COMMERCIAL TRUST (SCT)
SOROUSH SARAMIN ASATIR
SOUTH WAY SHIPPING AGENCY CO. LTD
SOUTH ZAGROS OIL & GAS PRODUCTION COMPANY
SPARKLE BRILLIANT DEVELOPMENT LIMITED
SPRINGTHORPE LIMITED
STATIRA MARITIME INCORPORATION
SUREH (NUCLEAR REACTORS FUEL COMPANY)
SYSTEM WISE LTD
TAMALARIS CONSOLIDATED LTD

TENTH OCEAN ADMINISTRATION GMBH
TENTH OCEAN GMBH & CO. KG
TEU FEEDER LIMITED
THETA NARI NAVIGATION
THIRD OCEAN ADMINISTRATION GMBH
THIRD OCEAN GMBH & CO. KG
THIRTEENTH OCEAN ADMINISTRATION GMBH
THIRTEENTH OCEAN GMBH & CO. KG
TOP GLACIER COMPANY LIMITED
TOP PRESTIGE TRADING LIMITED
TRADE CAPITAL BANK
TRADE TREASURE
TRUE HONOUR HOLDINGS LTD
TULIP SHIPPING INC
TWELFTH OCEAN ADMINISTRATION GMBH
TWELFTH OCEAN GMBH & CO. KG
UNIVERSAL TRANSPORTATION LIMITATION UTL
VALFAJR 8TH SHIPPING LINE
WEST OIL & GAS PRODUCTION COMPANY
WESTERN SURGE SHIPPING COMPANY LIMITED
WISE LING SHIPPING COMPANY LIMITED
ZANJANI, Babak
ZETA NERI NAVIGATION

ATTACHMENT 1 - PART II

LIST OF PERSONS, ENTITIES AND BODIES SET OUT IN ANNEX I TO COUNCIL DECISION 2010/413/CFSP AND ANNEX VIII TO COUNCIL REGULATION (EU) NO 267/2012

AGHA-JANI, Dawood
ALAI, Amir Moayyed
ASGARPOUR, Behman
ASHIANI, Mohammad Fedai
ASHTIANI, Abbas Rezaee
ATOMIC ENERGY ORGANISATION OF IRAN (AEOI)
BAKHTIAR, Haleh
BEHZAD, Morteza
ESFAHAN NUCLEAR FUEL RESEARCH AND PRODUCTION CENTRE (NFRPC) AND ESFAHAN NUCLEAR TECHNOLOGY CENTRE (ENTC)
FIRST EAST EXPORT BANK, P.L.C.:
HOSSEINI, Seyyed Hussein
IRANO HIND SHIPPING COMPANY
IRISL BENELUX NV
JABBER IBN HAYAN
KARAJ NUCLEAR RESEARCH CENTRE
KAVOSHYAR COMPANY
LEILABADI, Ali Hajinia
MESBAH ENERGY COMPANY

MODERN INDUSTRIES TECHNIQUE COMPANY
MOHAJERANI, Hamid-Reza
MOHAMMADI, Jafar
MONAJEMI, Ehsan
NOBARI, Houshang
NOVIN ENERGY COMPANY
NUCLEAR RESEARCH CENTER FOR AGRICULTURE AND MEDICINE
PARS TRASH COMPANY
PISHGAM (PIONEER) ENERGY INDUSTRIES
QANNADI, Mohammad
RAHIMI, Amir
RAHIQI, Javad
RASHIDI, Abbas
SABET, M. Javad Karimi
SAFDARI, Seyed Jaber
SOLEYMANI, Ghasem
SOUTH SHIPPING LINE IRAN (SSL)
TAMAS COMPANY

ATTACHMENT 2 - PART I

LIST OF PERSONS, ENTITIES AND BODIES SET OUT IN ANNEX II TO COUNCIL DECISION 2010/413/CFSP AND ANNEX IX TO COUNCIL REGULATION (EU) NO 267/2012

AEROSPACE INDUSTRIES ORGANISATION, AIO
AL YASIN, Javad
ALUMINAT
ANSAR BANK
ARAN MODERN DEVICES
ARAS FARAYANDE
ARFA PAINT COMPANY
ARFEH COMPANY
ARIA NIKAN,
ARMED FORCES GEOGRAPHICAL ORGANISATION
ASHTIAN TABLO
BABAEI, Davoud
BALS ALMAN
BANK SADERAT IRAN
BANK SADERAT PLC
BARGH AZARAKSH
BEHNAM SAHRIYARI TRADING COMPANY
BONYAD TAAVON SEPAH
BORBORUDI, Sayed Shamsuddin
DANESHJOO, Kamran
DARVISH-VAND, IRGC Brigadier-General Javad
ELECTRONIC COMPONENTS INDUSTRIES
ESNICO (EQUIPMENT SUPPLIER FOR NUCLEAR INDUSTRIES CORPORATION)
ETEMAD AMIN INVEST CO MOBIN

EYVAZ TECHNIC
FADAVI, Rear Admiral Ali
FAJR AVIATION COMPOSITE INDUSTRIES
FARAHI, IRGC Brigadier-General Seyyed Mahdi
FARASEPEHR ENGINEERING COMPANY
FATAH, Parviz
GHANI SAZI URANIUM COMPANY
HAERI, Engineer Mojtaba
HIRBOD CO
HOSEYNITASH, IRGC Brigadier-General Ali
HOSSEINI NEJAD TRADING CO.
INSTITUTE OF APPLIED PHYSICS
IRAN AIRCRAFT INDUSTRIES
IRAN AIRCRAFT MANUFACTURING COMPANY
IRAN CENTRIFUGE TECHNOLOGY COMPANY
IRAN COMMUNICATIONS INDUSTRIES
IRAN COMPOSITES INSTITUTE
IRAN ELECTRONICS INDUSTRIES
IRAN MARINE INDUSTRIAL COMPANY
IRAN POOYA
IRAN SAFFRON COMPANY OR IRANSAFFRON CO.
IRANIAN AVIATION INDUSTRIES ORGANIZATION
IRGC AIR FORCE
IRGC QODS FORCE
IRGC-AIR FORCE AL-GHADIR MISSILE COMMAND
ISFAHAN OPTICS
ISLAMIC REVOLUTIONARY GUARD CORPS
JAFARI, Milad
JAVEDAN MEHR TOOS
JELVESAZAN COMPANY
KARANIR
KARIMIAN, Ali
KHALA AFARIN PARS
KHANSARI, Majid
MAAA SYNERGY
MACPAR MAKINA SAN VE TIC
MAHMUDZADEH, Ebrahim
MARINE INDUSTRIES
MAROU SANAT
MATSA (MOHANDESI TOSEH SOKHT ATOMI COMPANY)
MECHANIC INDUSTRIES GROUP
MEHR BANK
MINISTRY OF DEFENSE AND SUPPORT FOR ARMED FORCES LOGISTICS
MOBIN SANJESH
MODERN TECHNOLOGIES FZC
MOHAMMADI, Mohammad
MOHAMMADLU, Brigadier-General Beik

MOVASAGHNIA, Mohammad Reza
MULTIMAT LC VE DIS TICARET PAZARLAMA LIMITED SIRKETI
NACCACHE, Anis
NADERI, Brigadier-General Mohammad
NAJJAR, IRGC Brigadier-General Mostafa Mohammad
NAQDI, BrigGen Mohammad Reza
NASERI, Mohammad Sadegh
NASERIN VAHID
NEDA INDUSTRIAL GROUP
NEKA NOVIN
NOAVARAN POOYAMOJ
NOURI, Ali Ashraf
OIL INDUSTRY PENSION FUND INVESTMENT COMPANY
ORGANISATION OF DEFENSIVE INNOVATION AND RESEARCH
PAKPUR, BrigGen Mohammad
PARCHIN CHEMICAL INDUSTRIES
PARTO SANAT CO
PASSIVE DEFENSE ORGANIZATION
PAYA PARTO
QASEMI, Rostam (a.k.a. Rostam GHASEMI)
RAAD IRAN
RAKA
RESEARCH CENTRE FOR EXPLOSION AND IMPACT
ROSMACHIN
SAIDI, Hojatoleslam Ali
SALAMI, BrigGen Hossein
SAMAN NASB ZAYENDEH ROOD; SAMAN NASBZAINDE ROOD
SAMAN TOSE'E ASIA
SAMEN INDUSTRIES
SCHILLER NOVIN
SEPANIR OIL AND GAS ENERGY ENGINEERING COMPANY
SHAFI'I RUDSARI, Rear Admiral Mohammad
SHAHID AHMAD KAZEMI INDUSTRIAL GROUP
SHAHID BEHESHTI UNIVERSITY
SHAKHESE BEHBUD SANAT
SHAMS, Abolghassem Mozaffari
SHAMSHIRI, IRGC Brigadier-General Ali
SHARIF UNIVERSITY OF TECHNOLOGY
SHETAB G.
SHETAB GAMAN
SHETAB TRADING
SHIRAZ ELECTRONICS INDUSTRIES
SIMATEC DEVELOPMENT COMPANY
SOLAT SANA, Abdollah
SOLTANI, Hamid
STATE PURCHASING ORGANISATION
STEP STANDART TEKNIK PARCA SAN VE TIC A.S.

SUN MIDDLE EAST FZ COMPANY
SURENA (A.K.A. SAKHD VA RAH-AN- DA-ZI)
TABA (IRAN CUTTING TOOLS MANUFACTURING COMPANY - TABA TOWLID ABZAR BORESHI IRAN)
TAGHTIRAN
TAJHIZ SANAT SHAYAN
TECHNOLOGY COOPERATION OFFICE OF THE IRANIAN PRESIDENT'S OFFICE
TEST TAFSIR
TIDEWATER
TOSSE SILOOHA
TURBINE ENGINEERING MANUFACTURING
VAHIDI, IRGC Brigadier-General Ahmad
WEST SUN TRADE GMBH
Y.A.S. CO. LTD
YARSANAT
YASA PART
ZADEH, Amir Ali Haji

ATTACHMENT 2 - PART II

LIST OF PERSONS, ENTITIES AND BODIES SET OUT IN ANNEX I TO COUNCIL DECISION 2010/413/CFSP AND ANNEXES VIII TO COUNCIL REGULATION (EU) NO 267/2012

7TH OF TIR.
ABBASI-DAVANI, Fereidoun
ABZAR BORESH KAVEH CO.
AGHAJANI, Azim
AHMADIAN, Ali Akbar
AMIN INDUSTRIAL COMPLEX
AMMUNITION AND METALLURGY INDUSTRIES GROUP
ARMAMENT INDUSTRIES GROUP
BAHMANYAR, Bahmanyar Morteza
BANK SEPAH
BANK SEPAH INTERNATIONAL
BARZAGANI TEJARAT TAVANMAD SACCAL COMPANIES
BEHINEH TRADING CO.
CRUISE MISSILE INDUSTRY GROUP
DASTJERDI, Ahmad Vahid
DEFENCE INDUSTRIES ORGANISATION (DIO)
DEFENSE TECHNOLOGY AND SCIENCE RESEARCH CENTER
DERAKHSHANDEH, Ahmad
DOOSTAN INTERNATIONAL COMPANY
ELECTRO SANAM COMPANY
ESLAMI, Mohammad
ESMAELI, Reza-Gholi
ETTEHAD TECHNICAL GROUP
FAJR INDUSTRIAL GROUP
FAKHRIZADEH-MAHABADI, Mohsen

FARASAKHT INDUSTRIES
FARAYAND TECHNIQUE
FATER (OR FAATER) INSTITUTE
GHARAGAHE SAZANDEGI GHAEM
GHORB KARBALA
GHORB NOOH
HARA COMPANY
HEJAZI, Mohammad
HOJATI, Mohsen
IMENSAZAN CONSULTANT ENGINEERS INSTITUTE
INDUSTRIAL FACTORIES OF PRECISION (IFP) MACHINERY
JOZA INDUSTRIAL CO.
KALA-ELECTRIC
KAVEH CUTTING TOOLS COMPANY
KETABACHI, Mehrdada Akhlaghi
KHATAM AL-ANBIYA CONSTRUCTION HEADQUARTERS
KHORASAN METALLURGY INDUSTRIES
M. BABAIE INDUSTRIES
MAKIN
MALEK ASHTAR UNIVERSITY
MALEKI, Naser
MINISTRY OF DEFENSE LOGISTICS EXPORT
MIZAN MACHINERY MANUFACTURING A.K.A.: 3MG
NAQDI, Mohammad Reza
NEJAD NOURI, Mohammad Mehdi
NIRU BATTERY MANUFACTURING COMPANY
OMRAN SAHEL
ORIENTAL OIL KISH
PARCHIN CHEMICAL INDUSTRIES
PARS AVIATION SERVICES COMPANY
PEJMAN INDUSTRIAL SERVICES CORPORATION
QODS AERONAUTICS INDUSTRIES
RAH SAHEL
RAHAB ENGINEERING INSTITUTE
REZAIE, Morteza
SABALAN COMPANY
SAD IMPORT EXPORT COMPANY
SAFARI, Morteza
SAFAVI, Yahya Rahim
SAFETY EQUIPMENT PROCUREMENT (SEP)
SAHAND ALUMINUM PARTS INDUSTRIAL COMPANY
SAHEL CONSULTANT ENGINEERS
SALIMI, Hosein
SANAM INDUSTRIAL GROUP
SEPANIR
SEPASAD ENGINEERING COMPANY
SHAHID BAGHERI INDUSTRIAL GROUP (SBIG)

SHAHID HEMMAT INDUSTRIAL GROUP (SHIG)
SHAHID KARRAZI INDUSTRIES
SHAHID SATARRI INDUSTRIES
SHAHID SAYYADE SHIRAZI INDUSTRIES
SHO'A' AVIATION.
SOLEIMANI, Qasem
SPECIAL INDUSTRIES GROUP
TABATABAEI, Ali Akbar
TIZ PARS
YA MAHDI INDUSTRIES GROUP
YAS AIR
YAZD METALLURGY INDUSTRIES
ZAHEDI, Mohammad Reza
ZOLQADR, General

ATTACHMENT 3

IRANIAN FINANCIAL INSTITUTIONS AND INDIVIDUAL AND ENTITIES IDENTIFIED AS GOVERNMENT OF IRAN (GOI) ON THE SDN LIST; DESIGNATED ENTITIES AND INDIVIDUALS ON THE SDN LIST AND ENTITIES AND INDIVIDUALS LISTED ON THE FSE LIST; INDIVIDUALS AND ENTITIES SANCTIONED UNDER ISA; BLOCKED PROPERTY OF THE FOREGOING

AA ENERGY FZCO*
ABAN AIR
ADVANCE NOVEL LIMITED
AFZALI, Ali
AGHA-JANI, Dawood
AL AQILI GROUP LLC
AL AQILI, Mohamed Saeed
AL FIDA INTERNATIONAL GENERAL TRADING
AL HILAL EXCHANGE
ALPHA EFFORT LIMITED
AMERI, Teymour
AMIN INVESTMENT BANK*
ANTARES SHIPPING COMPANY NV
ARASH SHIPPING ENTERPRISES LIMITED*
ARIAN BANK
ARTA SHIPPING ENTERPRISES LIMITED*
ASAN SHIPPING ENTERPRISE LIMITED*
ASCOTEC HOLDING GMBH*
ASCOTEC JAPAN K.K.*
ASCOTEC MINERAL & MACHINERY GMBH*
ASCOTEC SCIENCE & TECHNOLOGY GMBH*
ASCOTEC STEEL TRADING GMBH*

* Denotes Iranian financial institutions and individuals and entities identified as GOI by the Office of Foreign Assets Control (OFAC). U.S. persons and foreign entities owned or controlled by a U.S. person will continue to be prohibited from transactions with these individuals and entities, pursuant to the Iranian Transactions and Sanctions Regulations.

ASHTEAD SHIPPING COMPANY LIMITED
ASIA BANK
ASIA ENERGY GENERAL TRADING (LLC)*
ASIA MARINE NETWORK PTE. LTD.
ASSA CO. LTD.
ASSA CORP.
ATLANTIC INTERMODAL
ATOMIC ENERGY ORGANIZATION OF IRAN
AZORES SHIPPING COMPANY LL FZE
BAHADORI, Masoud*
BANCO INTERNACIONAL DE DESARROLLO, C.A.
BANDAR IMAM PETROCHEMICAL COMPANY*
BANK KARGOSHAEE
BANK KESHAVARZI IRAN*
BANK MARKAZI JOMHOURI ISLAMI IRAN*
BANK MASKAN*
BANK MELLAT*
BANK MELLI IRAN INVESTMENT COMPANY
BANK MELLI IRAN*
BANK MELLI PRINTING AND PUBLISHING CO.
BANK OF INDUSTRY AND MINE (OF IRAN)*
BANK REFAH KARGARAN*
BANK SEPAH INTERNATIONAL PLC
BANK SEPAH*
BANK TEJARAT*
BANK TORGOVOY KAPITAL ZAO*
BANK-E SHAHR*
BATENI, Naser
BAZARGAN, Farzad*
BEHSAZ KASHANE TEHRAN CONSTRUCTION CO.*
BEHZAD, Morteza Ahmadali
BELFAST GENERAL TRADING LLC
BEST PRECISE LIMITED
BIIS MARITIME LIMITED
BIMEH IRAN INSURANCE COMPANY (U.K.) LIMITED*
BLUE TANKER SHIPPING SA*
BMIIC INTERNATIONAL GENERAL TRADING LTD
BOU ALI SINA PETROCHEMICAL COMPANY*
BREYELLER STAHL TECHNOLOGY GMBH & CO. KG*
BUSHEHR SHIPPING COMPANY LIMITED
BYFLEET SHIPPING COMPANY LIMITED
CAMBIS, Dimitris*
CASPIAN MARITIME LIMITED*
CAUCASUS ENERGY
CEMENT INVESTMENT AND DEVELOPMENT COMPANY
CENTRAL INSURANCE OF IRAN
CISCO SHIPPING COMPANY CO. LTD.

COBHAM SHIPPING COMPANY LIMITED
COMMERCIAL PARS OIL CO.*
CONCEPT GIANT LIMITED
CREDIT INSTITUTION FOR DEVELOPMENT*
CRYSTAL SHIPPING FZE
CYLINDER SYSTEM L.T.D.*
DAJMAR, Mohhammad Hossein
DANESH SHIPPING COMPANY LIMITED*
DARYA CAPITAL ADMINISTRATION GMBH
DAVAR SHIPPING CO LTD*
DENA TANKERS FZE*
DERAKHSHANDEH, AHMAD
DETTIN SPA
DEY BANK*
DFS WORLDWIDE
DIVANDARI, Ali
DORKING SHIPPING COMPANY LIMITED
EDBI EXCHANGE COMPANY
EDBI STOCK BROKERAGE COMPANY
EFFINGHAM SHIPPING COMPANY LIMITED
EGHTESAD NOVIN BANK*
EIGHTH OCEAN ADMINISTRATION GMBH
EIGHTH OCEAN GMBH & CO. KG
ELEVENTH OCEAN ADMINISTRATION GMBH
ELEVENTH OCEAN GMBH & CO. KG
ESFAHAN NUCLEAR FUEL RESEARCH AND PRODUCTION CENTER
ESLAMI, Mansour
EUROPAISCH-IRANISCHE HANDELSBANK AG*
EUROPEAN OIL TRADERS
EVEREX
EXECUTION OF IMAM KHOMEINI'S ORDER*
EXPORT DEVELOPMENT BANK OF IRAN*
EZATI, Ali
FAIRWAY SHIPPING LTD
FAL OIL COMPANY LIMITED
FARNHAM SHIPPING COMPANY LIMITED
FARSOUDEH, Houshang
FAYLACA PETROLEUM
FERLAND COMPANY LIMITED
FIFTEENTH OCEAN GMBH & CO. KG
FIFTH OCEAN ADMINISTRATION GMBH
FIFTH OCEAN GMBH & CO. KG
FIRST EAST EXPORT BANK, P.L.C.
FIRST ISLAMIC INVESTMENT BANK LTD.
FIRST OCEAN ADMINISTRATION GMBH
FIRST OCEAN GMBH & CO. KG
FIRST PERSIA EQUITY FUND

FOURTEENTH OCEAN GMBH & CO. KG
FOURTH OCEAN ADMINISTRATION GMBH
FOURTH OCEAN GMBH & CO. KG
FUTURE BANK B.S.C.*
GALLIOT MARITIME INC
GARBIN NAVIGATION LTD*
GEORGIAN BUSINESS DEVELOPMENT
GHADIR INVESTMENT COMPANY*
GHAED BASSIR PETROCHEMICAL PRODUCTS COMPANY*
GHALEBANI, Ahmad*
GHARZOLHASANEH RESALAT BANK*
GHAVAMIN BANK*
GHEZEL AYAGH, Alireza
GOLDEN RESOURCES TRADING COMPANY L.L.C.*
GOLDENTEX FZE
GOLPARVAR, Gholamhossein
GOMSHALL SHIPPING COMPANY LIMITED
GOOD LUCK SHIPPING L.L.C.
GRACE BAY SHIPPING INC*
GREAT BUSINESS DEALS
GREAT METHOD LIMITED
HADI SHIPPING COMPANY LIMITED*
HAFIZ DARYA SHIPPING CO
HARAZ SHIPPING COMPANY LIMITED*
HATEF SHIPPING COMPANY LIMITED*
HEKMAT IRANIAN BANK*
HERCULES INTERNATIONAL SHIP*
HERMIS SHIPPING SA*
HIRMAND SHIPPING COMPANY LIMITED*
HODA SHIPPING COMPANY LIMITED*
HOMA SHIPPING COMPANY LIMITED*
HONAR SHIPPING COMPANY LIMITED*
HONG KONG INTERTRADE COMPANY*
HORMOZ OIL REFINING COMPANY*
HORSHAM SHIPPING COMPANY LIMITED
HOSSEINPOUR, Houshang
HTTS HANSEATIC TRADE TRUST AND SHIPPING GMBH
IDEAL SUCCESS INVESTMENTS LIMITED
IFIC HOLDING AG*
IHAG TRADING GMBH*
IMPIRE SHIPPING COMPANY*
INDUS MARITIME INC
INDUSTRIAL DEVELOPMENT AND RENOVATION ORGANIZATION OF IRAN*
INTERNATIONAL SAFE OIL
INTRA CHEM TRADING GMBH*
IRAN & SHARGH COMPANY*
IRAN & SHARGH LEASING COMPANY*

IRAN AIR
IRAN FOREIGN INVESTMENT COMPANY*
IRAN INSURANCE COMPANY*
IRAN O HIND SHIPPING COMPANY
IRAN O MISR SHIPPING COMPANY
IRAN PETROCHEMICAL COMMERCIAL COMPANY*
IRAN ZAMIN BANK*
IRANAIR TOURS
IRANIAN MINES AND MINING INDUSTRIES DEVELOPMENT AND RENOVATION ORGANIZATION*
IRANIAN OIL COMPANY (U.K.) LIMITED*
IRANIAN-VENEZUELAN BI-NATIONAL BANK / JOINT IRAN-VENEZUELA BANK*
IRASCO S.R.L.*
IRINVESTSHIP LTD.
IRISL (MALTA) LIMITED
IRISL (UK) LTD.
IRISL CHINA SHIPPING CO., LTD.
IRISL EUROPE GMBH
IRISL MARINE SERVICES & ENGINEERING COMPANY
IRISL MULTIMODAL TRANSPORT CO.
IRITAL SHIPPING SRL COMPANY
ISI MARITIME LIMITED
ISIM AMIN LIMITED
ISIM ATR LIMITED
ISIM OLIVE LIMITED
ISIM SAT LIMITED
ISIM SEA CHARIOT LIMITED
ISIM SEA CRESCENT LIMITED
ISIM SININ LIMITED
ISIM TAJ MAHAL LIMITED
ISIM TOUR LIMITED
ISLAMIC REGIONAL COOPERATION BANK*
ISLAMIC REPUBLIC OF IRAN SHIPPING LINES
JABBER IBN HAYAN
JAM PETROCHEMICAL COMPANY
JASHNSAZ, Seifollah*
JUPITER SEAWAYS SHIPPING*
KADDOURI, Abdelhak
KAFOLATBANK*
KALA LIMITED*
KALA PENSION TRUST LIMITED*
KARAFARIN BANK*
KASB INTERNATIONAL LLC*
KAVERI MARITIME INC
KAVOSHYAR COMPANY
KERMAN SHIPPING CO LTD
KHALILI, Jamshid
KHAVARMIANEH BANK*

KHAZAR SEA SHIPPING LINES
KISH INTERNATIONAL BANK*
KISH PROTECTION & INDEMNITY
KONING MARINE CORP*
KONT INVESTMENT BANK
KONT KOSMETIK
KSN FOUNDATION
KUO OIL PTE. LTD
LANCELIN SHIPPING COMPANY LIMITED
LEADING MARITIME PTE. LTD.
LEILABADI, Ali Hajinia
LISSOME MARINE SERVICES LLC
LOGISTIC SMART LIMITED
LOWESWATER LIMITED
MACHINE SAZI ARAK CO. LTD.*
MAHAB GHODSS CONSULTING ENGINEERING COMPANY*
MAHDAVI, Ali
MALSHIP SHIPPING AGENCY LTD.
MARANER HOLDINGS LIMITED
MARBLE SHIPPING LIMITED
MARJAN PETROCHEMICAL COMPANY*
MAZANDARAN CEMENT COMPANY
MAZANDARAN TEXTILE COMPANY
MCS ENGINEERING*
MCS INTERNATIONAL GMBH*
MEHR CAYMAN LTD.
MEHR IRAN CREDIT UNION BANK*
MEHRAN SHIPPING COMPANY LIMITED*
MELLAT BANK SB CJSC
MELLAT INSURANCE COMPANY*
MELLI AGROCHEMICAL COMPANY, P.J.S.
MELLI BANK PLC
MELLI INVESTMENT HOLDING INTERNATIONAL
MELODIOUS MARITIME INC
MERSAD SHIPPING COMPANY LIMITED*
MESBAH ENERGY COMPANY
METAL & MINERAL TRADE S.A.R.L.*
MID OIL ASIA PTE LTD
MILL DENE LIMITED
MINAB SHIPPING COMPANY LIMITED*
MINES AND METALS ENGINEERING GMBH*
MIR BUSINESS BANK ZAO
MOALLEM INSURANCE COMPANY
MOBIN PETROCHEMICAL COMPANY*
MODABER*
MODALITY LIMITED
MOGHADDAMI FARD, Mohammad

MOHADDES, Seyed Mahmoud*
MOINIE, Mohammad*
MONSOON SHIPPING LTD*
MOUNT EVEREST MARITIME INC
MSP KALA NAFT CO. TEHRAN*
N.I.T.C. REPRESENTATIVE OFFICE*
NABIPOUR, Ghasem
NAFTIRAN INTERTRADE CO. (NICO) LIMITED*
NAFTIRAN INTERTRADE CO. (NICO) SARL*
NAFTIRAN TRADING SERVICES CO. (NTS) LIMITED*
NARI SHIPPING AND CHARTERING GMBH & CO. KG
NASIRBEIK, Anahita
NATIONAL IRANIAN OIL COMPANY PTE LTD*
NATIONAL IRANIAN OIL COMPANY*
NATIONAL IRANIAN TANKER COMPANY LLC*
NATIONAL IRANIAN TANKER COMPANY*
NATIONAL PETROCHEMICAL COMPANY*
NAYEBI, Pourya
NEFERTITI SHIPPING COMPANY
NEUMAN LIMITED
NEW DESIRE LIMITED
NEW YORK GENERAL TRADING
NEW YORK MONEY EXCHANGE
NICO ENGINEERING LIMITED*
NIKOUSOKHAN, Mahmoud*
NIKSIMA FOOD AND BEVERAGE JLT
NINTH OCEAN ADMINISTRATION GMBH
NINTH OCEAN GMBH & CO. KG
NIOC INTERNATIONAL AFFAIRS (LONDON) LIMITED*
NIZAMI, Anwar Kamal
NOOR AFZAR GOSTAR COMPANY
NOOR ENERGY (MALAYSIA) LTD.*
NOURI PETROCHEMICAL COMPANY*
NOVIN ENERGY COMPANY
NPC INTERNATIONAL LIMITED*
NUCLEAR RESEARCH CENTER FOR AGRICULTURE AND MEDICINE
NUCLEAR SCIENCE AND TECHNOLOGY RESEARCH INSTITUTE
OCEAN CAPITAL ADMINISTRATION GMBH
OIL INDUSTRY INVESTMENT COMPANY*
OMID REY CIVIL & CONSTRUCTION COMPANY*
ONE CLASS PROPERTIES (PTY) LTD.*
ONE VISION INVESTMENTS 5 (PTY) LTD.*
ONERBANK ZAO*
ORCHIDEA GULF TRADING
P.C.C. (SINGAPORE) PRIVATE LIMITED*
PACIFIC SHIPPING DMCEST
PAJAND, Mohammad Hadi

PARDIS INVESTMENT COMPANY*
PARS MCS*
PARS OIL AND GAS COMPANY*
PARS OIL CO.*
PARS PETROCHEMICAL COMPANY*
PARS PETROCHEMICAL SHIPPING COMPANY*
PARS TRASH COMPANY
PARSAEI, Reza*
PARSIAN BANK*
PARTNER CENTURY LIMITED
PARVARESH, Farhad Ali
PASARGAD BANK*
PEARL ENERGY COMPANY LTD.
PEARL ENERGY SERVICES, SA
PERSIA INTERNATIONAL BANK PLC
PERSIA OIL & GAS INDUSTRY DEVELOPMENT CO.*
PETRO ENERGY INTERTRADE COMPANY*
PETRO ROYAL FZE*
PETRO SUISSE INTERTRADE COMPANY SA*
PETROCHEMICAL COMMERCIAL COMPANY (U.K.) LIMITED*
PETROCHEMICAL COMMERCIAL COMPANY FZE*
PETROCHEMICAL COMMERCIAL COMPANY INTERNATIONAL*
PETROIRAN DEVELOPMENT COMPANY (PEDCO) LIMITED*
PETROLEOS DE VENEZUELA S.A. (PDVSA)
PETROPARS INTERNATIONAL FZE*
PETROPARS LTD.*
PETROPARS UK LIMITED*
PIONEER ENERGY INDUSTRIES COMPANY
POLAT, Muzaffer
POLINEX GENERAL TRADING LLC*
POLYNAR COMPANY*
POST BANK OF IRAN*
POURANSARI, Hashem*
PROTON PETROCHEMICALS SHIPPING LIMITED*
PRYVATNE AKTSIONERNE TOVARYSTVO AVIAKOMPANIYA BUKOVYNA
QANNADI, Mohammad
QULANDARY, Azizullah Asadullah
RAHIQI, Javad
RASOOL, Seyed Alaeddin Sadat
REY INVESTMENT COMPANY*
REY NIRU ENGINEERING COMPANY*
REYCO GMBH.*
REZVANIANZADEH, Mohammed Reza
RISHI MARITIME INC
RISHMAK PRODUCTIVE & EXPORTS COMPANY*
ROYAL ARYA CO.*
ROYAL OYSTER GROUP

ROYAL-MED SHIPPING AGENCY LTD
SABET, Javad Karimi
SACKVILLE HOLDINGS LIMITED
SADAF PETROCHEMICAL ASSALUYEH COMPANY*
SAFDARI, Seyed Jaber
SAFIRAN PAYAM DARYA SHIPPING COMPANY
SAMAN BANK*
SAMAN SHIPPING COMPANY LIMITED*
SAMBOUK SHIPPING FZC*
SANDFORD GROUP LIMITED
SANTEX LINES LIMITED
SARKANDI, Ahmad
SARMAYEH BANK*
SARV SHIPPING COMPANY LIMITED*
SECOND OCEAN ADMINISTRATION GMBH
SECOND OCEAN GMBH & CO. KG
SEIBOW LIMITED
SEIBOW LOGISTICS LIMITED
SEIFI, Asadollah
SEPID SHIPPING COMPANY LIMITED*
SEVENTH OCEAN ADMINISTRATION GMBH
SEVENTH OCEAN GMBH & CO. KG
SEYYEDI, Seyed Nasser Mohammad*
SEYYEDI, Seyedeh Hanieh Seyed Nasser Mohammad
SHAHID TONDGOOYAN PETROCHEMICAL COMPANY*
SHALLON LIMITED
SHAZAND PETROCHEMICAL COMPANY*
SHERE SHIPPING COMPANY LIMITED
SHIPPING COMPUTER SERVICES COMPANY
SHOMAL CEMENT COMPANY
SIMA GENERAL TRADING CO FZE*
SIMA SHIPPING COMPANY LIMITED*
SINA BANK*
SINA SHIPPING COMPANY LIMITED*
SINGA TANKERS PTE. LTD.
SINO ACCESS HOLDINGS LIMITED
SINOSE MARITIME PTE. LTD.
SIQIRIYA MARITIME CORP.
SIXTH OCEAN ADMINISTRATION GMBH
SIXTH OCEAN GMBH & CO. KG
SMART DAY HOLDINGS GROUP LIMITED
SOKOLENKO, Vitaly
SORINET COMMERCIAL TRUST (SCT) BANKERS
SOROUSH SARZAMIN ASATIR SHIP MANAGEMENT COMPANY
SOUTH SHIPPING LINE IRAN
SPEEDY SHIP FZC
SPRINGTHORPE LIMITED

STARRY SHINE INTERNATIONAL LIMITED
SWISS MANAGEMENT SERVICES SARL*
SYNERGY GENERAL TRADING FZE*
SYSTEM WISE LIMITED
TABATABAEI, Seyyed Mohammad Ali Khatibi*
TABRIZ PETROCHEMICAL COMPANY*
TADBIR BROKERAGE COMPANY*
TADBIR CONSTRUCTION DEVELOPMENT COMPANY*
TADBIR ECONOMIC DEVELOPMENT GROUP*
TADBIR ENERGY DEVELOPMENT GROUP CO.*
TADBIR INVESTMENT COMPANY*
TAFAZOLI, Ahmad
TALAI, Mohamad
TAMAS COMPANY
TAT BANK*
TC SHIPPING COMPANY LIMITED*
TENTH OCEAN GMBH & CO. KG
THE EXPLORATION AND NUCLEAR RAW MATERIALS PRODUCTION COMPANY
THE NUCLEAR REACTORS FUEL COMPANY
THIRD OCEAN ADMINISTRATION GMBH
THIRD OCEAN GMBH & CO. KG
THIRTEENTH OCEAN GMBH & CO. KG
TONGHAM SHIPPING CO LTD
TOP GLACIER COMPANY LIMITED
TOP PRESTIGE TRADING LIMITED
TOSEE EQTESAD AYANDEHSAZAN COMPANY*
TOSEE TAAVON BANK*
TOURISM BANK*
TRADE TREASURE LIMITED
TRUE HONOUR HOLDINGS LIMITED
TWELFTH OCEAN ADMINISTRATION GMBH
TWELFTH OCEAN GMBH & CO. KG
UPPERCOURT SHIPPING COMPANY LIMITED
VALFAJR 8TH SHIPPING LINE CO SSK
VOBSTER SHIPPING COMPANY LTD
WEST SUN TRADE GMBH*
WIPPERMANN, Ulrich
WOKING SHIPPING INVESTMENTS LIMITED
YASINI, Seyed Kamal
YAZDI, Bahareh Mirza Hossein
ZADEH, Hassan Jalil
ZANJANI, Babak Morteza
ZARIN RAFSANJAN CEMENT COMPANY*
ZEIDI, Hossein
ZHUHAI ZHENRONG COMPANY
ZIRACCHIAN ZADEH, Mahmoud*

BLOCKED PROPERTY	PROPERTY OF	TYPE	IMO NUMBER
EP-CFD	IRAN AIR	Aircraft	
EP-CFE	IRAN AIR	Aircraft	
EP-CFH	IRAN AIR	Aircraft	
EP-CFI	IRAN AIR	Aircraft	
EP-CFJ	IRAN AIR	Aircraft	
EP-CFK	IRAN AIR	Aircraft	
EP-CFL	IRAN AIR	Aircraft	
EP-CFM	IRAN AIR	Aircraft	
EP-CFO	IRAN AIR	Aircraft	
EP-CFP	IRAN AIR	Aircraft	
EP-CFQ	IRAN AIR	Aircraft	
EP-CFR	IRAN AIR	Aircraft	
EP-IAA	IRAN AIR	Aircraft	
EP-IAB	IRAN AIR	Aircraft	
EP-IAC	IRAN AIR	Aircraft	
EP-IAD	IRAN AIR	Aircraft	
EP-IAG	IRAN AIR	Aircraft	
EP-IAH	IRAN AIR	Aircraft	
EP-IAI	IRAN AIR	Aircraft	
EP-IAM	IRAN AIR	Aircraft	
EP-IBA	IRAN AIR	Aircraft	
EP-IBB	IRAN AIR	Aircraft	
EP-IBC	IRAN AIR	Aircraft	
EP-IBD	IRAN AIR	Aircraft	
EP-IBG	IRAN AIR	Aircraft	
EP-IBH	IRAN AIR	Aircraft	
EP-IBI	IRAN AIR	Aircraft	
EP-IBJ	IRAN AIR	Aircraft	
EP-IBK	IRAN AIR	Aircraft	
EP-IBL	IRAN AIR	Aircraft	
EP-IBM	IRAN AIR	Aircraft	
EP-IBN	IRAN AIR	Aircraft	
EP-IBP	IRAN AIR	Aircraft	
EP-IBQ	IRAN AIR	Aircraft	
EP-IBS	IRAN AIR	Aircraft	
EP-IBT	IRAN AIR	Aircraft	

[x] Denotes blocked property of individual and entities identified as GOI by the Office of Foreign Assets Control. U.S. persons and foreign entities owned or controlled by a U.S. person will continue to be prohibited from transactions with these individuals and entities, pursuant to the Iranian Transactions and Sanctions Regulations.

EP-IBV	IRAN AIR	Aircraft	
EP-IBZ	IRAN AIR	Aircraft	
EP-ICD	IRAN AIR	Aircraft	
EP-ICE	IRAN AIR	Aircraft	
EP-ICF	IRAN AIR	Aircraft	
EP-IDA	IRAN AIR	Aircraft	
EP-IDD	IRAN AIR	Aircraft	
EP-IDF	IRAN AIR	Aircraft	
EP-IDG	IRAN AIR	Aircraft	
EP-IEB	IRAN AIR	Aircraft	
EP-IEC	IRAN AIR	Aircraft	
EP-IED	IRAN AIR	Aircraft	
EP-IEE	IRAN AIR	Aircraft	
EP-IEF	IRAN AIR	Aircraft	
EP-IEG	IRAN AIR	Aircraft	
EP-IRK	IRAN AIR	Aircraft	
EP-IRL	IRAN AIR	Aircraft	
EP-IRM	IRAN AIR	Aircraft	
EP-IRN	IRAN AIR	Aircraft	
EP-IRR	IRAN AIR	Aircraft	
EP-IRS	IRAN AIR	Aircraft	
EP-IRT	IRAN AIR	Aircraft	
EP-MDD	IRAN AIR	Aircraft	
EP-MDE	IRAN AIR	Aircraft	
UR-BXI	IRAN AIR	Aircraft	
UR-BXL	IRAN AIR	Aircraft	
UR-BXM	IRAN AIR	Aircraft	
UR-CGS	IRAN AIR	Aircraft	
UR-CGT	IRAN AIR	Aircraft	
UR-CHW	IRAN AIR	Aircraft	
UR-CHX	IRAN AIR	Aircraft	
UR-CHY	IRAN AIR	Aircraft	
UR-CHZ	IRAN AIR	Aircraft	
UR-CJQ	IRAN AIR	Aircraft	
UR-BHJ	PRYVATNE AKTSIONERNE TOVARYSTVO AVIAKOMPANIYA	Aircraft	
UR-BXN	PRYVATNE AKTSIONERNE TOVARYSTVO AVIAKOMPANIYA	Aircraft	
UR-CIX	PRYVATNE AKTSIONERNE TOVARYSTVO AVIAKOMPANIYA	Aircraft	
UR-CIY	PRYVATNE AKTSIONERNE TOVARYSTVO AVIAKOMPANIYA	Aircraft	
UR-CJA	PRYVATNE AKTSIONERNE TOVARYSTVO AVIAKOMPANIYA	Aircraft	

UR-CJK	PRYVATNE AKTSIONERNE TOVARYSTVO AVIAKOMPANIYA	Aircraft	
RIONA	HAFIZ DARYA SHIPPING CO	Vessel	9349588
MIRZA KOCHEK KHAN	ISLAMIC REPUBLIC OF IRAN SHIPPING LINES	Vessel	7027899
ASSA	ISLAMIC REPUBLIC OF IRAN SHIPPING LINES	Vessel	7632814
AMITEES	ISLAMIC REPUBLIC OF IRAN SHIPPING LINES	Vessel	7632826
HORMUZ 2	ISLAMIC REPUBLIC OF IRAN SHIPPING LINES	Vessel	7904580
PARMIDA	ISLAMIC REPUBLIC OF IRAN SHIPPING LINES	Vessel	8105284
BARSAM	ISLAMIC REPUBLIC OF IRAN SHIPPING LINES	Vessel	8107581
PANTEA	ISLAMIC REPUBLIC OF IRAN SHIPPING LINES	Vessel	8108559
IRAN AKHAVAN	ISLAMIC REPUBLIC OF IRAN SHIPPING LINES	Vessel	8113009
SARINA	ISLAMIC REPUBLIC OF IRAN SHIPPING LINES	Vessel	8203608
SABRINA	ISLAMIC REPUBLIC OF IRAN SHIPPING LINES	Vessel	8215742
ATTRIBUTE	ISLAMIC REPUBLIC OF IRAN SHIPPING LINES	Vessel	8309593
ALIAS	ISLAMIC REPUBLIC OF IRAN SHIPPING LINES	Vessel	8309608
AQUARIAN	ISLAMIC REPUBLIC OF IRAN SHIPPING LINES	Vessel	8309610
ADVENTIST	ISLAMIC REPUBLIC OF IRAN SHIPPING LINES	Vessel	8309622
AGEAN	ISLAMIC REPUBLIC OF IRAN SHIPPING LINES	Vessel	8309634
ANGEL	ISLAMIC REPUBLIC OF IRAN SHIPPING LINES	Vessel	8309646
AGILE	ISLAMIC REPUBLIC OF IRAN SHIPPING LINES	Vessel	8309658
AJAX	ISLAMIC REPUBLIC OF IRAN SHIPPING LINES	Vessel	8309672
ACROBAT	ISLAMIC REPUBLIC OF IRAN SHIPPING LINES	Vessel	8309684
SHADFAR	ISLAMIC REPUBLIC OF IRAN SHIPPING LINES	Vessel	8309696
AMPLIFY	ISLAMIC REPUBLIC OF IRAN SHIPPING LINES	Vessel	8309701
IRAN HORMUZ 21	ISLAMIC REPUBLIC OF IRAN SHIPPING LINES	Vessel	8314263
IRAN HORMUZ 22	ISLAMIC REPUBLIC OF IRAN SHIPPING LINES	Vessel	8314275
IRAN HORMUZ 23	ISLAMIC REPUBLIC OF IRAN SHIPPING LINES	Vessel	8319782
IRAN SHALAK	ISLAMIC REPUBLIC OF IRAN SHIPPING LINES	Vessel	8319940
IRAN YOUSHAT	ISLAMIC REPUBLIC OF IRAN SHIPPING LINES	Vessel	8319952
AEROLITE	ISLAMIC REPUBLIC OF IRAN SHIPPING LINES	Vessel	8320121
ADRIAN	ISLAMIC REPUBLIC OF IRAN SHIPPING LINES	Vessel	8320133
NAGHMEH	ISLAMIC REPUBLIC OF IRAN SHIPPING LINES	Vessel	8320145
RONAK	ISLAMIC REPUBLIC OF IRAN SHIPPING LINES	Vessel	8320157
ACCURATE	ISLAMIC REPUBLIC OF IRAN SHIPPING LINES	Vessel	8320169
TABANDEH	ISLAMIC REPUBLIC OF IRAN SHIPPING LINES	Vessel	8320171
GULAFSHAN	ISLAMIC REPUBLIC OF IRAN SHIPPING LINES	Vessel	8320183
ALAMEDA	ISLAMIC REPUBLIC OF IRAN SHIPPING LINES	Vessel	8320195
IRAN PARAK	ISLAMIC REPUBLIC OF IRAN SHIPPING LINES	Vessel	8322064
IRAN CHARAK	ISLAMIC REPUBLIC OF IRAN SHIPPING LINES	Vessel	8322076
IRAN HORMUZ 25	ISLAMIC REPUBLIC OF IRAN SHIPPING LINES	Vessel	8422072
IRAN HORMUZ 26	ISLAMIC REPUBLIC OF IRAN SHIPPING LINES	Vessel	8422084
DORITA	ISLAMIC REPUBLIC OF IRAN SHIPPING LINES	Vessel	8605234

IRAN SHALAMCHEH	ISLAMIC REPUBLIC OF IRAN SHIPPING LINES	Vessel	8820925
AAJ	ISLAMIC REPUBLIC OF IRAN SHIPPING LINES	Vessel	8984484
IRAN HORMUZ 12	ISLAMIC REPUBLIC OF IRAN SHIPPING LINES	Vessel	9005596
IRAN KONG	ISLAMIC REPUBLIC OF IRAN SHIPPING LINES	Vessel	9007582
VISTA	ISLAMIC REPUBLIC OF IRAN SHIPPING LINES	Vessel	9010711
VIANA	ISLAMIC REPUBLIC OF IRAN SHIPPING LINES	Vessel	9010723
IRAN HORMUZ 14	ISLAMIC REPUBLIC OF IRAN SHIPPING LINES	Vessel	9020778
HAMD	ISLAMIC REPUBLIC OF IRAN SHIPPING LINES	Vessel	9036052
SOBHAN	ISLAMIC REPUBLIC OF IRAN SHIPPING LINES	Vessel	9036935
SATTAR	ISLAMIC REPUBLIC OF IRAN SHIPPING LINES	Vessel	9040479
ABBA	ISLAMIC REPUBLIC OF IRAN SHIPPING LINES	Vessel	9051624
BEHDAD	ISLAMIC REPUBLIC OF IRAN SHIPPING LINES	Vessel	9051636
PARSHAN	ISLAMIC REPUBLIC OF IRAN SHIPPING LINES	Vessel	9051648
VALERIAN	ISLAMIC REPUBLIC OF IRAN SHIPPING LINES	Vessel	9051650
NEGEEN	ISLAMIC REPUBLIC OF IRAN SHIPPING LINES	Vessel	9071519
ATTAR	ISLAMIC REPUBLIC OF IRAN SHIPPING LINES	Vessel	9074092
PARIN	ISLAMIC REPUBLIC OF IRAN SHIPPING LINES	Vessel	9076478
TEEN	ISLAMIC REPUBLIC OF IRAN SHIPPING LINES	Vessel	9101649
GOWHAR	ISLAMIC REPUBLIC OF IRAN SHIPPING LINES	Vessel	9103087
IRAN DALEER	ISLAMIC REPUBLIC OF IRAN SHIPPING LINES	Vessel	9118551
PATRIS	ISLAMIC REPUBLIC OF IRAN SHIPPING LINES	Vessel	9137210
NARDIS	ISLAMIC REPUBLIC OF IRAN SHIPPING LINES	Vessel	9137246
KADOS	ISLAMIC REPUBLIC OF IRAN SHIPPING LINES	Vessel	9137258
ZOMOROUD	ISLAMIC REPUBLIC OF IRAN SHIPPING LINES	Vessel	9138044
BRELYAN	ISLAMIC REPUBLIC OF IRAN SHIPPING LINES	Vessel	9138056
NILDA	ISLAMIC REPUBLIC OF IRAN SHIPPING LINES	Vessel	9165786
JOVITA	ISLAMIC REPUBLIC OF IRAN SHIPPING LINES	Vessel	9165798
MANOLA	ISLAMIC REPUBLIC OF IRAN SHIPPING LINES	Vessel	9165803
GLADIOLUS	ISLAMIC REPUBLIC OF IRAN SHIPPING LINES	Vessel	9165815
ELYANA	ISLAMIC REPUBLIC OF IRAN SHIPPING LINES	Vessel	9165827
NEGAR	ISLAMIC REPUBLIC OF IRAN SHIPPING LINES	Vessel	9165839
SAVIZ	ISLAMIC REPUBLIC OF IRAN SHIPPING LINES	Vessel	9167253
GLOXINIA	ISLAMIC REPUBLIC OF IRAN SHIPPING LINES	Vessel	9167265
NESHAT	ISLAMIC REPUBLIC OF IRAN SHIPPING LINES	Vessel	9167277
BEHSHAD	ISLAMIC REPUBLIC OF IRAN SHIPPING LINES	Vessel	9167289
JAIRAN	ISLAMIC REPUBLIC OF IRAN SHIPPING LINES	Vessel	9167291
IRAN SHAHED	ISLAMIC REPUBLIC OF IRAN SHIPPING LINES	Vessel	9184691
GOLSAR	ISLAMIC REPUBLIC OF IRAN SHIPPING LINES	Vessel	9193185
ZARSAN	ISLAMIC REPUBLIC OF IRAN SHIPPING LINES	Vessel	9193197
ARVIN	ISLAMIC REPUBLIC OF IRAN SHIPPING LINES	Vessel	9193202
ARTAVAND	ISLAMIC REPUBLIC OF IRAN SHIPPING LINES	Vessel	9193214
TERESA	ISLAMIC REPUBLIC OF IRAN SHIPPING LINES	Vessel	9209324
GABRIELA	ISLAMIC REPUBLIC OF IRAN SHIPPING LINES	Vessel	9209336

SARITA	ISLAMIC REPUBLIC OF IRAN SHIPPING LINES	Vessel	9209348
SILVER CRAFT	ISLAMIC REPUBLIC OF IRAN SHIPPING LINES	Vessel	9209350
MAHNAM	ISLAMIC REPUBLIC OF IRAN SHIPPING LINES	Vessel	9213387
TERMEH	ISLAMIC REPUBLIC OF IRAN SHIPPING LINES	Vessel	9213399
MAHSAN	ISLAMIC REPUBLIC OF IRAN SHIPPING LINES	Vessel	9226944
HAMADAN	ISLAMIC REPUBLIC OF IRAN SHIPPING LINES	Vessel	9226956
TARADIS	ISLAMIC REPUBLIC OF IRAN SHIPPING LINES	Vessel	9245304
PARMIS	ISLAMIC REPUBLIC OF IRAN SHIPPING LINES	Vessel	9245316
ZAR	ISLAMIC REPUBLIC OF IRAN SHIPPING LINES	Vessel	9260160
ZIVAR	ISLAMIC REPUBLIC OF IRAN SHIPPING LINES	Vessel	9260172
VALILI	ISLAMIC REPUBLIC OF IRAN SHIPPING LINES	Vessel	9270646
SHAMIM	ISLAMIC REPUBLIC OF IRAN SHIPPING LINES	Vessel	9270658
IRAN SHAHR-E-KORD	ISLAMIC REPUBLIC OF IRAN SHIPPING LINES	Vessel	9270684
IRAN KASHAN	ISLAMIC REPUBLIC OF IRAN SHIPPING LINES	Vessel	9270696
SININ	ISLAMIC REPUBLIC OF IRAN SHIPPING LINES	Vessel	9274941
PARMIS	ISLAMIC REPUBLIC OF IRAN SHIPPING LINES	Vessel	9283007
AZARGOUN	ISLAMIC REPUBLIC OF IRAN SHIPPING LINES	Vessel	9283019
SALIS	ISLAMIC REPUBLIC OF IRAN SHIPPING LINES	Vessel	9283021
GOLBON	ISLAMIC REPUBLIC OF IRAN SHIPPING LINES	Vessel	9283033
PARDIS	ISLAMIC REPUBLIC OF IRAN SHIPPING LINES	Vessel	9284142
TANDIS	ISLAMIC REPUBLIC OF IRAN SHIPPING LINES	Vessel	9284154
SHERE	ISLAMIC REPUBLIC OF IRAN SHIPPING LINES	Vessel	9305192
UPPERCOURT	ISLAMIC REPUBLIC OF IRAN SHIPPING LINES	Vessel	9305207
TONGHAM	ISLAMIC REPUBLIC OF IRAN SHIPPING LINES	Vessel	9305219
VOBSTER	ISLAMIC REPUBLIC OF IRAN SHIPPING LINES	Vessel	9305221
GOLAFRUZ	ISLAMIC REPUBLIC OF IRAN SHIPPING LINES	Vessel	9323833
ADALIA	ISLAMIC REPUBLIC OF IRAN SHIPPING LINES	Vessel	9328900
SHABGOUN	ISLAMIC REPUBLIC OF IRAN SHIPPING LINES	Vessel	9346524
AGATA	ISLAMIC REPUBLIC OF IRAN SHIPPING LINES	Vessel	9346536
BENITA	ISLAMIC REPUBLIC OF IRAN SHIPPING LINES	Vessel	9346548
MARISOL	ISLAMIC REPUBLIC OF IRAN SHIPPING LINES	Vessel	9349576
ORIANA	ISLAMIC REPUBLIC OF IRAN SHIPPING LINES	Vessel	9349590
MERCEDES	ISLAMIC REPUBLIC OF IRAN SHIPPING LINES	Vessel	9349667
RAMONA	ISLAMIC REPUBLIC OF IRAN SHIPPING LINES	Vessel	9349679
GILDA	ISLAMIC REPUBLIC OF IRAN SHIPPING LINES	Vessel	9367982
SANIA	ISLAMIC REPUBLIC OF IRAN SHIPPING LINES	Vessel	9367994
SARIR	ISLAMIC REPUBLIC OF IRAN SHIPPING LINES	Vessel	9368003
SOMIA	ISLAMIC REPUBLIC OF IRAN SHIPPING LINES	Vessel	9368015
GLORY	ISLAMIC REPUBLIC OF IRAN SHIPPING LINES	Vessel	9369710
ARIES	ISLAMIC REPUBLIC OF IRAN SHIPPING LINES	Vessel	9369722
ABTIN 1	ISLAMIC REPUBLIC OF IRAN SHIPPING LINES	Vessel	9379636
ARSHAM	ISLAMIC REPUBLIC OF IRAN SHIPPING LINES	Vessel	9386500
PARSHAD	ISLAMIC REPUBLIC OF IRAN SHIPPING LINES	Vessel	9387786

HAADI	ISLAMIC REPUBLIC OF IRAN SHIPPING LINES	Vessel	9387798
RAAZI	ISLAMIC REPUBLIC OF IRAN SHIPPING LINES	Vessel	9387803
SAEI	ISLAMIC REPUBLIC OF IRAN SHIPPING LINES	Vessel	9387815
ARTMAN	ISLAMIC REPUBLIC OF IRAN SHIPPING LINES	Vessel	9405930
BASKAR	ISLAMIC REPUBLIC OF IRAN SHIPPING LINES	Vessel	9405942
BAHJAT	ISLAMIC REPUBLIC OF IRAN SHIPPING LINES	Vessel	9405954
HAAMI	ISLAMIC REPUBLIC OF IRAN SHIPPING LINES	Vessel	9405966
SHAADI	ISLAMIC REPUBLIC OF IRAN SHIPPING LINES	Vessel	9405978
SHAYAN 1	ISLAMIC REPUBLIC OF IRAN SHIPPING LINES	Vessel	9420356
TABAN 1	ISLAMIC REPUBLIC OF IRAN SHIPPING LINES	Vessel	9420368
YARAN	ISLAMIC REPUBLIC OF IRAN SHIPPING LINES	Vessel	9420370
AMIN	ISLAMIC REPUBLIC OF IRAN SHIPPING LINES	Vessel	9422366
AVANG	ISLAMIC REPUBLIC OF IRAN SHIPPING LINES	Vessel	9465746
KIAZAND	ISLAMIC REPUBLIC OF IRAN SHIPPING LINES	Vessel	9465758
BATIS	ISLAMIC REPUBLIC OF IRAN SHIPPING LINES	Vessel	9465760
WARTA	ISLAMIC REPUBLIC OF IRAN SHIPPING LINES	Vessel	9465849
SALIM	ISLAMIC REPUBLIC OF IRAN SHIPPING LINES	Vessel	9465851
ARDAVAN	ISLAMIC REPUBLIC OF IRAN SHIPPING LINES	Vessel	9465863
NAMI	LISSOME MARINE SERVICES LLC	Vessel	8419178
GAS CAMELLIA	LISSOME MARINE SERVICES LLC	Vessel	8803381
TESS	LISSOME MARINE SERVICES LLC	Vessel	8913564
KATERINA 1	LISSOME MARINE SERVICES LLC	Vessel	9031959
MARIA	LISSOME MARINE SERVICES LLC	Vessel	9110626
SUN OCEAN	LISSOME MARINE SERVICES LLC	Vessel	9408358
YOUNES [×]	NATIONAL IRANIAN TANKER COMPANY	Vessel	8212465
YOUSEF [×]	NATIONAL IRANIAN TANKER COMPANY	Vessel	8316106
YAGHOUB [×]	NATIONAL IRANIAN TANKER COMPANY	Vessel	8316168
TOLOU [×]	NATIONAL IRANIAN TANKER COMPANY	Vessel	8318178
VALFAJR2 [×]	NATIONAL IRANIAN TANKER COMPANY	Vessel	8400103
BADR [×]	NATIONAL IRANIAN TANKER COMPANY	Vessel	8407345
BANEH [×]	NATIONAL IRANIAN TANKER COMPANY	Vessel	8508462
SARDASHT [×]	NATIONAL IRANIAN TANKER COMPANY	Vessel	8517231
MARIVAN [×]	NATIONAL IRANIAN TANKER COMPANY	Vessel	8517243
BRIGHT [×]	NATIONAL IRANIAN TANKER COMPANY	Vessel	9005235
CARIBO [×]	NATIONAL IRANIAN TANKER COMPANY	Vessel	9011246
AURA [×]	NATIONAL IRANIAN TANKER COMPANY	Vessel	9013749
BICAS [×]	NATIONAL IRANIAN TANKER COMPANY	Vessel	9077850
MAHARLIKA [×]	NATIONAL IRANIAN TANKER COMPANY	Vessel	9079066
NAPOLI [×]	NATIONAL IRANIAN TANKER COMPANY	Vessel	9079078
NYOS [×]	NATIONAL IRANIAN TANKER COMPANY	Vessel	9079080
NAINITAL [×]	NATIONAL IRANIAN TANKER COMPANY	Vessel	9079092

NATIVE LAND ×	NATIONAL IRANIAN TANKER COMPANY	Vessel	9079107
ATLANTIC ×	NATIONAL IRANIAN TANKER COMPANY	Vessel	9107655
SPARROW ×	NATIONAL IRANIAN TANKER COMPANY	Vessel	9171450
SWALLOW ×	NATIONAL IRANIAN TANKER COMPANY	Vessel	9171462
SUPERIOR ×	NATIONAL IRANIAN TANKER COMPANY	Vessel	9172038
SPOTLESS ×	NATIONAL IRANIAN TANKER COMPANY	Vessel	9172040
SABRINA ×	NATIONAL IRANIAN TANKER COMPANY	Vessel	9172052
DESTINY ×	NATIONAL IRANIAN TANKER COMPANY	Vessel	9177155
HUMANITY ×	NATIONAL IRANIAN TANKER COMPANY	Vessel	9180281
ORIENTAL ×	NATIONAL IRANIAN TANKER COMPANY	Vessel	9183934
SHONA ×	NATIONAL IRANIAN TANKER COMPANY	Vessel	9187629
ABELIA ×	NATIONAL IRANIAN TANKER COMPANY	Vessel	9187631
ALERT ×	NATIONAL IRANIAN TANKER COMPANY	Vessel	9187643
SUNDIAL ×	NATIONAL IRANIAN TANKER COMPANY	Vessel	9187655
SILVER CLOUD ×	NATIONAL IRANIAN TANKER COMPANY	Vessel	9187667
HUWAYZEH ×	NATIONAL IRANIAN TANKER COMPANY	Vessel	9212888
HORIZON ×	NATIONAL IRANIAN TANKER COMPANY	Vessel	9212890
HAPPINESS ×	NATIONAL IRANIAN TANKER COMPANY	Vessel	9212905
MARINA ×	NATIONAL IRANIAN TANKER COMPANY	Vessel	9212917
HALISTIC ×	NATIONAL IRANIAN TANKER COMPANY	Vessel	9212929
DELVAR ×	NATIONAL IRANIAN TANKER COMPANY	Vessel	9218454
DAYLAM ×	NATIONAL IRANIAN TANKER COMPANY	Vessel	9218466
DAMAVAND ×	NATIONAL IRANIAN TANKER COMPANY	Vessel	9218478
DENA ×	NATIONAL IRANIAN TANKER COMPANY	Vessel	9218480
DARAB ×	NATIONAL IRANIAN TANKER COMPANY	Vessel	9218492
IRAN FAZEL ×	NATIONAL IRANIAN TANKER COMPANY	Vessel	9283746
FIANGA ×	NATIONAL IRANIAN TANKER COMPANY	Vessel	9283760
IRAN FAHIM ×	NATIONAL IRANIAN TANKER COMPANY	Vessel	9286140
IRAN FALAGH ×	NATIONAL IRANIAN TANKER COMPANY	Vessel	9286152
DECESIVE ×	NATIONAL IRANIAN TANKER COMPANY	Vessel	9356593
SANCHI ×	NATIONAL IRANIAN TANKER COMPANY	Vessel	9356608
MAJESTIC ×	NATIONAL IRANIAN TANKER COMPANY	Vessel	9357183
SUCCESS ×	NATIONAL IRANIAN TANKER COMPANY	Vessel	9357353
SUNEAST ×	NATIONAL IRANIAN TANKER COMPANY	Vessel	9357365
SPLENDOUR ×	NATIONAL IRANIAN TANKER COMPANY	Vessel	9357377
COURAGE ×	NATIONAL IRANIAN TANKER COMPANY	Vessel	9357389
HONESTY ×	NATIONAL IRANIAN TANKER COMPANY	Vessel	9357391
AMBER ×	NATIONAL IRANIAN TANKER COMPANY	Vessel	9357406
DAL LAKE ×	NATIONAL IRANIAN TANKER COMPANY	Vessel	9357717
JUSTICE ×	NATIONAL IRANIAN TANKER COMPANY	Vessel	9357729

HYDRA [×]	NATIONAL IRANIAN TANKER COMPANY	Vessel	9362059
DOVE [×]	NATIONAL IRANIAN TANKER COMPANY	Vessel	9362061
ZEUS [×]	NATIONAL IRANIAN TANKER COMPANY	Vessel	9362073
IMICO NEKA 455 [×]	NATIONAL IRANIAN TANKER COMPANY	Vessel	9404546
IMICO NEKA 456 [×]	NATIONAL IRANIAN TANKER COMPANY	Vessel	9404558
IMICO NEKA 457 [×]	NATIONAL IRANIAN TANKER COMPANY	Vessel	9404560
SUNSHINE [×]	NATIONAL IRANIAN TANKER COMPANY	Vessel	9569205
DOJRAN [×]	NATIONAL IRANIAN TANKER COMPANY	Vessel	9569619
ATLANTIS [×]	NATIONAL IRANIAN TANKER COMPANY	Vessel	9569621
FORTUN [×]	NATIONAL IRANIAN TANKER COMPANY	Vessel	9569633
SALALEH [×]	NATIONAL IRANIAN TANKER COMPANY	Vessel	9569645
SMOOTH [×]	NATIONAL IRANIAN TANKER COMPANY	Vessel	9569657
SKYLINE [×]	NATIONAL IRANIAN TANKER COMPANY	Vessel	9569669
INFINITY [×]	NATIONAL IRANIAN TANKER COMPANY	Vessel	9569671
DEMOS [×]	NATIONAL IRANIAN TANKER COMPANY	Vessel	9569683
YANGZHOU DAYANG DY905 [×]	NATIONAL IRANIAN TANKER COMPANY	Vessel	9575424
SUNRISE [×]	NATIONAL IRANIAN TANKER COMPANY	Vessel	9615092
ANTHEM	SIQIRIYA MARITIME CORP	Vessel	8310669
JAFFNA	SIQIRIYA MARITIME CORP	Vessel	8609515
OLYSA	SIQIRIYA MARITIME CORP	Vessel	9001605

ATTACHMENT 4

ABBASI-DAVANI, Fereidoun
ADVANCE ELECTRICAL AND INDUSTRIAL TECHNOLOGIES SL
ALUMINAT
ANDISHEH ZOLAL
ARIA NIKAN MARINE INDUSTRY
BUJAR, Farhad
DAYENI, Mahmoud Mohammadi
EYVAZ TECHNIC MANUFACTURING COMPANY
FAKHRIZADEH-MAHABADI, Mohsen
FARATECH
FARAYAND TECHNIQUE
FULMEN GROUP
IMANIRAD, Arman
IMANIRAD, Mohammad Javad
IRAN CENTRIFUGE TECHNOLOGY COMPANY
IRAN POOYA
JAHAN TECH ROOYAN PARS
JAVEDAN MEHR TOOS
KAHVARIN, Iradj Mohammadi
KALAYE ELECTRIC COMPANY

KHAKI, Parviz
MANDEGAR BASPAR KIMIYA COMPANY
MARO SANAT COMPANY
MODERN INDUSTRIES TECHNIQUE COMPANY
NEDA INDUSTRIAL GROUP
NEKA NOVIN
PARTO SANAT CO.
PAYA PARTOV CO.
PENTANE CHEMISTRY INDUSTRIES
PETRO GREEN
PISHRO SYSTEMS RESEARCH COMPANY
POUYA CONTROL
PUNTI, Pere
RAHIMYAR, Amir Hossein
SIMATIC DEVELOPMENT CO.
TAGHTIRAN KASHAN COMPANY
TANIDEH, Hossein
TARH O PALAYESH
THE ORGANIZATION OF DEFENSIVE INNOVATION AND RESEARCH
TOWLID ABZAR BORESHI IRAN
WISSER, Gerhard
YASA PART
ZOLAL IRAN COMPANY

JCPOA Annex III - Civil Nuclear Cooperation

A. General

1. Iran and E3/EU+3 decided to co-operate, among others, including through IAEA technical cooperation, where appropriate, and without prejudice to the existing bilateral agreements, in different areas of civil nuclear co-operation to be developed within the framework of this JCPOA, as detailed in this Annex. In this context, the Joint Commission will also support assistance to Iran, including through IAEA technical cooperation projects, as appropriate.

2. All civil nuclear cooperation projects under this JCPOA will be mutually determined by the participating states and will be consistent with the JCPOA and the national laws and regulations of the participating parties.

3. The civil nuclear and scientific cooperation projects envisioned between Iran and the E3/EU+3 as part of this JCPOA may be undertaken in a variety of formats, with a variety of potential participants. A given project undertaken by the E3/EU+3 will not necessarily include participation by all E3/EU+3 parties:

3.1. bilateral or multilateral cooperation arrangements with Iran. Such arrangements would be mutually determined by the participating states.

3.2. projects under the auspices of the IAEA, either through IAEA technical co-operation projects including through Project and Supply Agreements.

3.3. through International Science and Technology Centres.

Specifically, E3/EU+3 parties will undertake, to develop nuclear co-operation with Iran, in particular within the following areas:

B. Reactors, Fuels and Associated Technologies, Facilities and Processes

4. Modern light water power and research reactors and associated equipment, technologies and facilities

E3/EU+3 parties, as appropriate, will facilitate Iran's acquisition of light-water research and power reactors, for research, development and testing, and for the supply of electricity and desalination, with arrangements for the assured supply of nuclear fuel and the removal of spent fuel as provided for in relevant contracts, for each reactor provided. This may include the following areas for co-operation:

4.1. Construction as well as effective and safe operation of new light water power reactors and associated equipment, according to Generation III+ requirements, including small and medium sized nuclear reactors, including joint design and manufacturing, as appropriate.

4.2. Construction of state of the art light water moderated multipurpose research reactors capable of testing fuel pins, assembly prototypes and structural materials with associated related facilities, including joint design and manufacturing, as appropriate.

4.3. Supply of state-of-the-art instrumentation and control systems for the above research and power reactors, including joint design and manufacturing, as appropriate;

4.4. Supply of nuclear simulation and calculation codes and software solutions with regard to the above areas, including joint development, as appropriate;

4.5. Supply of first and second loop main equipment as well as core of the above research and power reactors, including joint design and manufacturing, as appropriate;

4.6. On-the-job training on fuel management scenarios and reshuffling for the above research and power nuclear reactors;

4.7. Joint technical review of Iran's current nuclear reactors, upon the request by Iran, in order to upgrade current equipment and systems, including concerning nuclear safety;

5. Arak Modernisation Project

5.1. As described in Section B of Annex I, an international partnership composed of E3/EU+3 parties and Iran, which may subsequently be enlarged to include mutually determined third countries will be established, to support and facilitate the redesign and rebuilding of the IR-40 reactor at Arak into a modernised, not exceeding 20MWth, heavy-water moderated and cooled research reactor, based on the agreed conceptual design (as attached to Annex I).

5.2. Iran will take the leadership role as the owner and as the project manager, and have responsibility for overall implementation of the Arak modernisation project. A Working Group composed of E3/EU+3 participants will be established to support and facilitate the redesigning and rebuilding of the reactor. An international partnership composed of Iran and the Working Group would implement the Arak modernisation project, with E3/EU+3 participants assuming responsibilities as described in Annex I. The Working Group could be enlarged to include other countries by consensus of the participants of the Working Group and Iran. E3/EU+3 participants and Iran will conclude an official document expressing their strong commitments to the Arak modernisation project in advance of Implementation Day which would provide an assured path forward to modernise the reactor and would define the responsibilities assumed by the E3/EU+3 participants, especially in the key areas such as redesign, design review and certification, reactor core manufacturing, fuel design, fabrication and supply, safety and security, spent fuel treatment or disposition, as well as concerning the supply of materials, equipment, instrumentation and control systems, and subsequently contracts would be concluded. The participants of the Working Group will provide assistance needed by Iran for redesigning and rebuilding the reactor, consistent with their respective national laws, in such a manner as to enable the safe and timely construction and commissioning of the modernised reactor.

5.3. Iran and the Working Group will cooperate to develop the final design of the modernised reactor and the design of the subsidiary laboratories to be carried out by Iran, and review conformity with international safety standards, such that the reactor can be licensed by the relevant Iranian regulatory authority for commissioning and operation.

5.4. Iran will continue to assume the primary responsibility for financing the modernisation project. Additional funding arrangements for the project, including for IAEA projects supporting the Arak modernisation project, will be determined based on the official document and contracts to be subsequently concluded.

6. **Nuclear Fuel**

6.1. E3/EU+3 parties, as appropriate, will support assistance to Iran, including through the IAEA, as appropriate, in meeting international qualification standards for nuclear fuel fabricated by Iran.

6.2. E3/EU+3 parties will seek to cooperate regarding the supply of modern fuels, including, as appropriate, joint design and fabrication, the relevant licenses and fabrication technologies and equipment and related infrastructure, for current and future nuclear research and power reactors, including technical assistance on purification processes, forming and metallurgical activities for different types of nuclear fuel clads and cladding for the modernised Arak heavy water research reactor.

C. **Research and Development (R&D) Practices**

7. To implement other aspects of this JCPOA and in support of a broader opening of scientific engagements between the E3/EU+3 and Iran, the E3/EU+3 and Iran will seek cooperation and scientific exchange in the field of nuclear science and technology:

7.1. Accelerator-based nuclear physics and nuclear astrophysics research, and stable isotope production in international collaboration at the nuclear, physics, and technology centre at the Fordow facility. Iran will request from the E3/EU+3 and other interested parties specific proposals for cooperative international nuclear, physics, and technology projects and will host an international workshop to review these proposals. The goal is to realise international collaborative projects within a few years. The transitioning to stable isotope production of two cascades will be conducted in a joint partnership between the Russian Federation and Iran on the basis of arrangements to be mutually agreed upon.

7.2. Plasma physics and nuclear fusion;

7.3. Research reactor applications at the TRR, modernized Arak reactor, or at other future research reactors in Iran, such as:

7.3.1. Training

7.3.2. Radio-isotope production and utilization

7.3.3. Nuclear desalination

7.3.4. Neutron transmutation doping

7.3.5. Neutron activation analysis

7.3.6. Neutron capture therapy

7.3.7. Neutron imaging and materials characterization studies using neutron beams

7.4. E3/EU+3 parties and Iran could also explore co-operation in the following additional areas:

7.4.1. Design, manufacture and/or assembly of in-core measuring instrumentation and technologies;

7.4.2. Nuclear instrumentation and control, systems and electronics design, manufacture and/or assembly;

7.4.3. Fusion technology and plasma physics and related infrastructure and facilitating contribution of Iran to the International Thermonuclear Experimental Reactor (ITER) Project and/or similar projects, including relevant IAEA technical cooperation projects;

7.4.4. Neutrino astronomy;

7.4.5. Design and manufacturing, and supply, of different types of accelerators and supply of related equipment including through relevant IAEA technical cooperation projects;

7.4.6. Data acquisition and processing software and interface equipment;

D. Nuclear Safety, Safeguards and Security

8. Nuclear safety

E3/EU+3 parties, and possibly other states, as appropriate, are prepared to cooperate with Iran to establish a Nuclear Safety Centre in Iran, engage in workshops and training events in Iran to support interactions between Iranian nuclear regulatory authorities and those from the E3/EU+3 and elsewhere to, among other things, share lessons learned on establishing and maintaining regulatory independence and effectiveness, and training on implementing nuclear safety culture and best practices; facilitate exchanges and visits to nuclear regulatory authorities and nuclear power plants outside of Iran focusing on best practices for safe operation; and enhance and strengthen domestic emergency preparedness and severe accident management capability.

Provide support and assistance to enable Iran to join relevant conventions on nuclear safety and security, e.g. through workshops or seminars furthering accession to such commitments. Such workshops or seminars could also take place under the auspices of the IAEA.

E3/EU+3 parties, and possibly other states, as appropriate, will co-operate with Iran in the following areas of nuclear safety, as well as in other areas to be mutually agreed:

8.1. Conclusion of bilateral/multilateral agreements with related organisations and research centres;

8.2. Supply of valid codes, instruments and equipment related to nuclear safety;

8.3. Facilitate exchange of knowledge and experience in the area of nuclear safety;

8.4. Enhance and strengthen domestic emergency preparedness and severe accident management capability;

8.5. Arrange on-the-job training and apprenticeship courses for reactor and facility operators, regulatory authority personnel and related supportive organizations in the area of nuclear safety inside and outside of Iran;

8.6. Establish a Nuclear Safety Centre in Iran, which shall be equipped with necessary tools, techniques and equipment, in order to support and facilitate technical and professional training and exchange of lessons-learned for reactor and facility operators, regulatory authority personnel and related supportive organizations;

9. Nuclear Safeguards

E3/EU+3 parties, and possibly other states, as appropriate, are prepared to cooperate with Iran on the effective and efficient implementation of IAEA safeguards and transparency measures in Iran. Co-operation in the following areas can be envisaged:

9.1. Cooperation in the form of on-the-job trainings and workshops to strengthen nuclear material accounting and control process, human resource development, and quality assurance/quality control processes;

9.2. E3/EU+3 parties, and other states, as appropriate, are prepared to cooperate with Iran for the effective and efficient implementation of IAEA safeguards and transparency measures in Iran.

9.3. This cooperation could take the form of training and workshops to strengthen Iran's safeguards regulatory authority, nuclear material accounting and control processes, human resource development, and quality assurance/quality control processes.

10. Nuclear Security

E3/EU+3 parties, and possibly other states, as appropriate, are prepared to cooperate with Iran on the implementation of nuclear security guidelines and best practices. Co-operation in the following areas can be envisaged:

10.1. Co-operation in the form of training courses and workshops to strengthen Iran's ability to prevent, protect and respond to nuclear security threats to nuclear facilities and systems as well as to enable effective and sustainable nuclear security and physical protection systems;

10.2. Co-operation through training and workshops to strengthen Iran's ability to protect against, and respond to nuclear security threats, including sabotage, as well as to enable effective and sustainable nuclear security and physical protection systems.

E. Nuclear Medicine and Radioisotopes, Associated Technologies, Facilities and Processes

11. E3/EU+3 parties, as appropriate, are prepared to cooperate with Iran to improve the utilization of nuclear medicine in Iran in order to enhance Iran's expertise in diagnostic imaging and radiotherapy, increase the availability of medical radioisotopes for diagnosis and treatment of Iranian citizens, and facilitate Iran's participation in the broader international scientific and nuclear medicine community. Such cooperation may include:

11.1. Upgrades to the infrastructure associated with existing cyclotron facilities, including for medical radioisotopes production.

11.2. Facilitating Iranian acquisition of a new cyclotron, and associated radio-pharmacy equipment, for medical radioisotopes production.

11.3. Acquisition of state-of-the-art diagnostic imaging and radiotherapy equipment for existing or new nuclear medicine centers, including co-operation between hospitals for the treatment of individual patients.

11.4. Cooperation on occupational and patient dosimetry procedures.

11.5. Improved target utilization to increase radioisotope production.

11.6. Acquisition of radioisotope sources for bracho therapy, and radiotherapy instrument calibration, and other medical and industrial applications.

11.7. Supply of state-of-the art radio-medicine center and necessary laboratories.

F. Waste Management and Facility Decommissioning

12. E3/EU+3 parties, as appropriate, are prepared to cooperate with Iran in the safe, effective, and efficient management and disposition of nuclear and radiological wastes derived from Iran's nuclear fuel cycle activities and nuclear medicine, radioisotope production and/or consumption activities.

13. E3/EU+3 parties, as appropriate, are prepared to cooperate with Iran in areas of safe, effective, and environmentally friendly best practices for facility decontamination and decommissioning, including co-operation on long term storage facilities for the repository of low and medium level waste.

14. E3/EU+3 parties, as appropriate, are prepared to facilitate exchanges and visits to relevant sites and locations outside of Iran related to effective waste management and best practices.

15. E3/EU+3 parties, as appropriate, will facilitate the supply of appropriate equipment and systems for waste management and depository facilities in Iran.

G. Other projects

16. Other projects may be implemented between the relevant E3/EU+3 parties and Iran, as mutually determined by the participants in the JCPOA, including in the following areas:

16.1. Construction of nuclear desalination and associated infrastructure in Iran;

16.2. Development of laser technology for medical applications (e.g. for eye surgery);

JCPOA Annex IV – Joint Commission

1. Establishment, Composition, and Coordinator

1.1. The Joint Commission is established to carry out the functions assigned to it in the JCPOA, including its Annexes.

1.2. The Joint Commission is comprised of representatives of Iran and the E3/EU+3 (China, France, Germany, the Russian Federation, the United Kingdom, and the United States, with the High Representative of the Union for Foreign Affairs and Security Policy), together, the JCPOA participants.

1.3. The Joint Commission may establish Working Groups in particular areas, as appropriate.

1.4. The High Representative of the Union for Foreign Affairs and Security Policy ('High Representative'), or his/her designated representative will serve as the Coordinator of the Joint Commission.

2. Functions

2.1. The Joint Commission will perform the following functions:

2.1.1. Review and approve the final design for the modernized heavy water research reactor and the design of the subsidiary laboratories prior to the commencement of construction, and review and approve the fuel design for the modernized heavy water research reactor as provided for in Section B of Annex I;

2.1.2. Review and approve, upon request by Iran, development, acquisition, construction or operation of hot cells (containing a cell or interconnected cells), shielded cells or shielded glove boxes with dimensions beyond 6 cubic meters in volume and specifications set out in Annex I of the Additional Protocol, as provided for in paragraph 21 of Annex I;

2.1.3. Review and approve plans submitted by Iran to initiate R&D on uranium metal based TRR fuel, as provided for in paragraph 26 of Annex I;

2.1.4. Review and approve, upon request by Iran, projects on new types of centrifuges to proceed to a prototype stage for mechanical testing, as provided for in paragraph 43 of Annex I;

2.1.5. Receive information in advance about the specific projects that will be undertaken at Fordow, as provided for in paragraph 44 of Annex I;

2.1.6. Receive information about the conceptual framework of stable isotope production at Fordow, as provided for in paragraph 46.1 of Annex I;

2.1.7. Assess and then approve, upon request by Iran, that fuel assemblies manufactured in Iran and their intermediate products cannot be readily reconverted into UF6, based on the objective technical criteria, with the goal of enabling fuel to be fabricated in Iran, as provided in paragraph 59 of Annex I;

2.1.8. Support assistance to Iran, including through IAEA technical cooperation as appropriate, in meeting international qualification standards for nuclear fuel produced by Iran, as provided for in paragraph 59 of Annex I;

2.1.9. Review and approve in advance, upon request by Iran, engagement by Iran, including through export of any enrichment or enrichment related equipment and technology, with any other country, or with any foreign entity in enrichment and enrichment related activities, including related research and development, as provided for in paragraph 73 in Annex I;

2.1.10. Provide consultation, and advise on the necessary means in the context of access as specified in paragraph 78 of Annex I;

2.1.11. Review and approve in advance, upon request by Iran, the design, development, fabrication, acquisition, or use for non-nuclear purposes of multi-point explosive detonation systems suitable for a nuclear explosive device and explosive diagnostic systems (streak cameras, framing cameras and flash x-ray cameras) suitable for the development of a nuclear explosive device, as provided for in paragraphs 82.2 and 82.3 of Annex I;

2.1.12. Review and consult to address issues arising from the implementation of sanctions lifting as specified in this JCPOA and its Annex II;

2.1.13. Review and decide on proposals for nuclear-related transfers to or activities with, Iran, in accordance with Section 6 of this Annex and the United Nations Security Council resolution endorsing this JCPOA;

2.1.14. Review, with a view to resolving, any issue that a JCPOA participant believes constitutes nonperformance by another JCPOA participant of its commitments under the JCPOA, according to the process outlined in the JCPOA;

2.1.15. Adopt or modify, as necessary, procedures to govern its activities;

2.1.16. Consult and provide guidance on other implementation matters that may arise under the JCPOA.

3. **Procedures**

3.1. The Joint Commission will meet on a quarterly basis and at any time upon request of a JCPOA participant to the Coordinator. The Coordinator will convene a meeting of the Joint Commission to be held no later than one week following receipt of such a request, except for consultations in accordance with Section Q of Annex I and any other matter that the Coordinator and/or a JCPOA participant deem urgent, in which case the meeting will be convened as soon as possible and not later than three calendar days from receipt of the request.

3.2. Meetings of the Joint Commission will be held in New York, Vienna, or Geneva as appropriate. The host country should facilitate entry formalities for those attending such meetings.

3.3. The Joint Commission may decide by consensus to invite observers to attend its meetings.

3.4. Except as provided in Section 6 of this Annex which will be subject to the confidentiality procedure of the UN, the work of the Joint Commission is confidential and may be shared only among JCPOA participants and observers as appropriate, unless the Joint Commission decides otherwise.

4. **Decisions**

4.1. Except as stated otherwise in this Annex, decisions by the Joint Commission are to be made by consensus.

4.2. Each JCPOA participant will have one vote. Decisions of the Joint Commission are to be taken by the Representative or the Deputy Representative or other such alternate as the JCPOA participant may designate.

4.3. The vote of each JCPOA participant will be made known to all other JCPOA participants if any JCPOA participant requests a recorded vote.

4.4. Matters before the Joint Commission pursuant to Section Q of Annex I are to be decided by consensus or by affirmative vote of five JCPOA participants. There is no quorum requirement.

4.5. The Coordinator will not take part in decision-making on nuclear-related transfers and activities as set out in Section 6 of this Annex.

5. **Other**

5.1. Each JCPOA participant will be responsible for its own costs of participating in the Joint Commission, unless the Joint Commission decides otherwise.

5.2. JCPOA participants may request that the Coordinator circulates a notification to the other JCPOA participants at any time. Upon such a request, the Coordinator will circulate such notification without delay to all JCPOA participants.

6. **Procurement Working Group**

6.1. With the purpose of establishing a procurement channel, the Joint Commission will, except as otherwise provided by the United Nations Security Council resolution endorsing this JCPOA, review and decide on proposals by states seeking to engage in:

6.1.1. the supply, sale or transfer directly or indirectly from their territories, or by their nationals or using their flag vessels or aircraft to, or for the use in or benefit of, Iran, and whether or not originating in their territories, of all items, materials, equipment, goods and technology set out in INFCIRC/254/Rev.12/Part 1, and, if the end-use will be for Iran's nuclear programme set out in this JCPOA or other non-nuclear civilian end-use, all items, materials, equipment, goods and technology set out in INFCIRC/254/Rev.9/Part 2 (or the most recent version of these documents as updated by the Security Council), as well as any further items if the relevant State determines that they could contribute to activities inconsistent with the JCPOA; and,

6.1.2. the provision to Iran of any technical assistance or training, financial assistance, investment, brokering or other services related to the supply, sale, transfer, manufacture, or use of the items, materials, equipment, goods and technology described in subparagraph (a) above;

6.1.3. acquisition by Iran of an interest in a commercial activity in another State involving uranium mining, production or use of nuclear materials and technologies as listed in INFCIRC/254/Rev.12/Part 1, and such investments in territories under their jurisdiction by Iran, its nationals, and entities incorporated in Iran or subject to its jurisdiction, or by individuals or entities acting on their behalf or direction, or by entities owned or controlled by them.

6.2. The Joint Commission will discharge its responsibility for reviewing and making recommendations on proposals for nuclear-related transfers to or activities with Iran through a Procurement Working Group.

6.3. Each E3+3 State and Iran will participate in the Procurement Working Group. The High Representative will serve as the Coordinator of the Procurement Working Group.

6.4. Except as otherwise provided by the Joint Commission or the United Nations Security Council resolution endorsing this JCPOA, the Procurement Working Group will consider proposals according to the following process:

6.4.1. Upon receipt of a proposal, including all necessary supporting information, by a State seeking to engage in transfers and activities referenced in Section 6.1, the Coordinator will forward the proposal, through appropriate means, without delay to the Procurement Working Group and, when the proposal relates to items, material, equipment, goods and technology intended to be used in nuclear activities authorized by the JCPOA, to the IAEA. The Procurement Working Group will have up to 30 working days to consider and decide on the proposal.

6.4.2. "Necessary supporting information" for purposes of Section 6.4.1 means: (a) a description of the item; (b) the name, address, telephone number, and email address of the exporting entity; (c) the name, address, telephone number, and email address of the importing entity; (d) a statement of the proposed end-use and end use location, along with an end-use certification signed by the AEOI or the appropriate authority of Iran attesting the stated end-use; (e) export license number if available; (f) contract date, if available; and (g) details on transportation, if available; provided that if any of the export license number, contract date, or details on transportation are not available as of the time of submittal of the proposal, such information will be provided as soon as possible and in any event as condition of approval prior to shipment of the item.

6.4.3. Each participant in the Procurement Working Group will have to communicate to the Coordinator, within 20 working days, whether it approves or rejects the proposal. The timeline for consideration may be extended for an additional period of 10 working days at the request of a participant of the Procurement Working Group.

6.4.4. The proposal will be recommended for approval as soon as the Coordinator receives formal approvals from all the Procurement Working Group Participants or if, at the end of the 30 working day period, the Coordinator has received no disapprovals from any of the Procurement Working Group Participants. If at the end of the 30 working day period, the proposal has not been recommended for approval, the proposal may, at the request of at least two Working Group Participants within 5 working days, be referred to the Joint Commission, which would decide on approval of the proposal by consensus within 10 working days. Otherwise the proposal will be recommended for disapproval. The disapproving JCPOA participant(s) should provide relevant information regarding the disapproval to the Joint Commission as appropriate, taking into account the need to protect confidential information.

6.4.5. The Coordinator will communicate the recommendation of the Joint Commission to the United Nations Security Council no later than 35 working days, or in case of referral to the Joint Commission no later than 45 working days from the date the Coordinator transmitted the proposal and all necessary supporting information to the Procurement Working Group.

6.4.6. Except as decided otherwise by consensus, the Procurement Working Group will meet every three weeks for reviewing the proposals. When some of the proposals to be reviewed relate to items, material, equipment, goods and technology intended to be used in nuclear activities authorized by the JCPOA, the IAEA may be invited to attend the meeting as an observer.

6.5. All JCPOA participants will act in accordance with the procurement channel and will only engage in transfers and activities referenced in Section 6.1 following approval by the Joint Commission and the United Nations Security Council. Iran will not use, acquire, or seek to procure the items, materials, equipment, goods, and technology referred to in Section 6.1 of this Annex for nuclear activities which are inconsistent with this JCPOA.

6.6. Any JCPOA participant may refer a procurement-related activity to the Joint Commission under the dispute settlement mechanism if it is concerned that such activity is inconsistent with this JCPOA.

6.7. Iran will provide to the IAEA access to the locations of intended use of all items, materials, equipment, goods and technology set out in INFCIRC/254/Rev.12/Part 1 (or the most recent version of these documents as updated by the Security Council) imported following the procedure under Section 6 of this Annex.

6.8. Iran will permit the exporting state to verify the end-use of all items, materials, equipment, goods and technology set out in INFCIRC/254/Rev.9/Part 2 (or the most recent version of these documents as updated by the Security Council) imported following the procedure under Section 6 of this Annex. Upon request of the exporting state, or if the Joint Commission deems necessary when approving a proposal for transfer, the Joint Commission will provide expertise to the exporting state, including experts, as needed, to participate in the end-use verification.

6.9. The Procurement Working Group will respond to requests for guidance on procurement activities from third parties, as communicated by the Coordinator. The Procurement Working Group will endeavor to respond to such requests for guidance within 9 working days from the date the Coordinator submits it to the Procurement Working Group.

6.10. The Joint Commission will report to the United Nations Security Council at least every 6 months on the status of the Procurement Working Group's decisions and on any implementation issues.

7. Working Group on Implementation of Sanctions Lifting

7.1. The Joint Commission will discharge its responsibilities for reviewing and consulting on issues related to the implementation of sanctions lifting as specified in this JCPOA assisted by a working group on the implementation of sanctions lifting.

7.2. The Joint Commission participants will participate in this working group. The High Representative will serve as coordinator of this working group.

7.3. If at any time following the implementation day Iran believes that any other nuclear-related sanction or restrictive measure including related designations of the E3/EU+3 is preventing the full implementation of the sanctions lifting as specified in this JCPOA, the JCPOA participant in question will consult with Iran with a view to resolving the issue. If they are not able to resolve the issue, Iran or any member of the E3/EU+3 may refer the issue to the working group.

7.4. The participants of the working group will review and consult, with a view to resolving the issue within 30 working days.

7.5. If after involvement of the working group, the issue remains unresolved, any participant of the JCPOA may refer it to the Joint Commission.

JCPOA Annex V - Implementation Plan[354]

1. This Annex describes the sequence of the actions specified in Annexes I and II to this JCPOA.

A. <u>Finalisation Day</u>

2. Upon conclusion of the negotiations of this JCPOA, the E3/EU+3 (China, France, Germany, the Russian Federation, the United Kingdom and the United States, with the High Representative of the European Union for Foreign Affairs and Security Policy) and Iran will endorse this JCPOA.

3. Promptly after the conclusion of the negotiations of this JCPOA, the proposed UN Security Council resolution referred to in Section 18 of this Annex will be submitted to the UN Security Council for adoption without delay.

[354] This Annex is only for the purpose of determining the sequence of implementation of the commitments described in this JCPOA and annexes thereto and does not restrict or expand the scope of these commitments.

4. The EU will promptly endorse the UN Security Council resolution referred to above through Council Conclusions.

5. Iran and the IAEA will start developing necessary arrangements to implement all transparency measures provided for in this JCPOA so that such arrangements are completed, in place, and ready for implementation on Implementation Day.

B. Adoption Day

6. Adoption Day will occur 90 days after the endorsement of this JCPOA by the UN Security Council through the resolution referred to above, or at an earlier date by mutual consent of all JCPOA participants, at which point this JCPOA comes into effect.

7. Beginning on Adoption Day, JCPOA participants will make necessary arrangements and preparations, including legal and administrative preparations, for the implementation of their JCPOA commitments.

8. Iran will officially inform the IAEA that, effective on Implementation Day, Iran will provisionally apply the Additional Protocol, pending its ratification by the Majlis (Parliament), and will fully implement the modified code 3.1.

9. Iran will implement paragraph 66 from Section M on "Past and Present Issues of Concern" of Annex I.

10. The EU and its Member States will adopt an EU Regulation, taking effect as of Implementation Day, terminating all provisions of the EU Regulation implementing all nuclear-related economic and financial EU sanctions as specified in Section 16.1 of this Annex, simultaneously with the IAEA-verified implementation by Iran of agreed nuclear-related measures.

11. The United States, acting pursuant to Presidential authorities, will issue waivers, to take effect upon Implementation Day, ceasing the application of the statutory nuclear-related sanctions as specified in Sections 17.1 to 17.2 of this Annex. The President will also take action to direct that all appropriate additional measures be taken to implement the cessation of application of sanctions as specified in Sections 17.1 to 17.4 of this Annex, including the termination of Executive orders as specified in Section 17.4, and the licensing of activities as specified in Section 17.5.

12. E3/EU+3 participants and Iran will begin discussions on an official document to be concluded in advance of Implementation Day which will express strong commitments of the E3/EU+3 participants to the Arak Heavy Water Reactor modernisation project and define the responsibilities assumed by the E3/EU+3 participants.

13. The EU, its Member States and the United States will begin consultation as appropriate with Iran regarding relevant guidelines and publicly accessible statements on the details of sanctions or restrictive measures to be lifted under this JCPOA.

C. Implementation Day

14. Implementation Day will occur upon the IAEA-verified implementation by Iran of the nuclear-related measures described in paragraph 15 below, and, simultaneously, the E3/EU+3 taking the actions described in paragraphs 16 and 17 below, and with the actions described in paragraph 18 below taking place at the UN level in accordance with the UN Security Council resolution.

15. **Iran will implement the nuclear-related measures as specified in Annex I:**

15.1. Paragraphs 3 and 10 from Section B on "Arak Heavy Water Research Reactor";

15.2. Paragraphs 14 and 15 from Section C on "Heavy Water Production Plant";

15.3. Paragraphs 27, 28, 29, 29.1 and 29.2 from Section F on "Enrichment Capacity";

15.4. Paragraphs 32, 33, 34, 35, 36, 37, 38, 39, 40, 41 and 42 from Section G on "Centrifuges Research and Development";

15.5. Paragraphs 45, 46, 46.1, 46.2, 47.1, 48.1 from Section H on "Fordow Fuel Enrichment Plant";

15.6. Paragraphs 52, 54 and 55 from Section I on "Other Aspects of Enrichment";

15.7. Paragraphs 57 and 58 from Section J on "Uranium Stocks and Fuels";

15.8. Paragraph 62 from Section K on "Centrifuge Manufacturing";

15.9. Complete the modalities and facilities-specific arrangements to allow the IAEA to implement all transparency measures provided for in Annex I;

15.10. Paragraphs 64 and 65 from Section L on "Additional Protocol and Modified Code 3.1";

15.11. Paragraphs 80.1 and 80.2 from Section R on "Centrifuge Component Manufacturing Transparency"; and

15.12. Within one year from Implementation Day, Iran will have completed the measures specified in paragraphs 47.2 and 48.2 of Section H on "Fordow Fuel Enrichment Plant".

16. **The European Union will:**

16.1. Terminate the provisions of Council Regulation (EU) No 267/2012 and suspend the corresponding provisions of Council Decision 2010/413/CFSP specified in Sections 1.1.1–1.1.3; 1.1.5–1.1.8; 1.2.1–1.2.5; 1.3.1, 1.3.2 (in so far as it concerns Articles 16 and 17 of Council Decision 2010/413/CFSP) and 1.3.3; 1.4.1 and 1.4.2; 1.10.1.2 (in so far as it concerns Articles 39, 43, 43a of Council Regulation (EU) No 267/2012) of Annex II. EU Member States will terminate or amend national implementing legislation as required.

16.2. Amend the provisions of Council Regulation (EU) No 267/2012 and the corresponding provisions of Council Decision 2010/413/CFSP specified in Sections 1.6.1–1.7.2 of Annex II, in connection with activities consistent with this JCPOA.

16.3. Remove individuals and entities set forth in Attachment 1 to Annex II of this JCPOA from Annexes VIII and IX to Council Regulation (EU) 267/2012. Suspend the provisions of Council Decision 2010/413/CFSP specified in Section 1.9.1 of Annex II in relation to individuals and entities set forth in Attachment 1 to Annex II.

16.4. Amend the provisions of Council Regulation (EU) No 267/2012 and Council Decision 2010/413/CFSP specified in Sections 1.5.1 and 1.5.2 of Annex II to implement the relevant provisions of the UN Security Council resolution referred to above.

17. **The United States will:**[355]

17.1. Cease the application of the sanctions set forth in Sections 4.1–4.5 and 4.7 of Annex II, with the exception of Section 211(a) of the Iran Threat Reduction and Syria Human Rights Act of 2012 (TRA);

17.2. Cease the application of the sanctions set forth in Section 4.6 of Annex II, in connection with activities consistent with this JCPOA, including trade with individuals and entities set forth in Attachment 3 to Annex II;

17.3. Remove individuals and entities set forth in Attachment 3 to Annex II from the Specially Designated Nationals and Blocked Persons List (SDN List), the Foreign Sanctions Evaders List (FSE List), and/or the Non-SDN Iran Sanctions Act List as set forth in Section 4.8.1 of Annex II;

17.4. Terminate Executive Orders 13574, 13590, 13622, 13645 and Sections 5–7 and 15 of Executive Order 13628 as set forth in Section 4 of Annex II; and

17.5. License activities as set forth in Section 5 of Annex II.

18. **UN Security Council**

18.1. In accordance with the UN Security Council resolution endorsing this JCPOA, the provisions imposed in UN Security Council resolutions 1696 (2006), 1737 (2006), 1747 (2007), 1803 (2008), 1835 (2008), 1929 (2010) and 2224 (2015) will be terminated subject to re-imposition in the event of significant

[355] The sanctions that the United States will cease to apply are those directed towards non-U.S. persons, as described in Section 4 of Annex II.

non-performance by Iran of JCPOA commitments, and specific restrictions, including restrictions regarding the transfer of proliferation sensitive goods will apply.[356]

18.2. The E3/EU+3 will take appropriate measures to implement the new UNSC resolution.

D. <u>Transition Day</u>

19. Transition Day will occur 8 years from Adoption Day or upon a report from the Director General of the IAEA to the IAEA Board of Governors and in parallel to the UN Security Council stating that the IAEA has reached the Broader Conclusion that all nuclear material in Iran remains in peaceful activities, whichever is earlier.

20. **The European Union will:**

20.1. Terminate the provisions of Council Regulation (EU) No 267/2012 and suspend the corresponding provisions of Council Decision 2010/413/CFSP specified in Sections 1.1.4, 1.3.2 (in so far as it concerns Articles 15 and 18 of Council Decision and Articles 36 and 37 of Council Regulation); 1.5.1 and 1.5.2 (in so far as it concerns Ballistic Missiles restrictions); 1.6.1–1.9.1 of Annex II.

20.2. Remove individuals and entities set forth in Attachment 2 to Annex II from Annexes VIII and IX to Council Regulation (EU) 267/2012.

20.3. Remove individuals and entities set forth in Attachment 1 to Annex II from Annexes I and II to Council Decision 2010/413/CFSP.

20.4. Terminate all provisions in Council Decision 2010/413/CFSP suspended on Implementation Day.

21. **The United States will:**

21.1. Seek such legislative action as may be appropriate to terminate, or modify to effectuate the termination of, the statutory sanctions set forth in Sections 4.1–4.5, 4.7 and 4.9 of Annex II;

21.2. Seek such legislative action as may be appropriate to terminate, or modify to effectuate the termination of, the statutory sanctions described in Section 4.6 of Annex II, in connection with activities consistent with this JCPOA, including trade with individuals and entities set forth in Attachments 3 and 4 to Annex II; and

21.3. Remove individuals and entities set out in Attachment 4 to Annex II from the SDN List and/or the FSE List as set forth in Section 4.8.1 of Annex II.

22. **Iran will:**

22.1. Seek, consistent with the Constitutional roles of the President and Parliament, ratification of the Additional Protocol.

E. <u>UNSCR Termination Day</u>

23. UNSCR (UN Security Council resolution) Termination Day will occur in accordance with the terms of the UN Security Council resolution endorsing the JCPOA, which is 10 years from Adoption Day, provided that the provisions of previous resolutions have not been reinstated.

24. On UNSCR Termination Day, the provisions and measures imposed in that resolution would terminate and the UN Security Council would no longer be seized of the Iran nuclear issue.

25. **The European Union will:**

25.1. Terminate all remaining provisions of Council Regulation (EU) No 267/2012 and Council Decision 2010/413/CFSP.

[356] The provisions of this Resolution do not constitute provisions of this JCPOA.

F. Other

26. The terminations described in this Annex V are without prejudice to other JCPOA commitments that would continue beyond such termination dates.

Annex B: Statement[357]

Statement

China, France, Germany, the Russian Federation, the United Kingdom, the United States, and the European Union have concluded with Iran a Joint Comprehensive Plan of Action (JCPOA) to reach a comprehensive, long-term and proper solution to the Iranian nuclear issue. To improve transparency and create an atmosphere conducive to the full implementation of the JCPOA, China, France, Germany, the Russian Federation, the United Kingdom, the United States, and the European Union have set forth below certain provisions. Their participation in the JCPOA is contingent upon the United Nations Security Council adopting a new resolution that would, acting under Article 41 of the UN Charter: terminate resolutions 1696 (2006), 1737 (2006), 1747 (2007), 1803 (2008), 1835 (2008), 1929 (2010), and 2224 (2015); require States to comply with the provisions in this statement for their respective durations; and facilitate, in cooperation with the Joint Commission established in the JCPOA, implementation of the JCPOA as provided in paragraphs 2 and 6(a) below.

As provided by a resolution so deciding, the following provisions would apply on the date on which the IAEA Director General submits a report verifying that Iran has taken the actions specified in paragraph 15.1–15.11 of Annex V of the JCPOA:

1. The term "all States" as used in this document, and as incorporated in the resolution, means "all States without exception."

2. All States may participate in and permit the following activities provided that approval is provided in advance, on a case-by-case basis, by the Security Council:

(a) the supply, sale or transfer directly or indirectly from their territories, or by their nationals or using their flag vessels or aircraft to, or for the use in or benefit of, Iran, and whether or not originating in their territories, of all items, materials, equipment, goods and technology set out in INFCIRC/254/Rev.12/Part 1 and INFCIRC/254/Rev.9/Part 2 (or the most recent versions of these documents, as updated by the Security Council), as well as any further items if the State determines that they could contribute to reprocessing or enrichment-related or heavy water-related activities inconsistent with the JCPOA;

(b) the provision to Iran of any technical assistance or training, financial assistance, investment, brokering or other services, and the transfer of financial resources or services, related to the supply, sale, transfer, manufacture or use of the items, materials, equipment, goods and technology described in subparagraph (a) above; and

(c) acquisition by Iran of an interest in a commercial activity in another State involving uranium mining or production or use of nuclear materials and technology as listed in INFCIRC/254/Rev.12/Part 1, and such investment in territories under their jurisdiction by Iran, its nationals, and entities incorporated in Iran or subject to its jurisdiction, or by individuals or entities acting on their behalf or at their direction, or by entities owned or controlled by them,

except that approval in advance by the Security Council shall not be required for the supply, sale, or transfer to Iran of equipment covered by B.1 of INFCIRC/254/Rev.12/Part 1 when such equipment is for light water reactors, low-enriched uranium covered by A.1.2 of INFCIRC/254/Rev.12/Part 1 when it is incorporated in assembled nuclear fuel elements for such reactors, as well as items, materials, equipment, goods and technology set out in INFCIRC/254/Rev.9/Part 2 only when for exclusive use in light water reactors.

[357] Circulated under the symbol S/2015/545.

For any items, materials, equipment, goods and technology that are approved by the Security Council pursuant to subparagraph (a) above, or are supplied, sold, or transferred subject to the exception stated above, States are to ensure that: (a) the requirements, as appropriate, of the Guidelines as set out in the referenced INFCIRC have been met; (b) they have obtained and are in a position to exercise effectively a right to verify the end-use and end-use location of any supplied item; (c) they notify the Security Council within ten days of the supply, sale or transfer; and (d) in the case of supplied items, materials, equipment, goods and technology listed in the referenced INFCIRCs, they also notify the IAEA within ten days of the supply, sale or transfer.

And except also that approval in advance by the Security Council is not required for the supply, sale, or transfer of items, materials, equipment, goods and technology, and the provision of any related technical assistance, training, financial assistance, investment, brokering or other services, that is directly related to the necessary modification of two cascades at the Fordow facility for stable isotope production, the export of Iran's enriched uranium in excess of 300 kilograms in return for natural uranium, and the modernization of the Arak reactor based on the agreed conceptual design and, subsequently, on the agreed final design of such reactor, provided that Member States ensure that: (a) all such activities are undertaken strictly in accordance with the JCPOA; (b) they notify the Security Council and Joint Commission ten days in advance of such activities; (c) the requirements, as appropriate, of the Guidelines as set out in the referenced INFCIRC have been met; (d) they have obtained and are in a position to exercise effectively a right to verify the end-use and end-use location of any supplied item; and (e) in case of supplied items, materials, equipment, goods and technology listed in the referenced INFCIRCs, they also notify the IAEA within ten days of the supply, sale or transfers.

This paragraph shall apply until the date ten years after JCPOA Adoption Day, as defined in the JCPOA, except if the IAEA submits a report confirming the Broader Conclusion before that date, then the requirement to obtain approval in advance by the Security Council shall be suspended immediately and, beginning on the date of this suspension, the exceptions provided for in this paragraph shall continue to apply and all States may participate in and permit the activities set forth in this paragraph if they notify the Security Council and the Joint Commission at least ten working days in advance of each such activity on a case-by-case basis.

3. Iran is called upon not to undertake any activity related to ballistic missiles designed to be capable of delivering nuclear weapons, including launches using such ballistic missile technology, until the date eight years after the JCPOA Adoption Day or until the date on which the IAEA submits a report confirming the Broader Conclusion, whichever is earlier.

4. All States may participate in and permit the activities described below *provided* that the Security Council decides in advance on a case-by-case basis to permit such activity:

   (a) the supply, sale or transfer directly or indirectly from their territories, or by their nationals or using their flag vessels or aircraft to or from Iran, or for the use in or benefit of Iran, and whether or not originating in their territories, of all items, materials, equipment, goods and technology set out in S/2015/546 and of any items, materials, equipment, goods and technology that the State determines could contribute to the development of nuclear weapon delivery systems; and

   (b) the provision to Iran of any technology or technical assistance or training, financial assistance, investment, brokering or other services, and the transfer of financial resources or services, or Iran's acquisition of an interest in any commercial activity in another State, related to the supply, sale, transfer, manufacture or use of the items, materials, equipment, goods and technology described in subparagraph a of this paragraph or related to the activities described in paragraph 3.

provided that in the event of an approval by the Security Council: (a) the contract for delivery of such items or assistance include appropriate end-user guarantees; and (b) Iran commit not to use such items for development of nuclear weapon delivery systems.

This paragraph shall apply until the date eight years after the JCPOA Adoption Day or until the date on which the IAEA submits a report confirming the Broader Conclusion, whichever is earlier.

5. All States may participate in and permit, *provided* that the Security Council decides in advance on a case-by-case basis to approve: the supply, sale or transfer directly or indirectly from or through their territories, or by their nationals or individuals subject to their jurisdiction, or using their flag vessels or aircraft, and whether or not originating in their territories, to Iran, or for the use in or benefit of Iran, of any battle tanks, armoured

combat vehicles, large caliber artillery systems, combat aircraft, attack helicopters, warships, missiles or missile systems, as defined for the purpose of the United Nations Register of Conventional Arms, or related materiel, including spare parts, and the provision to Iran by their nationals or from or through their territories of technical training, financial resources or services, advice, other services or assistance related to the supply, sale, transfer, manufacture, maintenance, or use of arms and related materiel described in this subparagraph.

This paragraph shall apply until the date five years after the JCPOA Adoption Day or until the date on which the IAEA submits a report confirming the Broader Conclusion, whichever is earlier.

6. All States are to:

(a) Take the necessary measures to ensure that any activities described in paragraphs 2, 4, and 5 occur on their territories, or involving their nationals or individuals subject to their jurisdiction, or involving their flag vessels or aircraft, only pursuant to the relevant terms of those paragraphs, and also to prevent and prohibit any activities inconsistent with these provisions, until the date ten years after the JCPOA Adoption Day or until the date on which the IAEA submits a report confirming the Broader Conclusion, whichever is earlier;

(b) Take the necessary measures to prevent, except as decided otherwise by the UN Security Council in advance on a case-by-case basis, the supply, sale, or transfer of arms or related materiel from Iran by their nationals or using their flag vessels or aircraft, and whether or not originating in the territory of Iran, until the date five years after the JCPOA Adoption Day or until the date on which the IAEA submits a report confirming the Broader Conclusion, whichever is earlier;

(c) For eight years after the JCPOA Adoption Day or until the date on which the IAEA submits a report confirming the Broader Conclusion, whichever is earlier, continue to freeze the funds, other financial assets and economic resources which are on their territories at the date of adoption of the JCPOA, and freeze the funds, other financial assets and economic resources which are on their territories at any time thereafter, that are owned or controlled by the individuals and entities that were specified on the list established and maintained by the Committee pursuant to resolution 1737 (2006) as of the date of adoption of the new resolution, with the exception of those individuals and entities specified in Attachment hereto, or that may be de-listed by the Security Council, and freeze those of additional individuals and entities that may be designated by the Security Council as: having engaged in, directly associated with or provided support for Iran's proliferation-sensitive nuclear activities undertaken contrary to Iran's commitments in the JCPOA or the development of nuclear weapon delivery systems, including through the involvement in procurement of prohibited items, goods, equipment, materials and technology specified in this statement; having assisted designated individuals or entities in evading or acting inconsistently with the JCPOA or the new resolution; having acted on behalf or at the direction of designated individuals or entities; or having been owned or controlled by designated individuals or entities, including through illicit means.

(d) For eight years from the JCPOA Adoption Day or until the date on which the IAEA submits a report confirming the Broader Conclusion, whichever is earlier, ensure that any funds, financial assets or economic resources are prevented from being made available by their nationals or by any individuals or entities within their territories, to or for the benefit of designated individuals or entities. These requirements shall not apply to funds, other financial assets or economic resources that have been determined by relevant States:

i. To be necessary for basic expenses, including payment for foodstuffs, rent or mortgage, medicines and medical treatment, taxes, insurance premiums, and public utility charges or exclusively for payment of reasonable professional fees and reimbursement of incurred expenses associated with the provision of legal services, or fees or service charges, in accordance with national laws, for routine holding or maintenance of frozen funds, other financial assets and economic resources, after notification by the relevant States to the Security Council of the intention to authorize, where appropriate, access to such funds, other financial assets or economic resources and in the absence of a negative decision by the Security Council within five working days of such notification;

ii. To be necessary for extraordinary expenses, provided that such determination has been notified by the relevant States to the Security Council and has been approved by the Security Council;

iii. To be necessary for the civil nuclear cooperation projects described in Annex III of the JCPOA, provided that such determination has been notified by the relevant States to the Security Council and has been approved by the Security Council;

iv. To be the subject of a judicial, administrative or arbitral lien or judgment, in which case the funds, other financial assets and economic resources may be used to satisfy that lien or judgment provided that the lien or judgment was entered into prior to the date of Security Council resolution 1737 (2006), is not for the benefit of a person or entity subject to the measures in this paragraph, and has been notified by the relevant States to the Security Council; or

v. To be necessary for activities directly related to the items specified in paragraph 2, or to any other activity required for the implementation of the JCPOA, provided that such determination has been notified by the relevant States to the Security Council and has been approved by the Security Council.

In addition, this provision shall not prevent a designated individual or entity from making payment due under a contract entered into prior to the listing of such individual or entity, provided that the relevant States have determined that the contract is not related to any of the prohibited items, materials, equipment, goods, technologies, assistance, training, financial assistance, investment, brokering or services referred to in this statement; the payment is not directly or indirectly received by an individual or entity subject to the measures in this paragraph; and after notification by the relevant States to the Security Council of the intention to make or receive such payments or to authorize, where appropriate, the unfreezing of funds, other financial assets or economic resources for this purpose, ten working days prior to such authorization.

In addition, States may permit the addition to the accounts frozen pursuant to this paragraph of interest or other earnings due on those accounts or payments due under contracts, agreements or obligations that arose prior to the date on which those accounts were frozen, provided that such interest, other earnings and payments continue to be subject to these measures and are frozen;

(e) For five years from the JCPOA Adoption Day or until the date on which the IAEA submits a report confirming the Broader Conclusion, whichever is earlier, take the necessary measures to prevent the entry into or transit through their territories of individuals described in paragraphs 6(c) above, although underlining that nothing in this paragraph shall oblige a State to refuse its own nationals entry into its territory. The measures imposed in this paragraph shall not apply when the Security Council determines on a case-by-case basis that such travel is justified on the grounds of humanitarian need, including religious obligations, or where the Security Council concludes that an exemption would otherwise further the objectives of the new resolution, including where Article XV of the IAEA statute is engaged;

(f) Take the required actions, in accordance with the resolution and guidance provided by the Security Council, with respect to items the supply, sale, transfer, or export of which is being undertaken contrary to the provisions contained in the JCPOA or this statement, and cooperate in such efforts.

7. All States are called upon to facilitate full implementation of the JCPOA by inspecting, in accordance with their national authorities and legislation and consistent with international law, in particular the law of the sea and relevant international civil aviation agreements, all cargo to and from Iran, in their territory, including seaports and airports, if the State concerned has information that provides reasonable grounds to believe that the cargo contains items the supply, sale, transfer, or export of which is being undertaken contrary to the provisions contained in the JCPOA or this statement; and are called upon also to cooperate in inspections on the high seas with the consent of the flag State, if there is information that provides reasonable grounds to believe the vessel is carrying items the supply, sale, transfer or export of which is being undertaken contrary to the provisions contained in the JCPOA or this statement.

China, France, Germany, the Russian Federation, the United Kingdom, the United States and the European Union note their understanding that, upon adoption of a resolution endorsing the JCPOA, the Security Council would make the practical arrangements to undertake directly the tasks specified in this statement, including to monitor and take action to support the implementation by Member States of these provisions, review proposals described in paragraph 2 of this statement, answer inquiries from Member States, provide guidance, and examine information regarding alleged actions inconsistent with the resolution. Furthermore, these states propose that the Security Council ask the Secretary-General to report to the Security Council on the implementation of these provisions every six months.

The duration of the provisions in this statement may be reviewed by the Joint Commission at the request of any participant at its biannual ministerial-level meetings, at which time the Joint Commission could make recommendations by consensus to the Security Council.

ATTACHMENT

1. AGHA-JANI, Dawood
2. ALAI, Amir Moayyed
3. ASGARPOUR, Behman
4. ASHIANI, Mohammad Fedai
5. ASHTIANI, Abbas Rezaee
6. ATOMIC ENERGY ORGANISATION OF IRAN (AEOI)
7. BAKHTIAR, Haleh
8. BEHZAD, Morteza
9. ESFAHAN NUCLEAR FUEL RESEARCH AND PRODUCTION CENTRE (NFRPC) AND ESFAHAN NUCLEAR TECHNOLOGY CENTRE (ENTC)
10. FIRST EAST EXPORT BANK, P.L.C.:
11. HOSSEINI, Seyyed Hussein
12. IRANO HIND SHIPPING COMPANY
13. IRISL BENELUX NV
14. JABBER IBN HAYAN
15. KARAJ NUCLEAR RESEARCH CENTRE
16. KAVOSHYAR COMPANY
17. LEILABADI, Ali Hajinia
18. MESBAH ENERGY COMPANY
19. MODERN INDUSTRIES TECHNIQUE COMPANY
20. MOHAJERANI, Hamid-Reza
21. MOHAMMADI, Jafar
22. MONAJEMI, Ehsan
23. NOBARI, Houshang
24. NOVIN ENERGY COMPANY
25. NUCLEAR RESEARCH CENTER FOR AGRICULTURE AND MEDICINE
26. PARS TRASH COMPANY
27. PISHGAM (PIONEER) ENERGY INDUSTRIES
28. QANNADI, Mohammad
29. RAHIMI, Amir
30. RAHIQI, Javad
31. RASHIDI, Abbas
32. SABET, M. Javad Karimi
33. SAFDARI, Seyed Jaber
34. SOLEYMANI, Ghasem
35. SOUTH SHIPPING LINE IRAN (SSL)
36. TAMAS COMPANY

PEACE CONSOLIDATION IN WEST AFRICA[358]

Decisions

On 11 September 2014, the President of the Security Council addressed the following letter to the Secretary-General:[359]

> I have the honour to inform you that your letter dated 9 September 2014 concerning your intention to appoint Mr. Mohammed Ibn Chambas, of Ghana, as your Special Representative for West Africa and Head of the United Nations Office for West Africa[360] has been brought to the attention of the members of the Security Council. They take note of the intention expressed in your letter.

At its 7357th meeting, on 8 January 2015, the Council considered the item entitled:

"Peace consolidation in West Africa

"Report of the Secretary-General on the activities of the United Nations Office for West Africa (S/2014/945)".

At the same meeting, the Council decided to extend an invitation, in accordance with rule 39 of its provisional rules of procedure, to Mr. Mohammed Ibn Chambas, Special Representative of the Secretary-General for West Africa and Head of the United Nations Office for West Africa.

At its 7480th meeting, on 7 July 2015, the Council considered the item entitled:

"Peace consolidation in West Africa

"Report of the Secretary-General on the activities of the United Nations Office for West Africa (S/2015/472)".

At the same meeting, the Council decided to extend an invitation, in accordance with rule 39 of its provisional rules of procedure, to Mr. Mohammed Ibn Chambas, Special Representative of the Secretary-General for West Africa and Head of the United Nations Office for West Africa.

NON-PROLIFERATION/DEMOCRATIC PEOPLE'S REPUBLIC OF KOREA[361]

Decision

At its 7397th meeting, on 4 March 2015, the Security Council considered the item entitled:

"Non-proliferation/Democratic People's Republic of Korea

"Note by the President (S/2015/131)".

Resolution 2207 (2015)
of 4 March 2015

The Security Council,

Recalling its previous relevant resolutions, including resolutions 825 (1993) of 11 May 1993, 1540 (2004) of 28 April 2004, 1695 (2006) of 15 July 2006, 1718 (2006) of 14 October 2006, 1874 (2009) of 12 June 2009, 1887 (2009) of 24 September 2009, 1928 (2010) of 7 June 2010, 1985 (2011) of 10 June 2011, 2050 (2012) of

[358] Resolutions or decisions on this question were first adopted by the Security Council in 2006.

[359] S/2014/662.

[360] S/2014/661.

[361] Resolutions or decisions on this question were first adopted by the Security Council in 2006.

12 June 2012, 2087 (2013) of 22 January 2013, 2094 (2013) of 7 March 2013 and 2141 (2014) of 5 March 2014, as well as the statements by its President of 6 October 2006,[362] 13 April 2009[363] and 16 April 2012,[364]

Recalling also the creation, pursuant to paragraph 26 of resolution 1874 (2009), of the Panel of Experts on the Democratic People's Republic of Korea, under the direction of the Security Council Committee established pursuant to resolution 1718 (2006), to carry out the tasks provided for in that paragraph,

Recalling further the interim report of the Panel of Experts appointed by the Secretary-General pursuant to paragraph 26 of resolution 1874 (2009) and the final report of the Panel of 23 February 2015,[365]

Recalling the methodological standards for reports of sanctions monitoring mechanisms contained in the report of the Informal Working Group of the Security Council on General Issues of Sanctions,[366]

Welcoming the efforts made by the Secretariat to expand and improve the roster of experts for the Security Council Subsidiary Organs Branch, bearing in mind the guidance provided in the note of the President of 22 December 2006,[366]

Emphasizing, in that regard, the importance of credible, fact-based, independent assessments, analysis and recommendations, in accordance with the mandate of the Panel of Experts, as specified in paragraph 26 of resolution 1874 (2009),

Determining that the proliferation of nuclear, chemical and biological weapons, as well as their means of delivery, continues to constitute a threat to international peace and security,

Acting under Article 41 of Chapter VII of the Charter of the United Nations,

1. *Decides* to extend until 5 April 2016 the mandate of the Panel of Experts on the Democratic People's Republic of Korea, as specified in paragraph 26 of resolution 1874 (2009) and modified in paragraph 29 of resolution 2094 (2013), expresses its intent to review the mandate and take appropriate action regarding further extension no later than 7 March 2016, and requests the Secretary-General to take the necessary administrative measures to this effect;

2. *Requests* the Panel of Experts to provide to the Security Council Committee stablished pursuant to resolution 1718 (2006), no later than 5 August 2015, a midterm report on its work, and further requests that, after a discussion with the Committee, the Panel submit to the Council its midterm report by 7 September 2015, and also requests a final report to the Committee no later than 5 February 2016 with its findings and recommendations, and further requests that, after a discussion with the Committee, the Panel submit to the Council its final report no later than 7 March 2016;

3. *Also requests* the Panel of Experts to provide to the Committee a planned programme of work no later than 30 days after the reappointment of the Panel, encourages the Committee to engage in regular discussions about this programme of work and to engage regularly with the Panel about its work, and further requests the Panel to provide to the Committee any updates to this programme of work;

4. *Expresses its intent* to continue to follow the work of the Panel of Experts;

5. *Urges* all States, relevant United Nations bodies and other interested parties to cooperate fully with the Committee and the Panel of Experts, in particular by supplying any information at their disposal on the implementation of the measures imposed by resolutions 1718 (2006), 1874 (2009), 2087 (2013) and 2094 (2013);

6. *Decides* to remain actively seized of the matter.

Adopted unanimously at the 7397th meeting.

---

[362] S/PRST/2006/41.

[363] S/PRST/2009/7.

[364] S/PRST/2012/13.

[365] See S/2015/131.

[366] See S/2006/997.

UNITED NATIONS REGIONAL CENTRE FOR PREVENTIVE DIPLOMACY FOR CENTRAL ASIA[367]

Decision

On 17 March 2015, the President of the Security Council addressed the following letter to the Secretary-General:[368]

> I have the honour to inform you that your letter dated 13 March 2015 concerning your intention to appoint Mr. Petko Draganov, of Bulgaria, as your Special Representative and Head of the United Nations Regional Centre for Preventive Diplomacy for Central Asia in Ashgabat[369] has been brought to the attention of the members of the Security Council. They take note of the intention expressed in your letter.

MAINTENANCE OF INTERNATIONAL PEACE AND SECURITY[370]

A. Conflict prevention

Decisions

At its 7247th meeting, on 21 August 2014, the Security Council decided to invite the representatives of Armenia, Azerbaijan, Botswana, Brazil, Canada, Colombia, Cuba, Denmark, Egypt, Ethiopia, Guatemala, India, Indonesia, Iran (Islamic Republic of), Ireland, Israel, Japan, Kazakhstan, Malaysia, Mexico, Montenegro, Morocco, Namibia, the Netherlands, New Zealand, Pakistan, Peru, Qatar, Slovakia, Slovenia, South Africa, Spain, Switzerland, the Syrian Arab Republic, Thailand, Turkey, Ukraine, Viet Nam and Zimbabwe to participate, without vote, in accordance with rule 37 of its provisional rules of procedure, in the discussion of the item entitled:

"Maintenance of international peace and security

"Conflict prevention

"Letter dated 5 August 2014 from the Permanent Representative of the United Kingdom of Great Britain and Northern Ireland to the United Nations addressed to the Secretary-General (S/2014/572)".

At the same meeting, the Council also decided to extend an invitation, in accordance with rule 39 of its provisional rules of procedure, to Ms. Navanethem Pillay, United Nations High Commissioner for Human Rights.

At the same meeting, the Council further decided to extend an invitation, in accordance with rule 39 of its provisional rules of procedure, to Mr. Ioannis Vrailas, Deputy Head of the Delegation of the European Union to the United Nations.

Resolution 2171 (2014) of 21 August 2014

The Security Council,

Recalling all its previous resolutions and the statements by its President on the prevention of armed conflict, preventive diplomacy, mediation and the peaceful settlement of disputes, in particular resolutions 1366 (2001) of 30 August 2001 and 1625 (2005) of 14 September 2005 and the statements by its President of 22 February 1995,[371]

---

[367] Resolutions or decisions on this question were first adopted by the Security Council in 2007.

[368] S/2015/189.

[369] S/2015/188.

[370] Resolutions or decisions on this question were first adopted by the Security Council in 2007.

[371] S/PRST/1995/9.

30 November 1999,[372] 20 July 2000,[373] 13 May 2003,[374] 20 September 2005,[375] 21 April 2009,[376] 22 September 2011[377] and 15 April 2013,[378]

Recalling also the determination of the peoples of the United Nations to save succeeding generations from the scourge of war and to reaffirm faith in fundamental human rights,

Recalling further all purposes and principles enshrined in the Charter of the United Nations,

Recalling the primary responsibility of the Security Council for the maintenance of international peace and security, and acting in accordance with the purposes and principles of the Charter,

Reaffirming the continuing commitment of the Council to addressing the prevention of armed conflicts in all regions of the world,

Expressing its determination to enhance the effectiveness of the United Nations in preventing and ending armed conflicts, their escalation, spread when they occur, and their resurgence once they end,

Recalling that the prevention of conflict remains a primary responsibility of States, and further recalling their primary responsibility to protect civilians and to respect and ensure the human rights of all individuals within their territory and subject to their jurisdiction, as provided for by relevant international law, and further reaffirming the responsibility of each individual State to protect its populations from genocide, war crimes, ethnic cleansing and crimes against humanity,

Acknowledging the role that civil society can play in contributing to conflict prevention,

Reiterating the need for a comprehensive approach to conflict prevention and sustainable peace, which comprises operational and structural measures for the prevention of armed conflict and addresses its root causes, including through strengthening the rule of law at the international and national levels and promoting sustained economic growth, poverty eradication, social development, sustainable development, national reconciliation, good governance, democracy, gender equality and respect for and protection of human rights,

Calling attention to the importance of early awareness and consideration of situations which may deteriorate into armed conflicts, and emphasizing that the United Nations, including the Council, should heed early warning indications of potential conflict and ensure prompt and effective action to prevent, contain or end conflicts, in accordance with the Charter,

Underlining the overriding moral, political and humanitarian imperatives as well as the economic advantages of preventing the outbreak, continuation, escalation or relapse into conflict,

Deeply concerned by the high human cost and suffering caused by armed conflicts, as well as the material and economic costs to the countries directly affected, the wider region and the international community, including through the inclusive rebuilding of States and societies in the aftermath of armed conflict, and recognizing that peace, security and development are mutually reinforcing, including in the prevention of armed conflict,

Affirming that a comprehensive conflict prevention strategy should include early warning, preventive diplomacy, mediation, preventive deployment, peacekeeping, practical disarmament and other measures to contribute to combating the proliferation of and illicit trade in arms, accountability measures as well as inclusive post-conflict peacebuilding, and recognizing that these components are interdependent, complementary and non-sequential,

Emphasizing the critical role of peacebuilding and the Peacebuilding Commission in support of countries emerging from conflict, in particular through the mobilization of sustained international support to critical national capacity needs,

---

[372] S/PRST/1999/34.

[373] S/PRST/2000/25.

[374] S/PRST/2003/5.

[375] S/PRST/2005/42.

[376] S/PRST/2009/8.

[377] S/PRST/2011/18.

[378] S/PRST/2013/4.

Stressing the essential role of the Secretary-General in the prevention of armed conflict, including through early warning,

Stressing also the importance of the efforts of the Secretary-General to enhance his role, in accordance with Article 99 of the Charter,

Taking note of the report of the Secretary-General entitled "Preventive diplomacy: delivering results"[379] and the recommendations contained therein on steps to maximize the prospects of success in United Nations preventive diplomacy efforts,

Noting that terrorism is an important element in an increasing number of conflict situations and that countering incitement to terrorism motivated by extremism and intolerance, and addressing the conditions conducive to the spread of terrorism, can complement conflict prevention efforts,

Stressing the importance of accountability in preventing future conflicts, avoiding the recurrence of serious violations of international law, including international humanitarian law and human rights law, and enabling sustainable peace, justice, truth and reconciliation, and emphasizing in this context the responsibility of States to comply with their relevant obligations to end impunity and, to that end, to thoroughly investigate and prosecute persons responsible for genocide, crimes against humanity, war crimes or other serious violations of international humanitarian law and international human rights law,

Stressing also that the fight against impunity and to ensure accountability for genocide, crimes against humanity, war crimes and other egregious crimes has been strengthened through the work on and prosecution of these crimes in the international criminal justice system, ad hoc and mixed tribunals as well as specialized chambers in national tribunals; and recognizing in this regard the contribution of the International Criminal Court, in accordance with the principle of complementarity to national criminal jurisdictions as set out in the Rome Statute of the Court,[380] towards holding accountable those responsible for such crimes; and reiterating its call upon the importance of State cooperation with these courts and tribunals in accordance with the States' respective obligations,

Reaffirming the important role of women in the prevention and resolution of conflicts and in peacebuilding, and reiterating its call to increase the equal, full and meaningful participation, representation and involvement of women in conflict prevention and mediation efforts in a mutually reinforcing manner in line with resolutions 1325 (2000) of 31 October 2000, 1820 (2008) of 19 June 2008, 1888 (2009) of 30 September 2009, 1889 (2009) of 5 October 2009, 1960 (2010) of 16 December 2010, 2106 (2013) of 24 June 2013 and 2122 (2013) of 18 October 2013,

1. *Expresses its determination* to pursue the objective of prevention of armed conflict as an integral part of its primary responsibility for the maintenance of international peace and security;

2. *Calls upon* all States to intensify efforts to secure a world free of the scourge of war and conflict;

3. *Stresses* that the prevention of conflicts remains a primary responsibility of States and actions undertaken within the framework of conflict prevention by the United Nations should support and complement, as appropriate, the conflict prevention roles of national Governments;

4. *Reaffirms* the duty of all States to settle their international disputes by peaceful means, inter alia through negotiation, enquiry, good offices, mediation, conciliation, arbitration and judicial settlement, or other peaceful means of their own choice;

5. *Recalls* Chapter VI, in particular Articles 33 and 34, of the Charter of the United Nations, and reaffirms its commitment to the settlement of disputes by peaceful means and the promotion of necessary preventive action in response to disputes or situations, the continuance of which is likely to endanger the maintenance of international peace and security;

6. *Recognizes* that some of the tools in Chapter VI of the Charter, which can be used for conflict prevention, have not been fully utilized, including negotiation, enquiry, mediation, conciliation, arbitration, judicial settlement and

[379] S/2011/552.

[380] United Nations, *Treaty Series*, vol. 2187, No. 38544.

resort to regional and subregional organizations and arrangements, as well as the good offices of the Secretary-General, and stresses its determination to make and call for the greater and more effective use of such tools;

7. *Acknowledges* the important role the following can play in contributing to the prevention of the outbreak, escalation, continuation and recurrence of conflict:

- United Nations regional offices;
- Special political missions;
- Peacekeeping operations;
- The Peacebuilding Commission;

as well as regional and subregional organizations and arrangements;

8. *Also acknowledges* that sanctions imposed under relevant provisions of the Charter are an important tool in the maintenance and restoration of international peace and security and can contribute to create conditions conducive to the peaceful resolution of situations that threaten or breach international peace and security, and support conflict prevention;

9. *Encourages* the Secretary-General to continue enhancing the use of his good offices, dispatching Representatives, Special Envoys and mediators, to help to facilitate durable, inclusive and comprehensive settlements, and further encourages the Secretary-General to continue his early engagement in the prevention of potential conflicts;

10. *Encourages* field-based special political missions and peacekeeping operations to enhance their assessment and analysis capabilities to prevent relapse into conflict within their existing mandates;

11. *Recognizes* that mediation is an important means for the pacific settlement of disputes, including, wherever possible, preventively and before disputes evolve into violence, and appreciates the efforts of the Secretary-General to continue to strengthen United Nations mediation support capacities, including the Mediation Support Unit as a provider of mediation support to the United Nations system, in accordance with agreed mandates;

12. *Expresses its willingness* to give prompt consideration to early warning cases brought to its attention by the Secretary-General, including to the dispatch, in appropriate circumstances, of preventive political missions, and encourages the Secretary-General to bring to its attention any matter which in his opinion may threaten the maintenance of international peace and security, in accordance with Article 99 of the Charter;

13. *Acknowledges* that serious abuses and violations of international human rights or humanitarian law, including sexual and gender-based violence, can be an early indication of a descent into conflict or escalation of conflict, as well as a consequence thereof; and calls upon States which have not already done so to consider ratifying the instruments of international humanitarian, human rights and refugee law and to take appropriate steps to implement these instruments domestically, which could contribute to timely prevention of conflicts;

14. *Encourages* the Secretary-General to continue to refer to the Security Council information and analyses which he believes could contribute to the prevention of armed conflict, including on cases of serious violations of international law, including international humanitarian law and human rights law, and on potential conflict situations arising, inter alia, from ethnic, religious and territorial disputes, poverty and lack of development;

15. *Expresses its commitment* to take early and effective action to prevent armed conflict and to that end to employ all appropriate means at its disposal, in accordance with the provisions of the Charter;

16. *Recalls* the important role of the Special Advisers to the Secretary-General on the Prevention of Genocide and on the Responsibility to Protect, whose functions include acting as an early warning mechanism to prevent potential situations that could result in genocide, crimes against humanity, war crimes and ethnic cleansing, as well as the important role the Special Representative of the Secretary-General on Sexual Violence in Conflict and the Special Representative of the Secretary-General for Children and Armed Conflict can play in contributing to conflict prevention; calls upon States to recommit to prevent and fight against genocide and other serious crimes under international law, and reaffirms paragraphs 138 and 139 of the 2005 World Summit Outcome[381] on the responsibility to protect populations from genocide, war crimes, ethnic cleansing and crimes against humanity;

[381] General Assembly resolution 60/1.

17. *Recognizes* the important role the Office of the United Nations High Commissioner for Human Rights and the Office of the Special Adviser on the Prevention of Genocide can play in conflict prevention, and also recognizes the role their briefings on human rights violations and hate speech play in contributing to early awareness of potential conflict;

18. *Emphasizes* the important role that women and civil society, including women's organizations and formal and informal community leaders, can play in exerting influence over parties to armed conflict; and reiterates the continuing need to increase success in preventing conflict by increasing the participation of women at all stages of mediation and post-conflict resolution and by increasing the consideration of gender-related issues in all discussions pertinent to conflict prevention;

19. *Reiterates its request* to the Secretary-General and his Special Envoys and Special Representatives to United Nations missions, as part of their regular briefings, to update the Council on progress in inviting women to participate, including through consultations with civil society, including women's organizations, in discussions pertinent to the prevention and resolution of conflict, the maintenance of peace and security and post-conflict peacebuilding;

20. *Expresses its commitment* to consider and use the tools of the United Nations system to ensure that early warning of potential conflicts translates into early, concrete preventive action, including towards the goal of protecting civilians, by or in coordination with the most appropriate United Nations or regional actor, in accordance with the Charter;

21. *Encourages* the peaceful settlement of local disputes through regional arrangements in accordance with Chapter VIII of the Charter, acknowledges the efforts undertaken to strengthen operational and institutional cooperation between the United Nations and regional and subregional organizations aimed at conflict prevention, and in this regard reiterates the need to continue strengthening strategic dialogue, partnerships and more regular exchanges of views and information at the working level, with the aim of building national and regional capacities in relation to preventive diplomacy;

22. *Calls for* enhanced cooperation and capacity-building with regional and subregional organizations and arrangements to help to prevent armed conflicts, their spread and impact, including through cooperation in early warning mechanisms, as well as to help to facilitate preventive action, consistent with Chapter VIII of the Charter;

23. *Reiterates its support* for the work of the Peacebuilding Commission, and expresses its continued willingness to make use of the advisory, advocacy and resource mobilization roles of the Commission in peacebuilding activities;

24. *Reaffirms its willingness* to strengthen its relationship with civil society, including, as appropriate, through, inter alia, meetings in an informal and flexible manner with civil society, to exchange analyses and perspectives on the issue of the prevention of armed conflict;

25. *Requests* the Secretary-General to submit a report to the Council on actions taken by him to promote and strengthen conflict prevention tools within the United Nations system, including through cooperation with regional and subregional organizations, by 31 August 2015;

26. *Decides* to remain actively seized of the matter.

Adopted unanimously at the 7247th meeting.

B. Inclusive development for the maintenance of international peace and security

Decisions

At its 7361st meeting, on 19 January 2015, the Security Council decided to invite the representatives of Argentina, Armenia, Austria, Azerbaijan, Benin, Brazil, Cambodia, Canada, Colombia, Croatia, Cuba, Cyprus, the Dominican Republic, Ecuador, Egypt, Estonia, Georgia, Germany, Greece, Guatemala, Haiti, Hungary, India, Indonesia, Iran (Islamic Republic of), Iraq, Ireland, Israel, Italy, Japan, Kazakhstan, Kenya, Luxembourg, Mexico, Montenegro, Morocco, the Netherlands, Nicaragua, Pakistan, Panama, Paraguay, Peru, Poland, the Republic of

Korea, Rwanda, Slovakia, Slovenia, Somalia, South Africa, Sweden, Thailand, Turkey, Uruguay and Viet Nam to participate, without vote, in accordance with rule 37 of its provisional rules of procedure, in the discussion of the item entitled:

"Maintenance of international peace and security

"Inclusive development for the maintenance of international peace a security

"Letter dated 6 January 2015 from the Permanent Representative of Chile to the United Nations addressed to the Secretary-General (S/2015/6)".

At the same meeting, the Council also decided to extend an invitation, in accordance with rule 39 of its provisional rules of procedure, to Mr. Antonio de Aguiar Patriota, Permanent Representative of Brazil to the United Nations, in his capacity as Chair of the Peacebuilding Commission.

At the same meeting, the Council further decided to extend an invitation, in accordance with rule 39 of its provisional rules of procedure, to Ms. Leymah Gbowee, President of the Gbowee Peace Foundation Africa.

At the same meeting, the Council decided to extend an invitation, in accordance with rule 39 of its provisional rules of procedure, to Mr. Thomas Mayr-Harting, Head of the Delegation of the European Union to the United Nations.

At the same meeting, following consultations among members of the Security Council, the President made the following statement on behalf of the Council:[382]

The Security Council reaffirms its primary responsibility under the Charter of the United Nations for the maintenance of international peace and security and its readiness to strive for sustainable peace in all situations under its consideration.

The Council underlines that security and development are closely interlinked and mutually reinforcing and key to attaining sustainable peace. The Council recognizes that their relationship is complex, multifaceted and case-specific.

The Council reiterates that, in order to support a country to emerge sustainably from conflict, there is a need for a comprehensive and integrated approach that incorporates and strengthens coherence between political, security, development, human rights and rule of law activities, and addresses the root causes of each conflict, including through strengthening the rule of law at the national and international levels, promoting sustainable economic growth and development, poverty eradication, political, religious and cultural tolerance, freedom of opinion and expression, social cohesion and inclusiveness, national reconciliation, good governance, democracy, gender equality, and respect for and protection of human rights, and facilitating reintegration and rehabilitation.

The Council affirms that national ownership and national responsibility are key to establishing sustainable peace. The Council reaffirms the primary responsibility of national authorities in identifying their priorities and strategies for post-conflict peacebuilding, with a view to ensuring national ownership.

The Council underlines that integrated action on the ground by security and development actors needs to be coordinated with the national authorities and can significantly contribute to stabilizing and improving the security situation and ensuring the protection of civilians. The Council also notes the importance of cooperation with civil society in this context. The Council affirms that sustainable peace and development cannot be achieved without the inclusion of all relevant stakeholders and underlines that women must be included as active participants in all stages of peacebuilding, peace agreements and development programmes. The Council expresses its willingness to engage in dialogue, where necessary, on specific situations on its agenda with other actors, including United Nations agencies, funds and programmes and international financial institutions.

The Council encourages Member States to consider developing a United Nations common approach to inclusive development as a key for preventing conflict and enabling long-term stability and sustainable peace.

[382] S/PRST/2015/3.

The Council highlights in this regard the importance of identifying and addressing social, economic, political, cultural and religious exclusion, intolerance, as well as violent extremism, which can be conducive to terrorism, as drivers of conflict. The Council further notes the importance of early awareness and consideration of situations of exclusion in post-conflict States and draws the attention of Member States to the contribution that mitigation actions, including those based on best available practices and models of inclusiveness at the local, national, regional and global levels, can make in this regard.

The Council recognizes the continuing need to increase women's participation and the consideration of gender-related issues in all discussions pertinent to the prevention and resolution of armed conflict, the maintenance of peace and security, and post-conflict peacebuilding and reiterates its intention, when establishing and renewing the mandates of United Nations missions, to include provisions on the promotion of gender equality and the empowerment of women in conflict and post-conflict situations.

The Council calls upon Member States to take concrete measures to further assist youth, particularly those in armed conflict situations, and encourages the involvement of young people, where appropriate, in activities concerning the protection of children and youth affected by armed conflict situations, including in conflict prevention, peacebuilding and post-conflict processes.

The Council recalls the need for inclusive and effective disarmament, demobilization and reintegration processes, including those relating to the release and reintegration of children formerly associated with armed forces or armed groups, with the involvement of affected individuals and local communities, while respecting the need to fight against impunity.

The Council stresses that terrorist groups benefiting from transnational organized crime may contribute to undermining affected States, specifically their security, stability, governance and social and economic development, complicating conflict prevention and resolution efforts. The Council emphasizes that the combined presence of terrorism, violent extremism and transnational organized crime may exacerbate conflicts in affected regions and notes that terrorist groups benefiting from transnational organized crime can, in some cases and in some regions, complicate conflict prevention and resolution efforts.

The Council encourages Member States to engage relevant local communities and non-governmental actors in developing strategies, including through interreligious, interethnic and intercultural dialogue, to counter the violent extremist narrative that can incite terrorist acts, address the conditions conducive to the spread of violent extremism, which can be conducive to terrorism, including by empowering youth, families, women, religious, cultural and education leaders, and all other concerned groups of civil society and adopt tailored approaches to countering recruitment to this kind of violent extremism and promoting social inclusion and cohesion.

The Council re-emphasizes the importance of considering and initiating peacebuilding activities from the earliest stages of planning and implementation of peacekeeping operations, as appropriate, including through clear and achievable mandates. The Council stresses the importance of clarity of roles and responsibilities of the United Nations peacekeeping operation and the United Nations country team and other relevant actors for the delivery of prioritized support to a country consistent with its specific peacebuilding needs and priorities, as outlined by national authorities, in order to ensure effective integration of efforts, in particular where peacekeeping missions and special political missions are operating alongside other United Nations peacebuilding actors and regional and subregional organizations. The Council further emphasizes the importance of integration of United Nations efforts during the transition process of Council-mandated operations.

The Council notes that successful implementation of the many tasks that peacekeeping operations could be mandated to undertake in the areas of security sector reform, disarmament, demobilization and reintegration, the rule of law, transitional justice and human rights requires an understanding of and acting with a perspective which takes into account the close interlinkage between security and development. In this context, the Council notes with appreciation the contribution that peacekeepers and peacekeeping missions make to early peacebuilding, including through creating a conducive environment which enables economic recovery and the provision of basic services. The Council acknowledges that this contribution can help to establish and build confidence in the mission.

The Council underlines that reconstruction, economic revitalization and capacity-building constitute crucial elements for the long-term development of post-conflict societies and in generating sustainable peace, and in this regard attaches special importance to national ownership and stresses the significance of international assistance.

The Council notes that, in matters relating to the maintenance of international peace and security under its consideration, conflict analysis and contextual information on, inter alia, social and economic issues is important, when such issues are drivers of conflict, represent a challenge to the implementation of Council mandates or endanger the process of consolidation of peace. In this regard, the Council requests the Secretary-General to ensure that his reporting to the Council contains such contextual information.

The Council recalls the role played by the illegal exploitation of natural resources in fuelling some past and current conflicts. In this regard, the Council recognizes that the United Nations can play a role in helping the States concerned, as appropriate, upon their request and with full respect for their sovereignty over natural resources and under national ownership, to prevent illegal access to those resources and to lay the basis for their legal exploitation with a view to promoting development, in particular through the empowerment of Governments in post-conflict situations to better manage their resources.

The Council encourages close cooperation within the United Nations system and with regional, subregional and other organizations on the ground and at Headquarters in order to properly engage in conflict and post-conflict situations, in accordance with its responsibilities under the Charter, and expresses its willingness to consider ways to improve such cooperation.

The Council calls for the rapid implementation, in consultation with regional organizations, of regional strategies encompassing security, governance, development, human rights and humanitarian issues such as the United Nations integrated strategy for the Sahel region.[383]

The Council encourages Member States, particularly those represented on the governance structures of the United Nations agencies, funds and programmes, to promote coherence in the work of the United Nations in conflict and post-conflict situations.

The Council recalls its resolution 1645 (2005) and acknowledges the important role of the Peacebuilding Commission in the peacebuilding architecture and stresses its willingness to strengthen its links with the Commission by, inter alia, making greater use of its advisory role. The Council calls upon the Commission to make further efforts in promoting improved coherence and alignment of partners' policies around national peacebuilding strategies and priorities, and ensure regional and international support and effective response through engagement and establishing partnerships with international financial institutions, neighbouring countries and regional and subregional organizations. The Council underscores the importance of the regional aspect of peacebuilding and the need for engaging and collaborating with regional actors in policy-related and country-specific issues in the advice made by the Commission

The Council highlights the contribution that the Economic and Social Council can make in addressing economic, social, cultural and humanitarian issues and underlines the importance of close cooperation in accordance with Article 65 of the Charter.

C. Reflect on history, reaffirm the strong commitment to the purposes and principles of the Charter of the United Nations

Decisions

At its 7389th meeting, on 23 February 2015, the Security Council decided to invite the representatives of Albania, Algeria, Armenia, Australia, Austria, Azerbaijan, Belgium, Bosnia and Herzegovina, Botswana, Brazil, Burundi, Canada, Colombia, Costa Rica, Cuba, Cyprus, the Democratic People's Republic of Korea, Ecuador, Egypt, Estonia, Ethiopia, Georgia, Germany, Guatemala, Hungary, India, Indonesia, Iran (Islamic Republic of), Ireland, Israel, Italy, Japan, Kazakhstan, Kenya, Kuwait, Latvia, Liechtenstein, Maldives, Mexico, Montenegro,

[383] S/2013/354, annex.

Morocco, the Netherlands, Nicaragua, Pakistan, Papua New Guinea, the Philippines, Poland, the Republic of Korea, Romania, Rwanda, Saudi Arabia, Serbia, Slovenia, South Africa, Sweden, Switzerland, the Syrian Arab Republic, Thailand, Tunisia, Turkey, Ukraine, the United Arab Emirates, Uruguay, Viet Nam and Zimbabwe to participate, without vote, in accordance with rule 37 of its provisional rules of procedure, in the discussion of the item entitled:

"Maintenance of international peace and security

"Reflect on history, reaffirm the strong commitment to the purposes and principles of the Charter of the United Nations

"Letter dated 3 February 2015 from the Permanent Representative of China to the United Nations addressed to the Secretary-General (S/2015/87)".

At the same meeting, the Council also decided to extend invitations, in accordance with rule 39 of its provisional rules of procedure, to Mr. Thomas Mayr-Harting, Head of the Delegation of the European Union to the United Nations, and Mr. Téte António, Permanent Observer of the African Union to the United Nations.

D. The role of youth in countering violent extremism and promoting peace

Decisions

At its 7432nd meeting, on 23 April 2015, the Security Council decided to invite the representatives of Albania, Australia, Austria, Azerbaijan, Belgium, Benin, Brazil, Canada, Colombia, Costa Rica, Croatia, Egypt, Georgia, Germany, Hungary, India, Indonesia, Iran (Islamic Republic of), Italy, Japan, Kazakhstan, Kenya, Lebanon, Luxembourg, Maldives, Malta, Montenegro, Morocco, the Netherlands, Pakistan, Poland, Portugal, Qatar, the Republic of Korea, Sweden, Switzerland, the Syrian Arab Republic, Thailand, Turkey, Ukraine and the United Arab Emirates to participate, without vote, in accordance with rule 37 of its provisional rules of procedure, in the discussion of the item entitled:

"Maintenance of international peace and security

"The role of youth in countering violent extremism and promoting peace

"Letter dated 27 March 2015 from the Permanent Representative of Jordan to the United Nations addressed to the Secretary-General (S/2015/231)".

At the same meeting, the Council also decided to extend invitations, in accordance with rule 39 of its provisional rules of procedure, to Mr. Peter Neumann and Mr. Scott Atran.

At the same meeting, the Council further decided to extend an invitation, in accordance with rule 39 of its provisional rules of procedure, to Mr. Nassir Abdulaziz al-Nasser, United Nations High Representative for the Alliance of Civilizations.

At the same meeting, the Council decided to extend invitations, in accordance with rule 39 of its provisional rules of procedure, to Mr. Téte António, Permanent Observer of the African Union to the United Nations, and Mr. Ioannis Vrailas, Deputy Head of the Delegation of the European Union to the United Nations.

At the same meeting, the Council also decided to extend an invitation to the Permanent Observer of the Observer State of the Holy See to the United Nations, in accordance with the provisional rules of procedure of the Council and its previous practice in that regard.

E. Peace and security challenges facing small island developing States

Decisions

At its 7499th meeting, on 30 July 2015, the Security Council decided to invite the representatives of Antigua and Barbuda, Argentina, Australia, Bahamas, Barbados, Belgium, Brazil, Colombia, Costa Rica, Cyprus, the Dominican Republic, Egypt, Estonia, Fiji, Georgia, Germany, Haiti, India, Indonesia, Israel, Italy, Jamaica, Japan, Kazakhstan, Kiribati, Luxembourg, Maldives, the Marshall Islands, Mexico, Micronesia (Federated States of), Morocco, Nauru, the Netherlands, Palau, Panama, Papua New Guinea, Poland, the Republic of Korea, Saint Vincent and the Grenadines, Samoa, Seychelles, Singapore, Solomon Islands, South Africa, Sweden,

Thailand, Timor-Leste, Tonga, Trinidad and Tobago, Turkey, Tuvalu, Ukraine and Uruguay to participate, without vote, in accordance with rule 37 of its provisional rules of procedure, in the discussion of the item entitled:

"Maintenance of international peace and security

"Peace and security challenges facing small island developing States

"Letter dated 15 July 2015 from the Permanent Representative of New Zealand to the United Nations addressed to the Secretary-General (S/2015/543)".

At the same meeting, the Council also decided to extend invitations, in accordance with rule 39 of its provisional rules of procedure, to Mr. Toke Talagi, Premier of Niue, and Mr. Mark Brown, Minister of Finance of the Cook Islands.

At the same meeting, the Council further decided to extend an invitation, in accordance with rule 39 of its provisional rules of procedure, to Mr. Thomas Mayr-Harting, Head of the Delegation of the European Union to the United Nations.

At the same meeting, the Council decided to extend an invitation to the Permanent Observer of the Observer State of the Holy See to the United Nations, in accordance with the provisional rules of procedure of the Council and its previous practice in that regard.

F. General matters

Decision

On 27 May 2015, the President of the Security Council addressed the following letter to the Secretary-General:[384]

> I have the honour to inform you that your letter dated 20 May 2015,[385] concerning your intention to move the award ceremony for the Captain Mbaye Diagne Medal for Exceptional Courage to coincide with the peacekeeping summit to be held in September 2015 and to extend the period of eligibility for the award of the Medal to 1 January 2007, has been brought to the attention of the members of the Security Council, who take note of the information provided and the intention expressed therein.

PEACE AND SECURITY IN AFRICA[386]

A. Ebola

Decisions

At its 7268th meeting, on 18 September 2014, the Security Council decided to invite the representatives of Afghanistan, Albania, Andorra, Angola, Armenia, Austria, Bangladesh, Belgium, Belize, Benin, Bhutan, Bosnia and Herzegovina, Botswana, Brazil, Bulgaria, Burkina Faso, Burundi, Cameroon, Canada, Colombia, the Congo, Côte d'Ivoire, Croatia, Cuba, Cyprus, the Czech Republic, the Democratic Republic of the Congo, Denmark, Djibouti, the Dominican Republic, Egypt, Equatorial Guinea, Eritrea, Estonia, Finland, Gabon, Georgia, Germany, Ghana, Greece, Grenada, Guinea, Guyana, Honduras, Hungary, Iceland, Iraq, Ireland, Israel, Italy, Japan, Kazakhstan, Kenya, Kyrgyzstan, Latvia, Lebanon, Liberia, Libya, Liechtenstein, Malawi, Malaysia, Maldives, Mali, the Marshall Islands, Mauritius, Micronesia (Federated States of), Monaco, Montenegro, Morocco, Mozambique, Namibia, Nauru, Nepal, the Netherlands, New Zealand, Nicaragua, Niger, Norway, Panama, Papua New Guinea, Poland, Portugal, Qatar, the Republic of Moldova, Romania, Saint Lucia, Samoa, San Marino,

---

[384] S/2015/386.

[385] S/2015/385.

[386] Resolutions or decisions on this question were first adopted by the Security Council in 2007.

Sao Tome and Principe, Senegal, Serbia, Seychelles, Sierra Leone, Slovakia, Slovenia, Solomon Islands, Somalia, South Africa, South Sudan, Spain, Sri Lanka, Suriname, Sweden, Switzerland, Thailand, the former Yugoslav Republic of Macedonia, Timor-Leste, Togo, Trinidad and Tobago, Tunisia, Turkey, Uganda, Ukraine, the United Republic of Tanzania, Uruguay, Vanuatu, Viet Nam, Yemen and Zambia to participate, without vote, in accordance with rule 37 of its provisional rules of procedure, in the discussion of the item entitled:

"Peace and security in Africa

"Ebola".

At the same meeting, the Council also decided to extend invitations, in accordance with rule 39 of its provisional rules of procedure, to Dr. David Nabarro, United Nations System Senior Coordinator for Ebola Virus Disease, Dr. Margaret Chan, Director-General of the World Health Organization, and Mr. Jackson K. P. Niamah, representative of Médecins sans frontières.

At the same meeting, the Council further decided to extend invitations, in accordance with rule 39 of its provisional rules of procedure, to Mr. Thomas Mayr-Harting, Head of the Delegation of the European Union to the United Nations, and Mr. Téte António, Permanent Observer of the African Union to the United Nations.

Resolution 2177 (2014)
of 18 September 2014

The Security Council,

Recalling its resolution 2176 (2014), adopted on 15 September 2014, concerning the situation in Liberia and its statement to the press of 9 July 2014,

Recalling also its primary responsibility for the maintenance of international peace and security,

Expressing grave concern about the outbreak of the Ebola virus in, and its impact on, West Africa, in particular Liberia, Guinea and Sierra Leone, as well as Nigeria and beyond,

Recognizing that the peacebuilding and development gains of the most affected countries concerned could be reversed in the light of the Ebola outbreak, and underlining that the outbreak is undermining the stability of the most affected countries concerned and, unless contained, may lead to further instances of civil unrest, social tensions and a deterioration of the political and security climate,

Determining that the unprecedented extent of the Ebola outbreak in Africa constitutes a threat to international peace and security,

Expressing concern about the particular impact of the Ebola outbreak on women,

Welcoming the convening of the Mano River Union Extraordinary Summit, held in Guinea on 1 August 2014, and the commitments expressed by the Heads of State of Côte d'Ivoire, Guinea, Liberia and Sierra Leone to combat the Ebola outbreak in the region, including by strengthening treatment services and measures to prevent the outbreak spreading across borders,

Taking note of the measures taken by the Member States of the region, especially Liberia, Guinea and Sierra Leone, as well as Nigeria, Côte d'Ivoire and Senegal, in response to the Ebola outbreak, and recognizing that the outbreak may exceed the capacity of the Governments concerned to respond,

Taking note also of the letter dated 29 August 2014 from the Presidents of Liberia, Sierra Leone and Guinea to the Secretary-General,[387] requesting a comprehensive response to the Ebola outbreak, including a coordinated international response to end the outbreak and to support the societies and economies affected by restrictions on trade and transportation during the outbreak,

Recognizing the measures taken by the Member States of the region, in particular Côte d'Ivoire, Cabo Verde, Ghana, Mali and Senegal, to facilitate the delivery of humanitarian assistance to the most affected countries,

[387] S/2014/669, annex.

Emphasizing the key role of Member States, including through the Global Health Security Agenda where applicable, to provide adequate public health services to detect, prevent, respond to and mitigate outbreaks of major infectious diseases through sustainable, well-functioning and responsive public health mechanisms,

Recalling the International Health Regulations (2005),[388] which are contributing to global public health security by providing a framework for the coordination of the management of events that may constitute a public health emergency of international concern, and aim to improve the capacity of all countries to detect, assess, notify and respond to public health threats, and underscoring the importance of States members of the World Health Organization abiding by these commitments,

Underscoring that the control of outbreaks of major infectious diseases requires urgent action and greater national, regional and international collaboration, and in this regard stressing the crucial and immediate need for a coordinated international response to the Ebola outbreak,

Commending Member States, bilateral partners and multilateral organizations for the crucial assistance, including financial commitments and in-kind donations, provided to and identified for the affected people and Governments of the region to support the scaling-up of emergency efforts to contain the Ebola outbreak in West Africa and interrupt transmission of the virus, including by providing flexible funds to relevant United Nations agencies and international organizations involved in the response to enable them and national Governments to purchase supplies and enhance emergency operations in the affected countries, as well as by collaborating with public and private sector partners to accelerate development of therapies, vaccines and diagnostics to treat patients and limit or prevent further infection or transmission of the Ebola virus disease,

Expressing deep appreciation to the first-line responders to the Ebola outbreak in West Africa, including national and international health and humanitarian relief workers contributed by the Member States of diverse regions and non-governmental organizations such as Médecins sans frontières and the International Federation of Red Cross and Red Crescent Societies, and also expressing appreciation to the United Nations Humanitarian Air Service for transporting humanitarian personnel and medical supplies and equipment, especially to remote locations in Guinea, Liberia and Sierra Leone, during the outbreak,

Welcoming the efforts of the African Union, in coordination with bilateral partners and multilateral organizations, to craft a united, comprehensive and collective African response to the outbreak, including through the deployment of health-care workers to the region, and also the efforts of the Economic Community of West African States to support steps to contain the spread of the Ebola virus, including through the support of the defence forces of its member States,

Expressing concern about the impact, including on food security, of general travel and trade restrictions in the region, and taking note of the call by the African Union upon its member States to lift travel restrictions to enable the free movement of people and trade to the affected countries,

Emphasizing the role of all relevant United Nations system entities, in particular the General Assembly, the Economic and Social Council and the Peacebuilding Commission, in supporting the national, regional and international efforts to respond to the Ebola outbreak, and recognizing in this regard the central role of the World Health Organization, which designated the Ebola outbreak a public health emergency of international concern,

Stressing the need for coordinated efforts of all relevant United Nations system entities to address the Ebola outbreak in line with their respective mandates and to assist, wherever possible, national, regional and international efforts in this regard,

Taking note of the World Health Organization Ebola response road map of 28 August 2014 which aims to stop transmission of the Ebola virus disease worldwide, while managing the consequences of any further international spread, and taking note also of the 12 mission-critical actions, including infection control, community mobilization and recovery, to resolve the Ebola outbreak,[389]

Taking note also of the World Health Organization protocols to prevent the transmission of the Ebola virus disease between individuals, organizations and populations, underlining that the Ebola outbreak can be contained,

---

[388] World Health Organization, document WHA58/2005/REC/1, resolution 58.3, annex.

[389] See S/2014/679.

including through the implementation of established safety and health protocols and other preventive measures that have proven effective, and commending the efforts of the United Nations Mission in Liberia to communicate, including through UNMIL Radio, such protocols and preventive measures to the Liberian public,

Reiterating its appreciation for the appointments by the Secretary-General of Dr. David Nabarro as the United Nations System Senior Coordinator for Ebola Virus Disease and of Mr. Anthony Banbury as the Deputy Ebola Coordinator and Operation Crisis Manager operating from the crisis response mechanism of the United Nations, which was activated on 8 September 2014 and which aims to consolidate the operational work of the United Nations system, Member States, non-governmental organizations and other partners focused on providing assistance to the affected countries in response to the Ebola outbreak, as well as to ensure United Nations system assistance to developing, leading and implementing an effective response to the broader dimensions of the outbreak that include food security and access to basic health services,

Welcoming the intention of the Secretary-General to convene a high-level meeting on the margins of the sixty-ninth session of the General Assembly to urge an exceptional and vigorous response to the Ebola outbreak,

1. *Encourages* the Governments of Liberia, Sierra Leone and Guinea to accelerate the establishment of national mechanisms to provide for the rapid diagnosis and isolation of suspected cases of infection, treatment measures, effective medical services for responders, credible and transparent public education campaigns, and strengthened preventive and preparedness measures to detect, mitigate and respond to Ebola exposure, as well as to coordinate the rapid delivery and utilization of international assistance, including health workers and humanitarian relief supplies, as well as to coordinate their efforts to address the transnational dimension of the Ebola outbreak, including the management of their shared borders, and with the support of bilateral partners, multilateral organizations and the private sector;

2. *Also encourages* the Governments of Liberia, Sierra Leone and Guinea to continue efforts to resolve and mitigate the wider political, security, socioeconomic and humanitarian dimensions of the Ebola outbreak, as well as to provide sustainable, well-functioning and responsive public health mechanisms, emphasizes that responses to the Ebola outbreak should address the specific needs of women, and stresses the importance of their full and effective engagement in the development of such responses;

3. *Expresses concern* about the detrimental effect of the isolation of the affected countries as a result of trade and travel restrictions imposed on and to the affected countries;

4. *Calls upon* Member States, including of the region, to lift general travel and border restrictions, imposed as a result of the Ebola outbreak, and that contribute to the further isolation of the affected countries and undermine their efforts to respond to the Ebola outbreak, and also calls upon airlines and shipping companies to maintain trade and transport links with the affected countries and the wider region;

5. *Calls upon* Member States, especially of the region, to facilitate the delivery of assistance, including qualified, specialized and trained personnel and supplies, in response to the Ebola outbreak to the affected countries, and in this regard expresses deep appreciation to the Government of Ghana for allowing the resumption of the air shuttle of the United Nations Mission in Liberia from Monrovia to Accra, which will transport international health workers and other responders to areas affected by the Ebola outbreak in Liberia;

6. *Calls upon* Member States, especially of the region, and all relevant actors providing assistance in response to the Ebola outbreak to enhance efforts to communicate to the public, as well as to implement, the established safety and health protocols and preventive measures to mitigate against misinformation and undue alarm about the transmission and extent of the outbreak among and between individuals and communities, and in this regard requests the Secretary-General to develop a strategic communication platform using existing United Nations system resources and facilities in the affected countries, as necessary and available, including to assist Governments and other relevant partners;

7. *Calls upon* Member States to provide urgent resources and assistance, including deployable medical capabilities such as field hospitals with qualified and sufficient expertise, staff and supplies, laboratory services, logistical, transport and construction support capabilities, airlift and other aviation support and aeromedical services and dedicated clinical services in Ebola treatment units and isolation units, to support the affected countries in intensifying preventive and response activities and strengthening national capacities in response to the Ebola outbreak and to allot adequate capacity to prevent future outbreaks;

8. *Urges* Member States, as well as bilateral partners and multilateral organizations, including the African Union, the Economic Community of West African States and the European Union, to mobilize and provide immediately technical expertise and additional medical capacity, including for rapid diagnosis and training of health workers at the national and international levels, to the affected countries and those providing assistance to the affected countries, and to continue to exchange expertise, lessons learned and best practices, as well as to maximize synergies to respond effectively and immediately to the Ebola outbreak, to provide essential resources, supplies and coordinated assistance to the affected countries and implementing partners, and calls upon all relevant actors to cooperate closely with the Secretary-General on response assistance efforts;

9. *Urges* Member States to implement relevant temporary recommendations issued under the International Health Regulations (2005)[388] regarding the 2014 Ebola outbreak in West Africa, and lead the organization, coordination and implementation of national preparedness and response activities, including, where and when relevant, in collaboration with international development and humanitarian partners;

10. *Commends* the continued contribution and commitment of international health and humanitarian relief workers to respond urgently to the Ebola outbreak, and calls upon all relevant actors to put in place the necessary repatriation and financial arrangements, including medical evacuation capacities and treatment and transport provisions, to facilitate their immediate and unhindered deployment to the affected countries;

11. *Requests* the Secretary-General to help to ensure that all relevant United Nations system entities, including the World Health Organization and the United Nations Humanitarian Air Service, in accordance with their respective mandates, accelerate their response to the Ebola outbreak, including by supporting the development and implementation of preparedness and operational plans and liaison and collaboration with Governments of the region and those providing assistance;

12. *Encourages* the World Health Organization to continue to strengthen its technical leadership and operational support to Governments and partners, monitor Ebola transmission, assist in identifying existing response needs and partners to meet those needs to facilitate the availability of essential data and hasten the development and implementation of therapies and vaccines according to best clinical and ethical practices, and also encourages Member States to provide all necessary support in this regard, including the sharing of data in accordance with applicable law;

13. *Decides* to remain seized of the matter.

Adopted unanimously at the 7268th meeting.

B. General matters

Decisions

At its 7249th meeting, on 27 August 2014, the Security Council considered the item entitled "Peace and security in Africa".

At the same meeting, following consultations among members of the Security Council, the President made the following statement on behalf of the Council:[390]

> The Security Council reiterates its continued concern about the alarming situation in the Sahel region and reaffirms its continued commitment to address the complex security and political challenges to the stability and development of the region despite the collective efforts undertaken by the region and the international community and reaffirms its continued commitment to address these challenges, which are interrelated with humanitarian and development issues as well as the adverse effects of climate and ecological changes. The Council reiterates the importance of a coherent, comprehensive and coordinated approach encompassing governance, security, humanitarian, human rights, development and environmental aspects to respond to the threats across the Sahel region as well as to address the root causes of these challenges.

[390] S/PRST/2014/17.

The Council reaffirms its strong commitment to the sovereignty, territorial integrity, political independence and unity of countries of the Sahel region and reiterates the importance of national and regional ownership of the United Nations integrated strategy for the Sahel.[391] The Council encourages further close consultation between Member States of the Sahel, West Africa and the Maghreb as well as with regional, multilateral and other bilateral donors and partners to enhance the efforts to implement the strategy. The Council commends the growing leadership role assumed by the countries of the region, and welcomes in this regard the establishment of the Group of Five for the Sahel, which aims to enhance ownership of the initiatives focused on addressing the threats to peace and security and development in the Sahel. The Council encourages the Office of the Special Envoy of the Secretary-General for the Sahel to work closely with the countries of the Group of Five as well as other countries of the region and regional and international actors to tackle these threats.

The Council welcomes the high-level visit to the region undertaken from 4 to 7 November 2013 by the United Nations Secretary-General, the Chairperson of the African Union Commission, the President of the World Bank Group, the President of the African Development Bank and the Commissioner for International Cooperation and Development of the European Union, which was an important mission to promote closer coordination and cooperation among the countries of the Sahel and their partners. The Council encourages the reinvigoration of the vision set out during the visit, in order to translate the will and commitment of the international community into tangible results. The Council, in this regard, welcomes the initiatives taken by the countries of the Group of Five for the Sahel to appoint national focal points to improve coordination with the Office of the Special Envoy of the Secretary-General for the Sahel, as well as the initiative to establish a follow-up group composed of the Permanent Representatives of the Group of Five and other Sahel countries in New York, to regularly meet, share information and follow up with the Secretariat on the implementation of the United Nations integrated strategy for the Sahel.

The Council welcomes the establishment of the Ministerial Coordination Platform for the Sahel, to discuss common priorities for initiatives in the Sahel under a rotating chairmanship, held by Mali from 2014 to 2015. The Council takes note of the conclusions of the two meetings of the Platform, held in Bamako on 5 November 2013 and 16 May 2014 and calls upon the international community, including the United Nations and the African Union, as co-Chairs of the technical secretariat, to support the functioning of the Platform. The Council welcomes the efforts made by Mali, as current Chair of the Platform, to consolidate these initiatives for the Sahel and looks forward to further progress in the months ahead.

The Council welcomes the establishment of the coordination mechanism within the United Nations system, including three United Nations inter-agency working groups on governance, security and resilience, to ensure a coordinated and coherent response to the challenges in the region. The Council welcomes the relocation of the Office of the Special Envoy of the Secretary-General for the Sahel to the premises of the United Nations Office for West Africa in Dakar, as part of its efforts to more fully and directly anchor the implementation of the United Nations integrated strategy for the Sahel in the region and maximize synergies with the relevant entities of the United Nations system.

The Council continues to be gravely concerned about the activities in the Sahel region of terrorist organizations, including the Organization of Al-Qaida in the Islamic Maghreb, Jama'atu Ahlis Sunna Lidda'Awati Wal-Jihad (Boko Haram), Ansar Eddine, the Mouvement pour l'Unification et le Jihad en Afrique de l'Ouest and Al Mourabitoun, and reiterates its strong condemnation of the recent terrorist attacks perpetrated in the region. The Council also reiterates its concern over the serious threats to peace and security posed by armed conflict, the proliferation of arms and transnational organized crime and other illicit activities such as drug trafficking in the Sahel region, and the increasing links, in some cases, with terrorism.

The Council recalls that sanctions are an important tool in countering terrorism and recalls that the groups mentioned in the paragraph above are included on the Al-Qaida Sanctions List and subject to the sanctions measures. The Council commends the initiative of the Al-Qaida sanctions committee and its Analytical Support and Sanctions Monitoring Team to engage with Member States of the Sahel, the Maghreb and adjoining regions to consider ways in which the sanctions regime can support and enhance the inputs of affected States, in order to be integrated into national and regional responses to the Al-Qaida threat in the region.

[391] S/2013/354, annex.

The Council welcomes the efforts of the Counter-Terrorism Committee and its Executive Directorate to ensure the full implementation of resolutions 1373 (2001) and 1624 (2005) and to facilitate technical assistance to Member States, and in this regard commends the focused approach of the Executive Directorate aimed at addressing the counter-terrorism needs of Member States in the Sahel and Maghreb regions, primarily in the area of border control and developing comprehensive counter-terrorism strategies. The Council encourages the Executive Directorate to continue to work with Member States, at their request, and to assess and facilitate technical assistance, in particular, in close cooperation within the Counter-Terrorism Implementation Task Force, as well as with all bilateral and multilateral technical assistance providers.

The Council welcomes the Nouakchott Process on the Enhancement of Security Cooperation and the Operationalization of the African Peace and Security Architecture in the Sahelo-Saharan Region, launched on 17 March 2013, and takes note of the conclusions of the ministerial meetings held in N'Djamena on 11 September 2013 and in Niamey on 19 February 2014, as well as of the five meetings of the Heads of Intelligence and Security Services organized by the African Union Commission. The Council also takes note of the conclusions of the Paris Summit for Security in Nigeria, held on 17 May 2014, as well as the London Ministerial on Security in Nigeria, held on 12 June 2014, which reaffirmed the commitment of the countries of the region and international partners to increase security cooperation to more effectively address the threat of terrorism in the region, including by efforts to contribute to the revitalization of the Multinational Joint Task Force to patrol the Lake Chad region and to create a Regional Intelligence Fusion Unit.

The Council reaffirms the sovereign prerogative of Member States to secure their borders and calls upon those of the Sahel region to strengthen border security and consider establishing special units to undertake regional patrols, to effectively constrain the spread of transnational threats in the region. The Council welcomes the commitment made by African leaders at the Malabo summit, held on 26 and 27 June 2014, and steps taken by the African Union to operationalize the African Capacity for Immediate Response to Crisis and encourages the States members of the African Union to generate substantive pledges to this initiative.

The Council, underscoring that terrorism, together with transnational organized crime and other illicit activities such as drug trafficking, are recurrent threats in the Sahel, encourages the Member States of the Sahel region to improve the coordination of their efforts to combat these threats more effectively. The Council welcomes the cooperation between the countries of the Sahel and their bilateral and multilateral partners in combating terrorism in the region and encourages international partners to provide support for the enhancement of their national and regional capabilities, including their capacity to conduct regional patrols, and to establish and maintain joint coordination centres and joint information-sharing centres. The Council recalls the importance of upholding human rights and the rule of law in the fight against terrorism. The Council calls upon the countries of the Sahel to intensify cross-border and interregional cooperation and coordination in order to counter more effectively the threats to peace and security in the region.

The Council takes note of the report of the Secretary-General on progress towards the United Nations integrated strategy for the Sahel[392] and stresses the importance of ensuring the implementation of all three pillars of the strategy, namely, security, governance and resilience, which are interdependent. The Council underscores the importance of including civil society in the implementation of the strategy and stresses the need for the Governments of the Sahel region to continue to demonstrate the sustained political will necessary to enable the effective and durable implementation of the strategy.

The Council remains concerned about the extremely fragile humanitarian situation in the Sahel region where at least 20 million people remain at risk of food insecurity and nearly 5 million children are at risk of acute malnutrition. The Council commends the efforts of the Regional Humanitarian Coordinator for the Sahel, with the support of the Office for the Coordination of Humanitarian Affairs of the Secretariat and other humanitarian actors and agencies, to build and strengthen resilience at the local, national and regional levels with the aim of mitigating the impact of such disasters. The Council, in this regard, commends the support provided by the countries of the region and other donors and calls upon the international community to strengthen its support in areas which require immediate attention.

[392] S/2014/397.

The Council expresses its appreciation to the former Special Envoy of the Secretary-General for the Sahel, Mr. Romano Prodi, for having facilitated the development of the United Nations integrated strategy for the Sahel and also expresses its appreciation for the efforts of the former Special Representative of the Secretary-General for West Africa, Mr. Said Djinnit, in supporting the implementation of the strategy.

The Council welcomes the appointment of the new Special Envoy of the Secretary-General for the Sahel, Ms. Hiroute Guebre Sellassie, and expresses its full support for the fulfilment of her mandate. The Council encourages the Special Envoy to pursue her efforts and good offices in order to enhance regional and interregional cooperation and strengthen coordinated international assistance to the countries of the Sahel region in close coordination with the Special Representative of the Secretary-General for West Africa.

The Council requests the Secretary-General to inform it of the progress toward the implementation of the United Nations integrated strategy for the Sahel through an oral briefing by 15 December 2014, and through a report and a briefing no later than 30 November 2015.

At its 7279th meeting, on 14 October 2014, the Council decided to invite the representatives of Guinea, Liberia and Sierra Leone to participate, without vote, in accordance with rule 37 of its provisional rules of procedure, in the discussion of the item entitled "Peace and security in Africa".

At the same meeting, the Council also decided to extend invitations, in accordance with rule 39 of its provisional rules of procedure, to Mr. Anthony Banbury, Special Representative of the Secretary-General and Head of the United Nations Mission for Ebola Emergency Response, Mr. Hervé Ladsous, Under-Secretary-General for Peacekeeping Operations, and Mr. Tayé-Brook Zerihoun, Assistant Secretary-General for Political Affairs.

At its 7318th meeting, on 21 November 2014, the Council decided to invite the representatives of Guinea, Liberia, Mali and Sierra Leone to participate, without vote, in accordance with rule 37 of its provisional rules of procedure, in the discussion of the item entitled "Peace and security in Africa".

At the same meeting, the Council also decided to extend invitations, in accordance with rule 39 of its provisional rules of procedure, to Mr. Anthony Banbury, Special Representative of the Secretary-General and Head of the United Nations Mission on Ebola Emergency Response, Dr. David Nabarro, Special Envoy of the Secretary-General on Ebola, and Mr. Thomas Mauget, Head of the French Red Cross in Guinea.

At the same meeting, following consultations among members of the Security Council, the President made the following statement on behalf of the Council:[393]

> The Security Council reiterates its grave concern about the unprecedented extent of the Ebola outbreak in Africa, which constitutes a threat to international peace and security, and the impact of the Ebola virus on West Africa, in particular Liberia, Guinea and Sierra Leone. The Council expresses its appreciation for the crucial contributions and commitments made by the Member States of the region to continue to lead the ground-level response against the Ebola outbreak, as well as to address the wider political, security, socioeconomic and humanitarian impact, including on food security, of the Ebola outbreak on communities and the need to plan for the longer-term recovery in the region, including with the support of the Peacebuilding Commission. The Council underscores the continued need for robust contact tracing, social mobilization and community-level engagement efforts, especially outside of major urban areas in the most affected countries.
>
> The Council stresses the importance for the United Nations Mission for Ebola Emergency Response to continue to strengthen coordination with the Governments of Guinea, Liberia and Sierra Leone and all national, regional and international actors, including bilateral partners and multilateral organizations, including the Mano River Union, the African Union, the Economic Community of West African States, the European Union, the World Bank Group and the United Nations system, in order to more readily identify gaps in the response effort and to utilize all Ebola response assistance more fully and efficiently, particularly at the local level. In this regard, the Council requests that the Secretary-General accelerate efforts to scale up the presence and activities of the Mission at the district and prefecture level outside of the capital cities.
>
> The Council expresses its concern about the recent reported Ebola infections in Mali. The Council recognizes the important steps taken by the Government of Mali, including by appointing an Ebola incident

[393] S/PRST/2014/24.

coordinator to lead a whole-of-government response. The Council affirms the importance of preparedness by all Member States to detect, prevent, respond to, isolate and mitigate suspected cases of Ebola within and across borders and of bolstering the preparedness of all countries in the region. The Council recalls the International Health Regulations (2005),[388] which aim to improve the capacity of all countries to detect, assess, notify and respond to all public health threats.

The Council welcomes the efforts undertaken by the Mission to provide overall leadership and direction to the operational work of the United Nations system, as mandated by the General Assembly. The Council underscores the need for relevant United Nations system entities, including the United Nations peacekeeping operations and special political missions in West Africa, in close collaboration with the Mission and within their existing mandates and capacities, to provide immediate assistance to the Governments of the most affected countries.

The Council lauds the critical, heroic and selfless efforts of the first-line responders to the Ebola outbreak in West Africa, including national health and humanitarian relief workers, educators and burial team members, as well as international health and humanitarian relief workers contributed by the Member States of diverse regions and non-governmental and intergovernmental organizations. The Council expresses its condolences to the families of the victims of the Ebola outbreak, including national and international first-line responders. The Council urges all Member States, non-governmental, intergovernmental and regional organizations to continue to respond to the outstanding need for medical personnel, as well as related critical gap areas such as personnel with expertise in sanitation and hygiene.

The Council underscores the critical importance of putting in place essential arrangements, including medical evacuation capacities and treatment and transport provisions, to facilitate the immediate, unhindered and sustainable deployment of health and humanitarian relief workers to the affected countries. The Council welcomes the steps announced by Member States and regional organizations to provide medical evacuation capacities for health and humanitarian relief workers, as well as other treatment options in situ.

The Council notes the considerable efforts of the international community to scale up its coordinated response to the Ebola outbreak and the important progress on the ground as a result of these contributions. In this regard, the Council commends those Member States, which, in concert with other actors on the ground, have opened Ebola treatment units and provided other crucial support in the affected countries. The Council urges all Member States, bilateral partners and multilateral organizations to expedite the provision of resources and financial assistance, as well as mobile laboratories; field hospitals to provide non-Ebola related medical care; dedicated and trained clinical personnel and services in Ebola treatment units and isolation units; therapies, vaccines and diagnostics to treat patients and limit or prevent further Ebola infection or transmission; and personal protective equipment for first-line responders. The Council calls upon Member States, especially in the region, to facilitate immediately the delivery of such assistance to the most affected countries.

The Council emphasizes that the dynamic needs on the ground in the most affected countries require that the response of the international community response remain flexible, in order to adapt to changing requirements and rapidly respond to new outbreaks.

The Council strongly urges Member States, as well as airlines and shipping companies, while applying appropriate public health protocols, to maintain trade and transport links with the most affected countries to enable the timely utilization of all efforts aimed at containing the Ebola outbreak within and across borders of the region. While recognizing the important role that appropriate screening measures can play in stopping the spread of the outbreak, the Council expresses its continued concern about the detrimental effect of the isolation of the affected countries as a result of trade and travel restrictions imposed on and to the affected countries, as well as acts of discrimination against the nationals of Guinea, Liberia, Mali and Sierra Leone, including Ebola survivors and their families or those infected with the disease.

At its 7335th meeting, on 11 December 2014, the Council considered the item entitled "Peace and security in Africa".

At the same meeting, the Council decided to extend an invitation, in accordance with rule 39 of its provisional rules of procedure, to Ms. Hiroute Guebre Sellassie, Special Envoy of the Secretary-General for the Sahel.

COOPERATION BETWEEN THE UNITED NATIONS AND REGIONAL AND SUBREGIONAL ORGANIZATIONS IN MAINTAINING INTERNATIONAL PEACE AND SECURITY[394]

Decisions

At its 7343rd meeting, on 16 December 2014, the Security Council decided to invite the representatives of Algeria, Brazil, Egypt, Ethiopia, India, Indonesia, Iran (Islamic Republic of), Ireland, Italy, Japan, Kazakhstan, Malaysia, Namibia, the Netherlands, New Zealand, Pakistan, Slovakia, Sweden, Tunisia, Turkey and Uganda to participate, without vote, in accordance with rule 37 of its provisional rules of procedure, in the discussion of the item entitled:

"Cooperation between the United Nations and regional and subregional organizations in maintaining international peace and security

"Peace operations: the United Nations-African Union partnership and its evolution

"Letter dated 8 December 2014 from the Permanent Representative of Chad to the United Nations addressed to the Secretary-General (S/2014/879)".

At the same meeting, the Council also decided to extend an invitation, in accordance with rule 39 of its provisional rules of procedure, to Mr. Pierre Buyoya, African Union High Representative for Mali and the Sahel.

At the same meeting, the Council further decided to extend an invitation, in accordance with rule 39 of its provisional rules of procedure, to Mr. Nick Westcott, Managing Director for Africa in the European External Action Service of the European Union.

At the same meeting, following consultations among members of the Security Council, the President made the following statement on behalf of the Council:[395]

The Security Council recalls its previous relevant resolutions and statements by its President which underscore the importance of developing effective partnerships between the United Nations and regional and subregional organizations, in accordance with the Charter of the United Nations and the relevant statutes of the regional and subregional organizations.

The Council recalls the purposes and principles of the Charter of the United Nations, and reaffirms its primary responsibility under the Charter for the maintenance of international peace and security.

The Council welcomes the briefing of the United Nations Secretary-General, Mr. Ban Ki-moon, and that of the African Union High Representative for Mali and the Sahel, former President Pierre Buyoya.

The Council acknowledges the progress made in the ongoing cooperation between the United Nations and the African Union, and stresses the importance of further strengthening cooperation and developing effective partnership with the Peace and Security Council of the African Union consistent with Chapter VIII of the Charter, to address common collective security challenges in Africa.

The Security Council reiterates that cooperation with regional and subregional organizations in matters relating to the maintenance of international peace and security and consistent with Chapter VIII of the Charter can improve collective security.

The Council recognizes that regional organizations are well positioned to understand the root causes of armed conflicts owing to their knowledge of the region, which can be a benefit for their efforts to influence the prevention or resolution of these conflicts.

The Council acknowledges the role of the African Union in efforts to prevent or settle conflicts on the African continent and expresses its support for the continued efforts of the African Union to promote peace initiatives conducted by the African Union, and similar initiatives of subregional organizations.

---

[394] Resolutions or decisions on this question were first adopted by the Security Council in 2007.

[395] S/PRST/2014/27.

The Council commends the increased contribution of the African Union to the maintenance of peace and security, including peacekeeping, in particular in the Sudan (Darfur), Mali, the Central African Republic and Somalia, as well as the African Union Regional Task Force, and efforts to further strengthen its capacity, including through the operationalization of both its African Standby Force and its Rapid Deployment Capability, and welcomes the United Nations-African Union continued cooperation on different components of the African Peace and Security Architecture, including on early warning, preventive diplomacy, mediation, electoral assistance, peacekeeping, conflict prevention and resolution, promotion of human rights and the rule of law, and post-conflict recovery and reconstruction.

The Council welcomes the decision by the African Union to declare 2014–2024 as the Madiba Nelson Mandela Decade of Reconciliation in Africa and to take appropriate measures to promote reconciliation as a means of securing peace, stability and development in Africa, as well as to also take appropriate steps in collaboration with its member States to promote the lessons learned from his indelible legacy in the areas of truth, reconciliation and peacebuilding.

The Council welcomes the efforts undertaken by the African Union to end impunity and ensure accountability, including by strengthening national justice institutions.

The Council stresses the importance of further strengthening cooperation with the African Union in order to assist in building its capacity to deal with common collective security challenges in Africa, including through the African Union's commitment of rapid and appropriate responses to emerging crisis situations, and the development of effective strategies for conflict prevention and resolution, peacekeeping and peacebuilding.

The Council reiterates that regional organizations have the responsibility to secure human, financial, logistical and other resources for their organizations, including through contributions by their members and support from partners and welcomes the valuable financial support provided by partners in this regard.

The Council recognizes that one major constraint facing the African Union in effectively carrying out the mandates of maintaining regional peace and security is securing predictable, sustainable and flexible resources.

The Council encourages closer coordination and cooperation on policing issues between the United Nations Secretariat and international, regional and subregional organizations, including through training, the sharing and exchange of knowledge, thematic expertise and operational support as appropriate.

The Council recognizes the role that the African Union can play in the protection of civilians, and in particular women and children affected by armed conflict, as well as in the prevention of and response to sexual and gender-based violence in armed conflicts and post-conflict situations and supports the critical role that women play in all peace and security efforts, including those to prevent and resolve conflict and mitigate its impact.

The Council welcomes the United Nations partnership in the field of peacekeeping, including support to the efforts of the African Union to develop policy, guidance and training, in particular in the areas of security sector reform, post-conflict reconstruction, women and peace and security and the protection of civilians, including child protection and the prevention of and response to sexual and gender-based violence in armed conflicts and post-conflict situations.

The Council recognizes the valuable contribution of relevant regional and subregional organizations and arrangements for the protection of children affected by armed conflict and commends in this regard the declaration signed on 17 September 2013 by the Office of the Special Representative of the Secretary-General for Children and Armed Conflict and the Peace and Security Department of the African Union Commission, in order to mainstream protection mechanisms in all peace and security activities of the African Union, in close partnership with the United Nations Children's Fund.

The Council encourages in this regard the African Union Commission to help to address the widespread impact of armed conflict on children, invites it to continue the mainstreaming of child protection into its advocacy, policies, programmes and mission planning, the development and expansion of guidelines to protect children affected by armed conflict as well as the training of personnel and the inclusion of child protection staff in its peacekeeping and field operations, and reiterates its call for the establishment of child protection mechanisms within its secretariat, including through the appointment of child protection focal points.

The Council urges Member States and relevant international organizations to contribute to strengthening the capacity of the African Union and its subregional organizations in conflict prevention and crisis management and in post-conflict stabilization, including through the provision of human, technical and financial assistance.

The Council reiterates the importance of establishing a more effective relationship between the Security Council and the Peace and Security Council, including through achieving more effective annual consultative meetings, the holding of timely consultations, and collaborative field missions of the two Councils, as appropriate, to formulate cohesive positions and strategies on a case-by-case basis in dealing with conflict situations in Africa.

The Security Council calls for the strengthening of cooperation between the United Nations Secretariat and the African Union Commission, including in the area of mediation efforts, and underscores the importance of developing the follow-up programme to the 2006 United Nations-African Union Ten-year Capacity-Building Programme, as an important contribution towards conflict prevention, management and resolution on the African continent. In this regard, the Council welcomes the United Nations-African Union joint decision during the fifteenth session of the Regional Coordination Mechanism for Africa, held in Abuja in March 2014 to establish a working group to start formulating a successor programme that will also reflect the support of the United Nations to Agenda 2063.

The Council welcomes the appointment of the high-level panel to review peace operations, and invites this panel to consult closely with the African Union.

The Council welcomes regular interaction between the United Nations Secretariat and the African Union Commission, through the United Nations-African Union Joint Task Force on Peace and Security, and encourages the Task Force to continue to focus on strategic and country-specific issues of the African continent that are of interest to both organizations and requests that the Task Force consider ways to enhance United Nations and African Union cooperation on conflict prevention in Africa and that it provide updates to the Council subsequent to its meetings.

The Council commends the transfer of authority from the African-led International Support Mission to the Central African Republic to the United Nations Multidimensional Integrated Stabilization Mission in the Central African Republic on 15 September 2014 and welcomes the ongoing lessons-learned exercise on the transitions from African Union to United Nations peacekeeping operations in Mali and the Central African Republic, pursuant to paragraph 13 of resolution 2167 (2014) and looks forward to concrete recommendations from this lessons-learned exercise, which would seek to strengthen the management of transitions from African Union to United Nations peacekeeping missions.

The Council stresses the importance of supporting the political role of the African Union, both during the transition from African Union to United Nations peacekeeping missions, as well as in the formulation and implementation of governance and other reforms to be carried out in addressing the root causes of conflict in Africa.

The Council encourages the United Nations and the African Union to take concrete steps to strengthen their relationships and develop a more effective partnership when addressing issues of mutual interest and underscores the need to enhance the United Nations and African Union predeployment joint planning and joint mission assessment processes to promote common understanding and increase effectiveness of peacekeeping missions.

The Council calls upon the Secretary-General to coordinate with and support the African Union Commission in its development of a list of needed capacities and recommendations on ways the African Union can further develop its military, civilian, police, technical, logistic and administrative capabilities, welcomes the practice of staff exchanges, especially between the United Nations and the African Union, and encourages its continuity, particularly for staff in the financial and logistic areas, and further encourages the African Union to identify its priorities in personnel training, particularly in those areas dealing with financial, logistic and administrative matters.

The Council notes the progress in the level and process of preparation for the eighth joint consultative meeting of the Security Council and the Peace and Security Council, held on 6 June 2014 in New York, including the finalization in advance of the agenda for the annual consultative meeting and the joint press briefing by the President of the Security Council and the Chairperson of the Peace and Security Council, and recommends that the ninth consultative meeting, scheduled to take place in Addis Ababa in 2015, address the issue of follow-up to and implementation of previous communiqués.

The Security Council welcomes the adoption of the Fiftieth Anniversary Solemn Declaration by African leaders on 26 May 2013, pledging to "end all wars in Africa by 2020" and "achieve the goal of a conflict-free Africa", expresses its readiness to contribute and calls upon all, in particular relevant United Nations entities to help to achieve this goal, including by considering defining a concrete five-year actionable plan in support of the goal of achieving a conflict-free Africa by 2020. The Council notes in that regard that instability and violence in the Central African Republic, the Democratic Republic of the Congo, Libya, the Sahel, Mali, Somalia, South Sudan and Sudan need to be addressed and resolved as a matter of urgency.

The Council recognizes the important role of the good offices of the Secretary-General in Africa, and encourages the Secretary-General to continue to use mediation as often as possible to help to resolve conflicts peacefully, working in coordination and closely with the African Union and its subregional organizations in that regard, as appropriate.

The Council takes note of the election of the new five members of the African Union Panel of the Wise and acknowledges the key preventive role that the Panel can play, and calls for increased political support to the Panel in the implementation of its mandate, and encourages the Panel's early engagement in deteriorating situations at risk of conflict.

The Council stresses the importance of strengthened African Union and United Nations capacities for early warning, conflict analysis, dialogue and mediation and increased African Union-United Nations collaboration in the area of good offices and between United Nations-African Union Envoys. The Council underscores the need to allocate resources to support and strengthen the Continental Early Warning System, the good offices role of Special Envoys and Representatives, as well as post-conflict reconstruction and development efforts, including through the African Solidarity Initiative.

The Council stresses the importance of a coordinated international response to causes of conflict and recognizes the need for the development of effective long-term strategies and emphasizes the need for all United Nations organs and agencies to pursue preventive strategies and to take action within their respective areas of competence to assist Member States and regional and subregional organizations to eradicate poverty, strengthen development cooperation and assistance and promote respect for human rights and fundamental freedoms.

The Council welcomes recent developments regarding cooperation between the United Nations, the African Union and the European Union, including the contribution of the European Union to the enhancement of African Union capacities, and further encourages regional and subregional organizations to strengthen and increase cooperation among them, including efforts to enhance their respective capacities, in the maintenance of international peace and security.

The Council reaffirms its previous resolutions and the statements by its President regarding the Prodi report,[396] including the statements of 26 October 2009,[397] 22 October 2010[398] and 6 August 2013,[399] as well as resolutions 1809 (2008), 1863 (2009), 2033 (2012), 2086 (2013) and 2167 (2014).

The Council stresses the need to secure more financial resources from within the African continent, without prejudice to the support from the United Nations and other partners.

The Council reiterates its resolve to give peacekeeping operations clear, credible and achievable mandates matched by appropriate resources.

[396] Report of the African Union-United Nations panel on modalities for support to African Union peacekeeping operations (see S/2008/813).

[397] S/PRST/2009/26.

[398] S/PRST/2010/21.

[399] S/PRST/2013/12.

The Council stresses the need to enhance the predictability, sustainability and flexibility of financing regional organizations when they undertake peacekeeping under a Council mandate, and recognizes the benefit of joint planning missions and assessment visits in determining the needs of regional peace support operations.

The Council welcomes the renewed efforts of the African Union for the full operationalization of the African Peace and Security Architecture, and looks forward to the finalization of the ongoing Architecture assessment report, as well as to the successful conduct in 2015 of the Amani Africa II Exercise, which will validate the full operational capability of the African Standby Force.

The Council welcomes the steps taken for the operationalization of the African Capacity for Immediate Response to Crises, including through enhanced decision-making to facilitate rapid deployment.

The Council stresses the importance for the United Nations of developing the ability of the African Union and its subregional organizations to deploy peacekeeping forces rapidly in support of United Nations peacekeeping operations or other Council-mandated operations, and welcomes recent initiatives taken in this regard by the African Union.

The Council takes note of the commitments made by the European Union and Africa at the European Union-Africa Summit held in Brussels on 2 and 3 April 2014 to strengthen the operationalization of the African Peace and Security Architecture, in particular by supporting the African Standby Force and its Rapid Deployment Capacity, supported and managed in a sustainable way, as reaffirmed by the European Union Political and Security Committee and the African Union Peace and Security Council in Brussels on 15 May 2014. The Security Council further encourages initiatives aimed at creating more synergies between the African Union, the European Union and the United Nations in this endeavour, and further takes note of close cooperation between the European Union and the African Union, with the relevant regional and subregional organizations, the United Nations and its agencies, and with other international coordination mechanisms. The Council commends all the efforts already achieved by the European Union to this end and further welcomes the expressed intention of the European Union to allocate increased funding, including through the African Peace Facility.

The Council also takes note of the first African Union-China Strategic Dialogue for Peace and Security in Africa, launched in October 2014, which considers further cooperation measures in the peace and security area, including supporting the African Capacity for Immediate Response to Crises.

The Council further takes note of the first United States of America-Africa Leaders Summit and welcomes the announcement of the African Peacekeeping Rapid Response Partnership, which seeks to strengthen the capabilities of African countries to rapidly deploy peacekeepers in response to emerging conflict.

The Council requests the Secretary-General to present an annual report to the Council on ways to strengthen the partnership between the United Nations and the African Union on issues of peace and security in Africa, including the work of the United Nations Office to the African Union.

At its 7402nd meeting, on 9 March 2015, the Council considered the item entitled:

"Cooperation between the United Nations and regional and subregional organizations in maintaining international peace and security

"European Union".

At the same meeting, the Council decided to extend an invitation, in accordance with rule 39 of its provisional rules of procedure, to Ms. Federica Mogherini, High Representative for Foreign Affairs and Security Policy of the European Union.

At its 7439th meeting, on 11 May 2015, the Council considered the item entitled "Cooperation between the United Nations and regional and subregional organizations in maintaining international peace and security".

At the same meeting, the Council decided to extend invitations, in accordance with rule 39 of its provisional rules of procedure, to Ms. Federica Mogherini, High Representative for Foreign Affairs and Security Policy of the European Union, and Mr. Téte António, Permanent Observer of the African Union to the United Nations.

At the same meeting, the Council also decided to extend an invitation, in accordance with rule 39 of its provisional rules of procedure, to Mr. Peter Sutherland, Special Representative of the Secretary-General for International Migration.

THE SITUATION IN LIBYA[400]

Decisions

On 12 August 2014, the President of the Security Council addressed the following letter to the Secretary-General:[401]

> I have the honour to inform you that your letter dated 8 August 2014 concerning your intention to appoint Mr. Bernardino León, of Spain, as your Special Representative for Libya and Head of the United Nations Support Mission in Libya[402] has been brought to the attention of the members of the Security Council. They take note of the intention expressed in your letter.

At its 7251st meeting, on 27 August 2014, the Council decided to invite the representatives of Germany, Italy and Libya to participate, without vote, in accordance with rule 37 of its provisional rules of procedure, in the discussion of the item entitled "The situation in Libya".

At the same meeting, the Council also decided to extend an invitation, in accordance with rule 39 of its provisional rules of procedure, to Mr. Tarek Mitri, Special Representative of the Secretary-General for Libya and Head of the United Nations Support Mission in Libya.

Resolution 2174 (2014)
of 27 August 2014

The Security Council,

Recalling all its resolutions on Libya since resolution 1970 (2011) of 26 February 2011, as well as the statement by its President of 16 December 2013,[403]

Reaffirming its strong commitment to the sovereignty, independence, territorial integrity and national unity of Libya,

Deploring the increasing violence in Libya, in particular around Tripoli and Benghazi, condemning ongoing fighting by armed groups and incitement to violence, and expressing its deep concern at its impact on Libya's civilian population and institutions, as well as the threat it poses to Libya's stability and democratic transition,

Welcoming the calls of the Government of Libya and House of Representatives for an immediate ceasefire, underlining the need for all parties to engage in peaceful and inclusive political dialogue and to respect the democratic process, and encouraging the Arab League, the African Union and all those with influence on the parties, in particular neighbouring and regional countries, to support an immediate cessation of hostilities and constructive engagement with such a dialogue,

Recalling its decision in resolution 1970 (2011) to refer the situation in Libya to the Prosecutor of the International Criminal Court, and reaffirming the importance of the Government of Libya's cooperation with the Court and the Prosecutor,

Reaffirming the importance of holding accountable those responsible for violations or abuses of human rights or violations of international humanitarian law, including those involved in attacks targeting civilians,

---

[400] Resolutions or decisions on this question were first adopted by the Security Council in 2011.

[401] S/2014/584.

[402] S/2014/583.

[403] S/PRST/2013/21.

Expressing deep concern at the threat posed by unsecured arms and ammunition in Libya and their proliferation, which poses a risk to stability in Libya and the region, including through transfer to terrorist and violent extremist groups, and underlining the importance of coordinated international support to Libya and the region to address these issues,

Concerned at the growing presence of Al-Qaida-linked terrorists groups and individuals operating in Libya, reaffirming the need to combat by all means, in accordance with the Charter of the United Nations and international law, including applicable international human rights, refugee and humanitarian law, threats to international peace and security caused by terrorist acts, and recalling in this regard the obligations under resolution 2161 (2014) of 17 June 2014,

Expressing its determination to use targeted sanctions in pursuit of stability in Libya, and against those individuals and entities that threaten its stability and obstruct or undermine its successful completion of the political transition,

Mindful of its primary responsibility for the maintenance of international peace and security under the Charter,

Acting under Chapter VII of the Charter,

1. *Calls upon* all parties to agree to an immediate ceasefire and an end to fighting, and expresses its strong support for the efforts of the United Nations Support Mission in Libya and the Special Representative of the Secretary-General for Libya in this regard;

2. *Condemns* the use of violence against civilians and civilian institutions, and calls for those responsible to be held accountable;

3. *Calls upon* the House of Representatives and the Constitutional Drafting Assembly to carry out their tasks in a spirit of inclusiveness, and calls upon all parties to engage in an inclusive Libyan-led political dialogue in order to help restore stability and to forge consensus around the next steps in Libya's transition;

4. *Reaffirms* that the measures specified in paragraphs 15, 16, 17, 19, 20 and 21 of resolution 1970 (2011), as modified by paragraphs 14, 15 and 16 of resolution 2009 (2011) of 16 September 2011, apply to individuals and entities designated under that resolution and under resolution 1973 (2011) of 17 March 2011 and by the Security Council Committee established pursuant to paragraph 24 of resolution 1970 (2011), decides that they shall also apply to individuals and entities determined by the Committee to be engaging in or providing support for other acts that threaten the peace, stability or security of Libya, or obstruct or undermine the successful completion of its political transition, and decides that such acts may include but are not limited to:

(*a*) Planning, directing or committing acts that violate applicable international human rights law or international humanitarian law, or acts that constitute human rights abuses, in Libya;

(*b*) Attacks against any air, land or sea port in Libya, or against a Libyan State institution or installation, or against any foreign mission in Libya;

(*c*) Providing support for armed groups or criminal networks through the illicit exploitation of crude oil or any other natural resources in Libya;

(*d*) Acting for or on behalf of or at the direction of a listed individual or entity;

5. *Reiterates* that individuals and entities determined by the Committee to have violated provisions of resolution 1970 (2011), including the arms embargo, or assisted others in doing so, are subject to designation, and notes that this includes those who assist in the violation of the assets freeze and travel ban in resolution 1970 (2011);

6. *Requests* the Panel of Experts on Libya established pursuant to paragraph 24 of resolution 1973 (2011), in addition to its current mandate, to provide information on individuals and entities that meet the designation criteria specified in paragraphs 4 and 5 of the present resolution;

7. *Requests* that the Committee give due regard to requests for delisting of individuals and entities who no longer meet the designation criteria;

8. *Decides* that the supply, sale or transfer of arms and related materiel, including related ammunition and spare parts, to Libya in accordance with paragraph 13 (*a*) of resolution 2009 (2011) as modified by paragraph 10 of resolution 2095 (2013) of 14 March 2013 must be approved in advance by the Committee;

9. *Calls upon* all States, in particular States neighbouring Libya, to inspect in their territory, including seaports and airports, in accordance with their national authorities and legislation and consistent with international law, in particular the law of the sea and relevant international civil aviation agreements, all cargo to and from Libya, if the State concerned has information that provides reasonable grounds to believe the cargo contains items the supply, sale, transfer or export of which is prohibited by paragraph 9 or 10 of resolution 1970 (2011), as modified by paragraph 13 of resolution 2009 (2011) and paragraphs 9 and 10 of resolution 2095 (2013), for the purpose of ensuring strict implementation of those provisions;

10. *Reaffirms* its decision to authorize all Member States to, and that all Member States shall, upon discovery of items prohibited by paragraph 9 or 10 of resolution 1970, as modified by paragraph 13 of resolution 2009 (2011) and paragraphs 9 and 10 of resolution 2095 (2013), seize and dispose (such as through destruction, rendering inoperable, storage or transferring to a State other than the originating or destination States for disposal) of such items, and further reaffirms its decision that all Member States shall cooperate in such efforts;

11. *Requires* any Member State ,when it undertakes an inspection pursuant to paragraph 9 of the present resolution, to submit promptly an initial written report to the Committee containing, in particular, explanation of the grounds for the inspections, the results of such inspections, and whether or not cooperation was provided, and, if prohibited items for transfer are found, further requires such Member States to submit to the Committee, at a later stage, a subsequent written report containing relevant details on the inspection, seizure and disposal, and relevant details of the transfer, including a description of the items, their origin and intended destination, if this information is not in the initial report;

12. *Affirms* its readiness to review the appropriateness of the measures contained in the present resolution, including the strengthening, modification, suspension or lifting of the measures, and its readiness to review the mandate of the Mission, as may be needed at any time in the light of developments in Libya;

13. *Decides* to remain actively seized of the matter.

Adopted unanimously at the 7251st meeting.

Decisions

At its 7264th meeting, on 15 September 2014, the Security Council decided to invite the representative of Libya to participate, without vote, in accordance with rule 37 of its provisional rules of procedure, in the discussion of the item entitled:

"The situation in Libya

"Report of the Secretary-General on the United Nations Support Mission in Libya (S/2014/653)".

At the same meeting, the Council also decided to extend an invitation, in accordance with rule 39 of its provisional rules of procedure, to Mr. Bernardino León, Special Representative of the Secretary-General for Libya and Head of the United Nations Support Mission in Libya.

At its 7306th meeting, on 11 November 2014, the Council decided to invite the representative Libya to participate, without vote, in accordance with rule 37 of its provisional rules of procedure, in the discussion of the item entitled "The situation in Libya".

At the same meeting, the Council also decided to extend an invitation, in accordance with rule 39 of its provisional rules of procedure, to Ms. Fatou Bensouda, Prosecutor of the International Criminal Court.

At its 7345th meeting, on 17 December 2014, the Council decided to invite the representative of Libya to participate, without vote, in accordance with rule 37 of its provisional rules of procedure, in the discussion of the item entitled:

"The situation in Libya

"Briefing by the Chair of the Security Council Committee established pursuant to resolution 1970 (2011) concerning Libya".

At its 7387th meeting, on 18 February 2015, the Council decided to invite the representatives of Algeria, Egypt, Italy, Libya and Tunisia to participate, without vote, in accordance with rule 37 of its provisional rules of procedure, in the discussion of the item entitled "The situation in Libya".

At the same meeting, the Council also decided to extend an invitation, in accordance with rule 39 of its provisional rules of procedure, to Mr. Bernardino León, Special Representative of the Secretary-General for Libya and Head of the United Nations Support Mission in Libya.

At its 7398th meeting, on 4 March 2015, the Council decided to invite the representative of Libya to participate, without vote, in accordance with rule 37 of its provisional rules of procedure, in the discussion of the item entitled:

"The situation in Libya

"Letter dated 23 February 2015 from the Panel of Experts established pursuant to resolution 1973 (2011) addressed to the President of the Security Council (S/2015/128)

"Report of the Secretary-General on the United Nations Support Mission in Libya (S/2015/144)".

At the same meeting, the Council also decided to extend an invitation, in accordance with rule 39 of its provisional rules of procedure, to Mr. Bernardino León, Special Representative of the Secretary-General for Libya and Head of the United Nations Support Mission in Libya.

At its 7399th meeting, on 5 March 2015, the Council decided to invite the representative of Libya to participate, without vote, in accordance with rule 37 of its provisional rules of procedure, in the discussion of the item entitled:

"The situation in Libya

"Special report of the Secretary-General on the strategic assessment of the United Nations presence in Libya (S/2015/113)

"Letter dated 23 February 2015 from the Panel of Experts established pursuant to resolution 1973 (2011) addressed to the President of the Security Council (S/2015/128)

"Report of the Secretary-General on the United Nations Support Mission in Libya (S/2015/144)".

Resolution 2208 (2015)
of 5 March 2015

The Security Council,

Recalling its resolution 1970 (2011) of 26 February 2011 and all its subsequent resolutions on Libya,

Taking note of the report of the Secretary-General of 26 February 2015 on the United Nations Support Mission in Libya,[404]

Taking note also of the special report of the Secretary-General of 13 February 2015 on the strategic assessment of the United Nations presence in Libya,[405] including the recommendations on the configuration of the United Nations presence made therein,

Supporting the ongoing efforts of the Special Representative of the Secretary-General for Libya to facilitate a political solution to the increasing challenges facing the country,

Recognizing, in the current circumstances, the need for a short extension of the mandate of the Mission,

Recognizing also the need for a short extension of the authorizations provided by and the measures imposed by resolution 2146 (2014) of 19 March 2014,

Determining that the situation in Libya continues to constitute a threat to international peace and security,

Acting under Chapter VII of the Charter of the United Nations,

1. *Decides* to extend until 31 March 2015 the authorizations provided by and the measures imposed by resolution 2146 (2014);

[404] S/2015/144.

[405] S/2015/113.

2. *Also decides* to extend until 31 March 2015 the mandate of the United Nations Support Mission in Libya, as set out in paragraph 6 of resolution 2144 (2014) of 14 March 2014, under the leadership of the Special Representative of the Secretary-General for Libya, in full accordance with the principles of national ownership;

3. *Further decides* to remain seized of the matter.

Adopted unanimously at the 7399th meeting.

Decision

At its 7420th meeting, on 27 March 2015, the Security Council decided to invite the representatives of Egypt and Libya to participate, without vote, in accordance with rule 37 of its provisional rules of procedure, in the discussion of the item entitled:

"The situation in Libya

"Special report of the Secretary-General on the strategic assessment of the United Nations presence in Libya (S/2015/113)

"Letter dated 23 February 2015 from the Panel of Experts established pursuant to resolution 1973 (2011) addressed to the President of the Security Council (S/2015/128)

"Report of the Secretary-General on the United Nations Support Mission in Libya (S/2015/144)".

Resolution 2213 (2015) of 27 March 2015

The Security Council,

Recalling its resolution 1970 (2011) of 26 February 2011 and all its subsequent resolutions on Libya,

Reaffirming its strong commitment to the sovereignty, independence, territorial integrity and national unity of Libya,

Welcoming the ongoing efforts of the United Nations Support Mission in Libya and the Special Representative of the Secretary-General for Libya to facilitate a Libyan-led political solution to the increasing challenges facing the country, and underlining the importance of agreement, in accordance with the principles of national ownership, on immediate next steps towards completing Libya's political transition, including the formation of a national unity government,

Welcoming also the ongoing United Nations-facilitated political dialogue, recognizing the contribution of Member States to host and support meetings of that dialogue, and emphasizing the necessity for the constructive participation of the elected House of Representatives and other Libyan parties to take forward the democratic transition, build State institutions and start the reconstruction of Libya,

Gravely concerned at the growing trend of terrorist groups in Libya to proclaim allegiance to Islamic State in Iraq and the Levant (also known as Da'esh) and the continued presence of other Al-Qaida-linked terrorist groups and individuals operating there, reaffirming the need to combat by all means, in accordance with the Charter of the United Nations and international law, including applicable international human rights, refugee and humanitarian law, threats to international peace and security caused by terrorist acts, and recalling in this regard the obligations under resolution 2161 (2014) of 17 June 2014,

Expressing deep concern at the threat posed by unsecured arms and ammunition in Libya and their proliferation, which undermines stability in Libya and the region, including through transfer to terrorist and violent extremist groups, and underlining the importance of coordinated international support to Libya and the region to address these issues,

Reaffirming the importance of holding accountable those responsible for violations or abuses of human rights or violations of international humanitarian law, including those involved in attacks targeting civilians,

Recalling its decision in resolution 1970 (2011) to refer the situation in Libya to the Prosecutor of the International Criminal Court, noting the decision of the Pre-Trial Chamber dated 10 December 2014, and emphasizing strongly the importance of the Government of Libya's full cooperation with the Court and the Prosecutor,

Recalling also the need for all parties to respect the relevant provisions of international humanitarian law and the United Nations guiding principles of humanitarian emergency assistance,

Taking note of the report of the Secretary-General of 26 February 2015 on the United Nations Support Mission in Libya,[404]

Taking note also of the special report of the Secretary-General of 13 February 2015 on the strategic assessment of the United Nations presence in Libya,[405] including the recommendations on the configuration of the United Nations presence made therein,

Taking note further of the final report of the Panel of Experts on Libya, submitted pursuant to paragraph 13 (*d*) of resolution 2144 (2014) of 14 March 2014[406] and the findings and recommendations contained therein,

Determining that the situation in Libya continues to constitute a threat to international peace and security,

Acting under Chapter VII of the Charter,

1. *Calls for* an immediate and unconditional ceasefire, underscores that there can be no military solution to the ongoing political crisis, and urges all parties in Libya to engage constructively with the efforts of the United Nations Support Mission in Libya and the Special Representative of the Secretary-General for Libya to facilitate, in accordance with the principles of national ownership, the formation of a national unity government and agreement on interim security arrangements necessary for stabilizing Libya;

2. *Calls upon* all Member States to fully support the efforts of the Special Representative of the Secretary-General;

3. *Encourages* Member States, particularly in the region, to urge all parties in Libya to engage constructively in the United Nations-facilitated dialogue and work quickly towards a successful outcome;

4. *Condemns* the use of violence against civilians and civilian institutions and the continuing escalation of conflict, including attacks on airports, State institutions and other vital national infrastructure and natural assets, and calls for those responsible to be held accountable;

5. *Calls upon* the Government of Libya to promote and protect human rights, including those of women, children and people belonging to vulnerable groups, and to comply with its obligations under international law, and calls for those responsible for violations of international humanitarian law and violations and abuses of human rights to be held accountable;

6. *Condemns* cases of torture and mistreatment, and deaths by torture, in detention centres in Libya, calls upon the Government of Libya to take all steps necessary to accelerate the judicial process, transfer detainees to State authority and prevent and investigate violations and abuses of human rights, calls for all Libyan parties to cooperate with government efforts in this regard, calls for the immediate release of all individuals arbitrarily arrested or detained in Libya, including foreign nationals, and underscores the Government's primary responsibility for promoting and protecting the human rights of all persons in Libya, particularly those of African migrants and other foreign nationals;

7. *Calls upon* the Government of Libya to cooperate fully with and provide any necessary assistance to the International Criminal Court and the Prosecutor as required by resolution 1970 (2011);

8. *Encourages* Libya and regional States to promote regional cooperation aimed at stabilization of the situation in Libya, to prevent former Libyan regime elements and violent extremist groups or terrorists from using the territory of Libya or such States to plan, fund or carry out violent or other illicit or terrorist acts to destabilize Libya or States in the region, and notes that such cooperation would benefit regional stability;

United Nations mandate

9. *Decides* to extend the mandate of the Mission until 15 September 2015 under the leadership of the Special Representative of the Secretary-General, and decides further that the mandate of the Mission as an integrated special political mission, in full accordance with the principles of national ownership, shall focus, as an

[406] See S/2015/128.

immediate priority, on support to the Libyan political process and security arrangements, through mediation and good offices, and further, within operational and security constraints, shall undertake:

(*a*) Human rights monitoring and reporting;

(*b*) Support for securing uncontrolled arms and related materiel and countering their proliferation;

(*c*) Support to key Libyan institutions;

(*d*) Support, on request, for the provision of essential services, and delivery of humanitarian assistance in accordance with humanitarian principles;

(*e*) Support for the coordination of international assistance;

10. *Recognizes* that the current security situation in Libya requires a reduction in the size of the Mission, but requests the Secretary-General to maintain the necessary flexibility and mobility to adjust Mission staffing and operations at short notice in order to support, as appropriate and in accordance with its mandate, implementation by the Libyans of agreements and confidence-building measures or in response to their expressed needs, and further requests the Secretary-General to keep the Security Council informed prior to such changes to the Mission in his reports pursuant to paragraph 27 of the present resolution;

Sanctions measures

11. *Reaffirms* that the travel ban and asset freeze measures specified in paragraphs 15, 16, 17, 19, 20 and 21 of resolution 1970 (2011), as modified by paragraphs 14, 15 and 16 of resolution 2009 (2011), apply to individuals and entities designated under that resolution and under resolution 1973 (2011) and by the Security Council Committee established pursuant to paragraph 24 of resolution 1970 (2011), and reaffirms that these measures also apply to individuals and entities determined by the Committee to be engaging in or providing support for other acts that threaten the peace, stability or security of Libya, or obstruct or undermine the successful completion of its political transition, and decides that such acts may include but are not limited to:

(*a*) Planning, directing or committing, acts that violate applicable international human rights law or international humanitarian law, or acts that constitute human rights abuses, in Libya;

(*b*) Attacks against any air, land or sea port in Libya, or against a Libyan State institution or installation, including oil facilities, or against any foreign mission in Libya;

(*c*) Providing support for armed groups or criminal networks through the illicit exploitation of crude oil or any other natural resources in Libya;

(*d*) Threatening or coercing Libyan State financial institutions and the Libyan National Oil Corporation, or engaging in any action that may lead to or result in the misappropriation of Libyan State funds;

(e) Violating, or assisting in the evasion of, the provisions of the arms embargo in Libya established in resolution 1970 (2011);

(*f*) Acting for or on behalf of or at the direction of a listed individual or entity;

12. *Reiterates* that individuals and entities determined by the Committee to have violated the provisions of resolution 1970 (2011), including the arms embargo, or assisted others in doing so, are subject to designation, and notes that this includes those who assist in the violation of the assets freeze and travel ban in resolution 1970 (2011);

13. *Condemns* the continued violations of the measures contained in resolution 1970 (2011), and directs the Committee, in line with its mandate and guidelines, to consult as soon as possible with any Member State about which the Committee deems there is credible information that provides reasonable grounds to believe the State is facilitating such violations or any other acts of non-compliance with these measures;

Prevention of illicit oil exports

14. *Decides* to extend until 31 March 2016 the authorizations provided by and the measures imposed by resolution 2146 (2014) of 19 March 2014;

15. *Urges* the Government of Libya to provide regular updates to the Committee on ports, oil fields and installations that are under its control and to inform the Committee about the mechanism used to certify legal exports of crude oil;

Arms embargo

16. *Stresses* that arms and related materiel, including related ammunition and spare parts, that are supplied, sold or transferred as security or disarmament assistance to the Government of Libya in accordance with paragraph 8 of resolution 2174 (2014) of 27 August 2014, should not be resold to, transferred to or made available for use by parties other than the designated end user;

17. *Urges* the Government of Libya to improve further the monitoring and control of arms or related materiel that are supplied, sold or transferred to Libya in accordance with paragraph 9 (*c*) of resolution 1970 (2011) or paragraph 8 of resolution 2174 (2014), including through the use of end user certificates, and urges Member States and regional organizations to provide assistance to the Government to strengthen the infrastructure and mechanisms currently in place to do so;

18. *Reiterates its call upon* Libya, with the assistance of international partners, to address the illicit transfer, destabilizing accumulation and misuse of small arms and light weapons in the country, and to ensure the safe and effective management, storage and security of their stockpiles of small arms and light weapons and the collection and/or destruction of surplus, seized, unmarked or illicitly held weapons and ammunition;

19. *Calls upon* all Member States, in order to ensure strict implementation of the arms embargo established by paragraphs 9 and 10 of resolution 1970 (2011) and modified by subsequent resolutions, to inspect in their territory, including seaports and airports, in accordance with their national authorities and legislation and consistent with international law, in particular the law of the sea and relevant international civil aviation agreements, vessels and aircraft bound to or from Libya, if the State concerned has information that provides reasonable grounds to believe that the cargo contains items the supply, sale, transfer or export of which is prohibited by paragraphs 9 or 10 of resolution 1970 (2011), as modified by paragraph 13 of 2009 (2011), paragraphs 9 and 10 of 2095 (2013) and paragraph 8 of 2174 (2014) for the purpose of ensuring strict implementation of those provisions, and calls upon all flag States of such vessels and aircraft to cooperate with such inspections;

20. *Reaffirms* its decision to authorize all Member States to, and that all Member States shall, upon discovery of items prohibited by paragraph 9 or 10 of resolution 1970 (2011), as modified by paragraph 13 of resolution 2009 (2011), paragraphs 9 and 10 of resolution 2095 (2013) and paragraph 8 of resolution 2174 (2014), seize and dispose (such as through destruction, rendering inoperable, storage or transferring to a State other than the originating or destination States for disposal) of such items, and further reaffirms its decision that all Member States shall cooperate in such efforts;

21. *Requires* any Member State, when it undertakes an inspection pursuant to paragraph 19 of the present resolution, to submit promptly an initial written report to the Committee containing, in particular, explanation of the grounds for the inspections, the results of such inspections, and whether or not cooperation was provided, and, if prohibited items for transfer are found, further requires such Member States to submit to the Committee, at a later stage, a subsequent written report containing relevant details on the inspection, seizure and disposal, and relevant details of the transfer, including a description of the items, their origin and intended destination, if this information is not in the initial report;

Assets

22. *Welcomes* the efforts of the Libyan authorities to implement measures to increase transparency of government revenues and expenditures, including salaries, subsidies and other transfers from the Central Bank of Libya, and welcomes the efforts of the Libyan authorities to eliminate the duplication of payments and to guard against the illegal diversion of payments, and encourages further steps in this regard that ensure the long-term sustainability of Libya's financial resources;

23. *Supports* the efforts of the Libyan authorities to recover funds misappropriated under the Qadhafi regime, and in this regard, encourages the Libyan authorities and Member States that have frozen assets pursuant to resolutions 1970 (2011) and 1973 (2011) as modified by resolution 2009 (2011) to consult with each other regarding claims of misappropriated funds and related issues of ownership;

Panel of Experts

24. *Decides* to extend until 30 April 2016 the mandate of the Panel of Experts on Libya, established pursuant to paragraph 24 of resolution 1973 (2011) and modified by resolutions 2040 (2012), 2146 (2014) and 2174 (2014), expresses its intent to review the mandate and take appropriate action regarding further extension no later than 12 months from the adoption of the present resolution, and decides that the Panel shall carry out the following tasks:

(*a*) Assist the Committee in carrying out its mandate as specified in paragraph 24 of resolution 1970 (2011), and modified in resolutions 2146 (2014), 2174 (2014) and the present resolution;

(*b*) Gather, examine and analyse information from States, relevant United Nations bodies, regional organizations and other interested parties regarding the implementation of the measures decided in resolutions 1970 (2011), 1973 (2011) 2146 (2014) and 2174 (2014), and modified in resolutions 2009 (2011), 2040 (2012), 2095 (2013), 2144 (2014) and the present resolution, in particular incidents of non-compliance;

(*c*) Make recommendations on actions that the Council, the Committee, the Government of Libya or other States may consider to improve implementation of the relevant measures;

(*d*) Provide to the Council an interim report on its work no later than 180 days after the appointment of the Panel, and a final report to the Council, after discussion with the Committee, no later than 15 March 2016, with its findings and recommendations;

25. *Urges* all States, relevant United Nations bodies, including the Mission, and other interested parties to cooperate fully with the Committee and the Panel of Experts, in particular by supplying any information at their disposal on the implementation of the measures decided in resolutions 1970 (2011), 1973 (2011), 2146 (2014) and 2174 (2014), and modified in resolutions 2009 (2011), 2040 (2012), 2095 (2013), 2144 (2014) and the present resolution, in particular incidents of non-compliance, and calls upon the Mission and the Government of Libya to support the investigatory work of the Panel inside Libya, including by sharing information, facilitating transit and granting access to weapons storage facilities, as appropriate;

26. *Calls upon* all parties and all States to ensure the safety of the members of the Panel of Experts, and that all parties and all States, including Libya and countries of the region, provide unhindered and immediate access, in particular to persons, documents and sites the Panel deems relevant to the execution of its mandate;

Reporting and review

27. *Requests* the Secretary-General to report to the Council on the implementation of the present resolution at least every 60 days;

28. *Affirms* its readiness to review the appropriateness of the measures contained in the present resolution, including the strengthening, modification, suspension or lifting of the measures, and its readiness to review the mandate of the Mission, as may be needed at any time in the light of developments in Libya, particularly outcomes of the United Nations-facilitated dialogue;

29. *Decides* to remain actively seized of the matter.

Adopted unanimously at the 7420th meeting.

Resolution 2214 (2015)
of 27 March 2015

The Security Council,

Recalling its resolutions 1267 (1999) of 15 October 1999, 1373 (2001) of 28 September 2001, 1624 (2005) of 14 September 2005, 1989 (2011) of 17 June 2011, 2161 (2014) of 17 June 2014, 2170 (2014) of 15 August 2014, 2174 (2014) of 27 August 2014, 2178 (2014) of 24 September 2014, 2195 (2014) of 19 December 2014 and 2199 (2015) of 12 February 2015, and the relevant statements by its President,

Reaffirming its primary responsibility for the maintenance of international peace and security in accordance with the Charter of the United Nations,

Reaffirming also that terrorism in all its forms and manifestations constitutes one of the most serious threats to international peace and security and that any acts of terrorism are criminal and unjustifiable regardless of their motivations, whenever and by whomever committed, and remaining determined to contribute further to enhancing the effectiveness of the overall effort to fight this scourge on a global level,

Reaffirming further the need to combat by all means, in accordance with the Charter and international law, threats to international peace and security caused by terrorist acts, and stressing in this regard the important role the United Nations plays in leading and coordinating this effort,

Recognizing that development, security and human rights are mutually reinforcing and are vital to an effective and comprehensive approach to countering terrorism, and underlining that a particular goal of counter-terrorism strategies should be to ensure sustainable peace and security,

Reaffirming that terrorism cannot and should not be associated with any religion, nationality or civilization,

Emphasizing that sanctions are an important tool under the Charter in the maintenance and restoration of international peace and security, including countering terrorism, and underlining the importance of prompt and effective implementation of relevant resolutions, in particular Security Council resolutions 1267 (1999) and 1989 (2011) as key instruments in the fight against terrorism,

Reaffirming its resolution 1373 (2001) and in particular its decisions that all States shall prevent and suppress the financing of terrorist acts and refrain from providing any form of support, active or passive, to entities or persons involved in terrorist acts, including by suppressing recruitment of members of terrorist groups and eliminating the supply of weapons to terrorists,

Recognizing the significant need to build capacities of Member States to counter terrorism and terrorist finance,

Reaffirming its determination to combat by all means, in accordance with the Charter and international law, threats to international peace and security caused by terrorist acts, including those committed by Islamic State in Iraq and the Levant (also known as Da'esh) everywhere, and urging all Member States to actively cooperate in this regard,

Expressing grave concerns over the growing trend of terrorist groups in Libya that proclaim allegiance to Islamic State in Iraq and the Levant,

Expressing grave concern about Islamic State in Iraq and the Levant, groups that have pledged allegiance to Islamic State in Iraq and the Levant, Ansar al Charia Benghazi and Ansar al Charia Derna (hereinafter collectively referred to as Ansar al Charia), and all other individuals, groups, undertakings and entities associated with Al-Qaida operating in Libya, and about the negative impact of their presence, violent extremist ideology and actions on stability in Libya, neighbouring countries and the region, including the devastating humanitarian impact on the civilian populations,

Deploring the terrorist acts being committed by Islamic State in Iraq and the Levant, groups that have pledged allegiance to Islamic State in Iraq and the Levant, Ansar al Charia and all other individuals, groups, undertakings and entities associated with Al-Qaida operating in Libya, including the recent cowardly and heinous kidnapping and killing of a number of Egyptian citizens in Sirte and the killing of Libyan civilians in Al-Qoba,

Expressing grave concern over the acute and growing threat posed by foreign terrorist fighters in Libya and the region which increase the intensity, duration and intractability of the conflict in Libya, and who also pose a serious threat to their States of origin, the States they transit and the States to which they travel, as well as States neighbouring to Libya that are affected by grave security burdens,

Recognizing that addressing the threat posed by foreign terrorist fighters requires comprehensively addressing underlying factors, including by preventing radicalization to terrorism, stemming recruitment, inhibiting foreign terrorist fighter travel, disrupting financial support to foreign terrorist fighters, countering violent extremism, which can be conducive to terrorism, countering incitement to terrorist acts motivated by extremism or intolerance, promoting political and religious tolerance, economic development and social cohesion and inclusiveness, ending and resolving armed conflicts, and facilitating reintegration and rehabilitation,

Noting with grave concern the continued threat posed to international peace and security by Islamic State in Iraq and the Levant, Ansar al Charia and all other individuals, groups, undertakings and entities associated with Al-Qaida operating in Libya, including in southern Libya, and reaffirming its resolve to address all aspects of that threat,

Expressing concern at the increased use, in a globalized society, by terrorists and their supporters of new information and communications technologies, in particular the Internet, for the purposes of recruitment and incitement to commit terrorist acts,

Commending the efforts undertaken by the Special Representative of the Secretary-General for Libya to facilitate a political solution to the political and security crisis in Libya,

Reaffirming its strong commitment to the sovereignty, independence, territorial integrity and national unity of Libya,

1. *Condemns* all terrorist acts committed by Islamic State in Iraq and the Levant, groups that have pledged allegiance to Islamic State in Iraq and the Levant, Ansar al Charia and all other individuals, groups, undertakings and entities associated with Al-Qaida operating in Libya, and emphasizes in this regard the need for a comprehensive approach to fully combat them;

2. *Stresses* the necessity of the full implementation of Security Council resolutions 1267 (1999), 1373 (2001), 1624 (2005), 1989 (2011), 2161 (2014), 2170 (2014), 2174 (2014), 2178 (2014), 2195 (2014) and 2199 (2015), including with respect to Islamic State in Iraq and the Levant, Ansar al Charia and all other individuals, groups, undertakings and entities associated with Al-Qaida operating in Libya;

3. *Urges* Member States to combat by all means, in accordance with the Charter of the United Nations and international law, threats to international peace and security caused by terrorist acts, including those committed by Islamic State in Iraq and the Levant, groups that have pledged allegiance to Islamic State in Iraq and the Levant, Ansar al Charia and all other individuals, groups, undertakings and entities associated with Al-Qaida operating in Libya, in coordination with the Government of Libya;

4. *Encourages* the submission of listing requests to the Security Council Committee pursuant to resolutions 1267 (1999) and 1989 (2011) by Member States of individuals and entities supporting Islamic State in Iraq and the Levant, Ansar al Charia and all other individuals, groups, undertakings and entities associated with Al-Qaida operating in Libya, and further encourages the Committee to urgently consider additional designations of individuals and entities supporting Islamic State in Iraq and the Levant, Ansar al Charia and other listed entities in Libya;

5. *Expresses its strong determination* to consider listing pursuant to resolution 2161 (2014) individuals, groups, undertakings and entities associated with Islamic State in Iraq and the Levant, Ansar al Charia and Al-Qaida operating in Libya who are financing, arming, planning or recruiting for them, or otherwise supporting their acts or activities, including through information and communications technologies, such as the internet, social media or any other means;

6. *Reaffirms* that Member States must ensure that any measures taken to counter terrorism comply with all their obligations under international law, in particular international human rights law, international refugee law and international humanitarian law, underscores that respect for human rights, fundamental freedoms and the rule of law are complementary and mutually reinforcing with effective counter-terrorism measures and are an essential part of a successful counter-terrorism effort, and notes the importance of respect for the rule of law so as to effectively prevent and combat terrorism, and notes that failure to comply with these and other international obligations, including under the Charter, is one of the factors contributing to increased radicalization and fosters a sense of impunity;

7. *Calls upon* the Security Council Committee established pursuant to paragraph 24 of resolution 1970 (2011) to consider expeditiously requests under paragraph 8 of resolution 2174 (2014) for the transfer or supply of arms and related materiel, including related ammunition and spare parts, to the Government of Libya for the use by its official armed forces to combat Islamic State in Iraq and the Levant, groups that have pledged

allegiance to Islamic State in Iraq and the Levant, Ansar al Charia and all other individuals, groups, undertakings and entities associated with Al-Qaida operating in Libya, and urges relevant States to provide relevant information for such a request;

8. *Emphasizes* the importance of providing support and assistance to the Government of Libya, including by providing it with the necessary security and capacity-building assistance;

9. *Calls upon* Member States to help build the capacity of other Member States, where necessary and appropriate and upon request, to address the threat posed by Islamic State in Iraq and the Levant, groups that have pledged allegiance to Islamic State in Iraq and the Levant, Ansar al Charia and all other individuals, groups, undertakings and entities associated with Al-Qaida operating in Libya, and welcomes and encourages bilateral assistance by Member States to help build such national, subregional or regional capacity;

10. *Expresses strong support* for the efforts of the Government of Libya to combat Islamic State in Iraq and the Levant, groups that have pledged allegiance to Islamic State in Iraq and the Levant, Ansar al Charia and all other individuals, groups, undertakings and entities associated with Al-Qaida operating in Libya, and of members of the international community assisting the Government in this regard upon its request;

11. *Recognizes* the important roles of the African Union, the League of Arab States and Libya's neighbouring countries with regard to finding a peaceful solution to the crisis in Libya, and commends their efforts in countering the threats to international peace and security posed by Islamic State in Iraq and the Levant, groups that have pledged allegiance to Islamic State in Iraq and the Levant, Ansar al Charia and all other individuals, groups, undertakings and entities associated with Al-Qaida operating in Libya;

12. *Expresses its support* to the United Nations-led political dialogue between the Government of Libya and all Libyan parties that renounce violence, and calls upon them to engage constructively with the initiative of the Special Representative of the Secretary-General for Libya with the purpose of forming a national unity government, and commends their continued participation in the dialogue;

13. *Directs* the Analytical Support and Sanctions Monitoring Team of the Committee pursuant to resolutions 1267 (1999) and 1989 (2011) to report, within 180 days, and provide a preliminary oral update to the Committee within 90 days, on the terrorism threat in Libya posed by Islamic State in Iraq and the Levant, Ansar al Charia and all other individuals, groups, undertakings and entities associated with Al-Qaida operating in Libya, and on their sources of arms, funding, recruitment, demographics, connections to the terrorist networks in the region, and recommendations for additional actions to address the threat, and requests that after a Committee discussion of these reports, the Chair of the Committee brief the Council on its principal findings;

14. *Decides* to remain actively seized of the matter.

Adopted unanimously at the 7420th meeting.

Decisions

At its 7441st meeting, on 12 May 2015, the Security Council decided to invite the representative of Libya to participate, without vote, in accordance with rule 37 of its provisional rules of procedure, in the discussion of the item entitled "The situation in Libya".

At the same meeting, the Council also decided to extend an invitation, in accordance with rule 39 of its provisional rules of procedure, to Ms. Fatou Bensouda, Prosecutor of the International Criminal Court.

At its 7485th meeting, on 15 July 2015, the Council decided to invite the representative of Libya to participate, without vote, in accordance with rule 37 of its provisional rules of procedure, in the discussion of the item entitled "The situation in Libya".

At the same meeting, the Council also decided to extend an invitation, in accordance with rule 39 of its provisional rules of procedure, to Mr. Bernardino León, Special Representative of the Secretary-General for Libya and Head of the United Nations Support Mission in Libya.

THE SITUATION IN MALI[407]

Decisions

At its 7274th meeting, on 8 October 2014, the Security Council decided to invite the representative of Mali to participate, without vote, in accordance with rule 37 of its provisional rules of procedure, in the discussion of the item entitled:

"The situation in Mali

"Report of the Secretary-General on the situation in Mali (S/2014/692)".

At the same meeting, the Council also decided to extend an invitation, in accordance with rule 39 of its provisional rules of procedure, to Mr. Hervé Ladsous, Under-Secretary-General for Peacekeeping Operations.

On 12 December 2014, the President of the Security Council addressed the following letter to the Secretary-General:[408]

> I have the honour to inform you that your letter dated 10 December 2014 concerning your intention to appoint Mr. Mongi Hamdi, of Tunisia, as your Special Representative for Mali and Head of the United Nations Multidimensional Integrated Stabilization Mission in Mali[409] has been brought to the attention of the members of the Security Council. They take note of the intention expressed in your letter.

At its 7355th meeting, on 6 January 2015, the Council decided to invite the representative of Mali to participate, without vote, in accordance with rule 37 of its provisional rules of procedure, in the discussion of the item entitled:

"The situation in Mali

"Report of the Secretary-General on the situation in Mali (S/2014/943)

"Letter dated 23 December 2014 from the Secretary-General addressed to the President of the Security Council (S/2014/944)".

At the same meeting, the Council also decided to extend an invitation, in accordance with rule 39 of its provisional rules of procedure, to Mr. Hervé Ladsous, Under-Secretary-General for Peacekeeping Operations.

At its 7378th meeting, on 6 February 2015, the Council decided to invite the representative of Mali to participate, without vote, in accordance with rule 37 of its provisional rules of procedure, in the discussion of the item entitled "The situation in Mali".

At the same meeting, following consultations among members of the Security Council, the President made the following statement on behalf of the Council:[410]

> The Security Council urges the Malian parties, namely the Government of Mali and the signatory and adherent armed groups of the Ouagadougou preliminary agreement, to resume without delay the inter-Malian negotiation process in Algiers. The Council urges the Malian parties to engage through senior and fully empowered representatives in order to reach as soon as possible a comprehensive and inclusive peace agreement that addresses the root causes of the crisis in Mali. The Council urges the parties to engage with sustained political will, a spirit of compromise and in good faith on substantive discussions towards such an agreement. In this regard, the Council further calls upon the Malian parties to make the necessary concessions, while respecting the sovereignty, unity and territorial integrity of the Malian State.

[407] Resolutions or decisions on this question were first adopted by the Security Council in 2012.

[408] S/2014/890.

[409] S/2014/889.

[410] S/PRST/2015/5.

The Council urges the parties to seize the historic opportunity offered by the inter-Malian negotiation process in Algiers, in which all neighbouring countries and relevant regional and international partners are involved, to support lasting peace in Mali. Recognizing the legitimate aspiration of all Malian citizens to enjoy lasting peace and development, the Council stresses that the Malian parties have a responsibility to the Malian people and the international community to reach a durable peace agreement.

The Council reiterates its full support to the facilitation efforts of Algeria and all the members of the international mediation team. The Council calls upon all actors who have influence on the Malian parties to urge them to negotiate seriously and in good faith towards a comprehensive and inclusive peace agreement. The Council also expresses its full support to the Special Representative of the Secretary-General for Mali, Mr. Mongi Hamdi, and requests him to use his good offices mandate and actively engage to play a key role in the inter-Malian negotiation process in Algiers.

The Council urges all parties to refrain from any action, whether direct or conducted through proxies, that jeopardizes prospects for peace and, in this regard, expresses its readiness to consider appropriate measures, including targeted sanctions, against those who resume hostilities and violate the ceasefire.

The Council reiterates its full support to the United Nations Multidimensional Integrated Stabilization Mission in Mali and its contribution to peace and security in Mali, and welcomes the sustained efforts of the French forces supporting it. The Council commends the continued commitment and sacrifices of troop- and police-contributing countries of the Mission. The Council reiterates its strongest condemnation of all attacks against Mission peacekeepers, personnel and property, and underlines that attacks targeting peacekeepers may constitute war crimes under international law. The Council recalls the obligations in paragraph 2 (*e*) of resolution 1373 (2001).

The Council requests the Mission to fully implement its mandate, and in this regard recalls its authorization that the Mission use all necessary means, within its capabilities and its areas of deployment, in accordance with resolution 2164 (2014), including to deter threats and take active steps to prevent the return of armed elements, to protect civilians under imminent threat of physical violence and to respond to attacks against its personnel, installations and equipment.

The Council underscores that only a comprehensive and inclusive peace agreement can bring lasting security to Mali. The Council deplores the continued violence in the north of Mali, which causes the loss of human lives and casualties. The Council therefore demands that all parties, including those who are not signatories to the Ouagadougou preliminary agreement, cease immediately all hostilities and reject violence. The Council demands that all parties fully respect the ceasefire agreement signed on 23 May 2014, as well as the declaration of the cessation of hostilities signed in Algiers on 24 July 2014. The Council further urges all parties to swiftly implement all agreed confidence-building measures, in particular the mechanisms established by the declaration of the cessation of hostilities, to facilitate the implementation of the ceasefire, with the support of and in coordination with the Mission.

The Council welcomes the decision of the Secretary-General to launch an independent inquiry to determine the facts surrounding the tragic incidents that took place on 27 January 2015 during a violent demonstration in front of the Mission base in Gao, in the north of Mali, and the reported death of at least three protesters, and expresses its sincere condolences to the families of those who have died.

Drawing on lessons from the previous peace agreements signed by the Malian parties, which did not achieve a durable peace in Mali, the Council urges the Malian parties – and calls upon the members of the international mediation team – in Algiers to devise concrete oversight mechanisms that will ensure the full, faithful and immediate implementation of a future comprehensive and inclusive peace agreement. The Council calls for all relevant parties to ensure that provisions relating to participation of women, sexual violence and child protection are taken into account during the ongoing negotiations and any possible outcome.

The Council stresses the critical importance that such an agreement be Malian-led and Malian-owned and calls upon the Malian parties to demonstrate commitment to its complete implementation. The Council emphasizes that the Special Representative and the Mission should play a leading role, in conjunction with the other members of the international mediation team and other relevant partners, to support and oversee the implementation of such an agreement, for which primary responsibility rests with the Malian parties.

On 6 March 2015, the President of the Security Council addressed the following letter to the Secretary-General:[411]

> I have the honour to inform you that your letter dated 4 March 2015 concerning your intention to appoint Major General Michael Lollesgaard, of Denmark, as Force Commander of the United Nations Multidimensional Integrated Stabilization Mission in Mali[412] has been brought to the attention of the members of the Security Council. They take note of the intention expressed in your letter.

At its 7425th meeting, on 9 April 2015, the Council decided to invite the representative of Mali to participate, without vote, in accordance with rule 37 of its provisional rules of procedure, in the discussion of the item entitled:

"The situation in Mali

> "Letter dated 2 January 2015 from the Secretary-General addressed to the President of the Security Council (S/2015/3)
>
> "Letter dated 16 March 2015 from the Secretary-General addressed to the President of the Security Council (S/2015/187)
>
> "Report of the Secretary-General on the situation in Mali (S/2015/219)".

At the same meeting, the Council also decided to extend an invitation, in accordance with rule 39 of its provisional rules of procedure, to Mr. Hervé Ladsous, Under-Secretary-General for Peacekeeping Operations.

At its 7468th meeting, on 23 June 2015, the Council decided to invite the representative of Mali to participate, without vote, in accordance with rule 37 of its provisional rules of procedure, in the discussion of the item entitled:

"The situation in Mali

> "Report of the Secretary-General on the situation in Mali (S/2015/426)
>
> "Letter dated 16 June 2015 from the Secretary-General addressed to the President of the Security Council (S/2015/444)".

At the same meeting, the Council also decided to extend an invitation, in accordance with rule 39 of its provisional rules of procedure, to Mr. Mongi Hamdi, Special Representative of the Secretary-General for Mali and Head of the United Nations Multidimensional Integrated Stabilization Mission in Mali.

At its 7474th meeting, on 29 June 2015, the Council decided to invite the representative of Mali to participate, without vote, in accordance with rule 37 of its provisional rules of procedure, in the discussion of the item entitled:

"The situation in Mali

> "Report of the Secretary-General on the situation in Mali (S/2015/426)
>
> "Letter dated 16 June 2015 from the Secretary-General addressed to the President of the Security Council (S/2015/444)".

Resolution 2227 (2015) of 29 June 2015

The Security Council,

Recalling its previous resolutions, in particular resolutions 2100 (2013) of 25 April 2013 and 2164 (2014) of 25 June 2014, the statements by its President of 23 January[413] and 28 July 2014[414] and 6 February 2015[410] and its statements to the press of 10 April, 1 and 29 May and 18 June 2015,

---

[411] S/2015/167.

[412] S/2015/166.

[413] S/PRST/2014/2.

[414] S/PRST/2014/15.

Reaffirming its strong commitment to the sovereignty, unity and territorial integrity of Mali, emphasizing that the Malian authorities have primary responsibility for the provision of stability and security throughout the territory of Mali, and underscoring the importance of achieving national ownership of peace- and security-related initiatives,

Reaffirming the basic principles of peacekeeping, including consent of the parties, impartiality and non-use of force except in self-defence and defence of the mandate, and recognizing that the mandate of each peacekeeping mission is specific to the needs and situation of the country concerned,

Recognizing the legitimate aspiration of all Malian citizens to enjoy lasting peace and development,

Welcoming the signing of the Agreement on Peace and Reconciliation in Mali (the Agreement)[415] in 2015 by the Government of Mali, the Plateforme coalition of armed groups and the Coordination des mouvements de l'Azawad coalition of armed groups as a historic opportunity to achieve lasting peace in Mali, and commending the signatories to the Agreement for the courage they demonstrated in this regard,

Considering the Agreement as balanced and comprehensive, aiming to address the political, institutional, governance, security, development and reconciliation dimensions of the crisis in Mali, respecting the sovereignty, unity and territorial integrity of the Malian State,

Underscoring that the responsibility for the full and effective implementation of the Agreement, which has to be Malian-led and Malian-owned, rests with the Government of Mali and the Plateforme and Coordination armed groups, and will be crucial to contribute to lasting peace in Mali, drawing lessons from previous peace agreements,

Commending the role played by Algeria and other members of the international mediation team to facilitate the inter-Malian dialogue, which led to the signing of the Agreement by the Government of Mali and the Plateforme and Coordination armed groups, welcoming the signing of the Agreement by the members of the international mediation team, and calling upon the members of the Agreement Monitoring Committee and other relevant international partners to support the implementation of the Agreement and to maintain close coordination to support lasting peace in Mali,

Stressing the need for clear, detailed and concrete oversight mechanisms to support the implementation of the Agreement, notably through the Agreement Monitoring Committee and its four subcommittees dealing with political and institutional issues, defence and security, economic, social and cultural development, and reconciliation, justice and humanitarian issues,

Strongly condemning the violations of the ceasefire by the Malian parties that occurred in Mali, which led to loss of life, including of civilians, and displacement and undermined the peace process, welcoming the signing of the security arrangements for the cessation of hostilities on 5 June 2015 by the Government of Mali and the Coordination armed groups, and recalling the ceasefire agreement of 23 May 2014 and the declarations of cessation of hostilities of 24 July 2014 and 19 February 2015 signed by the Malian parties,

Reiterating its strong support for the Special Representative of the Secretary-General for Mali and for the United Nations Multidimensional Integrated Stabilization Mission in Mali to assist the Malian authorities and the Malian people in their efforts to bring lasting peace and stability to their country, and noting the development of the protection of civilians strategy of the Mission, bearing in mind the primary responsibility of the Malian authorities to protect the population,

Commending troop- and police-contributing countries of the Mission for their contribution, paying tribute to the peacekeepers who risk their lives in this respect, strongly condemning attacks against peacekeepers, and underlining that attacks targeting peacekeepers may constitute war crimes under international law,

Expressing its concern at the slow pace of deployment of Mission personnel and equipment, which has seriously hindered the ability of the Mission to fully implement its mandate since its establishment on 25 April 2013 by Security Council resolution 2100 (2013), and welcoming efforts by the Secretary-General to accelerate the deployment of troops and equipment, as well as to provide adequate training, to improve the security and safety of Mission personnel in a complex security environment that includes asymmetric threats, notably the use of mines and improvised explosive devices,

[415] See S/2015/364 and Add.1.

Strongly condemning the activities in Mali and in the Sahel region of terrorist organizations, including Al-Qaida in the Islamic Maghreb, Ansar Eddine and the Mouvement pour l'unicité et le jihad en Afrique de l'Ouest, which continue to operate in Mali and constitute a threat to peace and security in the region and beyond, and human rights abuses and violence against civilians, notably women and children, committed in the north of Mali and in the region by terrorist groups,

Stressing that terrorism can be defeated only by a sustained and comprehensive approach involving the active participation and collaboration of all States and regional and international organizations to impede, impair and isolate the terrorist threat, and reaffirming that terrorism cannot and should not be associated with any religion, nationality or civilization,

Recalling the listing of the Mouvement pour l'unicité et le jihad en Afrique de l'Ouest, the Organization of Al-Qaida in the Islamic Maghreb, Ansar Eddine and its leader, Iyad ag Ghali, and Al-Mourabitoune on the Al-Qaida Sanctions List established by the Security Council Committee pursuant to resolutions 1267 (1999) and 1989 (2011), and reiterating its readiness, under the above-mentioned regime, to sanction further individuals, groups, undertakings and entities that are associated with Al-Qaida and other listed entities and individuals, including Al-Qaida in the Islamic Maghreb, the Mouvement pour l'unicité et le jihad en Afrique de l'Ouest, Ansar Eddine and Al-Mourabitoune, in accordance with the established listing criteria,

Welcoming the continued action by the French forces, at the request of the Malian authorities, to deter the terrorist threat in the north of Mali,

Noting with growing concern the transnational dimension of the terrorist threat in the Sahel region, underscoring the importance of achieving regional ownership and response in this regard, welcoming in this context the establishment of the Group of Five for the Sahel and the Nouakchott Process on the enhancement of security cooperation and the operationalization of the African Peace and Security Architecture in the Sahelo-Saharan region, as well as the commitment made by the African leaders at the Malabo summit of 26 and 27 June 2014 and steps taken by the African Union to operationalize the African Capacity for Immediate Response to Crises, and welcoming the efforts of the French forces to support the States members of the Group of Five for the Sahel to increase regional counter-terrorism cooperation,

Expressing its continued concern over the serious threats posed by transnational organized crime in the Sahel region, including arms and drug trafficking and human trafficking, and its increasing links, in some cases, with terrorism, underlining the responsibility of the countries in the region in addressing these threats, and welcoming the stabilizing effect of the international presence in Mali, including the Mission,

Strongly condemning the incidents of kidnapping and hostage-taking with the aim of raising funds or gaining political concessions, reiterating its determination to prevent kidnapping and hostage-taking in the Sahel region, in accordance with applicable international law, recalling its resolution 2133 (2014) of 27 January 2014, including the call upon all Member States to prevent terrorists from benefitting directly or indirectly from the payment of ransoms or from political concessions and to secure the safe release of hostages, and in this regard noting the publication by the Global Counterterrorism Forum of the Algiers Memorandum on Good Practices on Preventing and Denying the Benefits of Kidnapping for Ransom by Terrorists,

Strongly condemning also all abuses and violations of human rights and violations of international humanitarian law, including those involving extrajudicial and summary executions, arbitrary arrests and detentions and ill-treatment of prisoners, sexual and gender-based violence, as well as killing, maiming, recruitment and use of children, and attacks against schools and hospitals, calling upon all parties to respect the civilian character of schools as such in accordance with international humanitarian law and to cease unlawful and arbitrary detention of all children, and calling upon all parties to bring an end to such violations and abuses and to comply with their obligations under applicable international law,

Reiterating, in this regard, that all perpetrators of such acts must be held accountable and that some of the acts referred to in the paragraph above may amount to crimes under the Rome Statute of the International Criminal Court[416] and noting that, acting upon the referral of the transitional authorities of Mali dated 13 July 2012, the

[416] United Nations, *Treaty Series*, vol. 2187, No. 38544.

Prosecutor of the Court opened, on 16 January 2013, an investigation into alleged crimes committed on the territory of Mali since January 2012, and recalling the importance of assistance and cooperation, by all parties concerned, with the Court,

Emphasizing the need for all parties to uphold and respect the humanitarian principles of humanity, neutrality, impartiality and independence in order to ensure the continued provision of humanitarian assistance, the safety and protection of civilians receiving assistance and the security of humanitarian personnel operating in Mali, and stressing the importance of humanitarian assistance being delivered on the basis of need,

Underscoring that Malian civilian control and oversight, as well as further consolidation of the Malian Defence and Security Forces, are important to ensure the long-term security and stability of Mali and to protect the people of Mali,

Commending the role of the European Union Training Mission in Mali in providing training and advice for the Malian Defence and Security Forces, including contributing to the strengthening of civilian authority and respect for human rights, and of the European Union Capacity-Building Mission in Sahel Mali in providing strategic advice and training for the police, gendarmerie and national guard in Mali,

Calling upon the Malian authorities to address immediate and long-term needs, encompassing security, governance reform, development and humanitarian issues, to resolve the crisis in Mali and to ensure that the Agreement translates into concrete benefits for the local populations, notably through the priority projects outlined in the Agreement, calling upon the international community to provide broad support in this regard, and stressing the need for enhanced coordination of these international efforts,

Commending the contributions already made following the donors conference held in Brussels in May 2013 and towards the 2015 consolidated appeal for Mali, and urging all Member States and other donors to contribute generously to humanitarian operations,

Remaining seriously concerned over the significant ongoing food and humanitarian crisis in Mali, and over the insecurity which hinders humanitarian access, exacerbated by the presence of armed groups and terrorist and criminal networks, and their activities, the presence of landmines as well as the continued proliferation of weapons from within and outside the region that threatens the peace, security and stability of States in the region, and condemning attacks against humanitarian personnel,

Determining that the situation in Mali continues to constitute a threat to international peace and security,

Acting under Chapter VII of the Charter of the United Nations,

Framework for peace and reconciliation and the implementation of the Agreement on Peace and Reconciliation in Mali

1. *Urges* the Government of Mali and the Plateforme and Coordination armed groups to fulfil their commitments under the Agreement on Peace and Reconciliation in Mali (the Agreement),[415] and in this regard further urges them to continue to engage constructively with sustained political will and in good faith to achieve the full and effective implementation of the Agreement;

2. *Also urges* the Government of Mali and the Plateforme and Coordination armed groups to immediately and fully respect and uphold the ceasefire agreement of 23 May 2014, the security arrangements for the cessation of hostilities of 5 June 2015 and the declarations of cessation of hostilities of 24 July 2014 and 19 February 2015;

3. *Expresses its readiness* to consider targeted sanctions against those who take actions to obstruct or threaten the implementation of the Agreement, those who resume hostilities and violate the ceasefire, as well as those who attack and take actions to threaten the United Nations Multidimensional Integrated Stabilization Mission in Mali;

4. *Demands* that all armed groups in Mali put aside their arms, cease hostilities, reject the recourse to violence, cut off all ties with terrorist organizations and recognize, without conditions, the unity and territorial integrity of the Malian State;

5. *Urges* the Malian authorities to further combat impunity and, in this regard, to ensure that all perpetrators of violations and abuses of human rights and violations of international humanitarian law, including those involving sexual violence, are held accountable, and also urges the Malian authorities to continue to cooperate with the International Criminal Court, in accordance with the obligations of Mali under the Rome Statute of the Court;[416]

6. *Urges* all parties in Mali to cooperate fully with the deployment and activities of the Mission, in particular by ensuring the safety, security and freedom of movement of Mission personnel with unhindered and immediate access throughout the territory of Mali to enable the Mission to carry out fully its mandate;

7. *Requests* the Special Representative of the Secretary-General for Mali to continue to use his good offices, in particular to play a key role to support and oversee the implementation of the Agreement by the Government of Mali and the Plateforme and Coordination armed groups, notably by heading the secretariat of the Agreement Monitoring Committee, and in particular, to assist the Malian parties in identifying and prioritizing implementation steps, consistent with the provisions of the Agreement and with paragraphs 14 (*b*) and (*c*) below, and affirms its intention to facilitate, support and follow closely the implementation of the Agreement;

8. *Urges* the Government of Mali and the Plateforme and Coordination armed groups to cooperate fully and coordinate with the Special Representative and the Mission, in particular on the implementation of the Agreement;

9. *Calls upon* the members of the Agreement Monitoring Committee and other relevant international partners to support the implementation of the Agreement, and to coordinate their efforts with the Special Representative and the Mission in this regard, and recognizes the role of the Committee to reconcile disagreements between the Malian parties;

10. *Encourages* the Government of Mali to take the steps necessary for the effective implementation of the Agreement, including political and institutional reforms;

11. *Calls upon* all relevant United Nations agencies, as well as regional, bilateral and multilateral partners, to provide the technical and financial support necessary to contribute to the implementation of the Agreement, in particular its provisions pertaining to socioeconomic and cultural development;

Mandate of the Mission

12. *Decides* to extend the mandate of the Mission until 30 June 2016, within the authorized troop ceiling of 11,240 military personnel, including at least 40 military observers to monitor and supervise the ceasefire, as well as reserve battalions capable of deploying rapidly within the country, and 1,440 police personnel;

13. *Authorizes* the Mission to take all means necessary to carry out its mandate, within its capabilities and its areas of deployment;

14. *Decides* that the Mission shall perform the following tasks:

(*a*) *Ceasefire*

To support, monitor and supervise the implementation of the ceasefire arrangements and confidence-building measures by the Government of Mali and the Plateforme and Coordination armed groups, to devise and support, as needed, local mechanisms with a view to consolidating these arrangements and measures, as well as to report to the Security Council on any violations of the ceasefire, consistent with the provisions of the Agreement, especially part III and annex 2 thereof;

(*b*) *Support to the implementation of the Agreement on Peace and Reconciliation in Mali*

(i) To support the implementation of the political and institutional reforms provided for by the Agreement, especially in part II thereof;

(ii) To support the implementation of the defence and security measures of the Agreement, notably to support, monitor and supervise the ceasefire, to support the cantonment, disarmament, demobilization and reintegration of armed groups, as well as the progressive redeployment of the Malian Defence and Security Forces, especially in the north of Mali, taking into account the security conditions, and to coordinate international efforts, in close collaboration with other bilateral partners, donors and international organizations, including the European Union, engaged in these fields, to rebuild the Malian security sector, within the framework set out by the Agreement, especially part III and annex 2 thereof;

(iii) To support the implementation of the reconciliation and justice measures of the Agreement, especially in part V thereof, notably the establishment of an international commission of inquiry, in consultation with the parties;

(iv) To support, within its resources and areas of deployment, the conduct of inclusive, free, fair and transparent local elections, including through the provision of appropriate logistical and technical assistance and effective security arrangements, consistent with the provisions of the Agreement;

(*c*) *Good offices and reconciliation*

To exercise good offices, confidence-building and facilitation at the national and local levels, in order to support dialogue with and among all stakeholders towards reconciliation and social cohesion and to encourage and support the full implementation of the Agreement by the Government of Mali and the Plateforme and Coordination armed groups, including by promoting the participation of civil society, including women's organizations, as well as youth organizations;

(*d*) *Protection of civilians and stabilization*

(i) To protect, without prejudice to the primary responsibility of the Malian authorities, civilians under imminent threat of physical violence;

(ii) In support of the Malian authorities, to stabilize the key population centres and other areas where civilians are at risk, notably in the north of Mali, including through long-range patrols, and in this context to deter threats and take active steps to prevent the return of armed elements to those areas;

(iii) To provide specific protection for women and children affected by armed conflict, including through child protection advisers and women's protection advisers, and address the needs of victims of sexual and gender-based violence in armed conflict;

(iv) To assist the Malian authorities with the removal and destruction of mines and other explosive devices and weapons and ammunition management;

(*e*) *Promotion and protection of human rights*

(i) To assist the Malian authorities in their efforts to promote and protect human rights, including to support, as feasible and appropriate, the efforts of the Malian authorities, without prejudice to their responsibilities, to bring to justice those responsible for serious abuses or violations of human rights or violations of international humanitarian law, in particular war crimes and crimes against humanity in Mali, taking into account the referral by the transitional authorities of Mali of the situation in their country since January 2012 to the International Criminal Court;

(ii) To monitor, help to investigate and report to the Council and publicly, as appropriate, on violations of international humanitarian law and on violations and abuses of human rights, including violations and abuses against children and sexual violence in armed conflict committed throughout Mali, and to contribute to efforts to prevent such violations and abuses;

(*f*) *Humanitarian assistance and projects for stabilization*

(i) In support of the Malian authorities, to contribute to the creation of a secure environment for the safe, civilian-led delivery of humanitarian assistance, in accordance with humanitarian principles, and the voluntary, safe and dignified return or local integration or resettlement of internally displaced persons and refugees, in close coordination with humanitarian actors;

(ii) In support of the Malian authorities, to contribute to the creation of a secure environment for projects aimed at stabilizing the north of Mali, including quick-impact projects;

(*g*) *Protection, safety and security of United Nations personnel*

To protect United Nations personnel, notably uniformed personnel, installations and equipment, and ensure the safety, security and freedom of movement of United Nations and associated personnel;

(*h*) *Support for cultural preservation*

To assist the Malian authorities, as necessary and feasible, in protecting from attack the cultural and historical sites in Mali, in collaboration with the United Nations Educational, Scientific and Cultural Organization;

Deployment and capacities of the Mission

15. *Requests* the Secretary-General to take all steps necessary, including through the full use of existing authorities and at his discretion, to enable the Mission to reach its full operational capacity without further delay;

16. *Also requests* the Secretary-General to take all appropriate additional measures to enhance the safety and security of, and basic services for, Mission personnel, in particular uniformed personnel, including through enhancing the intelligence capacities of the Mission, providing training and equipment to counter explosive devices, the generation of adequate military capabilities to secure the Mission's logistical supply routes, as well as more effective casualty and medical evacuation procedures, to enable the Mission to execute effectively its mandate in a complex security environment that includes asymmetric threats;

17. *Urges* the troop- and police-contributing countries of the Mission to expedite the procurement and deployment of remaining contingent-owned equipment and urges Member States to provide troops and police that have adequate capabilities, training and equipment, including enablers, specific to the operating environment, in order for the Mission to fulfil its mandate, and welcomes the assistance of Member States to the troop- and police-contributing countries of the Mission in this regard;

18. *Calls upon* Member States, especially those in the region, to ensure the free, unhindered and expeditious movement to and from Mali of all personnel, as well as equipment, provisions, supplies and other goods, which are for the exclusive and official use of the Mission, in order to facilitate the timely and cost-effective delivery of the logistical supply of the Mission;

19. *Encourages* the Secretary-General to keep the Mission concept under review in order to maximize the positive impact of Mission resources, and requests the Secretary-General to keep the Council informed on its implementation;

Cross-cutting issues in the mandate of the Mission

20. *Requests* the Mission to further enhance its interaction with the civilian population, as well as its communication with the Malian Defence and Security Forces, including through the development of an effective communication strategy and Mission radio, to raise awareness and understanding about its mandate and activities;

21. *Also requests* the Mission to ensure that any support provided to non-United Nations security forces is provided in strict compliance with the human rights due diligence policy on United Nations support to non-United Nations security forces;[417]

22. *Requests* the Secretary-General to ensure full compliance of the Mission with the United Nations zero-tolerance policy on sexual exploitation and abuse and to keep the Council fully informed if such cases of misconduct occur;

23. *Requests* the Mission to take fully into account gender considerations as a cross-cutting issue throughout its mandate and to assist the Malian authorities in ensuring the full and effective participation, involvement and representation of women at all levels and at an early stage of the stabilization phase, including the security sector reform and disarmament, demobilization and reintegration processes, as well as in reconciliation and electoral processes, and further requests the Mission to assist the parties to ensure the full and active participation of women in the implementation of the Agreement;

24. *Also requests* the Mission to take fully into account child protection as a cross-cutting issue throughout its mandate and to assist the Malian authorities in ensuring that the protection of the rights of children is taken into account, inter alia, in disarmament, demobilization and reintegration processes and in security sector reform in order to end and prevent violations and abuses against children;

25. *Further requests* the Mission to consider the environmental impacts of its operations when fulfilling its mandated tasks and, in this context, to manage them as appropriate and in accordance with applicable and relevant General Assembly resolutions and United Nations rules and regulations, and to operate mindfully in the vicinity of cultural and historical sites;

[417] S/2013/110, annex.

Inter-mission cooperation in West Africa

26. *Authorizes* the Secretary-General to take the steps necessary in order to ensure inter-mission cooperation, notably between the United Nations Multidimensional Integrated Stabilization Mission in Mali, the United Nations Mission in Liberia and the United Nations Operation in Côte d'Ivoire, and appropriate transfers of troops and their assets from other United Nations missions to the United Nations Multidimensional Integrated Stabilization Mission in Mali, subject to the following conditions: (i) the information and approval of the Council, including on the scope and duration of the transfer, (ii) the agreement of the troop-contributing countries, and (iii) the security situation where these United Nations missions are deployed, and without prejudice to the performance of their mandates, and in this regard encourages further steps to enhance inter-mission cooperation in the West African region, as necessary and feasible, and to report thereon for consideration as appropriate;

French forces mandate

27. *Authorizes* French forces, within the limits of their capacities and areas of deployment, to use all means necessary until the end of the mandate of the Mission as authorized in the present resolution, to intervene in support of elements of the Mission when under imminent and serious threat, upon the request of the Secretary-General, and requests France to report to the Council on the implementation of this mandate in Mali and to coordinate its reporting with the reporting by the Secretary-General referred to in paragraph 35 below;

Group of Five for the Sahel and African Union contribution

28. *Encourages* the Member States of the Sahel region to improve coordination to combat recurrent threats in the Sahel, including terrorism, together with transnational organized crime and other illicit activities such as drug trafficking, welcomes the efforts of the Member States of the Sahel to strengthen border security and regional cooperation, including through the Group of Five for the Sahel and the Nouakchott Process on the enhancement of security cooperation and the operationalization of the African Peace and Security Architecture in the Sahelo-Saharan region, as well as the commitment made by the African leaders at the Malabo summit of 26 and 27 June 2014 and steps taken by the African Union to operationalize the African Capacity for Immediate Response to Crises, and encourages the States members of the African Union to generate substantive pledges to the African Capacity for Immediate Response to Crises;

International cooperation on the Sahel

29. *Calls upon* all Member States, notably Sahel, West Africa and Maghreb States, as well as regional, bilateral and multilateral partners, to enhance their coordination to develop inclusive and effective strategies to combat, in a comprehensive and integrated manner, the activities of terrorist groups crossing borders and seeking safe havens in the Sahel region, notably Al-Qaida in the Islamic Maghreb, the Mouvement pour l'unicité et le jihad en Afrique de l'Ouest, Ansar Eddine and Al-Mourabitoune, and to prevent the expansion of those groups as well as to limit the proliferation of all arms and transnational organized crime;

30. *Reiterates its call for* the rapid and effective implementation, in consultation with regional organizations, of regional strategies encompassing security, governance, development, human rights and humanitarian issues, such as the United Nations integrated strategy for the Sahel,[418] and recalls in this regard the good offices role of the Special Envoy of the Secretary-General for the Sahel in order to enhance regional and interregional cooperation, in close coordination with the Special Representative of the Secretary-General for West Africa;

European Union contribution

31. *Calls upon* the European Union, notably its Special Representative for the Sahel, and its European Union Training Mission in Mali and European Union Capacity-Building Mission in Sahel Mali, to coordinate closely with the United Nations Multidimensional Integrated Stabilization Mission in Mali and other bilateral

[418] S/2013/354, annex.

partners of Mali engaged to assist the Malian authorities in security sector reform, as provided for by the Agreement and consistent with paragraph 14 (*b*) (ii) above;

Obligations under international humanitarian and human rights law

32. *Urges* all parties to comply with obligations under international humanitarian law to respect and protect humanitarian personnel, facilities and relief consignments, and take all required steps to allow and facilitate the full, safe, immediate and unimpeded access of humanitarian actors for the delivery of humanitarian assistance to all people in need, while respecting the United Nations humanitarian guiding principles and applicable international law;

33. *Reiterates* that the Malian authorities have primary responsibility to protect civilians in Mali, further recalls its resolutions 1265 (1999) of 17 September 1999, 1296 (2000) of 19 April 2000, 1674 (2006) of 28 April 2006, 1738 (2006) of 23 December 2006 and 1894 (2009) of 11 November 2009 on the protection of civilians in armed conflict, its resolutions 1612 (2005) of 26 July 2005, 1882 (2009) of 4 August 2009, 1998 (2011) of 12 July 2011, 2068 (2012) of 19 September 2012, 2143 (2014) of 7 March 2014 and 2225 (2015) of 18 June 2015 on children and armed conflict and its resolutions 1325 (2000) of 31 October 2000, 1820 (2008) of 19 June 2008, 1888 (2009) of 30 September 2009, 1889 (2009) of 5 October 2009, 1960 (2010) of 16 December 2010, 2106 (2013) of 24 June 2013 and 2122 (2013) of 18 October 2013 on women and peace and security, and calls upon the Mission and all military forces in Mali to take them into account and to abide by international humanitarian, human rights and refugee law, and recalls the importance of training in this regard, and urges all parties to implement the conclusions on children and armed conflict in Mali adopted by the Security Council Working Group on Children and Armed Conflict on 7 July 2014;[419]

Small arms and light weapons

34. *Calls upon* the Malian authorities, with the assistance of the Mission, consistent with paragraph 14 above, and international partners, to address the issue of the proliferation of and illicit trafficking in small arms and light weapons, in accordance with the Economic Community of West African States Convention on Small Arms and Light Weapons, Their Ammunition and Other Related Materials and the Programme of Action to Prevent, Combat and Eradicate the Illicit Trade in Small Arms and Light Weapons in All Its Aspects,[420] in order to ensure the safe and effective management, storage and security of their stockpiles of small arms and light weapons and the collection and/or destruction of surplus, seized, unmarked or illicitly held weapons, and further stresses the importance of the full implementation of its resolutions 2017 (2011) of 31 October 2011, 2117 (2013) of 26 September 2013 and 2220 (2015) of 22 May 2015;

Reports by the Secretary-General and review of the mandate

35. *Requests* the Secretary-General to report to the Council every three months after the adoption of the present resolution on the implementation of the resolution, focusing on the progress in the implementation of the Agreement and on the efforts of the Mission to support it;

36. *Affirms its intention* to consider reviewing the mandate of the Mission before 30 June 2016, as necessary, especially in the light of progress made in the implementation of the Agreement;

37. *Decides* to remain actively seized of the matter.

Adopted unanimously at the 7474th meeting.

---

[419] S/AC.51/2014/2.

[420] *Report of the United Nations Conference on the Illicit Trade in Small Arms and Light Weapons in All Its Aspects, New York, 9–20 July 2001* (A/CONF.192/15), chap. IV, para. 24.

ITEMS RELATING TO UKRAINE

A. Letter dated 28 February 2014 from the Permanent Representative of Ukraine to the United Nations addressed to the President of the Security Council (S/2014/136)[421]

Decisions

At its 7239th meeting, on 8 August 2014, the Security Council decided to invite the representative of Ukraine to participate, without vote, in accordance with rule 37 of its provisional rules of procedure, in the discussion of the item entitled "Letter dated 28 February 2014 from the Permanent Representative of Ukraine to the United Nations addressed to the President of the Security Council (S/2014/136)".

At the same meeting, the Council also decided to extend an invitation, in accordance with rule 39 of its provisional rules of procedure, to Mr. Ivan Šimonović, Assistant Secretary-General for Human Rights.

At its 7253rd meeting, on 28 August 2014, the Council decided to invite the representative of Ukraine to participate, without vote, in accordance with rule 37 of its provisional rules of procedure, in the discussion of the item entitled "Letter dated 28 February 2014 from the Permanent Representative of Ukraine to the United Nations addressed to the President of the Security Council (S/2014/136)".

At the same meeting, the Council also decided to extend an invitation, in accordance with rule 39 of its provisional rules of procedure, to Mr. Jeffrey Feltman, Under-Secretary-General for Political Affairs.

At its 7287th meeting, on 24 October 2014, the Council decided to invite the representative of Ukraine to participate, without vote, in accordance with rule 37 of its provisional rules of procedure, in the discussion of the item entitled "Letter dated 28 February 2014 from the Permanent Representative of Ukraine to the United Nations addressed to the President of the Security Council (S/2014/136)".

At the same meeting, the Council also decided to extend invitations, in accordance with rule 39 of its provisional rules of procedure, to Mr. Oscar Fernandez-Taranco, Assistant Secretary-General for Political Affairs, and Mr. Ivan Šimonović, Assistant Secretary-General for Human Rights.

At its 7311th meeting, on 12 November 2014, the Council decided to invite the representative of Ukraine to participate, without vote, in accordance with rule 37 of its provisional rules of procedure, in the discussion of the item entitled "Letter dated 28 February 2014 from the Permanent Representative of Ukraine to the United Nations addressed to the President of the Security Council (S/2014/136)".

At the same meeting, the Council also decided to extend an invitation, in accordance with rule 39 of its provisional rules of procedure, to Mr. Jens Anders Toyberg-Frandzen, Assistant Secretary-General ad interim for Political Affairs.

At the same meeting, the Council further decided to extend invitations, in accordance with rule 39 of its provisional rules of procedure, to Mr. Ertuğrul Apakan, Chief Monitor of the Organization for Security and Cooperation in Europe Special Monitoring Mission to Ukraine, and Ms. Heidi Tagliavini, Special Representative of the Organization for Security and Cooperation in Europe Chairperson-in-Office in Ukraine and in the Trilateral Contact Group.

At its 7365th meeting, on 21 January 2015, the Council decided to invite the representative of Ukraine to participate, without vote, in accordance with rule 37 of its provisional rules of procedure, in the discussion of the item entitled "Letter dated 28 February 2014 from the Permanent Representative of Ukraine to the United Nations addressed to the President of the Security Council (S/2014/136)".

At the same meeting, the Council also decided to extend an invitation, in accordance with rule 39 of its provisional rules of procedure, to Mr. Jeffrey Feltman, Under-Secretary-General for Political Affairs.

At its 7368th meeting, on 26 January 2015, the Council decided to invite the representative of Ukraine to participate, without vote, in accordance with rule 37 of its provisional rules of procedure, in the discussion of the

[421] Resolutions or decisions on this question were first adopted by the Security Council during the period from 1 January to 31 July 2014.

item entitled "Letter dated 28 February 2014 from the Permanent Representative of Ukraine to the United Nations addressed to the President of the Security Council (S/2014/136)".

At the same meeting, the Council also decided to extend an invitation, in accordance with rule 39 of its provisional rules of procedure, to Mr. Jeffrey Feltman, Under-Secretary-General for Political Affairs.

At its 7395th meeting, on 27 February 2015, the Council considered the item entitled "Letter dated 28 February 2014 from the Permanent Representative of Ukraine to the United Nations addressed to the President of the Security Council (S/2014/136)".

At the same meeting, the Council decided to extend invitations, in accordance with rule 39 of its provisional rules of procedure, to Ms. Heidi Tagliavini, Special Representative of the Organization for Security and Cooperation in Europe Chairperson-in-Office in Ukraine and in the Trilateral Contact Group, and Mr. Ertuğrul Apakan, Chief Monitor of the Organization for Security and Cooperation in Europe Special Monitoring Mission to Ukraine.

At its 7400th meeting, on 6 March 2015, the Council decided to invite the representative of Ukraine to participate, without vote, in accordance with rule 37 of its provisional rules of procedure, in the discussion of the item entitled "Letter dated 28 February 2014 from the Permanent Representative of Ukraine to the United Nations addressed to the President of the Security Council (S/2014/136)".

At the same meeting, the Council also decided to extend invitations, in accordance with rule 39 of its provisional rules of procedure, to Mr. Jeffrey Feltman, Under-Secretary-General for Political Affairs, Mr. John Ging, Director of the Coordination and Response Division of the Office for the Coordination of Humanitarian Affairs of the Secretariat, and Mr. Ivan Šimonović, Assistant Secretary-General for Human Rights.

At its 7457th meeting, on 5 June 2015, the Council decided to invite the representative of Ukraine to participate, without vote, in accordance with rule 37 of its provisional rules of procedure, in the discussion of the item entitled "Letter dated 28 February 2014 from the Permanent Representative of Ukraine to the United Nations addressed to the President of the Security Council (S/2014/136)".

At the same meeting, the Council also decided to extend an invitation, in accordance with rule 39 of its provisional rules of procedure, to Mr. Jeffrey Feltman, Under-Secretary-General for Political Affairs.

At the same meeting, the Council further decided to extend an invitation, in accordance with rule 39 of its provisional rules of procedure, to Mr. Alexander Hug, Deputy Chief Monitor of the Organization for Security and Cooperation in Europe Special Monitoring Mission to Ukraine.

At its 7498th meeting, on 29 July 2015, the Council decided to invite the representatives of Australia, Belgium, Canada, Germany, Indonesia, Ireland, Israel, Italy, the Netherlands, the Philippines, Romania, Ukraine and Viet Nam to participate, without vote, in accordance with rule 37 of its provisional rules of procedure, in the discussion of the item entitled "Letter dated 28 February 2014 from the Permanent Representative of Ukraine to the United Nations addressed to the President of the Security Council (S/2014/136)".

At the same meeting, the Council voted on a draft resolution contained in document S/2015/562. The result of the voting was as follows: 11 votes in favour (Chad, Chile, France, Jordan, Lithuania, Malaysia, New Zealand, Nigeria, Spain, United Kingdom of Great Britain and Northern Ireland and United States of America), 1 against (Russian Federation) and 3 abstentions (Angola, China and Venezuela (Bolivarian Republic of)). The draft resolution was not adopted, owing to the negative vote of a permanent member of the Council.

B. Letter dated 13 April 2014 from the Permanent Representative of the Russian Federation to the United Nations addressed to the President of the Security Council (S/2014/264)[421]

Decisions

At its 7234th meeting, on 5 August 2014, the Security Council decided to invite the representative of Ukraine to participate, without vote, in accordance with rule 37 of its provisional rules of procedure, in the discussion of the item entitled "Letter dated 13 April 2014 from the Permanent Representative of the Russian Federation to the United Nations addressed to the President of the Security Council (S/2014/264)".

At the same meeting, the Council also decided to extend an invitation, in accordance with rule 39 of its provisional rules of procedure, to Mr. John Ging, Director of the Coordination and Response Division of the Office for the Coordination of Humanitarian Affairs of the Secretariat.

At its 7269th meeting, on 19 September 2014, the Council decided to invite the representatives of Canada, Germany, Indonesia, Malaysia, the Netherlands and Ukraine to participate, without vote, in accordance with rule 37 of its provisional rules of procedure, in the discussion of the item entitled "Letter dated 13 April 2014 from the Permanent Representative of the Russian Federation to the United Nations addressed to the President of the Security Council (S/2014/264)".

At the same meeting, the Council also decided to extend an invitation, in accordance with rule 39 of its provisional rules of procedure, to Mr. Jeffrey Feltman, Under-Secretary-General for Political Affairs.

At its 7384th meeting, on 17 February 2015, the Council decided to invite the representatives of Germany and Ukraine to participate, without vote, in accordance with rule 37 of its provisional rules of procedure, in the discussion of the item entitled "Letter dated 13 April 2014 from the Permanent Representative of the Russian Federation to the United Nations addressed to the President of the Security Council (S/2014/264)".

Resolution 2202 (2015)
of 17 February 2015

The Security Council,

Recalling the purposes and principles enshrined in the Charter of the United Nations, and reaffirming its full respect for the sovereignty, independence and territorial integrity of Ukraine,

Expressing its grave concern at the tragic events and violence in eastern regions of Ukraine,

Reaffirming its resolution 2166 (2014) of 21 July 2014,

Firmly convinced that the resolution of the situation in eastern regions of Ukraine can only be achieved through a peaceful settlement to the current crisis,

1. *Endorses* the Package of Measures for the Implementation of the Minsk Agreements, adopted and signed in Minsk on 12 February 2015 (annex I);

2. *Welcomes* the Declaration by the President of the Russian Federation, the President of Ukraine, the President of the French Republic and the Chancellor of the Federal Republic of Germany in support of the Package of Measures for the Implementation of the Minsk Agreements, adopted on 12 February 2015 in Minsk (annex II), and their continuing commitment therein to the implementation of the Minsk Agreements;

3. *Calls upon* all parties to fully implement the Package of Measures, including a comprehensive ceasefire as provided for therein;

4. *Decides* to remain seized of the matter.

Adopted unanimously at the 7384th meeting.

Annex I

Package of Measures for the Implementation of the Minsk Agreements[422]

Minsk, 12 February 2015

1. Immediate and comprehensive ceasefire in certain areas of the Donetsk and Luhansk regions of Ukraine and its strict implementation as of 15 February 2015, 12 a.m. local time.

[422] Circulated under the symbol S/2015/110.

2. Withdrawal of all heavy weapons by both sides by equal distances in order to create a security zone of at least 50 km wide from each other for the artillery systems of calibre of 100 and more, a security zone of 70 km wide for MLRS and 140 km wide for MLRS "Tornado-S", Uragan, Smerch and tactical missile systems (Tochka, Tochka U):

- for the Ukrainian troops: from the de facto line of contact;
- for the armed formations from certain areas of the Donetsk and Luhansk regions of Ukraine: from the line of contact according to the Minsk Memorandum of 19 September 2014;

The withdrawal of the heavy weapons as specified above is to start on day 2 of the ceasefire at the latest and be completed within 14 days.

The process shall be facilitated by the OSCE and supported by the Trilateral Contact Group.

3. Ensure effective monitoring and verification of the ceasefire regime and the withdrawal of heavy weapons by the OSCE from day 1 of the withdrawal, using all technical equipment necessary, including satellites, drones, radar equipment, etc.

4. Launch a dialogue, on day 1 of the withdrawal, on modalities of local elections in accordance with Ukrainian legislation and the Law of Ukraine "On interim local self-government order in certain areas of the Donetsk and Luhansk regions" as well as on the future regime of these areas based on this law.

Adopt promptly, by no later than 30 days after the date of signing of this document a Resolution of the Parliament of Ukraine specifying the area enjoying a special regime, under the Law of Ukraine "On interim local self-government order in certain areas of the Donetsk and Luhansk regions", based on the line of the Minsk Memorandum of 19 September 2014.

5. Ensure pardon and amnesty by enacting the law prohibiting the prosecution and punishment of persons in connection with the events that took place in certain areas of the Donetsk and Luhansk regions of Ukraine.

6. Ensure release and exchange of all hostages and unlawfully detained persons, based on the principle "all for all". This process is to be finished on day 5 after the withdrawal at the latest.

7. Ensure safe access, delivery, storage and distribution of humanitarian assistance to those in need, on the basis of an international mechanism.

8. Definition of modalities of full resumption of socioeconomic ties, including social transfers such as pension payments and other payments (incomes and revenues, timely payments of all utility bills, reinstating taxation within the legal framework of Ukraine).

To this end, Ukraine shall reinstate control of the segment of its banking system in the conflict-affected areas and possibly an international mechanism to facilitate such transfers shall be established.

9. Reinstatement of full control of the State border by the Government of Ukraine throughout the conflict area, starting on day 1 after the local elections and ending after the comprehensive political settlement (local elections in certain areas of the Donetsk and Luhansk regions on the basis of the Law of Ukraine and constitutional reform) to be finalized by the end of 2015, provided that paragraph 11 has been implemented in consultation with and upon agreement by representatives of certain areas of the Donetsk and Luhansk regions in the framework of the Trilateral Contact Group.

10. Withdrawal of all foreign armed formations, military equipment, as well as mercenaries from the territory of Ukraine under monitoring of the OSCE. Disarmament of all illegal groups.

11. Carrying out constitutional reform in Ukraine with a new constitution entering into force by the end of 2015 providing for decentralization as a key element (including a reference to the specificities of certain areas in the Donetsk and Luhansk regions, agreed with the representatives of these areas), as well as adopting permanent legislation on the special status of certain areas of the Donetsk and Luhansk regions in line with measures as set out in the footnote until the end of 2015 (see note).

12. Based on the Law of Ukraine "On interim local self-government order in certain areas of the Donetsk and Luhansk regions", questions related to local elections will be discussed and agreed upon with representatives of certain areas of the Donetsk and Luhansk regions in the framework of the Trilateral Contact Group. Elections will be held in accordance with relevant OSCE standards and monitored by OSCE/ODIHR.

13. Intensify the work of the Trilateral Contact Group including through the establishment of working groups on the implementation of relevant aspects of the Minsk Agreements. They will reflect the composition of the Trilateral Contact Group.

Note:

Such measures are, according to the Law on the special order for local self-government in certain areas of the Donetsk and Luhansk regions:

- Exemption from punishment, prosecution and discrimination for persons involved in the events that have taken place in certain areas of the Donetsk and Luhansk regions;
- Right to linguistic self-determination;
- Participation of organs of local self-government in the appointment of heads of public prosecution offices and courts in certain areas of the Donetsk and Luhansk regions;
- Possibility for central governmental authorities to initiate agreements with organs of local self-government regarding the economic, social and cultural development of certain areas of the Donetsk and Luhansk regions;
- State supports the social and economic development of certain areas of the Donetsk and Luhansk regions;
- Support by central government authorities of cross-border cooperation in certain areas of the Donetsk and Luhansk regions with districts of the Russian Federation;
- Creation of the people's police units by decision of local councils for the maintenance of public order in certain areas of the Donetsk and Luhansk regions;
- The powers of deputies of local councils and officials, elected at early elections, appointed by the Verkhovna Rada of Ukraine by this law, cannot be terminated early.

Participants of the Trilateral Contact Group:

Ambassador Heidi Tagliavini
Second President of Ukraine, L. D. Kuchma
Ambassador of the Russian Federation to Ukraine, M. Yu. Zurabov
A.W. Zakharchenko
I.W. Plotnitsky

Annex II

Declaration of the President of the Russian Federation, the President of Ukraine, the President of the French Republic and the Chancellor of the Federal Republic of Germany in support of the Package of Measures for the Implementation of the Minsk Agreements, adopted on 12 February 2015 in Minsk[422]

The President of the Russian Federation, Vladimir Putin, the President of Ukraine, Petro Poroshenko, the President of the French Republic, François Hollande, and the Chancellor of the Federal Republic of Germany, Angela Merkel, reaffirm their full respect for the sovereignty and territorial integrity of Ukraine. They firmly believe that there is no alternative to an exclusively peaceful settlement. They are fully committed to undertake all possible individual and joint measures to this end.

Against this background, leaders endorse the Package of Measures for the Implementation of the Minsk Agreements adopted and signed on 12 February 2015 by all signatories who also signed the Minsk Protocol of 5 September 2014 and the Minsk Memorandum of 19 September 2014. Leaders will contribute to this process and will use their influence on relevant parties to facilitate the implementation of that Package of Measures.

Germany and France will provide technical expertise for the restoration of the segment of the banking system in the conflict-affected areas, possibly through the establishment of an international mechanism to facilitate social transfers.

Leaders share the conviction that improved cooperation between the European Union, Ukraine and the Russian Federation will be conducive to the crisis settlement. To this end, they endorse the continuation of trilateral talks between the European Union, Ukraine and the Russian Federation on energy issues in order to achieve follow-up stages to the winter gas package.

They also support trilateral talks between the European Union, Ukraine and the Russian Federation in order to achieve practical solutions to concerns raised by the Russian Federation with regard to the implementation of the Deep and Comprehensive Free Trade Agreement between Ukraine and the European Union.

Leaders remain committed to the vision of a joint humanitarian and economic space from the Atlantic to the Pacific based upon full respect for international law and the Organization for Security and Cooperation in Europe principles.

Leaders will remain committed to the implementation of the Minsk Agreements. To this end, they agree to establish an oversight mechanism in the Normandy format which will convene at regular intervals, in principle at the level of senior officials from the foreign ministries.

THE SITUATION IN THE DEMOCRATIC PEOPLE'S REPUBLIC OF KOREA

Decisions

At its 7353rd meeting, on 22 December 2014, the Security Council considered the item entitled:

"The situation in the Democratic People's Republic of Korea

> "Letter dated 5 December 2014 from the representatives of Australia, Chile, France, Jordan, Lithuania, Luxembourg, the Republic of Korea, Rwanda, the United Kingdom of Great Britain and Northern Ireland and the United States of America to the United Nations addressed to the President of the Security Council (S/2014/872)".

Following statements made by two members of the Council, the provisional agenda was adopted by 11 votes in favour (Argentina, Australia, Chile, France, Jordan, Lithuania, Luxembourg, Republic of Korea, Rwanda, United Kingdom of Great Britain and Northern Ireland and United States of America), 2 against (China and Russian Federation) and 2 abstentions (Chad and Nigeria).

Upon resumption of the 7353rd meeting, the Council decided to extend invitations, in accordance with rule 39 of its provisional rules of procedure, to Mr. Tayé-Brook Zerihoun, Assistant Secretary-General for Political Affairs, and Mr. Ivan Šimonović, Assistant Secretary-General for Human Rights.

Part II. Other matters considered by the Security Council

CONSIDERATION OF THE DRAFT REPORT OF THE SECURITY COUNCIL TO THE GENERAL ASSEMBLY

Decision

At its 7283rd meeting, on 22 October 2014, the Security Council considered the item entitled "Consideration of the draft report of the Security Council to the General Assembly".

The decision of the Council was reflected in the following note by the President:[423]

> At its 7283rd meeting, held on 22 October 2014, the Security Council considered its draft report to the General Assembly covering the period from 1 August 2013 to 31 July 2014. The Council adopted the draft report without a vote.

SECURITY COUNCIL DOCUMENTATION AND WORKING METHODS AND PROCEDURE

A. Implementation of the note by the President of the Security Council (S/2010/507)

Decisions

On 4 August 2014, the President of the Security Council issued the following note:[424]

> The members of the Security Council reaffirm that the work of the Council is a collective endeavour and responsibility, and that enhanced cooperation and consultation among all Council members is vital for the efficient and transparent functioning of the Council.
>
> The members of the Council also reaffirm the importance of continuing to improve intra-Council dialogue, communication and exchange of information, especially in crisis or fast-evolving situations.
>
> The members of the Council therefore agree to continue to enhance dialogue among all Council members, in particular in crisis or fast-evolving situations, so that the Council may respond more efficiently and therefore better fulfil its responsibility of maintaining international peace and security.
>
> The members of the Council, in this context, recognize the important role of the President of the Council, including in facilitating communication and exchange of information.

At its 7254th meeting, on 28 August 2014, the Council considered the item entitled "Implementation of the note by the President of the Security Council (S/2010/507)".

On 15 October 2014, the President of the Security Council issued the following note:[425]

> The members of the Security Council reaffirmed their commitment to enhancing the efficiency and transparency of the work of the Council and to implementing all previously agreed documents, including the provisional rules of procedure of the Council and the note by the President of the Council of 26 July 2010,[426] and have agreed on the following:
>
> 1. The speaking order for meetings of the Council as a general practice is established by a draw. In certain cases, the speaking order is established by the use of a sign-up sheet.

---

[423] S/2014/750.

[424] S/2014/565.

[425] S/2014/739 and Corr.1.

[426] S/2010/507.

2. The President of the Security Council, as a general practice, makes his or her national statement last of all Council members. In certain cases, he or she may make a single statement comprising introductory remarks and his or her national statement before the other members take the floor.

The President is encouraged to inform the other members in advance of his or her wish to do so in order to ensure that there are no objections.

3. In certain cases, the President of the Security Council may adjust the list of speakers and inscribe first the delegation(s) responsible for the drafting process in order to allow it or them to make an introductory or explanatory presentation. In cases when an unscheduled or emergency meeting is convened, the President may also adjust the list so that the delegation having requested the meeting can speak before the other Council members in order to present the reasons for convening the meeting.

4. The President of the Security Council may inscribe first the Chairs of the subsidiary bodies of the Council when presenting to the Council their work or reporting on outstanding issues within their mandate.

5. Members of the Council can trade slots in the list of speakers. It is recommended that delegations involved inform the Secretariat as to what was agreed.

Members of the Council are encouraged to inform the Secretariat of such changes as soon as possible, especially if the meeting has already started, in order to allow the interpreters to be ready to interpret from the language which will be used.

6. When high-level officials are representing Council members at a meeting, the list of speakers will be entitled "The list of speakers, after the draw and adjusted for protocol". For each category of high-level officials, the speakers will be listed within that category according to the order of the draw. The speakers within each category will speak after those in a category of higher-level officials and before those in a category of lower-level officials.

If, after the list of speakers has been circulated, there is a change in the level of a delegation's representative, that representative's speaking order will be readjusted according to protocol and his or her place within categories of same-level officials will be determined according to the order of the original draw.

7. The permanent representative of a Council member who also holds a post at the Cabinet or ministerial level within his or her Government will speak by order of the draw, without adjustment for protocol.

For meetings announced as high-level in advance, where higher-level officials are representing other Council members, a permanent representative serving at the Cabinet or ministerial level may request an adjustment by protocol of his or her place on the list of speakers. The delegation concerned is encouraged to inform the Secretariat and the other Council members in advance of its request to have that representative's speaking order adjusted by protocol. After being informed of such a request, the Secretariat will add, beside the name of the representative on the list of speakers, that he or she is speaking as a member of his or her Cabinet. When a permanent representative at the Cabinet or ministerial level has spoken in that capacity at a formal meeting, it will be noted in appendix II to the annual report of the Council.

For meetings not announced as high-level in advance, visiting higher-level officials may be accorded a speaking slot before permanent representatives as a matter of courtesy where there is no objection by members of the Council.

At its 7285th meeting, on 23 October 2014, the Council decided to invite the representatives of Algeria, Bosnia and Herzegovina, Botswana, Brazil, Costa Rica, Côte d'Ivoire, the Czech Republic, Egypt, Estonia, Germany, Guatemala, Hungary, India, Indonesia, Iran (Islamic Republic of), Ireland, Italy, Japan, Kazakhstan, Liechtenstein, Malaysia, Maldives, Mexico, Montenegro, Morocco, the Netherlands, New Zealand, Nicaragua, Norway, Pakistan, Peru, Poland, Portugal, Romania, Saint Lucia, Spain, Sweden, Switzerland, Thailand, Ukraine and Uruguay to participate, without vote, in accordance with rule 37 of its provisional rules of procedure, in the discussion of the item entitled:

"Implementation of the note by the President of the Security Council (S/2010/507)

"Security Council working methods

"Letter dated 8 October 2014 from the Permanent Representative of Argentina to the United Nations addressed to the Secretary-General (S/2014/725)".

At the same meeting, the Council also decided to extend invitations, in accordance with rule 39 of its provisional rules of procedure, to Ms. Kimberly Prost, Ombudsperson appointed pursuant to Security Council resolution 1904 (2009), and Ms. Fatou Bensouda, Prosecutor of the International Criminal Court.

At its 7294th meeting, on 30 October 2014, the Council considered the item entitled "Implementation of the note by the President of the Security Council (S/2010/507)".

At its 7325th meeting, on 26 November 2014, the Council considered the item discussed at the 7294th meeting.

At its 7352nd meeting, on 22 December 2014, the Council also considered the item discussed at the 7294th meeting.

At its 7373rd meeting, on 29 January 2015, the Council further considered the item discussed at the 7294th meeting.

At its 7422nd meeting, on 30 March 2015, the Council considered the item discussed at the 7294th meeting.

At its 7479th meeting, on 30 June 2015, the Council also considered the item discussed at the 7294th meeting.

B. General matters

Decision

On 12 May 2015, the President of the Security Council issued the following note:[427]

Pursuant to paragraph 4 (*b*) of the note by the President of the Security Council dated 30 October 1998,[428] and after consultations among the members of the Council, it was agreed to elect the Chairs and Vice-Chairs of subsidiary bodies for the period ending 31 December 2015 as follows:

Security Council Committee pursuant to resolutions 751 (1992) and 1907 (2009) concerning Somalia and Eritrea

Chair: Rafael Darío Ramírez Carreño (Venezuela (Bolivarian Republic of))
Vice-Chairs: Chad and Jordan

Security Council Committee pursuant to resolutions 1267 (1999) and 1989 (2011) concerning Al-Qaida and associated individuals and entities

Chair: Gerard van Bohemen (New Zealand)
Vice-Chairs: Chile and Russian Federation

Security Council Committee established pursuant to resolution 1373 (2001) concerning counter-terrorism

Chair: Raimonda Murmokaitė (Lithuania)
Vice-Chairs: Angola, France and Russian Federation

Security Council Committee established pursuant to resolution 1518 (2003)

Chair: U. Joy Ogwu (Nigeria)
Vice-Chair: Malaysia

Security Council Committee established pursuant to resolution 1521 (2003) concerning Liberia

Chair: Dina Kawar (Jordan)
Vice-Chairs: Angola and Spain

[427] S/2015/2/Rev.4. Previously issued on 2 and 21 January, 19 March and 23 April 2015 as documents S/2015/2 and Rev.1–3.

[428] S/1998/1016.

Security Council Committee established pursuant to resolution 1533 (2004) concerning the Democratic Republic of the Congo

Chair: Dina Kawar (Jordan)
Vice-Chairs: Chile and Lithuania

Security Council Committee established pursuant to resolution 1540 (2004)

Chair: Román Oyarzun Marchesi (Spain)
Vice-Chairs: New Zealand, Nigeria and United Kingdom of Great Britain and Northern Ireland

Security Council Committee established pursuant to resolution 1572 (2004) concerning Côte d'Ivoire

Chair: Cristián Barros Melet (Chile)
Vice-Chairs: Angola and New Zealand

Security Council Committee established pursuant to resolution 1591 (2005) concerning the Sudan

Chair: Rafael Darío Ramírez Carreño (Venezuela (Bolivarian Republic of))
Vice-Chairs: Nigeria and Spain

Security Council Committee established pursuant to resolution 1636 (2005)

Chair: Mahamat Zene Cherif (Chad)
Vice-Chairs: Lithuania and New Zealand

Security Council Committee established pursuant to resolution 1718 (2006)

Chair: Román Oyarzun Marchesi (Spain)
Vice-Chairs: Chad and Jordan

Security Council Committee established pursuant to resolution 1737 (2006)

Chair: Román Oyarzun Marchesi (Spain)
Vice-Chair: Chad

Security Council Committee established pursuant to resolution 1970 (2011) concerning Libya

Chair: Ramlan Bin Ibrahim (Malaysia)
Vice-Chair: Spain

Security Council Committee established pursuant to resolution 1988 (2011)

Chair: Gerard van Bohemen (New Zealand)
Vice-Chairs: Chile and Russian Federation

Security Council Committee established pursuant to resolution 2048 (2012) concerning Guinea-Bissau

Chair: U. Joy Ogwu (Nigeria)
Vice-Chair: Venezuela (Bolivarian Republic of)

Security Council Committee established pursuant to resolution 2127 (2013) concerning the Central African Republic

Chair: Raimonda Murmokaitė (Lithuania)
Vice-Chair: Jordan

Security Council Committee established pursuant to resolution 2140 (2014)

Chair: Raimonda Murmokaitė (Lithuania)
Vice-Chair: Jordan

Security Council Committee established pursuant to resolution 2206 (2015) concerning South Sudan

Chair: Cristián Barros Melet (Chile)
Vice-Chairs: Malaysia and New Zealand

Working Group on Peacekeeping Operations

Chair: Mahamat Zene Cherif (Chad)
Vice-Chair: United Kingdom of Great Britain and Northern Ireland

Ad Hoc Working Group on Conflict Prevention and Resolution in Africa

Chair: Ismael Abraão Gaspar Martins (Angola)
Vice-Chair: Chad

Working Group established pursuant to resolution 1566 (2004)

Chair: Raimonda Murmokaitė (Lithuania)
Vice-Chairs: Angola, France and Russian Federation

Working Group on Children and Armed Conflict

Chair: Ramlan Bin Ibrahim (Malaysia)
Vice-Chair: Nigeria

Informal Working Group on Documentation and Other Procedural Questions

Chair: Ismael Abraão Gaspar Martins (Angola)
Vice-Chair: Lithuania

Informal Working Group on International Tribunals

Chair: Cristián Barros Melet (Chile)
Vice-Chair: Spain

INTERNATIONAL COURT OF JUSTICE[429]

Election of five members of the International Court of Justice (S/2014/520, S/2014/521 and S/2014/522)

Decisions

At its 7297th to 7304th and 7313th meetings, on 6, 7 and 17 November 2014, the Security Council considered the item entitled “Election of five members of the International Court of Justice (S/2014/520, S/2014/521 and S/2014/522)”.

On 6 and 17 November 2014, the Council, at its 7297th and 7313th meetings, and the General Assembly, at the 39th and 53rd plenary meetings of its sixty-ninth session, elected five members of the International Court of Justice to fill the vacancies occurring on the expiration of the terms of office of the following judges:

Mr. Mohamed Bennouna (Morocco)

Ms. Joan E. Donoghue (United States of America)

Mr. Kenneth Keith (New Zealand)

[429] Resolutions or decisions on this question were first adopted by the Security Council in 1946.

Mr. Bernardo Sepúlveda-Amor (Mexico)

Mr. Leonid Skotnikov (Russian Federation)

The following were elected were elected as members of the International Court of Justice for a term of office beginning on 6 February 2015:

Mr. Mohamed Bennouna (Morocco)

Mr. James Richard Crawford (Australia)

Ms. Joan E. Donoghue (United States of America)

Mr. Kirill Gevorgian (Russian Federation)

Mr. Patrick Lipton Robinson (Jamaica)

Items included in the agenda of the Security Council for the first time from 1 August 2014 to 31 July 2015

NOTE: The practice of the Security Council is to adopt at each meeting, on the basis of the provisional agenda circulated in advance, the agenda for that particular meeting; the agenda as adopted for each meeting held during the period from 1 August 2014 to 31 July 2015 will be found in the records of the 7233rd to 7499th meetings (S/PV.7233–7499).

The following list of items shows also the meetings at which the Council decided, during that period, to include in the agenda items that had not been inscribed previously.

Item	*Meeting*	*Date*
The situation in the Democratic People's Republic of Korea	7353rd	22 December 2014
Meeting of the Security Council with the troop- and police-contributing countries pursuant to resolution 1353 (2001), annex II, sections A and B		
United Nations Multidimensional Integrated Stabilization Mission in the Central African Republic	7424th	8 April 2015

Checklist of resolutions adopted by the Security Council from 1 August 2014 to 31 July 2015

Draft resolutions considered at a formal meeting and not adopted

Checklist of statements made by the President of the Security Council from 1 August 2014 to 31 July 2015

www.ingramcontent.com/pod-product-compliance
Lightning Source LLC
Chambersburg PA
CBHW061151240926
51846CB00006B/983